Withdrawn
University of Waterloo

Gaudí

Withdrawn
University of Waterloo

César Martinell

Gaudí

His Life · His Theories · His Work

Translated from the Spanish by
Judith Rohrer

Edited by
George R. Collins

The MIT Press
Cambridge, Massachusetts

Originally published by the Colegio Oficial de Arquitectos de Cataluña y Baleares,
Comisión de Cultura, Barcelona, under the title
GAUDI: Su vida, su teoría, su obra (Biografías I).

Copyright © 1967 by Colegio Oficial de Arquitectos de Cataluña y Baleares
English translation copyright © 1975 by Editorial Blume, Barcelona
First MIT Press edition
Printed and bound in Spain   Depósito Legal: B. 17970-1975
Printed by Grafos, S. A. Arte sobre papel. Paseo Carlos I, 157 - Barcelona 13

All rights reserved. No part of this book may be reproduced in any form or by any means,
electronic or mechanical, including photocopying, recording,
or by any information storage and retrieval system,
without permission in writing from the publisher.

Library of Congress Cataloging in Publication Data

Martinell y Brunet, César, 1888-1973.
    Gaudí: his life, his theories, his work.

    Translation of Gaudí: su vida, su teoría, su obra.
    Bibliography: p. 476.
    Includes indexes.
    1. Gaudí y Cornet, Antonio, 1852-1926. I. Title.
NA1313.G3M2813   1975   720'.92'4   74-109
ISBN 0-262-13072-6

CONTENTS

APPENDICES

SOURCES FOR THE PRESENT STUDY

INDICES

PREFACE TO THE ENGLISH-LANGUAGE EDITION

This is the most complete, detailed study that has yet been made of the architect Antonio Gaudí. Its special value resides in the familiarity with which the author, as a young man, knew Gaudí during the last decades of his life, and in the perspective which César Martinell—who was both a practicing architect and an experienced historian—gave to the remarks which he and others heard from Gaudí's lips. The book also contains a wealth of new data and illustrations which the author had unearthed in recent years and made available here for the first time. Martinell performed a particulary valuable service in achieving a more precise dating of many of Gaudí's works and in his discussion of the various attributions that have been made to Gaudí since his death.

The present volume will supplement all the previous definitive accounts of Gaudí's career. The first of these, still a classic, was published in 1928-29, only two years after Gaudí's death, by José F. Ráfols and Francisco Folguera; Ráfols, the principal author, was an architect and art historian who had known the master well for many years and had worked as his assistant. Another of the young associates of Gaudí, Juan Bergós, supplied a major biography in 1954, and still another, Isidro Puig Boada, published the basic monograph on Gaudí's major work, the Church of the Sagrada Familia. The only prior study of Gaudí that approximates the present one in size, breadth of data, and quantity of illustrations was published by the Neapolitan architectural historian Roberto Pane in 1964. None of these has been translated into English. Martinell's interest in Gaudí has always been personal—a fascination with his master's manner of thinking and architectural theory. His first book on Gaudí was a collection of the architect's sayings, particulary about the Sagrada Familia church, published in 1951; as it was written in Catalan it has always seemed a little inaccessible, but it has recently been revised and translated into Spanish. Martinell kept careful notation of his exchanges with his mentor, and since Gaudí wrote nothing himself during most of his career, Martinell's notes are valuable evidence of his thought. In this book, however, the author has not limited himself to his own materials; he has interviewed all others who knew Gaudí in any capacity, and we profit from their insights as well.

The organization of this book evolves directly out of Martinell's own professional interests and the nature of his association with Gaudí. Part I, for instance, about Gaudí's life, reflects the mystique that they both shared about the innate qualities of those who, like themselves, grew up in the hinterland (Campo de Tarragona) of the city of Tarragona on the eastern littoral of Spain. Part II, on Gaudí's theory, is indeed strictly theoretical in nature and, among other things, explores for the first time Gaudí's own early writings. Part III, which inventories and analyzes Gaudí's individual works and projects, is comprehensive and scrupulous, as we would expect from an author who has produced pioneering studies of the Medieval and Baroque monuments of Catalonia. Lengthy, discerning discussion, like Martinell's, of each major work is essential in cases such as Gaudí's where each design is unique and significantly different from its predecessors. The chronological organization of this section makes it possible for the author to keep his readers aware at all times of the extraordinary devotion of this single human being to one overriding and lifelong project: the designing and building of the Sagrada Familia, to be one of the world's largest churches. Gaudí's somewhat irascible and totally unmaterialistic dedication to this cause can be sensed in nearly every other project in which he was involved, and the author makes this clear.

Martinell insists on our recognition of Gaudí as primarily an architect, and he is clearly impatient with those who would see him as some sort of modern painter, abstract artist, or surrealist. An absorbing feature of this book is the way in which the author shows how the many innovative features of Gaudí's designs were a natural result of the pains he took with the details of the building programs with which he was faced. Aspects which at first sight might strike us as bizarre or pure fantasy emerge, after explanation, as perfectly rational, sensible, even inevitable results of the tireless scrutiny and research that Gaudí gave to every project. Martinell sees Gaudí's ultimate intention to be the realization of a sense of overall balance of equilibrium in his work; his use of materials, ol polychromy, his deployment of building masses and internal spaces, and his search for an «equilibrated» structure employing the traditional Catalan masonry techniques, are all described by the author as being in keeping with the desire to achieve a harmonious relation between the edifice he was building and the laws of nature. The universal interests of Gaudí enriched this search; especially fascinating are Martinell's descriptions of the involvement of Gaudí in problems of music and sound in the Sagrada Familia project and the way in which he infused all his works with underlying geometrical harmonies and proportions—usually of a dynamic rhythmical character.

The present book will do much to correct the image of Gaudí as an eccentric and isolated visionary diverting architecture into private, sculptural, folkloric channels. We are beginning to realize that his long career was dedicated to a dogged exploration of the nature of the art of building and of the very purpose of architecture. Martinell's mass of data and reminiscences is an absolutely necessary basis to our understanding of the question that Gaudí posed, and even more is needed as he himself suggests. At last there is taking place a serious archival investigation of Gaudí's works, to which Martinell has contributed, and the new information—especially that lately uncovered by Professor Juan Bassegoda of the *Amigos de Gaudí* of Barcelona—has been so substantial that as recent a text as the present one was in some parts out of date by the time we translated it. I have made no effort to update Martinell's book by adding later discoveries, but I have revised such passages of the text and the dating where it is known that we were previously wrong.

The reader will notice—and indeed the author himself warns us—that the three-part organization of the book tends to go over the same material three different times, with inevitable repetition. We have tried to reduce this to a minimum by the elimination of certain passages and the substitution of cross-references. Also, the author himself, in preparation for this English-language edition, had cut out material which he felt to be of purely local—that is, Catalan—interest, especially in Part I, and he had encouraged us to do more of this. We have not indicated these deletions in the main text but have done so in the appendices because of the documentary character of the latter. Several of these documents have been shortened. Our Appendix IV (Appendix V in the Spanish edition) represents only a fraction of Gaudí's youthful diary, and his Memorial on the street-lamps (Appendix IV in the Spanish text) has been eliminated altogether by the author who does, however, retain important passages from it in his text. The index of Works of Gaudí and the List of Illustrations that appeared in the Spanish edition have been combined into what is essentially a chronological checklist of buildings (and their illustrations); this the reader will, I hope, find useful.

This volume represented the first—and a very auspicious beginning—of a substantial series of biographical studies of Catalan architects in which a number of us from Spain and abroad are collaborating. The series has been commissioned by the *Colegio Oficial de Arquitectos de Cataluña y Baleares*, the Catalan architectural association, whose forerunner had brought out a succession of valuable monographs when it was founded in the late nineteenth century. Already published, besides this present one, are studies of two Gothic architects: Reinard des Fonoll (1969) and Guillem Sagrera (1970) and of the twentieth-century architect Rafael Masó (1971) as well as a comprehensive historical atlas of Barcelona (1972). In preparation are volumes on Jujol, Vilaseca, Guastavino, Rubió, Rogent, and Gallissá, all of whom impinge in one way or another on the career of Gaudí. It his hoped that the books will bring the vast accomplishments of these architects to the attention of a public outside the peninsula.

Speaking personally, I knew César Martinell for many years, and I have respected and have made frequent use of his numerous publications on Gaudí. His efforts, through his *Centro de Estudios Gaudinistas*, to put the study of Gaudí's oeuvre on a scientific, scholarly basis was estimable, and I am proud to have been able to contribute papers to that entity on more than one occasion. In the summer of 1966, when I was residing in the Casa Milá, I was able to assist him in the making of the spectacular new photographs of its interior which were here published for the first time. So I was delighted to accept the task of overseeing the translation of this, his *opus magnum*.

The new material Martinell has released in this book is almost overwhelming, and I have only enough space to comment on one or two items. On the whole I agree with his new dates; dating of buildings is often arbitrary, and the chronology of Gaudí's works is especially fluid because of the complete destruction of his atelier and files in 1936. Martinell's attribution of the Dr. Robert monument to Gaudí and his removal of both of the Compañía Trasatlántica's exposition pavilions and the work in the Parque de la Ciudadela are interesting but still, I think, debatable. His use of our friend Juan Matamala's drawing to introduce the idea of a gigantic New York hotel as being Gaudí's does not do justice to the matter; the original drawings by Gaudí which Matamala owns and associates with the project are not convincing, either. Also, in his enthusiasm for Gaudí's essay on «Ornamentation»—which he was the first to publish—Martinell would seem to have given overmuch weight to immature and not yet well formed ideas of the young architect. In general the thoughts in the essay sound second-hand—a quality we never associate with Gaudí's architecture after 1878.

In the work of converting César Martinell's monumental study into English I am indebted to many persons, primarily to Judith Rohrer for the remarkable industry and persistance she displayed in the long job of translation. Friends in Barcelona have assisted with many details—Juan Bassegoda, David Mackay, Enric Jardí, the Bonet and Casanelles families, in particular. Without the archive of the *Amigos de Gaudí* of Barcelona, which was assembled by the tireless and unselfish efforts of the late Enric Casanelles, neither this book nor its translated edition would have been possible. I have myself been aided in the reading of proofs by my sons Lucas and Nicolas and have been reinforced in the whole project by the patience of the Spanish publisher, and by the high standards of the editors of the MIT Press. It should perhaps be mentioned that a quantity of modern illustrations of Gaudí's work that one finds in this and other recent publications were commissioned or in part financed by our own Archive of Catalan Art and Architecture at Columbia University through a grant from the American Council of Learned Societies. Among these used here are all the photographs of the materials in the Reus Museum, some of those of Comillas, Astorga, and León, and the interior details of the Casa Vicens—all taken by the photographer Francisco Aleu. The same should be said for the measured drawings of the Casa Batlló executed in the office of the architect Luis Bonet Garí.

The above was written in the fall of 1970. For a variety of financial reasons production of the English edition was interrupted and was only able to get underway again three years later. To our sorrow, the author César Martinell died on 19 November 1973 just as we were again at work, and it has not, therefore, been possible to check certain final details with him. Although considerable new material has continued to come to light in the interim—especially drawings, which Professor

Bassegoda and I are incorporating into our portfolio of Gaudí drawings soon to be published—I have made no effort to include these, or to update other parts of the present volume except where it seemed absolutely necessary.

George R. Collins
COLUMBIA UNIVERSITY in the
City of New York

AUTHOR'S PREFACE

There already has been published abundant anecdotal material—some of it contradictory—on Gaudí. In some cases the facts correspond to the master whom I had the honor of knowing during the last decade of his life, while others present us with a mysterious Gaudí from someone's imagination; the imaginary myths would provoke a lengthy discussion, so I did not feel it proper to include them in what I hope is a compendious treatise; I have left the discussion of them for some future time.

Once I had collected the basic information, I decided that it would be a good idea to look over my own collection of anecdotes—some of them provided by Gaudí himself—and tie them in with his architectural ideas, considering the avid enthusiasm that readers have for such tales even when they reveal a more conventional Gaudí. And it was thus that this book came about, sponsored by the *Colegio Oficial de Arquitectos de Cataluña y Baleares;* here I have attempted the difficult task of writing the biography of a man for whom no really complete biography exists, despite his tremendous stature as an architect.

In Part One, «His Life,» which is divided into 24 chapters and 109 sections, I have included information relating to his personal life from birth and early schooling to his death, including psychological traits—transitory or otherwise, such as his youthful secularism, sentimental adventures, sympathies with the working class—and those circumstances which contributed to the formation of his mature personality (details which I had originally planned to omit). The result is, I hope, a clear and accurate description of Gaudí's personal characteristics. I have also tried to describe those incidents in which the architect's personality played an appreciable role in his works, even though such intervention might not be significant in the development of his architecture per se.

Despite the gruffness which has been attributed to the master, we young architects who visited him in his studio were always received in a warm and friendly manner, and we never found him reserved in his opinions. He talked freely and openly, usually about his all-absorbing work on the Church of the Sagrada Familia which he already knew that he would not be able to complete. His simple forthrightness gave credence to the idea that his explanations may have been intended to impress on us certain principles which would be difficult to understand—once he was gone—from drawings or models alone.

To a certain extent, I feel that those of us who had the benefit of his illuminating explanations have the duty to transmit them—as several of us, myself included, have already done—as an aid to the orientation of the critics and simple *aficionados.* Thus, in Part Two, «His Theory,» I have collected Gaudí's esthetic ideas in 10 chapters and 42 sections, so that the interested reader can find the questions and frustrations that motivated the various novel solutions found in his work.

The personal—and the most interesting—stage of Gaudí's architecture makes necessary such a clarification of his theory. Some of his innovations, as well as his work as a whole, become more accessible when his motives are known. This clarification is especially necessary given the manner in which the subject has been treated in the past, with erroneous attributions, lamentable oversights, etc. An objective revision with as much documentation and clarity as possible is required.

This is what I have attempted in Part Three, where «His Work» is studied in 17 chapters and 52 sections. Here I have presented a detailed and concise examination of each work with maximum fidelity and precision as far as concepts and attributions are concerned. Several early works attributed to the great architect—the Montserrat *camarín,* imaginary projects for an underground temple and pantheon at the same monastery, the cascade in Parque de la Ciudadela, the balustrade of the Salón de San Juan, the railing of the Aribau monument, pavilions for the Cádiz exposition of 1887 and that of Barcelona the next year—were in need of re-examination; writers of recent years have taken them for granted without looking at the basis for the original attributions or checking their accuracy.

Such transgressions are understandable in the early biographies, but not in the latest ones where, in the eager quest for new discoveries, even more erroneous attributions have been made based on the earlier arbitrary ones. On the other hand, some works quite obviously by Gaudí have been overlooked, such as several aspects of his first plans for Mataró, the monument to Dr. Bartolomé Robert which stood for 30 years in the center of the popular Plaza de la Universidad in Barcelona, and the interesting sketch of the monument to the bishop Torras y Bages important for its geometric expressionism which along with the monuments to fire and water was a part of the Sagrada Familia project. Such omissions, in contrast to the excessive attributions listed above, indicated the most logical and responsible direction to take in the careful analysis of the master's work which I have attempted in Part Three.

At the end of this study I have included 10 documentary Appendices, some of which amplify or confirm points treated in the text as in the case of two interesting letters with sketches attached from the architect Villar y Carmona which prove his authorship of the Montserrat *camarín*. Others are writings by Gaudí himself, most of which have not been published elsewhere.

Following this is a list of the archives consulted, a very brief bibliography of the basic studies of Gaudí—some of which are very hard to find—and a list of the books in which I have myself previously examined, in a more detailed manner, certain aspects which are therefore only briefly covered in the present book. I have preferred clarity to attractiveness in the illustrations, and therefore have paid more attention to relating the overall views with· details than to mere abundance of pictures.

My objective has been to present as clear as possible an all-inclusive exposition of the master's work. Thus I have undertaken research in many archives which were previously untouched in this respect; I have further researched the contemporary press, and have consulted witnesses to the facts or their descendants, as well as carefully examining each of the works and its documentation in the substantial bibliography. At times I have relied on what I saw with my own eyes at the master's side and on my memory of his invaluable words. The sources of information are so varied that, however many aspects are covered, the necessity to choose precludes my considering the present book to be exhaustive.

It gives me great pleasure to bring new data to light in this book, as well as new criticism and commentary which I believe of interest, and I hope that these will be valuable contributions to the study of the master and his work—a study which still leaves much to be done.

I would like to say that my purpose has been objective study rather than any sort of defense of Gaudí's work. If at times my admiration for the architect or my affection for the man make it seem as if the latter were true, it was not my intention; nor on the other hand, did I feel it necessary to conceal those sentiments. I have proceeded in a sincere manner, without apology. Proof of this can be found in the anecdotes compiled in the section *To err is human* (XXIII-104) and the observations which I throw out from time to time as material for discussion, which could be converted into adverse commentary depending on the severity with which they are judged.

Faithful to this criterion and taking into consideration the intimate, introverted manner in which the most interesting of his works were produced, I have avoided making chronological and esthetic relationships with the great contemporary masters from whom he did not received personal influence and on whom he possibly did not have any influence himself. Such a comparative study would be more proper to a general study of modern architecture than to the particular case of Gaudí.

Before closing the introduction, I would like to say that if there is any value in my work I must share this value with all those who have helped me to realize it. First of all the *Colegio de Arquitectos* which, under the deanship of Manuel de Solá-Morales, took up the idea and encouraged me in this publication with which the present dean Antonio M. de Moragas Gallissá and the Cultural Commission recently created chose to inaugurate the series of biographies of Catalan architects that it proposes to publish; also, the Municipal Museum of Reus and its director Salvador Vilaseca who facilitated the study of the objects preserved there, as well as the *Junta de Obras* of the Sagrada Familia, the Abbeys of Montserrat and Poblet with respect to their archives, and all other public and private archives that I have had occasion to consult. I would also like to remember gratefully the following for their help: the architect Juan Rubió, Rosario Segimón widow of Sr. Milá, the architect Jaime Bayó, the master ironsmith Luis Badía, and Bernardo García Galán, all of whom have numerous impressions and memories of the master with whom they lived. Also to my good friends Sr. Alonso Luengo, Pedro M. de Basáñez, Prof. J. Bassegoda Nonell, who particulary collaborated, along with his students, in the graphic work, Juan Bergós, Oriol Bohigas, Sr. Bonet Garí, Reinald Bozzo, O.S.B., Miguel Brullet, Sebastián Buxó Calvet, J. M. Camps Arnau, Felipe de Dalmases, Señores Gomis-Prats who have a most exquisite photographic archive, the sculptor Antonio R. González, J. M. Guix Sugrañes, Juan A. Maragall, Juan Matamala Flotats, Francisco de P. Quintana, José M. Pericas, J. Puig Boada, M. Ribas Piera, Juan Rogent, Prof. J. Ruiz Vallés and his students, Antonio L. Savall, A. Trías Maxenchs, and all of those who, in addition to these, are cited in the notes or who are not mentioned in my notes but were helpful in my work. To all I express my sincere appreciation for the manner, often spontaneous, with which they brought me their information, pouring forth their admiration for the master, and giving their contributions the aspect of a collective collaboration of stimulating cultural and patriotic significance in the undertaking to know better the work of the talented architect.

C. M. B.

part one / HIS LIFE

1. ANCESTORS
2. A DOUBLE LINE OF COPPERSMITHS
3. BIRTH, BROTHERS AND SISTERS, BIRTHPLACE

1. ANCESTORS (Fig 1)

In any introduction to the life of Gaudí, one must refer back to his ancestors, for the simple reason that he himself did so on several occasions, considering that his lineage had a definite influence on his qualities as an architect. We can trace these ancestors—at first merchants, later farmers, and finally coppersmiths—to Reus and its surrounding countryside in the early years of the XVII century, where they had recently arrived from France along with a number of other smiths and tradesmen («marxants») who had settled in the Campo de Tarragona. Mentioned as coppersmiths in contemporary documents of commercial transactions are the names Mascombes, Gaudí, Longavernia, La Pierre, and Brunel. [1]

Juan Gaudí, a merchant by trade, whom Armengol Viver supposes to have lived in Riudoms, being originally from Auvergne, married María Escura of Riudoms in that same city in 1634. [2] The buying and selling of merchandise led this Juan Gaudí to set up a shop in his new home, the family house of his wife; for in his will of 1638 he is classified as «dealer» and «shop-keeper». In that same will he left a legacy of thirty Barcelona pounds to his father Antonio and chose to be buried in whatever parish he died, indicating that he did not consider his situation in Riudoms to be permanent.

Nevertheless, his son Juan, who had given up his father's trade to become a weaver, continued living in the same town. The son and grandson of this second Juan, both named José,

1. Luisa Vilaseca, «A propósito de la calle del Vidre... y de los Gaudí en Reus,» in the weekly *Reus* N.º 222 (July 14, 1956). Information from the Reus archives.

2. J. M. Armengol Viver, «La gènesi de Gaudí,» *El Matí* (Barcelona: June 21, 1936); an article minutely documented from study in the parish archive of Riudoms.

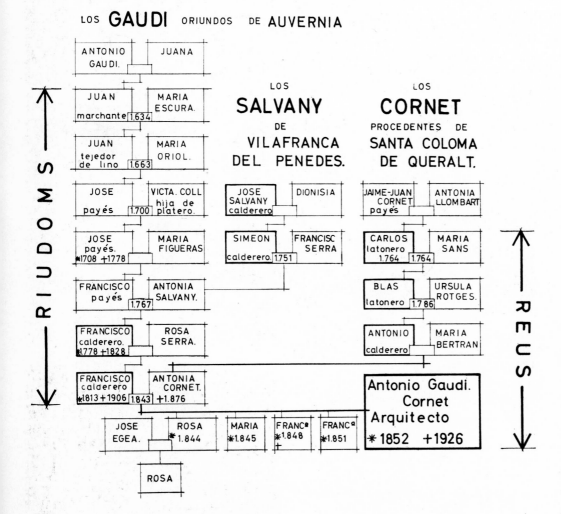

LOS **GAUDI** ORIUNDOS DE **AUVERNIA**

1. Gaudí's family tree. The more heavily outlined boxes indicate the coopersmiths and braziers.

were farmers by trade, a circumstance which would suggest the acquisition of a small amount of land, the fruit of savings acquired from a modest life's work. This property, in the possession of their descendants, kept the Gaudís in agriculture for three generations.

2. A DOUBLE LINE OF COPPERSMITHS (Fig. 1)

The son of the second José, Francisco Gaudí Figueras, was also a farmer, but in 1767 he married Antonia Salvany Serra, whose father Simón and grandfather José were both from Vilafranca del Penedés; this trade was transmitted from them to their Gaudí descendants who gave up farming for the industry of the maternal grandparents. The son of Francisco and Antonia, Francisco Gaudí Salvany, took up the coppersmith practice, and the grandson, Francisco Gaudí Serra, the father of the architect, carried it on. This Gaudí Serra, born in Riudoms, married Antonia Cornet Bertrán of Reus, also from a family of coppersmiths and brassworkers in the region of Santa Coloma de Queralt.

Gaudí was convinced that this abundance of coppersmiths in his immediate background influenced the ease with which he was able to visualize space as well as his plastic sensitivity —the qualities which he considered basic to the architect's practice.

In addition to these craftsmen, he also had a maternal grandfather who was a sailor and a great-grandfather, on his mother's side, who was a cooper—all people acquainted with space and working in situations intimately involved in manipulation and visualization in three dimensions. So many generations of people involved with space before him had prepared the way and had sharpened his sensitivity to such training. Gaudí jokingly called this facility to visualize space «copper kettlery.» [3]

3. César Martinell, *Conversaciones con Gaudí* (Barcelona: Ediciones Punto Fijo, 1969), p. 98. This book transcribes various conversations with the architect.

2. The now-destroyed house at No. 4, Calle de San Juan in Reus, where Gaudí was probably born.

3. The baptismal font where our architect was baptized in the parish church of San Pedro in Reus. The font was preserved until July, 1936. From *La Ilustración Artística*, 1888, p. 2.

The first Gaudí coppersmith in Riudoms, descendant of farmers, carried out his trade—most probably influenced by the tradition of his maternal grandparents the Salvanys of Vilafranca—on a modest scale, but when his son, the father of our architect, was married in 1843 to the daughter of the coppersmith Cornet in Reus, the business grew; this son became an industrialist, manufacturing the complex distilling apparatus for making alcohol from wine —a flourishing industry in the Campo de Tarragona during the middle of the last century.

The town of Riudoms turned out to be too restricted for the new industrialist, and he was drawn to the nearby urban center of Reus, where he was registered as resident in September, 1851. [4]

3. BIRTH, BROTHERS AND SISTERS, BIRTHPLACE (Figs. 2, 3)

Gaudí was the youngest of five children born to the Gaudí-Cornet couple. Rosa, the eldest, was born in 1844. The next year another daughter María (who died when still in her youth) was born. Then came a son named Francisco who died shortly afterwards, and following his death in 1851, another was born and given the same name. In 1852 the architect was born. His baptismal certificate, now preserved in the archives of the parish of San Pedro of Reus says, «The twenty-sixth day of June of eighteen fifty-two: in aforesaid baptismal fonts: by me Joseph Casas, Priest and Vicar of said Church, was baptised Anton, Plácito, Guillem, born yesterday at nine-thirty in the morning, son of Francisco Gaudí, coppersmith of Riudoms, and Antonia Cornet of Reus, married. Pat. grandparents Francisco Gaudí, coppersmith of Riudoms and Rosa Serra of Reus; M. Antonio Cornet, coppersmith of Reus and María Bertrán of Tarragona. Godparents Plácido Gaudí, turner of Riudoms and Raimunda Gaudí y Tarragó of Barcelona. Advised of Doctrine and Relationship Josep Casas, vicar.» Signed.

From this we can deduce that Gaudí was born in Reus at 9:30 a. m. on June 25, 1852. The baptismal certificate does not implicitly state the place of birth, but as no observation to the contrary is made, it is only normal to assume that the child came into this world within the boundaries of the parish in which he was baptized. This supposition is confirmed by a great number of the architect's official documents which have been preserved relating to school records, military service, notarized court appearances, as well as the last testament which he made out in Puigcerdá on June 9, 1911. [5]

While we can take for granted then that Gaudí was born in the town of Reus, we cannot be equally precise so far as the exact house is concerned.

Possible birthplaces include the Calle de la Amargura (now Cervantes), the Calle de San Vicente y Alegre, and No. 8 of the Calle de San Juan. Nevertheless, No. 4 on the Calle de San Juan seems to prevail. The old houses which formerly stood at 2 and 8 on this same street were torn down, and on the cleared land was constructed a building belonging to the Hispano-American bank. On its façade they have fixed a commemorative plaque saying: «Antonio Gaudí Cornet was born in this house on June 25, 1852.»

4. Jordi Elias, *Gaudí, Assaig Biogràfic* (Barcelona: 1961), p. 17; J. M. Guix Sugrañes, *Defensa de Gaudí* (Barcelona: 1960), pp. 57, 58, 59.

5. These details, some of which will be repeated in successive pages, would not be necessary if it were not for the fact that it has been argued that the birthplace of the famous architect was Riudoms since he seems to have said on one occasion that he «was from Riudoms.» If he did indeed say this, we must interpret it figuratively, considering the great amount of time spent in that village as a child. The fact that I was from Valls, in the same Campo de Tarragona, gave rise to several conversations on our respective places of birth. I most concretely recall that in 1917, after they had organized in Valls several ceremonies to raise money for the temple of the Sagrada Familia with satisfactory results, he told me that they had been superior to those obtained shortly before for the same cause in Reus, «in spite of the fact that it's my home town.» I can't imagine that Gaudí would falsely declare himself a native of Reus at a loss to Riudoms. The allegations pro and con for the two conflicting opinions can be found in a publication by the town of Riudoms in 1960 entitled *La verdad sobre Gaudí: conjunto de pruebas que revalidan el hecho histórico del nacimiento de Gaudí en el «Mas de la Calderera» de Riudoms*, and another by Guix Sugrañes entitled *Defensa de Gaudí* which transcribes two lectures in which the author defended the Reusian thesis (1960).

II. CHILDHOOD AND ADOLESCENCE

4. SICKNESS AS A CHILD

The well-defined and sharply characterized personality of Gaudí's maturity had, in its beginnings, to struggle with an infirm body that demanded extra parental care, at first forcing a prolongation of the weaning period [1] and later requiring extended periods to be spent on the Riudoms farm to take advantage of the country atmosphere for the benefit of the baby's health. [2] Before he was six, he suffered from attacks of articular rheumatism which at times made walking so difficult that he was obliged to get around on a little donkey. [3] These attacks reappeared from time to time throughout his life.

We find, then, a frail child whose delicate health forced him to refrain from the usual children's games of his companions. If this created in him certain complexes, they would certainly have been only of physical limitation, for intellectually his lack of activism was compensated for by an exceptional development of his sense of observation—a quality innate in him—and by the stimulation of a precocious mind.

In his tiny home in Riudoms he could not roam about much, but he would often observe the hens, free in the fields, and would watch their movements. Whatever he saw he took in rapidly and made it his own. One day he would hear his teacher explain in class that «birds have wings to fly,» and remembering his observations, he quickly replied: «The hens on our farm have great big wings and they can't fly at all. They use them to run faster.» [4]

5. PRIMARY SCHOOLING

Gaudí's primary education took place in a school set up by the teacher Francisco Berenguer in a loft on the Calle de Monterols (now Calle Fortuny) where, around 1860, he met Eduardo Toda; as the latter does not allude in any special way to the health of the future architect, we can suppose that, his body strengthened, Gaudí led a life normal for boys his age. [5] It appears that later he transferred to a school run by Mr. Rafael Palau in the same building that housed the Reus Hospital. [6]

6. SECONDARY EDUCATION (Fig. 4)

Once his childhood infirmity was conquered, Gaudí, under his father's tutelage, embarked upon the studies which would serve as the basis for a future profession. Although this could have caused difficulties for a family of limited means, I can not share the opinion of some biographers who would have Gaudí's father in a situation just short of poverty, forced to place his son as a factory apprentice and to seek outside sources of funds in order to get the boy's studies underway. [7]

Gaudí's older brother was a doctor, so that when the future architect began secondary school, his brother was already attending classes there, and it seems only logical that the modest manufacturer felt the typical desire to insure that his sons would enjoy a higher position in

1. Joan Bergós, *Antoni Gaudí, l'home i l'obra* (Barcelona: 1954), p. 14.

2. Guix, *op. cit.*, p. 35. Notarial declaration of Vicente Gaudí Jauma, the architect's nephew; that Gaudí was born in Reus «although they took him to Riudoms when he was very little.»

3. Bergós, *op. cit.*, p. 14.

4. José F. Ráfols, *Antonio Gaudí* (Barcelona: 1929), p. 10.

5. Eduardo Toda, «Records d'Antoni Gaudí a Reus, fins l'any 1870.» *El Matí*, June 21, 1936.

6. Ráfols, *op. cit.*, p. 9.

7. Elías, *op. cit.*, p. 29.

4. The cloister of the convent of San Francisco in Reus which was converted in 1866 into the secondary school where Gaudí studied. The future architect is among this group of students accompanied by several professors.

society, even at the cost of economic strain. Moreover, obtaining a secondary education in Reus in those days was no great problem. In 1858 the «Escuela Pía» had been established, and two years later it began to function as an Institute of Secondary Education incorporated with the one in Tarragona [8] so that official examinations could be taken at the Institute in Reus, thus saving the parents the cost of room and board away from home.

Once his elementary education was over, Gaudí's father, always thinking of his sons' future, set to work to make conditions favorable for both to pursue advanced studies if they felt up to it. As his older brother Francisco had done, Antonio entered secondary school—a year beyond the legal age, perhaps because of his less than robust childhood. He probably began his studies without any preconceived idea of what he wanted to be. At eleven years he was still too young to choose a vocation although we can assume that several were suggested to him. The natural development of his intelligence and the diversity of the studies typical of secondary education, with their various difficult and attractive aspects, would serve as the compass to orient him in his choice.

Although we have found only vague references to Gaudí's primary schooling, the archives of the Institute of Tarragona provide us with valuable data by which we can follow the next stages of our student with certainty (Appendix I). In 1863 he applied for and was granted an entrance exam to the secondary level (on September 14.) He was questioned about Christian doctrine, Castilian grammar and arithmetic; he answered correctly and was admitted to the first year class. [9]

Gaudí registered for the year, listing himself in his application as a native of Reus, living at No. 4 on the Calle San Vicente, fourth floor, first door. He gave as his guarantor (a necessity for all schools in those days) the Scolapian father Valentín Oliver, who had served as secretary on his examining board. In the first two years he earned average grades, suspending arithmetic the first year and failing it in the following September. He was suspended in Descriptive Geography the second year, but received a passing grade the following September. His registration card for the second year gives his home address as No. 8 Calle San Juan, with his father serving as guarantor (September 14, 1864).

When he reached the third year he came to life, perhaps influenced by the example of his companions Eduardo Toda and José Ribera, both of whom had the same classes and outstanding grades, and with whom Gaudí formed an inseparable trio. That year [10] he received grades of «Notable» («Remarkable») and «Sobresaliente» («Outstanding») in Geometry and Arithmetic, «Notablemente Aprovechado» («Remarkably Diligent») in Arithmetic Principles, and a surprising «Notablemente Aprovechado» («Extremely proficient») in Greek, an omen of his special but well-concealed inclination for letters. The next year he maintained this with «Notablemente Aprovechado» in Psychology, Descriptive Geography, World History, Rhetoric, and Poetics and «Bueno» («Good») in Religion and Ethics.

The fifth year [11] he only took three subjects in Reus: Mathematics «Notablemente Aprovechado» and Christian Doctrine and History with a simple «Aprobado» («Passed»). The other two subjects, Natural History and Elementary Physics, were taken the next year in the Institute of Barcelona. In order for him to transfer there, his father had requested the son's transcript on September 16, 1868. [12] The reason for the transfer is not clear, nor is the reason why he would spend an entire year for only these two subjects unless it was that he already had to support himself in his fifth year. His friend Toda noted that Gaudí's family had some trouble financing two professional students. [13]

We must note, however, that by the next year that difficulty was resolved. We must also remember that Isabel II was dethroned in 1868—a fact which both that year and the next had grave repercussions in Reus.

These two subjects necessary to finish his secondary education were passed by Gaudí as a special student at the Institute of Barcelona in June of 1869, the first subject on the third and the second on the 25th. [14]

8. Calasanz Bau, *Historia de las Escuelas Pías en Cataluña* (Barcelona: 1951), p. 351.

9. As a curiosity, we transcribe the set of questions for this exam which is contained in the school record, in Appendix I.

10. He gives as his address Calle San Vicente, 4, and his guarantor is Ramón Mañé, on September 14, 1865.

11. In his registration application of September 7, 1867, his father served as his guarantor and it simply says, «living in Reus» without specifying an address.

12. In the documents contained in this record, Gaudí's Reusian birth is expressed in his own hand or that of his father.

13. Toda, *op. cit.*

14. Archive of the «Instituto Jaime Balmes» in Barcelona. Minutes of the exam for the year 1868-1869. These minutes only give those passed and those suspended.

III. REUS AND THE CAMPO DE TARRAGONA

7. THE CITY (Figs. 5-8)

Gaudí's exam grades testify to the reputation for being good students that was enjoyed by the Gaudí-Ribera-Toda trio.[1] But this did not prevent the three friends from finding time to roam around Reus and the surrounding countryside with an eagerness natural to adolescent boys «discovering» the world.

By age 16 Gaudí's preference for art had become apparent. He discovered this slowly, in the classroom and after school, perhaps more the latter than the former. Toda reports[2] that the inseparable trio loved to wander through the Reusian countryside: the river beds, roads, beautiful landscapes, all evoking the romantic sentiments then in vogue. While Ribera and Toda composed poems or prose in a literary vein, Gaudí was attracted by the ruins of the Roman kilns on the road to Monterols—the so-called «clergymen's trail»—or other such places where art and nature joined forces.

Gaudí exhibited no inclination toward literature, and his two friends never knew him to write a word. When, in 1867, the three had the idea of publishing a little magazine, *El Arlequín,* of which they finally put out ten handwritten issues in «printings» of twelve copies each, Gaudí wanted only to be in charge of the illustrations which he engraved in wood and printed as if with a stamp and pad. Whenever he was asked to take part in amateur theatricals set up in the garrets or patios of his friends' houses he would only volunteer to paint the decorations on strips of old newspaper to be mounted on bamboo poles. They could never get him out onto the stage, not even as a member of the chorus. This consistent anti-exhibitionism as well as a disdain for popular literature lasted throughout his lifetime, to the point that he always opposed having his picture taken and he employed the word «literary» in a pejorative sense.

The boy, sickly and perhaps introverted from his early childhood days, began to communicate; according to Toda who listened to him eagerly, he loved to talk about art, the only subject which seems to have really interested him.[3] In his youthful activities we can already detect traits that were to characterize him in later life, such as his *independence* and his *feeling for «place»:* he knew where he could best fit in, given his particular temperament and aptitudes. His *plastic sensitivity* was manifest in a preference for visible and material things; his *manual dexterity* prompted him to engrave the illustrations for *El Arlequín* and in his late years to fashion figure models of extreme intricacy, in wire; and his *genius at synthesis* co-ordinated the multiple observations of his everyday life toward a specific end.

Of all of these qualities—which we will examine more closely later—Gaudí gave prime importance to the gift of synthesis which, he claimed, grew keener over the years. He also stated that this, like all of the other qualities, came to him through the combination of light, atmosphere, and landscape which formed the setting for the development of his first impressions. The Reus of his childhood was for him a world in miniature: there he found on a reduced scale everything that existed in the real world, and his observations provided him with valuable lessons in reality.[4]

The country hikes which Toda mentions had their urban counterpart in the street ramblings to which he also makes reference. In my essay *The Reusian Roots of Gaudí's Work,*[5] I have mentioned the endless number of observations which he made in these formative years and which produced in him a precocious understanding of life's many facets. From his everyday environment he learned such things as how, after multiple and varied processes, the tender shoots of hemp were converted into the tough soles of sandals, how wheat became bread; how cast iron was turned into machinery; clay on the potter's wheel into pitchers and other vessels; the skins of pressed grapes into alcohol in the complicated distilleries which his father manufactured. One of his uncles, who was a turner by trade, could make pieces of wood into beautiful banisters, just as stones and bricks could be turned into houses, as if in a game of masons.[6]

With such activities in plain sight during his early days in Reus, we can be sure that—Gaudí's character being what it was—by the time he was fifteen he had learned all of those technical lessons about how things worked that could possibly be drawn from his immediate experience.

If he was attracted by the utilitarian aspects of everyday life, he had even greater reason to admire the works of art which past ages had accumulated in his tiny city, such as the Gothic church of San Pedro, at that time disguised on the interior along Renaissance lines, with rich Baroque reredoses and a Gothic campanile. He admired the palatial homes of the March, Bor-

1. Toda, *op. cit.* I know Toda's scholastic record which abounds in «sobresalientes»; I am not familiar with Ribera's which I imagine to have been similar.

2. *Ibid.*

3. Eduardo Toda i Güell. *El Doctor Josep Ribera y Sans* (Escornalbou: 1930), p. 6.

4. César Martinell, *La raíz reusense en la obra de Gaudí* (Reus: 1952), pp. 275 ff. This book won the Reus Reading Center Contest for that year.

5. Cited in previous note.

6. These and other crafts and occupations indicated in the text were visible to all in Gaudí's Reus of the 1860's, just as they were in the neighboring city of Valls during my adolescent years at the beginnings of the present century.

5. The hollow-centered spiral staircase of the Reus campanile which was imitated in the Sagrada Familia Church.

6. Lower part of the sumptuous *camarín* of the Virgin of Mercy in Reus, a work of the 18th-century sculptor Luis Bonifás whom Gaudí admired.

7. The Reus bell tower with its separate entrance from the street —in case of public disturbances, according to the young Gaudí's notes.

rás, and Bofarull families, the last sumptuously decorated by the painter Pedro Pablo Montaña; the Courthouse by the architect Pujades; the Sanctuary of the Misericordia with its richly sculptured *camarín*, the work of the sculptor Bonifás—a splendorous setting which Gaudí would remember in his later years as a work of art of unsurpassed elegance. [7]

8. AN EXULTANT COUNTRYSIDE (Figs. 9, 10)

All of Gaudí's early observations were made through an atmosphere of light and color which, as he was completely immersed in it at the time, he could not fully appreciate. But it became part of his being, and later when he was older and looked back on it he never tired of reminiscing and never ceased to feel homesick for it: the ambience of reddish earth, green hazelnut trees and plentiful vineyards, the silvery olive trees contrasting with the evergreen shrubbery, and the luminous blue of the Mediterranean in the distance.

For Gaudí, the urban district of Reus with all of its complexity and activity was simply the center of a whole fertile zone of vegetation and light that extended far out from the city, marked

7. Martinell, *Conversaciones con Gaudí...*, p. 56.

8. Present-day remains of one of the Roman pottery kilns near Reus which Gaudí enjoyed visiting in his adolescence.

9. The «Puente del Diablo» aqueduct, one of the many examples of Roman architecture preserved in the Campo de Tarragona.

here and there with small towns, country homes, and streams. There was the Riudoms of his infancy, the robust walled town of Alcover, with a Romanesque church containing beautiful examples of Gothic painting and handicrafts, the villages of Morell, Borges, Alforja, the last with a tall bell tower, and the Hermitage of San Antonio. He probably extended his excursions into the Priorato as far as the mountains of Arbolí, Mussara, Cornudella, the Montsant range and Ciurana; and most certainly as far as Masroig where his parents had property.

The first time that he returned from the Priorato, his eyes filled with mountains and hills which seemed to be a succession of geological waves, he discovered the exultant beauty of the Campo de Tarragona that opened at his feet as he came over the «Coll Negre» with all its own inimitable richness and delicacy of color. He would have seen Reus in the foreground, and beyond it Tarragona with Salou to the right—all bordered by the blue sea meeting the sky: the granddaughters of the ancient *Reddis, Tarraco,* and *Salauris* surrounded by those same beauteous delights which were sung by the poet Martial, who valued them higher than those of Rome.

As he descended to the plain, those diaphanous colors, pure vibrations of light, would become tangible and full of life. The panorama takes on detail and substance. Tarragona attracted him; he submerged himself in that imprecise note of color which, from the top of the «Coll Negre», looked like a bouquet of flowers on a blue mantle, and entered the cathedral with its classical volumes and Mediterranean light; he roamed along the golden tonalities of the so-called «Cyclopean» walls, the Iberian ones, and the Roman ones; Pilate's Castle, the Chapel of San Pablo; further on, the Tower of the Two Scipios and the arch of Bará, and closer by, the Roman aqueduct—the «Devil's Aqueduct» (Fig. 9)— and the ancient fortifications of Salou, very close to Reus.

Without leaving the Campo de Tarragona he could see examples of art and architecture which awaken the innate sensibility in one's soul. But perhaps most of all he was attracted by the sight of the sea. In the sea he found a synthesis of space, beauty, and movement which he equated with life. In the water one could see, all at once, the two dimensions of surface, and the third of depth which reflected the sky, all in motion and bathed in «that light» which he would remember for the rest of his life and never find anywhere else. [8]

In addition to its luminosity, the Campo de Tarragona had in its favor a nearness of the Mediterranean; furthermore, six centuries of Roman domination had left the natives with certain ethnic characteristics which included an especial clarity of vision. Gaudí was especially proud of this natural aptitude which he said came to him from his Tarragonese origin.[9]

9. SQUALLS (Fig. 11)

This peaceful pocket of tranquility and light did not always remain so pacific. The weather was not without its gray and rainy days, and strong gusts of wind often shook the trees while heavy rains inundated the land. At the same time these were a blessing, for they irrigated the land and purified the atmosphere. Gaudí never mentioned to me the possible effects of

8. Gaudí's own statement, repeated on several occasions.

9. During the 11 years in which I knew Gaudí, from 1915 when I was still a student, to 1926 when he died. I heard him comment several times on this subject which appears in various places in my already mentioned book, *Conversaciones con Gaudí.*

these tempestuous periods of squalls and storms on his character or on the moral fiber of his countrymen—frank, independent, concise in their speech, and imaginative—each carrying inside, perhaps, his own potential storm. These storms, while they exist, rarely come to the surface for they are subdued by the ethnic Romanism and the luminosity of the atmosphere. An ordinarily peaceful country, it will rebel against injustice and oppression, and in popular uprisings the people of the country are outstanding for their fearlessness and independence.

10. PRIM

In precisely the same decade that Gaudí was pursuing his secondary education, Reus took on a special significance in Spanish politics, due to the personality of General Prim, also a native of that town. On the 18th of September, 1868, two days after the student Gaudí had applied for a transfer of credits to Barcelona, Prim, returned from exile, proclaimed in Cádiz the end of the reign of Queen Isabella II, as a prelude to the revolution which would indeed dethrone her before the end of the month. [10] Once the Revolutionary Junta which was to direct the progress of the «revolution of salvation» amid looting, fires, and assassinations was constituted in Reus, there followed a wave of secularism which suppressed all outward signs of religion; the first civil marriage in Spain was celebrated at that time, and the Escuela Pía was converted into a lay institute.

At that same time another Reusian native, the painter Fortuny, was conquering Paris with the success of his painting «The Vicarage.» On the 27th of December, 1870, Prim died, treacherously assassinated, having brought the House of Savoy to the Spanish throne.

This contrasting array of symbolic events, some bloody, some joyful, against the rainbow-colored backdrop of the polychrome light of the Reusian countryside, set the stage for Gaudí, when in the years between 16 and 18 he prepared himself to take his place in the world.

10. Panoramic view of the Campo de Tarragona whose light and coloring were so often praised by Gaudí.

11. A strong southwester on the Campo de Tarragona. Drawing by José Pons.

10. Ferran Soldevila, *Història de Catalunya* (Barcelona: 1926), p. 1368.

IV. THE RUINS OF POBLET

11. INCIPIENT VOCATION
12. ILLUSORY RESTORATION
13. VOCATION DECIDED

11. INCIPIENT VOCATION (Fig. 12)

Within this world saturated with political inquietude, the interior world of the future architect was also in a state of unrest. He had almost earned his secondary school diploma, and for any conscientious student, the termination of these studies represented a definite responsibility as well as a relative liberation. Ended was the preparatory stage which readied him to start along the professional path which he would follow for the rest of his life.

His father was a coppersmith, and his older brother was studying to be a doctor, a rather naturally chosen career. Gaudí felt that he would like to become an architect; the idea came to him little by little, but with conviction.

When José Ribera moved to Reus in 1865, he came from Espluga de Francolí where his father had been teaching since 1860; [1] he therefore was acquainted with the Cistercian monastery of Poblet, 3 kilometers from Espluga, which at that time was abandoned. Its deteriorating state of ruin had impressed the boy so much that he could not forget it on moving to Reus. On coming across architectural vestiges in their rambles through the country, he would frequently tell his friends of its abandoned magnificence. Through his enthusiastic commentaries he revealed to his two Reusian companions the importance of the famous monastery and the necessity for immediate action.

1. Toda, *El Doctor Josep Ribera...*, p. 7.

12. Preparatory drawing in watercolor for the restoration of Poblet which was not carried out. Executed from an outline map drawn up for legal purposes without correct measurements or proportions.

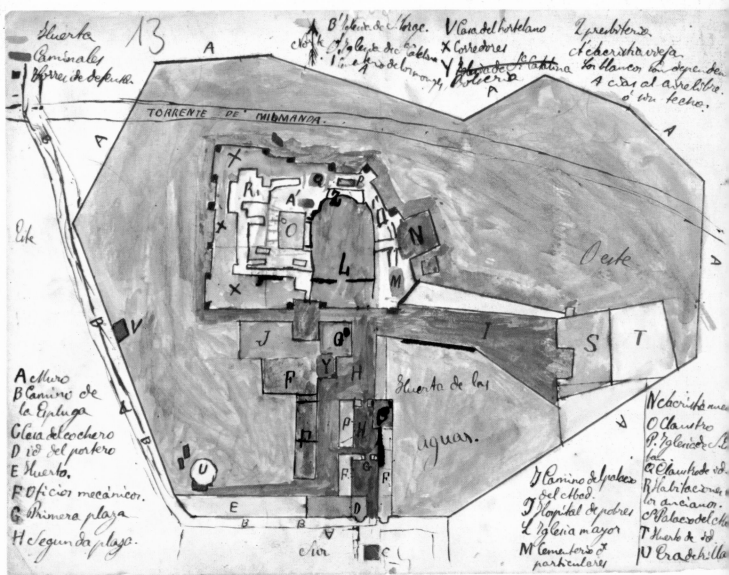

13. The lantern and the back part of the ruined monastery of Poblet which the future architect planned to restore when still in high school.

14. Tombstone of the Abbot Alferic of Poblet, now in the capitular hall, as restored by Gaudí and his friends Toda and Ribera.

This awakened their desire to visit the monastery, something they were able to do in the summer of 1867 on the invitation of one of Ribera's sisters who continued to live in Espluga after the death of the father. [2]

12. ILLUSORY RESTORATION (Fig. 13)

The vision of the imposing ruins invaded by vegetation which repossessed the patios, walls, and half-fallen vaults, so impressed the three friends that they swore in their generous adolescent enthusiasm to spare no effort necessary to achieve total restoration.

Given the age of the protagonists—Gaudí was 15 as was Ribera, and Toda was a year and a half younger—the project was pure illusion, yet it is interesting for us to examine. The three boys from 13 to 15 years in age proposed to restore Poblet, and took the restoration as the basis for a whole model town which we will discuss later * (XXXVI-155). The future architect was put in charge of the material reconstruction of the walls and vaults. Ribera was to research the history in order to arouse public interest, and Toda was to assemble an archive and library as well as to write a monograph, the profit from which would provide the capital to begin the work [3] (Appendix II).

Before leaving Poblet, they began their restoration work by putting together the fragments of the tombstone of the Abbot Alferic which they found scattered about the capitular hall. The restoration has survived to this day (Fig. 14).

13. VOCATION DECIDED

It is easy to imagine how the spectacular abandoned ruins would impress the three youths, especially Gaudí. The crumbling vaults and arches revealed in skeletal form the mechanics of architectural structure which he had never seen so explicitly in well-preserved buildings. The dramatic effect of such desolation impelled him to intervene. He imagined himself confronted with a dying person who called out for help. A case of burning architectural passion: without title or formal studies, but laden with juvenile optimism, he began to work. He himself would attribute to that month of July 1867 the beginning of his professional activity —beginning with nothing less than the prodigious restoration of the ruins of Poblet. From this moment on he was an anointed architect. All that was left were the tedious academic studies, and even they could not deter him nor dampen his enthusiasm.

Needless to say, the illusions remained in the project stage. Toda reports that of the three friends only Gaudí remained in Reus, firm in his plans for Poblet which he revised every day in order to make execution more easy. [4] In November, 1870, he was still in his native city and wrote the following letter to his friend:

«Señor Eduardo Toda.

Dear Friend: Greetings.

Don't be surprised that I haven't written, because as you might imagine, I have had nothing to say; but I write you now so that you can let me know what has become of Ribera, and whether you have told him of our plans, which hopefully he has not turned cold on, though I'm not sure.

When you write you can tell me how things are there, now that you've seen the place ,but don't do as you did with the paintings of Goya where you neither described them nor gave me your opinion.

Early this month Bassedas left to study in Zaragoza.

I have nothing more to say since nothing much of importance has occurred here, except for what happened with Quichu, which you must already know about from other people here.

Regards from my brother. I remain at your disposition,

Antonio Gaudí.

Reus, November 26, 1870.

P. S. Write about the student situation.» [5]

The three restoration enthusiasts slowly abandoned the undertaking. Gaudí embraced the idea for two whole years, but once left alone and absorbed by other obligations, he realized how illusory the idea had been, and he too finally gave it up. [6]

The generous spirit with which Gaudí planned to carry out the restoration of Poblet loses some importance in retrospect when we consider the transcendental catalytic influence which Poblet may have exercised on him, revealing once and for all the indeflectable architectural urge which Gaudí carried within himself.

---

* Reference to other parts of this book is indicated by chapter and section, in roman and arabic numerals, in parentheses.

2. Toda, «Records d'Antoni Gaudí...,» says that this excursion took place in 1869. Nevertheless, in Ribera's biography published in 1930 he says that his friend left for Almería to pursue his studies in 1867, the year in which the trip was probably made.

3. Toda, op cit.

4. Toda, El Doctor Josep Ribera..., p. 16.

5. Toda, «Records d'Antoni Gaudí...» Toda explains that Bassedas and Quichu mentioned in the letter were a schoolmate and a controversial local politician, and «the student situation» referred to university disturbances in favor of the candidacy of Amadeo of Savoy for king of Spain. This letter is the first known document written by Gaudí after that of the Memorial for the restoration of Poblet which was a collaborative effort.

6 When the government undertook this restoration years later, the near octogenarian Toda headed it as president of the foundation which was formed for that purpose.

14. AT THE SCHOOL OF SCIENCES (Fig. 15)

After he passed the two subjects that he needed for his diploma in Barcelona in June of 1869, Gaudí returned to Reus for his summer vacation. He was caught unaware by renewed political disturbances which kept him from returning to Barcelona during the registration period for the School of Sciences—which ended September 30—where he wanted to enroll in those subjects which were prerequisites for admission to the School of Architecture.

When he finally reached the city on October 11, he went immediately to the ancient Convento del Carmen on the street of the same name, which with its beautiful Renaissance and Gothic cloisters then served as the University, in order to draw up a petition for late admission, since «political circumstances» had not permitted him to make the journey in time. [1] In the petition, written in his own hand, he states that he is 17 years old, a native of Reus, and that he wishes to study those subjects necessary to enter the architecture program. Admission was granted and he was enrolled in Advanced Algebra, Geometry, Trigonometry, and Analytical Geometry.

In the year 1871 the student Gaudí passed Differential Calculus, Integral Calculus, and Descriptive Geometry, but suspended Rational Mechanics, a course which he did not pass until 1874.

During the 1871-72 school year he passed Natural History, Advanced Algebra, Plane and Solid Trigonometry, and Plane and Solid Analytical Geometry, and on September 25, 1873, he requested a certificate of approbation for these subjects along with those of Descriptive Geometry and Calculus which, as we have seen, he had passed in 1871, with the intention of entering the School of Architecture.

1. University Archive of the School of Sciences, (App. III).

15. Entrance to the now-demolished convent of the Carmelitas in Barcelona which was converted into the University and the School of Sciences when Gaudí attended the latter from 1869 to 1872. Water-color by Soler y Rovirosa.

15. AN ERRATIC STUDENT

In this phase of his life, the great architect's independent personality began to appear in his frank manner, dissenting as he did whenever room was not allowed for his opinions and intuitively revising taken-for-granted methods of procedure. He admitted in principle the validity of the program of studies by which he was to broaden the basic knowledge of his secondary school training. Being a conscientious student, he understood the advantages, and even the necessary character, of what he was studying, but his temperament led him to favor the artistic disciplines over those which were more theoretical in nature. Abstractions bored him; he could not bear them. For Gaudí, Analytical Geometry which converted the geometric plasticity of forms into algebraic formulas—«abstractions of abstractions,» he called them—was pure torture. He himself confessed that when the professors would expound theoretical «doctrine» he was bored, but when they stuck to concrete practical material he would listen with enthusiasm.

Gaudí once said that he never went beyond Elementary Geometry, and that he intuited the geometric properties of masses through his innate three-dimensional vision. This need not be taken literally. It is obvious that in his Advanced Geometry class he naturally and without difficulty grasped the concepts which the professor explained, but in the classroom he was able, in addition, to pull together the loose ends of his knowledge. There were several professors whose observations and suggestions left their mark on his architectural formation.

He remembered especially one of the professors with whom he studied when he was 18. It was under his influence that Gaudí was attracted to the geometry of warped surfaces, which he would later employ with amazing results. He once told me: «He was a very good professor and a friend of Monge. He didn't explain all of the properties of such surfaces because he didn't know them, but he had a definite feeling for them and explained what he did know with such enthusiasm that it was contagious.» [2] This memory of his school days, 54 years later, indicates that he followed his classes with interest—when in attendance.

2. Martinell, *Conversaciones con Gaudí*, p. 85. Monge was a famous geometrician who developed the study of Descriptive Geometry by means of a system of projections which is still followed today.

16. THE OLD STOCK EXCHANGE (Fig. 16)

When Gaudí sought admission to the Provincial School of Architecture, in September, 1873, it was still functioning on the second floor of the Neo-classic Stock Exchange building, (La Lonja) and it was there that he presented his certificate of prerequisites, lacking Rational Mechanics which he had suspended in June and September, 1871.

Nevertheless, he was admitted to the School to take courses in Line and Figure Drawing, additional prerequisites for admission, both of which he passed in September, 1874. At the same time he finally passed the pending Rational Mechanics class at the School of Sciences which cleared the way for his full admission to Architecture School.

From the transcript which is preserved in the School archives, we see that besides the two mentioned drawing courses he also passed the first-year course in Drawing of Architectural Groupings which put him two years ahead of his entering class in this respect; it seems remarkable that he was even allowed to take this exam. The next September he passed the preparatory-year subjects of Plaster Casting and Architectural Detailing in the School of Architecture.

These five passing marks in design in only two exam periods demonstrate Gaudí's artistic aptitudes as well as the fact that he entered his new professional studies on the right foot.

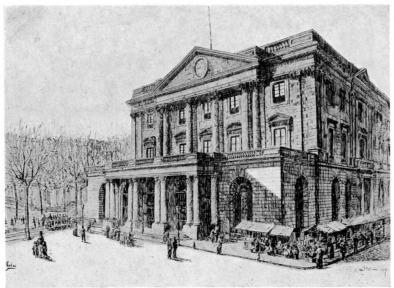

16. Exterior view of the Casa Lonja (Stock Exchange building) where Gaudí studied his first years of Architecture, 1873-1875. From an engraving of the period.

17. The new University building where the School of Architecture was located from 1875 until 1962. In the early days classes were held in the second floor of the clock-tower and in the adjoining classrooms.

17. THE NEW UNIVERSITY (Fig. 17)

The Board of Public Instruction in Madrid had ordered the transfer of the School of Achitecture from the old building to the new in March, 1874, but certain difficulties in the Barcelona Provincial Commission, on which the school depended more directly, delayed the move so that it only took place a year after the inauguration of the new building. In the beginning, the director, Rogent, held his Projects class on the second floor of the clock-tower, according to Buenaventura Bassegoda who was a student there in the years 1884-1886. [1] And so Gaudí realized the greater part of his professional studies in that part of the Neo-medieval building.

During these years he continued the formula of rebellion which we have observed in the School of Sciences, but in this new stage his personality became more concretely defined. For Gaudí, passion always took precedence over discipline, and on entering the School his passion for architecture was clearly apparent. What before could have been a simple interest was now firmly oriented toward a preconceived goal.

He was passionately fond of certain of his studies, and the architectural library established in the School was a spiritual feast. [2] Gaudí never tired of reading and re-reading books concerned with imposing buildings which he retained in his mind as if he had actually seen them. Several conjectural ideas which he had kept to himself were now brought to the surface and encouraged, and he set forth new problems to be solved.

Gaudí avidly studied the dictionaries of French architecture and furniture by Viollet-le-Duc, which were then quite novel. The first impressed him deeply as is apparent in certain details of his early works. The book *Carpintería de lo Blanco* by López de Arenas also influenced him, with its drawings of *mudéjar* pattern work which was supposed to have had its source in the School of Alexandria and later spread by the Arabs. After school he attended the Philosophy classes of Llorens y Barba and the Esthetics lectures of Milá y Fontanals. He visited monuments in the city on trips organized by Rogent—visits which he would continue on his own after finishing his course work, extending them to monuments in other parts of Catalonia and Southern France. He enjoyed theater and the opera and was fond of reading the classics. [3]

As a student, Gaudí acquired a solid cultural basis for his aptitudes and inclinations, and already showed promise for the future. He himself began to have presentiments of things to come, but without vanity. His profound knowledge of certain subjects did not alienate him from his fellow students, and despite his modest dress, borrowed books, and free hours spent drafting, he appears to have been jovial and smiling. [4] According to his classmate Joaquín Bassegoda, he had a wild character and enjoyed a good joke; he told his own and would laugh heartily in response to those related to him, especially those with clever double meanings—whatever their color. [5]

He was a student of unquestionable merit, but nevertheless, because of his lack of discipline, his academic performance had its ups and downs. His self-confidence seems to have protected him from being ashamed of his suspensions. He later commented on this characteristic, rating himself as a «bad student.» [6]

He recalled that almost all of his professors «had flunked him.» Or course, such a recollection at the height of his fame could have reflected more a lack of understanding on the part of the professors than a lack of intelligence on the part of the student, but that was not Gaudí's intention for he made it clear that the suspensions were justified since he did not study those subjects that he disliked. It has been said that he gloried in these suspensions, even to the point of requesting a certificate for them. This is certainly hard to believe. He simply did not care one way or the other.

1. B. Bassegoda y Amigó, *El arquitecto Elías Rogent* (Barcelona: 1929), p. 61. The other classes were given in the neighboring classrooms.

2. Bergós, *op. cit.*, p. 17.

3. *Ibid.*, p. 18.

4. *Ibid.*

5. Lluís Bonet Garí, «L'espiritualitat en l'arquitectura de Gaudí,» *Critèrion* n.º 23, p. 42.

6. Martinell, *Conversaciones con Gaudí*, p. 70.

18. Apse of the Church of Montserrat by the architect Villar y Lozano. Gaudí worked as a draftsman on the plans in late 1876.

18. A SALARIED DRAFTSMAN (Fig. 18)

Gaudí had to work to support himself, and it even appears that the family's limited means necessitated the sale of some of his mother's property to pay for his studies in Barcelona. Bergós says [7] that during the first year of his academic career he worked with Don Francisco de P. Villar, a professor at the School, having formerly worked as a draftsman for the firm Padrós and Borrás. His classmates had the impression that he worked to help his parents economically. [8] The places of residence listed in his school record corroborate this modesty of means. [9]

In addition to the mentioned bibliographical references, we have access to a primary document which gives us an idea of how Gaudí played his double role of student and draftsman in his last years of architecture school, torn between the obligation to attend classes and the necessity to work in order to make his life easier. This document consists of several handwritten notes jotted down hastily in pencil (which makes several of the phrases illegible) in a notebook which is preserved in the Reus Municipal Museum. In these he recorded his hours of work for various professional architects during the period from November 21 or 22, 1876, to the sixth of January of the following year (Appendix IV).

From these notes we infer that he was not so unconcerned about attending his classes at the School as he would have us believe in his later recollections alluding to his student days; they reflect an intensive and heterogeneous extra-curricular activity, working primarily for Fontseré and Villar at the same time, as well as for Serrallach and the already mentioned firm of Padrós and Borrás.

Besides his work as a draftsman, the notes indicate the young Gaudí's involvement in official business and his sense of responsibility for the jobs that were entrusted to him. On recording two and one half hours of work for Serrallach on «a summer house,» he warns that «much work is necessary to get out of trouble.» It is most probable that this phrase refers concretely to his work as a draftsman, rather than to the future architect's economic difficulties as one writer has suggested.

19. A FORTUITOUS EXAM

During the 1874-75 school year, Gaudí worked for the *maestro de obras* (master builder) José Fontseré Mestre, director of the works at the Ciudadela Park then under construction, who entrusted to the student the continuation of a project involving the calculation of a water depository which had been begun by another assistant. [10] The latter had copied the calculations of a depository in Lyon, France, from a French magazine. Gaudí, however, felt that the French solution was not applicable in this case and preferred to set up and solve the problem in his own way. Fontseré did not trust the scanty experience of his young employee,

7. *Op. cit.*, p. 19.

8. Ráfols, *op. cit.*, p. 16.

9. In addition to the addresses already mentioned of his preparatory years, we can add that in the 1873-74 school year he lived at 2 bis Calle de Copons where he continued living alone with his parents the next year, once his brother had finished his studies. When he finished his own studies he lived at 11 Calle de Call, third floor, and shortly thereafter we find him living with his father at number 370, Consejo de Ciento, on the fourth floor.

10. Ráfols and Bergós say in their cited works that this deposit was that of the cascade in the Park of the Ciudadela. This may have been so, although the deposit was separate from the cascade itself. When he told me the story, he did not identify the deposit in question. *Conversaciones con Gaudí*, p. 70.

19. Project for the central patio in a building to be used by a Provincial Government. School project by Gaudí.

and asked the architect Juan Torras, professor of Resistance of Materials at the School of Architecture, for his opinion of the calculations. The latter found the study to be correct and was curious to know the name of the author.

That very year, Gaudí was enrolled in Resistance of Materials, but he seldom attended class; nevertheless, the professor found so much merit in the depository project that he considered it worthy of a passing grade, and he made a note to grant him such at the end of the course after a token exam.

This was in June, 1875, during his second year of Architecture School when he was almost 23. Bergós says that when he worked as an assistant to Villar he was still in his first year. When we consider his age and experience it becomes clear that the work of Gaudí in the offices of these established professionals was more that of an inferior subordinate than that of an adjunct director as has been supposed by some.

20.   PROJECTS CLASS (Figs. 19 - 24)

In the theoretical subjects with their formulas and derivations of remote importance to him, our student was rather indolent; such was not the case with the more artistic subjects to which he devoted himself with enthusiasm. He was particularly fond of Projects class which served to summarize the content of each year's courses. We have already seen that he received a mark of «Outstanding» in his first year of Projects. Ráfols relates the anecdote that on a project for a cemetery gate (Fig. 20) which was given them as an exam theme, Gaudí was suspended for having paid more attention to the funeral procession and to the coffin than to the architecture. We will discuss this project later (XXXVI-156).

If the anecdote is true, he may have been reprimanded, but not suspended. Although Ráfols does not indicate the year, we must guess that it was the second since he was «outstanding» the first year, and we will look at his third year project shortly. The humorous story reveals the student's deep self-confidence and even a youthful euphoria as a result of his first year

20.   School project for a cemetery entrance.

21.   Cascade of the Parque de la Ciudadela, often mistakenly attributed to Gaudí, but actually the work of José Fontseré with some assistance by Gaudí.

mark, a state of mind which also led him to compete for the second year prize—something he would not have been able to do in the case of a suspension.

In order to compete for the prize, a student had to have received a mark of «Outstanding» on his project. As he did not receive such a high mark that year, he petitioned the director requesting re-examination in second-year Projects «which was passed last June, in order to attempt to better the mark in hopes of entering the competition should the attempt be successful.» [11] He was allowed to take the exam in September, but only received a «Notable», and was therefore disqualified for the prize competition.

This indicates that Gaudí did not disdain academic honors, and also is proof of his application and enthusiasm: he was eager to take a second exam despite his extra work as a draftsman and his service in the Military Administrative Service which he was doing at the same time.

21. MILITARY SERVICE

Gaudí became eligible for military service in July, 1874. [12] From documents in the School archives we know that this service kept him from taking his Applied Mechanics and Stereotomy exams during the first exam period in June, 1875, but on the 23rd of the same month, having been given leave to attend to his academic affairs, he asked to be allowed to take exams in those subjects. Later, on September 30 of the same year he petitioned the director asking to be allowed to pay the second half of his registration fee in Art Theory which he was unable to do on time «due to being completely tied up in the military service to which he

11. Archive of the Escuela Técnica Superior de Arquitectura de Barcelona.
12. Ráfols, op. cit., p. 21.

22. Comprehensive Exam project for a university auditorium, in the archives of the School of Architecture of Barcelona.

PARANINFO.

23. Detail of the paintings in the cupola of the previous project.

24. Student project for a monumental fountain in the Plaza de Cataluña which is preserved in the archives of the Architecture School.

is subject [*sic*], but which now allows me to do so.» We know from Ráfols that he went into the Tortosa reserve unit in January, 1879, once his studies were over.

22. A WORD FROM DIRECTOR ROGENT

In the four years from 1873-74 when Gaudí entered the School, still located in the old stock exchange building, until 1876-77, he passed those several subjects necessary for admission, the subjects of the preparatory year, and those of the three years of the professional program, all in regular June exams except for the first and second year of Projects, both of which he completed in September.

When it came to the third and final Projects exam, he was interested in passing in June, for immediately after the September exams would come the comprehensive exam which would last for three months. He was understandably anxious to avoid having two long exams so close together. The June Projects exam each year consisted in developing a theme given by the professor at the end of the course, with a time limit of one month.

That year Professor Rogent, the director of the School, had assigned a hospital project about which Gaudí was not very enthusiastic. As a result, when it came time to turn in the finished work, it was still lacking the façade. He solved this problem by taking paper home with him and finishing it in a night. This was against the academic regulations and displeased the professor. As a punishment, he passed all of the other students and held Gaudí over until September, without any special publicity. When the latter learned of this and realized that the two long exams would come back-to-back, he decided to appeal to the director, bringing to his attention the fact that what he had done was not incompatible with the purpose of the exam which was to test the students' ability. Rogent was convinced and granted him a new exam on the theme of a monumental fountain (Fig. 24), a project which merited extremely high praise from Professor Villar who was a member of the jury. [13]

With this Projects exam out of the way in June Gaudí was virtually finished with his academic curriculum (except for the comprehensive exam) a final satisfaction which he was able to give his mother before she died on September 8th of that year.

The various incidents and anecdotes which have been related illustrate the numerous problems (scholastic, financial, familial, social, bureaucratic, and temperamental) which Gaudí had to overcome before obtaining the title of architect. His comprehensive exercises were held between October 22, 1877, and January 4, 1878; his title was issued in Madrid on March 15, 1878.

In spite of the problems with suspensions and excessive regulations, Gaudí left behind a good impression at the School. We have seen the esteem in which he was held by Torras and Villar who were not the only ones to appreciate his personality, with all of its ups and downs. Even the director Rogent who had only fleeting official contact with him was impressed by his brilliant talent, and it appears that, once Gaudí was passed by a majority (it was not unanimous) on his comprehensive examination on January 4, 1878, the director told his fellow professors that they had passed «either a madman or a genius.»

13. Martinell, *op. cit.*, p. 69.

23.   AN EVENTFUL DECADE

Gaudí was an attentive student during his years at Architecture School, but at the same time both he and the university were very much involved in the affairs of the world around them. On the one hand his academic obligations demanded his attention, but on the other his youthful enthusiasm for anything new kept him up-to-date on scientific advances, new philosophical theories, and the prevailing political controversies of his day. As has already been indicated, the decade crucial to Gaudí's intellectual formation (1867 - 1877) was a period extremely rich in transcendental events for the Spanish nation.

This decade of political and labor activity was enveloped in an atmosphere of secularism and non-belief that was encouraged by the various governments, all generally hostile to the Church. Persecution in some quarters was carried to the point where theological schools were closed down and religious instruction was prohibited in the secondary schools.

Such was the ideological environment, this mixture of doubt, atheism, substitute ideals and despair, which served as the incubator for Gaudí's spirit, so eager for perfection and novelty, in his late formative years. It should also be remembered that these were the years in which free-thinking and progressive ideas were prevalent in the field of philosophy, establishing the two-pronged slogan «Freedom and Progress» which must have intellectually appealed to Gaudí, eager as he was for learning, with his sentiments inclined toward kindness and charity to those in need. Given his passionate temperament and his relative inexperience, it is logical that the young Gaudí would be swept up in the current of liberal-progressive aspirations then prevalent.

24.   A PHASE OF ANTICLERICALISM (Fig. 25)

For those of us who knew the deeply religious Gaudí of the later years, it is hard to imagine him as a restless youth with anticlerical tendencies which he is reputed to have been in his student years. Nevertheless, given the ideological ambience of the time, we can understand it as a cultural and humanitarian reaction on Gaudí's part, a logical attitude for an energetic youth with progressive ideas.

Even in adolescence, when he and his friends Toda and Ribera planned the restoration of Poblet, the three showed signs of the fashionable anticlericalism of their day in the preamble of the memorial which they composed and which is preserved in the monastery archives. At the same time they revealed their noble intentions in a paragraph in the «enfant terrible» manner betraying more a mimetic ingenuousness than a convinced commitment. They wrote: «Yes, Poblet must be restored; here nevermore must nest the ominous power of the black vultures which once devoured the mind of the Spanish people in order to eradicate the

25.   The corner where the Barcelona Rambla meets the Calle de Pelayo, site of the Café Pelayo which served as a gathering place for intellectuals. Gaudí was a frequent visitor to the Café in his early student years. From an engraving of the period in *Barcelona Retrospectiva 1800-1900*.

memory of their own evil deeds. In marked contrast with those days of old, it must now be newly elevated as the sublime temple of humanity, where Science and Art have their museums and academies, where the farmer finds his means...»

The anticlericalism which spread throughout Spain in the middle of the last century was taken up as a protest against the absolutism of Fernando VII, and against the dominant role of the clergy in the reign of his daughter—a role more political than religious. The people instinctively linked the dynasty with the clergy: thus when Isabel was dethroned, the following couplet came out:

«We have torn down the throne,
Now on to the priests
Who devour the nation
Like the wildest of beasts.»

Such were the lyrics accepted by the masses and proclaimed by progressive opinion. As progressivism took root among the young people, especially in politically advanced Reus, as we have seen (III - 10), it is not surprising that the three lads would follow the ideological current without necessarily forswearing their religious ideas; indeed, in their restoration project they did not forget the church, for which they planned to provide a set of velvet mourning curtains as well as others of damask to serve as wall hangings.

The architect Bonet Garí discussed his religiosity with Gaudí's classmate, Professor Joaquín Bassegoda, who felt that one must not give much credence to the manifestations of religious disdain so often suggested in discussing the great architect's youth. [1] Bassegoda always assumed that his dominant feelings were religious ones and never once heard him speak against religion. «He went to Christmas Eve mass at the Cathedral to hear the music of Vilanova, and he said that the music was not appropriate for the celebration of the Sacrifice.» Though the argument is admittedly weak, the testimony of a person as respected as Bassegoda is always important.

We see, then, an impetuous youth (a bit wild, Bassegoda said) who enthusiastically participated in an effervescent ideological moment that denied respect to the traditional values which were losing ground at the time.

25. THE EMBERS OF FAITH

I am certain that Gaudí never felt himself cut off from religion. His anticlerical outburst was something superimposed which could dull, but not destroy, the principles of faith which he had inherited from his elders and nourished throughout childhood and adolescence, those periods which usually leave a profound mark on one's life The story is told that when a Viaticum Holy Procession would pass by his house at night or in the early hours of the morning, the architect's father used to follow the then-common tradition of placing a light in the window in homage to the Holy Father.[2]

The feelings of his innocent boyhood days spent in the *Escuelas Pías* would come back to him from time to time, like a warning voice amidst the whirlwind of those tumultuous times. Gaudí's humanism, stimulated by the workers' movements of the period, caused him to sympathize with anything which proved beneficial to the needy classes. Thus one of his first professional jobs was for a co-operative society in Mataró called «La Obrera Mataronense» for which he drew up the plans for a meeting-house which was never built. Apparently the commission developed out of his friendship—made while still in school—with the co-operative's director who had attempted to interest Gaudí in his labor organization. Years later he would remember with admiration the impressive personality and humanitarian qualities of the director, yet Gaudí was apparently reluctant to join in his group's activities because of the director's notorious atheism, [3] proof that, despite his youthful turbulence, the embers of faith nested always in his soul.

26. SECULARISM ABANDONED

We do not know how long this phase of his youth lasted, but it must have been short-lived, for his manner and social position were soon to change as he adapted himself to the customs of high society while still maintaining for the moment, his advanced ideas.

When he took over as architect of the Sagrada Familia in 1883, his irreligiosity worried the temple's extremely devout founder, José María Bocabella, for some time. The religious nature of this work and his relationship with Bocabella and with Martorell for whom he had worked as an assistant, and later his relationship with the bishop of Astorga, Dr. Grau, were all influential in re-igniting the temporarily buried embers of his faith. When, in 1889, he became friendly with the bookseller Antonio Palau y Dulcet, the latter described him as «a humble, hard-working man of faith,» and found his manner of speaking so sweet that he imagined «Saint Francis must have spoken that way.» [4] Faith and Will had finally triumphed over the destructive elements of his temperament and ideas.

1. Bonet Garí, *loc. cit.*
2. J. M. Guix Sugrañes, «La casa natalicia de Gaudí en Reus,» *La Vanguardia* (September 14, 1965).
3. Jordi Elias, *Gaudí*, p. 51.
4. Antoni Palau i Dulcet, *Memòries d'un llibreter català* (Barcelona: 1935), p. 84.

VIII. HIS FIRST COMMISSION

We have seen that, in spite of a supposed carelessness while a student at the School of Architecture, Gaudí left behind a favorable impression of his outstanding aptitude (VI - 22). This impression of his worth went beyond the classrooms of the university. Before long he was considered to be a highly competent architect, and very few weeks after passing his comprehensive exam he received his first official commission—from the City of Barcelona. Though of little material importance, the circumstances involved made this work the pat on the back which marked his entrance into the inner sanctum of the architectural profession.

The symbolic character attributable to this first job and the abundant documents at hand [1] will permit us a detailed acquaintance with this episode in the architect's life, showing his painstaking nature, as well as a spirit of modishness which he was soon to lose.

27. HONORIFIC SUBSTITUTION

The commission in question consisted of the model for a single decorative lamppost for the city streets. This model had previously been entrusted to the painter and decorator Jaime Serra y Gibert—an artist famous for his work as well as for his academic responsibilities and distinctions—who died before he could carry out the commission. As a substitute for the respected artist, the City proposed «the young and proficient architect D. Antonio Gaudí,» whose appointment was approved on the 19th of February, 1878, and communicated to Gaudí on the 27th of that month.

The young architect, 25 years old, felt a logical satisfaction in the confidence thus shown in him, as well as a desire to be worthy of the considerable responsibility despite the relative modesty of the theme. In the documents one notes professional dignity in the desire to excel, as well as a definite interest in elevating the theme in order to give it a technical and artistic grandness far beyond its dimensions. The meticulous care taken with the plans, details, and documents in the manner of a student contrasts with the looseness evident in his last works.

28. PAINSTAKING WORK (Figs. 161, 162, 189, 190)

Accompanying his design, Gaudí submitted a watercolor drawing, at a scale of one tenth the actual size, which must have made a good impression, for it was honored with a frame and was hung on the Department's office wall. He also presented a memorial which he titled «CANDELABRA: Descriptive Notes on the Project for Grouped Candelabras for Plazas and Public Avenues of the City of Barcelona». The document is well thought-out, and one detects a desire to establish his professional standing. It begins with considerations of an urbanistic sort; then he presents judicious general observations on the use of materials, and later moves on to the description of the proposed «candelabra». He speaks of the appropriate placement of such fixtures, of their construction, and of the way they can be executed within the specified cost.

The design and the memorial were presented in June, and approved on the 17th of July. The order to build the candelabra or lamppost which was to serve as a model was given on the 29th of the same month, alloting a budget of 3.605 pesetas for the first model. On the 25th of October he was urged to speed up completion of the project as the City was in need of a lamppost to replace the one in the Plaza de San Sebastián which was in very bad condition. Gaudí was concerned about time, but even more about perfection. In spite of this on December 14 he was on the point of finishing the model which the city authorities wished to see mounted before ordering its definitive installation.

The designer of the model felt that it lacked the importance proper to a single monumental candelabra, having been projected with more thought to illumination than to monumentality. He explained this to the mayor, adding that in order to use his design effectively a minimum of two such lampposts should be installed. At the same time he apologized for having taken more time than he had expected on the model out of a desire to execute all of the details with extreme care. The authorities (who probably found the model superior to their expectations) were convinced by these arguments and ordered the construction of another candelabra for 2.000 pesetas, which was the price stipulated for successive copies, planning to put them both in the Plaza Real to replace those already there which did not meet «the esthetic conditions necessary in such a noble and heavily frequented place.»

The young architect continued his services without interruption. On the 14th of January, 1879, he presented two different projected solutions for the installation of either two or four lamp-

1. Administrative archives of the Ayuntamiento de Barcelona, certificate n.º 794. All information in this chapter is taken from this source unless otherwise indicated.

40

posts in the Plaza Real. The second had certain inconveniences, and so the first was accepted. The decision was communicated to the architect on the 31st of January.

Evidence that the clients were pleased by the lamppost can be found in the proposal made by the councilor José Denis that two of the new models be placed in the Plaza del Palacio and two more at the entrance to Barceloneta. The officials, however, felt that they were too luxurious for such commercial sites and, in accord with the architect, it was decided that for this purpose they should be simplified. Thus, the six lamps were reduced to three, the helmet and gilded decoration omitted, and the cost consequently diminished. On February 22 it was confirmed that the design of these lamps should also be entrusted to Gaudí.

Once the lampposts were ready, they were inspected and approved, and it was decided that they should be placed in the Plaza Real to be inaugurated during the forthcoming festival of the Merced. At that time they were greeted by laudatory comments from both the public and the press.

29. UNCOMPENSATED DEDICATION

From what has been said it becomes obvious that the young architect undertook his first public work with great interest, seeing to it that the various craftsmen involved carried out their work in the most perfect manner possible. His professional dignity insisted that the first of his projects to be put on public view, small as it was, should be executed with the greatest possible perfection without regard for his expenditure of effort or for personal profit, despite the extreme care put into the work.

For such carefulness Gaudí was to have been paid 336 pesetas, according to the official rate. Feeling that this amount was entirely too low for the amount of work carried out, he tried to appraise the work with the following adjustment which does not include the urbanistic projects for the Plaza Real.

Candelabra Project. Study. Watercolor in possession of the most excellent City Government. Memorial and Budget	500 pesetas
Definitive Studies for the project. Lifesize details. Idem. of Execution	800 pesetas
Direction. Details of Decoration and Auxiliary Apparatus and Supervision	900 pesetas
Budget Distribution	100 pesetas
Total	2300 pesetas

Public administration being a serious business, the bill had to proceed through required channels. As it dealt with a matter of lighting, it was sent for confirmation to the Chief Engineer, Conrado Cintas y Orfila, who, on March 3, 1880, approved the materials and execution of the candelabra. Concerning the fees, he was of the opinion that payment for a job such as this should not be regulated by prevailing tariffs, but rather by an appraisal such as the one which Gaudí had submitted, and that this bill should be sent to the Chief Architect of Building and Ornamentation for his assessment. The Chief Architect then was Antonio Rovira y Trías who, once he had studied the case, reported—on the 24th of March—that some of the items in Gaudí's statement seemed superfluous to him, estimating the fees for the project at 850 pesetas, distributed in the following manner: 350 pesetas for the project, memorial, and budget; 200 pesetas for the watercolor; and 300 pesetas for the direction of the work.

The municipal commission accepted the increase in the cost of the lampposts, and because of the «immense difference» of 1,450 pesetas between the finding of the Municipal Architect

26. Caricature placing the Gaudí lampposts of the Plaza Real, inaugurated in 1879, above the «Three Graces» group which is there, too. From satirical review, *L'Esquella de la Torratxa*.

41

27. The young Gaudí when he finished his studies and still dressed fashionably. Photograph by Audouard & Co., in the Reus Museum.

and the amount requested in the bill, they had the deference to consult with Gaudí who, on April 5, let it be known that he still felt that the amount that he had requested was only fair; but in order to «avoid delay» and argument he accepted the Municipal Architect's budget.

30. THE BEGINNING OF VALUABLE FRIENDSHIPS

From August 1878 when he was able to begin the construction of the first candelabra, until May 1880 when the last were completed, almost two years passed during which Gaudí frequented Eudaldo Puntí's carpentry workshop, a spacious shed which easily accommodated the various workmen involved in constructing the lampposts It was there that he made his professional debut, his particular way of interpreting new artistic forms and technical processes catching the attention of the workers themselves and also of several important clients on their visits to the well-equipped Puntí workshops.

The young architect, warmed by this enthusiasm and by the interest which his work had aroused, got to know several of the visitors. One of these was the proprietor of the Comella glove shop—a client of Puntí's—who commissioned Gaudí to do a display window for the Paris Exposition, to be built in this same workshop. It was there, too, that he met his future maecenas and close friend Eusebio Güell. [2]

In addition, he met the sculptor Lorenzo Matamala who, as an assistant in the workshop, modeled the ornamental parts of the lampposts. The moral and artistic character of the sculptor who was two years younger than Gaudí made a good impression and several years later, in 1885, when the architect was put in charge of the Sagrada Familia, he proposed that Matamala collaborate with him on the work on the Temple, guaranteeing him that he would be thus employed for the rest of his life. [3]

2. Communicated to me by Juan Matamala.
3. Related by the same J. Matamala who had heard it from his father Lorenzo.

31. SIGNIFICANT MANUSCRIPTS

Gaudí was not fond of writing. He himself stated this in his later years, and his friend Toda is witness to the fact during his adolescence. Nevertheless, there exist in the Museum at Reus two manuscripts which reveal a certain satisfaction in expressing his ideas on paper. These are a study of Ornamentation, and a very brief resumé of the «casa pairal» (the manorial home of the Catalan countryside) (Appendices IV, V) which, along with the Memorial for the candelabra of the Plaza Real, constitute an exception—examples of a scant literary activity of which no other evidence is known to exist. [1]

The most important of these manuscripts is that which deals with ornamental theory, and which we will be more concerned with when we study the theoretical aspect of Gaudí's architecture in Part Two. This is a thick student notebook in clearly pencilled lettering with the exception of a few final pages in ink (Appendix IV). These studies were begun on the fourth page when he was already working on the lampposts—«August 10, 1878» is noted—but the notebook contains fading notes from his student days on the preceding sheets. One of them says: «3 May '73—Decreasing Inclined Sundial,» with a drawing of this problem in Gnomonic Theory which formed part of the subject «Shadows» that he passed in the year 1874-75. On another page we read «Cascante begins December 14,» along with some notes dated 1876 which seem to refer to hours worked on what he calls «Villar's camarín.» This was probably the project of the structure of the *camarín* at Montserrat where the stonecutters began working under Villar's orders in November, 1878. This note is testimony to the fact that Gaudí was working as a draftsman for Villar in 1876, and that he was interested in noting the work of a companion, Cascante—who was to serve as the builder of El Capricho at Comillas—of whom we will have more to say in a later chapter (XXXIX - 164).

When the young architect finished his studies, perhaps having extra time on his hands, he reviewed what he had learned at the school and what he had thought and seen on his own relating to ornamentation. Perhaps stimulated by his first commissions, which were mainly ornamental in nature, he decided to make a broader study of the subject which he entitled «Ornamentation.»

He begins: «I propose to study ornamentation seriously. My goal is to make it interesting and intelligible.» This proposal to make architectural ornamentation «interesting and intelligible,» somewhere between ingenuous and conceited, would seem to indicate that what he had been taught in the school did not meet such qualifications, and that he felt it would be useful to restructure and broaden it, adding his own observations, some of which predict the later Gaudí.

These didactic concerns did not last for long: in the 67 pages filled by this study and written between August 10, 1878 and March 20, 1879, we note that the exposition diminishes as time passes. In the beginning, some concepts are tediously explained, whereas at the end, all are abbreviated.

The content is interesting. Some ideas were probably taken from student or scholarly studies. He states that «some of the ideas expressed come from Viollet-le-Duc's *Entretiens sur l'Architecture.*» At other times there are ingenious original ideas which he was later to carry into practice. His ideas of this sort can be divided into those dealing with esthetic principles and those concerning practical procedures, and will be discussed in the corresponding sections of this study.

The theme which is most extensively developed is that of the nature of the Catholic church and from his reflections on religion we can deduce an acquaintance with the articles of faith which he treats with respect. Regarding the nature of the Catholic church he says, it «tends always toward the more grandiose, for its objective is a mystery,» adding that «the time is past when faith and enthusiasm could build an infinite number of cathedrals, perhaps indicating that religious nature is a bit indecisive, that religious objects are the slaves of a profane idea—art.» He believed that the stylistic imitation of the great ancient temples responded more to «romantic ideas than religious ones, giving rise to religious protection of the art of past ages and an art which imposes itself as a style rather than an art which identifies with the religion in order to give it expression, as should be the case.»

Regarding the sculptures that decorate such buildings, he writes: «Now nothing but saints are represented, and even these are only an excuse to put up a pedestal or a little ornamental dais, i. e., a pretext to introduce an irrelevant, purely plastic form.» Such a merely

1. In 1973 Judith Rohrer discovered an actual printed article by Gaudí, hitherto unnoticed although it appeared in an influential magazine of the Catalan movement. It is a review of an exhibition of decorative arts with which he was involved (see p. 49), written in straightforward fashion, «L'Exposició d'Arts Decorativas en l'Institut del Foment del Travall Nacional», *La Renaixença,* XI, no. 51 (1 Feb. 1881), 709-11); XI, no. 53 (3 Feb. 1881), 739-40. Signed «Antoni Gaudí, Barcelona Janer de 1881.» — G. R. C.

28. Gaudi's friend the diplomat Eduardo Toda at 28 in a simulated contemplative pose, practicing for for a historical evocation at Poblet which was never realized.

ornamental function of images did not correspond to the grandiosity of the idea which he felt to be represented by the temple, whose portal should be «of great size, not made for individual men, but for all Humanity which comfortahly fits in the bosom of its Creator.»

Religious concepts are more common than materialistic ones in the manuscript, supporting our image of a youth from a Christian family, educated in the Escuela Pía, carried away by progressivism in his youthful years.

In other parts of the manuscript he provides us with a basis for judging the radical changes which, in various aspects, affected the architect in his passage from youth to maturity. For example, in one section he sets forth a method of drawing up projects and of calculating accurate budgetary estimates. For him the mission of the architect lay «not only in designing grand projects, but also in making them possible... economically speaking, and consequently in being aware of contemporary production methods and systems.» This paragraph ironically brings to mind the various works of the master, designed at the height of his career, which were to remain unfinished as a result of their prohibitive expense.

Another aspect of this differentiation is provided by the paragraph which says «March 20, '79 — As I see it, in order to establish a clientele and a name, it is necessary to insist on payment in terms of what the jobs are worth; for this reason I consider the German tariff to be completely wrong.» This desire for profit and for making a name for himself, logical in the beginnings of a professional career, would have been unimaginable knowing the later Gaudí had it not been found written in his own hand in this manuscript.

Another fact which contradicts his life style as we knew it is that he would at age 26 write these notes in Castilian, at a time when he was already an active excursionist with *Catalanista* tendencies. This is even more surprising when we recall the obstinancy with which he later used his vernacular tongue, even with non-Catalans.

He terminated his study with a brief commentary on private and public buildings in Barcelona, covering to some extent the cost of cheap housing for workers and their rents. In this too we could find a contradiction if we were to consider how, despite his early preference for the cause of labor, all of his later works were in the service of families of high society.

This manuscript, the most extensive one that we possess by Gaudí, is interesting as an example of the changes which took place after his early youth. Certain characteristics and qualities persisted, but others, when compared to his later ways, seem hardly to relate to the same person. But even more than for the specific value of these contradictions, the manuscript is interesting for the generic significance which can be inferred from the whole of it and which suggests tolerance in accepting those religious, moral, and artistic deviations of his youth which are not in agreement with the later Gaudí.

The manuscript is also interesting for the ideological concerns of the author, recently graduated from architecture school, in dealing respectfully with religion and for the insistence with which he speaks of a great temple, as if in presentiment of the one which would later make him famous.

We can deduce that the manuscript was written with care but that it responded more to a momentary state of mind than to speculative or pedagogical objectives on the whole.

This aspect of his literary activity becomes even more evident in another very brief manuscript (four pages) which is kept in the same museum (Fig. 171). It is written on a folded sheet of letter paper which must have belonged to him, judging from the initial «G» which serves as a letterhead (in relief, and very ornamental—a possible manifestation of his youthful dandyism). This manuscript is undated. It must have been written sometime after the notebook as it is in Catalan, but not much later since it is written in the same theoretical vein, as can be seen in the description and praise of the *casa pairal* presented with definite ethnic overtones:

The house is the small nation of the family.»
«The family, like the nation, has its history, external relations, changes of government, etc.»
«The independent family has its own home; that which is not independent must rent a home.»
«One's own home is his native country; a rented home is the country of immigration: thus to own his own home is every man's dream.»
«One cannot imagine his own home without the family; only a rented house can be imagined in that manner.»
The family home has been given the name *casa pairal*. On hearing this name, who does not recall some beautiful place in the country or in the city?»

He then considers the causes for the decadence of these homes so necessary to everyone and to all times; he formulates a program and a description of one—which we will discuss in the theoretical section (XXXII - 143)—and he finishes up, with definitive literary delectation, by describing those elements which serve to exert a moral influence on the inhabitants of the house (Appendix V).

This short manuscript is completely saturated with a strong feeling for family and for one's own home, possibly reflecting desires which it is logical that the architect would have entertained in the optimism of his youth. In his old age he was to tell us that he never felt any desire for marriage, but it is possible that behind this «never» was hidden a period of forgotten disillusionments which twisted the path of his aspirations (XII - 43 and 46).

32. EARLY WORKS

We have seen that the technical aspect of the profession was no problem for Gaudí when he graduated from architecture school. His practical experience as an assistant to other professional architects and his own intuition taught him how to put academic theory into practice.

Usually in such cases the impatience to begin professional work is not satisfied because of the normal scarcity of clientele for a debutant architect. The disproportion may have been even more accentuated in Gaudí's case, given his industrious spirit and the passion which he felt for architectural work. However, we have already seen that very shortly he was given the honorable commission by the City of Barcelona which permitted him to demonstrate his capabilities and to establish professionally advantageous relationships.

One such relationship resulted from a window which he designed on a commission from the Comella glove firm to exhibit their goods at the Paris International Exposition (Fig. 194). This job, like that of the Barcelona lampposts, was of great importance despite its material pettiness, both because of its success at the exposition and because it confirmed Don Eusebio Güell's high estimate of the architect's talents. Previous biographies have attributed Güell's high esteem for Gaudí exclusively to the window at Paris without reference to the encounters in the Puntí workshops.

Another of Gaudí's works was presented at the Paris Exposition of 1878—a work born of his concern for the working man's cause which had put him in contact with the directors of the «Obrera Mataronense», a co-operative for which he drew up a plan for a working-class district.

One of Gaudí's constant concerns was that of relating his works to the end which they were to serve, and in this work—perhaps coinciding with his social preoccupations of the moment—he carefully researched the question of the workers' demands and rights by studying the contemporary treatises and taking note of salaries and statistics.[2] In the decoration of the auditorium, created by Gaudí himself, we get a taste of the ingenious «redeemerism» of the Mataró co-operativists in the slogans which they asked the architect to include «Nothing is greater than fraternity»; «Comrade, be sound, practice kindness!»; «Do you wish to be an intelligent man? Be kind»; «Too much courtesy is proof of a false education.» The memory of the last slogan may have influenced Gaudí's manner at times.

That same year he constructed a retable for the Sisters of Jesus and Mary in Tarragona (Fig. 195). The architect's niece Rosa was a scholarship student in the Sisters' school, and it appears that the commissions grew out of this relationship, indicating that his anticlericalism was not extreme.[3]

After spending five years working boldly and without paying too much attention to the economic results of his labors, the time arrived when Gaudí decided to limit his free work and not to accept jobs which did not represent an assured return. This was evident when his friend Timoteo Padrós proposed that he draw up some plans for a textile factory which he was thinking of setting up in Madrid. Gaudí explained to him in a letter that he was familiar with the type of building desired and that he would make similar studies which he had already completed available to him, adding: «as you know very well, I live by my work and cannot dedicate myself to projects that are vague or exploratory, and I am sure that you yourself would not want me to give up the certain for the uncertain.» [4]

This period of optimistic and to some extent lucrative work culminated in the construction of the Vicens house in Gracia, and of the country house known as «El Capricho» (The Caprice) on the outskirts of Comillas (Santander), owned by Sr. Díaz de Quijano. For the latter he only drew the plans, directing the work without visiting the construction site—out of fear of disagreement with the client, according to Bergós.[5] In addition there was an altar for the Sisters of Jesus and Mary in San Andrés del Palomar (which is dated 1876 by Ráfols, and 1879-81 by Bergós), another already mentioned for Tarragona, and the decoration of the Gibert Pharmacy at number 2 Paseo de Gracia, which no longer exists. These and several pieces of furniture for his own use constitute all of the known works of the first years of the great architect's career. In the third part of this study where we deal directly with his work, we will see how the most outstanding technical characteristics of the works here enumerated are exemplary of Gaudí's bit-by-bit achievement of a professional reputation—a reputation which soon became frankly apparent.

29. Gaudí and other excursionists at the Cathedral of Elne in 1883. First row; next to the arches, from left to right: Alvaro Verdaguer, Alejandro de Riquer, Arturo Masriera, Pedro Vidal, Rev. Collell, M. Serra y Solé. Second row; Emilio Vilanova, Narciso Oller, Cayetano Cornet, Jacinto Verdaguer, Luis Cutxet, GAUDÍ, Angel Guimerá, Justino Pepratx, Francisco X. Tobella, J. Torruella. Third row, seated: Tomás Forteza, Ramón Arabia, Rev. Bonafont, and N. Pepratx.

2. Ráfols cites: Dacich, *Economie Politique des Atheniens;* Moreau, *Du Probleme de la Misère;* and Lavasceur, *Histoire des Classes Ouvrières en France,* *op. cit.,* p. 69.
3. The cronology of these first works and some of the details are taken in general from Ráfols, *op. cit.,* pp. 22, 30, 34-40, and from Bergós, *op. cit.,* p. 69.
4. Ráfols, *op. cit.,* p. 36.
5. *Op. cit.,* p. 72.

33. DANDYISM AND LABOR SYMPATHIES (Fig. 27)

In this first stage of establishing himself as an architect he never forgot his humble origins and his rather difficult life as a student with an outside job. These memories produced in him a desire to compensate for past privations in the deserved state of well-being and refinement—perhaps as a reaction shaded with a bit of enthusiasm for revenge—which his present possibilities put within reach.

6. For this description I rely on the reports of Ráfols, Bergós, and Elías in their already cited works. Once Gaudí told me that when he was young he didn't like to wear new shoes. In the interest of comfort he let his brother (who wore the same size as he) break in those which he had to buy. This detail could either contradict or sustain the stylish dress attributed to him. Dr. Trias has saved a «form» in the shape of Gaudí's cranium which was used to adapt hats to his head, from the «Arnau» hat shop where Gaudí must have bought several hats. The high class of this shop, which was one of the most distinguished in all of Barcelona at the time and was located on the then-booming Calle del Conde del Asalto across from the Güell palace, supports the thesis of an elegant Gaudí. It is also supported by the carefully penned calling card for his architectural offices on the Calle del Call which is preserved in the Reus Museum and the youthful photograph where touches of gray can be seen in his beard, taken in the luxurious studio of Audonard and Company (Fig. 27).

It was with this attitude, apparently, that he introduced himself into the distinguished society of Barcelona. He was of medium stature and full of youth and energy, with a blond beard and hair worn long in the fashion of the times. Of light complexion, his blue eyes were in contrast to his penetrating stare, and he had the full lips of a man who loves life. His appearance was generally moderate and reflective, always dressed with care in morning coat and top hat. He cultivated the sometimes ostentatious manners of high society. He drove in an open carriage (it was thus that he visited his works in progress, and without descending he would consult plans and give orders). When his schedule permitted he practiced horsemanship. He enjoyed good food and good tobacco, attended concerts, legitimate theater and the opera, and frequently went to the Liceo.[6]

In his youth he was far from the retiring man of his later years, rubbing elbows with writers and artists to whom he sometimes had recourse for the decoration of his works. Such was to be the case with Torrescasana in the Vicens house and with Clapés in the Güell palace and later in «La Pedrera.» Such company provided the perfect climate for his high spirits and usually exalted sentiments.

As Gaudí breathed this new social atmosphere, his sharp sense of observation revealed to him the wide range of values embraced by the various sectors of the aristocracy —those born to nobility, those who had earned a place through wealth, and the intellectual aristocracy. He realized that although he would professionally have to seek clients among the

47

wealthy, it was in the shelter of intelligence and sensitivity that his artistic concepts would best blossom.

He knew from experience in upper bourgeois circles that it was from these that his commissions would come, yet he truly disliked the ambience of these people to whom he felt himself superior. He was much more attracted to the intellectual art world with its shades of Bohemia and raw discussions of the over-riding problems of the day. While he promoted himself in bourgeois society in hopes of finding work, he criticized its economic principles and consistently defended the workers' movements. On the other hand, while he felt himself to be a worker he did not cease to attend the society parties and to enjoy delicate foods.[7] This was not really a contradictory attitude, but rather was born of his non-conformist temperament and of his revisionist spirit. He felt sympathy for the workers in their struggle for a better way of life which he himself hoped to find in the select surroundings which he frequented —an ambience whose defects he recognized and censured.

From a humanitarian and social point of view, Gaudí felt that work should guarantee a state of well-being for the worker and that the comforts of the wealthy class should be legitimized by a life of work and generosity. He admired the select and refined worker whom he found in his friend Salvador Pagés, the manager of the Mataró co-operative, and the industrious aristocrat whom he had seen in Eusebio Güell, and he hoped for a fraternal integration of the two living side by side. He expounded and discussed this vision of social problems with convincing ability, making his opinion respected by differing ideologies. In later years he retracted his liberal ways, but he never abandoned his laborist ideals, though he did cease to flaunt them. What he did was to substitute Christian charity for secular philanthropy.

34. EXCURSIONISM AND POLITICS (Figs. 28, 29)

Once his formal studies were over, Gaudí continued on his own to investigate the ancient monuments of Catalonia. This study had been carefully fomented by the architect Rogent as director of the School of Architecture by means of the already mentioned excursions which served as lessons in the history of architecture. With characteristic enthusiasm Gaudí sought the company of other architects with similar leanings and of those excursionist groups which included notable monuments on their itineraries with the object of reviving a love for the country and its heritage.

A resurgence of patriotic consciousness had been taking root in Catalonia from the beginning of the century, at first being mainly literary, but later taking up the defense of the Catalan economy and even later becoming structured into a political party. Until that time, excursionism was considered to be a political sort of activity, nourished by the study and admiration of local monuments and the cultivation of the Catalan language which had been suppressed since the days of Philip V.

The end of Gaudí's formal studies coincided with the basically romantic—but decidedly active—resurgence of political Catalanism. In May, 1879, Valentín Almirall founded the *Diari Català,* the first daily newspaper publisher in Catalan, which adhered to an ideology which he called «provincialism.» During the paper's two-year existence, its editor convoked the first *catalanista* congress in 1880 and founded the «Centre català» with the expressive slogan «Catalunya i Avant» (Catalonia and Forward!).

The intellectual community hummed with the new ideology which was enthusiastically adhered to by the younger element, each person participating in the activities most in line with his own interests.

In November, 1876, the «*Catalanista* Association of Scientific Excursions» was founded; in November, 1879, Gaudí was a member, taking part in excursions throughout Catalonia as well as in a famous one to Roussillon.

On these artistic-historical excursions his feelings of Catalan-ness were solidified—sentiments which had perhaps begun to form as he stood before the grandiose ruins of Poblet in his early years, and which were later encouraged in the classes of Pablo Milá y Fontanals who shared similar *catalanista* feelings and who exerted a strong influence on his students.[8]

Gaudí was never affiliated with any party, nor was he a political militant, despite repeated entreaties later made to him by Prat de la Riba and Cambó with whose ideas he sympathized,[9] but he always shared the unrest and idealism which served to elevate a sense of Catalanism throughout his lifetime. Above all he promoted the use of the Catalan language which he considered to be the ideal expression of this personality. When Catalanism passed from being merely romantic-literary into politics, there were moments of struggle when the language was the object of severe attacks which offended the patriotic sentiments of the Catalans and inflamed Gaudí's passionate spirit, leading him to take part in the struggle with the simplest means available to him: a stubborn adherence to his vernacular tongue, which absolutely excluded the official Spanish language as a protest against attacks that were

7. Jordi Elías, *op. cit.,* p. 45.
8. Manuel Benach Torrents, *Pablo Milá y Fontanals: gran figura del romanticismo artístico catalán* (Vilafranca del Penedés, 1958).
9. Bergós, *op. cit.,* p. 31.

proceeding from official sources. This was the only active political manifestation which he kept up throughout his lifetime. The excursions lasted for only a short time.

Gaudí's fellow excursionists soon noticed that he was already well acquainted with the monuments visited, and he was sometimes entrusted with projects to enhance the visits. He reconstructed the ground plan of the age-old hospital at Olesa de Bonesvalls, and in nearby Vilafranca he made drawings of a valuable and artistic silver mace. He was asked to prepare studies on the important subject of which parts of the old city should be preserved when discussion began about the reformation of Barcelona,[10] and on the exposition of decorative arts that had been planned by the National Institute for the Advancement of Labor. In 1880 and 1881 he served as a member of the board of directors of the «Catalanista Association of Scientific Excursions» and he continued to be a member of the organization until 1889 (and perhaps beyond that time though we cannot be sure for later membership lists have been lost). At the end of 1890 this group joined together with another of similar nature giving rise to the «Excursionist Center of Catalonia» whose membership lists of 1890 do not, however, include the name of Gaudí.[11]

Among other excursions he of course visited Montserrat. In addition, he visited Mallorca and also climbed to the top of the Maladetta, descending all the way to Toulouse. It seems that he was disappointed by the famous church of Saint Sernin in comparison to similar buildings which he knew in Catalonia, and is said to have jokingly remarked on seeing it, «Let's go home,» renouncing foreign excursions for the rest of his life, with the exception of one trip to Morocco in 1887 with the Marquis of Comillas during which he also took the opportunity to visit Andalusia.

His precise knowledge of the most famous monuments of architectural history, to which he would at times refer in great detail, was principally the result of studying illustrated books. Nevertheless, the maestro showed great interest in the medieval *Cité* of Carcassonne at the time of its restoration by Viollet-le-Duc. During the time he spent there he examined the triple wall so closely that the neighboring villagers took him for the director of the restoration and wanted to honor him. [12] He found the restoration work of the brilliant French architect too scenographic, in spite of the rigorous archaeological criteria employed. [13]

On the occasion of a visit by a group of Valencian writers to Catalonia, a trip to Poblet was arranged. Gaudí had the idea of giving the visitors a novel vision of those glorious ruins which had early excited his imagination, by illuminating the vaults of the temple and the cloisters with Bengal lights.

Gaudí loved the spectacular optimism which could be obtained through lighting and color effects in already existing monuments, and in addition they stimulated his imagination with respect to the works he was designing, whose frequently polychromed surfaces were calculated to achieve maximum beauty in the play of light and shade, as we shall see.

10. J. Elías, *op. cit.*, p. 67.

11. Lists prior to this year have not been kept and therefore we cannot know if Gaudí was a member in its early years. J. Elías, *op. cit.*, p. 63.

12. Ráfols, *op. cit.*, p. 22.

13. Francisco Quintana says that Gaudí told him that his visit to Carcassonne was a question of «arriving in the morning and leaving in the afternoon.» It seemed to him to be a *Castell dels tres dragons.* (Castle of the three Dragons.)

X. THE BOOKSELLER BOCABELLA

35. A DEVOUT FOLLOWER OF SAINT JOSEPH (Figs. 30-33)

José María Bocabella y Verdaguer was the initiator of the idea to erect a temple to the Holy Family in Barcelona. The idea came to him on a trip to Rome and Loreto, and the thought was that it should reproduce the architectonic forms of the church thus dedicated in the latter city. He was an extremely devout person, the owner of a religious book shop. Carried along by his fervor, he founded the «Spiritual Association of Devout Followers of Saint Joseph,» and published *El Propagador de la Devoción a San José* in order to counteract the damage to the people's piety being brought about by revolutionary ideas. He possessed a small fortune, and was a very close friend of the now venerated Father Claret; when the latter, as bishop, came to Barcelona, he rode in Bocabella's carriage.

On returning to Barcelona after his trip to Italy, Bocabella met with several obstacles, and slight variations were made in the original plan for the church before the project was entrusted to the diocesan architect, Francisco del Villar. On St. Joseph's Day, 1882, the first stone was solemnly put in place in a ceremony attended by the official authorities and the Bishop Urquinaona who was assisted by the later bishop Morgades.

Gaudí appears to have attended the ceremony. Although, as we have seen, he did work as an assistant for Villar, he was not so employed at that time. In 1882 he was working with Juan Martorell instead (VII - 26) and it is possible that he may have gone to the ceremony with him, Martorell being a friend and technical advisor to Bocabella.

Work was hardly begun on the church when discrepancies arose between the administration and the director which soon escalated to the point of provoking the latter's resignation. When Villar withdrew from the job, Bocabella proposed that Martorell occupy the vacant post. However, this architect did not feel that he was really free to accept under the delicate circumstances—having been Bocabella's technical advisor in the mentioned discrepancies—and he recommended his young assistant Gaudí as a substitute, recognizing him to be excellently qualified to carry out this new commitment.

36. THE GREAT TEMPLE IS ENTRUSTED TO GAUDÍ

Thus it was that Gaudí, at the age of 31, was put in contact with this profoundly religious man on November 3, 1883. The devout Bocabella, prime mover and guiding spirit of the expiatory temple, had faith in the talent of the young architect recommended by Martorell, but was bothered by his lack of interest in religion. Yet from the beginning he was confident of overcoming this lack through divine intercession.

Gaudí, on the other hand, ignored the confessional aspect of the task and concerned himself with the revision of procedures employed in the work in progress. The crypt had been begun, but none of the columns were yet in place. The new director, with his fashionable appearance and independent spirit, sporting a blond beard, a low top hat, and gray morning coat, would visit the construction site—at that time far removed from the city—in an open carriage. Apparently, without getting down from his coach he would examine the plans and give orders to the foreman.

This novel manner was not the only difference occasioned by the change of directing architect. At times Gaudí would get down from his carriage and go down into the hollow of the crypt. On such occasions he would observe detailing, would test materials, and take notes; it was not long before he was to impose a radical change in the construction that was already begun. Esthetically, he was in complete disagreement with what had been previously done, and administratively he wished to introduce new directives which produced a tense relationship with the contractor, Macario Planella. The latter, on March 3, 1884, designated the architect Elías Rogent as an arbitrator to settle the matter in agreement with the new director. Gaudí wanted the finalization of all work accomplished to that point so that he could break radically with the previous phase and be able to work with absolute freedom. The contractor was willing to accede, as long as certain contract requirements were fulfilled—and these were the subject of contention. [1]

This incident must have worried Bocabella who was forced to intervene. Nevertheless, his chief concern continued to be the new architect's beliefs.

37. ARCHITECTURE AS THE PRECURSOR OF FAITH

In spite of his lukewarm religiosity, the commission to do the new temple had an impact on Gaudí's spirit. Perhaps at first it was simply a feeling of professional satisfaction with the

1. Information from the archive of J. Rogent y Massó, to whom I am most grateful for his co-operation.

30. José M. Bocabella y Verdaguer, founder of the temple of the Sagrada Familia, who was influential in Gaudí's religiosity. Original portrait by Alejo Clapés preserved by the sitter's descendents.

31. The Church of Loreto which Bocabella planned at first to imitate in his temple to the Holy Family in Barcelona. Author's archive.

step forward which the work represented, and which he would remember gratefully all of his life. Speaking of this in his last days he said, «What more could an architect wish than to take command of the construction of a great temple?» He held his entrance into the Sagrada Familia project to be providential, beginning with the resignation of Villar who he claimed had never before renounced a single job, and he attributed this exception to the intervention of Saint Joseph.[2]

It is possible that he felt that such supernatural influence in the new commission was also responsible for the change which took place in his spirit, turned from skepticism to faith through Bocabella's dedication and the religious content of the project.

2. Martinell, *Conversaciones con Gaudí*, p. 71.

3. Told to me by the architect Juan Rubió who served as Gaudí's assistant on the Temple, in 1915 when I was working as Rubió's draughtsman.

4. Told to me by D. Felipe de Dalmases, the great-grandson of Bocabella, on January 6, 1962 and November 22, 1965.

The devout book-dealer and moving force behind the projected expiatory temple never let his young collaborator out of sight, practicing on him with apostolic efficiency, and presenting him with a copy of *El Año Cristiano* (The Christian Year) which he had edited. Bocabella recommended that he read it, and Gaudí did so with care, finding therein many of the symbols which he later applied in the Sagrada Familia.[3] Bocabella's descendants have corroborated this fact which is a part of the family tradition, and add that their great-grandfather always had faith that with the intercession of St. Joseph, the architect would become a true believer. Probably in hopes of assisting this conversion, he commissioned Gaudí to design a reliquary to house the great number of saints' relics which he owned, and later, a private oratory for his home, both of which still exist (Figs. 196, 197).[4]

It seems logical that Bocabella would exert influence to awaken the faith of the carefree architect when we recall that the idea of founding the Sagrada Familia responded to expiatory motives. The legend placed on the first stone stated that the temple was being built «to the greater honor and glory of the Holy Family, so that all sleeping hearts may be awakened from their indifference, that faith may be exalted and warmth instilled in charity...»

Even considered from a purely human point of view, it is natural that the architect would, in this critical stage of giving artistic form to such spiritual goals, feel himself influenced by the effects of the prayer on the cornerstone, and that the general atmosphere of faith and expiation which surrounded the temple and its founder would evaporate the tendencies toward secularism which only a few years before had caused him to have no reservation about mixing with the atheism of the Mataró co-operative.

In this first phase his concept of the temple lacked the compulsion of his later ideas. Grandiosity and perfection developed from the circumstances. The majestic and worthy church which he set out to build in the beginning was later inflated by his passion and by the new ideas suggested by his faith so that a project far superior to that foreseen took shape. And by virtue of that harmonious law which relates ethics to esthetics, in following the path of art he came to religion. Once he was committed to it, art and religion collaborated in the grandiose conception which would make him famous.

When Bocabella died in 1891, he could feel the satisfaction of having seen and contributed to the spiritual metamorphosis of our architect.

32. The architect Villar's project for the Sagrada Familia in the neo-Gothic style. Frontal view. Author's archive.

33. Lateral view of the same project.

XI. YESTERDAY A SHEPHERD, TODAY A NOBLEMAN

38. WORK AND NOBILITY (Figs. 34, 35)

We have seen how Gaudí came to know Eusebio Güell, and how the latter admired the architect's first completed work—the window for the Comella glove shop at the 1878 Paris Exposition. With his discerning vision Güell was able to discover in that work of little importance the seed of a new art, and in its creator, the artist friend whose praises he loved to sing.

When Gaudí made the acquaintance of the man who later was to become the first Count Güell, he found in him the ideal aristocrat that he had dreamed of: active, generous, paternal toward his subordinates, and with a mind that was sensitive to artistic values. His father, Juan Güell y Ferrer, had been born in Torredembarra, near Tarragona, in 1800 to a modest family. After nautical studies in Barcelona, he left at the age of 18 for America, returning at 36 with a small capital which formed the basis of the family's later prosperity.

Don Eusebio was a man of Catholic faith, highly cultured and of fine sensitivity. He liked to surround himself with intellectual and literary figures, and to support worthy artists. His house was filled with works of art of museum quality. He did not enjoy holding representative posts, in spite of which he served as a city counsellor, provincial representative, president of the Floral Games in 1890, Gentleman to the King, and was named a count in 1910. He also was a founder and president of the first «Centre Català» begun, as we have seen, by Almirall in 1880.[1]

At mid-century the class struggle had broken out in Catalonia—at times in a violent manner—and questions provoked by this situation were the order of the day. Thus, when Gaudí considered the modest and exemplary origin of the Güells, he saw them to personify the rational solution to the socio-economic problems disturbing the country's industry—the worker who succeeds on his own, and the patron who knows how to be a friend to his workers, in contrast to the widespread bourgeois practices that he wished to combat.

The interpenetration of conflicting interests was graphically portrayed on the coat of arms of nobility which Don Eusebio asked Gaudí to design for him when he became a count (Fig. 34). There the architect placed an owl on a quarter-moon as a symbol of prudence and wisdom through changing temporal conditions, coupled with the phrase «today a nobleman» *(avui senyor)*. On the other half the concept was completed with the words «yesterday a shepherd,» *(ahir pastor)* and a dove with a gear wheel alluding to Güell's industrial colony, Santa Coloma. The intention was to unite labor and nobility.

Gaudí considered his friend and maecenas to be the «true nobleman», and said so at every opportunity. One day while speaking with the then bishop of Barcelona, Cardinal Casañas, the maestro was asked what he meant by the term «true nobleman.» He answered: «A nobleman is a person of excellent sensitivity, excellent manners, and excellent position. Excelling in everything, he knows no envy and no one bothers him; he is pleased to see that those

1. Bergós, *op. cit.*, p. 168, notes 36, 37.

34. The Güell coat-of-arms designed by Gaudí, in which allusion is made to the hard-working and noble qualities of the creator of the industrial colony of Santa Coloma, and also to the colony's name.

35. Eusebio Güell y Bacigalupi, an artistically sensitive and hard-working person. A portrait contemporary with the construction of his palatial residence. Published in *Ilustració Catalana* in 1888.

36. View of the hall of the Palacio Güell published in *Ilustración Hispano-Americana* in 1891 in reporting its inauguration.

around him display their capabilities.» He ended by saying, «Weren't the Medici like that?» The cardinal was convinced.[2]

39. MUTUAL ADMIRATION (Figs. 36-39)

His faith in Güell's noble conduct was founded in Don Eusebio's dealings with himself and with the other artists who worked for him. Gaudí soon became his architect—first for some projects that were never executed, then for the pavilion, gatehouse, and stables in Les Corts, and in 1885 for the palatial house on the Calle del Conde del Asalto, his first important civil work. This last commission came only two short years after he had been entrusted with the building of the Sagrada Familia. Just as in the case of the temple his responsibilities as directing architect had led him to delve into the problems of religion, in designing this seignorial house, he penetrated deeply into the social and private habits of his client in order to better adapt the new building to them.

Through this professional procedure, the architect incorporated himself into the ranks of high society without especially proposing to do so, with a building which, once finished, attracted the attention of those intellectuals who saw in it a reflection of the aristocratic Barcelona bourgeoisie. The press reported the termination of this original work, stressing and praising it as a great artistic event—in several cases, however, without mentioning the name of the architect.[3]

Another noble characteristic of the maecenas became evident to Gaudí some years later when he generously sponsored an exposition of photographs of Gaudí's architectonic work in the Paris Architecture Salon in 1910—including the polychromed model of the Nativity façade of the Sagrada Familia. Güell sent his son to tell the architect that if he was planning to accompany his work to Paris, he would be welcome to travel with the father. Gaudí understood this as his way of informing him that the trip would be paid for and that in Paris he would be introduced to Güell's friends (the industrialist made yearly trips to the French capital and was very well-connected), and that he would otherwise enjoy the advantages of such a distinguished traveling companion. The maestro acknowledged the deference and answered that he had already thought it over and decided not to go. The nobleman and the architect met together or were in close contact every day, but nothing more was ever said on this matter. When Gaudí related this incident, he further remarked: «Doesn't that strike you as princely procedure? He and I had reached the point where we understood each other without words. He didn't come to me personally so that I would not feel compelled by his presence; rather, he sent a high-ranking ambassador to see me—this indeed is a prince!»[4]

40. A PATRIOT AND A MAN OF FAITH

In addition to his nobility and artistic sensitivity, Güell possessed two other traits which the architect admired. One of these was his affectionate openness about all problems relating

37. Palacio Güell. The central salon with the chapel door closed and decorated with shell appliqués and paintings by Clapés. *La Ilustración Hispano-Americana*, 1891.

38. Palacio Güell. Sitting room and library next to the dining room. Engraving in *La Ilustración Hispano-Americana*, 1891.

2. Told to me by Gaudí himself on December 13, 1924. See my *Conversaciones con Gaudí...*, p. 97; see also, *Revista de Catalunya* N.º 25 (July 25, 1926).

3. *Ilustración Hispano-Americana* 532, 533, 535, (January 11 and 18 and February 1, 1891).

4. Martinell, *op. cit.*, p. 97.

39. Palacio Güell. Chapel attached to the salon which becomes an oratory when the doors are opened. Engraving in *La Ilustración Hispano-Americana*, 1891.

to Catalonia, not only those involving protectionist tariffs, but also those questions concerned with the region's historical and political prestige. The other quality was his religiosity which in the beginning was perhaps not so important to the architect; yet it must have impressed him and may even have influenced him: the Güell palace was dignified with an oratory chapel which the architect seems to have designed not only with care, but with delight.

41. FORESIGHTED VISION OF GAUDÍ'S WORTH

If our architect was a fervent admirer of the nobility and other characteristics of this distinguished man, the latter had equal admiration for Gaudí, even when he was still little-known. Güell had a penetrating vision that enabled him to discover the architect's unsuspected qualities in the very beginning. Although the name of Gaudí was not even mentioned in the commentaries on his work for Güell—in spite of the original solutions which we will see in discussing their technical aspects—Güell maintained unwavering faith in his talent in the face of adverse critics and overly-jealous administrators.

The story goes that on one occasion Don Eusebio had to be away during the work on the house on the Calle del Conde del Asalto. When he went to see the progress on his return, the administrative secretary—alarmed by the expense which seemed exorbitant to him—nervously prepared the proprietor's spirits before telling him the amount that had been spent to that point. When Güell heard the sum he simply said, «Is that all?» The jealous administrator apparently looked with misgiving on the activities of Güell's architect, and he is said to have murmured, «I fill the pockets of Don Eusebio, and Gaudí empties them for him.»

There is another saying which refers to the house on the Calle del Conde del Asalto that goes: given its originality, the larger it grew, the less people liked it. The owner and the architect, while both sensitive to public opinion, felt that the most important thing was for both of them to like it. Once the work was finished, Gaudí—always desiring to outdo himself—felt that it could have been better, and he is supposed to have told his client that if before it had only pleased the two of them, now *he* didn't like it either. To this the owner replied that it still pleased him immensely.

I doubt that there is much truth to the anecdote. Nevertheless it characterizes Güell's fidelity to Gaudí's work—a fidelity which brought commissions for his most important constructions: the church at his industrial colony and the well-known park, both of which, though created by Gaudí, were suggested and made possible by Güell.

Knowing these works, we can see in retrospect how valuable this patronage was. But when we consider that in the beginning Gaudí was unknown and his great works still unprojected so that not even Güell could imagine them, the insight involved in Güell's protection of Gaudí acquires an even greater value. It is to this relationship that we owe three of the master's most representative works, and we can be grateful for Güell's discovery and encouragement of Gaudí's work just as it was being born.

XII. FROM LOVE TO CHARITY

42. THE LOFTINESS OF CHARITY (Fig. 40)

Gaudí's passionate temperament was not without its manifestations of physical love. In the optimistic illusions of his youth he dreamed of creating a family; later such worldly illusions were discarded and sublimated in a love for virtue which, in turn, gave life to his art. In the three Sagrada Familia façades—the one that he built and the other two which he left in the design stage—he glorified the three theological virtues, always giving Charity preference over Faith and Hope. He justified this precedence with the words of St. Paul: Faith and Hope terminate in salvation; but Charity will live forever.

43. ON MARRIAGE

His amorous restlessness did not last long. Once his younger years were past he not only had no love affairs, but also had a reputation among the women as being unfriendly. Sebastiana Corts, who knew him and his family, says that «from his youth on he always led a very austere—almost monk-like—life, without girl friends or love affairs, for he never even looked at women.» [1]

In the same vein we have the somewhat more definitive testimony of Don Felipe de Dalmases y de Dalmases, Bocabella's great-grandson, who had it from his aunt Dolores that the architect had «anti-women» tendencies. Bocabella's grandchildren observed that he would treat the boys in a friendly manner, but not the girls—a fact which gave the latter cause for complaint. When Clapés painted portraits of the Bocabella couple, Gaudí did not wish to look at that of the wife, and when the daughter Francisca criticized the father's likeness, he remarked: «women don't understand anything,» adding that a likeness of features was not necesary in a good portrait.[2]

This coldness was confirmed for me when, as I was a bachelor, he made some pointed observations in advising me to marry. He then interrupted himself and said to me, «You may wonder why I didn't take my own advice. Well, I'll tell you.» (I must admit that for an instant I expected some sort of sensational revelation, but he merely said:) «Because I never felt any vocation for the married life.» The simplicity of the reply disappointed me at the time, but afterwards, thinking it over, it seemed to me the perfect synthesis of his inner character.

His all-consuming passion tied him more closely to his art, and his work on the Sagrada Familia, saturated as it was with the Christian spirit, carried him to God. Without realizing it, without proposing to do so, and without special vows, he gave himself to religion and architecture; and as is common to all such deliverances, his was complemented by celibacy. This was perhaps the most logical solution in Gaudí's case, as his character—once he had chosen this double ideal of religion and art—would have made life with him little less than impossible for any woman.

Gaudí had illusions, but he was not deluded. He knew perfectly well what happiness human love could bring, and I am certain that his judgment was correct in appraising his apparent failures and converting them into a spiritual triumph.

After having extolled the advantages of marriage in the reflections which I have mentioned above, he added that those who seek in it complete happiness will be deceived. Matrimony is a mixture of hazards and contradictions, and prudence therefore counsels that it be considered more as a cross to bear than a panacea of happiness if disappointments are to be avoided. I remember what he told me almost word for word: «Disillusionment always has as its antecedent some illusion which if avoided will also avoid the effect. Therefore it is best not to have illusions about such important things.»

Human love cannot help but egotistically demand love in return. Gaudí, freed of such sentimental attachment, could give himself entirely to the selfless love of charity, born in God and reverting back to Him.

Some of his mannerisms and certain anecdotes told about him could argue for a lack of charity. This is entirely possible. He himself confessed to having defects like all other human beings, and among these were the egoistic capriciousness, unfriendly manner, and shortness which we were able to observe, but which were less apparent in the last years of his life. It is possible that his dislike for women which we have mentioned came about as a defensive reaction born of memories which crystallized in this mannerism.

40. Nativity façade, emblem of Charity, the virtue which the architect planned to represent in each of the other two façades as well.

1. Guix Sugrañes, *Defensa de Gaudí*, p. 169. Declaration before the notary Pagés Giner with the purpose of proving Gaudí's Reusian origin.
2. Stated by Don Felipe de Dalmases on January 6, 1962.

In renouncing physical love, he prudently renounced illusions which might lead to disillusionment. With his spirit forged in this renunciation which was replaced by charity—not as a derivative, but as a superlative—his lack of vocation for marriage and his exemplary life in its religious and artistic aspects are more easily understood.

This intimate sentimental transition from the human to the divine should be emphasized, for it is one of the least known and most edifying episodes in the architect's life.

44. SENTIMENTAL STABILITY

Someone has suggested that perhaps some of the aspects of Gaudí's architecture which appear especially tormented were the result of inner torment produced by a mature life devoid of family love. The logic of this assumption escapes me, for such torment was not evident. He was loved by his mother and his brother until he was 24 years old, by his father until he was 55, and by his neice Rosa for six years more. He enjoyed the affection of such good friends as the Llimona brothers, the poet Maragall, the conductor Millet, Dr. Torras y Bages, Father Ignacio Casanovas, and Dr. Santaló among others. And then there were his collaborators whom he considered also as his friends: Berenguer, Matamala, Rubió, Sugrañes... As far as the loves which we will speak of, they must certainly have momentarily awakened certain hopes for the future, and yet it is certain that once he had renounced them, Gaudí, who so strongly believed in providence, was thankful that such fleeting illusions had been sacrificed on the altars of other more permanent and elevated loves.

It is my belief that our architect enjoyed perfect temperamental and sentimental stability. Once his early youth was past, he directed his life in a conscious manner, and day after day would analyze the complex factors influencing him until he reached the conclusion that he «did not feel a vocation for marriage.»

45. AMOROUS VENTURES

Gaudí's friend the poet Maragall has related in a literary manner several of the architect's romantic loves, which he himself must have revealed—first in a story in Catalan entitled *Una calaverada* («A Foolish Act»), [3] republished in the book *Vides al pas* (1912), and later translated into Castilian and expanded to serve as the «Introduction» to his *Elogios*. He does not name the architect, and there is a lyrical tenor to the story, yet certain details leave little room for doubting the reality of the tale.

Several artist friends—a painter, a sculptor, a poet, a musician, an architect—have told of their amorous exploits. The architect with his «unkempt gray-blond beard and eyes of violet on a palely colored face» has remained silent, and his friend the painter, «shaking him by the shoulder in friendly violence—for he was quite fond of him—says, 'Here he is ... the hermit forever!'» and impells him to tell of his exploits as well.

We will follow the story as the poet tells it. On a trip which he made to look at cathedrals, the architect met a girl with whom he was already acquainted at the home of some friends. She was a foreigner, and was about to be married to a boy from her country who had had to go to America... and she was here awaiting his return. She was pretty and very intelligent, and he fell in love with her. But, she being engaged, and her fiancé away ... it would have been a lowly deed. She took a liking to him and enjoyed his conversation. She curiously looked into his heart without duplicity or coquetry, as a child draws near the water to see himself in it. One day they had been talking longer than usual—he so inspired that he dared not recognize the words as his own. The mother came in to tell her that it was time to go to bed; she got up, flushed, and embraced her mother with great effusion saying: «Oh, Mother, what an hour I've had!» «Come on, come on,» the woman replied, «get to bed: you're all tired out...» And the next day they decided to leave... He knew about it, but did not have the courage to see them off; at the hour of their departure he lay in bed, stretched out like a corpse...

For two or three years she remained fixed in his thoughts. One day he took a quick trip to the city where she lived, in hopes of catching a glimpse of her. He was unsuccessful until his time of departure. Then, from the train in the station he figured out which was the couple's house, and with the train already in motion he saw a figure in one of the galleries dressed in white—a white so white that it outshone the sun... and he fell back into the cushions of the car, sobbing like a child. «There you have my amorous exploit» he said in closing.

He stood up, transfigured and erect, his face strangely rosy, and his violet colored eyes sparkled. He looked like a twenty-year-old youth... and he hurried out of the salon, apparently ashamed. But those who had listened to him stared at the door for a while in silence, as if a bit of splendor had been left behind.

This subtle and inspired narration might seem to be a figment of the poet's imagination, but such is not the case: in addition to the details already mentioned, Maurici Serrahima has

3. *Ilustració Catalana*, November 20, 1904.

vouched for the truth of the story which he knew through verbal tradition, and has provided the names of the artists there assembled: the Llimona brothers, painter and sculptor, the musician Enrique Morera, Maragall himself, and Gaudí with his assistant Juan Rubió.[4] This is confirmed by the poet's sons for whom it is family tradition.[5] Such was the romantic adventure of the great architect which, clouded in mystery, seems a condensation of his human love affairs.

Bergós, who is usually well-informed, alludes to two other loves, and in the case of the second is more precise, as far as time and people involved.[6] «After digressions involving a frivolous flirtation and a frustrated pretense of love, his aspirations crystallized when he was 32 in his formal engagement to an extremely pious young woman who finally decided to become a Sister of Jesus and Mary.» In a footnote Bergós explains that the «frustrated pretense of love» refers to the wooing of a French girl from a distinguished family who was already engaged. [7]

The flirtation which Bergós mentions is probably that mentioned by Jorge Elías who says that while Gaudí was involved with the Mataró Co-operative he fell in love with the elder of two sisters who served as teachers in the organization. They belonged to a well-to-do family which held meetings in their home every Sunday; the architect attended these, and was frequently asked to stay for dinner. The girl was almost an adolescent, very beautiful, and educated with care by the nuns of the Sacred Heart. She played the piano, sang, and—rare as it was for girls in that day—was a proficient swimmer. The enamored architect shone in these Sunday get-togethers, with his pleasant conversation on erudite, and particularly artistic, subjects. But he could not maintain his fluent ease in talking of artistic matters when it came to the matter of love. Here instead he showed a certain timidity which caused him to go slowly in his relationship with his loved one, who one fine day showed off the engagement ring given her by a local businessman. From then on Gaudí was absent from the meetings which lasted for three or four years, and similarly he abandoned his trips to Mataró after he was put in charge of the Sagrada Familia.[8] There exists a different version of the story which says that Gaudí stopped seeing the teacher on his own initiative because he was displeased with things which he had heard about her.

46. A CHANGE OF DIRECTION

According to Elías, «Gaudí subconsciously felt his life to be a great failure. The sense of defeat would always be with him.» I feel that this is a gratuitous statement, for Gaudí was anything but a failure and a loser, even in the sentimental area.

If we consider one by one the three apparent failures at love we will see that such failure did not, in truth, exist. In the Mataró idyl he never even declared his love, and there remains some doubt as to whether the break was initiated by him or by her. In that related by Maragall, the girl is captivated by Gaudí's word and spirit and exclaims, «Oh, Mother, what an hour I've had!» And the cautious mother took the girl away in order to avoid the irresistible attraction which might upset the wedding plans. More than a defeat this could be construed as a triumph for someone who, out of delicacy of feeling, wished to respect a previously made wedding pact. He may have been left with nostalgia or a momentary desolation, but certainly not with blighted hope or a sensation of failure. As for the third idyl with the young woman who later preferred the religious life, this may nave caused some irritation or disappointment, but not defeat or failure—especially not if we recall that at the same time Gaudí was engaged in a return to religious practices.

Whatever was fragile or capricious in his youth was soon put at the back of his memories which day by day seemed farther away. Painstaking care in his dressing style, attendance at the theater and concerts, a liking for good food, excursions and get-togethers, pleasures —all such worldliness was purged from his customs, which became marked by a rigorous asceticism that at one point even endangered his health.

All of this was without affected piousness, in a silent struggle with himself. It was a constant struggle because the only thing that he was not able to annul from his ardent youth was his vehement temperament which he always fought to control without completely achieving his aim. His impulsive character was the enemy contained within—an enemy which was usually conquered, though at times this proved impossible. He himself was to tell us in his later years: «All of my life I have made an effort to control my character; I am usually successful, but at times my character is stronger than I am.»

4. Maurici Serrahima, *Butlletí de la Societat Catalana d'Estudis Històrics* II, (1953).

5. Told to me by Juan Antonio Maragall Noble in February, 1964.

6. *Op. cit.*, p. 50.

7. José Pla, in the literary sketch «Gaudí,» in his books *Homenots*, says that the young lady was of German nationality (p. 217).

8. Elias, from whom I have borrowed the foregoing account, adds that once this young lady was married she went into the hat-making business in Barcelona. When I was a student, a friend of mine at the Architecture School was the son of a hat-designer who was known to have aroused Gaudí's sentiments. I cite this fact because of the coincidence which may reinforce the credibility of the basic facts presented. M. Ribas y Piera clarifies that the teacher sisters were named Agustina and Pepita Moreu, the latter being the one with whom Gaudí was in love (*Serra d'Or*, December, 1965).

XIII. ASTORGA: THE BISHOP AND HIS PALACE

41. The Bishop of Astorga, Juan Bta. Grau, whose virtues and gifts of administration had great influence on the architect's spirit.

47. A LABORIOUS PROJECT (Figs. 41, 266-277)

When the architect received the commission to design the Episcopal Palace at Astorga in 1887, he was involved in intensive work on the crypt of the Sagrada Familia and in the termination of the Güell house. He therefore did not feel that the moment was opportune for the postponement of work on these projects, which would be involved in any orientation visit to Astorga to familiarize himself with the terrain before beginning the job. Instead, he wrote to the bishop, Dr. Grau—a fellow Reusian—thanking him soundly and requesting technical information and data about the site which would allow him to prepare the work in the meantime. For this project, in addition to designing a program for the building, he had to take into account the environment of a place unfamiliar to him and also how he could best give the palace the look of an episcopal residence. Thus he also requested photographs of the most important buildings in the city and of the cathedral which stood next to the future palace; he consulted books of Spanish monuments and the unpublished photos which his friend Ixart had assembled for a series of books which he was preparing entitled *España: sus monumentos y artes*. With this preparation he drew up the plans which were submitted in August, 1887. [1] The bishop was pleased by the project and telegraphed his reply: «Received magnificent plans. Like very much. Congratulations. Await letter.» [2]

The success of the plans and the episcopal congratulations gave the work a new priority, and the architect decided to travel to Astorga in order to confirm his interpretation of the documentation which he had received.

In spite of the fact that Gaudí drew up detailed plans in order to earn a favorable report from the Academy of San Fernando in Madrid, it appears that the Academy was bothered by the unusual solutions adopted by the architect. This was certainly not the last time that Gaudí, with his independent—and later ungovernable—character, would find himself in disaccord with the authorities. The problems which arose in regard to the Astorgan palace are documented in the Acts of the Academy of San Fernando. [3] (Appendix VI).

From these Acts we know that on the 14th of November, 1887, the Academy received from the Ministry of Justice the project for the Episcopal Palace at Astorga, which was passed on to the Department of Architecture for its report. This department, meeting on February 20, 1888, approved Gaudí's presentation «with several additions relating to the narrowness of the main stairway, to prices, expenses and salary, and to the need for details of the proposed construction work.» On December 3, the Academy again received the plans «revised in accordance with the modifications proposed by the Architecture Section in its previous report» which was again passed on to that section for its opinion.

The second report, issued on January 11 next, found that Gaudí had added to the project «a new Document Number 6 containing: a notebook of observations on the findings of the cited Royal Academy; a sheet of onionskin paper with several structural details at various scales...» It appears that the author of the project revised it to meet all of the criticisms in the previous report which he found to be well-taken; those which he did not, he rebutted, maintaining his points of view, as can be seen in the document reproduced in Appendix VI.

The project consisted of five parts: the Memorial, plans, specifications, a list of quantities, and résumé of measurements with an estimate of cost which was amplified in the cited Document Number 6. In spite of this, the second review reiterated the points of view taken in the first except in one question of unitary prices, which Gaudí had resolved according to customary practice instead of complicated official prescriptions. Perhaps taking into account his alleged motives, the report states that «dealing as we are with a project formulated under special circumstances, the authorities can resolve this particular case to their own convenience,» and it closes by recommending for the second time that the project be returned to the author for the prescribed rectifications, some of which were included in new plans dated 1888. The architect showed his vexation at such intermeddlings in a letter to Dr. Grau of March 3, 1889.

48. THE BISHOP AND THE LITURGY (Fig. 42)

During these preparatory stages he was able to continue work on the Güell mansion and also travel to Astorga in order to give shape to the palace whose construction symbolically

1. Ráfols, *op. cit.*, pp. 57, 58.
2. *Ibid.*, p. 61.
3. Library of the Real Academia de Bellas Artes de San Fernando; *Libro de Actas*, 1884-88, and *Boletín de la Real Academia de Bellas Artes de San Fernando IX*, 82 (1888).

42. The main altarpiece of the Cathedral of Astorga by the sculptor G. Becerra, whom Gaudí admired. The sacrarium is in the center.

began on June 24, the prelate's saint's day. The bishop was provisionally living in the seminary—the previous palace having been destroyed by fire—and the architect also stayed there during his Astorga sojourns.

Thus Gaudí became acquainted at close range with the impressive Dr. Grau, whom he admired for his gift of good government and for the dexterity with which he was able to solve the difficult problems of the diocese. Speaking years later with the architect and historian José Pijoan about this palace in Astorga and of the bishop's part in it Gaudí said: «His effort to arouse the town was tremendous, but hopeless. He undertook that work in order to set an example and to stimulate the region's activity. He ended up fighting with everyone: with his superiors in León and with the parishioners of Astorga. Everyone, from the mayor, who was contractor for the materials, to the cathedral chapter, set up obstacles. We (Gaudí) [4] went there for a large part of each year, and that revived Dr. Grau's spirit. Never have I seen a firmer nor more well-intentioned will than his. While he lived we overcame all bitterness.» [5]

The bishop kept up with and gave life to the religious questions of the day. He made all of them the subject of polemics, lectures, and colloquia which were then later taken up by the magazine *El Criterio Tridentino* which he founded. This atmosphere of religious discussion had an influence on the architect whose irreligious ideology of previous years was rapidly disappearing. It is understandable that the prelate would take advantage of the situation in hopes of fitting his spirit into a perfectly orthodox framework.

Of the many problems which concerned Grau, the one which most influenced Gaudí was that of the restoration of the liturgy—a subject which frequently came up in their conversations. One day after having spent part of the morning in the cathedral contemplating the main altarpiece—a magnificent work by the sculptor Gaspar Becerra—the architect proposed to his friend and fellow countryman the Bishop that it might be advantageous to get rid of the canopy which then concealed the sacrarium, so beautifully sculpted with figures of the prophets and the resurrection of Jesus. The prelate reminded him that the canopy had a precise function in expressing the regal dignity of the Holy Sacrament, a fundamental dogma of the Church. Gaudí insisted: in that sacrarium the royalty had been sufficiently indicated by the hand of the artist by means of the royal mantle, sustained by angels, that was permanently sculpted around it.

Alonso Luengo who relates the episode reports the dialogue to have gone as follows: [6]
«Perhaps you are right in this, at least a little bit right.»
«In this and in everything!» Gaudí exclaimed.

He immediately softened his attitude and the bishop, in a gesture of cordiality, suggested that he carry a petition to the Sacred Congregation on Ritual asking that the canopy be removed for the reason which Gaudí himself would set forth in the argument.

«The answer from the Sacred Congregation was final; under no pretext whatsoever could they allow the suppression of the canopy, a liturgical piece of irreplaceable expressiveness.»

«The impact made by this decision on Gaudí's mind was enormous. He often recounted the anecdote throughout his lifetime and, in a chat with the penitential canon of Barcelona, Dr. Ballester, when quite old, he pointed to that moment in his youth as a turning point—the most important in his creative development.» [7]

This incident marked the beginning of the interest which later led him to study the multiple aspects of the liturgy and to become one of the most effective campaigners for liturgical

4. In referring to himself, Gaudí used the first person plural.
5. J. Elias, *op. cit.*, p. 91.
6. Luis Alonso Luengo, *Gaudí en Astorga*, (Astorga: 1954), p. 14.
7. *Ibid.*, p. 15.

restoration in Barcelona. In later years, conversing with the prelate of Málaga, Don Manuel González, Gaudí called these years «the most productive in his liturgical formation.» [8]

49. THE AMBIENCE

For Gaudí, the Astorgan setting had two well-differentiated aspects. One, that which radiated from the person of the bishop, was agreeable to him, as was the post of diocesan architect which had been conferred on him and which gave him the opportunity to make important reforms in the seminary as well as to study the village churches and buildings which, like some of those in the town itself, impressed him favorably. On the other hand, he could not get along with the other side—not with the canons, nor with the people, nor with anyone for that matter who saw things in a way different from his own.

Dr. Grau was a great man who stood out from the crowd of which he never felt himself a part. One day after a somewhat tedious exchange of impressions between the bishop and the vicar general with the architect present, the prelate lamented to Gaudí once they were alone that not even the vicar general could understand him. [9]

This general situation put Gaudí in a state of hypersensitivity. On one of his visits to Astorga, he was joined at the bishop's table by the ex-minister Pío Gullón who throughout the meal extolled the brilliant oratory in the *Cortes*, [10] finishing up with high praise for Castelar —a model of grandiloquence at the time; the architect intervened to point out the celebrated orator's emphatic mannerisms. [11] On another occasion he was invited to sit in on the exams of an excellent seminary student who was to expound upon archaeological themes. The student was the illustrious Astorgan Antolín López Peláez, who years later became famous as a political speaker in the Senate while at the same time bishop of Jaca, and who died while serving as archbishop in Tarragona. Gaudí was not satisfied with him either. He found his facile diction to be lacking in content.

50. THE WORK AND PAYMENT

In 1891 and the following years, construction of the palace progressed rapidly. Once the lower floors were built and the general structure underway, the architect had to return to Barcelona where, with the crypt of the Sagrada Familia now covered, he planned to begin the apse in a more personal vein than he had been able to follow in the crypt. This did not mean that he forgot the work in Astorga; he followed its progress closely by means of photographs sent to him every week showing how the columns and vaults of the halls and chapel were erected under the care of the two foremen whom he had taken there with him at the beginning of the work. It appears that this last detail displeased some of the industrialists in the town, but this did not keep Gaudí from being so enthusiastic about the job that at one point he personally took part in the building work.

The case of the mounting of the triple arch of the portico which is related in the cited chronicles is significant in demonstrating the obstinate diligence which he applied to all of his affairs. These unusually shaped arches which broadened out to one side involved a complex wooden cradle system which he wished to simplify. The task turned out to be difficult, and the voussoirs caved in twice halfway through the construction. «Half of the town crowded into the area surrounding the construction site, contemplating the spectacle, and architects all over Spain awaited with ironic smiles the result of that *madness*, while Gaudí, mounted on a platform and withdrawn from all that surrounded him, throwing up his arms at every movement of the stone, took on the aspect of an impetuous flame.»

The bold deed was accomplished at sunset, but snow and a strong southwesterly wind again destroyed it. Far from flagging, Gaudí's energy grew, and he personally—with the aid of his second assistant Pedro Luengo—rebuilt the arches which were finally consolidated and held. «The architects hands, the skin blistering, were for a moment one with the stone and his pulse one with the workman who, many years later in recalling that moment with emotion, was to proudly claim that the most valued recognition of his noble craftsmanship had been Gaudí's embrace, once the last stone of the portico was put in place never to move again.» [12]

Gaudí was not well paid for his efforts. Toward the end of 1892 he realized that after four years of work he hadn't received a single cent of his salary on this job which was being financed by the Ministry of Justice with the funds administered by a diocesan Committee for the Reparation of Churches over which the bishop presided. An official petition in his own hand was sent to the bishop expressing his personal thanks for the attention afforded him during his three sojourns in Astorga—the only material benefit which his work had produced to that point. He complained of the neglect shown by the state which «contrasts in a sorry way» with the treatment he had received from other private clients. And he attached a bill for his salary which had climbed to 3.433,88 pesetas, requesting that the bishop carry his petition to the ministry.

8. *Ibid.*, p. 11.
9. Unpublished notes on a conversation with Gaudí.
10. The national legislature in Spain.
11. Martinell, *op. cit.*, p. 74.
12. Alonso Luengo, *op. cit.*, pp. 17, 18.

Once the petition had been considered and numerous reports sent out, the ministry responded with excuses and it was not until years later that the architect was successful in collecting what was owed him.[13]

51. THE DEATH OF THE BISHOP

In 1893 Gaudí was again in Astorga. The bishop fell ill while making his pastoral visitation rounds in the diocese and called for him. The prelate did not feel that his sickness was very important, but the architect knew intuitively that he was dying, and said so to those around him. He told the architect Pijoan who has recorded his words: «Do you know why I knew that the bishop was dying? I found him so beautifully transformed that I had the idea that he couldn't live. He was beautiful, too beautiful. All of his personal character had disappeared: the lines of his face, his color, his voice. And perfect beauty cannot live. The abstract face of the Greek divinity could never have lived.»[14]

The bishop was not to return to Astorga alive. He died during that pastoral visit. Gaudí was profoundly affected by the death of his friend, to whom he paid concrete tribute in his sorrow by personally erecting a small tabernacle in the church of the seminary; at the back there was a sober catafalque on which the box with the prelate's remains was placed. The funeral procession was attended by Gaudí who knelt devoutly beside the ornamental tabernacle. It was also the architect who prepared his sepulcher for him: a rough funeral urn in six pieces of the same granite as the palace, with only the humble inscription «JOANNES, 1893» below. The slab which covers the ashes bears the prelate's coat of arms which, according to tradition, Gaudí sculpted with his own hands.[15]

52 DISAGREEMENTS WITH THE CHAPTER (Figs. 43, 44)

The chronicler Alonso Luengo reports Gaudí's renunciation of the direction of the work on the palace in the following manner, which I transcribe in its entirety, being an Astorgan view which coincides with that which Gaudí held regarding the disagreeable end:

43. The state of the Episcopal Palace in Astorga when Gaudí resigned as director of the works on the prelate's death.

13. *Ibid.*, p. 22.

14. *La Veu de Catalunya,* January 20, 1906.

15. Alonso Luengo, *op. cit.,* p. 25, and complementary reports from Pedro Rodríguez López, *Episcopologio Asturicense* (1908).

44. Rear view of the bishop's palace at Astorga, just as it was at the bishop's death.

«Construction was interrupted shortly after the death of the prelate, for the chaplains who took the vacated leadership of the Diocesan Committee for the Restoration of Churches, lacking the bishop's extraordinary vision, tried to abide by more practical norms. Incapable of understanding the latent liturgical symbolism of Gaudí's work, they tangled with him in heated arguments over the difficulty of adapting the building to the needs of an Astorgan residence—which they definitely considered to be its sole purpose—and over the cost of labor, materials, etc.

«Gaudí, thus deprived of the confidence and comprehension which had been unlimited with Dr. Grau, was extremely irritated; he withdrew the craftsmen that he had originally brought with him from Catalonia and he took back the plans. From León he sent the Committee the following official statement: 'As there no longer exists the complete conformity of point of view and value standards which existed between my respected friend the late prelate of your diocese, His Excellency Don Juan Bautista Grau, and myself—a circumstance which I consider essential and indispensable for the successful completion of the work on the Episcopal Palace of your city—I find myself in the position of placing in your hands as president of the Diocesan Committee my resignation as directing architect of the same.'

«The local press decried the chapter's incomprehension, exalting the genius of Gaudí; the chaplains defended themselves through agreements and letters which were passed from hand to hand, and the small city became for several months the stage setting for the most passionate discussions.»

It is reported that Gaudí, growing angrier day by day, burned the plans of the palace in order that he never again be tempted to continue it, and that he made the following declaration with which he considered the whole affair terminated: «They will be incapable of finishing it, and capable of leaving it unfinished.» [16]

The chronicler explains later that Gaudí did not burn the plans—as we can well imagine. It would have been an act of theatricality out of keeping with his manner. Besides, it would have been useless as there always remained the copies for the official record. In order to clear up these lamentable disagreements, he appealed to the head of the archdiocese in Va-

16. Alonso Luengo, *op. cit.*, pp. 25, 26.

63

45. Gaudí at 36. From an exhibitor's pass to the Universal Exposition in Barcelona in 1888.

17. Unpublished notes on a conversation with Gaudí.

18. Told to me by Bernardo M. Galán who, from age 17 to age 20, worked as timekeeper on the work of Gaudí in León and heard the phrase from the maestro himself. Communicated in April, 1961.

19. Martinell, *op. cit.*, pp. 66, 67.

20. J. Pijoan, «L'Obra de la Sagrada Família,» *Forma* (1907), pp. 128 ff.; Martinell, «La Sagrada Família, Temple de Catalunya,» *El Pirineu Català* (Ripoll), March 20, 1915.

21. Alonso Luengo, *op. cit.*, p. 27.

22. When the Centro de Estudios Gaudinistas visited this palace in April, 1960, we were accompanied by the bishop who fully explained his adapted plan then in progress.

lladolid, but the archbishop would not receive him.[17] Seeing this hostile indifference on the higher level, and being aware of the desire proclaimed by some Astorgans to «sweep away the Catalans,» he decided with sorrow to abandon Astorga with the intention of never returning. He told a friend of his from León that he never again wanted to pass through the city, «not even in a balloon.» [18] Years later he still vividly remembered the incomprehension on the part of the Astorga chapter toward his work, as is confirmed by the anecdote which I have published elsewhere concerning a chaplain «who knew a lot about construction work,» and tried to modify Gaudí's building with lamentable results.[19]

As Gaudí had foreseen, the palace remained without a roof for 20 years until the bishop Julián de Diego Alcolea in 1904 understood the value of the work begun and wished to bring it to a worthy conclusion. To this end he sent various emissaries to the architect to commission him to finish it, always receiving the same negative answer.[20] A dinner set up for this purpose by Eusebio Güell at his house in Barcelona, with Gaudí and Alcolea present, was no more sucessful. «A delicious after-dinner conversation,» Alcolea commented later, «but definitively disappointing.»[21]. In view of the architect's irreversible negative, the bishop entrusted the termination of the work to another architect who did not follow the original plans. The palace was not inhabited until 1961, when the bishop Castelltort undertook its total completion. But even he was not able to carry this out, due to his sudden death.[22]

53. A LARGE BUILDING FOR A SMALL CITY (Figs. 278 - 284)

In the late 1890's, the city of León had about 16,000 inhabitants (one-fifth of its present population), and except for the cathedral, the grandiose monastery of San Marcos, and the collegiate church of San Isidoro, the rest of the city—save the sober Renaissance palace of the Guzmán family (XVI century)—was made up of simple and structurally unpretentious residential buildings. Years before, an important textile trade had been established by Juan Homs y Botinás who came from Catalonia. One of his employees, Simón Fernández, married Homs' sister-in-law, and the company of «Homs and Fernández» was founded. It later became «Fernández and Andrés,» when another of Homs' employees was taken into partnership. The company also had a banking house of the sort common in those days, annexed to the textile warehouse and based on the buying and selling of securities and the exchange of gold. Most of the textiles were bought in Barcelona where the partners frequently travelled, being on very good terms with the manufacturers «Güell, Parellada, & Co.» to whom they revealed their plans to construct a new building. It was Eusebio Güell who recommended Gaudí as the architect.[1]

Gaudí submitted the plans in December, 1891, a time hardly suited for open-air masonry work in that climate. He took advantage of the winter months to gather the necessary materials together in storage near the construction site. He went to León to give pertinent instructions and also to take notes on the foundations of the building, which were to be laid on land which did not seem firm enough to support the huge building which he planned to erect.

The messrs. «Fernández and Andrés» were mainly interested in several large business warehouses which the architect designed for the street floor and basement, adding four other floors that were designed for residential use and which turned the building into an apartment house as well, making it the largest building in the city after the three mentioned above. As the building was unusual for this city and because he had his suspicions concerning the firmness of the ground, Gaudí set about studying the site and possible precedents with care; he studied the ruins of an existing Roman building and also the cathedral, where he found that in both the problem was solved by expanding the area of the base—a solution which he decided to adopt in his work as well.[2]

When he felt that the opportune moment had come, the architect moved to León, taking with him a team of skilled workmen and craftsmen. There were no specialized workers in the city except for the stonecutters who were working on the restoration of the cathedral. He was also aided by Claudio Alsina, a highly able assistant who visited the construction site every few months to see that Don Antonio's orders were carried out, and to keep him posted on the state of the work.[3] When the good weather came, the previously planned and prepared construction work was put into motion and the house grew rapidly before the astonished eyes of the Leonese people who admired the grandiosity of the building.

54. TECHNICAL BACKBITING (Figs. 45, 46)

By the time that Gaudí began to work in León he had overcome his religious indifference. After he had begun the palace at Astorga he had lived for periods with the bishop there; in the León project he gave the image of St. George a position of prominence on the main façade. In the get-togethers at the Barcelona Ateneo he was impressing people with his modest ways and gentle manner of speaking; nevertheless he was still only at the beginning of his «metamorphosis». He had lost the elegant air of his youth along with his blond beard and fashionable long hair, and had taken on the bourgeois aspect which is apparent in the photograph on his pass to the Barcelona Exposition of 1888: his head is shaved and he has the full face of a man who enjoys good food. Perhaps the attentions which he enjoyed during his stays in Astorga, to which he alludes in his official petition on salary claims as the only material benefit which his work there had brought him, referred to the meals in the bishop's company. He lived there with him in cordial friendship which was not without its arguments; but with everyone else but the construction workers, the disagreements were continuous.

In going to León he hoped not to pursue a similar path, and so he decided not to .mingle with the Leonese people, whose customs he judged to be different from his own. He gave an indication of his nascent religiosity by taking lodging in the house of the Catalan canon, Cayetano Sentís Grau, who was a friend of his and was also the ecclesiastical governor. He showed his independent character in periods of disdainfulness, refusing to make a single courtesy visit or to return those made to him, in order to avoid wasting time.[4]

46. Corbelled stones of the corner tower of the Casa Fernández Andrés in León whose construction gave rise to adverse comments.

1. Information communicated in April, 1961, by Bernardo Martínez Galán of León.

2. Martinell, *Conversaciones con Gaudí*, p. 66.

3. Statement by Bernardo M. Galán in May, 1961.

4. Martinell, *op. cit.*, p. 66.

Such scarcely sociable procedure created an atmosphere of ill-will around him, especially among the local technicians who did not look with pleasure on the presence of a foreign architect in their midst. Thus, when they saw the foundations which he laid for this house in the most central spot in the town—foundations different from the kind commonly employed in the region—several of the engineers spread the word in the cafés and informal get-togethers of the town that the foundations were poorly done, since «piles, piledrivers, and other such things» [5] had not been employed.

As it happened, to hold in place the corbel stones which were to support the four corner towers, they had to be propped up before being actually built in; with the atmosphere prepared, people believed that the house was indeed about to collapse and needed to be propped up. The town, stirred up as it was by the opinions of the technicians, filled with the murmured false alarm until even the little children coming out of school would clamor, «The house of the Botines is falling down!»

Gaudí was informed that an engineer who had been consulted on the case had answered, «I don't know... I just don't know...» The architect turned sharply on the man who gave him the news, saying that if the engineer knew so little about his profession, then he was ignorant. [6] He added that he would be willing to admit any opposing technical opinions on the condition that they be presented in writing and signed, so that once the house was finished they could be exhibited in a prominent place in the vestibule. And thus the impertinent chatter of the technicians was silenced. [7]

55. AN EXEMPLARY WORK

In the third part of this book we will discuss the architectural aspects of the León house. Here we can note the exemplary value of the work carried out under Gaudí's orders. The architect himself was seldom in León since he was busy in Barcelona working out the new structure which he planned to use on the Sagrada Familia, and was also working on the Teresan School which he had been commissioned to do at the same time as the Leonese house. These affairs obliged him to space out his visits to the construction site, but the gaps were effectively filled by the more frequent trips of his deputy, Alsina, who transmitted his instructions.

Although the architecture of the building produced no descendants in León, due to the great difference in building traditions at the time in that area, the town did, on the other hand, receive the benefit of the stay of several of the craftsmen whom Gaudí took with him to work on the building. One of the master builders, Mariano Padró, stayed on to practice creditably in León for several years as a contractor before returning to Barcelona. Another, Vicente Simó, married and remained as a contractor in that city where his sons now reside.

In spite of the many modern buildings which have embellished the Leonese capital in the last half-century, this house which presides over the central Plaza de San Marcelo has lost none of its primacy. An example of the esteem with which León regards that great building was the general protest which was heard around 1950 over the plan to replace Gaudí's image of St. George with another one. The Gaudinian image continues to stand over the entrance to the building which is today owned by the Caja de Ahorros y Monte de Piedad bank of León which has its offices there.

5. Ibid.
6. Ibid.
7. Told to me by Gaudí himself on November 9, 1915.

56. A NEW ARCHITECTURAL THEME (Figs. 285 - 295)

In these chapters we do not intend to follow the master's work exclusively in terms of the jobs themselves, but rather in terms of those people related to them who may have had a spiritual or personal influence on his life. We have seen how Bocabella and Bishop Grau influenced his religious life, and Güell his social. In his work on the convent-school of the mother house of the Order of Sta. Teresa de Jesús, he became impressed by the Reverend Enrique de Ossó, whose influence was exerted more through his exemplary virtue than by a direct apostolate in the style of Bocabella and Dr. Grau.

In 1888, Gaudí was put in charge of the construction of the mother house for the Order of Sta. Teresa de Jesús on the Calle de Ganduxer, thanks to the good offices of his friend, the illustrious Francisco Marsal who recommended him to Reverend Ossó. It is possible that Gaudí was more interested in the new architectural theme than in the religious quality of the patronage. In this new trust he saw a recognition of his merits and the assurance of prestige as a worthy architect; he was, of course, pleased with it as a professional triumph, and also as a new area for the development of the architectonic passion which possessed him. Nevertheless, if we use the work itself as our criterion, we see that it is in this building that his Catholic orthodoxy begins to operate in an overt manner, judging from the abundance of religious symbols which will be discussed later (XLIII - 175).

Thus, after having designed the aristocratic home for the Güells, the palace in Astorga, and the great Temple which was still in the beginning stages, he was given the opportunity to do an important academic building as well as its church and a residence for the nuns. The theme was complicated by the necessity to respect the Order's scarcity of economic resources; Gaudí took this shortage of funds into account, but his constant desire for perfection

47. A religious motif on the entrance gate to the Teresan convent, Calle Ganduxer, Barcelona.

and the artistic criteria which he felt applicable in this case seem to have produced at least some friction, if not a strained relationship, in his dealings with Reverend Ossó who would have preferred less art and more economy.

57. TO EACH HIS OWN

In order to repay Dr. Marsal's friendship, the architect hastened the construction work as much as possible so that by April, 1890 (the first stone having been placed on August 27, 1888), the building was well enough along to allow the community and school to move in, which they did on the 19th of that month. Many of the artistic details projected by the architect were left unfinished because of the pressure of time and also because of their expensiveness which would have exceeded the funds at the Order's disposal.

The present nuns recall that when the venerable founder protested the growing number of bills for brick needed by the architect for the proper completion of the building, Gaudí, undisturbed, replied: «To each his own, Reverend Enrique. I'll build houses, you say mass and preach sermons,» demonstrating that with Father Ossó he felt himself to be more an architect than a catechumen.[1]

He admired Father Ossó for his virtue and for his organizational spirit which became apparent during the construction period, but this admiration, with all of the beneficial effects which it had on him, could not make him renounce his intentions in relation to the building. His independent and unconventional dealings with the venerable priest reveal a facet of Gaudí's character which was later to become more marked, even in his period of the most purified religiosity—i.e., his sharp manner of address, even used sometimes with priests.

The school and residence built by Gaudí is only a part of the overall plan. When, in 1912, the Order wanted to build the projected church, they approached the architect once more and asked him to make certain simplifications and modifications of a liturgical sort. He would not yield,[2] and it was he himself who proposed that they hire another architect for the job.

1. I am indebted to Mother Donata of this same college who supplied me with the historical details of this chapter in a note written in February, 1964.
2. Bergós, *op. cit.*, p. 54.

58. A SENSE OF RESPONSIBILITY (Figs. 48, 49)

When the first stage of the convent-school of Sta. Teresa was finished in 1890, the crypt of the Sagrada Familia which had been used for services since 1885 was almost covered, although the vaults remained open until 1891. The first years of work on the temple marked a remarkable change in the architect. He already had works of great importance to his credit which had brought him fame while still a young man, but this church was to confirm his potentialities while at the same time awakening responsibility for the new commitment—not as a laborious charge, but as the spur which would enliven his constant desire for perfection. For a short while he even felt within him the egotistical desire for the perfect temple but it was beyond his capabilities, given his preparation at the time.

A church must carry out a program of spiritual goals and motifs that demand meticulous preparation in order to be effective. Although Gaudí may not have aspired to achieve such results in an ideological sense, as an architect he nevertheless felt the responsibility of this delicated function, and he decided to prepare himself by studying the authoritative texts. Such texts soon became «documents» for meditational thought, and it was not long before Gaudí's half-dormant faith was revived.

Once he had completed the crypt—which he was forced to continue in the style already established—he began work on the apse in which he was able to exhibit his more personal talent, and which was to serve as the first step toward a grandiosity in the new church which each day he envisioned more profoundly.

59. THE SPIRIT OF THE TEMPLE CATCHES FIRE IN THE ARCHITECT (Figs. 50-52)

The religious, evangelical, and liturgical themes which were perhaps at first merely norms for the structuring of the building program, soon took fire in the architect and left a profound impression on him. It was impossible for his sensitive soul to ponder with indifference upon the tenderness of the Divine Infant's nativity, the cruel pain of the Passion, and the triumphant splendor of the Glory. All of it—glory, pain, and tenderness—suggested a cer-

48. Nativity façade at the end of the last century. The lighter-colored figures and elements are plaster models that the architect put up provisionally as a sort of experiment before their definitive execution.

tain grandiosity which he dreamed of making clearly visible in his work; he wanted the stones placed one on top of another to form verses of a magnificent poem which would be perceived by the eyes of the people and repeated through the centuries.

But this monument which he imagined would have to serve as an effective church in addition to projecting poetic beauty; it would have to be a place of prayer, where man could make contact with God through the sacraments and ceremonies of the cult. The discussions and colloquia on the liturgy which Gaudí had had with Dr. Grau in Astorga came back to him, and he read and re-read the treatise by Father Guéranger, which was to remain with him for the rest of his life; in this he discovered that the liturgy was the source of beauty in religious ceremonies, in addition to its religious significance. The architect often stated that by letting himself be guided by liturgical prescriptions, he would obtain the most beautiful solutions.

He carefully weighed each solution which he might apply to the temple in order to assure that it would be an exemplar in its artistic aspects, structural techniques, and religious effectiveness. He experienced again the tenets of what he had been taught as a child: that the church is where the Heavenly Father receives his earthly children and sanctifies them in order to lead them into heaven. As an architect he liked to steep himself with such ideas and then apply them to his work. We have seen that the devout Bocabella gave him *El Año Cristiano* and recommended that he read it. Gaudí followed it day by day, and to this reading he added others of greater amplitude, determined to convert their substance into stone in order to ennoble his total conception.

THE GREAT POEM IN STONE. The crypt and apse, finished in 1893, served as a sort of prologue while he prepared to begin the first canto of the great poem which he felt should commence with the Nativity façade, following logical chronological order. Someone argued that it would be preferable to begin with the Passion which was to face the city and which therefore would attract people to the work in progress. But the architect could «see» both façades and was of the opposite opinion. He had a feeling that the average person would not like the Passion façade which he intended to give angular and severe forms in keeping with the drama of Calvary—especially not if that façade were erected before that of the Nativity. The latter, on the other hand, though facing away from the center of the city, would be attractive because of its flowing and optimistic forms in harmony with the Birth of Christ. The new and architecturally unusual surfaces which were as yet imprecisely forming themselves in the imagination of the artist would lend themselves to the service of a cheerful theme, in contrast to the opposite façade with its anguished subject and details. The birth of the great temple and the canto of the Nativity, bathed in the rays of the rising sun, were one and the same thing to Gaudí.

49. State of the work on the Sagrada Familia seen from the inside in 1900.

The Nativity façade as originally planned was not to have had the dimensions which he later gave to it. Villar had designed a large church, but no greater than others in Barcelona. That which Gaudí first envisioned and realized in the apsidal part was to be larger, but not to the point of the grandiose conception which he eventually was able to project. The final grandeur of the Temple was due to a circumstance which Gaudí saw as providential, coming as it did at an opportune early moment.

This «providential» circumstance involved the receipt of a donation for the building fund of such proportions that Bishop Catalá considered it too great for one single work, and was inclined to turn part of it over to other pious businesses. Knowing or suspecting the bishop's point of view, the Temple Junta indicated to the architect that he should invest the donation money in construction as rapidly as possible; coming as he was about to begin work on the façade, this moved him to expand its projected size.[1] This economic leeway, along with the contemporary *modernista* vogue for symbols, gave rise to the wealth of ornament which set the tone for Gaudí's creation.

60. FROM SECULARISM TO FAITH

Concerning as it does an intimate process of which Gaudí never spoke, it is difficult to know exactly how the change from the young irreligious and care-free dandy to the austere man of faith of the later years came about. However, it does seem safe to assume a spiritual crisis which must have taken place at the same time as his incorporation into the work on the church.

It is probable that the architect vacillated between his secular ideas and his revived faith. A first stage of human, social, and sectarian considerations would have kept his religious life separate from the professional aspect of his work. A busy man has no reason to involve his private beliefs in the objectives of his occupation, even if it is centered on a church which he hopes to make a model of beauty and effectiveness. Faced with such a desire for perfection, it was logical that his God, who had carried him to that point, would then concede to him the grace of faith which he accepted.

The Reverend Joseph Thomas, S. J., who has studied a generically similar case writes: «He wanted to believe. He had accepted the faith. He believed that the choice was made once and for all, and he considered himself to be a man of faith; and in his eyes, the only problem was to continue thus. Little by little he was to discover that that was not the most essential thing. One does not spontaneously become a Christian. To be a Christian is something that is won, bit by bit, unceasingly, in all that one does. It concerns a difficult fidelity and a permanent ratification. Far from being played out in a single decision, the conversion is transformed into the ordinary course of our lives. Faith is a victory, a day-by-day victory over the world.» «This is the victory which has conquered the world, our faith.»[2] I believe that a similar process was at work on Gaudí—a process which he confirmed each day with greater fidelity and perseverance, replacing all of the secular and worldly bad habits of his spirit with religious truths and practices.[3]

1. Statement taken down from Gaudí himself.

2. Joseph Thomas, S. J., *Creer en Jesucristo*, p. 96.

3. He did not limit himself to those of the simple practitioner, but extended them to other areas. We know from L. Bonet y Punsoda that in 1913 and 1918 (and we can suppose that this was also true for the intervening years) he was a member of the San Magín confraternity in Tarragona (*Semana Santa*, Barcelona).

50. The grand Expiatory Temple in 1906, with plaster sculpture in the portal of Hope.

51. The towers under construction in 1904 when, in the course of the work, the architect changed them from square to circular plan, which seemed like a more nearly perfect solution. The *modernista* projection conceals this transition.

52. Overall idea of the great expiatory temple. Pen drawing by the architect Juan Rubió for a publicity pamphlet in 1915.

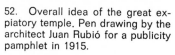

53. The architect confined to his bed because of excessive fasting during Lent, 1894. Drawing by R. Opisso to illustrate his article «Gaudí, una rigorosa abstinencia cuaresmal», *Diario de Barcelona*.

61. HIS OWN MOST EXACTING CRITIC

He earnestly struggled to achieve a perfection which he realized that he had not attained because of an untamed nature which spattered his life with intemperances. He was bothered by this, and to control himself better he became an exacting critic of his own behaviour, judging his actions more harshly than those around him would.

The Reverend Francisco Baldelló tells us that in the early days of the Spiritual League of Our Lady of Montserrat, of which Gaudí was a member, one secretary took the initiative of making a list of those members whose conduct was most edifying; among those listed was our architect. As the inquiring secretary observed defects in the people listed, he would cross them off until the day arrived when the only members remaining were the composer Millet and the architect Gaudí. When the latter heard of this he told the note-taker: «Would you please erase my name as well? Don't you know the *Tu solus sanctus* that we say in mass? There is only one who is perfect, and he is not in this world.»

62. CONVERGENT ACTIVITIES

If on the one hand an enemy lurked in his own character which turned him away from the mild manner which he would have liked, on the other, he had the compensation of his work, so intimately bound to the truths of faith which were the themes embodied in the Temple. The other jobs on which he worked often served as preliminary experiments which he would later use in the greater perfection of his favorite project. Such was the case with the interesting funicular study which he did for the church at the Güell colony between 1898 and 1908. According to his own admission, this study was undertaken more with the idea of using it on the Sagrada Familia than on the Colonia Güell church where he applied the system in only a partial manner.

63. EXTREME AUSTERITY (Fig. 53)

During Lent of 1894, Gaudí's fasts became so extreme that, his strength exhausted, he stayed huddled in his residence on the Calle Diputación 339, fourth floor, second door, where his assistant Francisco Berenguer visited him almost every day to consult with him concerning details of the work. He grew weaker by the day, and on Palm Sunday his assistants on the temple decided to pay a collective visit. They found him in a lamentable state of collapse, stretched out on the bed with all of his clothes on, an old overcoat serving as a blanket, in a scantily furnished room with strips of wallpaper hanging from the walls and a modest crucifix without artistic merit above a «Viennese» style sofa. His assistant Opisso said that never as in those moments had he seen «in the weak face of Gaudí, such nobility and saint-like majesty.»

The pleas of his father—now in his 70's—with whom he lived, and who sought the help of his friend Dr. Santaló, were not successful in dissuading him from his abstinence, nor was his niece who also lived with him, nor his visitors.

Fearing a fatal end, his collaborators Rubió and Berenguer decided to go to his intimate friend, Dr. Torras y Bages, who lived nearby. After prudent reflection and a difficult inner struggle over whether to continue his sacrifice or give in to the spiritual reasoning of the wise Doctor, Gaudí «awakened as if by miracle from that profound lethargic sleep into which he had sunk, and an expression of extreme thankfulness illuminated his features.» [4]

Just as he was able to free himself from human sentimentality and from the material comfort of dressing fashionably as he used to, he also discarded the protection of wealth and of

4. Ricardo Opisso, «Gaudí: una rigurosa abstinencia cuaresmal,» *Diario de Barcelona*, March 24, 1951.

the dominating spirit which had characterized him in his youth. He donated his properties in Reus and Riudoms to pious or altruistic causes and he refused to accept payment for his work on the Sagrada Familia, save the rudimentary meal cooked for him daily at noon by the caretaker of the office pavilion—a meal of ascetic sobriety.

64. AUTHORITARIAN, INSPIRED, AND HUMBLE

He refused payment, and would not tolerate adulation. Most difficult for him was to control his dominating spirit. He imposed his criteria not out of pride, but out of the conviction that he was right; perhaps also because for him one of the conditions of being an architect was to «direct», a task almost always synonymous with command—and his command was quick and without diplomatic circumlocutions. He would not tolerate anyone's opposing him, though he would listen to reason if it was adequately presented.

As a counterpoint to these bursts of domination, the rest of his life and personal behaviour were saturated with such extreme humility that more than once he was offered alms by people on the street who took him for a poor shy beggar. He continued steadfastly along this road of abnegation for the rest of his life, without ever renouncing the light of inspiration which he considered to be a gift of God which should be put to His service in the greater perfection of the temple. The church was his only temporal concern, and someone wrote that he was a visionary who walked the streets carrying the Temple inside of him; indeed, it filled his whole being and his thoughts. He conceived of a magnificent temple of which he could see only the façade—a model of what the rest was to have been, always growing in perfection; and that Temple, even before it was born, acted upon him in a beneficial way, opening his eyes to the light of faith—perhaps in answer to the supplication sealed in the first stone which he had watched being laid, perhaps with a tinge of worldly skepticism, in 1882. Through this great work he offered his life and his person to God.

65.   INCOMPREHENSION

By the beginning of the last decade of the nineteenth century, Gaudí's personal and professional selves were fully consolidated. His architecture still moved about in historial styles, but the novelty of several of the solutions which he adopted in addition to their technical perfection had earned him fame as an eminent architect. The general public was perplexed by his accomplishments. They wanted to understand him, but it was not an easy task. Nevertheless, his forms were imposing. Those who did not understand them were at least respectful, and an intellectual minority frankly admired them. Along with this admiration by the intellectuals, several wealthy people with artistic sensitivity and a love of the new entrusted to him their commissions.

One such job came to him from the Marquis of Comillas—possibly influenced by his brother-in-law, Eusebio Güell—who hired him to design a monastery for the Franciscan missions in Tangiers, which was never executed. In this project, which was lost in 1936, he employed various towers similar in silhouette to those which he later constructed for the Sagrada Familia. The work in Tangiers was never carried out. According to Gaudí, this was due to the fact that the Marquis did not comprehend the magnitude of the Franciscan Legation in Tangiers, nor did he understand his project (Fig. 296).

66.   THE CALVET HOUSE (Figs. 54, 313-330)

In 1898 the heirs of the highly reputed Pedro Mártir Calvet, Pedro, Eduardo and Elisa, commissioned Gaudí to do the house at No. 52 (now No. 48) Calle de Caspe whose decorative detailing he resolved in a baroque style. The choice of Gaudí was based on the guarantee of excellence and modernity which his name had come to represent; perhaps another influential factor was his affinity in political ideas with Eduardo Calvet, a militant Catalanista and deputy to the *Cortes*. Proof that the choice was a good one came when the house was terminated in 1899 and awarded the prize which the City of Barcelona had just created to honor annually the building considered to be most artistically worthy. [1]

In the carefully delineated drawings for this building, of artistic value in themselves, we see signs of the architect's independent character. He exceeded the maximum height indicated in the city ordinances with the two gables crowning the main façade. When this was noticed in the municipal offices, they warned the architect in the customary manner, so that he could adapt the project to the prescribed regulations. When he was informed of the situation, Gaudí delegated his collaborator Juan Rubió to see the municipal officer concerned and to draw, in his presence, a horizontal line across the drawing at the maximum height permitted by the City, and to refuse to build higher than that point—leaving the facade abruptly interrupted. The architect's stubbornness, and perhaps the political prestige of the co-owner Eduardo, got the house built just as it had been designed.

Another indicative incident occurred during construction of this building, when the nun's convent next door (No. 54) got a court injunction against the violation of their privilege of a clear view from the windows of their patio along the property line. Accepting the nuns' just complaint, Gaudí invented an ingenious arrangement of inclined arches which we will discuss in the technical study of the house (XLV - 180).

Gaudí usually put one or more crosses on top of his buildings, and in this case, he put one of wrought iron on each of the two gables capping the façade. Toward the end of the construction work, the Güells stopped by for a visit, being friends of both the proprietors and the architect, and admirers of the latter as we have seen. From below it was difficult to distinguish the crosses, and the wife, seeing those motifs in twisted iron and feeling close enough to speak frankly with the architect, asked him what that «entanglement» of iron was up there; to which the architect, with equal frankness and a double meaning replied that that was a cross which «indeed is an entanglement and a nuisance to many.» [2]

Sometimes, as in the case just mentioned, Gaudí gave play to his sense of humor, often using it to put forward important moral or religious points of view, as here, or for political persuasion, or at times simply as a joke. In this same Casa Calvet, the knocker of the main door is an extremely interesting work in wrought iron whose symbolism has both political and comical character (Fig. 319).

1. My information about the family of this house was facilitated on February 28, 1964, by Don Sebastián Buxó Calvet, the son of Doña Elisa Calvet. According to this information, certain details mentioned by Sr. Elías in his book *Gaudí*, (pp. 163 ff.) are incorrect.
2. Bergós, *op. cit.*, p. 97.

54. Emblem over the entrance portal to the Casa Calvet, with the initial of the proprietors and a cypress, the symbol of hospitality.

67.   MINOR WORKS, EXPERIENCES, AND CONSULTATIONS (Figs. 55, 56)

As work continued on the Calvet house, he also worked intensively on several minor projects. One of these was a fencing wall and gate with a daring marquee for the property of Hermenegildo Miralles, a manufacturer of stamped relief articles in cardboard and bookbindings (Fig. 349-352).[3] Gaudí was on good terms with the manufacturer who let him use the powerful presses of his workshops to test resistance to compression in untried materials. At this same time he decorated one of the salons of the «Torino» bar with plaques similar to those used on the gate (Fig. 353) and also remodelled the first floor apartment of No. 3 Calle Puertaferrisa, where the Marquises of Castelldosrius moved from their house on the Calle Mendizábal.

In this period he also decorated the grottos of the «Sala Mercé» which were set up by his friend the painter Luis Graner as an attraction on the Rambla de los Estudios, showing himself to be an able scenographer of fantastic effects. He also designed the tiny entertainment hall which still exists in the Cinema Atlántico on the Rambla de los Estudios, 122, and designed a house for the same artist in 1904 which got no further than the foundations (Figs. 354, 355).

At the end of the last century, he spent several summer days on the ancient family estate of Francisco Ullar at Sant Feliu de Codines. On that occasion the proprietor asked Gaudí to design a textile factory which he was planning to build there. The architect designed a banner for the factory's choral society (Figs. 347, 348), but the actual building project was never completed by him; only a few general suggestions which gave a maximum of openings to the façade and reduced the filling to pillars and supporting arches—a novel solution at that time when traditional windows still prevailed in such buildings. The factory was completed

3. Regarding the present disposition of the work, see Note XLVI-4.

in 1901 and still exists with its huge circular arches, suggested by Gaudí, but without Gaudinian forms. [4]

In September 1900, the «Lliga Espiritual de la Mare de Déu de Montserrat» for which Gaudí served as a member of the board of directors, commissioned him to direct the monumental First Mystery of Glory of the Rosary on that holy mountain, which we will discuss in greater detail in Part Three.[5] Some of his trips to the site were made in the company of his father who retained incredible health and agility for his 90-odd years.

It appears that he was not pleased with his work at Montserrat, judging from what I have been told by the architect Pericas to whom he described it with severe criticism for the monks. He censured them among other things for not having realized what a magnificent natural spire the so-called «pierced rock» could have formed, had it housed a great bell which would have become the voice of the mountain. Pericas later developed this idea graphically in a commercial prospectus for a bell foundry (Figs. 55, 56).

The most insignificant facets of Gaudí's life, both professional and private, were always somehow related to his artistic ideals. Everything was related to his architectural work which he constantly submitted to the most rigorous self-criticism. Whereas on the one hand he respected architectural tradition, on the other he did not rely on routine structural solutions and his revisionist spirit constantly posed questions which he tried to work out through direct observation.

For a period in these decades he was concerned with the internal stresses which were produced within the mass of all materials subjected to compression —a phenomenon which he interpreted in a manner different from the treatises on the Resistance of Materials. It was here that his friendship with Miralles came in handy, for he could use his compressors in his experiments. José Pijoan tells us of one such experiment to which he was invited by Gaudí.

«He was technically concerned with the fact that materials will support weights up to their breaking point, and that when they do break it is not with a single length-wise fissure, but rather it begins with little cracks halfway up. One day he took us to the Miralles book bindery which contained the most enormous hydraulic press to be found in Barcelona. In preparation, he had cut out meter-high prisms from the stone which he wanted to use, and now set about subjecting them to pressure in order to observe how they would react under greater loads. Gaudí was excited and satisfied as he watched the behaviour of the prisms of various stones. 'You see? You see how they swell in the middle rather than splitting from top to bottom? The Greeks understood this mechanical phenomenon and enlarged their columns at the center making the diameter larger than above or below. That is the *entasis*. Our instinct also tells us that cylindrical columns are wrong when we see them.' And indeed, the blocks which Gaudí had brought along to the Miralles workshop now looked as if they were smiling, with the wrinkles which formed at their centers.» [6]

Many years later I heard him sustain the theory: that materials do not break by simple compression or extension, but rather by flexion.

As proof of the architect's growing reputation, we can cite the fact that his opinion was often sought in difficult situations. For example, when the architect Jaussely was drawing up his plan for the general urbanization of the city, he came to Gaudí to ask his opinion on the area surrounding the Sagrada Familia, and incorporated it into his project.[7]

He was also consulted by his friend Dr. Torras y Bages in two outstanding instances when the latter was serving as bishop of Vich. On the first occasion, he included Gaudí on the committee presided over by the canon Dr. Collell which was appointed in 1905 to advise on the sketches submitted by the painter José María Sert for the decoration of the Vich cathedral. The canon and the architect disagreed on the paintings, and the latter told Sert directly that in order to produce paintings that would harmonize with the pious climate of the district, or art which would respectfully portray the history of the diocese, it was «absolutely impossible to do so from Paris or New York» where the painter resided. Gaudí expressed the opinion that Sert, rather than a painter, was a «dealer in paintings.» [8]

The second counsel sought by Dr. Torras came years later when he named Gaudí to the commission which also included the architects Font y Gumá and José María Pericas and was to report on Alejandro Soler y March's project for the renovation of the cathedral of Manresa.

Several years earlier, in 1908, Gaudí had been consulted by the official architects commissioned by the City to draw up a project in memory of Jaime I, who asked him for his opinion concerning a monument to the «conqueror» king. When the chapter of the cathedral of Barcelona decided, in 1911, to illuminate their temple electrically, Gaudí was consulted by one of the canons. Dealing as he was with the most important church of the city whose splendor is all-imposing, he answered in writing despite his usual reluctance to do so, but his advice was not followed.[9]

4. Information supplied by Don Josep Umbert y Rosés who published it in part in the Program of the Fiesta Mayor of San Feliu de Codines in 1966.

5. The documentation on this «Mystery» comes from the monastery archive. I am grateful to the monk Dom Reinald M. Bozzo for facilitating and collaborating in the research. See XLVI-185.

6. José Pijoan, «Algo sobre Gaudí,» *Destino* No. 1229, (February 25, 1961).

7. Isidro Puig Boada, *El Templo de la Sagrada Familia*, (Barcelona: 1952), p. 22.

8. Told to me by the architect José M. Pericas (July 20, 1964) who had heard it from Gaudí.

9. Martinell, *op. cit.*, pp. 77, 78.

55. The «roca foradada» of Montserrat which Gaudí suggested could be made into a grand natural bell tower.

56. Drawing by the architect José M. Pericas interpreting the previous suggestion.

In addition to these cases and others which could be cited of a public nature, his opinion was solicited in private works as well, and he usually acceded even though due attention was not always paid to his advice.

68. TWO SIGNIFICANT WORKS (Figs. 331-346, 485-489)

A work of outstanding personality was that commissioned by Doña María Sagués, the widow Figueras, a great admirer of Gaudí's work, and which was realized from 1900 to 1902 on the site known as Bellesguard in the Bonanova section above Barcelona, where the king Martin the Humane had made his summer home; from there he could see the boats as they neared the coast. This historical framework suggested the medieval style adopted by the architect, and the look of a feudal castle which he chose to give to the building.

During the summer of 1901, the Bishop of Mallorca, Dr. Campins, was in Barcelona and he discussed with Gaudí his project for the liturgical restoration of his Balearic Island cathedral. Gaudí's feeling for the liturgy and artistic culture immensely impressed the prelate.[10] The consequence of this exchange of opinions was a trip to Mallorca where the architect spent several days in the cathedral studying the delicate problem of moving the choir from the center of the nave where it was to the more appropriate site in the presbytery. The rapid manner in which he carried out the necessary modifications caused much talk among the Mallorcan canons who were not favorably inclined toward innovation. Gaudí nevertheless effected the restoration with enthusiasm, and he could always count on the prelate's confidence for support.

In spite of his busy schedule, Gaudí made several extended trips to Palma in order to study conscientiously this difficult commitment. On one of his visits, he worked out the models for some angels which he planned to put on the baldachin, and which were executed using a personal process which we will discuss later (XXVIII - 121). This process was later repeatedly applied in the Sagrada Familia. He was a guest at the episcopal palace, and, as in Astorga, he took his meals at the bishop's table though here with greater frugality for he had adopted a vegetarian diet in the meantime. On the other hand, the after-dinner conversations were sometimes animated by guests who enjoyed talking with the maestro, and there were fascinating discussions of subjects of art and liturgy.

In the third part of this book we will discuss Gaudí's restoration work in detail. Here we limit ourselves to the personal aspects of his stay in Palma which was reminiscent of that in Astorga as he mingled with the prelate and quarreled with the «ambience» (XLIX - 194).

On the Day of the Immaculate Conception in 1904, the first part of the restoration was inaugurated. At the ceremony, Miguel Costa y Llobera preached a sermon which highly praised the work accomplished. In reality, however, this praise was shared by only a select few; the other souls felt terrorized by the decisions of the restorer. Gaudí's plans pleased the majority less and less, including King Alfonso XIII, who had offered to aid in the restoration of the royal mausoleums in the chapel of the Trinity. Kerrigan notes that «the longer Gaudí's presence remained in the cathedral, the less he was considered in any way as the total restorer.»[11]

Nevertheless, the architect continued his visits to Palma and kept busily at work. Kerrigan reports that one day in 1914, after a dispute or quarrel with the masons, the architect went

10. Emilio Sagristá, pbro., *Gaudí en la Catedral de Mallorca,* (Castellón de la Plana: 1962).

11. Anthony Kerrigan, «Gaudí Restaurador,» *Papeles de Son Armadans,* 35 bis, (December 1959), p. 121.

straight to the episcopal palace and the next day embarked for Barcelona. It has been said that this action coincided with a lack of funds for the continuation of the work. Whatever the case, the architect never returned. The next year his friend and admirer Bishop Campins died.

69. A TRANSCENDENTAL MODEL

We see then, that in the transition over the turn of the century our architect reached a high level of professional activity considering both the extent of his work and his intense creativity, developed in a quiet and conscientious manner. This was the incubational period for the ingenious works which were soon to appear, as we can see by the study which he made for the church which his friend Güell asked him to design for the industrial colony of Santa Coloma de Cervelló.

The variety of the works entrusted to him, each with its own special characteristics, did not divert him from those architectonic problems which had obsessively percolated in his mind since his youth. He had just finished the Nativity façade, and he was preparing to erect the four towers of the Sagrada Familia. He was not yet ready to undertake the covering of the great nave, but he was considering the most logical manner to do so. This problem had preoccupied him for some time, and although he saw the road to the solution intuitively, he wanted to assure himself that he stood on firm ground before undertaking a project of such large dimensions.

The commission to do the little church, coming as it did from such a close and understanding friend as Don Eusebio, gave him the opportunity to work out to his satisfaction the mechanical problems of its support in order to apply his findings later to the Sagrada Familia. Thus it was that instead of beginning his studies for the new job with paper and pencil, he proceeded to construct a three-dimensional model using cords and sacks of weighed birdshot in a manner which we will explain in more detail later. Through this process he arrived at the structurally equilibrated forms which he had intuited beforehand.

Ten years were spent in study and calculation before the construction work began in 1908; work was suspended six years later with only the crypt and its porch completed. The results of his studies gave Gaudí much to think about. The carefully considered funiculars of his model produced unquestionably logical inclined pillars. The fact that such pillars had never been used in construction before revealed to him the supreme importance of his model. After some initial hesitancy he adopted the model, believing it to represent a structural advance which it was his duty to put into practice.

In those same years, the same patron also commissioned him to layout the venerable «Montaner de Dalt» property which he converted into the Park Güell—testing as he did the applicability here of the inclined piers, with successful artistic and structural results. Along with this innovation came others, making the park a showplace for the original and sensitive Gaudí who had not, up to that point, asserted himself and his powerful personality to the extent which would be demonstrated from here on.

XVIII. PROFESSIONAL PLENITUDE

Gaudí's clients were necessarily wealthy persons with selective taste, and not easily frightened—persons willing to allow works of such astounding originality. Such were the characteristics, as we have seen, of his friend Güell, in whose project for a park he tried out the inclined pillars of roughly cut stone in bold tectonic expression and unusual form as prescribed by the funicular model we have mentioned.

In spite of the fact that by the beginning of the century European architecture in general was seeking new forms (Secessionism, Art Nouveau) which would put an end to the previously dominant historical eclecticism, the average man in the street was confused by the vigorous originality of the master Gaudí. The public could allow superficial decorative novelties such as Gaudí himself employed in some of his earlier works, but not those which went deeper, such as the obviously revolutionary innovations of the works just mentioned and those which were yet to come. It is not surprising that prospective clients of the architect would think twice before engaging him—for both economic and esthetic reasons.

1. Pedro Ricart, «Gaudí en la Casa Batlló,» unpublished lecture given in the Centro de Estudios Gaudinistas on May 21, 1963, at the Official College of Architects of Catalonia and Baleares.

2. Administrative Archive of the Ayuntamiento of Barcelona, certificate 9612 of the Expansión Commission. All data referring to this house come from this source unless otherwise noted.

70. AN AVANT GARDE HOUSE (Figs. 57, 433-459)

The house at 43 Paseo de Gracia (then no. 103) was built in 1877, in line with the impersonal standards of its day,[1] and in 1901 the proprietor, José Batlló, asked the City's permission to tear it down.[2] This proposal was not carried out, however, and in May 1904 the proprietor sought to construct underground cellars and to roof the interior rooms of the main floor ac-

57. Upper part of the Batlló façade, lowered on either side to adapt it to the height of the neighboring house. House on the right was recently heightened.

58. Column on the ground floor of the Casa Milá which projects into the Paseo de Gracia beyond the distance allowed by the Municipal Ordinances.

59. Caricature of the Casa Milá published in the weekly *Cu-cut*, January, 1909.

cording to plans signed by Gaudí on April 6. On November 7 he clarified in writing that he had given up the plans for demolition and that he wanted to build underground cellars, remodel the four existing floors and construct a fifth floor with servants' quarters above the flat roof. We can attribute this change of plan to Gaudí who had been recommended to Batlló by his friend Pedro Milá, who soon would himself commission another building on the same avenue. This renovation gave impetus to the blossoming of Modernismo on the grand Barcelona *paseo*—a style of which Gaudí became the most unusual exponent.[3]

On April 18, 1906, when work was already well advanced on the construction of the lower part of the façade which had been begun from scratch, the City ordered that the work be halted as it had been advised by a warden that the socles had been built 60 centimeters into the public right-of-way. Work was not suspended, and after various legal maneuvers, the order was repeated on April 30. On June 5 there was another denunciation, this time for the construction of an interior mezzanine and two rooms on the roof not mentioned in the application, and therefore not authorized. This must have been taken care of in spite of the architect's lack of concern for such procedures, for the house was finished without further incident, and on October 13 of the same year, authorization to rent out apartments was requested.

When the remodelling was finished, the house became the topic of general conversation due to its unusual forms, and the object of caricature in the humor magazines which called it the «house of the yawns,» referring to the rounded shape of the tribune openings, and the «house of the bones,» referring to the small columns in the shape of shin bones.

71.   AN ACT OF SOLIDARITY (Fig. 57)

Some writers do not understand, and have even criticized, the asymmetry of the upper portion of the Batlló façade, with the «unmotivated» presence of the little terrace and the lateral turret with the cross on top. When Gaudí observed the Casa Amatller next door, built by the architect Puig y Cadafalch in 1901, with its façade terminating in a medieval manner in the stepped pediment springing from the fourth floor, he felt that the five floors of the Batlló house would create a contrast that would prove detrimental to the neighboring façade. In order to avoid this, he pulled his back, leaving the tiny gallery or terrace almost on a level with the contiguous house; in order to compose and justify the resultant empty space he introduced the little tower topped with the four-armed cross characteristic of many of his other works which he had originally planned for the center.[4]

72.   A HOUSE BEYOND THE ORDINANCES   (Figs. 58-60, 450-483)

As we have seen, the Casa Batlló awakened general curiosity, and for the *diputado* Pedro Milá who had recommended the architect to his friend and who had made frequent visits to the construction site, it was the decisive proof that he should entrust to Gaudí the design of the large building which he was planning to erect on the same *paseo,* at the corner of Calle de Provenza. Gaudí was the only person who could conceive the delightfully modern building that he wanted. In addition, his wife and the proprietor of the building, Doña Rosa-

3. At the same time, Doménech y Montaner was building the Lleó Morera house at number 35 on the same *paseo*. It was in the *modernista* style and was terminated in 1905.

4. Communicated by the architect Jaime Bayó Font, executive contractor of the remodelling job, on April 25, 1953.

60. Caricature of the Casa Milá which appeared in the weekly *L'Esquella de la Torratxa.*

rio Segimón, also preferred him as she had been born in Reus like the architect, and recalled with sympathy his modest origins.

This big building was his last private commission, and it came about 30 years after the tiny lamppost in the Plaza Real. Comparing these two extremes, we find in them both the same structural dignity and the same ideal of perfection. What had explicitly changed, apart from the size of the two works, was the operational procedures and his professional expertise. In the first, we noted the meticulous drawings, carefully executed and water-colored with life-sized details which were faithfully followed, as well as the explicit instructions and the absolute compliance with rules of the authorities. This was characteristic of his method for quite some time—until the Casa Calvet. In the last two works, and especially in the latter one, he offers us plans which seem to have been done free-hand—drawings of sketchy quality which he did not follow in practice; subtracting here and adding or varying elements and dimensions there, ignoring completely the ordinances, he provoked denunciations by the authorities and suspensions of the construction work.

Gaudí signed and dated the plans in February, 1906; on the second of that month they were presented to the City; they were approved on June 15.[5] That year and the next, work proceeded normally without interruption, but on January 28, 1908, work was suspended on account of a column that stuck out a meter too far into the sidewalk of the Paseo de Gracia. Although informed of the infraction, the architect decided not to correct the position of the column. The City then authorized the cutting off of that portion that was in excess of the ordinance. Gaudí said that he would respect the cut but that he would also add an inscription explaining the reason for the defacement.[6] The building of the column was terminated on February 7 of that year and the column still exists intact.

On September 28, 1909, when work on the house was well along, a city inspector filed a complaint against several structures on the roof which exceeded the maximum height allowable by ordinance. The city's chief architect, Plantada, reported that «infringement of Article 118 of the Municipal Ordinances cannot be tolerated,» and as a consequence, on the 21st of October the mayor ordered that the work be suspended. The building appeared to be already finished, but an inspection by Plantada revealed that the servants' quarters «which are still quite far from completion» were involved in the roof structures, and on November 6 a period of 24 hours was allowed for the suspension of building activity.

Another report by the chief architect as to whether the house had been constructed in accordance with the approved plans found affirmatively as far as the surface area and the number of floors were concerned, but negatively as far as height, which exceeded that indicated in the plans and also that permitted by the ordinances. This was due to the fact that the height of each floor had been increased, exceeding the permitted maximum by some 4.4 meters altogether. In addition there were various penthouses for the use of the servants of varying heights above the fourth floor and six towers some six meters in height scattered over the roof. On November 13, 1909, the architect presented his opinion that the demolition of the excessive parts should be ordered.

5. The information relating to the City comes from the Administrative Archive, certificate 10526 of the Expansion Commission.

6. Told to me by Gaudí himself.

Fortunately, some of those who were to judge the issue realized the artistic importance of this work, and when the Committee on Expansion met on December 20, it was proposed that, in view of the fact that what constituted the infractions gave artistic value to the building, it be listed among those already provided for in the ordinances as artistic landmarks, by which means it would be possible to legalize the transgressions; the city agreed to do so on December 28. At the end of December, 1910, the owner Doña Rosario Segimón de Milá announced that the house was finished, and asked permission to rent out apartments and take up residence on the main floor. Permission was granted on January 31, 1912.

GAUDÍ'S ATTITUDE. Our architect paid little attention to the official requirements, believing that his criterion would win in the end—as indeed it did. Not only did it win, but that case served as a precedent for others of a similar nature. It was followed by the Vicente Ferrer building at the corner of the Ronda San Pedro and the Plaza Cataluña.

Telling me of this incident years later he compared it to what happens in the ports of Northern Europe where ice immobilizes the boats in the winter. When melting begins, the first to go out are the biggest that have the power to break the ice. The less powerful follow behind. He said this without snobbery or arrogance: simply stating a fact.

73. OTHER EPISODES

In July of 1909 there occurred in Barcelona the events which later came to be known as the «Semana Trágica» (Week of Tragedy) and which, although basically political in origin, took on an anti-religious aspect as all of the convents in Barcelona went up in flames.

The anti-religious demonstrations lasted from July 26 to July 30, and caused the Milás to decide to omit all external religious symbolism on their building in order to avoid any confusion about its purpose in future disorders. This decision produced great disgust on the part of the architect who resolutely insisted on maintaining his original proposals. The husband had conveyed the order to him on one of his trips from Blanes to Barcelona, and the architect almost succeeded in convincing him; however, he made his consent conditional, depending upon the agreement of his wife who was in Blanes. Gaudí traveled to that coastal town one afternoon in the hopes of persuading the owner with religious arguments. But it was useless: Doña Rosario felt that religion was a private matter which did not call for external signs, and even less so under the circumstances. The suppression of the image of the Virgin which Gaudí had wanted to include provoked a definite tension in the relationship between the proprietors and the architect, which in turn led to an inferiority in some of the interior detailing at variance from the original design.

The architect Jaime Bayó, contractor for this house, told me that for the undulating cornice of the interior patios, designed to catch the water from the roof, Gaudí ordered that the projecting parts be executed without iron reinforcing. One day the director noticed that in the forge installed at the construction site they were working on T-irons which he suspected to be a sort of reinforcement, and he repeated to Bayó his order that they not be employed in that spot. Nevertheless, taking advantage of a trip by Don Antonio to Mallorca, the contractor ordered that the reinforcements be put in place. Gaudí, seeing this on his return, reproached Bayó for having disobeyed his order. A short time later a workman happened to slip on the mansard roof and landed in the gutter—22 meters above the ground—and supported himself there thanks to the irons. When Gaudí heard of this, from Bayó himself, he admitted that he had done well in reinforcing the cornice.

Once the building was finished and the tall barricade which had hidden it from view was removed, the general public's reaction was one of perplexity; no one dared to take a stand on its beauty or artistic value. In spite of its air of evident superiority, most people did not like it, being unprepared for such an intense and unexpected design. Nevertheless, a select minority of intellectuals and artists appreciated it from the beginning [7] and there appeared commentaries and caricatures in the press to please all tastes.

74. GAUDÍ IN REUS: FRUSTRATED WORKS

The commissions for two of Gaudí's most important works (the Casa Milá and the Episcopal Palace at Astorga) may have come to him, at least in part, through the influence of the Reusian origins of the commissioners, Sra. Segimón de Milá and Dr. Grau. Nevertheless, the city of Reus itself does not possess a single work in spite of the architect's natural desire to construct something in his native city—especially in honor of the Virgin of Mercy of whom, as a man of faith and as a Reusian, he was a devoted worshipper.

In 1904, when the canonical coronation of this image was celebrated, he attended the religious ceremony and took advantage of the occasion to stay with his relatives for several days, expressing to them more than once his desire to build a new sanctuary for the Virgin of Mercy.

7. *Revista Nova* dedicated issue no. 7 (May 23, 1914) to this house and the architecture of Gaudí. As an exception, «Xenius» (Eugenio d'Ors) from his «Glosari» column in *La Veu de Catalunya*, established himself in opposition to that architecture.

Two years later, Gaudí's dream was almost realized. The administrative committee of the sanctuary solicited several designs for either a new building or the remodeling of the existing one, and of these they selected one presented by Gaudí.[8] In order to discuss the project with the members of the committee, Gaudí met with them and the two Reusian architects, Rubió and Sugrañes one summer morning in 1906 in the furniture store of Fusté, Sugrañes' uncle. There they went over the plans for the new building to be constructed.[9]

Between this first reunion and another which took place in the afternoon, something occurred which remains a mystery, as a result of which the committee, in the second meeting, expressed its surprise at the extent of the project and its cost (XLVI - 184) saying that they would be unable to undertake the work. When the three architects went to Fusté's house around five to pick up a suitcase that Gaudí had left there, the latter showed his disgust saying «Let's go. In our own town they don't want our plans, our models or our direction.» And he added «even if we had raised the money they wouldn't have wanted it. From morning to afternoon there was a change. I don't understand what could have happened.»

According to Gaudí, the plans were accompanied by a model, and the project was apparently not accepted by the committee because of pressure from other architects living in Reus at the time.

If on the one hand the architect wanted to leave examples of his work in Reus, the citizens of that town felt the same way, and the above-mentioned incident was not his only attempt to realize this mutual desire. Guix Sugrañes tells us how a wealthy commercial and banking firm, desiring a work of the illustrious son of Reus, commissioned him to design a new building which they planned to erect in a central spot in that city.[10] This time the proposed project was not carried out because they were unable to acquire a neighboring building which stood in the way of the new one. Guix says, «when the committee of the Banco de España was ready to erect its building on the Arrabal de Santa Ana, they commissioned Gaudí to do the project. But the latter refused any limitations and would not give an estimate, for he wanted to construct a building so original that people would come even from abroad to admire it.»[11]

It is too bad that such proposals did not become reality. Their rejection must have caused some disenchantment in the sensitive spirit of the architect, considering the contrast with the appreciation which his work had received in Barcelona. Nevertheless, he was above such personal disappointment, and his affection for his native town was not weakened on this score. This is confirmed by the fact that he donated to the Municipality of Reus the house which he owned on what is now the Calle del Maestro de Anta and which was later torn down for urbanistic reasons; he designed the standard for the Reusian colony in Barcelona (lost in 1936) for their pilgrimage to the Virgin of Mercy; and he donated an image of the Virgin of Montserrat to the priory of San Pedro which was venerated there until 1936.

His trips to Reus were not very frequent, and were always hurried so that he would be away as little as possible from his work in Barcelona. Nevertheless, he attended the ceremony of the laying of the first stone of the Riudecanyes Dam—a highly important event for Reus—and through the son of a nephew, Antonio Ciré y Montserrat, who administered his land in Riudoms, he acquired ten shares in the dam enterprise in 1909.[12]

75. AN UNREALIZED GRANDIOSE PROJECT

Another proof of the fame achieved by Gaudí is the reported commission in 1908 from an American who admired his architecture, to design a hotel building for the United States which would surpass in dimension and in originality anything seen to that time. The idea remained up in the air, and we know of its grandiosity only from drawings which Juan Matamala made from memory of the preliminary project, any originals having been lost during the war in 1936 (XLVIII - 192).

Gaudí apparently remained enthusiastic about the commission for some time, not only because of its size and the original technical solutions by which he planned to carry it out, but also because he intended to donate his earnings on this commission to his favorite project —the Sagrada Familia.[13]

8. The notarial document which provides this information, cited by Guix Sugrañes, *op. cit.*, pp. 49, 50, speaks of a project for a new Sanctuary.» In spite of this we believe that it was actually only a remodelling job, given the good condition of that standing and the sumptuous *camarín* which Gaudí admired.

9. Declaration of Juan Fusté Gras, the son of the store owner. Guix Sugrañes, *op. cit.*, pp. 49, 50.

10. *Op. cit.*, pp. 196, 197.

11. *Idem.*

12. *Ibid.*, p. 169.

13. Information facilitated by Juan Matamala who lived almost as a member of the family with Gaudí.

XIX. THE GENIUS AT WORK AND AN AUSTERE LIFE

76. REDEMPTIVE LABOR (Fig. 61)

The last years of the 19th century and the first ones of this century marked a period of triumph for the architect in both the professional and spiritual fields. Those first cautious observations on esthetics in his student days had taken life in a new form of architectonic expression; his return to a more orthodox faith put an end to his youthful skepticism. This double triumph came as the result of an intense internal struggle, and a great deal of thought. His intelligence and optimism helped him in the battle, but the dangers and adversities provoked a profound crisis in his spirit, resulting in a deterioration of his health.

After careful study, both through inspiration and calculation, Gaudí had discovered new directions for architecture, on roads wider and more satisfying to his own sense of logic and plasticity. Perhaps with an inner pride, he recognized that he had taken the great step which we will study in Part Two of the present volume. He arrived at this stage by the persistent struggle to turn his material into idea, and in the fight he took a great deal of punishment. [1] Such punishment did not bother him, however, for it is necessary in redemptive labor and it brought him closer to the achievement of his ideal.

The air of mysticism which accompanied his successes placed the architect on a social level below that of his standing as a professional. Had he been an architect who operated like a businessman, or had he advertised himself in relation to the public, he could have situated himself socially on a higher level. But he was no longer interested in these material things; he was concerned rather with the purification of his art and of his spirit, which he felt could proceed only in the erection of his great church.

Having found his new architecture along the path to his God, he was anxious not to betray the divine generosity, and he planned all of his works within new standards. It soon became apparent to him that he owed all of his energies to the temple. That double vow of art and religion which he took in the fullness of youth would now, as he began to age, be perfected in a renunciation of all that was not his Sagrada Familia. He would see to his current commitments, but little by little he would disentangle himself from all worldly duties to live out his days in the service of the church which he was erecting in honor of Jesus, Mary, and Joseph—becoming himself a sort of living stone in the overall fabric.

77. AT THE PARK GÜELL (Fig. 62)

During the years in which Gaudí dedicated himself actively to his profession, his social life was appropriate to his professional prestige and in his everyday life he was in constant contact with the common people. In 1900 work was begun on the park commissioned by his friend Don Eusebio, and in the first years the project advanced rapidly. This was originally to have been a garden community, but only two houses were ever constructed —one in the upper part, by the lawyer Don Martín Trías Doménech, and another designed by Francisco Berenguer, the builder's technician for the park and Gaudí's assistant. Gaudí bought the latter house in 1906 and lived there with his reduced family. The places where he had lived up to that point had not offered any personal distinction—something he wanted less and less as his customs grew more simple. Nor did he buy the chalet in the new park out of a desire for greater social prestige or well-being, but rather in the interest of saving his aging father from the necessity of climbing to a fourth floor apartment and of providing him with a more healthy atmosphere and a more tranquil life than that of the city. The architect, also, wanted to flee from the ever-increasing bustle and noise of the city streets.

He went there to live with his father who was 93 and his niece, Rosa Ejea. The latter was the daughter of a sister who had died young and who had been married to an Andalusian musician who was both a Bohemian and an excessive drinker and had passed on to his daughter a certain lack of mental stability which, though not really constituting a deficiency, preoccupied her uncle during those six years which she outlived her grandfather. Gaudí's satisfaction in being able to provide his father with a tranquil old age did not last long, however, for he died after only eight months in the new house, leaving the architect alone with his niece and a servant girl.

1. Letter from Maragall to Pijoan, May 25, 1903.

In the early days in his new home he would dress with a certain amount of tidiness, and when he went home for the night he would sometimes do so in a covered coach.

He demanded of his niece a definite care in the appearance and services of the dining room, as well as of the entire house. He would not compromise with trivial conversation nor with the loving couples in the park, for which reason he ordered that such carrying-on not be permitted.[2] Nor did he make concessions for Rosa's romancing, but he did take her to the folkloric and children's shows that were presented in the park, as well as to religious functions and the decidedly moral «Espectacles Graner,» organized by his friend the painter.

Apart from the few worldly luxuries which he allowed himself, he led a generally ordered and exemplary life. Rising around seven, he would go without breakfast to his parish church of San Juan de Gracia where from the beginning he had been eager to take part as an active parishioner. There he would hear mass and receive the sacrament, a custom which he had followed for some time. When he died in 1926 he had taken the sacrament daily for over 30 years.

On certain holy days he would attend the services at the cathedral because there, he said, mass was celebrated for the entire city. Always in the same position, leaning against the column that supports the pulpit with hands folded and without sitting, he followed the ceremony with complete attention. He was bothered if anyone distracted him, and especially if they wanted to speak to him of architecture for there he felt himself to be neither architect nor artist, but simply a Christian.[3]

On workdays, when he had finished his devotions, he would dedicate himself fully to his professional work. At nightfall, almost always on foot, he headed for downtown Barcelona, usually to the oratory of San Felipe Neri where he attended meditations read by one of the Fathers and followed with enthusiasm the Litanies of the Saints which were recited daily after the meditation. [4]

2. Arturo Llopis, *Gaudí en la Villa de Gracia*, p. 13.
3. From some unpublished notes facilitated by Reverend Francisco Baldelló.
4. Baldelló, notes cited.

61. The architect in his Sagrada Familia office. Drawing by Ricardo Opisso.

To return to the park he took the tram which left from the little Plaza of Santa Ana, and when this was removed he took the one which left from Ausias March, next to the Plaza de Urquinaona. There was a newspaper stand where he customarily bought the evening edition of his favorite paper *La Veu de Catalunya,* which served him as reading matter during the trip. If it had not yet been delivered, he would await its arrival.

He would stand quietly, his back to the corner, awaiting the paper and looking very insignificant—or perhaps more than insignificant, humble. So humble did he appear that one day he was taken for one of those poor shy beggars who await a gift from some kind soul among the passers-by; someone approached him with a gesture offering money. For a moment, in order not to disappoint the donor, he was tempted to accept the alms, but he realized that this would have made a joke out of a charitable act and he delicately refused the gift.[5] On another occasion, according to Juan Matamala, the son of «senyor Llorenç,» he and Gaudí were standing one evening taking cover from the rain beneath a balcony on the Paseo de Gracia, and a passer-by gave him two pesetas, indicating that they were to be shared by the two of them. That day he accepted the donation, deciding to put the coins the next morning in the alms box for the Temple, which he did in the presence of «senyor Llorenç.»

If it seemed to him that he had not walked the distance which he considered necessary to his health during the day, he would return home on foot, accompanied in his last days by the Sagrada Familia model-maker, his good friend Lorenzo Matamala.

In his early years of living at the park, when Pope Pious X ordered that the people should participate in liturgical singing, Gaudí received the news of the reform with enthusiasm, and tried to use his influence to get his parish to establish the new liturgical practice as soon as possible, as had already been done in other parishes. He contacted other parishioners who felt the same way, and together they expressed to the priest, Reverend Salvador Barone, their desire. The priest cited certain obstacles, and with a few excuses put an end to the matter. This attitude aroused Gaudí who lost his serenity and said to the priest, «Well then, we will have to ask our Lord that he take you away as soon as possible; then the obstacles will begin to disappear and reform will take place more quickly.» Those assembled hid their surprise with smiles that attempted to make a joke out of the incident. It so happened that shortly thereafter the parishioners of San Juan participated in the singing of the high mass on holidays.[6]

78. HIS FRIEND MARAGALL

Gaudí's occasional obstreperous manner provided him with quite a few adversaries. Perhaps some of the enmities and hostilities which arose during his lifetime originated in judgments that were delivered in a sharp manner and without mitigating circumstances. On the other hand, he also had many good friends among the higher echelons of culture, religion, and politics, which dispel the image of him as being always intemperate.

One such friend was the poet Juan Maragall who was constantly in contact with him, and was one of the first persons to proclaim the importance of the Temple of the Sagrada Familia, when most people had not yet noticed it. As early as 1900, in the *Diario de Barcelona* for which he frequently wrote articles, he published the piece «A Temple is Born», announcing that it was something marvelous.

Maragall had great love and admiration for the architect who visited him on May 20, 1903, to ask him to write a speech aimed at raising money for the Mystery of Glory which he was directing for Montserrat. The poet gratefully received the petition and enthusiastically set about to satisfy Gaudí.[7] About the same time the architect invited the poet to visit Park Güell. They spoke a great deal about the meaning of ornamentation in southern countries, until they arrived at metaphysical conclusions which Maragall did not share, but neither the harmony of their discussions nor the poet's admiration were affected.[8] In an undated letter to Pijoan, Maragall tells him of a visit to the Sagrada Familia, where Gaudí expressed himself every day in a more expansive and more personal manner. It was «a sort of lecture on what is the measure of things, referring especially to architecture,» the poet writes, «which left me enchanted and full of ideas. I went home with the sensation of carrying away a treasure.»

It was perhaps this visit which gave rise to the article in the *Il·lustració Catalana* of 1905 in which he again speaks of the temple and of its architect. And that same year, in the *Diario de Barcelona,* he published his famous article «*Una Gràcia de Caritat...!*» to proclaim loudly and pathetically the precarious economic situation of the temple and how humiliating it would be should construction have to be halted for lack of alms donated to a work which would bring prestige to Catalonia; he repeated the same message the next year with another article in the same *Diario.*

62. Gaudí's residence in the Park Güell; designed by his assistant Berenguer. [This house, purchased by the *Amigos de Gaudí* of Barcelona in the early 1960s to serve as a museum of Gaudí memorabilia, now also houses the archival collection of that entity—one of the prime research tools for Gaudí and the Catalan architectural movement. — G. R. C.]

5. Told to me by Gaudí himself.
6. Baldelló, notes cited.
7. Letter from Maragall to José Pijoan dated May 20, 1903. *Obras Completas de Maragall,* XXIII.
8. *Idem.*

63. View of Barcelona with the convents burning during the *Semana Trágica*, July, 1909.

In 1907, the poet again praised the spiritual and artistic meaning of the temple in the art magazine *Forma* and that same year José Pijoan published an article entitled «*L'Obra de la Sagrada Familia*» in the same magazine.

Such articles demonstrate his friends' admiration for his work and the affection which they felt for him and to which Gaudí responded. In addition to these friendships we could mention that of Dr. Torras y Bages, both before he was elevated to the seat of bishop of Vich and during his bishopric; that which we have seen with the bishop Grau of Astorga; and that with Dr. Campins of Palma de Mallorca. There were also the wise Jesuit Casanovas, Dr. Santaló, Luis Millet, Cambó, Prat de la Riba, Martín Trías...

79. THE TRIAS FAMILY

The lawyer Don Martín Trías Doménech was the first and only man to buy real estate in the new park. He commissioned the architect Julio Batllebell to design the house that he was planning to build, for the two had been fellow students in secondary school, and in their subsequent friendship had taken advantage of each others' reciprocal professional services whenever necessary.[9]

Gaudí was surprised at the intervention of another architect in the area which he was developing, and he mentioned this to Sr. Trías who explained the situation to him. Gaudí accepted his reasons as justified. He had hoped to design this house himself because of the special topography of the lot which he had planned to take into account by making the entrance be by way of the roof, placing the kitchens with their smoke and fumes on the top floor and the other services on the lower floors; all would be connected by a comfortable interior stairway and exterior inclined ramps. This incident did not for one moment cloud the relationship between the architect and the lawyer, and the friendship grew when the architect went to live in the park and their visits became mutual and frequent during the summer months that the Trías family spent there.

Gaudí's friendship was strongest with the son Alfonso, despite the great difference in age, and the latter felt from the beginning a great admiration and affection for the brilliant artist. In order that he would not have to cross the solitary roads of the park alone when he arrived at nighttime, Alfonso would go out to meet him when he came, whether by tram to the Plaza de Rovira, or by carriage to the foot of the Calle Larrard.

There his young companion would be every night, ready to undertake the climb which Gaudí tempered with frequent stops at friendly houses along the way—an example of the characteristic affable treatment which the architect enjoyed. The first stop was usually at either the house of the Valls or the Codorniu at the entrance to the street. Further up he would enter the «El Caballo Blanco» snack bar which was also the grocery store where the neighbors of the park did their shopping and whose owner was a friend.

9. Information from Dr. Alfonso Trías Maxenchs, son of Don Martín Trías.

And finally they would stop to talk to the milk-selling goatherds, two brothers fond of music and literature with whom he chatted on these subjects, discussing the new Wagnerian music which was then the fashion in the philharmonic circles of Barcelona. An hour and sometimes more was spent in such conversations, but at the entrance to the park there was always a period of small talk with Carlos the gatekeeper who was an intelligent botanist and the cultivator of the nursery for the park's plant supply; he cared for and protected them jealously with numerous signs saying «respect the flowers,» and «do not stray from the paths.» When the journey was over, the young Alfonso—today the eminent doctor, Trías Maxench, to whom we are grateful for the tale—would leave the architect at his house and continue the climb up to his own.[10]

Sometimes on Sunday mornings the boy would accompany Gaudí to the religious services at the cathedral and when they came out they would take the older man's favorite walk —along the jetty where he delighted in the sight of the sea. They would return along the same wharf, always next to the water and contemplating it until they reached the Puerta de la Paz and the foot of the monument to Columbus which Gaudí admired for the size of its statue, so well adjusted to the distance from which it was to be seen.

The conversation was a monologue by Gaudí who enjoyed commenting on political and artistic events. The Sunday crowds which surrounded them were of no interest. When they arrived at the end of the Rambla de Canaletas, they would cross the Plaza de Cataluña on the diagonal and continue up the Paseo de Gracia, more elegant and less crowded. The monologue continued, hardly interrupted by the discreet interventions of the adolescent who only broke in to suggest new subjects. These led to others: the supply was inexhaustible—from his professional or personal life, or from his extensive readings, recalled in a vivid and lively manner in the conversation. He seldom spoke of travel which he did not enjoy.

At the Calle de Aragón they would turn to the right and proceed to the nearby convent of teaching nuns, where the architect would stop in a manner which would terminate the walk; with an affable gesture he held out his hand to say good-bye to the boy. It was time to eat. In this house the architect found his frugal repast some Sunday afternoons.

80. THE «WEEK OF TRAGEDY» (Fig. 63)

The first decade of this century in Catalonia was filled with political and social disturbances. The region was attempting to recover from the collapse of Catalan industry and commerce as a result of the recent loss of the colonies of Cuba, Puerto Rico, and the Philippines in 1898. Economic energy was channeled into strategies of a political sort sometimes disguised as social demands. The central government meanwhile found itself obliged to repress insurrections and attacks by Moroccan Berbers who were disputing Spanish sovereignty in North Africa, making it necessary to send troops which were embarked from the port of Barcelona. This was all that was needed by the anarchist elements who, with the help of the workers' organizations, ordered a general strike as a protest against the embarcation.

This event paralyzed the working life of Barcelona, and the city was tragically illuminated by the fires that rose up from the convents. Gaudí, secluded in Güell Park in forced inactivity, contemplated the flames and quantities of smoke which dotted the city with heavy heart from his house on the hill. We can imagine how these events must have reverberated in the architect's religious and civic-oriented soul.

The sad spectacle evoked for him similar cases in history, and to calm his nerves he read of the burning of Constantinople in the early middle ages. The emperor, in a critical moment of his flight from the city, contemplated it from the other side of the Bosporous, and Gaudí established a parallel between the emperor who believed that surrender was imminent and the Barcelona authorities who were not certain that they could control the uprising. The emperor also saw many churches in flames—among them that of Santa Sophia with its wooden roof. When order was restored, he ordered that a new basilica be erected to Santa Sophia with an incombustible structure. The new temple was directed by three main architects with another two hundred at their orders, and an army of workers. Even so, the construction went on for over two centuries...[11] And Gaudí thought of the slow progress of *his* church which, with so few workers, could very well also turn out to be a work of centuries.

Those afternoons he would visit the Trias house where his young friend was sick in bed, and while he thus returned the long hours of companionship that he owed to the boy he also found comfort from his forced reclusion, disclosing his fears that the temple might become a victim of the revolt. The boy soothed him, prophesying that they would not destroy that work which could potentially give jobs to many workers. Gaudí thanked him for the prediction with a «May God hear you!»[12]

The anti-religious vandalism of that «Semana Trágica» left a strong impression on Gaudí and he felt that it should be taken as a lesson for the future, especially by the clergy, many of

10. Told to me by Dr. Alfonso Trías Maxenchs on the 2nd and 20th of June, 1964, at which time he also related information in the following paragraphs.
11. Recollections provided by Gaudí himself in a conversation on January 23, 1915, reproduced in *Conversaciones con Gaudí*, pp. 23, 24.
12. Reported by Dr. Trías.

64. Lampposts at Vich commemorating the centenary of Balmes, suggested by Gaudí and executed by the architects Canaleta and Jujol.

whose number had been assassinated. In spite of his religious nature, Gaudí was often hard on the priests. Much to his displeasure, Reverend Brasó, who was at that time directing the parish of San Juan de Gracia, experienced one of the architect's outbursts. Gaudí was advising certain measures to guard against the dominant anti-clericalism when the priest replied, «That is not my business.» Gaudí countered: «Then wait until they kill you, too, and put someone in your place who *will* tend to business.» Perhaps the Reverend realized the importance of what he was trying to say, but the bad impression left by the rude response stayed with him for the rest of his life.[13]

81. AN EXHIBITION IN PARIS

Gaudí's fame was established, and despite his natural anti-exhibitionism and his opposition to publicity, his name crossed the border, and a number of admirers from neighboring France, including the ex-minister of foreign affairs, Hanotaux, the painter Bouche, and the writer Marius-Ary Leblond, organized an exhibition of the maestro's work in the spring of 1910 at the «Société Nationale des Beaux Arts» in Paris. This idea was enthusiastically supported by the architect's friend and admirer Eusebio Güell who took care of the cost of photographs, models, transportation, and the rest of the exposition.[14]

It would seem that Gaudí was not opposed to the idea, for he assisted in the preparation of the material and he directed the polychromy of the model of the Nativity façade which was executed by Jujol. But in spite of his acquiescence, the exhibition project caused more skepticism than enthusiasm on his part because he imagined that the French would be unable to comprehend his work.[15]

He was accorded special treatment by the «Société,» with a special hall in the architecture section dedicated to his work alone, and everything that he sent was accepted without having to pass a jury of admission. But Gaudí's apprehensions were still not assuaged. Güell himself, recently distinguished with the title of Count, invited the architect to accompany him on one of his frequent trips to Paris. We have described in chapter XI the delicate manner in which the invitation was made, and how Gaudí declined.

In order that the exhibition would not be without the explanations that were considered necessary given the novelty of Gaudí's forms and structures, it was decided that the architect Jerónimo Martorell should go to Paris at the expense of the exhibition to explain the directions of the new architecture. Before leaving, he had a long conversation with Gaudí who warned him that in Paris they would not understand his architecture and that the public would be disturbed by the parabolic profile of the four bell towers. The explanation that he should give was that that form assumed «a perfection of the Gothic bell towers.» Such an explanation was bound to cause protests, and Gaudí recommended that Martorell not argue, but rather wait until the opponents had exhausted their arguments and when they had finished, to reply without flinching «that it was a perfection of the Gothic» and nothing more.[16]

The exhibition was a success in terms of numbers of visitors, and it stirred up lively polemics. While some persons, more or less understanding it, admired the new architecture, others attacked it zealously and «at one point they even feared disagreeable and violent consequences,» according to a report in the paper La Veu de Catalunya. Parisian criticism reflected the two tendencies: some papers printed adverse articles while other, more artistically reliable publications, such as L'Art et les Artistes, contained articles such as that of

13. Told to me by the sculptor J. M. Camps Arnau on April 27, 1955.

14. *Anuario de la Asociación de Arquitectos de Cataluña,* 1911.

15. Stated by Gaudí on several occasions.

16. Martinell, *op. cit.,* p. 104.

Marius-Ary Leblond which studied the outstanding works of the exposition in a conscientious manner. Although the opinions were not all laudatory, Gaudí's architecture received the blessing of international criticism, and along with the art of Catalonia it emerged triumphant from the test.

When the criticism of that exhibition of 1910 is seen in retrospect, in comparison with the general esteem which Gaudí's work enjoyed in exhibitions celebrated later in Paris itself, in New York, and in numerous foreign cities, it becomes clear that the detracting elements at that time were a lack of preparation and clear vision of the future. Time, the great truthsayer, has since given its verdict.

In spite of the fact that Gaudí never thought much of «northern» criticism, he could not help but have been influenced, as a sensitive individual, by the adverse opinions, and above all by the incomprehension of his architecture. This, along with a bout with Maltese fever, which aflicted him for many years, and his persistent spiritual tension—not in concern for the external success of his work, but rather for its perfection—produced in the architect a state of depression which forced him to take several weeks of rest far from his habitual tasks. His friend Father Ignacio Casanovas advised that he go to Vich and found him adequate lodging there.

82. A REST IN VICH

The pharmacist Joaquín Vilaplana who was Gaudí's companion during his stay in Vich told me in a letter of May 11, 1955, written at the age of 86, that the architect's affliction was «an obstinate anaemia contracted through an excess of intellectual work» and that his trip took place in 1910; at the recommendation of Father Ignacio Casanovas, S. J., he was a guest in the house «of the noble and pious Sra. Rocafiguera,» where he stayed for some three weeks. Once settled in that palatial mansion, it seems that he was intent on passing unnoticed and on being as little bother as possible. Thus he refused the luxurious apartment that had been readied for him and preferred one of the most modest in the house. Every morning he went to mass and to take the sacraments, and then would breakfast on a piece of bread toasted almost to the point of being burned.[17] Reverend Puigneró informs us that after breakfast he would usually spend long hours in the Diocesan Museum, contemplating the valuable objects housed there and chatting with the conservator, Reverend José Gudiol.[18] On occasion he would visit the bishop, Dr. Torras y Bages, whose friendship he had enjoyed in Barcelona and with whom he ate lunch several times. His meals at Sra. Rocafiguera's were of a most frugal sort within the limits of his vegetarian diet.

Sra. Rocafiguera was worried by the architect's personal habits, and in order to make his stay more pleasant, she solicited the aid of a friend, the pharmacist Vilaplana, to serve as a companion in the afternoons on his walks through the city and the surrounding area. From the record of these walks, preserved in the statements of the companion himself, it appears that their discussions became difficult, possibly due to their mutual intolerance of each others' opinions on art. According to what can be deduced from the end of the pharmacist's letter when he says, «I, too, have painted and drawn a great deal, and I have read an infinite number of books on art and seen innumerable famous buildings,» Sr. Vilaplana must have felt himself artistically prepared and with a right to his own opinions—something which was difficult for Gaudí to accept unless one took into account his esthetic points of view.

The Vich pharmacist was left with an unpleasant recollection of these promenades on which Gaudí «never spoke of his works nor of those of other Barcelona architects. He said that true art had been developed only in Rome and on the shores of the Mediterranean.» This resumé of Gaudí's opinions must have been deduced from the diatribes and attacks most probably produced when the pharmacist attempted to impose his points of view on the architect.

83. THE BALMES CENTENNIAL (Fig. 64)

It seems that Gaudí's presence in the capital of the Ausonensian Plain aroused certain expectations among those who knew of his customs and independent opinions, which he made no effort to conceal. Vich was at that time preparing to celebrate the centennial of the birth of Balmes, and the local authorities, appreciating the importance of a famous architect in such circumstances, sought his advice on a design for the monument which they were planning to erect in honor of the famous philosopher next to the house where he died. Gaudí studied the problem and came to the conclusion that the large monument that the authorities desired was not appropriate for the location due to the reduced dimensions of the little plaza, and he felt that it would be more fitting to erect something with urbanistic benefits, such as a fountain, which could be given a commemorative character.

The idea developed and became two obelisks of basalt and forged iron which could also be used as lampposts and which were placed at the Calle de Verdaguer entrance to the Plaza Mayor. The architect Canaleta was in charge of the structural part, and Jujol did the poly-

17. Jordi Elias, *Gaudí*, p. 168.
18. Told to me by the Rev. Gaspar Puigneró Bofill at 72, at his home in Vich on June 5, 1964.

chromy. These two obelisks, so original in form and structure, were the outstanding note in the preparations for that solemn ceremony, and even later they continued to draw a great diversity of comment, not all of it favorable.

In spite of the fact that the apparent authors of the work were the two above-mentioned architects who had just worked with Gaudí on the Casa Milá, everyone imagined that these obelisks were inspired by the brilliant master himself. It is possible that this was so, given the similarity of technique and materials to the basalt pillars used in the crypt of the church at the Güell colony, and to the balconies of the Milá house which Jujol had also painted.[19]

84. MORE REST AND A WILL IN PUIGCERDÁ

Once he had terminated his rest period in Vich, Gaudí returned to his normal life; but the next year the Maltese fever reappeared. This, together with his past debility, forced him to take another rest trip, this time to Puigcerdá in the company of his friend, Dr. Santaló. They stayed in the Hotel de Europa and spent several days in walks and placid conversation which were quite different from those of Vich due to the understanding on the part of the intimate friend.

On one of those days, June 9, 1911, Gaudí dictated his will before the notary of the town, a certain Cantó, in which he provided for the disposition of his material goods after his death.[20] In the will he left his house in Güell Park to the Sagrada Familia building fund, and also left a fund to his collaborator and friend the architect Juan Rubió.

19. These lampposts were torn down in 1923 at the beginning of the dictatorial regime of Primo de Rivera. It was an act of reaction against the politics of the people who had promoted the idea: the bishop Torras y Bages, the canon Collel, the archaeologist Rev. Gudiol, Gaudí himself — all in the *Catalanista* camp. When the dectruction was accomplished it was inspected personally by the Captain General, Emilio Barrera and the Civil Governor, Milans del Bosch.

20. Guix, *op. cit.*, p. 205.

XX. A RECLUSE IN "HIS" TEMPLE

At times I wonder if Gaudí realized the great responsibility which he had taken on when he gave the initial impulse to such magnificence for the Temple. I think that he was more likely carried away by his genius, and that he dreamed and created this great work without thinking of the consequences of carrying it out—consequences which would soon become apparent, i.e., the scarcity of alms and the long duration of the construction work which went even slower after the implementation of his newly invented system. These were problems which never ceased to worry him. Disappointments and personal inconveniences may also have induced him to leave off all that was not the Sagrada Familia and to dedicate to his favorite work all of the energies and years of his life that remained. Always before he had given the Temple precedence, but from here on he would devote himself exclusively to this work. He made his home in the workshop and offices of the Temple and he would watch the growth of his creation with the loving interest of a father watching the growth of a son.

85. VISITORS (Figs. 65, 66)

The exclusive dedication which Gaudí desired, without interferences of any sort, was nevertheless disturbed by the very interest which his work aroused in itself and as a result of the procedures employed which had never before been used in other works. As early as 1894 the press reported the unusual gesso reliefs which had been provisionally put in place to be studied *in situ* as models of the definitive sculptures, and mention was made of column bases in the form of turtles and huge snails seen in the architect's studio.[1] Such news items called attention to the author of the new façade which grew with an unknown quantity of original and expressive forms. Even before the silhouette of the towers began to appear, no single illustrious visitor could visit Barcelona without feeling himself obliged to visit the new temple... and its architect who would have preferred to remain peacefully absorbed in his studies and his stone.

The visits which he disliked the most were those of an official nature with their complicated protocol and people talking about architecture without understanding it; especially not his architecture which was completely esoteric for so many people. When King Alfonso XIII visited the temple in April 1904 he was received according to protocol, but it seems that Gaudí was quite uncommunicative with him. It is not true, however, that he refused to speak to him because he preferred not to speak Castilian as has been said. I don't know who served as the guide for that visit, but when the king asked the architect what style the temple was in he answered «gótico» in Castilian.[2] He spoke in Catalan to those who accompanied the retinue. As they moved from one place to another, someone asked where they were going, and Gaudí replied «ara anirem a veure el senyor Llorenç.»[3]

He was a bit more pleasant with the high dignitaries of the Church. On November 20, 1899, the bishop of Mallorca, Dr. Campins, visited the temple and was amiably received by the architect who spent over two hours with him, explaining the meaning of the work in complete detail: «his words were fascinating for their overflowing fantasy and great intelligence, in many areas beyond the field of his specialty.»[4] When Cardinal Ragonesi visited the temple he sustained an animated dialogue with the architect whom he called «the Dante of architecture.»

If his visitor was an American prelate who spoke Castilian, Gaudí would usually speak to him in that language.[5]

The anonymous and humble persons who had to speak with the master for some reason or other were usually received in an amiable way, but if the visitor was a famous personality preceded by his distinctions, or especially by a reputation of heterodox ideology, it was certain that the conversation would turn into an argument.

In 1901 the ex-president of the Republic, Francisco Pi y Margall, presided over the Barcelona «Jocs Florals» (Floral Games). His presidential discourse, read in Catalan by his fellow party member Vallés y Ribot, was a heroic poem to the Catalan tongue, to the liberty of the various Iberian peoples, and to the right which all had to govern themselves. During the stay of the illustrious Barcelona-born statesman, his friends took him to visit the already famous temple. When Gaudí was notified of his presence he came out with pleasure, prepared to explain the details of the work's structure and design—in Catalan as was his custom, especially since he was dealing with a compatriot who only a few days before had exalted the excellences of his vernacular tongue in public.

65. Cardenal Ragonesi and other dignitaries are amiably received by Gaudí on a visit to the Temple.

---

1. *Diario de Barcelona*, November 9, 1894.

2. Told to me by Quintana who heard it from Gaudí himself.

3. «Now we will go to see Sr. Lorenzo.» Sr. Lorenzo was the chief of the model workshop. From the unpublished notes of Reverend F. Baldelló.

4. Emilio Sagristá, *op. cit.*, p. 7. Reverend Sagristá was present on the visit concerned.

5. Rev. F. Baldelló, notes cited.

66. The bishop of Barcelona, Dr. Reig, and the president of the *Mancomunitat de Catalunya*, Prat de la Riba, visit the Temple construction in the company of the architect.

67. Gaudí praying in the Cathedral of Barcelona. Drawing by the sculptor Juan Matamala in 1924.

6. M. Comas Esquerra, «Coses d'En Gaudí,» *El Matí,* June 21, 1936.

7. *La Veu de Catalunya,* June 12, 1926.

8. Ramón Menéndez Pidal, who knew Unamuno well, defined him as «a restless man with a question that has no answer and always eager to contradict,» *La Vanguardia,* February 7, 1965.

9. J. Elias, *op. cit.,* pp. 184, 185; also related by J. M. Pericas.

10. Rafael Marquina, *Gaceta Literaria,* (Madrid), March 15, 1930, and José Tarín Iglesias, *La Vanguardia,* February 7, 1965.

The politician answered in Castilian, but the architect did not think it wise to give in and continued in the vernacular. The two Catalans seemed unable to understand each other, but each adhered to his original position. One of the others present intervened, making a joke out of it, to serve as interpreter for Gaudí's interesting explanations and for the observations and suggestions by the leader of Spanish Federalism and president of the grand festival of Catalan literature.[6]

When they went down into the crypt which was being used for religious services, the architect took some holy water and offered it to the politician who professed the secularist ideas which at that time seemed to go along with Republicanism. As the ex-president made no gesture of acceptance, Gaudí underlined his offering with a «Don Francisco!» of serene reproach which he repeated twice more until, on the third, the high-ranking man took the water and crossed himself with it, «much to the surprise of his young companions who looked on.»[7]

Another memorable visit was that of the president of the University of Salamanca, Miguel de Unamuno, in October of 1906. He had come to Barcelona at the invitation of the *Ateneo Enciclopédico Popular* to give a lecture coinciding with the celebration of the First International Congress on the Catalan Language, at a time when there was an atmosphere of political excitement due to the Catalan Solidarity movement and provoked by the recent Law of Jurisdictions. The guest from Salamanca, a perennial protester, could see the great vitality of Barcelona which he publicly recognized in his lecture, but he differed in his view of her problems.

Unamuno's friend Maragall took him to the Sagrada Familia so that he could admire the architecture and meet its creator. The common friendship with the poet was not enough to unite the two strong characters, however. Gaudí, at 54, had found a sure spiritual path which carried him farther and farther from his restless youth. The writer, on the other hand, was 12 years younger and although originally a man of faith, now seethed with tortured spirit in search of a truth that his privileged intelligence did not yet provide him. The first with his vehement temper which he tried to soften, was often unsuccessful; the second, a hardened non-conformist, made no attempt to hide his unsociable manners.[8] Another difference was essential for the architect: he was Mediterranean and the visitor Cantabrian. They couldn't possibly understand one another. The latter, in spite of his Basque origin, was always opposed to regionalist demands and he mocked the respective languages as «espingardas» (Bedouin rifles)—a synonym for things unserviceable and antiquated. These opinions, voiced in public, were all the reason that Gaudí needed to strengthen his custom of speaking Catalan which put Maragall in the position of having to translate the words of the architect. It was an uncomfortable visit and ended on a cold note. In the conversation a mathematical subject came up which the professor side-stepped, confessing his scanty preparation in that area. The architect recalled the incident with ironic surprise many years later—what a situation for one who professed to cultivate Philosophy, a science which in Classical Greece had included all branches of learning!

Well into the visit, the poet asked the philosopher for his opinion of the Temple, and the latter replied quite directly, «I don't like it, I don't like it, I don't like it.» The architect, as if addressing a non-existent audience, dauntlessly translated «No li agrada, no li agrada, no li agrada.» Neither of the two made any attempt to soften the situation. In fact, on the contrary, Unamuno characterized the Sagrada Familia as «drunken art» and referred to the religious symbols and motifs employed by saying that he was surprised that Gaudí, being so intelligent, would believe in «such things.» The architect put down the objection in a joking manner, but he very soon had the opportunity to answer the attack in all seriousness when the writer asked his opinion of his philosophical essays. To this Gaudí replied that those essays «reminded him of garbage from a nobleman's house, where fragments of silk, velvet, valuable and glittering things are stacked up, but all are definitely to be thrown out.»[9]

In the cloudy evening the bell of the Angelus rang out, separating the two men even further. «Don Antón took off his hat and, interrupting his reply, began to pray, withdrawn and devout. Don Miguel, standing at his side, contemplated him in mute solemnity. Don Antón finished his oration and exclaimed, putting his hat back on his head: 'Laus Deo. Good afternoon, gentlemen.' Don Miguel who could read deeply into people's hearts did not say another word. One wonders how great was the influence of that vibrant page in the burning epic of his soul.»[10]

In spite of the characteristic tension of the interview, it was not without its easy moments, and the Salamantine rector was permitted to show off his curious ability to make little birds and other figures out of paper. As an example of this talent he left a stool of folded paper which the architect kept for some time on a shelf in his studio as a souvenir of the famous visitor.

To justify his obstinacy in speaking Catalan to non-Catalans, Gaudí said in a half-joking manner that speaking thus everyone could understand him. When in 1921 the Alsatian organist Schweitzer visited the temple in the company of the director of the Orfeó Català, Luis Millet, our architect began by speaking French, but he did so with difficulty, and he himself

68. The office with the table where don Antonio used to eat. In the bag hanging from the lamp he used to keep raisins so that the rodents could not get at them. 1926.

69. Workroom with plaster models on the ceiling and walls. Two Argand lamps in the background, and on the left an electric tulip lamp and charcoal stove. 1904.

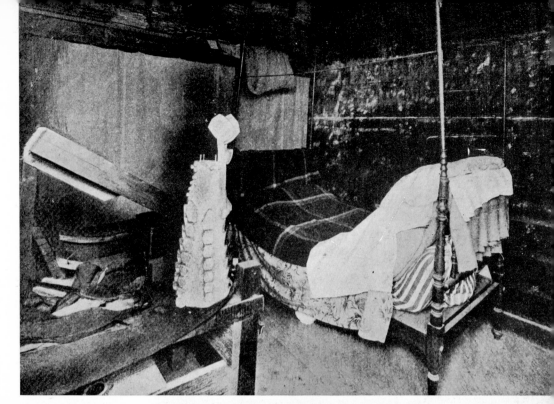

70. The bedroom in the office pavilion of the Temple was a simple cell cluttered with work utensils and models.

71. Gaudí taking communion at an open-air religious service.

72. Model workshop in the basement of the Temple with the model of the façade that was included in the 1910 Exposition in Paris to the right, showing the original solution for the towers.

interrupted to say, «You'll see: just let me speak Catalan and I'll do better.» When the visit was over, the eminent musician said that he had, indeed, understood him. [11]

Visits in general displeased him, with very few exceptions. Once when some English architects who were interested in his work were in Barcelona and visited the Sagrada Familia at length, he confessed that he was very happy that «they had the discretion not to ask for him.» [12]

86. THE LITURGIST (Figs. 67, 71, 74)

Though Gaudí was disturbed by external distractions of a social sort related to the Temple, such was not the case with the diversions of a religious nature, even though they were not properly architectural.

He was concerned with the Temple's upward growth, above the ground; and he felt that the service in the crypt—the spiritual root of its religious essence—should predict the great development which the future temple would acquire. Thus, besides his architectural activities, he became actively involved in the services held in the crypt and their liturgical aspects.

In this he would not tolerate the slightest transgression. From his early years with Bishop Grau in Astorga he had never ceased to perfect his knowledge through the reading of the *Bishop's Ceremonial*, the *Roman Missal*, *The Liturgical Year* written by the Benedictine Dom Prospère Guéranger, and through his own observations. [13] For him, the liturgical standards not only had religious significance, but he also considered that they must be esthetically effective. [14]

Gaudí took great pains to insure that the design of the new temple would respond to the most demanding liturgy in so far as providing solutions of a sculptural or spatial type as in the furniture, and those of an acoustic or temporal type for chants and recitals. That which he planned on a large scale for tomorrow's temple he delighted in applying as far as possible in the tiny crypt.

According to the Reverend Gil Parés who was chaplain of the crypt in Gaudí's day, besides being the architect he acted as a sort of master of ceremonies, insisting that all details be complied with in the ceremony and the utensils. If something was lacking, it was made *ex profeso* with the care revealed by so many of the liturgical objects which he designed. He personally took part in those ceremonies where he could be of service, such as the vigil before the Eucharist during the Forty Hours' devotions.

One day he observed that a certain priest was reading the Epistle from the Gospel pulpit, and he forced him to change; [15] and in a Corpus procession he objected to the fact that some laymen had been invited to carry the poles of the canopy which by liturgical protocol should be carried only by priests. The tact of Reverend Parés resolved the conflict, and the latter was called on more than once again to smooth over troubles caused by the architect's purism. [16]

Gaudí knew the significance of all of the ceremonies of the Church, and he believed that in the liturgy no detail was negligible for, as Balmes had said, the omission of small details could lead to the weakening of the religion.

Whenever he heard the chiming of the Angelus, whether he was alone or in company and whether the company be Catholic or not, a famous person or humble, he would invariably suspend the conversation and recite the angelical salutation with his head bared; if the others did not answer, he would continue the prayer alone, as we have seen was the case with Unamuno.

87. ASCETICISM (Fig. 68)

Gaudí's only practical activity was study in his quest to discover more perfect solutions and to turn them into architectural form in his work; and as it grew, he became more humble. His material life was reduced to a minimum in the certainty that in this manner his spiritual faculties would be sublimated and he would be able to make a more perfect labor of his temple.

His diet, already sober to begin with, due to the vegetarian system that he followed, became one of extreme frugality. He ate and slept only as much as was necessary to live, and he always left the table hungry, having at times to help himself get by between meals with raw almonds which he always carried in his pockets for such occasions. [17] He was equally moderate as far as sleeping, limiting himself to the rest necessary to maintain mental efficiency.

His usual meal was based on a salad with dressing which he held to be the perfect way of providing his body with vegetable oil. He also would eat fruits with milk—even citrus fruits—which he found easy to digest; these were accompanied by a little bread, and nothing to drink except for the milk. Nor did he use sugar; when he could not get fresh fruit, he would sometimes have a dessert of bread lightly spread with honey. [18]

11. Baldelló, notes cited.
12. Martinell, *op. cit.*, p. 96.
13. Statements by Gaudí to Bergós, *op. cit.*, p. 52.
14. Martinell, *op. cit.*, p. 49.
15. Elias, *op. cit.*, p. 188.
16. Baldelló, notes cited.
17. Bergós, *op. cit.*, p. 30.
18. *Idem.*

Reverend Gil Parés who sometimes sat with him during dinner without sharing in his meal corroborated this frugality and added a vignette of charming Franciscanism which he witnessed several times. The architect would sit at the end of one of his studio drawing tables to eat his lunch, and he would lift a little mouse up to the other end with his foot; the animal would then scurry across the table and arrive at the master's plate from which Gaudí would let him eat several crumbs of bread.[19] The scene surprised the clergyman the first time, but on successive days he admired more and more how well the architect and the trusting rodent got along together.

Just as he simplified his food, he also renounced all that was superfluous in dress, to the point that he stopped wearing underclothes and always wore the same suit—until it grew so old that the pleas of his closest friends forced him to replace it with another. The new one was bought for him by Sugrañes at a bazaar, using an old one to know the size.

Gaudí enjoyed pain and poverty as a counterbalance to the joys of life which for him were embodied in artistic creation which, if uncontrolled, could lead to an exuberance dangerous to its very beauty.[20] After his friends Maragall, Count Güell, and Dr. Torras y Bages died, he found himself even more alone, and he complemented his professional activity with edifying acts of charity. For over a year he offered his hospitality to the Tarragonese sculptor, Carlos Mani—a man who was of rather ungracious temperament and customs and was plagued by frequent illnesses. He also made visits to certain of the Temple stonecutters who had contracted tuberculosis as a result of not following precautions in their work.[21]

This conduct earned for the maestro the love of all of the Temple workers; and *senyor Llorenç*, the chief of the plaster model makers, who felt special affection for him, offered, against the will of his relatives, to spend nights with the architect so that he would not have to stay alone in his house at Güell Park.

In his last years he left his home in the park and slept in a small apartment in the office building at the Temple, invaded as was the rest of it by models, rolls of drawings, and books. His entire life was based on the Temple. He hardly left the site except for his prayers and for duties related to the same building. Without external distractions he felt his old age reinforced by greater spiritual agility.

88. «UNA GRÀCIA DE CARITAT!»

Not only did Gaudí not collect payment for his work on the temple, but when in 1914, the funds for the work reached a deficit of some 30,000 pesetas and construction was in danger of being paralyzed as the result of a lack of alms, the architect went into action. With work halted in that same year on the church at the Güell colony, and with no plans to take on any new work, he decided to put a maximum effort into pushing the growth of the great Temple in every way he could. He took advantage of the necessarily slow progress on the work to study carefully the problem of its overall structure, and in order to alleviate the economic problem he decided to follow up an article that Maragall had written in 1905 —«¡Una Gràcia de Caritat!»—and he went out to ask alms for the huge project.

Together with Dalmases Bocabella, the grandson of the Temple's initiator and a member of the administrative board, the architect went out for long periods to visit and ask assistance from people who seemed likely to lend a helping hand to the construction work. It was an apostolic and civic task which the master carried out in a sacrificial manner—certain that his act would thus yield more fruit.

On these visits the persuasive power of his words centered on the precarious economic situation, the religious, artistic, and patriotic significance of the new temple, and the civic duty of those who found themselves in a financial position to aid in the campaign, each one making his own sacrificial contribution.

To one of the persons visited, Gaudí insinuated the amount of the contribution which they were hoping to get from him for a certain objective; he was granted this with great pleasure, the donor saying that it did not represent any great sacrifice for him. Gaudí asked him to increase the contribution to the point that it would represent a sacrifice, saying that without such the gift had little worth in God's eyes and ran the risk of leading to vanity.[22]

These visits to people's homes tired him physically and spiritually, and the moral fatigue was even greater, due to the scanty results of the visits, which gave him the feeling that he was not satisfactorily fulfilling his commitment.

19. Baldelló, notes cited.
20. Bergós, *op. cit.*, p. 56.
21. *Ibid.*, p. 57.
22. Told to me by Gaudí.

XXI. MEETING WITH THE MASTER

89. COLLECTIVE VISITS

As a further stage of the newly-undertaken «pro Sagrada Familia» activities, the offices and workshops which were usually closed to the public opened their doors to collective visits led by the architect himself, in order to demonstrate the artistic and social, as well as the religious, importance of the famous temple. It was a highly interesting series of lectures, even though the architect did not wish to call them by that name.

The general public had turned Gaudí into an imaginary being. On the one hand, his fame, which was by then enormous, surrounded him with an aura of mysterious prestige. On the other hand, his reputation as being diffident and ill-humored surrounded him with a wall that was practically insurmountable. Therefore, when the collective visits were announced I decided to sign up for them to observe him at close range and to hear the voice of that man whom I had seen only twice on the street, not really certain if it was he or not.

The first visit was held on the afternoon of January 23, 1915. We gathered at the Temple —students from all of the Barcelona University schools— and were met by the chairman of the building committee, the canon Dr. Mas who soon after was promoted to be Bishop of Gerona. The master received us in the model workshop located in the basement, and his modest air and soft voice of an inspired prophet were quite different from the harsh man that I expected from what I had been told. His words flowed rich in content and familiar in tone.

Using the polychromed model of the Nativity façade which had been included in the Paris show, he explained to us the esthetic and symbolic aspects of the color. He spoke to us of the influence of geographical latitude on the feeling for Beauty; of the superior excellence of the sense of sight in comparison with the other human senses; of long construction periods for other temples in history; and of other interesting topics.[1] This general discussion before the model was supplemented by the reality of the constructed façade and an ascent to the top of the half-built towers. The architect did not accompany us—he said that he had always been a man of little muscular strength and that he avoided as much as possible climbing the bell towers.

When we came back down and went into the crypt, he extolled the beauty of the liturgy and spoke to us of lighting in temples. Afterwards, in his studio, he showed us sketches and drawings, explaining the general plan and the symbolism of the overall construction with clarity and an admirable sense of plasticity.

At the end of the visit I felt myself anointed with a new vision of architecture, as if my spirit had been enriched, and I hurried to my student rooming house to write down all that I had heard from the master, afraid that something might be forgotten. I did the same on successive visits with various other student groups, to which Gaudí showed the different facets of the work with admirable adaptation to the interests of the visitors. (It was from those notes that I compiled the book *Gaudí y la Sagrada Família explicada per ell mateix*—to which I refer several times in this book—when I was 25 although it was not published until 1951.)[2]

On February 3, during another visit, he showed students from the Business School unsuspected relationships between business and the fine arts, which he saw to be a source of wealth. Four days later, the students of engineering gave the architect the opportunity to speak of the sustaining structure of the temple, its hyperbolic paraboloid roof, the procedures of calculation, and a curious system for directly finding the intersection of warped forms with a plane. When I went with the School of Fine Arts on the 21st of the same month, he emphasized, among other things, the means he used to obtain the sculptures of the Temple through casts and studies of expression in the human skeleton, and he spoke of his concept of Art in relation to Beauty and Truth. For the visit by the Association of Architects of Catalonia on March 21, he lectured on general concepts of architecture and on the double roof of the temple, on the size of monumental sculpture and the way to achieve the monstruous expressions sometimes required by iconography; he spoke to us of the liturgy, of the excellence of the work, of the general and symbolic composition of the Temple—a wealth of knowledge revealing profound meditation from a decidedly architectonic point of view.

90. THE ARCHITECT IN HIS STUDIO (Figs. 69, 70, 72)

One day when I was coming out of the School of Architecture after the collective visits were over, my friend Folguera told me that he was going, on a mission that I do not remember, to see Gaudí. I recalled what Gaudí had told us when he said goodbye to us at the end of the

1. In my book, *Conversaciones con Gaudí*, I go into greater detail concerning the content of these visits.

2. In 1969, Ediciones Punto Fijo of Barcelona published the Castilian version of this work, corrected and enlarged by the author himself, under the title *Conversaciones con Gaudí* and this is the edition to which the present references relate. (Ed.)

first visit, after having offered himself to each and every one of us: that his offer was not mere courtesy, that we should take advantage of it according to the sincerity that we found in his words. As I did not doubt this sincerity, I proposed to Folguera that I accompany him and that he introduce me to the maestro so that I could confirm that I was not mistaken. That inaccessible and mysterious being which the general public had predicted had vanished from my eyes, and in his stead stood the frank and communicative man whom I always found Gaudí to be.

Once I had obtained his permission, I visited him other times on my own. He could usually be found in his studio at the temple. This was located in a pavilion destroyed during the Civil War, that stood in the same spot as the present one. One reached the upper floor where the studio was located by way of a wooden stair that led to a spacious section with well-connected compartments of agreeable appearance and simple furniture made of unpainted wood. Through a glass door you passed into another spacious office of irregular form. The outer walls of the area were mostly glass, and the light sifted through vines which grew on the exterior. The whole, in spite of its traditional elements, exhibited a spatial concept unsurpassed by the most advanced architecture today. One section of the roof could be moved by counterweights, like the double leaf of a huge door, and on sunny winter days it was opened to inundate the room with light. Beyond was a small room which I saw very few times, filled with rolls, models, and plans, among which was hidden the humble bed where he spent the night when inclement weather or other circumstances kept him from going to Güell Park during the time that he still lived there. The essence of this place was the architect himself, with the patriarchal appearance that belied his lack of bodily bulk, and his unkempt beard and hair which haloed his serene and prominent features that were marked by the blue luminous eyes and slightly bent nose; [3] his torso was bent by the years to accentuate the humble aspect of his deliberate movements. His hands would alternately stroke each other's back, or, during cold weather they would be put each in the opposite sleeve opening. The centripetal movements of his figure were concentrated in his penetrating stare which could be felt without one's knowing it, and which was softened by the color of his eyes; he captured even the slightest action within his range and would then analyze it and judge it with accurate precision. His intelligent glance—always gentle and energetic when necessary—was second only to his edifying and insistent voice which communicated his high ideals to his listeners.

He was not always to be found in his studio. At times he was in the model workshop in the basement, which would in the future become the conservation shop for the Temple. There he studied the plaster models of the structure under the care of Lorenzo Matamala who, besides being the interpreter and executor of the architect's complex conceptions, also became his companion, as we have seen, in order that he not be left alone at night in Güell Park. It was there that I heard Gaudí first explain the polychromed Nativity façade which he kept in a place of honor and there he also had fragments of his earliest solutions for the vaulting of the Sagrada Familia.

During the years which I frequented his studio and workshops, I saw how the pillars of the temple evolved from the use of square bases twisting in helix-forms—first with sharp salient angles and later with rounded ones of a parabolic form—to the novel columns of star-shaped plan and parabolic points rotating in two directions at once (Figs. 518, 519).

There was a time when he thought of making the column bases also serve as seats which would be comfortable only when one was sitting up straight: if the seated person tried, for example, to cross his legs, the discomfort would force him to sit correctly. He made life-size studies of these seats in plaster, and one day when I arrived he was involved in this task and asked me to sit down, as he had done before with others of different sizes, to test the general applicability to the results that he wanted. He later gave up the idea of the seats. Other models of his last years were those of the paraboloid sectional roofs of the sacristies, totally different from those he had designed earlier, and the large windows which were basically hyperboloids joined by paraboloids—the latter being the surfaces that he employed with preference (Fig. 515).

Wherever he was, in the model workshop which was an extension of his studio or in the studio itself annexed to the offices, the maestro was always busy at something that had to do with the temple; either he was engaged in work by himself or in orienting his assistants with detailed instructions that reflected his clear-sightedness in all aspects of the work from the most profound theory to the extremely superficial details.

91. PRECISION AND DEPTH

I was present once when he was giving instructions to his assistant Bertrán, and I was amazed by his minute precision. They were working on perfecting a tiny piece with a small firmer-chisel. He began with the warning that the operation would be a long one and that Bertrán should be careful to avoid tiring his hands; that he should hold the object with the left and keep the right free for the chisel. «Hold the object with three fingers;» Gaudí told him,

3. The fullness of his hair and beard which grew freely was shaved to a minimum at intervals of several weeks, in order to avoid frequent trips to the barber.

«three points will give the piece immobility, whereas two will not. With these fingers—those most accustomed to work—you will get less tired. With the one which remains free you can move the piece easily and the comfort will be translated into the perfection of the work...»

Gaudí related one's anatomical or physiological aptitudes to the results which one could obtain. Speaking of his own eyes, he said that the visual image painted on the retina took longer to erase than was normal (he was precise to the fraction of a second which I don't recall). This forced him to read slowly in order to avoid the confusion of superimposing the next word on the retina before the previous one had disappeared. Through the necessary slowness his reading was more efficient.

Another peculiarity of his eyes was that he had different vision in each: myopia in one and far-sightedness in the other, so that he enjoyed good vision at a distance and also close up without needing glasses which he disliked. He summarized the advantage as he saw it by saying «the Greeks never wore glasses.»

This precision had great artistic importance at times. He observed that people's appearance and features were intimately related to certain invariable points on the skeleton. The triangle of the forehead and the shoulders of each individual and its position give everyone his own particular and unique expression. For the facial features there exist certain muscles in the skull which remain invariable even when the individual gains or loses weight, and which cause him to maintain the same appearance by which he is recognized in spite of such changes.

At times his quest for exactitude reflected a physico-psychological profundity. Speaking of the tolling of bells, he explained the famous phenomenon that the older the bells, the better they sound; with the repeated percussion the molecular structure of the bronze becomes fibrous, improving its sound. But the bell loses resistance until the moment arrives when it cracks and ceases to be useful. And he went beyond this fact to draw a sentimental analogy: the best sound of the bell is given out immediately before cracking, that is, dying. Thus he deduced that the special emotion of the tolling bells at the end of each day came from this relation between the day that dies and the best sound that the bronze can give as a goodbye on ending its life.

In apparently unimportant subjects he was equally precise and knowledgeable in regards to causes and effects. He said that laziness is always more mental that physical. Resistance to undertaking a job usually has its origin in not knowing *how* it should be done. Once the initial intellectual problem is resolved, the physical execution is a simple thing. He defined jokes or anecdotes as brief stories with unforeseen and light conclusions in which use is made of synonyms with disparate meanings and incongruous backgrounds. It is the unexpected contrast of the ending which produces the hilarity.

In addition to such didactic explanations, he himself had great manual ability which he exercised and put to the service of his logic, thus maintaining dexterity in the articulations of his hands. During one period he worked out, in wire, models of the angels which were to adorn the columns of the temple, using the procedures invented in Palma de Mallorca, for he planned to make extensive use of such figures in the Sagrada Familia. In wire he reproduced a skeleton on a very small scale which he could then bend to give the desired expressions.

XXII. SEEN AND HEARD

During the period that I knew the master, the rhythm of his life was always the same, only occasionally distracted by small incidents from his daily professional work on the Sagrada Familia; he carried the weight of his fame in a noble and exemplary manner, in spite of what has been said of his natural temperament. His life, more than exemplary, was edifying. Sometimes I visited him merely to take advantage of the beneficial influence of his conduct and his conversation which, without his intending it thus, always served as advice for me.

92. SOBER DIET AND EXPANSIVE CONVERSATION

On Sunday December 19, 1915, I visited Gaudí late in the afternoon. I found him eating and offered to come back later. He said to me in a joking tone: «Haven't you ever seen an architect eat?» He insisted that I sit down across from him, and I did. The table was small, tucked in among the rolled plans and the models—very clean, and of great simplicity. He was eating a raw vegetable, perhaps escarole, which he mashed with a knife and stirred for a long time. It looked somewhat like a non-liquid *gazpacho*. His chest was protected by a napkin whose corners were stuck in the slits of his suit lapels, threatening to fall off at any moment. When he had finished the vegetable, he drank a glass of milk with a lemon slice, peel and all, floating in it; and for dessert he had a baked apple and half a mandarine orange. He served himself from the things laid out on the table with no servant to attend him. Such was the meal of the great architect on that December Sunday.

I had come to say goodbye before leaving for my home town after having passed my licensing exam. He showed interest in my comprehensive design project, and taking off from this scholastic subject, he spoke to me during the meal with complete familiarity of his own school days and of the suspensions which I have referred to in Chapter VI.[1] After lunch he wanted to show me the experiments that he was doing with tubular bells in the unheated room next door. He put on a coat before entering; the day was cold and he had been feeling a bit ill since early morning so that we came quickly back to the first room which was precariously heated by an ancient coal stove.

We stood there talking, he with his back to the stove warming his hands behind him. He spoke to me of a variety of things, with ease and simplicity: of how he had been hired to direct the Temple; of how providence was watching out for the progress of its construction; of measures that were being taken to obtain a government subsidy, and of how I could work in his studio if it should come through and I should want the job; of the natural gifts of natives of the Campo de Tarragona; of a new orientation for the apsidal chapels... all in a pleasant and frank manner.

We went out to the street. A fine rain was falling. We took a tram and stood out on the platform. With the same pleasantness as before he spoke of the ethnic differences that could be observed between people of the east and those of the interior of the Peninsula, and the influence which the sea and land exerted on this general phenomenon. These qualities, he said, were reflected in architecture and in prayer which is emphatic in the interior and sober on the coast. When we got off the tram he invited me to continue walking with him to the door of the chapel of San Severo where he stopped as if inviting a goodbye. He had come to the church to celebrate the Forty Hours' devotions.

93. ADVICE FROM THE MASTER

When I began to practice professionally in 1916 in the midst of the European War, the price of wood had gone up five times, and that led me to replace the skeletal gable frames usual in warehouses and factories with the equilibrated arches which Gaudí had put into use. I had built quite a few of them when in 1919 I was required to build several arches of greater dimensions (13.3 meters wide by 14 meters high) for the wine cellars Pinell de Bray which, compensating for the temporary loads of wind and snow, turned out to be of a thickness which seemed excessive and un-esthetic to me. After a great deal of indecision, I decided to consult with Gaudí concerning my doubts and feelings on the matter; he thought that I could do without the excessive thickness and that I could adopt the solution that I preferred as more esthetic. One can imagine my delight in the fact that my guesses coincided with the mechanical intuition of the great architect.

---

1. This conversation is more fully covered in Chapter VI, section 20 and in my book, *op. cit.*, p. 68.

He was not only a man of intuition, but also of responsibility. Without changing his criteria, he thought later about the case and discovered a structural trick which would absolutely guarantee the chosen solution; the next day he asked his assistant, the architect Quintana, who was a friend of mine, to indicate to me a way of making those apparently daring arches absolutely safe without varying their form. The procedure gave the arches a safety coefficient which removed any danger (Figs. 545, 546).

This anecdote would be unimportant if it were not indicative of the generosity with which the great architect put his talent at the service of a beginner. This giving of advice was not rare for him. Something similar happened with my friend the architect Bonet Garí who submitted to him a design for a monument to Prat de la Riba, which Gaudí commented on and modified with his pencil. We can imagine that these were not isolated cases.

94. CHILBLAINS AND REGIONALISM

On January 16, 1923, I visited the maestro in passing to greet him on his Saint's Day which was to be celebrated the foollowing day. He had chilblains on his hands, and he spoke to me of them. He said that they were just for old folks and children, and he explained why: they are congestions caused by the difficulty of blood circulation in the capillary tubes in the extremities of the body (feet, hands, ears). As the heart which pumps the blood in circulation was weakest in childhood and in old age, he deduced his theory. In order to facilitate circulation, he bathed in hot water which he himself warmed with a «meta» tablet [2] during the cold season.

Shortly before, he had been visited by Father Casanovas and another Jesuit who had come from the Philippines where the natives felt extremely cold at only 60 degrees F. —a fact surprising to us. He said that such differences justified the concept of regionalism because however much men continued to insist on unifying laws and customs, Nature would follow her course, maintaining insurmountable differences.

95. THE SCULPTURE CRITIC

The *Anuario de la Asociación de Arquitectos de Cataluña* of 1924 published a study of mine on the choir of the cathedral of Lérida as sculpted by the artist Bonifás whom I had studied with special interest. Gaudí praised the sculptor and my essay, and I took advantage of this generous disposition to ask his opinions regarding some of my ideas of which I still was not certain; I asked him if I might bring him some photographs and two images which I owned of the sculptor in order that we could discuss them and that I could refine my thoughts in that light.

He kept the sculptures and the photos in his studio for several weeks, and he showed himself to be a definite admirer of the Baroque artist. He praised the elegance of his images, and he remembered those that Bonifás had sculpted for the *camarín* of the Virgin of Mercy in his native Reus, which he classified among the most graceful sculptures in the world. He said that the sculptor possessed his sense of plasticity because he had been born in the Campo de Tarragona. He concluded that just as he admired the 18th century artist born in Valls, the latter would like his architecture if he could see it (Fig. 6).

In the photographs he admired the *paso* of the Dormition of the Virgin in the cathedral of Gerona with its baldachin covered by a great imperial crown with four festoons sustained by angels. He said that this was the most accurate portrayal that he had ever seen of the *Regina Mater Misericordiae* and he was inspired by it for the design of the baldachin which he planned for his temple, dedicated to the Assumption of the Virgin (Fig. 511).

One of the images that I took him was that of a Saint John which was missing his symbolic lamb and one arm, and which I was planning to restore. I consulted him on the restoration and he gave me enlightening advice concerning the positioning of the masses in the figure whose resultant weight should pass through the left heel on which the image rested.

96. A DISAGREEABLE EPISODE (Fig. 73)

I wouldn't allude to the present episode if it were not for the fact that one of Gaudí's biographers has deformed it to the point that only the coincidence of the main character and the flexion of the iron tube make it recognizable. In that version, of which I know no evidence, Gaudí is presented as lacking in mechanical understanding and moral sentiments, for which reason I feel obliged to tell the event just as I witnessed it.

We have already seen the mechanical intuition of the great architect. He intuited cases of equilibrium that were derived from the compression, extension, and flexion of materials, but he always preferred to confirm these phenomena through experimentation. One day he set out to test iron tubes under axial pressure in order to observe how and when flexion would occur as the load was progressively increased. He believed the experiment would prove in-

2. A handy combustible substance in common use at that time.

teresting, and he invited a few young architects to watch; among them those I remember being, myself, Puig Boada, Ráfols, Bonet, Qintana, and Folguera.

The test was carried out in the ditch that surrounded the crypt of the Sagrada Familia so that he could have easy access to the top of the tubes which he had placed in a vertical position. Gaudí directed and explained the experiment and pointed out the phenomena that resulted in order to draw his conclusions later. He often used to recall the aphorism that «experience is the mother of science;» and that the two together were the feet on which human knowledge strode forward. He emphasized that the first was the *mother,* and the second the *daughter,* i.e., that the former had greater category and for that reason he believed more in happenings than in books on science.

Folguera, who was extremely well prepared in rational mechanics, alluded several times to analytical formulas related to the case and Gaudí stated his preference for the teaching of experimental facts. He said that books usually wandered off in «discourses» which were not always trustworthy. Folguera persisted, citing a law of flexion which was applicable within certain limits, but not in such extreme cases. Gaudí answered by branding as «discourse» the arguments in the mechanics textbooks: a law which is not good except in certain circumstances is not a law but a «discourse.» The young architect, on seeing the books which were his intellectual daily bread put down in such a manner, forgot the circumstances of the moment and the importance of his adversary and openly exclaimed that in order to explain ideas, what Gaudí called «discourse» was necessary, and that even the master himself could not avoid it in expressing himself. The reply stunned everyone. There was a tense moment which Gaudí terminated by saying, in a measured tone, that he had obviously been mistaken in inviting the studious architect. The younger man realized that this was an invitation to leave but, recognizing that his words had been impetuous, and perhaps also wanting to avoid a sour ending, he asked if, in spite of the incident, he might be allowed to continue to watch the test. Gaudí acceded to his request.

97. IN JAIL AT 72

The master enjoyed attending important civic functions as if he were fulfilling a responsibility, even though in so doing he exposed himself to the riotous situations that frequently came about in the political atmosphere of his day. That was the case during the Floral Games of 1920 which were presided over by the French marshal, Joffre, whose wife reigned as queen of the festival. Due to a rivalry between the Mayor and the Chief of Police,[3] the latter ordered with little tact that his men move into action, giving rise to disturbances as the crowd left the literary festivities. Gaudí was in the vestibule when the fracas occurred, and was almost arrested. It seems that he was hit by the police and that he reacted by calling them «miserable» and «blood-thirsty.» Two Brothers of the Christian Doctrine intervened on the part of the architect and he was allowed to go free.[4]

3. Manuel Ribé carefully explains the incident in his book *Memorias de un Funcionario,* p. 83.

4. Told to me by my friend Isidro Magriñá who was present.

73. The architect in the ditch outside the crypt during the experiments of tube flexion under compression which were witnessed by several of us young architects.

74. In the Corpus Christi procession of 1924, when he walked with the members of the Círculo Artístico de Sant Lluch.

I cite this case as an antecedent to that which occurred four years later when he wanted to attend a mass which was celebrated on September 11 in the Church of Santos Justo y Pastor, in memory of those who fell in the siege of Barcelona in the year 1714. That date, the anniversary of the surrender of Barcelona to Felipe V which ended the War of Succession, was customarily commemorated by the *Catalanistas* by laying flowers on the statue of the councillor Rafael Casanova who was wounded in that siege while defending the city. The monument was taken down at the orders of the dictator Primo de Rivera in order to avoid such celebrations, and any other demonstration leading to that end was prohibited. The suffrage mass was allowed, however, and continued to be celebrated according to custom.

Word spread rapidly around Barcelona that Gaudí had been arrested by the police for wanting to go to mass, and that he had been taken to the police headquarters. On the next day I visited him to express my regrets over what had happened. He told me in complete detail —for an hour and a half—exactly what had happened. The notes which I made when I got home have been used in transcribing this previously unpublished episode in the master's life.[5]

When I arrived at his studio, he was seated with his back to the door and I asked permission to enter. He recognized my voice and said to me:

«Come in, Martinell. Make yourself at home. What good news do you bring? Not on that stool, it's too high. You'll be more comfortable over there.»

«So now they've let you go free?» I asked. «They told me that you were arrested yesterday.»

5. Unpublished notes of the author.

75. The state of the Nativity façade at Gaudí's death in 1926, with the tower of St. Barnabas completely terminated.

«Yes, they let me go. I was in custody for four hours—two locked in the jail cell with bars from which I could have gotten out if I had paid 10 *duros* (50 pesetas). They arrested me arbitrarily and violently. They insulted me. They told me twice to 'go to H...,' and called me 'shameful' several times. In all of this I didn't lose my calm, but I answered them in a manner that confused them and they didn't know what to say. What happened has caused me great sorrow since, as I reflect on what the world is like which orders us around. At the time I was very serene, but now, when I recall it, it gets to me and I try to forget it. There is so much agressiveness that goes against Catalonia—her language which is mine, and for that reason in those moments of persecution I didn't want to abandon it. The agressiveness that they felt against me was because I spoke to them in Catalan.»

«That's what I heard; and that another man who was there wanted to be arrested with you and they didn't take him.»

«Because he spoke to them in Castilian. Today he came to visit me and left his card. He said that he did not notice my insistence on speaking Catalan and that if he had realized he would have done the same. There you have it: a man over 60, well-educated who has a son who is an engineer, found himself in the same danger. I had gone to mass at San Justo. The door of the church was open, and as I entered my way was blocked by a policeman. There the civil authorities have no rights; the only authority is that of the bishop. I insisted, and they told me to go through another door. I went there and found other guards who also refused to let me enter. I told them that they had no right to do that, and they told me to respect the law. I answered that it was they who had the first obligation to use it justly; that

76. The pinnacle of the tower of Saint Barnabas, decorated with Venetian mosaic; Gaudí planned to vary the polychromy in the others, which he was not able to realize.

their authority was not law here and was in opposition to the ecclesiastical authority which was the only legitimate one in that holy place. I said all of this in Catalan. They asked me if I didn't know how to speak Castilian, and I answered that I could but that I didn't feel like it. I would have felt like a coward if I had abandoned my mother tongue in that moment of persecution. That was when they arrested me and took me to the police station.[6] Many people came along and offered to notify my family. I told them that I had no one; that I lived alone; that nevertheless they should advise Reverend Parés (the chaplain of the Sagrada Familia), Sr. Dalmases (of the Building Committee), and the Spiritual League of the Virgin of Montserrat.

«When we arrived at the police station, a good woman came up to me, dismayed: 'You, Don Antón?' She knew me for she had years before been the companion to one of my nieces, then elderly and now dead. The poor woman, on seeing me in custody, became a Veronica and ran to help me however she could. She cried disconsolately. I said to her: 'Don't cry; don't you see how calm I am? Nothing will happen to me.' She asked me if I needed anything, and as I was without food since eight when I had left my home to go to take the sacrament, I asked her to bring me a glass of milk. She brought it to me from a store nearby with a little bread which I ate right there. The poor woman could not get it through her head that I was under arrest. She cried like a Magdalene.» (As he described the scene a tear came to his eye.)

«All this in front of the police?» I asked.

«Yes sir, right before the chief himself.»

«It seems impossible that, even without knowing who you were, seeing this scene they would not reflect and be a bit more civil.»

«Ha! They didn't even want to let the woman through, nor those who came later to pay the fine! They are ignorant and stupid. The whole thing affected me like a miniature Hell: skinny guards with the sort of appearance that people call that of a 'poor devil;' the chiefs, better paid, with massive bellies, are the Lucifers who give the orders. They had their disagreements among themselves, but they were united in their remarks against me because I wouldn't speak to them in Castilian. They asked me what my profession was, and I told them that I was an architect. They said: 'Then you hold a title that was issued in Castilian.' I said that was so, and that I also paid my taxes in Castilian, but that the title had not been received from the state but rather from a school subsidized by a Catalan body. (Diputación de Barcelona.)

«They put me in a jail cell with double bars and a bench to sit on. There were two other arrested people there, and to introduce myself my greeting was: 'I am a man of 72 years, and I carry no other arms than these' (and he held up some thick rosaries and wooden crucifix with a metal Christ which he took out of the interior pocket of his jacket. Later I learned from Quintana that the crucifix had been blessed by the Pope.) As I had left home in order to go to mass and had not been allowed to do so, I spent a while with my prayers before starting up a conversation with my cell-mates.

«One told me that he had spent five or six months in the Model Prison and that he was here now because he was about to be released, and indeed he was after a short while. I was left alone with the other man who was a street peddler who had been caught without the required license; they were asking five *duros* fine for his freedom. I asked him if he knew someone who could lend him the five *duros* and he said yes in such a confused manner that I knew he meant no. It made me sad to think that for lack of means he would remain alone in the cell while I was let go. I sent a message to the parish priest of the church of La Merced to send me 75 pesetas because I had no money on me, and he himself came immediately. Meanwhile, Quintana, who knew of what had happened, had paid my fine.

«Then I told that man that I would pay his fine so that he could leave because it made me sad (there were tears in his eyes when he said it.) He was grateful and asked for my name and address in order to return the money to me when he could. I didn't give them to him. I only told him: 'my name is not important; when you have it to return to me, give the money in the spirit of charity to another who needs it, just as I have done now with you.' As I left, I told the commissioner, 'I trust that if I return another day you will not insult me as you have done today.'»

«And when they heard your name did they give any indication of knowing who you were?»

«No, that shows how ignorant they are. Yesterday when all of this happened I felt very calm. All in all, at noon I was free; but now when I think about what has happened it bothers me to think that we are going up a dead-end alley and that a radical change must definitely come.»

After relating the events as I have summarized them, he went on citing political, social, and economic cases which confirmed his point of view, and gave his thoughts on governmental censorship of the press which did not allow news to get out.

6. The architect Quintana, Gaudí's assistant, told me later that the police arrested him brusquely and with force. His arm still hurt that evening.

The architect Sugrañes arrived, and Gaudí continued the conversation with the two of us. He said that he preferred that the newspapers not speak of the case; but that that would be worse because if it were not allowed to be reported in Spain, the foreign press would explain it in their own way, as happened with the Floral Games when Joffre was president and the French press misrepresented the occurrences. In Barcelona itself, what happened was rumored from mouth to mouth without reliable information and became a legend in its own time.

98. THE FIRST TOWER AND THE LAST INTERVIEW (Figs. 75, 76)

On January 22, 1926, I visited Don Antonio for the last time. The motive was again his Saint's day which had been on the 17th, and I also wanted to see the first of the four bell towers which had just been finished. With this tower he had achieved the first important goal of his great Temple. The silent work over the years, day after day, to excel in his art, to exalt religion, and to bring prestige to Barcelona, had finally become a concrete reality in that gold cross which stood atop the high crown and which would soon be accompanied by three others which he would never see.

I found him more talkative and expressive than usual, as if in private celebration of the success of this first shining light of his great ideal which he discussed with enthusiasm.[7] He said that the termination «d'aquella punxa» (of that spire) had taken four years. Such things go slowly and one must know how to be patient. When the bishop of Vich visited the temple shortly before and learned that the shipment of mosaics from Venice was such a slow process, he suggested that they be ordered from Valencia in order to save time; but since they were not dealing with a matter of doctrine, Gaudí ignored the bishop's suggestion and waited for the Venetian mosaics. Those made in Valencia with a clay base would have turned earthy; the Venetian pieces were based on resistant colored glass or were gilded with fine gold incorporated into the glass at the time of fusion, and were unchangeable and higher in quality. He ordered only enough mosaic for one pinnacle, hoping that some Catalan industrialist would want to undertake the relatively easy job of the three remaining bell towers.

Gaudí went on to explain that some letters were missing on the spire which were to be of different sizes so that the observer would discover them as he drew closer. As an example of the precision which has been mentioned in the preceding chapter, he said that he had calculated that objects are visually distinguishable at 500 diameters distance and that if the object is shining, the distance increases to 1,000 diameters. The letters would measure from 40 centimeters to one meter, the small ones to be seen close up and the others at greater distances. He had discovered that the cross at the top, which was 3 meters in diameter and shiny, could be easily distinguished at 2,000 meters. He also observed that since he had topped the Güell Palace and other buildings with pinnacles, several architects had imitated him; their results were not successful because of their use of inadequate materials.

He took me out on a little second-floor terrace off the studio from which we could comfortably observe the recently completed tower top. The sunny morning of that winter day went well with the warm and optimistic words of a genius at the end of his life. He extended himself in speaking of his work. He explained the relationship of this spire (the one farthest to the south) to the three that were missing which would also have metallic reflections and a greater abundance of gold. The four «punxes» (he always used that Catalan word) about to be completed would be the culmination of the fragment which he trusted he would leave behind as a sample of the future Temple. He spoke extensively of his work which could be distributed around another, taller, central spire encircled by four lower ciboria and the 12 bell towers of the three façades...

As if he had a presentiment that this would be the last time, he spoke to me of the future temple with an emotion and a plasticity which I had never heard him use before. The whole temple took form in his graphic words which were nothing more than an explanation of his inner vision. He said that all the mosaic business was Greek, as were many other aspects of the Sagrada Familia. He felt that when the spires were finished, foreigners would detect them from afar as they approached the city by sea, and that people from all over the world would come to see them and they would be very influential in art.[8] He added that the essence of Greek art was innate in him; that he carried it within him and that when they had explained about the Greeks to him in school, none of it was new and he learned rapidly.

Gaudí attributed his Hellenism to the Mediterranean, and he said that he could tell me such things because I was from Valls on the same Campo de Tarragona where he was born.

As we admired the singular beauty of the Sagrada Familia pinnacle, Gaudí observed that the perfect descriptive phrase had been uttered by a humble man: a clockmaker who had been in charge, for quite some time, of winding the three clocks of the Sagrada Familia, for which he was paid 25 pesetas a year. He usually went about his work without saying anything. The day that he saw the completed tower without its scaffolding, he said simply: «Now I have seen the tower finished—fa goig.» This «fa goig» (it gives pleasure) tells it all: it is the gaudeum

---

7. As on other occasions, I took note of the conversation that very day and have utilized my notes in preparing the present text.

8. The passage of time has fully confirmed this prediction.

magnum of the Three Kings when they saw the star again, which was light and therefore joy. It inspires joy. It can't be expressed in a better way. The man was not saying words; he was expressing what he felt. Really, this brilliance makes you happy. This phrase which hit the mark was spoken by a modest man who for 25 pesetas went 52 times a year to wind 3 clocks. Gaudí never tired of commenting on this «fa goig,» and he didn't hide the happiness which he himself also felt in contemplating this fragment of his work, the anticipation of the great temple that lived in his imagination.

Before I left he showed me some alabaster and metal lamps which he was considering for the crypt (Fig. 512) and I said goodbye with the admiration which he always inspired, without suspecting that that would be my last visit.[9]

99. A CORDIAL AND EDIFYING MANNER

In the many times that I visited the master from January 1915 to January 1926, I never found him to be in a bad humor, nor did I find myself in uncomfortable situations. At the most I encountered cutting but good-natured remarks which never interrupted the friendly tone of the conversation nor detracted from its instructive and exemplary value which was almost that of an apostolate; any outbursts were abundantly compensated for by these positive aspects.

Our conversation would usually begin with subjects related to the Sagrada Familia, but it would then usually detour off into other artistic fields with Gaudí expressing his personal opinions which were sometimes quite surprising. He felt that the prestige of Gothic architecture was more romantic than plastic, for the poets extolled its maximum expression when it was in ruins by moonlight and covered with ivy, i.e., when it was scarcely to be seen and was reduced to a mere literary evocation. For him all that was literary was suspected of lacking in plasticity and of vain wordiness.

Gaudí's favorite art was the Greek, and after that, the Renaissance as represented by Saint Peter's in the Vatican—a well-proportioned work with numerous plastic and spatial qualities. He admired Leonardo whom he cited with praise, saying that it was impossible to deal with the theme of the Last Supper without being influenced by his fresco in Milan. He also admired Benvenuto Cellini for the carefully studied anatomy of his statues and reliefs, and he censured Michelangelo for the mannered musculature in some of his paintings, born more of the facility of his brush than of study. He said that a work of art should be based on truth in addition to esthetical emotion; without truth the work is incomplete.

Sometimes I wonder if the great interest that Gaudí felt for the Sagrada Familia and its continuation could have influenced the warm reception which he gave to the young architects who admired his work, perhaps in the hopes of stimulating a body of guardians to look after it when he could no longer do so. The great detail with which he explained new solutions as he discovered them, his advice on structure and certain artistic effects, and even on everyday life, may have been, from his point of view, disguised lessons on the continuity of the great Temple.[10] Looking back, those simple and productive chats—which were indeed important for their technical content—impressed me most for the humane and edifying reverberations which always flowed from the situation. Whatever the subject, be it simple or elevated, the tiniest details were an indication of his formidable and instructive personality.

Another exemplary aspect of his life was his indifference toward the use of publicity to promote his work. He imagined that his art would have effects elsewhere but he never fomented them. He lived a life isolated within himself, seeking only the attainment of his own ideals and absolutely withdrawn from any propagandist action which could have resulted in flattering himself or in the attraction of an abundant clientele.[11] His constant devotion to God and to the Art with which He was exalted was most edifying.

9. The late architect Quintana, who was kind enough to review the present narration, reminded me that the alabaster of these lamps, like that of the doves in the cypress of the façade, was provided by myself. Indeed, when I knew that the temple needed alabaster, I offered to negotiate with my friend Mateu who owned some quarries in Sarreal (Tarragona) to get him to supply the stone on the best possible terms. When the idea was accepted by the architect and the proprietor, I decided to defray the modest contribution, in spite of which Gaudí insisted several times that I get reimbursed by the temple administration.

10. He used to say that he had faith in the contribution which his successors would bring to enrich the work. The concrete studies on future themes were «in case God gave them better ideas» and probably also as a guide to follow.

11. The only publicity that he allowed was that which aimed at augmenting the income for the temple construction, with absolute exclusion of his professional work outside of that.

XXIII. THE MASTER'S DISPOSITION

So much has been said about Gaudí's stubborn character that, in spite of the fact that I consider it incidental, I feel that it is preferable to go fully into the subject in order to evaluate it on the basis of facts. We have just seen that his character and his manner were usually amiable and that he possessed a great reserve of kindness. Nevertheless, it must be recognized that whenever someone set out to contradict him with sufficient airs, his answer was full and sometimes aggressive. He himself recognized this defect and it bothered him, as we have seen and will discuss further (XXXIII - 145). He did not conceal his impetuous character and his desire to correct it. That desire probably began to show itself after his early youth, and when we consider the artist's temperament and the type of work which he carried out as an architect, it seems logical and even beneficial—though somewhat paradoxical—that such perfection was never achieved.

100. JUSTIFICATIONS FOR HIS BAD HUMOR

Gaudí carried within him an ideal that he had to translate into works, something which would not have been possible without an energetic and quick temperament. Architectural practice demands energy and the ability to command. He himself explained that the architect does not personally execute any of his works. He must realize everything through orders given to his subordinates, and this frequently forces him to speak *loudly, clearly,* and *directly;* this was especially so in the case of Gaudí, who broke with tradition and had to swim against the current.

If we knew nothing of the character and disposition of the great architect, we would have to assume a character with continuous intemperance which rarely saw a work fully accomplished. A genius which produces such works needs to overcome obstacles without taking the time to ponder over them. Similarly a general is tolerated as a means when an end is to be gained—even at the cost of cruel and bloody sacrifices. His disposition and his outbursts were unimportant when compared with the admirable work which he realized.

He began his professional work with a thirst for innovation. He possessed the necessary passion and dynamism to reach the envisioned ideal which, though he tried to explain it with words, he preferred to demonstrate in his works. He also had the necessary orientation to advance along a road strewn with obstacles which had to be levelled in an expedient manner if necessary. As an avid reader of Balmes, he followed his advice not to argue uselessly when persuasion was not feasible. Since he could not resign himself to just stop talking, it was in such situations that the curt disconcerting phrase would emerge which cut down the adversary at the risk of augmenting his reputation for intemperance.

Nevertheless, these agile and stinging rejoinders often had more cunning than bite. There were those who accepted them as lessons while others took offence. The latter usually joined the ranks of his numerous detractors.

In the preceding chapters we have related anecdotes which could have been included under the present heading. I don't pretend to give exhaustive treatment to any single aspect of this biography, and much less to this matter of anecdote which is only of relative importance but by way of example I will select several stories which illustrate the facet of his personality which concerns us here.

101. OUTBURSTS

There were those who were afraid of him—some perhaps out of lack of sympathy, and others because of some unfortunate experience. One of these was the blacksmith Uñoz, who did the ironwork for the Güell house and who would avoid the architect whenever he saw him coming and would make his brother attend to him. When Gaudí commissioned him to do the iron stair rail going down into the crypt of the temple and explained to him how it had to be, Uñoz objected that «it couldn't be done;» the architect told him «I'm through with you,» and Uñoz was fired.[1]

The blacksmith Badía who told me this story was the brother of the foreman of the Uñoz factory, and he worked on various jobs under Gaudí's orders without conflict. He did not recall any brusqueness. Whenever he received an order which seemed difficult or impossible,

1. Told to me by the blacksmith Luis Badía on May 3, 1955.

he would attempt it anyway, and if a difficulty did arise he would communicate it to Gaudí who would modify the plan if necessary.

Once, shortly after building the church for a convent, the contractor who had worked on it thought he saw some cracks in the cupola which warned of impending destruction. Although the nuns had confidence in the work and in the architect, the contractor's insistence led them to consult with Gaudí who immediately realized that the alarm was unfounded. During the inspection, the contractor wore a face that seemed to indicate he was in physical pain for some reason. With a few words confirming his suspicions, Don Antonio proclaimed his verdict: «Here we have the cracks and the ruin of the cupola. The entire problem lies in the stomach of this gentleman.» [2]

Among those who did not take Gaudí's indispositions badly I will cite the architect C. whom I happened to meet several times in the maestro's studio. Once the talk got onto rather intricate geometric concepts which Gaudí explained with great clarity. The architect C. interrupted: «Don Antonio, I don't understand why...» Don Antonio interrupted: «Don't worry, you wouldn't understand it. We are speaking of solid geometry, *spatial* geometry, and you have not advanced beyond the plane.» I was more shocked than my colleague who, according to what I later learned from Quintana, often got such responses, in spite of which he continued to visit the master.

In spite of the fact that his opinions were usually in disagreement with the majority, personal dealings with the maestro were not difficult, and I have already noted how agreeable they could be. Nevertheless, for certain people it was extremely easy to convert a conversation with him into a dispute. Some say that during his stays in Palma de Mallorca there were continuous arguments with the canons who dined with the bishop, and that this influenced the fact that he was not called back after his last departure for Barcelona.[3]

102. HUMILITY

The sculptor Camps Arnau told me that at the death of his collaborator, Francisco Berenguer, Gaudí went to express his sympathies to the family; he said to the widow: «You have lost a husband, but I have lost my right arm.» Among those assembled there was Dr. Martí y Juliá, an anti-religious man who told the architect—most probably in order to disturb his religious sentiments—that «those who show off their modesty so that people will take notice are the most proud of all.» Several of the people present were unsympathetic with the master and rejoiced at the doctor's words.

This leads us to consider another facet of the architect which has also been the object of much discussion: his pride. It is logical that a man whose critical spirit was so sharp concerning everything around him and who was wont to apply the magnifying glass of observation to his own behaviour would also realize the high qualities of his own architecture. He recognized and valued his superiority, as we know from some of his own statements, but that did not make him proud.

Admittedly, in his youth, at the very beginning of his professional life, there was an element of pride, and he took on a certain presumptuousness as a result of his first successes, but later, when he oriented his life along new channels, he could count on two antidotes to liberate him from this pride. The first was his conviction that everything that he did could be more perfect, and the second, his belief that his merits were not his own but rather things which were owed to God.

One day someone told him that his work on the Sagrada Familia would confer on him a special place in heaven: that he would shine like an arc lamp among common lights. Gaudí answered that even if that superiority were certain, it would be annulled before the brilliance of the Glory of God. And he added, «Have you ever noticed the sad role that an arc lamp must play in direct sunlight? It practically becomes the same as the light of a candle.» [4]

This could be taken as an isolated incident if we did not know of repeated cases which prove his authentic modesty. One day I visited him with a friend who, impressed by the perfect explanation he gave of a certain problem, labeled it «definitive.» Gaudí wouldn't hear of such a thing. He said that human affairs, however perfect they may appear, can always be better and that in this world there it nothing that is definitive. He consistently applied this criterion in his work, and although he arrived at solutions which produced a justified satisfaction, such as the first bell tower, he hoped to better them in parts yet to be built. The desire for perfection which he felt made him realize how limited was his human intelligence which could only resolve plastic problems in the two dimensions of the plane, in contrast to the angelic intelligence which he imagined would solve them directly in space.[5]

When he set forth the system of equilibrated structure which he had worked out for the church at the Güell colony and which he planned to adopt in the Sagrada Familia, he was evidently worried by the fact that the system was without precedent and that he was the first to apply it. The new procedure constituted an obvious advance in architecture, and the

77. The modest manner of the great architect caused him to be taken more than once for a shy beggar by passers-by. Drawing by J. Renart, March, 1925.

2. Related by the sculptor José M. Camps Arnau on April 27, 1955.
3. Related by the same sculptor on December 22, 1961.
4. I heard this myself, one of the first times that I spoke with him.
5. Martinell, *op. cit.*, pp. 85, 98.

discovery could have filled him with well-deserved pride. Nevertheless, it bothered him that he had to be the innovator, and he was only convinced to use it by the perfection and advantages which he felt it his duty to incorporate into architecture. Originality, which is usually the pride of any artist, was borne by him as if it were a painful obligation. He was pleased by his discovery as he analyzed its advantages, but he never translated that unconcealed superiority into empty conceit.

If there were numerous occasions when his character gave off sparks which could have been confused with pride, there were also many occasions when he voluntarily humiliated himself. Reverend Baldelló [6] recalls that for the Constantinian Festivals of the year 1913 they planned to celebrate a High Mass in the grounds of the Sagrada Familia, sung by the boys and girls of the parish schools. In a preparatory practice session in the Belén parish church, there arose a difference of opinion between the architect and the parish priest, Rvd. Ramón Garriga. The latter became irritated and told Gaudí that he was in the way with his eccentricities and dismissed him, taking him by the arm and leading him out of the meeting. Don Antonio humbly lowered his head, put his hands inside his jacket sleeves as he was wont to do, and went to sit down among the children. After the practice, as if nothing had happened and with great humility and energy, he reiterated his points of view and convinced everyone, including the rector who excused himself for his earlier action.

One notable aspect of this humility was the fact that he never willingly allowed his picture to be taken. Apart from the portrait which we have seen from his early youth and that of the Universal Exposition pass of 1888, all of the others that are known were made without his realizing it, or during visits of important people to the Sagrada Familia.

103. SENSE OF HUMOR

A little-known aspect of the architect was his sense of humor. It can not be said that he was a comedian because he was habitually quite serious, but he did have a full sense of humor and he permitted good-natured jokes. He laughed with frank though somewhat contained laughter, and he even expressed himself at times in a comical way. This was not unimportant to him. We have already seen his definition of a joke and his explanation of the psychological mechanism of laughter (XXI - 91).

He used his sense of humor several times in defense against unjust attacks. As a student we saw him «give atmosphere» to a project for the entrance to a cemetery, drawing the funeral cortege more carefully than the architecture—a humorous touch which angered the professor. As an architect, when he was beginning to stand out for his originality, he attended a professional dinner. After the banquet there were speeches, one of them by the professor of Architectural History who had just built a house on the Ramblas with balcony brackets imitating gear wheel quadrants. The theme of his speech was the need for every architect to respect historic styles and not permit himself innovations of a personal sort. Those in attendance realized that the invective was directed, toward the young innovator, and some adhered to the opinion of the professor until in a quiet moment Gaudí raised his voice to ask the orator: «Would you please tell me to which style the consoles of that new house on the Ramblas belong?» Ráfols, who picked up the anecdote, said that «a burst of laughter spread throughout the dining room—a burst of laughter which made the unhappy architect-turned-speaker look ridiculous.» [7]

In previous chapters when speaking of the «coppersmithery» of his ancestors (I - 2) we have sensed a humoristic vein which he himself confirmed with the following tale:

Once a visitor showed great interest in seeing a stair vault built «a la catalana,» —something new for the stranger. When Gaudí showed him one he was filled with wonder at how the mason could place the fine tiles in mid air, held only on the sides. The reasons of a structural order which the architect gave him did not convince the spectator who took the whole thing as little short of a miracle. To better convince him Gaudí «confided» to him that the mason «hypnotized» each tile by staring at it for a moment (while he was actually waiting for the mortar to set). It seems that the perplexed spectator was more convinced by the joke of hypnotism than with the masonry explanations.[8]

Speaking of the mannered anatomies of the people and angels in Michelangelo's paintings, he said that it looked as if the artist had turned them out continuously with the same lack of care with which a sausage maker turns out links in a series in whatever size you want.

Another case of humor—here used in a practical sense—was provoked by a madman who claimed to have found the formula for squaring the circle, and expressed his desire to dedicate it to the Virgin of Mercy without anyone's discovering the secret. This occurred at the time when Gaudí was working on the project for the restoration of the Reusian sanctuary, and it seemed logical that he would continue to direct the work. The madman visited him frequently with the hope of engraving the said formula on the first stone of the reformation, and he was not to be dissuaded by sensible reasoning. Tired of arguments, the architect decided to beat his adversary at his own game, and he pretended to be convinced; at the same time, he

6. Unpublished notes cited.
7. Ráfols, *Gaudí*, (1929), p. 80.
8. Told to me by Gaudí himself.

suggested to the madman the danger that some worker might reveal the secret and rob his formula. By using this strategy he freed himself from the annoying siege.[9]

104. TO ERR IS HUMAN

As I have said, I am not too enthusiastic about anecdotes, but while we are on the subject —and recognizing the great eagerness with which some people greet such tales—I will cite some relatively unimportant ones which point out no special aspect of the great architect except perhaps his involvement in the universal *errare humanum est* of simple everyday affairs.

When Gaudí lived with his niece in Güell Park, he would sometimes go to mass and take the sacrament downtown, and afterwards he would breakfast in the cloister of the cathedral on a raw egg which he had put into his pants pocket on leaving home. His niece warned him of the danger that the egg might break, but he protested that women didn't know anything about such matters, since the form of the egg has such conditions of resistance that it was impossible to crush it by pressing strongly on the two ends. His niece was silenced, and he put the egg in his pocket. Nothing happened until one day on coming out of mass at the cathedral he met his friend Alberto Bastardas, recently named as mayor of Barcelona, who was pleased to see him and crossed the street to embrace him. This was done moderately, but a hurried passer-by with an inopportune push on Gaudí's back ruined the egg's resistance and its contents ran down the famous architect's leg.[10]

Other more important anecdotes show that the architect was fallible not only in a superficial way but also in some professional areas where he would let himself be guided by a hardly justified obstinacy. Here I am referring to the episode of the placing of the large hanging baldachin in the cathedral of Mallorca which one biographer has recorded in a form which does not coincide with the version of the same event given by the Rvd. Sagristá who was present.[11]

It was December 7, 1912, the eve of the Feast of the Immaculate Conception, when the great crown-shaped lighting fixture was to make its debut. The architect Juan Rubió, who was acting as Gaudí's assistant on the job, had calculated the weight of the great crown and the resistance of the rope which was to hold it, and seeing that the latter was insufficient, he had repeatedly called it to the master's attention.

Gaudí paid no heed, and when the director went after dinner to lift the lighting fixture into place, the assistant preferred not to be present for the operation. In lifting the great weight, the cord broke and Gaudí attributed this to the condition of the rope. This was then replaced by another one approved by the architect, and it broke again; and when a steel cable substitute broke a third time, Gaudí, faced with the triple failure, didn't say a word. He simply picked up his hat and went to the nearby episcopal palace where he and Juan Rubió were staying and went to bed. Canon Llobera, church warden for the chapter and among those present, went to Rubió who had retired for the evening; he got up and took over the difficult operation in which the cable broke several more times. He was on the point of giving up when Miguel Sans, the foreman of the construction, informed him of the existence in Palma of another cable of higher caliber which they were able to secure at that late hour, finally resolving the danger. The cable suffered a slight deformation, in spite of which it stayed in place, and for its inauguration the next day it was reinforced with nine other tie-rods which held the fixture to the vault.

105. A CHARACTER SYNTHESIS

In this section I've tried to set down actions and phrases of Gaudí which, together with those previously seen, help us to formulate a more exact idea of his character. Without intending to reduce them to a system, I have grouped the anecdotes into categories: violent, humble, humorous, and mistaken. These could be broadened to include the others of a religious, political, esthetic, and cultural type which the reader will have picked up throughout the present biography and which would complete the picture of the great architect whom I had the honor of knowing in the last years of his life.

I have already stated in Chapter IX that it is not my intention to stray into the realm of psychoanalysis. My purpose is simply to provide some examples and commentary that may help understand this independent character, obstinate as it sometimes was in certain points of view—not out of egoism, but because of a conviction of correctness. Once he formed an opinion he defended it in great haste, often with a sharpness that contrasted with his other opposing characteristics. The injudicious actions of our architect were simply exaggerations of an energetic temperament, and he would even with frequency soften his outbursts with humorous phrases tinted with imperceptible irony and cleverly elegant expression.

Gaudí had a great architectural mission to carry out. He did not lack the genius's intelligence, dynamism, and constancy (a synonym for vocation) necessary to do so. It was a difficult task

9. Related by Gaudí.
10. Told to me by the architect Quintana who heard it from Gaudí himself.
11. Emilio Sagristá, *op. cit.*, pp. 58, 59. The praise and discrepancies in this book concerning Gaudí prove for me its historical veracity. The other tale to which I refer is that given by J. Elias on p. 120 of his cited book, which does not always stick to the facts.

only insofar as it was a lofty task which demanded a rhythm of pressure which was not easy to achieve.

He discarded human love early in his life. Reflection revealed to him through disillusionment that his independent and impulsive ways were not in keeping with matrimony. The sexual aspects did not stimulate him. If this was a problem in his youth, it was soon absorbed by his art and tempered by religion; and he knew how to convert a human sentiment full of intranquility into a theological virtue with lasting effect.

The decisive factors that count in the development of Gaudí's psyche followed a straight line. Once his love was converted into charity, his only human concern was Architecture which encompassed everything for him.

He reduced all of human knowledge to Architecture, and he hoped to sublimate this by putting it at the service of God—an idea that he made apparent in crowning his private works with crosses and by purifying to the maximum the art of his Temple. He related the plastic to the divine, saying that sight was the sense of the *Gloria* which consisted in *seeing* and enjoying God for all eternity. The most characteristic aspect of the personality of the master was his faith, founded on art and the liturgy. We must not forget that he arrived at his faith by the way of architecture and that for him it had such an extremely wide base that in the second half of his life, together with piety and sacrifice, it absorbed him totally.

In a more broadly social and human sense, Gaudí wisely advised taking advantage of circumstances when they were propitious and fighting them when they were adverse. He considered the circumstances to be a manifestation of Providence, and all of his action was directed toward doing good and serving the truth. Along these roads of work, reflection, and sacrifice, with his good qualities and his defects, through favorable and adverse circumstances, illuminated by the faith that continued to grow until his very last breath, this man who at times seemed so stubborn sought to put his art and his life at the service of the Glory of God.

106. THE ACCIDENT

In the architect's last years his life unfolded in a regular and methodical manner which was absolute, centering on his activities in the direction of the temple, and his devotions as a man of faith. On the afternoon of Monday June 7, 1926, he left his studio where he was working on one of the alabaster and metal lamps which he was going to put in the crypt of the Temple. He worked with his usual inspiration and optimism, and on taking leave of the worker who was helping him he said, «Vicente, come early tomorrow for we shall make very beautiful things.» He headed as usual toward the chapel of San Felipe Neri for his evening meditation.

He usually ate dinner and slept in his office at the Temple and so, when Father Parés saw that the customary hour for his return was past and he had not yet come back, he called the architect Sugrañes to communicate the anomaly. When he still had not come after ten, they imagined that he had either been arrested by the police in some altercation or that he had had an accident. Believing the latter to be the most logical, the chaplain set out on a survey of the dispensaries and first-aid stations along the route that Gaudí must have followed; in one of the first, on the Ronda de San Pedro, they told him that they had treated an old man of Gaudí's description who carried a Gospel book in his pocket and had his underwear held together with safety pins, for a traumatism produced on being hit by a tram. The details left no doubt that it was the architect, and informed that they had taken him to the *Hospital Clínico,* he advised Sugrañes, and the two went there together to find that nobody knew anything about what had happened. A second consultation by telephone corroborated the fact that the ambulance had been given orders to take the anonymous wounded man to the *Clínico,* but since he was not there, they headed for the Hospital de la Santa Cruz where they found him.

Gaudí had been run down between six and seven in the evening in the Calle de las Cortes Catalanas (today the Avenida de José Antonio) by Number 30 tram which then passed through the center of the avenue which had two tracks running in opposite directions together, separated by a small island.

No one knew him. The famous architect was nothing more than an anonymous old man whom several passers-by regarded with indifference until one who was moved by compassion attended him. Several taxi drivers refused to help, but another more merciful one was hailed by the passer-by and he drove him to the dispensary on the Ronda de San Pedro. The merciless cabbies were later fined by the mayor.

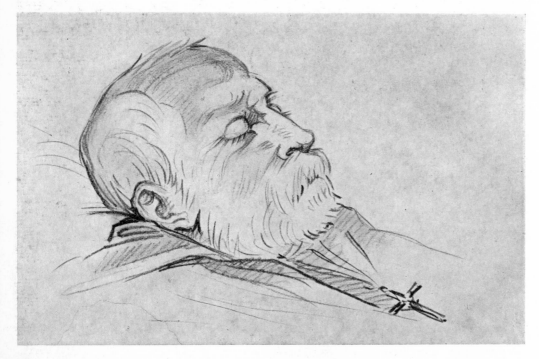

78. Gaudí on his death-bed. Drawing by J. Renart.

79. Death mask of Gaudi executed by the sculptor Juan Matamala Flotats.

107. IN THE HOSPITAL

At the dispensary the damage was diagnosed as a strong contusion on the right side, cerebral concussion, fracture of three ribs and a traumatism of the right ear. After administering first aid, they sent him to the *Hospital Clínico,* but the ambulance men—to shorten the distance or for other unknown reasons—took him to the Hospital de la Santa Cruz. Gaudí more than once had expressed his desire to die precisely in that hospital; for this reason some believed that the ambulance men's transgression may have had some sort of providential significance.

When Reverend Gil Parés and the architect Sugrañes arrived at the hospital and asked for Gaudí, the doctors on duty said that if the celebrated architect were there, the whole staff would know about it. «Nevertheless he is here and you don't realize it,» they answered. The admittance slip said «Antonio Sandí» and he had been taken to the general traumatics ward. The chaplain and the architect found the victim in a state of semi-unconsciousness and ordered that he be given the greatest of care. He was moved to the Immaculate section for preferential patients, and in a tiny room with an iron bed, a night table and chair, with space for nothing more, a pious painting at his head, he lived out the three remaining days of his life.

When the Reverend Parés and Sugrañes, accompanied by the maestro's other assistant, Quintana, returned to visit him the next morning, the patient regained consciousness after a night's prostration and requested the Last Rites which he fervently received. He appears to have been lucid until he entered his last agony, but he did not converse with anyone. When a high city official went to offer that he be moved to a private clinic at the Corporation's expense, he thanked him with a gesture indicating that he was fine where he was.[1]

The patient was visited by the eminent doctors Esquerdo, Gallard, and Corachán who agreed in their pessimistic report, in spite of which they felt it opportune to set his fractured ribs. The entire staff showed maximum diligence in attending him, and when the sad news spread through the city, the parade of friends, admirers, and eminent personalities was continuous. Cardinal Vidal y Barraquer, Bishop Miralles, Cambó, Puig y Cadafalch, Raimundo Abadal Calderó... They set up a book for the visitors to register, and the hallway outside the sick man's room was constantly animated from Tuesday evening and Wednesday when the press published the news with its deserved importance.

I was there on Wednesday morning and on Thursday at the same time. There were more people in the hallway on the second day. In my notes from that time I find the names of several other people who were there: the architects Juan Rubió, Sugrañes, Folguera, Bonet Garí, Cunill; the canon Cardó; the politician Abadal; the locksmith Mañach who proposed the creation of a Gaudí Museum; the poet Melchor Font who was dressed in military uniform and was working as a reporter for the newspaper *La Publicitat.* It was reported that Gaudí was in great pain. I drew near to see him from the door. He breathed with the loud respiration of death, and his eyes were open. He stared with his usual expression, but without recognition. Someone said that during those days he never altered his serene aspect, not even for the most lofty visitors. Only from time to time did he say «*Jesús, Déu meu!*». This led to the belief that he was conscious but that he wished to avoid all dialogue with the world in that supreme hour. On the pillow to his left he had a crucifix, and below it a handkerchief.

If it is true that he was conscious in his last hours, he would have used them in thanking God for the death which he had hoped for: in a hospital. «In the hospital,» he had said, «they take care of the sick for the love of God, not out of obligation as sometimes happens in the family, nor for pay as is the case in the clinics.»

There he lay, in the hospital which for more than five centuries had been under the protection of the Holy Cross which he himself always exalted, putting it as the finishing touch on his works. There he lay in a model cell open to the public which approached him without barrier in a spontaneous selection of friends and admirers who respectfully accompanied him as he took his leave with serene face and spaced out sighs of «*Jesús, Déu meu!*»

Amid whispers, in the outer room a press reporter began to interview those present, foreseeing the imminence of a special edition dedicated to the death of the great architect, and the spirit of the vigilant multitude became depressed as the hours passed, faced with the ineluctable event.[2] Around five in the afternoon of the 10th of June he gave up his soul to the Lord. The temple building committee took care of the necessary paperwork. Photographs of the cadaver were forbidden out of respect for his will which was never in favor of being photographed; but a death mask was allowed (Fig. 79) and an artist friend was authorized to make sketches (Fig. 78).

In a room on the lower floor next to the central patio, normally used by the house doctors, a funeral parlor was set up and soberly draped in black. Part of it contained a platform and two altar tables, and in the center there was a litter of the so-called imperial type with three

1. This is told by the chief himself, Manuel Ribé, who made the offer at the orders of the Mayor, the Barón de Viver. *Diario de Barcelona,* July 8, 1952.
2. Martinell, *op. cit.,* p. 115.

80. The architect's funeral cortege as it passed through the Puerta del Angel.

low prayer stools in front. The temple committee and that of the hospital made arrangements for members of the family and architects to keep vigil.

108. THE WAKE

When I arrived at the hospital at 10:30 at night, Gaudí's body was on the sepulcher, dressed in the habit of Good Death and covered with a white sheet. The young sculptor Juan Mata- mala, the son of *senyor Llorenç* the architect's friend and helper, was preparing to make a death mask. He himself had also been a friend of the architect and worked under him. Also present were the chaplain of the hospital Reverend Eduardo Royo, the young Dr. Alfonso Trías, who so often in his adolescence had been the master's companion, and the architects Ráfols, Puig Boada, Truñó, Pelayo Martínez, and myself, all ready to help the artist in his endeavor.

There was something anomalous about the hospital in its nocturnal silence. Vicars, doctors, students on duty, and nurses, entered from time to time to see the funeral chapel as work progressed on the mask. People from out of town like the artist Ricardo Opisso who had worked for the master for 12 years on the Temple, and the publicist Pedro Corominas, entered to pay their respects to the great architect. The operation was finished at about one in the morning.

We stayed on in vigil over the dead soul. The agitation of the first hours put off the Holy Rosary which was customary in such cases. That day Rosary was said only in the memories that the present situation evoked of the admired maestro, in tones of maximum respect.

The next morning mass was celebrated at the two altars of the chapel. The Temple commit- tee rightly believed that the architect should be buried next to his favorite work (a privilege that until then had only been granted to the descendents of the founder Bocabella), and the wait for permission which had to be obtained by entreaty from Rome and Madrid, delayed the burial for one day. For that reason, on Friday the 11th he was still present, and the pub- lic was permitted to file by and view the cadaver.[3]

3. It was a heterogeneous parade. The majority filed by devoutly, aware of the dead man's personality; some were there out of pure imitative instinct. As a side- light of pure authenticity, I can say that I heard some, with Andalusian ac- cents, ask who the dead person was. They weren't sure but they thought he was a bullfighter.

119

In the afternoon he was embalmed using the so-called «Eternitas» method by which an atmosphere which makes life for microbes and bacteria impossible is produced in the hermetically sealed-zinc coffin.[4] The zinc had a window in its upper face which allowed the cadaver to be seen. The coffin was placed on the platform between the two altar tables.

This was where it lay on the second night when less people stood vigil than the night before. Among those present, besides myself, were Jaime Bayó and José M. Jujol who had collaborated with him. On the suggestion of the second we said the Rosary. As the hours passed the crowd dwindled until only Pelayo Martínez, a plumber who had worked for Don Antonio, and myself were left.

109. THE BURIAL (80)

The small silent wake of the last hours contrasted strikingly with the magnificent demonstration of public bereavement at the burial ceremony which took place the next afternoon. Participating were representatives of official corporations and artistic organizations from Barcelona and other Catalan cities, and numerous bodies representing the cultural life of Barcelona.

Behind the coffin thousands of voices sang the Psalms of David and the responses of the dead without pause, all along the way. The parade followed a special route, singing some responses *corpore insepulto* in the cathedral and later continuing on to the Sagrada Familia. The huge attendance at the ceremony and the number of people who watched the parade from sidewalks and balconies were proof of the general esteem which the master enjoyed. Some balconies along the way were draped in mourning, and near the temple there were hangings on almost every house. Some of them—simple bedspreads with a black scarf or shawl superimposed—were even more impressive for their modesty and the love which they revealed. They were the spontaneous condolences of the good neighbors who for years had seen the great architect pass by with utmost simplicity.

When the Orfeó Català arrived at the temple led by master Lluís Millet, they rendered homage before the coffin, deposited below the place of the future altar, with the *Responsorio* of Victoria, alternating with the singing by the clergy. Night fell. The silence of the multitude was imposing and only interrupted by the tolling of the funeral bells and the chirping of the birds flocking overhead.

4. According to my friend Jacinto Torner, chief of funeral services for the *Diputación* who directed the embalming.

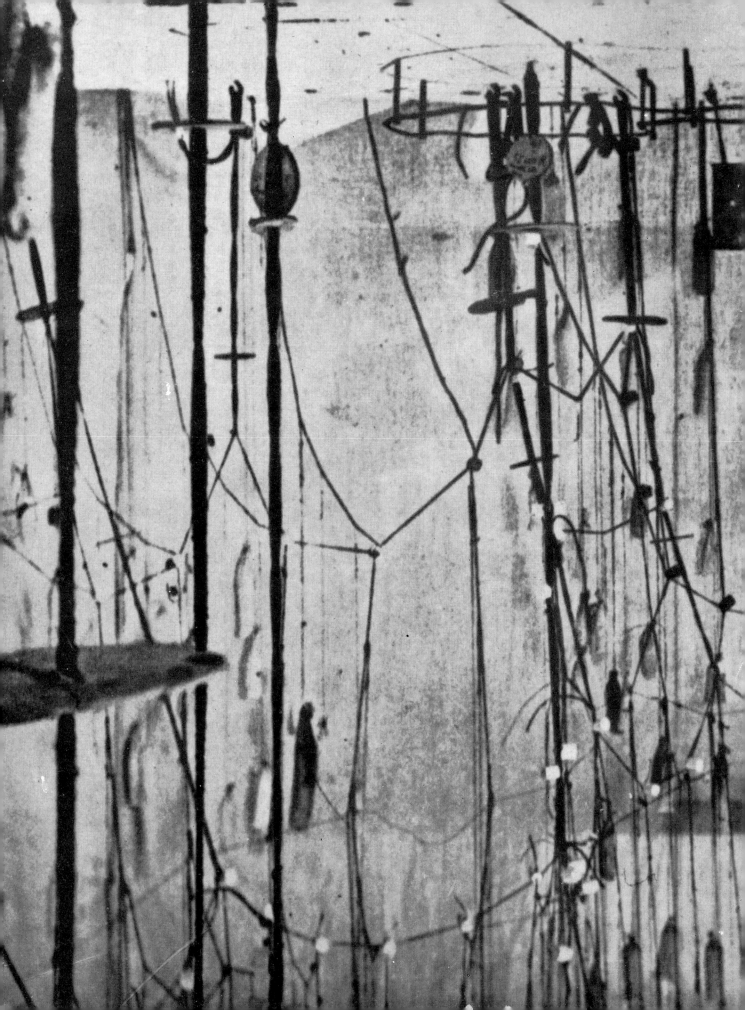

part two / HIS THEORIES

110. THE MASTER'S OPINION

Whereas in Part One it was necessary to search through archives, publications, and personal references for sufficient data to formulate an overall picture of the maestro's life, in this part where we study his architectural theory, the search will be easier and more effective, for it can be limited primarily to his own statements. He used to rationalize with his open loquacity the architectural problems on which he was working, using esthetic, structural, and functional principles to make clear the rationale of his new solutions.

Critics in recent years have generally divided writers on Gaudí into two camps: one made up of a sort of «old guard» composed of those of us who knew the maestro directly and can report his principles from personal contact, and the other consisting of the new theoreticians who focus on his works in the light of recent architectural trends, being unaffected by the sentimental power which the strong personality of such a genius was able to exert.

Such a classification is usually accompanied by a show of respect for the first group, but a veiled preference for the greater relevance of the second, in spite of the fact that some of the modern opinions fail to relate the artistic reality to the idea which inspired it. In other words, they judge Gaudí's works without taking his motives into account.

I prefer not to take sides in favor of either of the two groups, for it is possible that both are needed and that they complement each other. Yet I would like to make it clear that while not excluding recent critical analysis, I will in these chapters give first place to the opinions of the innovative architect himself, in the hope that certain problems in the interpretation of his work may finally be solved.

There exists enough evidence to judge and appreciate the evolution of Gaudí's esthetic ideas from his youth to his latest years, and thus to understand the relationship between cause and effect—the ideas and the works of art—during each phase of his life. In the book *Conversaciones con Gaudí*, we see certain esthetic ideas of his last years which serve as guides to the most personal phase of his production, and the Municipal Museum at Reus possesses a notebook which has been often cited but never analyzed (some writers, in fact, have even considered it lost)[1] and which provides us with a clear picture of his esthetic ideas as he himself jotted them down on finishing his professional studies.

As a youth he was already interested in standards of beauty. Despite his impetuous temperament and wild imagination, he was aware of the fact that the mysterious element which makes objects pleasing to the eye corresponds to specific physical stimuli which, once understood and properly applied, can effectively bring about a desired result. Such was his conviction about this that at 26, having recently completed Architecture School, one of the first things that he did was to write out the previously mentioned «Notes on Ornamentation;» this consisted of a melange of ideas proceeding from both classroom lectures and his own intensive reading, as well as others which reveal the author's forceful personality and which would be presented again later in his life in a more completely developed and definitive form.

111. A DIDACTIC ESSAY (Fig. 81)

The manuscript on ornamentation, although written in the very year that Gaudí finished school, deserves consideration as a serious and carefully thought-out study. His comprehensive exam was over on January 4 and his title issued on March 15. In the meantime, on February 27, the City of Barcelona had commissioned him to design a type of lamppost for the city streets, a project on which he spent considerable time and effort, confronting several of the problems which he later dealt with in the mentioned manuscript. From this it becomes obvious that the essay was not simply a theoretical or academic exercise for the author, but rather an explanation of carefully considered points of view, some taking off from school materials and others originating in his own intuition (Appendix IV).

The first lines of the essay allude to a discussion with his friend Oliveras, the architect, and to certain first-hand studies in the cathedral, aswell as to some photographs which he had examined of the Alhambra, after which he broadens out into more general esthetic considerations. Here we will examine those which seem most representative of his thought.

BASIC PRECEPTS: «To be interesting, ornamentation should represent objects which remind us of poetic ideas, and which constitute motifs.»

---

1. This manuscript was mentioned in Chapter IX, Section 31. Roberto Pane in his *Antonio Gaudí* (Milan: 1964), p. 12, says that it has disappeared.

«In order that an object be very beautiful, it is necessary that its form contain nothing superfluous, but only the material conditions which make it useful; we must take into account both the material and the use which will be made of it...»

«The most important requirement for an object that is to be considered beautiful is that it fulfill the purpose for which it is destined, not as if it were a matter of gathering together problems solved individually and assembling them to produce a heterogeneous result, but rather with a tendency toward a unified solution where the material conditions, function, and character of the object are taken care of and synthesized, and once the good solutions are known it is a matter of taking that one which is most fitting to the object as deduced from the need to attend to its function, character, and physical conditions.»

CHARACTER. He speaks of the character of a work of art which he says is «the definition of its esthetic-moral condition,» adding that it is also the criterion for ornamentation which should reveal the form that is «dictated solely by the complete satisfaction of some need.» Public objects should be severe in character, and he finds geometric ornamentation to be preferable, with the use of natural forms from time to time for contrast. He demonstrates this by citing Greek examples, in particular the Erechtheum, and further states that «common sense tells us that simple forms are characteristic of magnificence and that abundant ornamentation is more properly found in small masses.»

In dealing with the character of churches he advises: «do not conceal the great masses, but rather, on the contrary, keep their magnitude in mind, dissolving, if necessary, their imposing effect by means of fitting and simple ornamentation.»

He unpretentiously heralds the importance of equilibrated forms which will later become more apparent in his work, saying: «The forms of the exterior should mirror those of the interior; arches and vaults of equilibrated form, brick ribs, and rubble or tabicada spandrels can be raised on great pillars.» Further on he praises the esthetic and structural advantages of the dome.

He does not squarely face the problem of simple equilibrated forms, still conceiving of them as elevated on great pillars. It is apparent, however, that he senses their importance.

In a later section he explains that «forms expressed simply have more grandeur,» and that «the multiplication of the number of moldings necessarily induces a complexity of ornamental motifs.» And he continues: «Those forms derived from geometry produce great distinctness and clarity.» He was to develop this theme further in the course of his lifetime, and here he sums it up by saying that «the more perfect the forms, the less ornamentation that is necessary.»

He applied this principle to historical styles, saying that «the forms used by the Egyptians, the Greeks, and the Middle Ages did not require so much decoration as those derived from the Renaissance or the Byzantine itself; in styles which are not original and are therefore derived from others, decoration is of great importance—e.g., the Roman, laden with varied forms and sculptures and the Baroque which in this respect leaves the Roman far behind.» He was obviously referring to the historical Baroque style which developed out of the Renaissance, and not to the baroque in the sense of expansive expressiveness, which he himself sometimes made use of, omitting the superimposed ornamentation.

He goes on to explain that «the esthetic structure is one which reveals the varied means employed and the numerous problems resolved in its construction, making the objects pleasant in themselves, i.e., the object becomes an entity, whereas those covered by ornaments and without structure can be admired only for their expensiveness...»

«It is obvious that it is necessary to create an ornamentation based on our way of life which will interest the wise as well as the not-so-wise. This ornamentation must be determined by structure, material, and economy.»

PROPORTION. «Proportion, or the law of the relationship between the parts and the whole and between each part and each other part, is a subject with which we are well enough acquainted to state clearly and without digression that while we can derive a certain intuition from the study of nature, the study of technical progress and of new materials stamps each age and each building with a special character all its own.»

«...Isolated supports of iron are called on to play a great part, and we have—in the formulas of Love and Hodgkinson—the means of determining the aforementioned ratio (diameter to height).» In other words, he related the esthetics of the object to the mechanical properties of the material employed.

COLOR. In the course of the manuscript he speaks several times of color. In the beginning he says that «Ornamentation has been, is, and will be polychromatic; nature does not present us with any object that is monotonously uniform... therefore we must necessarily color, partially or completely, all architectonic members.» And in the «archaic and Greek [styles] where color, far from being omitted, enters greatly into the formation of artistic character... the forms are more elegant, more distinguished, and the animation of the color gives them great luster.»

PERSONAL ESTHETIC. Gaudí never abandoned this concern for esthetics which was apparent from his first moments as an architect, and even in his later years his conversation was liberally strewn with comments of an esthetic sort which expressed his personal ideas on the subject. While I do not wish to reduce them to a system, I will here attempt to assemble those memories and reports which I feel are useful to judge his work correctly—i.e., those which clarify certain of the maestro's points of view and shed light on his thought.[2]

I would first like to explain that Gaudí's esthetic system had its origin in the inspiration of his genius. The ideas and rationalizations were developed *a posteriori* as a consequence of his innovations. These usually were not matrix ideas, but commentaries. An idea valid one day could be replaced the next by another, better one and it was in this progressive manner that the Gaudinian esthetic was born—an esthetic which, once established, could influence artistic production external to itself, but not create it in a premeditated way. Gaudí's ideas illuminate and explain his motives in a manner which was supplementary for him but which is indispensable for the writers who wish to relate what he found in tradition to the original things which he created.

BEAUTY AND TRUTH WITHOUT PROFIT. I heard him say various times, basing himself on Saint Augustine and Saint John, that «Beauty is the radiance of Truth» or, in other words, without Truth there can be no Beauty... The fundamental mission of the artist is to produce «beautiful works, without worrying too much about economic compensation...» He linked Art and Business by their common qualities of synthesis and of situation, but he differentiated them in the fact that for the businessman it is allowed—and even considered meritorious—to let himself be influenced by profit goals, while for the artist it is repugnant to give preference to anything which might make him swerve from the path to Beauty.

ELEGANCE. Beauty must not be overloaded with elements but rather should display a sobriety by which Elegance is achieved—i.e., Elegance is Beauty obtained with minimal means. Elegance allows an imperceptible increase or decrease in one of its parts or characteristics to obtain a greater agility or a certain desired expression in the work of Art.

EXPRESSION. At times plastic or formal beauty is best sacrificed on the altar of a preconceived idea that can be obtained through formal expressiveness, replacing it with a sort of intellectual or moral beauty. This was the case with the Passion façade of the Sagrada Familia which Gaudí conceived in angular, deliberately austere forms in order to express the pathetic death of Jesus.

HELLENISM. Forms must be combined wisely so that each enhances the effect of the others. In this the Greeks were masters. In the folds of the drapery of the Venus de Milo one finds no detailed concavity, whereas the convex parts are quite intricately detailed. The value of the latter is enhanced by the former.

This same criterion dominates the Sagrada Familia, even in the Gothic elements. The expressionist austerity of the Passion façade as a contrast to the gentle optimism of the Nativity is an application of the same principle.

Another Hellenic element is the use of color which, as in the Greek temples, he planned to use throughout the Sagrada Familia, and did apply to the upper parts of the completed towers.

The Hellenism that Gaudí attributed to his Temple does not have to be taken in a literal stylistic sense, for it refers more to the elevated esthetic which is the molder of styles. We note here a coincidence with Viollet-le-Duc who said that «the masters who built a number of our western buildings in the Middle Ages were more profoundly imbued with those principles which were the essence of the Greek genius than those who merely imitated coldly Greek form could ever have been.» [3]

Gaudí summarized his admiration for Greek art by saying, «the Greeks never felt remorse.»

LATITUDE AND THE MEDITERRANEAN AS FACTORS OF BEAUTY. He said that the properties of Beauty were proportion, harmony, color; properties which reach a higher level of perfection in the middle geographic regions of the earth than they do in the extreme areas.

The inhabitants of the countries bathed by the Mediterranean Sea sense Beauty with greater intensity than do those of the Nordic countries, and they themselves are aware of this. The most notable works of Art have come from the Mediterranean peoples: Egyptians, Greeks, Italians, Spaniards, who have a more deeply rooted vision of Beauty due to their proximity to this privileged sea and due to the angle of the solar rays—almost 45 degrees—which is that most appropriate to the perfect viewing of Nature and its elements.

This Mediterraneanism which Gaudí extolled and practiced did not prevent him from being aware of Central European artistic movements—as we will see later (XLVI - 182)—which led

2. Many of what I call «memories» can be found in my book *Conversaciones con Gaudí*, and others are cited from memory. I will give the sources for those originating elsewhere.

3. Viollet-le-Duc, *Entretiens sur l'Architecture*, II, p. 181.

81. Scale drawing of the Passion façade done by Gaudí, in which the pathetic expression is more important than beauty of form.

him to extremely personal realizations, at times anticipating the Art Nouveau and the Jugendstil which in Catalonia were translated into so-called «Modernismo» with our architect being one of its outstanding exponents.

IMAGINATION AND FANTASY. In the equatorial regions and in those near the poles, people are conditioned to see things falsely—in the first because of an excess of light and in the second because of a light deficiency—and they do not perceive images as they are but rather get a somewhat fantastic version of them. For this reason, the people of such regions have a more advanced sense of fantasy and abstraction, and these qualities are manifest in their art, literature, philosophy, and even science.

In the intermediate zones, the heightened light and climate bring about a more real perception of images which is inborn in the habitants. These people have a more developed imagination and create works based on images born of a reality which is Truth.

Gaudí made a distinction between *fantasy* which is born of a deformed reality and peopled by ghosts, and *imagination* which is the product of real images, and he considered the two terms to be contradictory. Those who wish to praise the master—as many do—by attributing to him great fantasy, actually insult him in his own terminology. A similar slight is commited by those who seek Central African or other non 45-degree latitude sources for Gaudí's work. His inspiration was always close to the shores of the *Mare Nostrum* and more especially in that fertile Campo which enjoyed the legacy of the ancient *Tarraco*.

112. TRUTH ACHIEVED THROUGH STUDY (Figs. 82-84)

Gaudí took off from the idea that without Truth there can be no Beauty, and that in order to know the Truth, profound study was necessary.

Beauty is Life, and Life is found in the Creation whose most perfect work is man. Man does not create: he discovers and builds on his discoveries.[4] The work of art must have Life and therefore must subject itself to Truth.

FALSE EMOTION. Without Truth there is no complete art. But some works produce a false emotion which can be either exaggerated or infantile as in the case of the woman in the New Testament who, on finding the drachma that she had lost, was so overcome with emotion that on this small pretext she called in all of her neighbors to partake of her happiness.

The architect cited this parable on the occasion of an exposition by the painter Celso Lagar —a follower of the new tendencies in painting of the time which were the beginnings of those current today—at the Dalmau Galleries on the Calle de Portaferrisa. He felt that the painter had transferred to his canvas «an emotion of the vision of lights; but he has placed in the

4. Bergós, *op. cit.*, p. 35.

127

82. Detail of the tribune of the Casa Batlló in which the continuous forms serve to unite the supporting and supported elements. The mullions are of naturalistic bone-like forms combined with plant-like elements.

foreground what belongs to the distance. Here there is emotion but not Truth, without which there can be no work of Art.»

In spite of his originality and spirit of innovation, Gaudí always retained a classic conception of Art, finding in Nature the most certain guide for artistic renovation which was subject to Truth.[5]

From this it will be clear that he never basically accepted the informalist tendencies which have sometimes been attributed to him for certain fragments of his works which we will discuss later. The chromatic or plastic solutions which motivate such attributions were not intended by the architect as pictorial or sculptural works in the traditional sense, but rather as decorative elements of a secondary nature.

SYNTHESIS. To know the Truth, profound study is necessary. For this purpose one must have recourse to both analysis and synthesis. Analysis is necessary but incomplete; it is necessary for the partial appreciation of each element, but it loses sight of the whole and is therefore inferior to synthesis which coordinates these elements and produces unity.

There are various levels of synthesis. The line is a synthesis of points; the surface is a more general synthesis and the volume more general still. The volume is greater and has more plastic possibilities than the surface; the latter in turn is greater than the line which is itself superior to the point which is a mere abstraction and therefore artistically sterile.

If we imagine them to be infinite in extension the generatrices of ruled warped surfaces constitute infinite space. Such surfaces are the paraboloid, the hyperboloid, and the helicoid. All three have the same elementary structure which is represented by the tetrahedron. A tetrahedron, with unlimited faces, is the synthesis of infinite space.

The first of these surfaces could symbolize the Trinity while the second represents light and the third, movement. The paraboloid is generated by a straight line that slides along two others. If we imagine the three straight lines to be infinite, the first can symbolize the Holy Ghost which is the union between the Father and the Son represented by the other two straight lines. The infinite three form a totality which is one, indivisible and infinite—qualities which coincide with the essence of the Holy Trinity.[6]

The hyperboloid, because of its regular and gradual form with the generatrices spreading out from the throat, represents the radiation of light. The helicoid, due to its resemblance to the growth and development of certain plants, is movement incarnate. (Mechanically employed as a propeller, this form communicates movement to boats and airplanes.)

5. Ibid., p. 35.
6. Gaudí pointed out this coincidence which some writers have considered to be original with him. I do not know if he ever attributed this idea to anyone else, but I have reason to doubt that it was his.

83. The diverse textures of the porch of the crypt of the Colonia Güell.

UNITY. Synthesis must lead to unity—a condition of all works of architecture and of artistic composition in general. To compose means to unite, to relate parts, not to subdivide. The goal is the formation of a harmonic whole based on diverse elements with an overall criterion of *unity*.

Here we can recall the delight which he took in the synthesis of space, light, color, movement, and life which he found in the sea where the mobile surface of the transparent water and the third dimension of depth combined with the reflection of the sky were all enclosed in a single vision (!II - 8).

GEOMETRIC FORMS. When speaking of geometric forms, we usually think of those that are polyhedral, with flat faces. But there is no reason to exclude other geometrically generated forms which are more perfect. The polyhedral forms, which have been labelled «geometric» in a mindless exclusivism, are hardly abundant in Nature.[7] Even those which man constructs as a plane (doors, tables, boards) tend with time to warp into parabolic forms.

Gaudí had a strong intuition for resolving geometric problems, and they never gave him any trouble despite his not having studied (according to him) anything beyond elementary geometry. In his student days he began to feel the suggestiveness of those forms which he later was to make popular (V - 15). In the Batlló and Milá houses and in Güell Park he used continuous three dimensional forms without subjecting them to geometry. In the church for the Güell colony, he tended to geometrize them, and in the termination of the towers of the Temple he subjected them to a rigid geometry of previously determined forms of expression and movement.

In spite of the importance of form in the plastic arts, the maestro assigned it fourth place in an architectural work. He gave first importance to *situation*, second to *size*, third to *material* or *color*, and fourth to *form*. After that came *stability* and other properties.[8]

SUPPORTING AND SUPPORTED ELEMENTS. The traditional designation of supporting and supported elements in a building is arbitrary. In reality, only the element next to the ground is supporting and that at the top, supported. The rest are both supports for those elements above them and supported by those below.

This gratuitous distinction creates an imperfect continuity at the point of passage from that element which is taken to be supporting to the supported element. In openings, at the corner that joins the jambs to the lintel, it is usual to find some adornment (such as a capital, an impost, or a console) which serves to distract the attention from the mechanically unre-

7. Only in crystallography are they common. In that science they are divided into six systems and lend themselves to marvelous combinations.

8. Bergós, *op. cit.*, p. 39.

solved point. A conceptual deficiency is thus hidden by a detail which is agreeable to the eye, and the problem is diverted from the structural to the decorative field.

A possible way of resolving this is through the use of continuous forms adapted to function, structure, and beauty. In the Batlló and Milá houses where such continuous forms were adopted, they effectively enhance the overall sense of unity.

113.   LIFE IN THE WORK OF ART (Fig. 85)

LIFE, MOVEMENT, AND COLOR. The artist must give life to his works, and the most ostensible manifestations of life are movement and color.

As has been said, movement is best represented by helicoidal forms. Many trees grow in spiral fashion. Creeping vines twist along a helicoidal path. The solomonic column, which is the most mobile element in the history of architecture, obeys the same generating rule.

As for color, it can be said that its lack is the most visible manifestation of the lack of life. When a dead person in exceptional cases does not lose his color, it is said that he seems to be alive. The artist must not renounce the use of color. The Egyptians and Greeks polychromed their temples in spite of the rich Pentelic marble they used, and both cultures polychromed their sculpture as well.

In order to give chromatic richness to his buildings, Gaudí made use of colored materials such as stone and brick and of ceramic or glazed facings. In the Sagrada Familia he planned to use stucco in those archivolts of the Nativity façade which were protected from the rain; and on the spires of the towers he used Venetian mosaic as we have seen. In the Casa Milá he painted the ironwork of the balconies and the patios, combining this in his plans with the natural color of the foliage and flowers in carefully placed pots and boxes.

THE LITURGY. The Christian liturgy is a living lesson in the most purified esthetics. All of these lessons can be found in the book *Ceremonial de Obispos* (The Bishops' Ceremonial), bishops having all of the priestly prerogatives including that of consecrating other bishops.

84.   Interior of funicular model by which Gaudí studied the structure of the Colonia Güell church.

The liturgy has foreseen numerous details which produce greater beauty and a clear expression of the meaning of those liturgical objects to which it gives spiritual life. It specifies, for example, that nothing should be placed on top of the sacrarium, not even the crucifix, for the sacrarium houses the very body of Jesus Christ which cannot be placed below anything —not even its own image. In the primitive liturgy, only the image of Christ was granted a canopy. Later, this prescription fell into disuse, and niches and canopies were allowed for all of the saints. If it were not for this tolerance, a simple inspection would reveal the hierarchy of a temple's venerated saints, and the hierarchical order would heighten the overall beauty. When the liturgy prescribes a color for the ornaments in a given ceremony it recommends that this be the dominant color throughout the church, thus assuring chromatic harmony in the services; we can also observe the use that the liturgy makes of light which is the basis of all ornamentation.

The liturgy states that on Good Friday the holy oils should be consecrated on a table that is covered with natural flowers, and for important ceremonies it prescribes that the temples should be adorned with strongly-scented flowers and plants—both of these being details of exquisite taste.

TECHNICAL AND FUNCTIONAL SINCERITY. An obvious sincerity in the application of materials and a logical arrangement with regard to their properties was necessary in order to put the esthetic principles presented here into practice. In his first completed work, when he was 26, he had already established the premise of «the greatest frankness in the use of materials, leaving their structure and arrangement completely exposed, and absolutely disallowing any layer of color that might attempt to give an illusion of other, non-existent materials and objects and which would disappear at the hands of intemperate weather to reveal the true material as the nudity of the beggar is seen through his rags.» [9]

Gaudí was not only sincere in applying exposed and visible materials, but also he would frequently extract a certain tectonic expression from the nature of such materials which would serve to enhance the character of his works. In the church at the Colonia Güell we find a great variety of textures obtained from the various qualities of iron mineral slag, different

9. [This is quoted from Gaudí's memorial about street lamps, eliminated from the English edition. Ed.]

85. Park Güell, details showing the esthetic expression achieved with equilibrated structures and the carefully chosen rough stone textures.

arrangements of brick, and the robustly expressive mallet-hewn basalt pillars. In the Güell Park a good example of this—apart from the great textural variety which we will examine later—can be found in the flower stands in the form of pots above the small stone merlons which decorate one of the viaducts (Fig. 426). When we discuss the Casa Milá we will see how in several cases he used industrial iron shapes with admirable artistic results.

The use to which each object was to be put also influenced its technical characteristics. This can be seen in the iron front gate and the spiral ramp from the stables in the Güell palace; the patio of the Batlló house and the flexible plans and balconies of «La Pedrera;» and the wall of the Casa Calvet looking onto the convent.

Once the work program and the elements available for its realization were determined, he would solve the problem in his own manner, taking advantage of the teachings of experience but not subjecting himself to them. Guided by his powerful imagination and wisdom, he obtained solutions which were admired for their great originality. We can here recall the phrase that the maestro repeated several times and which none of the writers ever forget, yet which none completely explained: *«Originality means to return to the origin.»* To serve an end with given means, using their intrinsic qualities to the maximum and without stylistic prejudice —such was the simple path to originality when one had imagination and talent.

XXVI. STRUCTURE AND DECORATION

114. UNRESOLVED PROBLEMS

Knowing the importance that Gaudí gave to Truth as a necessary element of every work of art, and the intense critical spirit which was always with him, we can assume that he made a decided effort to invest his architecture with that Truth which would result in Beauty. His revisionist spirit was most intense in the case of Gothic structures whose mechanical inconveniences had been denounced by the theoreticians. Nevertheless, they never thought of directly correcting those inconveniences, and merely sought to compensate for them by using auxiliary structures.

When Gaudí took charge of the Sagrada Familia which had been begun in the Gothic style which was then almost obligatory for religious buildings, his first concern was to decrease those inclined forces which made the construction of buttresses, flying buttresses, and pinnacles necessary to act as supports and dead weights to verticalize the thrusts. His desire for synthesis could not permit the complex centrifugal forces at work in the Gothic temple, which favor the disintegration of its elements, and are compensated for by parasitic superstructures of dead weights and counter-thrusts.

He used to say to the assistants in his studio that «the Gothic is an art of formulas; my aim is to improve that style—to give to the Gothic a life which its compass tricks do not achieve.» And he would add: «But for one single man to conquer three centuries of building is a titanic task...!»[1]

TOWARDS THE SOLUTION. When the laws of mechanics were unknown, it was understandable that architecture, ideally a harmonic synthesis of structure, geometry, and mechanics could ignore the last to a certain extent; but once the methods for calculating internal thrusts were established, mechanics could no longer be ignored and should even take precedence in the synthesis just described.

Gaudí appreciated the necessity of such a unity, and from his earliest works he employed mechanically equilibrated forms that are not ordinarily to be found in our artistic tradition, first in Mataró where he used a somewhat empirical solution, and later in the Güell Palace with a look of great solidity on the façade and of summary svelteness and lightness on the interior; still lacking strict mechanical precision, as if he were trying out the wide varieties of esthetic expression possible with such forms. In the stables for the same patron in Les Corts, he also used these arches, here with a more utilitarian than esthetic end.[2]

These instances were basically planimetric. The cupola of the central salon of the Güell Palace and its supports were developed in a more spatial manner, but were still easily reducible to planes. He first confronted the situation in all of its complexity in the small church at the Güell colony which he began to study in 1898, with the idea of later applying his findings to the Sagrada Familia.

The calculation of these complex structures, especially in the necessary preparatory tests, would be extremely tedious when using the method of graphic statics usually employed. In order to facilitate his study, Gaudí set up the problem in a three-dimensional way, on a smaller scale and inverted, beginning with a drawing of the plan and replacing the pillars and arches with cords, and the loads with small proportional weights. In this way he obtained a funicular model by which rough estimates can be easily obtained to arrive at the closest approximation which then must be verified by calculation before carrying the solution into practice.

115. SYNTHETIC STRUCTURES

The forms that result from the acting loads and the constructional necessities, and which Gaudí was the first to use, have the advantage of producing no unresolved thrusts, the active elements of the construction being no more than a revelation of the internal thrusts which must necessarily be contained within these elements; therefore there is no dispersion, but rather an overall cohesion which strengthens the feeling of unity, and dispenses with auxiliary elements of support which, however beautiful they may be, esthetically confuse the work and make it more expensive.

With this new theory, the three formerly divorced principles of architecture were united: the *mechanical* fact is *geometrically* demonstrated and is translated into three-dimensional mate-

1. Ráfols, *Modernismo y Modernistas* (Barcelona: 1949), p. 310.
2. Gaudí used these arches in 1885, some 25 years before the engineer Vierendeel cited this form as the most appropriate in his Applied Mechanics text.

86. Naturalistic and capricious forms in the wrought-iron work of the Palacio Güell.

87. Example of cast iron in naturalistic forms in the Casa Vicens fence.

rial, making it *structural*. Mechanics, geometry, and structure have been synthesized to produce a logical architecture in which each active element fulfills its function in an equilibrated way and with the least effort.

The new theory created new solutions—such as slanting columns which scandalized the unprepared critics—and other procedures that gave a breath of fresh air to the exhausted canons in use for so many centuries. He was able to guide successfully his theory which, had it not been so carefully worked out and tested, might have seemed foolhardy although it did overcome inconveniences which were clearly to be seen in Gothic structures.

Gaudí had foreseen from the beginning the possibility of this theory and its transcendental implications. Nevertheless, when he had verified it and he realized its importance on such large scale, he understood the weighty responsibility involved in travelling such an unknown road, and there was a moment's hesitation before he started out, despite his usually decisive character. The novelty which would have excited so many other men produced in Gaudí an increased prudence; it was only the consideration that it represented an advance for architecture which led him to apply the theory in his work at the Sagrada Familia, feeling it his duty to help in the perfection of the building arts through his own work.

The theory was fully expounded by the architect in his conversations and in the models that he worked out for the church, but he applied it only in a part of the completed work. Nevertheless, it was obviously valuable in the general development of architecture because it marked a new direction and progress in structural concepts and processes. Architectural theory had not evolved much since the Gothic period. The Renaissance and 19th-century eclecticism were nothing more than erudite versions of earlier concepts, with the only sign of uneasiness coming with the Baroque esthetic. In the middle of the last century, with the development of iron and, later, of reinforced concrete, structural advances occurred which left stone architecture unaffected. Without a new theory, the latter would still be in the same or a similar state as when the Gothic architects of the 12th century established their procedures.

We must note, however, that the new theory is not limited to stone structures; this can be seen by Gaudí's first application of parabolic arches in wood, and his last projects for reinforced concrete vaults in the Sagrada Familia, and the use of this same material by other architects in buildings based on Gaudinian theory.

116. A NEW ESTHETIC

As proof of the validity of Gaudí's principle which related Truth to Beauty, if we can extricate ourselves from the forms which have been categorized as beautiful by tradition, we will observe that the equilibrated structures usually result in forms and rhythms of great beauty within a new esthetic.

Gaudí's intuition told him as early as the first applications of his theory in the Palacio Güell that these new forms were incompatible with traditional ornamental vocabulary, and he himself created the forms which would give proper emphasis to the basic structures without interfering with their mechanical and utilitarian function that are the truth of the building.

These equilibrated structures do not comprise the entirety of the master's architectural ideas which were so vigorous in other areas as well, but because they were his most personal and concrete innovation, we can consider them to be a representative example of Gaudí's architecture.

88. Another aspects of wrought-iron work, as used in the school of Santa Teresa.

89. Ironwork evoking vegetal forms combined with industrial profiles in the sill and translucent floor of a balcony in the Casa Milá.

The new forms which Gaudí discovered are most important structurally, but in architecture one cannot do without artistic considerations, and we have already seen the careful attention which he paid to this aspect of his works. He was not deterred by the fact that his new solutions and forms were without tradition in architecture; instead, convinced of their effectiveness and motivated by an absolute structural honesty, he created the esthetic which would suit them.

During his period of historicism, before he employed the new forms with a conviction, Gaudí used motifs of geometric, and above all naturalistic, ornament which he had accepted and praised in the essay on esthetics that we have examined; already in this first stage his basic principle was that decoration is not only for the pleasant entertainment of the eye, but also should give expression to a form or an idea. His ideal was that whatever was visible in his architecture should correspond to its function and to its structural essence, and he achieved this through form, material, textures, color, and light.

In the descriptive part of the present study, we will see some examples of this aspect of his work, but the complete application of his theory was never realized; he only set it forth in some of the three-dimensional models which he worked out. These were based on *a priori* warped surfaces, geometrically generated, which in themselves have artistic expression and allow decoration along their generatrices, thus accentuating their geometric origin to an even greater extent. What concerned him was the quest for an adequate language to express the new esthetic required by his new mechanics. With the hyperbolic paraboloid he achieved original decorative solutions which he later completed and beautified with hyperboloids. He used the conoid and the helicoid more sparingly, and with all of these he employed a geometrically expressive system that was rich in possibilities.

Gaudí only reached this level of purification in the upper parts of the towers of the Sagrada Familia and in the aforementioned models. More and more in his works he avoided any unessential element, infusing them with the spirit of synthesis which he had striven for from his youth. His goal was to emphasize the lines of force in an expressive and beautiful manner. After having taken care of the *utility, mechanics,* and *logic* which he considered basically important, he hoped to instill his works with an expression of *life* which was for him the source of *beauty* and of *truth.* He said that Architecture, like Sculpture and Painting, should give life to its works and that in order to obtain this life the architect must make use of all of the means at his command; among these, after the primary element of *form,* one must pay close attention to the *quality of the materials,* and to *light* and *color.*

117. TEXTURES (Figs. 86-89)

In regard to materials, Gaudí not only used those which were most appropriate to every project, but he also took special pains to put them to work in such a manner that they would enhance the desired effect. In the Sagrada Familia we can observe a variety of finished surfaces of the stone, depending on the character desired in each case. In the Colonia Güell and in Güell Park we see walls and pillars of brick or rubblework which in the mere choice of materials and in their rusticity acquire a variety of rich textures and are surprising in their structural expressiveness and their harmony with the landscape.

Gaudí used this expressive variety not only with stone materials, but also with glass, ceramic, and enamel revetments which he employed freely and with great diversity, at times achieving a «collage-like» quality; he also used the same criteria for wood and metallic revetments. With wrought iron he achieved works of great mastery which are valuable for their good taste, originality, and the technical difficulties which he was able to overcome. He frequently combined different materials to obtain the expressive effects that he desired as we will see in the Palacio Güell, where wrought iron is coupled with stone on the exterior and with wood and stone on the interior; in addition, these compositions have an architectonic interest in themselves.

IRON. Gaudí's professional beginnings coincided with the vogue for the artistic use of cast and rolled iron in construction, and with a renaissance of wrought iron which had enjoyed an extensive medieval tradition in Catalonia. The most outstanding Catalan architects of this time (Doménech y Montaner, Antonio Gallisá, Vilaseca, Puig y Cadafalch) were making an effort to re-establish these and other artistic crafts which had fallen into disuse, and soon Gaudí stood out among them for the originality of his forms and the logic of the solutions in which he employed each material according to its properties. He did not disdain cast iron, and we will see several examples of its use in Part Three.

Nevertheless, he excelled most admirably in his work of iron forging in which he realized objects that were exemplary in their composition and technique. The early works are generally of a more geometric composition—as in the dragon gate of the Finca Güell, the lower part of the front door gratings of the Güell Palace, and the window openings at the Teresan school. In this early stage we can observe certain naturalistic fragments and capricious curves which relate to the Art Nouveau.

90. Sacristy wardrobe for the Sagrada Familia Church, which can be transformed into an altar, a masterful work in iron and wood destroyed in 1936.

As time passed, expressionism was accentuated, and while he almost always simplified his solutions, at times he indulged in a delightful technical virtuosity such as that which we will see in the Calle Provenza grating of the Casa Milá (Fig. 473). In this building he employed factory-made elements with great success, revealing the mechanical structure artistically without recourse to hand-forged work.

WOOD. In the interests of constructive sincerity, Gaudí frequently employed unpainted wood with only faint moldings, leaving the artistic effect of the work to basic structure and perfection of execution. Already in his first works at the Casa Vicens and at Comillas (in spite of the fact that he did not direct the latter personally) we note—although these are not luxurious works—the special attention paid to the wooden objects (doors, windows) which become more artistic than functional. If he showed so much concern in these buildings of a run-of-the-mill sort, it is understandable that upon being entrusted with the noble mansion of the Güell family he would take extreme care in the doors, balustrades, wood-working, and decorative motifs which were always sober, elegant, and well-built. In the Calvet house he constructed the ceilings of uncarved wood.

Notable examples of wood construction were the portal of the Rosary at the Sagrada Familia, (Fig. 308) which was destroyed during the Civil War and later reconstructed as a gift by the carpenters guild of Barcelona, and the great wardrobe in the sacristy of the Temple, which was also destroyed and not remade (Fig. 90).

Sometimes he combined wood with iron, in rare cases as a simple superimposed ornamentation which he justified by giving it some sort of practical use as in the doors to the sacristies of the Temple crypt where the large curved iron straps serve as hinges (Fig. 260), but more frequently to form part of a mixed structure where the iron serves to consolidate or stiffen, as we will see in some of the furniture.

Until the Casa Batlló, Gaudí's wooden structures, whether fixed or movable, were essentially two-dimensional (although the carving of the ceilings in the Palacio Güell does give a spatial feeling; here for the first time they operate in three dimensions in a new, more plastic, expressiveness Figs. 238, 248).

118. SMALL STRUCTURES: FURNITURE (Figs. 90-95)

Needless to say, a great part of Gaudí's interest in architecture was in its social aspect as shelter for human beings. But in order to function, architectural works must be complement-

91. A dressing table for the Palacio Güell which introduces *modernista* forms.

92. An emphatically *modernista* detail of the dressing-table, decorated with incised patterns.

93. Wrought-iron lectern for liturgical use in the Sagrada Familia.

94. Portable, folding steps in the Cathedral of Mallorca.

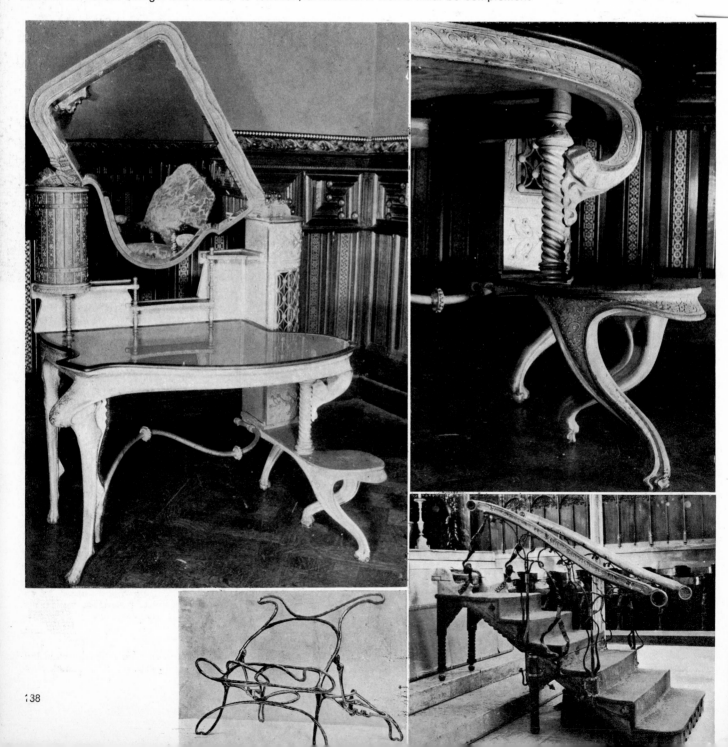

95. A bench of Baroque influence in the offices of the Casa Calvet.

ed by small interior structures—the furniture—which come into more intimate contact with man than does the house itself. Our architect was aware of this, and gave such structures priority, with designs and solutions that converted them into useful and sumptuous objects of bodily and artistic comfort in the special purposes which they are destined to serve.

We have already seen him working out chairs in which one could only be seated correctly (XXI - 90); in designing some of his liturgical furniture he took their material function, religious purpose, and artistic aspect into account in such an admirable manner that these pieces became true collector's items.

In these small objects—perhaps more easily than in the great building masses—one notices Gaudí's domination of surfaces and volumes which he links with space in an expressive and harmonious manner. In addition, we can observe his great understanding of his materials and their properties, his constant concern for beauty and functional logic. These were the principal factors which, combined with his fecund imagination, gave such a notable personality to his furniture, making it stand out among the best and most original of the Art Nouveau period.

His passion for functional synthesis came to him early. Already in his youthful notes on esthetics he states: «It can be said that use is the purpose for the creation of an object; character is the definition of its esthetic-moral condition; the physical conditions are those which concern such matters as durability, conservation, etc.» He knew from his earliest years as an architect how to incorporte all of the structural, utilitarian, tectonic, and esthetic properties which are at work in an object into the furniture which he designed. His special care and interest in this area is demonstrated in his notes when he speaks of a desk which he built for himself. He says: «In creating the central motif of my desk top, I have considered it to be like an album leaf where an object which is interesting for both its content and its form is desired. The surface is of cedar wood and is therefore a sort of yellowish red: the ornamental material is wrought iron. The way I formulated the motif is the following: I took up an idea which I found to be adaptable to the materials, i.e., the vegetation on the earth and scenes of the animals which reside therein...»; «let us suppose that the water is represented by two horizontal lines—the level of the water that is—and that two leaves... twisted incline toward the water, and then above the horizontals we see the leaves which grow up to the surface of the water, in the midst of which a dragonfly flits about.»

Although this discussion is abruptly interrupted, we can sense the enjoyment with which he elaborates on the ornamental part and some of the technique suggested by the cedar wood and the tempered iron which he used. Also from this first period (1878) is another desk table which is freely resolved with naturalistic ornamentation (Fig. 191),[3] and the prayer stools of the chapel for the Marquis of Comillas, designed with the liturgical purpose of fitting into the Gothicism of the chapel. The reliefs which adorn this furniture, while appearing to be merely naturalistic, obey norms of Gaudinian esthetics in their basic forms and undulating outlines (Figs. 192, 193).

The ornamental richness of this sort of furniture conceals a basic sobriety of forms. Once his debut as a furniture designer was over, but still within his first phase, we find a type of furniture of «great comfort» in a drawing for a covered armchair that has great ampleness of forms and a certain structural originality within traditional lines, and in a «chaise longue» for the Palacio Güell covered in leather and with orientalizing wrought-iron fittings (Fig. 240).

This pompousness of forms lasted for only a short while. In the Casa Calvet which he designed in the baroque style, he remained faithful to his theme in designing the furniture. In the owners' living room he produced the last examples of that style in a set of chairs covered in green silk and velvet with gilded helicoidal legs of carved wood, using gilded iron to decorate and reinforce the other elements (Fig. 328). On the other hand, in the office furniture he recalls the lightness and optimism of Louis XV without necessarily imitating it. The table and chairs are constructed of carved oak which adapts perfectly to the body and gives a sensation of softness. These are decorated with incised flowers and elegantly flowing openwork. In the Casa Batlló the furniture is similarly conceived though much more simplified, and more closely tied to its practical ends with very few ornamental concessions (Figs. 447-449).

Gaudí's liturgical furniture forms a chapter by itself in his production. Beyond some retables of his early years (Figs. 195-197), and other objects which we will have more to say about later, we are especially attracted to the pieces which he made for the services in the crypt of the Sagrada Familia, such as the confessionals and the portable pulpit—masterpieces of carpentry as were the wardrobes of the sacristy, especially one which could be converted into an altar (Figs. 258-263). Notable too were the massive and collapsible pedestal that supported the paschal candle, the candlestick, the extremely elegant wrought-iron lectern, the bishop's chair and bench for the officiating priests, the lantern which accompanied the Holy Viaticum, and various alabaster and metal lamps which he worked on up until his very last days (Fig. 512). Also there were crucifixes, various types of candelabra, and the benches for the parishioners whose seats were reinforced with ingeniously arranged iron ties as braces. He made similar benches for the crypt of the Colonia Güell church (Fig. 377), using some of the patterns employed in the Casa Calvet, where wedges of iron reinforce the seats which are arranged in such a way that the two people seated in them find themselves in a position which makes conversation uncomfortable—an application of the functional criteria explained earlier. The furniture which he used in the Cathedral of Mallorca constitutes another phase, moving in the direction of greater robustness and simplicity accomplished with great artistic purity (Figs. 485-497).

3. [There is a confusion here. Gaudi, we know, did design two early desks for himself (or a desk and a table). But Fig. 191 *is* the desk described in the above passage, because on the diary page he illustrates his ideas with two tiny sketches of the ornament which we see in Fig. 191. — G.R.C.]

XXVII. COLOR AND LIGHT

119. THE IMPORTANCE OF COLOR
120. ILLUMINATION

119. THE IMPORTANCE OF COLOR (Figs. 96 - 98)

We have already noted Gaudí's high esteem for color and his opinion that architecture, as a work of art, must produce a sensation of life. Life and Beauty are two concepts which demand color (XXV - 112), and despite the fact that most architecture in Gaudí's time used to do without it, the master's keen artistic sensibility made this an absolute necessity.

From his early youth, in the notes which we have so often alluded to, he stated clearly the case for a polychromed architecture (XXV - 111). As a devoted naturalist he takes a lesson from Nature in which «the contrast [of color] is always more or less vivid; it follows that therefore we must necessarily color, partially or completely all architectonic members; this coloration may disappear, but then the hand of time will see that it is replaced by that proper and precious one of antiquity.» He later goes on to consider the greater beauty of those ancient buildings which exhibit the coloring of time, when compared to those recently completed which display a «repellent coldness.»

In these notes he shows himself to be tolerant of the historical disappearance of polychromy, but also convinced of its effectiveness, not only because it was used by the Greeks and Egyptians, but also because «in certain places it has the great value of making the outlines and structural planes seem more energetic, and of giving a clearer idea of the object.» In his earliest works he made use of procedures which insured the permanence of the coloring, and he resolved with courage and ability this esthetic subtlety of architectural technique.

As elements of polychromy he preferred the natural coloration of materials, such as stone (often without any additional finishing) or reddish or clinker brick, the latter being employed with optimum results in the crypt of the Güell Colony church, and in the pinnacles of the Sagrada Familia towers. Sometimes he faced the stone and brick elements with small smooth-glazed ceramic tiles an in the Casa Vicens or with tiles ornamented in relief as in «El Capricho» at Comillas.

At other times he used patterned tiles broken into pieces to form a mosaic so as to adapt them to concave and convex surfaces without losing the pattern, as in the lateral walls of the Güell Park stairway, or to form the mosaics of mixed pieces of colored tiles, which we see in the curving bench of the grand plaza and in the roofs of the entrance pavilions in the same park, as well as in the elements on the roof terrace of the Güell Palace. These mosaics of thick fragments mixed in a capricious way were put together by the masons themselves following the directions of Gaudí or of his assistants.

The mosaic centers of the vaults of the Doric colonnade in the same park are based on ornamental motifs designed by the assisting architect José M. Jujol who was a highly-talented colorist and delineator. In the surfaces, he utilized colored glass and other materials such as fragments of porcelain plates, bottles, and other such things. In one of the pinnacles of the concierge's pavilion, embedded chocolate cups are used as the dominant surface detail. Throughout the principal façade of the Batlló house, he used glass and ceramic disks, and on the roof he used special varnished pieces that give off metallic reflection; in the one Sagrada Familia tower which he himself was able to complete, he adopted a glass mosaic manufactured especially for that purpose in Venice.

In addition to his wide repertoire of revetments and the freedom with which they were employed, he planned to use white-wash and other convenient kinds of painting in the Nativity façade and to take advantage of the patina of the stone and natural vegetation in the places where this was possible. We could say that Gaudí used color to a decorative end, without the intention of creating a painting as he has later been credited with doing. The broad yet delicate sensitivity of the architect employed all of the resources and chromatic effects contained in the modern painting movements, but it is probable that he did not foresee this development in painting. It would indeed have surprised him to see that these revetments which he created in collaboration with his masons and workmen would acquire the artistic significance which some have since attempted to attribute to them.

We recall the impression which the Lagar exposition at the Dalmau galleries made on him, and his remark of having found emotion, not the truth «without which there can be no work of art» (XXV - 112). In his most famous and often-discussed polychrome surfaces (this is probably due to the ease with which they can be photographed)—those of the bench in Güell Park—the architect sought a decorative note that might be called «emotion,» but he never felt the necessity to complete it with that naturalistic «truth« which would elevate the polychromy in itself to the level of a work of art. For him, the work of art was the bench which possessed a socially meaningful, utilitarian «truth.»

Those who write on abstract art, who see no need to complete the emotion with that truth which Gaudí esteemed absolutely necessary, have tried to strengthen their argument by making him the precursor of the same. If this were true, it would have to be noted that Gaudí did not intend it so: he cultivated the concrete and fled from the abstract. If he adopted a style which later was called abstract, it was by virtue of the decorative quality of its coloristic force; it was a complement that would lend life to his architectural work while using methods that would break the tradition of the «assumed nobility» of previous materials and procedures. He wished to give decorative expression to objects never before used. With these he obtained collage effects of great plastic and polychromatic feeling, but he was not thinking in terms of earthshaking innovation.

Those who attempt to demonstrate through subtle psychoanalysis that this polychromy which he invented, directed, and even worked on with his own hands, could have responded to a subconscious desire unsuspected by even the architect himself which was to make him the involuntary creator of abstract art, have a disputable thesis. Whatever the conclusions may be, we must admit that Gaudí did initiate an effective procedure for the use of lively and tectonic materials with multiple possibilities, to the point that portions of his polychrome revetments became masterpieces of non-figurative art, even though the artist conceived of them as mere secondary elements of his works.

As we have said, the run-of-the-mill architecture in Gaudí's time usually left out that factor of beauty represented by color, more because of the difficulties involved in its use and of incompetence on the part of the architects than for any logical reasons. Our architect was able to demonstrate how color completes the beauty of a form and gives a breath of life which non-colored architecture does not have.

120. ILLUMINATION (Figs. 99, 100)

LIGHT AND THE EXCELLENCE OF VISION. Light is necessary for a clear vision of all that surrounds us, and it also makes that vision possible while influencing greatly the esthetic results by its intensity and the direction from which it comes.

Light gives birth to the various colors into which it can be decomposed, and it is the basis of all ornamentation. Light reigns in the plastic arts, whereas painting does no more than copy it with its colors; the movement of architecture and sculpture allow the light to play on surfaces that produce an infinite number of shades and variations.

Without light, the plastic arts which we appreciate through our sense of vision—the most exalted of the senses—could not exist. The ear—one of the two so-called «noble» senses—needs time to act. Touch has no extension: it is an analytic sense. Through it we can appreciate form but not situation or color. Sight is synthetic. With it we appreciate form, size, situation, color, and life in general. It is with this sense that one best comprehends the omnipotence of God.

Gaudí had great admiration for the sense of sight and that light which makes it possible, with its effects augmented or diminished according to the intensity or direction of its rays, to the point of visually influencing the form of objects. He said that the forms of art are interesting both for their own configuration and as a pretext for the play of light over them. A beautiful figure can appear different and even the expression of its parts can vary as a result of

96. Decorative surface in the ceiling of the Doric colonnade of the Güell Park.

97. Decorative polychrome portion of the great sinuous bench.

whether or not it is bathed in light, which demonstrates the importance of illumination in the esthetic effect of all works of plastic art.

EXTERIORS. On flat surfaces, the chiaroscuro is usually restrained in expression, a situation which can be somewhat enlivened through the arrangement of the openings and protruding elements; but on three-dimensional surfaces where smooth convexity and concavity alternate in a decided manner, the shades and variants of the chiaroscuro can achieve a great expressive richness.

Elsewhere, referring to the Sagrada Familia, Güell Park, and above all to the Casa Milá, I have written that here «one can study how, at diverse times of the day, according to how the sun hits the facade, certain diverse expressions are achieved, all of great beauty; now the light colors dominate, now the dark; now the great projections are emphasized, now it is shaded in half-tones. These fluidly undulating surfaces, which renounce the immobile adornment of applied relief, are able to take on the living adornment of the light which every day from morning to night, and every day from summer to winter, offers its rays in diverse ways to pattern them with interminable arabesques.» [1]

1. Martinell, *Gaudinismo*, (Barcelona: 1954), p. 56.

98. Stairway in Güell Park with polychrome decoration.

99. Decorative chiaroscuro effect of the Casa Milá balconies.

100. The same decorative effect in another section of the same façade.

Gaudí always preferred solar light for the illumination of his architecture. Nevertheless, he was the first to think up the idea of electric beams which would project the rays against the darkness of the night (which three years after his death were spectacularly applied in the Barcelona International Exposition of 1929). These were not to be used for the illumination of surfaces, but to highlight the great cross pinnacle of the temple while projecting another great luminous cross over the city of Barcelona on certain nights.

INTERIORS. The great care with which the architect considered exterior illumination under the direct light of the sun was echoed in the interiors, as will be evident when we refer to some of his completed buildings and even more so in the studies that he made for the Expiatory Temple, in all of which he used natural light in an ingenious and logical manner, preferring it to electric illumination.

When using artificial light, of more easy gradation, he maintained the same principles for giving value and expression to his forms and took advantage of the sources themselves as a decorative element. He was opposed to the uniform and monotonous effect of central illumination. He advised putting lights next to walls, thus achieving a greater range of tones. In cases where uniform illumination was desired, he found it preferable to make the sources invisible, anticipating indirect lighting systems which had not yet come into use. He also advised discretion in taking advantage of the great facility afforded by electric lighting so as not to fall into presumptuous solutions. One should stop short of the available means—i.e., prefer a simple, easily-realized system to an ostentatious solution.[2]

Gaudí applied this criterion most rigorously in the case of churches where light should be moderate, providing only that which is necessary for the worshippers to read comfortably, and without overly powerful sources which distract and cause uneasiness, considering that the altar, which the liturgy says must be illuminated with candles, must not be outshone. To obtain such a result he advised the use of an unlimited number of old lamps or ones with a voltage greater than the electric current, making sure only that each lamp's intensity not surpass that of the candles at the altar. He stated that these candles, in spite of their weak light, when aided by the mobility which is given to them by the air, acquire a life which electricity cannot have.

He affirmed that such means could embellish new works and also those already in existence. He suggested that the neo-classic cathedrals might display the glass chandeliers proper to the 18th century or, better, the cornucopias which have more beautiful properties. Instead of the secular themes which usually adorned such temples, representations could be introduced which have iconographic or symbolic meaning and which, duly illuminated, would gave the churches decorative effects of great beauty.[3]

2. Martinell, *Conversaciones con Gaudí*, p. 77.
3. *Ibid.*, pp. 76, 77.

XXVIII. SCULPTURE

121. SCULPTURE AS ARCHITECTURE'S AID (Fig. 101)

In the often-cited notes on ornamentation, Gaudí distinguishes clearly between the objects, or the structures, and the ornamentation that enriches them and which seems superfluous to him. He says that «the esthetic structure is one which reveals the varied means employed and the numerous problems resolved in its construction, making the objects pleasant in themselves...» and he adds: «complication in ornamentation is nothing but a poor and expensive solution which only succeeds in making the object indifferent.» Referring to statuary as an ornamental element he writes: «Representative sculpture should be given some *ex profeso* place or placed in the least important parts of the structure, i.e., in the passive parts.»

The statuary of his time was based on a study of nature, and should have been completed with color when it existed in the natural object; Gaudí's passion for naturalistic truth made him affirm that «then movement is lacking, and then sensitivity and life, so that the best end for this sort of thing is scenography rather than ornamental sculpture.»

From his notebook we know that he was concerned from his youth with the relationship which should exist between statuary and the point of view of the observer. Years later this led him to design «sculpted scenography» for the Passion façade as opposed to the «ornamental sculpture» that he had used on the Nativity façade. For the later one he grouped the images in realistic episodes from the Lord's Passion which could be observed on a level through accesses on the interior of the façade in a near co-existence on the viewer's part with the characters represented.

He had said before that «common sense tells us that simple forms are characteristic of magnificence and that abundant ornamentation is more properly found in small masses.» This criterion does not prevail in the Nativity façade where the object is to accentuate the optimistic significance of the subject, which he achieved without taking away its grandeur. It was rather an application of the special case which he foresaw further on in his notes when he said that «ornamentation is a means by which certain qualities of form are used to dress an object in order to infuse it with a predetermined character, in some cases making the massiveness disappear to achieve a spiritual result, and in others accentuating it to make its nature felt in all of its rudeness and simplicity.» He later refers to the traditionally employed natural forms of ornamentation which «once had a meaning which we do not understand well

101. Detail of sculpted architecture with symbolic representations on the Nativity façade.

102. The apostle St. Barnabas in one of the towers where it passes from the square plan to the circular.

103. Pedestal, niche, and canopy for St. Barnabas on the edge of the square part of the tower with a pinnacle-mirador which ties it in to the cylindrical part of the same.

enough today» and he felt that «putting the vegetables of the garden in our cathedrals» was a way of thanking God for these gifts.

In his notes he shows a preference for what he calls «esthetic structure» unassisted by traditional sculpted forms, which goes along with the concurrent tone of his architecture, in spite of which he occasionally turned to figurative sculpture. We see this in the three large angels which he planned for the roof of the Episcopal Palace in Astorga, and which were later executed in zinc plate, in the image of St. George which he placed over the main door of the building in León, in the First Mystery of Glory, in the monument to Dr. Robert, and in the statue which he hoped to place at the top of the façade of the Casa Milá. For all of these he resorted to other artists; the images which he placed all over the façade of the Nativity were realized by Gaudí himself, however.

In Gaudí's time sculpture was still bound by the historical concept of imitative art, or rather, the idea that isolated or relief sculpture should represent something, and this is the concept to which our architect refers when speaking of sculpture. Nevertheless, we have already seen his passion for giving life to the forms which he created. First this manifested itself in the exteriorization of interior forces of mechanical origin, and soon after was accompanied by a smoothness or harshness of texture which would reinforce the expressiveness. Sometimes these would recall natural forms, but usually they would not recall anything: they were the simple esthetic version of a state of mind.

In his first works, Gaudí used decorative elements which modern writers classify as abstract sculptures—a name which would perhaps displease the maestro who tried so hard to be concrete by using well-defined forms whenever he had recourse to geometry or when he took his inspiration from natural forms. Later he used expressionistic forms which can be more easily classified within the abstract category.

122. SCULPTURAL PROFUSION (Figs. 102, 103)

Gaudí had an intense and highly sensitive feeling for form, and for him what was essential was to give it life and beauty. Sometimes he worked within certain norms, other times he leaned on different principles, depending on the advice of his fertile inspiration or the given circumstances. One such circumstance was the bountiful legacy which the Sagrada Familia committee had to spend quickly just as work on the Nativity façade was about to begin, which produced in the architect a joyful optimism which he had not known before. Thus that type of architectonic sculpture or sculpted architecture in which structure and decoration are united in the service of religious symbolism emerged. The pinions curl around icicles of snow; the central archivolt is filled with the signs and constellations of the Zodiac, while the lateral ones contain tropical animals and a swarm of bees, with naturalistic palm leaves serving as capitals; innumerable symbols completely cover the three archivolts and the lanterns above, setting the stage for scenes relating to the birth of Jesus.

It seems as if in this façade he hoped to make up for the non-conformity that he showed at age 26 when he lamented that those who built temples did not seek the profound religious meaning «but rather all [importance] is conceded, ridiculous as it seems, to the cabbage leaf, to the acanthus, to the openwork, and to the molding—to all of these as purely plastic form. Perhaps such accessories, which as details do not conform to our way of life, are supposed to infuse religiosity? Where are those expressive reliefs which remind us here of martyrdom and there of mystery, charity, or contemplation? Now nothing but saints are represented, and even these are only an excuse to put up a pedestal or a little ornamented dais, i.e., a pretext to introduce an irrelevant, purely plastic form.» (Appendix IV). In this façade, despite its abundance of sculpture, there is nothing that is «superimposed.» It could be said that everything «comes from within.» He applies the principle, also set forth in his youth, by which sculptural ornamentation should always have as its object, «to increase the importance of surfaces without weighing them down» and it should, in addition, give them a religious meaning or the effect of simple naturalism, recalling that «by studying vegetation and botany we discover highly ornamental properties in the most common plants»—something he had already demonstrated in the spires of the apse where simple grasses are monumentalized (Fig. 265).

A CLEVER STRATEGY. The images of holy persons or angels which decorate this façade and could be criticized as being superimposed, are conceived completely in unison with the surfaces that surround them and thus form with them a single whole; the four seated apostles, placed on the pedestals and covered by the canopies which he had censured in his youth, are executed in such a masterful manner that we cannot overlook their importance.

Anticipating ideas which will be explained later, I will mention that halfway along, Gaudí decided to change the square towers that he had begun into circular ones. These four apostles, which are over 15 meters tall with their pedestals and canopies and the galleries above them, cover the most visible parts of the intersections of the square towers which should be hidden; and the leftover triangles of the squares are absorbed into the apex gal-

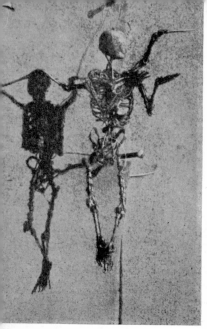

leries, being converted into circles. This was an extremely clever strategy that he later explained to me: distract the attention of the observer by detouring the question from the structural field to the decorative.

Other free-standing sculptures are the four angels which announce the good tidings and which are extremely well placed, with perfect scale and mobility.

123. A NEW TECHNIQUE (Figs. 104 - 109)

In order to give this Nativity façade the religious expression which he wanted—that of popular enjoyment similar to the Christmas-tide family «pessebres» (manger scenes)—he needed to spread a large number of statues throughout his work and to take extreme care in their *distribution, size,* and *expression.* The first two are the concern of the architect, and the last is usually left in the hands of the sculptor, a division of labor which Gaudí felt could prejudice the expressive unity of the work; for this reason he decided to take care of all three elements by himself.

Gaudí argued that it is difficult for good sculptors to renounce their own particular personality and point of view; in addition, each sculptor uses live models which, without realizing it, adopt comfortable attitudes which falsify the artist's intent. And so, in the interest of maximum effectiveness in all details of the temple work, Gaudí could not delegate the direction of this highly important element, and he himself became the executor of the sculpture as well.

He took advantage of his great manual dexterity to construct tiny schematic wire models of the figures which he planned to make, and with these he worked out the positioning of his characters to give them a maximum expressiveness. Once he had found the desired attitude he would reproduce it in a clay model in which he was aided for a short period by the sculptor Carlos Mani,[1] and then he would again study the figure using a skeleton which he possessed, coming as close as possible to the expression that he desired. To achieve this he would place the skeleton between two vertical mirrors placed on a dihedral angle, with another above and another below, which would then reflect all sides, permitting him to control the tiniest details of his study.

In addition to this natural skeleton, he had another completely articulated metal one, a fifth of the size, which was more comfortable to use in studying the models. He considered the skeleton to be a combination of lever systems which are moved by the muscles functioning as motors. The muscles were ingeniously represented in his mannequins through fine metallic sheets rolled on the diagonal and inserted in the anatomical muscle sites without permitting any but natural movements, so that when these rolls were contracted they would swell like real muscles.[2]

He emphasized the great importance of the study of the skeleton, for which he recommended two procedures: one was the direct study of skeletons obtained in the cemeteries, and the other the study of the movements of living persons. He said that the Greeks had achieved this knowledge thanks to their Olympic Games and that, by the Renaissance, artists had lost interest in the study of the skeleton, as had the artists of the Greek decadence.

He cited Benvenuto Cellini as someone who had studied anatomy well, recalling that he once restored a Greek statue with such perfection that it was difficult to distinguish the restored part. Michelangelo was inferior to Cellini in this respect for he preferred the muscular parts

104, 105. Models used by Gaudí to study expression in human figures.

106. Live model between mirrors for better studying the human figure.

107. Models of figures and plants in plaster as they stood in his office in 1917. In the background are the sounding tubes used to work out the bells.

---

1. Told to me by Quintana.
2. These concepts and those which follow are developed with greater detail in my book *Conversaciones con Gaudí,* pp. 43-46.

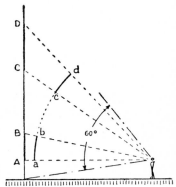

108. Diagram used to determine the foreshortening of figures at great heights, a system already contained in ancient treatises.

109. Statue of the child Jesus preaching in the temple flanked by Saints Zachariah and John in stone. Below, a plaster model of Jesus in the workshop at Nazareth, to be studied and corrected.

of the anatomy. The Spanish silver sculptor Juan de Arfe had recommended the study of the skeleton and lamented that this was not a more widespread custom, given the ease with which specimens could be found in the cemeteries.

In order to refine the expression of images, Gaudí advised the study of diverse ethnic types which could be found in their most pure state in regions away from the coast since the facility of communication on the sea and along the rivers of the coast had mixed up the various natural types. In spite of this he noted that in Catalonia there still existed ancient types such as the «Ilergetas» in the province of Lérida, the «Iberians» in Tortosa and Cuenca del Ebro, the «Romans» in the Campo de Tarragona, the «Greek» type in the Ampurdán, and the «Phoenicians» on the island of Ibiza. He suggested that these ethnographic characteristics be classified by means of photographs, and differentiated not only by features but also by bone structure.

He used to say that a figure's expression was given to it by the skeleton and that everything else was secondary in monumental sculpture which must be seen at a distance, where muscles, features, and other details have little influence on the overall expression. Once the attitude was decided he would fix its base points through a system of triangulation which made them invariable. Given the emotive expression that he was able to achieve in the plain and unattractive skeleton, it is not hard to understand that the expression gained plastic beauty when completed with musculature, clothes, and hair.

After the initial preparation, Gaudí would chose the human model most fitting in each case (fat, thin, man, woman, adolescent, or aged, etc.) and who would at the same time allow himself to be cast in underclothes after being arranged, again using the mirrors, in the exact position previously arrived at.[3] Once a final model was obtained in this manner, he would dress it with canvas or burlap soaked in gesso whitewash so that once the folds of the drapery had been arranged they would harden to produce a first life-size version of the desired image. Hair was simulated with threads of hemp which were also soaked in gesso and combined with wire to make it seem as if it were moved by the wind.

3. He was very talented in supervising the making of casts from living beings. The little donkey in the Flight into Egypt group was done from a life cast.

Then he would call in a proper sculptor—the above-mentioned Mani and later, between 1910 and 1921, Juan Matamala, the son of the model-maker «Senyor Llorenç»—to amplify the figure cast and dressed in clay to the desired size which was determined after lengthy study, taking into consideration the height to which it was to be raised.

Scale was the object of careful study. He established a law that would regulate the size of figures located at various heights depending on the visibility of the building which he assumed to be within an angle of 60 degrees on the exterior and 90 degrees on the interior, fixing the minimum distance to take in the whole and the maximum to appreciate its details. From this he determined the dimensions of the figures based on the principle that a face can be easily distinguished at a distance of 500 diameters. In addition to dimension based on distance, the length had to be exaggerated in proportion to the height at which the figure is to be placed in order to compensate for the effect of foreshortening.

He achieved this lengthening by selecting tall and slender models and the amount of longitudinal extension compared with those sculptures on a lower level was determined by the vertical projection of the arch containing the figure which has its center at the point of observation. He cited as examples of well-proportioned statues those of the Columbus monument in Barcelona and that of the Virgen de la Merced on the cupola of her basilica [4] which he compared favorably with the Saint Helen at the base of the cathedral dome which, though higher, is smaller, and therefore invisible.

When he had the full-scale model in clay with its form simplified to the maximum, he would reproduce it in gesso and place the reproduction at the site foreseen in order to observe it over a long period and to make the corrections and simplifications which such extended observation suggested. It was not until these corrections were made and had time to be studied that the model was given to the sculptor-copyist who was to execute the definitive image in stone. [5]

Ráfols has found Gaudí's sculpture somewhat tragic. Gaudí loved nature and in it he sought truth; he knew and «saw» what he wanted, but he did not have time to master sculptural technique; and yet he lacked confidence in the interpreting sculptor. Therefore he sought natural truth by making use of photographs and casts, mechanizing that which should be faithfully copied from nature, and submitting to his own taste that which comes from artistic inspiration. In this way he obtained images of surprising expressiveness that were in harmony with their surroundings. We see, as examples, the Child Jesus arguing with the Learned Doctors on the Faith portal and He seems to emerge from the stone in which He is created; the herald angels who, two on each side, flank the Charity portal; and the temptation of the woman by money on a small cloister *mensula*. On the other hand, there are times when his mechanistic procedures do not measure up to the idea which inspired them.

He did not use this procedure because he wanted to innovate or to create sculpture, but rather simply to avoid outside intervention in such a personal work. For the first Mystery of Glory at Montserrat he went to his friend the sculptor José Llimona to do the main sculpture work (Figs. 358, 359).

Here we must make it clear that not even in the hands of Gaudí is this procedure always successful. Nevertheless, the best statues obtained by such means are those realized in the architect's lifetime and some that were executed immediately after his death under the direction of the younger Matamala who had been for years in charge of that task while working for the master.

124. UNREALIZED STATUES IN MOTION

So great was Gaudí's desire to lend life to his works through color, or with forms that give an impression of movement while in reality remaining static, or through authentic movement as we have mentioned at the beginning of the present chapter, that in November 1915 he conceived the idea of placing at the tops of the Sagrada Familia towers several cherubim which would move their wings and thus incorporate the time factor into the artistic sensation of his work. [6] Above each of the elements which cap the towers he planned to place one of the cherubim of the Apocalypse—some five years old and four meters high—each with six wings: two to shelter the head, two to cover the body, and two to fly. By interweaving the latter he would form a railing for a gallery in which the towers would terminate. This railing was to have been triangular in form with the sides curving in and with the cherubim at the vertices; the wings were susceptible to a gentle motion in the wind which, besides giving life to the sculptures, would have recalled the movement of bell tower vanes of old. He planned to construct these figures by using a non-deformable metallic cloth mold which he would have filled, leaving the exterior face covered with mosaic.

The idea of giving movement to his figures has a precedent in the gate of the Finca Güell where the foot of the dragon moved whenever the door was opened.

4. Juan Matamala tells me that Cayetano Boigas, the architect of the Columbus monument, increased the size of the statue after it was already designed, on the advice of his friend Gaudí. The image and the cupola of La Merced were the work of the architect Juan Martorell.

5. Gaudí himself explained to me that he had tried out this system with figures for angels at the cathedral of Mallorca when he was there once with little work to do.

6. Statement by Gaudí on November 9, 1915. See *Conversaciones con Gaudí*. p. 64.

110. A monstruous figure hands an explosive bomb to a worker on the Rosary portal.

111. Flamingo on the exterior of the loggia of the Coronation of the Virgin.

112. Domestic birds alluding to the Christmas season under a corbel of the Nativity façade.

125. DECORATIVE FORMS

Aside from the free-standing figures which we have indicated, the naturalistic sculpted work which he left behind on this façade is copious and varied, and we can subdivide it into various groups. There are the animals, some cast or copied from life, and others taking on monstruous forms to symbolize sin or infernal beings. To best do this he represented persons «with the attitudes and proportions of beasts, for the monster is the person who forgets his proper dignity and approaches bestiality.» [7] Other animals present are the domestic fowl evoking the days of Christmas, and exotic birds used for decorative purposes. The plant kingdom is represented by flowers, foliage, palms, and the tall cypress which tops the entrance triptych. The minerals are there in a representation of the mountain of Montserrat, and in the snow and zodiacal stars; incense sends stylized smoke to the Sacred Heart of Jesus... various objects, inscriptions... all have a religious symbolism and are very much within the stylistic norms of Modernismo.

7. Martinell, *op. cit.*, p. 48. One such representation can be seen in the Rosary portal in the form of a figure which hands a bomb to the worker (Fig. 110).

113. Vegetal forms and snow-covered icicles sculpturally represented on the Nativity façade.

All three archivolts—below the snow and above it, in the lanterns and in their pinnacles—are filled to the brim with symbols in a way which reminds us of those contracts for Baroque altarpieces which stipulated that no surface should be left without ornamentation. Indeed, the sculpture of this façade is Baroque in several aspects. In spite of the Gothic framework, Gaudí shows his sympathy for that ostentatious and dynamic style while taking special care in the contrast of convexities and concavities so that the latter would enhance the relief of the former similar to the effect he saw in the drapery of the Venus de Milo (XXV - 111). It was due to this consideration which guided his work on the Sagrada Familia that he called his art Hellenic, to the surprise of the non-initiates.[8]

We could not speak of his decorative technique without alluding to a peculiar ornamental system of pre-established surfaces covered with naturalistic interlaced motifs executed in low relief which recall traditional arabesques. We find these reliefs in some of the borders and friezes of the lower parts of the Faith, Hope, and Rosary portals—in the last they are more

8. *Ibid.*, p. 46.

114. Incense smoke interpreted in stone on the same façade.

115. Detail of the monument to Dr. Bartolomé Robert with sentimentally modelled expressionistic forms.

116. Splay of the Rosary portal sculpted in imitation of basketwork.

highly developed and he employs motifs never before used. The drapery of the prophets which are included in this portal are enriched with small-scale geometric themes which recall the sumptuousness of the Castilian sculpture of the XVth century.

The refinement of these surfaces modeled in low relief, which he seems to have enjoyed working on at the time, was of short duration, and was not widespread in his work. In addition to the places indicated, he used it in some of the metallic repoussés of the Güell palace and in the concrete floor tiles, several interior columns, and the modeled plaster ceilings of the Casa Milá—these latter having frankly *modernista* characteristics, executed by Jujol.

126. ARCHITECTURE OR SCULPTURE?

In addition to the naturalistic forms which abound in the temple and which he used sparingly in other buildings, such as the fleur-de-lis in the Palacio Güell, the novel bone motif in the mullions of the Batlló house, leaves and animals in cast or wrought iron, in addition to such manifestations of traditional figurative sculpture, he was the fecund creator of forms which today are called sculptural but which Gaudí called simply decorative.

This is a question of nomenclature which I do not wish to argue, but I would like to comment on it in order to clarify certain misconceptions. In the historical classification of the arts, architecture is presented as an interpretative art whereas sculpture and painting are imitative and auxiliary to it. The fact that sculpture and painting can also be interpretive does not present a problem. Gaudí, in his passion to give life to his works, found himself creating forms which have later been called abstract many years before the restless movements of contemporary art led sculptors and painters to non-figuration.

The sculptor Subirachs, in a lecture on Gaudí's sculpture,[9] has said that the abstract polychrome sculptures which the architect realized in the projections of the roof of the Güell pal-

9. «Escultura figurativa y no figurativa de Gaudí,» a lecture sponsored by the Centro de Estudios Gaudinistas at the Ateneo Barcelonés, March 7, 1961.

ace anticipated the work of Kandinsky in his first non-figurative experiments by 25 years, and he added that in his opinion the Casa Milá was one of the most important *sculptural* works of all time, both taken as a whole and in the chimney and ventilator details which he praised most highly. Whereas Subirachs was careful to limit his judgment to the exterior of the building and did consider other aspects of the residence including the structural ones so important to Gaudí's work, I have also heard the Sagrada Familia referred to as *sculpture* in a less complimentary tone.

I will allow that the visible aspects of the last works of Gaudí are indeed *sculptural* in the widest sense, but the work cannot for that reason be considered merely as sculpture. The sculptor is an artist who needs talent, sensitivity, and a precise manual ability to carry out his work. The architect requires talent, sensitivity, and perhaps less manual ability, but also many other artistic, mathematical, and building techniques without which he could not successfully realize his work. Architecture is more spatial, sculpture more concise. A «sculpture» which requires laborious construction, calculations, stone junctures, pillars and beams, and which is inhabited and serves a social function, will be more an architectonic than a sculptural work, however modeled its surface may be. Such works on a reduced scale —e.g., Gaudí's models—could be called sculptures; in their final reality they are true architecture which, in the interests of «decor» allow surface decoration, be it figurative or not. Where sculpture permits greater freedom of movement, architecture requires precision; and—to be frank—I do not consider it admissible that a work of architecture be catalogued as sculpture no matter how decorated its exterior may be.

127. THE ABSTRACT: SCULPTURAL AND GEOMETRIC (Figs. 115 - 118)

Again we recall that Gaudí, in addition to using traditional sculpture in his statuary and decoration, was the creator of forms which today are considered abstract. We have already said that such a name would not be to his liking. I once heard him classify the figurative capitals of the cloister of Barcelona Cathedral as abstract because of the fact that the reduced size of the figures does not allow us to make out the subjects represented. Similarly he classified the Saint Helen of the dome as abstract because of the visual inconcreteness of the form at that height; and he held the figure of Columbus, clearly visible on his monument, to be the epitome of the concrete. Concrete and abstract were determined for him by the appreciable clarity of the object's characteristics, independent of what was represented. He held that the hyperbolic paraboloid—which could serve as a subject for abstract sculpture—was a concrete form, whose generation could be «concretely» determined through its directrices and generatrices, its geometric properties, material, thickness, luminous points, shadows, half-shadows, reflections, and dimensions, with complete exactitude, and without that vagueness which would place it on the side of abstraction.

As I have said, I do not propose to argue over names, but rather to clarify concepts and to such an end I allow today's «abstract» as a label for the last forms employed by our architect; within this category we can distinguish two phases: one merely sculptural, without geometric control, and another which was rigorously geometric.

Gaudí's first use of three-dimensional surfaces in an urban work came in the Casa Batlló. (He had previously used them very sparingly in the gate and wall for the Finca Miralles. Fig. 352.) He later used them on a wider scale in the Casa Milá. In these works his surfaces are sculpturally modeled, as if a giant had fashioned delightfully smooth-to-the-eye caves and projections, causing the light sliding over them to enrich the chiaroscuro effects. These forms were worked out in three-dimensional models, and once blown up to life-size they were the object of additional retouching according to visual demands. These were the concrete versions of the effects which he imagined and which led to those forms now called abstract.

Partly because of his desire for perfection, perhaps also due to technical circumstances, but more especially because of the strong geometrical roots within him, these forms were geometrized without losing their rhythmic freedom.

In the drawing of the Passion façade with its markedly plastic expressionism—a scale drawing done by the architect himself shortly after completing the Casa Milá—all of the elements have concretely geometric forms: the great slanting columns of the portico and the smaller ones of the pediment, the façade wall, and the monument to the bishop Torras which he designed for this frontal area (Fig. 520). In the succinct drawing on paper, the plastic concept which he had set forth with such valor earlier in the Batlló and Milá houses was reduced to a geometric one.

From paper it became reality in the pinnacles of his temple towers to which he disliked climbing, thus making the finishing strokes difficult. To transmit his orders to the assistants, he used the precise concrete language of mathematics, in which error was impossible. Thus those geometrically generated forms took shape, and far from producing any sort of rigidity, the geometry has rather put them more in tune with the laws of artistic harmony. An example of such forms can be found in the tower tops which we will discuss in dealing with rhythm in the master's work,[10] and again in the descriptive study of the Sagrada Familia.

10. Next chapter, Section 133.

117. Decoration of one of the columns of the main floor of the Casa Milá. Compare Fig. 476.

118. Pinnacles of the towers of the Sagrada Familia with geometrized «abstract» forms.

XXIX. GEOMETRIC RHYTHMS

In retrospect, Gaudí's artistic personality appears to be fraught with genius, and his works seem to have been a spontaneous effervescence. But we have seen in preceding chapters how all of his creation was preceded by thorough esthetic and mechanical analysis as well as by studies of the materials to employ, of the natural surroundings, and above all, of the ends which the work was to serve.

Another aspect of his work was the decorative and geometric one—frequently independent of the mechanics and the structure—which he mentions in his youthful notes and which he had probably learned from treatises about ornamental technique. He sometimes applied such geometric studies in traditional ways, but at other times he introduced innovations of a very personal sort. From these were born his variety of rhythms, some of which are characteristic of different stages of his development.

128. STRAIGHT LINES AND PLANES (Figs.119 - 132 and 159)

In the earliest phase of his career, Gaudí showed a preference for rectangular and triangular rhythms. The first were influenced by structure, and the second were merely decorative, being frequently converted into a framework of hexagonal forms. In the mixed fabric of rubble and

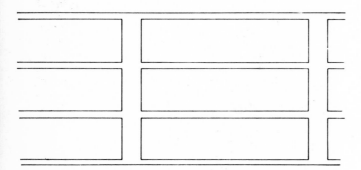

119. Horizontally rectangular geometric rhythms. Güell stables.

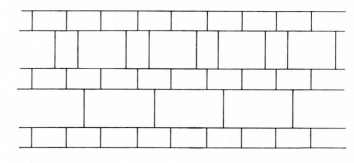

120. Ashlar junctures in the Sagrada Familia.

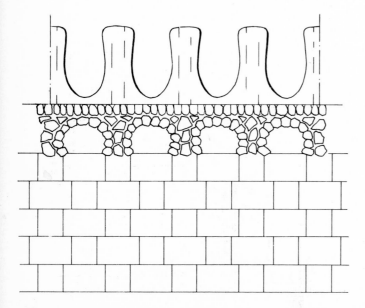

121. Güell Park. Rectangular pattern of the ceramic facing with repetitive rhythms in the upper part.

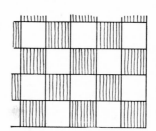

122. Checkerboard pattern at «El Capricho» in Comillas.

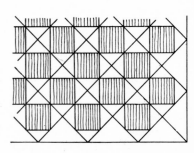

123. Quadrangular network pattern in the lower part of the Dragon Gate at the Güell stables in Les Corts.

brick which he employed without facing in order to take advantage of its chromatic qualities, he used the brick in a logically layered form to produce the system of bands which we see in the house on the Calle de las Carolinas (Figs. 207, 208); it is intersected by other vertical brick elements, creating horizontally positioned rectangles. The iron fence at the same house is composed of a structural network of squares; and in the upper part of the house, the rectangular rhythm becomes vertical rather than horizontal, and its decorative facing of glazed tile is enriched with colors which alternate in a checkerboard pattern. He continued with this tendency to enrich the upper parts by availing himself of sets of repetitive rhythms joined by different ones right up to beginning of his last period, not only in his buildings, but also in the subsidiary elements contained within them. In the front door grate at the Güell palace (Fig. 244), and in the dragon gate of the stables in «Les Corts», the upper parts display complex and mobile rhythms in contrast to the more severely geometric lower parts (Fig. 223).

In the stables themselves, we see that the horizontal rectangular reticulation is more structural than decorative, in what is basically a mud-wall fabric, reinforced with pillars and layers of brick which produce the rectangles. At some points the mud-wall is replaced by rubble-work. In other parts of these pavilions we see brickwork in hexagonally grouped triangular networks of Arabic derivation, and in the house at Comillas purely decorative horizontal banded rhythms abound, emphasized in the basement by vigorous stone junctures, and in the main body by appliqués of ceramic tile on the brick surface. In the gables and in the cylindrical tower the checkerboard pattern dominates in yellow and green ceramic-tile facing (Fig. 214).

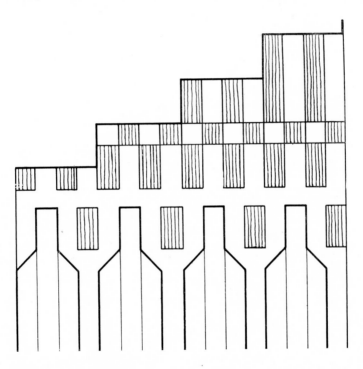

124. Casa Vicens, upper part of the facade with a vertically rectangular pattern.

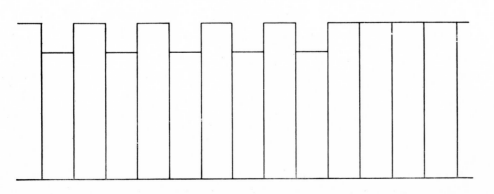

125. Palacio Güell, vertically rectangular rhythm in the façade tribune.

126. Palacio Güell, structure of an interior door, with a vertical rectangular pattern.

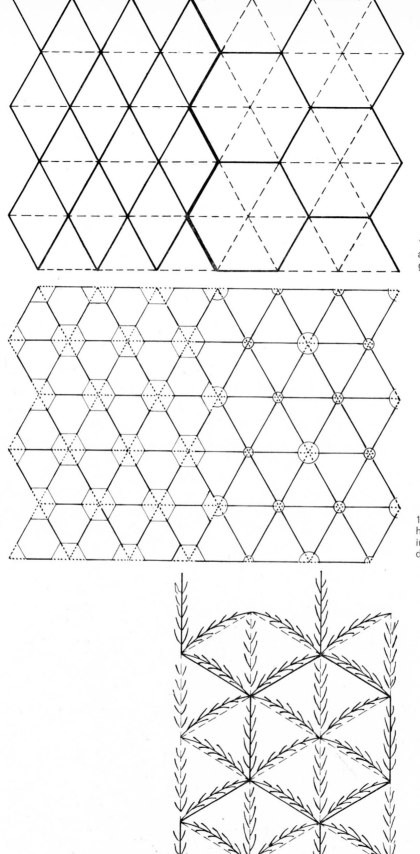

127. Rhythm of lozenges and hexagons over a framework of triangular nets.

128. A rhythm of triangles and hexagons with simple decoration in the Güell stables and the windows of the Colonia Güell church.

129. Curvilinear triangular pattern in the Cathedral of Mallorca.

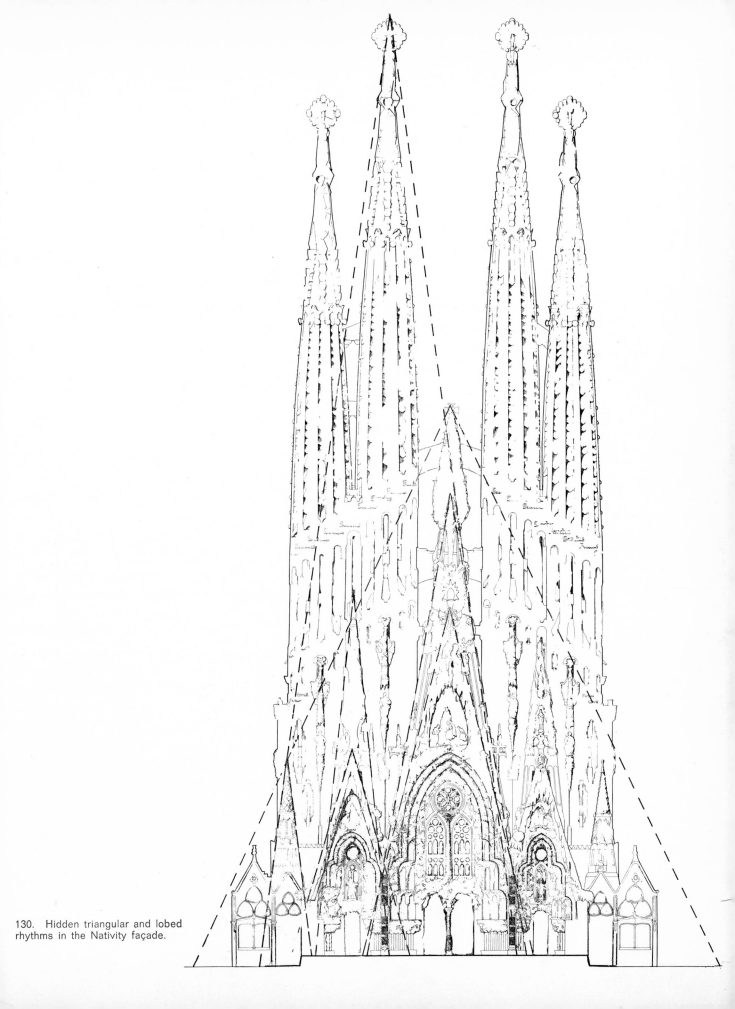

130. Hidden triangular and lobed rhythms in the Nativity façade.

Among the rectangular network-like patterns that he used, we should mention the alternation of rectangles and squares in both horizontal bands and in a vertical direction; in the stones of the Sagrada Familia bell towers and in the ceramic facing on the lateral retaining walls of the Güell Park stairway he alternates concave surfaces of squares with convex rectangles (Fig. 397).

In these latter walls we can observe the rhythmic repetitions which the architect lavished on the park. I refer to the uniformly distributed oval hollows in the upper part of the rubblework which contrasts with the ceramic veneer and the ceramic merlons which crown them. Similar merlons adorn the entrance pavilions, echoing the same repetitive pattern that we find in the decorative elements of the surrounding wall, in the viaducts, and —in more ostensible form— in the rustic monoliths or menhir-jardiniers of that Viaduct which we have designated by letter C (Figs. 419 - 424).

He employed square reticulation as the skeleton for circular rhythms (in the imbrication of the Güell stables [Fig. 228] and in the ironwork of the Calvet house [Fig. 316]) and triangular reticulation as the basis for hexagonal rhythms (the Güell stables and Güell colony church [Fig. 128], the Cathedral of Mallorca [Fig. 129], papier-mâché appliqués, and relief hydraulic mosaics [Fig. 159]) and for rounded triangles.

129. PARABOLIC AND LOBED ARCHES (Figs. 133 - 137 and 147 - 149)

Gaudí's initial preference for the Moslem was superseded by a preference for the Gothic, probably because of his commissions to direct the Sagrada Familia and the Episcopal Palace at Astorga. From this same period is the Palacio Güell, conceived in rectangular rhythms here vertically arranged to give a Gothic spirit while the elements of carpentry in the interior still reflect an Arabic influence in their quadrangular network patterns combined with triangles.

In his building we note for the first time the structurally efficient parabolic arches of the two main doors which were later to characterize his architecture and which he lavishly employed in a more elongated form in the interior along the main floor tribune, in the dining room, and in the central hall (Fig. 147).

The Convent of Santa Teresa on the Calle Ganduxer, of similar stylistic filiation but constructed with more modest materials—visible rubblework and brick—follows the same rhythmic patterns as the Güell Palace in the graceful parabolic arches of the interior (Fig. 149) and the triangular-hexagonal reticulation of the projecting portion of the façade.

The Gothic style is more obviously recalled in the Episcopal Palace at Astorga and in the house at León which has more the character of secular Gothic than does the Astorga building. The León house is basically a cube, similar to the Teresan convent, and Gaudí emphasizes the four corners of both edifices with pointed elementos rising above the body of the whole (Figs. 283 - 287).

In these two Leonese buildings we see for the first time—in addition to the Gothic elements of the general composition—the trilobate and pentalobate rhythm of the openings which he would frequently apply in the works of this and his following period (at Bellesguard, the Sagrada Familia, and Güell Park). Such rhythms can be found in the arcades of the Gothic cloister of San Pablo del Campo in Barcelona, but it would seem more logical to seek precedence of the motif in the fashion for such forms established by Art Nouveau architecture which Gaudí has been credited with revitalizing. He often applies this rhythm in an open manner as at Astorga, León, in the Rosary portal of the Sagrada Familia, and in Güell Park; at other times he uses it as the ordering schema or underlying framework, as in the Nativity façade where it regulates the naturalistic ornamentation of the three portals (Fig. 130).

The rhythms enumerated here were not simply a decorative resource, for he used them to give his works the expression he desired as well. He would use straight lines when he wanted to obtain a severity of expression, and curves to achieve an optimistic note. As we have said, he applied them consistently from his first years as an architect until the turn of the century when he built the Casa Calvet in the Baroque style, tenuously including the trilobulate motif in the upper opening of the façade (Figs. 314, 315). In the solomonic columns of the Calvet stairway wee see the rhythm of helicoidal movement (which he had also used sparingly in the Nativity façade) but it does not spread to the rest of the building (Fig. 317).

At the beginning of this century, Gaudí bid farewell to historical styles with a building whose compositional expression resides solely in its silhouette and the distribution of the openings. This was, of course, the country house called «Bellesguard», designed in a very personal Gothic style with its great pentalobulate window outlined above the entrance and the novel element of the audacious spire, here rising to a height double that of the rest of the building, and terminated with the four-armed cross which he had already used at the corners of the Teresan convent. The dominant height of this spire and the sacred symbol which tops it give the building the sense of unity which the architect was constantly seeking. He repeated this rhythm of the prominent spire in one of the Park entrance pavilions.

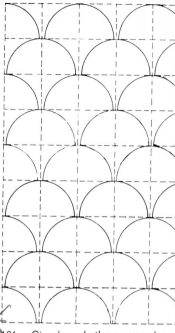

131. Circular rhythms superimposed on a square network pattern in the imbrications on the façades of the Güell stables.

132. Circular rhythms superimposed on a square network in the elevator door of the Casa Calvet.

133. Trilobed rhythms in the Palacio Episcopal of Astorga.

135. Trilobed rhythms in the Rosary door of the Sagrada Familia.

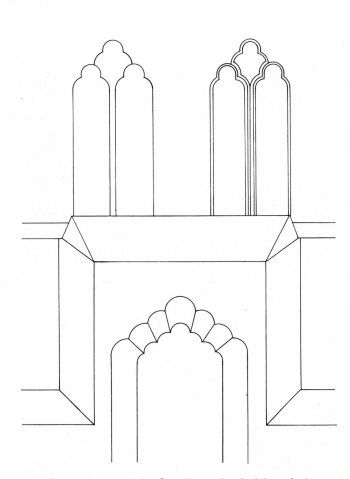

134. Lobed rhythms of the Casa Fernández Andrés, in León.

136. Five-lobed rhythm in the large window at Bellesguard.

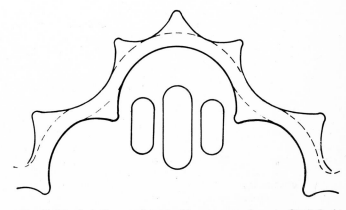

137. Trilobed rhythm combined with a sinuous form in Güell Park.

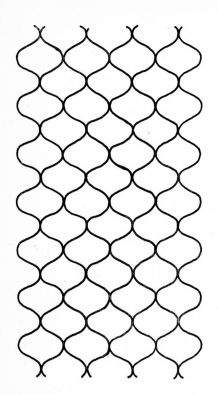

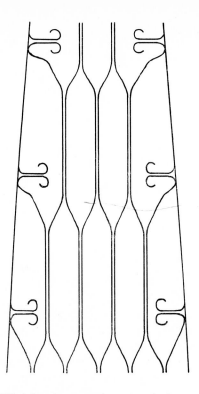

138. Regular vertical sinuous rhythm in the Palacio Güell entrance grating.

139. Regular vertical sinuous rhythm in the Teresan convent.

140. Regular semi-free sinuous rhythm in the Sagrada Familia.

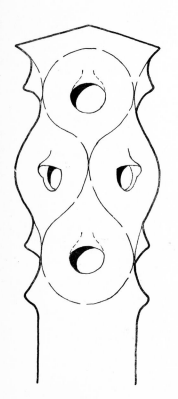

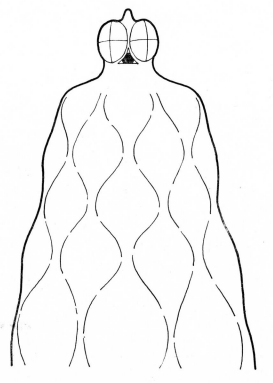

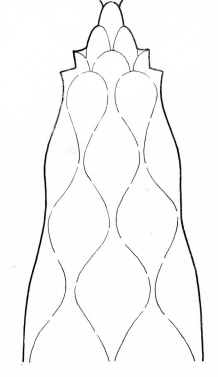

141. Regular semi-free sinuous rhythm in the Casa Milá roof elements.

142. Regular semi-free sinuous rhythm in the project for the Colonia Güell church.

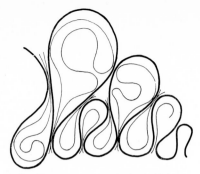

143. Free sinuous rhythm: Palacio
Güell, upper part of the gratings.

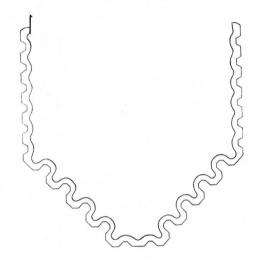

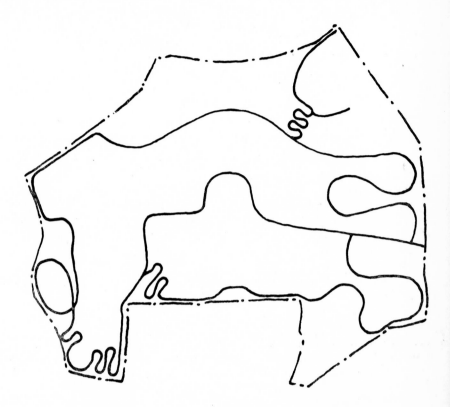

144. Free sinuous rhythms: Güell Park,
bench around the grand plaza.

145. Free sinuous rhythms: Güell Park viaducts in plan.

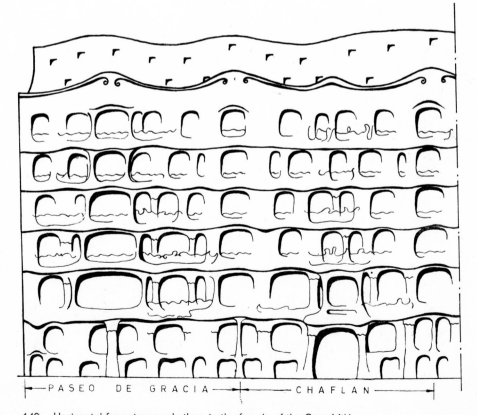

146. Horizontal free sinuous rhythms in the façade of the Casa Milá.

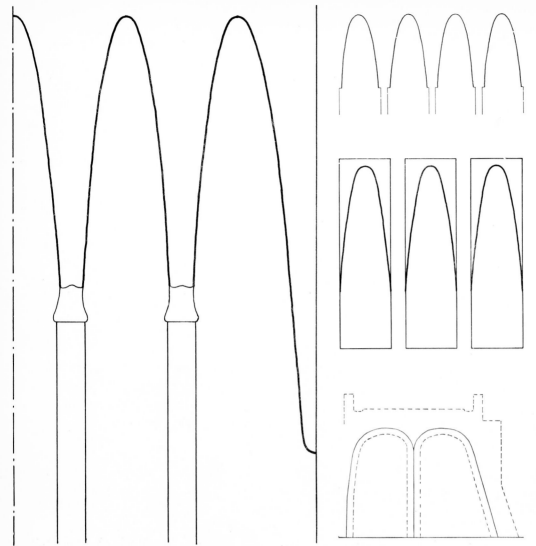

147. Decorative parabolic arches. Palacio Güell.

148. Decorative parabolic arches. Güell Stables.

149. Decorative parabolic arches. Teresan school.

150. Structural rhythm in Güell Park.

130. SINUOUS RHYTHMS: REGULAR AND FREE (Figs. 138 - 146)

In his historical phase which we have just examined, the master generally adhered to the dominant styles, even though he submitted them to the crucible of his critical sense and to the fire of his genius. Gaudí's rebellious temperament found encouragement in the Secessionist movement which had begun in Munich and Vienna, proclaiming the principle of opposition to established norms, and which took root in Catalonia with the name of «Modernismo.» It is possible that even without the support of the Secessionist iconoclasm, the impetus and restlessness of our architect would have led him to escape his historical fetters, but we must admit that the *modernista* movement acted as a liberating force which freed him from stylistic preoccupations and allowed him to forget rectilinear rhythms or outlines drawn with a compass in his search for dynamic rhythms implying movement; the results were sometimes completely free, but also frequently subject to geometrical order.

Gaudí's most typical *modernista* work, with the arbitrary curves proper to that style, was the sinuously outlined entrance gate to the Miralles property, and the fluid termination of the surrounding wall (Figs. 349 - 352).

He had already used this rhythmic type, without giving it the *modernista* character, in the iron gratings of the Güell Palace (Fig. 143), and in the window screens of the Teresan convent (Fig. 139). The upper section of the palace gratings and other ironwork of the second floor were definitely designed in the new artistic mode and, given the date of their execution, were prior to the general European movement. In the same style he conceived some of the Nativity façade details, such as the brackets that support the four evangelists and the balconies where the towers change from their square bases into a circular plan (Figs. 103, 140). The latter have become veritable classics of *modernismo*, due to their perfect combination of freer undulating rhythms with more regulated geometric norms, which gives them an especially attractive freedom and balance. He used such sinuous *modernista* rhythms lavishly in the lower floor grilles (now removed) and the roof of the Casa Milá, and also in Güell Park.

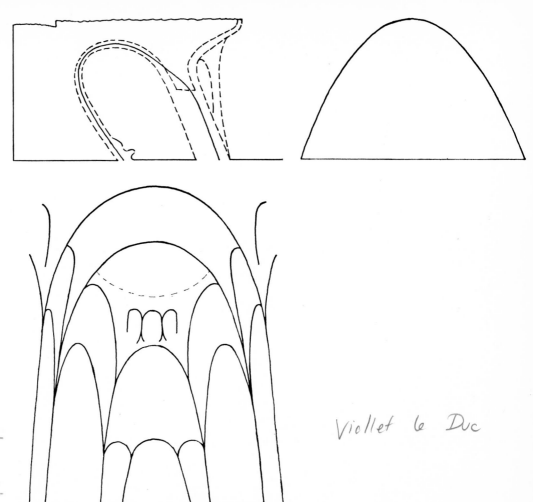

151. Structural rhythm in Güell Park.

152. Structural parabolic rhythm in the mansard of the Casa Milá.

153. Colonia Güell. Rhythm of equilibrated forms resulting from the funicular study with wires and weights.

Viollet le Duc

The Nativity façade, which falls within the new style, generally follows three rhythmic patterns: a hidden free triangulation, a partially apparent polylobulation, and a helicoidal composition. Gaudí had seen the medieval triangulated drawings which were used to proportion the Gothic temples in Viollet-le-Duc,[1] and most likely in other treatises. This was one of the factors which led him to label this architecture «industrial» (i.e., mechanical), and I am certain that he did not have faith in them. It appears that his confidence lay rather in his own artistic intuition in relation to the general expression that he wished to achieve. Nevertheless, the fact that he was dealing with unusual height[2] which was therefore difficult to correct, plus his usual prudence, forced him to submit the overall façade to his own triangulation in order to harmonize the parts. It seems to be no accident that the five lantern tops can be inscribed in the two sides of a tall isosceles triangle, as can certain lower elements and the upper part of the towers. This geometric framework could be responsible for the fine harmony evident in the façade as a whole.[3]

Though this hidden triangular rhythm must remain a hypothesis on my part, such is not the case with the lobulate rhythms which are quite apparent and regulate the profuse ornamentation of the three portals (Fig. 130).

In the bell towers, combined spatial helicoidal rhythms dominate in the ordering of the openings whereas mechanical ones determine the profile of the towers (Figs. 509, 510).

131.   STRUCTURAL AND HELICOIDAL RHYTHMS (Figs. 150 - 158)

Whereas we have been able to refer to historical styles and familiar rhythms up to this point, from here on we almost completely lose sight of them. We have seen that in the church for the Colonia Güell, of which only the crypt was built, Gaudí worked out and applied his new architectural theory. As a result, the inclined pillars and supports dictated by mechanical forces—which he decided to employ despite their unprecedented nature—make their first appearance. The diverse inclined resultant forces at the periphery of the church were to have been contained within curtain walls which would also not be vertical, and in some cases not even planar, but which would tend instead to be warped surfaces.

1. *Dictionaire raisonné de l'architecture française*, VII, pp. 531-561.

2. The pinnacle of the central element of the Nativity façade is 35 meters high, the lower towers, 70 meters, and the tall ones, 76.5 meters.

3. In the figure which shows the rhythms of this façade (fig. 130) the triangulation is sketched in a purely tentative manner.

The architect did not conceal his admiration for the hyperbolic paraboloid form and its multiple advantages: facile structure, good reflective properties for light and sound, adaptability to endless situations, esthetic qualities, etc. With these forms he solved a wide variety of architectural problems, and there was even a period when he used them in his design for the future Expiatory Temple. Such forms are to be found in the beautiful model for the sacristy cupolas, and with them he planned to resolve the nave vaulting.

Without concern for style, a new art and new rhythms were born which could be adapted to any mechanical needs and to all esthetic effects.

In the Güell Park, the new composition of equilibrated forms and inclined supports is more apparent; it is a design which, if we want to give it a stylistic label, we must call by the name of the maestro. In this park a geometrical, structurally determined rhythm predominates and is most evident in the galleries below the viaducts, in the helicoidally descending supports, and in the continuous sloping retaining wall with its inclined frontal colonnade.

This rhythm of equilibrated structural forms was most highly developed in the park, since his extensive use of the same rhythmic patterns projected for the Sagrada Familia never got beyond the model stage. Along with this rhythm, he also used purely decorative geometric ones as in the rectangular patterns which we have indicated in the lateral wall facings, the menhirs of one of the passageways, and in the Doric colonnade where the inclined columns at the perimeter and the entablature which recedes between the columns meet the great winding bench of the upper plaza (Fig. 402).

The sinuous rhythm which is clearly seen in the polychrome bench that encloses this plaza is echoed in several of the viaducts and retaining walls. In these the winding quality is not so apparent, but the waviness of the lines gives movement and optimism to those elements in which it is employed. (This sinuous rhythm which he had already used in an incipient manner in the ironwork of the Güell Palace and in the Teresan convent as well as in the Sagrada Familia was to reach its peak of expressiveness in the Casa Milá.) In the two park entrance pavilions he used some of these rhythms, dominated by the extremely free composition of the finely polychromed roof.

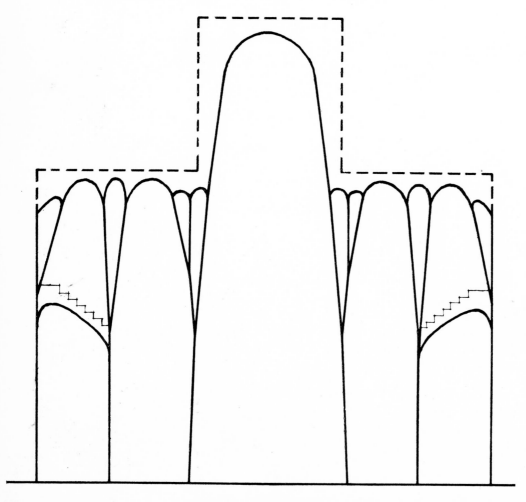

154. Structural rhythm in the transversal supports of the Sagrada Familia.

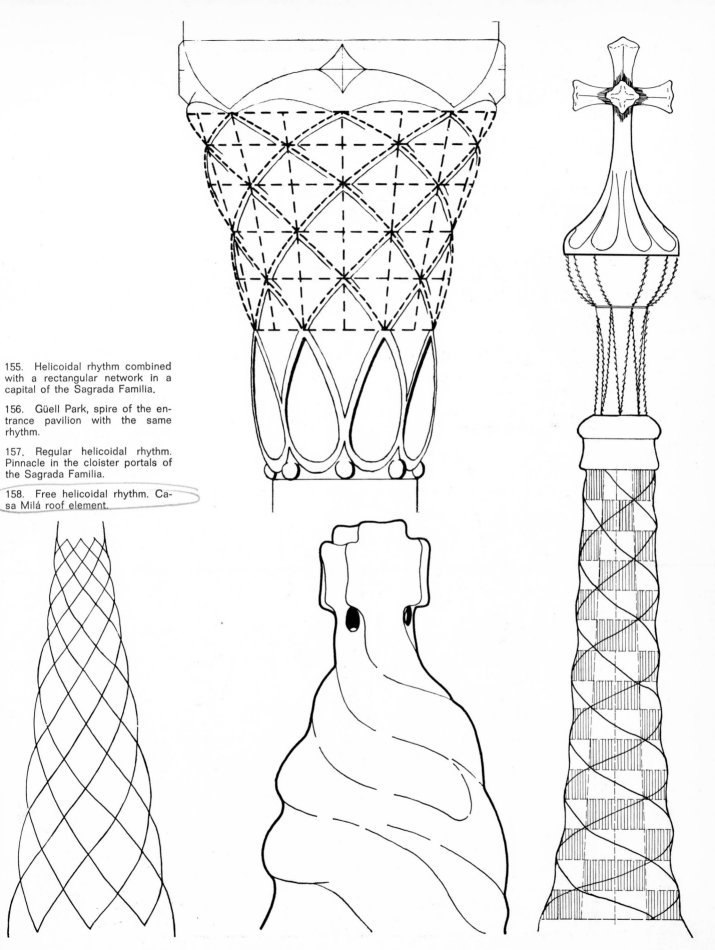

155. Helicoidal rhythm combined with a rectangular network in a capital of the Sagrada Familia.

156. Güell Park, spire of the entrance pavilion with the same rhythm.

157. Regular helicoidal rhythm. Pinnacle in the cloister portals of the Sagrada Familia.

158. Free helicoidal rhythm. Casa Milá roof element.

Worthy of mention here is the complex geometric design of the spire which upholds the characteristic four-arm cross (Fig. 156). Its form is that of an extremely elongated semi-hyperboloid with a throat at the top, and its decoration responds to two rhythms: one consists of two helices which cross each other from opposite directions in relief, and the other of a rectangular network of alternating colors, white and blue, in glazed mosaic which harmonizes marvelously with the sky in the background. This rectangular network is composed of equidistant horizontal lines (the parallels) while the verticals (the meridians) get closer as they move from the greater diameter of the base to the lesser one at the peak, causing the oblong rectangles at the base to become squares at the top.

It seems probable that he used the double helix in the spire because of the property of ascending movement which he attributed to this form, here intended to give the idea of ascension to the cross which it was to sustain. This idea of ascension is emphasized further by supporting the cross on an extremely open iron stand, and thus making it appear disconnected from all that is earth-bound.

He had used these same forms of the spire in an inverted position in the decoration of one of the Sagrada Familia capitals, which shows that he incorporated such rhythms into his decorative system in a conscious and meditated manner (Fig. 155).

132. FREE SPATIAL RHYTHMS

As Gaudí gradually discovered the new theory of which we have spoken he found himself, and he became aware of the infinite possibilities of the new system. The two park buildings, built outside of town, received from this an expressive strength which coupled them with nature without their imitating it by way of techniques and spatial rhythms which had nothing to do with the stereotomy of rectangular forms generally employed up to that time. His freedom of movement had reached fulfillment. He had seen the excellence of spatial forms and decided not to limit himself any longer to the two dimensions of the plane.

It was in this moment of his esthetic development that he was commissioned to do the two apartment houses on the Paseo de Gracia—an area where there was always the danger of falling into mannered stereotypes—which he gladly accepted, adapting them to his new plastic theory in order to prove that it was apt for all types of architectural construction.

The Casa Batlló was actually a remodeling job where he used continuous forms on the façade in a completely free and three-dimensional rhythm that gave the building a sense of unity. On the less remodeled floors he undulated the façade wall and covered in with a polychromatic ceramic mosaic.

Such was his enthusiasm at that moment for three-dimensional forms that he invented a device for making relief tile floors in concrete. It was a daring idea, and the solution was not easily obtained. He spent two years in the working out of the model and manufacturing the molds which were available only after the Batlló house had been finished (1906). For this reason, they were not used here but were instead incorporated into his plans for the Casa Milá which he built immediately afterwards.

These tiles are hexagonal in form (Fig. 159), and in order to achieve a maximum spatial illusion, their decoration symbolizes the earth, the sea, and the heavens using plants, marine animals, and star motifs in low relief. Originally he foresaw three different types of tiles, but in the course of his study he decided to reduce the three to one which would contain a third of each of the three motifs. As each tile was composed in triangular radial symmetry, the three motifs would be completed by putting the tiles together, as can be seen in those illustrated; [4] the covering of the Torino Bar ceiling was also made up of hexagonal pieces in relief, though these were less complex than the Milá floor tiles (Fig. 353).

In the house known as «La Pedrera» (the quarry), commissioned by the Milá-Segimón family, he wanted to escape the customary subdivision of an exterior façade into rectangular openings in the hope of giving unity to the great mass of free and smooth-flowing surfaces devoid of superimposed ornamentation. We get the impression that in these two buildings on the Paseo de Gracia the architect wanted to avoid a priori geometric rhythms and to let himself be carried away by a spontaneous outpouring of free forms in space with the single-minded end of giving expression and life to his works. This spontaneity of conception is confirmed by the drawings which he presented to the city government and which display a certain carelessness of outline, as if this were only a first draft, subject to change. In reality this was indeed the case for both houses, as we can see by comparing the projects which were the basis for municipal permission to build with the works as actually executed. Gaudí said several times that a project could not be something «on paper,» meaning that any such drawings were merely for convenience and should be open to revision (Figs. 57, 434, 453, 456).

Thus it was that these two buildings on passing from paper into reality were to acquire greater structural coherence, and in the Casa Milá we can see a nostalgic reappearance of the rhythms based on horizontal bands and rectangular networks which we saw in his earliest

4. These tiles were manufactured by the Escofet firm of Barcelona, to the exact specifications of the architect indicated on two Swedish steel molds. The relief was worked out in such a way that it would not be difficult to walk on. Proof of its success and of the relevancy of the design today is that in a recent contest of the Fomento de las Artes Decorativas it was awarded the highest distinction, the Delta de Oro. The pieces for the «Torino» ceiling were of a very hard pasteboard construction and merely decorative.

A   B

159. Interaction of complex rhythms with hexagonal patterns and triangular networks: A) Ceiling of the «Torino» bar, B) Floor of the Casa Milá.

works and which were not contained in the presentation drawings. In the actual building, these rhythms are emphasized by the sinuous edges between the floors which remind us of the traditional imposts, but here instead of dividing they unite the general composition; these undulating rectangles are crowned by the building's wavy upper silhouette and mansard roof, above which, in vertical contrast, emerge the smoke outlets, ventilators, and stairwells visible from below and following undulating and helicoidal rhythms which lend mobility and unity to the whole. In the molding of both of these houses the architect achieved an important aspect of that ideal which he had intuited from his early years as a student of geometry, and which he had sought after all of his life. It was only a phase; he had realized this plastic achievement as a sculptor, not as a geometrician which was his ideal. He had obtained plasticity in both buildings by *modeling* surfaces which he *organized* according to geometric rhythms, but the surfaces tend to slip away from the geometry. The synthesis to which he aspired was to be realized in his beloved Sagrada Familia church.

133. GEOMETRIZED PLASTICITY (Fig. 160)

Once the Nativity façade was completed along the Gothic-Modernista lines already indicated, the four towers were slowly erected; their silhouette was straight at the bottom and parabolical above, and the openings were distributed in a pattern of 12 vertical bands with another helicoidal rhythm that moved along them. These towers follow Gaudí's architectural theory in which forms correspond to structural forces, giving them a sense of unity where there is not an element too many or too few (Fig. 509).

In the decorative terminations of these towers he achieved the formal concept toward which he had been working throughout his life and which we have seen him attain in earlier buildings only as a result of sentimental inspiration, working as a sculptor; here the concept was made reality by the architect working in pure geometry.

Before reaching the pinnacle, the twelve vertical rib-like elements of the towers are joined in pairs to form six converging elements which in turn make up the base of the triangular pyramid with chamfered edges which is the main body of the pinnacle; the latter is then combined with other geometrical forms which are illustrated in the following diagram (Fig. 160). Toward the top, the elongated pyramid curves to form a bishop's crozier and becomes intertwined with the mosaic-covered terminal cross, which fulfills the chromatic aspect of the Gaudinian theory in more agile and delicately formed rhythms than in any of those he had previously projected.

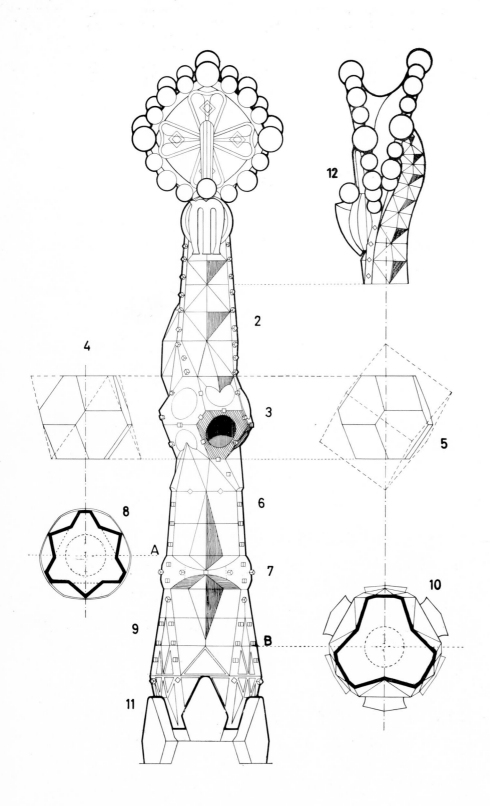

160. Free geometric rhythm in the top
pinnacles of the Sagrada Familia.

When we consider the compositional variety which we have just summarized, we realize the strength of Gaudí's creative maturity—and at the same time the sense of responsibility which kept him from relying completely upon his own inspiration and forced him to submit his conceptions to disciplines of a technical sort in his desire for a higher unity. We can see the immense distance that has been travelled between the rectangular or triangular rhythms of the first works or even the later lobulated ones and those of his last creation which elude categorization but which contain the fluidity of a completely free conception along with the scientific rigor of a mechanical and geometric solution to a problem.

GEOMETRIC ANALYSIS OF THE ADJOINING DIAGRAM

1. Two curvilinear squares standing on end and united on an angle at one corner, with a floriated cross on the exterior faces and bordered by spheres of various sizes.

2. Pyramidal trunk with triangular base and chamfered edges with angular joints in the lower part and quadrangular pyramids on the faces.

3. Pseudo-regular polyhedron obtained by cutting off the vertices of a cube or an octahedron through whose faces projects a sphere which is perforated in two places to provide for spotlights.

4. Formation of a polyhedron by cutting off the vertices of a regular octahedron.

5. Formation of a polyhedron by cutting off the vertices of a regular hexahedron or cube.

6. Pyramidal trunk with a triangular base with chamfered edges (it is not the prolongation of that seen in No. 2) with angular joints uniting it with the upper and lower sections.

7. Trunk of a cone with its bases beveled in a triangular arrangement.

8. Section at point A.

9. Conical trunk casing with a hexagonal lower section and triangular upper one.

10. Section at Point B.

11. Inverted hexagonal pyramidal trunk.

12. Very sharp pyramid with triangular base and chamfered edges, curved in the form of a crozier, the faces being extremely reduced pyramids with square bases which perforate the center of two squares seen in No. 1.

134. TWO RELATIVELY UNIMPORTANT WORKS

LA OBRERA MATARONENSE. We have already seen, in discussing our architect's sympathies for the working class (IX - 33), how this co-operative society commissioned him to design a project for a workers' neighborhood with 30 houses, a thread and textile factory, a residence for the director, and a social hall —a project which was never realized except for a very minimal part, but upon which he worked conscientiously, sending it to the Paris International Exposition.

The architect M. Ribas y Piera, who was the first to publish these plans (Figs. 163, 182-186), has carefully studied the project and feels that Gaudí's urbanistic ideas reflected the double path of utopian progressivism and romantic paternalism so manifest in the nineteenth century.

In the project for the Plaza Real which followed immediately afterwards, we see the architect concerned with the monumental and decorative aspects of urban planning, but in Mataró he was mainly preoccupied with the parceling of land, the distribution of spaces, and the living conditions for the worker residents. Although we cannot deduce the arrangement of the industrial sector from the data existing in the Municipal Archives, we can determine that of the residential quarters. There were to be thirty residences, grouped by twos in three long rows, with the intermediate streets oriented in a NW - SE direction. The houses of the middle row were placed in such a manner that each of them faced into the spaces between the other rows, thus augmenting their frontal exposure.

Ribas says that although the new architect's lack of experience can account for a certain ingenuousness in his urbanistic layout, it is perfectly acceptable within the context of other analogous projects of the period, and he cites similar colonies promoted in France 20 years earlier which also used small twinned houses with simple peripheral gardens similar to Gaudí's that link up with the «hygienist» concepts involving air, sun, and vegetation which prepared the way for the garden city movement in which Gaudí would in a sense participate when he constructed Güell Park.[1]

1. M. Ribas i Piera, «Gaudí i la Cooperativa Obrera de Mataró,» *Serra d'Or,* (December, 1965).

THE PLAZA REAL. If we admit Gaudí's propensity—more than facility—to see things in their total sense, it is easy to imagine his inborn qualifications as a planner, something which he demonstrated from his first stages as an architect. The utilitarian qualities or urbanism

161. Project for the layout of the Plaza Real, drawn up by Gaudí for the placement of two lampposts.

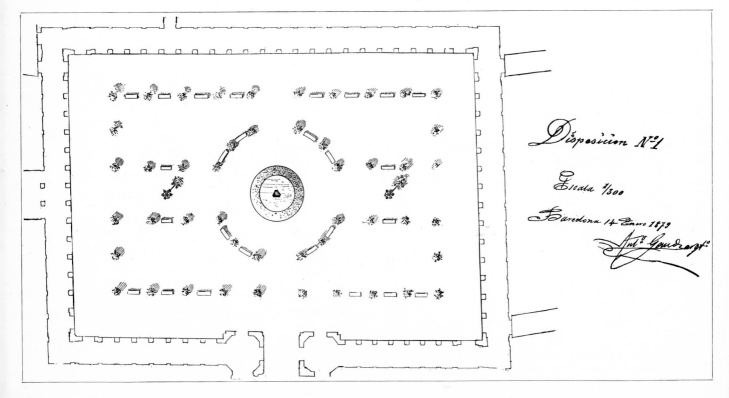

which concerned him in Mataró were complemented by the care with which he attended to the monumental, or, better, decorative character of this Barcelona square.

When he was commissioned by the City of Barcelona to design a decorative street lamp only a few weeks after his comprehensive exercises at the University, he immediately realized the urbanistic importance of the commission and he was not willing to limit himself to the simple purposes of illumination and decorativeness, but rather conceived of his work as a living element of the public way. He set forth his urbanistic ideas on the project in the careful memorial which accompanied it. In this memorial he incidentally suggests the adoption of street refuges «at multidirectional intersections of frequent transit,» and he suggests several appropriate sites: the plazas del Angel, del Pino, del Beato Oriol, de Junqueras, and Santa Ana. In addition, he shows off his historical knowledge of urban planning in a section which would seem to be of merely academic content if it were not for the practical use which he soon was able to make of it.[2]

This opportunity presented itself at the end of that same year, when he was about to terminate the lamp model and he made known to the Mayor his opposition to its being publicly displayed as a «monument» since he had designed it with the purpose of illumination foremost in his mind. Gaudí felt that in order to give it such a character either he would have to supplement it with ornamental additions which would lend greater relief or, better, he could erect a minimum of two together since one single lamp would not have the necessary stature.

As a consequence of this consideration it was decided that the lamp would be placed in the Plaza Real, which was then only partially developed, instead of the Plaza de San Sebastián as originally designated, so that there would be room for two or four lamps. Gaudí worked out various solutions for the location of either two or four lamps which he presented to the City on January 14, 1879. The project for two lamps was selected (Fig. 161).

135. TRADITION AND CHARACTER

In the universal vision which Gaudí maintained in every job which he was commissioned to do, he tended to become involved in urbanism even without proposing to do so in a specific manner. Thus in the country house of Bellesguard for the Figueras family which was located on the ancient site of the summer residence of King Martin the Humane, he worked from a premise of maximum respect for the previous tradition and character of the site in such aspects as the location of the new building, dignification of the remains of the old one, environment, and a new access road—all of which he resolved with an urbanistic skill which can still be admired today, along with the use of inclined pillars and arches to sustain the new

2. Municipal Administrative Archives of Barcelona, document 794.

162. The same project showing a solution with four lampposts.

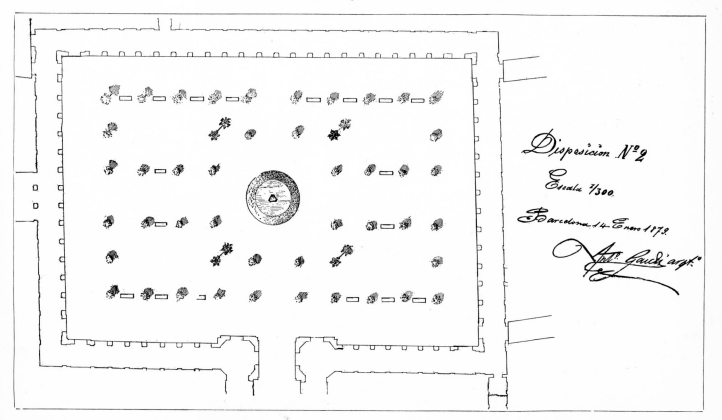

177

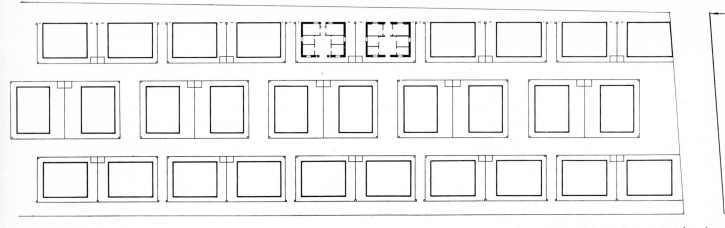

163. Urbanization project for «La Obrera Mataronense» of which only two of the planned 30 houses were built.

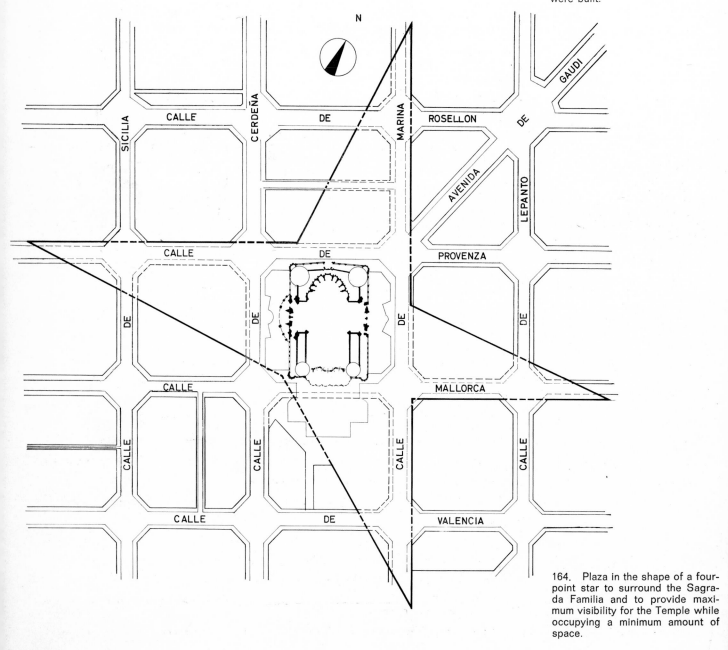

164. Plaza in the shape of a four-point star to surround the Sagrada Familia and to provide maximum visibility for the Temple while occupying a minimum amount of space.

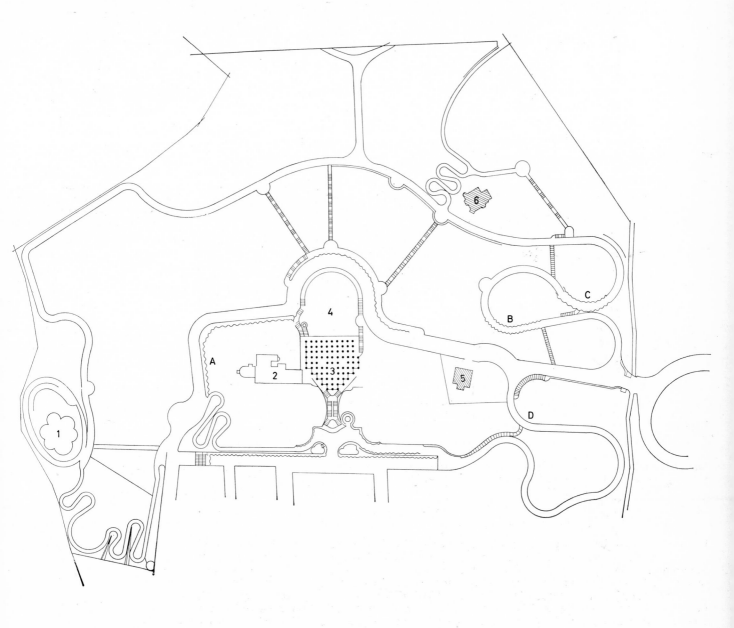

165. Overall plan of the Güell Park.

1. Hill where the Calvary has been erected, originally to have been the site of a chapel.

2. The former Güell residence which today has been converted into a municipal elementary school.

3. Hall of pseudo-Doric columns, to have been the market for the colony.

4. The grand plaza, partly of solid ground and partly resting on the above-mentioned hall.

5. Gaudi's house.

6. Dr. Trias' house.

A   Portico adjoining the Güell residence with an upper roadway.

B   Portico with three series of columns and an upper roadway.

C   Portico with three series of columns in a triangular arrangement and with an upper roadway bordered by rustic seats and tall jardinieres.

D   Portico with a double series of columns in a triangular arrangement and an upper roadway.

road. This will be discussed in greater detail in the descriptive part of the present study. (XLV - 181).

Gaudí clearly demonstrated his concern for things urbanistic to Ráfols [3] on the occasion of the death of the bishop Torras y Bages whom he praised for having stood in the way of a certain reform in Vilafranca which threatened the character of the village. He sustained this when his opinion was asked before the urban reform of Barcelona was begun; in this he favored respecting the character of the various neighborhoods over the introduction of long, grand, and uniform avenues which would destroy interesting old buildings and urban groupings.

When the replanning of Barcelona was being carried out in 1907-8, a commission was appointed to work out a plan to commemorate the figure of Jaime el Conquistador. The architect Puig y Cadafalch, who was a member of this commission, visited Gaudí to get his opinion on the matter of a monument to the «Victorious King.» Ráfols reports his reply:«Aren't they reforming the city now? Well then, this is just the time to restore, to the Plaza del Rey the atmosphere of those ancient times when the sovereign used to pass through it. Tear down the houses that have been built up against the church of Santa Agueda, and then tear down those which still stand on the Calle de la Tapinería and build a grandiose stairway which will join the Plaza del Rey with the great new avenue. Next to the door of the palace could be placed a sculptural group representing Jaime I and his court and men-at-arms so that the historic plaza could speak to us even more intensely of the great monarch.» [4] He did not feel that «a monument with a pedestal and a statue» would be appropriate «because however much the contemporary King, Louis IX of France, surpassed him in holiness, our monarch made up in political acumen.» [5]

He did not actually draw this project, except for some sketchy outlines on photographic blow-ups where he indicated which houses should be torn down to open the arches beneath Santa Agueda and a plaza in front of them, and he drew the pointed pyramidal pinnacles of the cathedral bell towers with the gallery of King Martin behind. Of his idea the commission only incorporated the open space indicated in one of the sketches which today carries the name of the Plaza de Berenguer el Grande, and carried out the demolition of some of the houses which hid the wall. The memory of the Conqueror King was entrusted to two beautiful polychrome inscriptions painted by Jujol on the eastern wall of Santa Agueda which have now disappeared.

Gaudí's collaborator, Domingo Sugrañes, says that the architect also advised that all of the buildings of interest destroyed by the reformation should be moved to the area surrounding the Cathedral and the Palacio Mayor, thus creating a complete history of Barcelona architecture from the thirteenth to the nineteenth century in a monumental urbanistic arrangement of the highest quality.[6] The advice was only followed later in the case of the Casa Padellás which serves as the present Museum of the History of the City and, recently, with some ancient façades in the Plaza de San Felipe Neri.

136. A STAR-SHAPED PLAZA (Fig. 164)

When the architect Jaussely was commissioned in 1906 to do the plan for the linking of Barcelona with its surrounding municipalities, he asked Gaudí to decide on an arrangement for the area surrounding the Sagrada Familia in order to incorporate it into his general plan. Gaudí designed a star-shaped plaza for the purpose of allowing people to contemplate the temple's central dome, which would be 170 meters high, within the normal visual angle of 30 degrees, and arranged it in such a manner as to allow two façades to be observed simultaneously with similar foreshortening. Because of the high cost of the land which this plaza would have occupied, Gaudí felt himself obliged to reduce the star to four points (combining them with the streets of the Cerdá gridiron plan) from which the temple mass could be seen at its four vertices.[7]

137. AN ORIGINAL PARK (Fig. 165)

Gaudí's most complete, and at the same time most representative, work is the park which he designed on a commission from Eusebio Güell on the grounds of the ancient Can Muntaner de Dalt on the Montaña Pelada (Bald Mountain) to the northwest of Barcelona. This arid spot—as the name indicates—is situated some 150 meters above sea level [8] and was converted into one of the most attractive in Barcelona, contemporary with and even anticipating in certain aspects the English idea of the garden suburb.

The purpose of the urbanization was to set up a residential zone of some 60 lots with their homes, roads, and general services such as a church, a plaza-theater, a market, etc., surrounded by pleasant vegetation. The development was oriented along the roads which the erratic topography of the site caused to be outlined in sinuous curves, but these roads were in turn regulated by two approximately perpendicular axes. One of these, running in a SE-NW direction, was determined by the Calle Olot entrance, the main stairway which opens onto it,

3. Ráfols, Gaudí, (1929), p. 132.
4. Ibid., p. 115.
5. Bergós, op. cit., p. 22.
6. D. Sugrañes, «Gaudí i l'Urbanisme,» El Matí, (July 31, 1932). The painted inscriptions mentioned here are ilustrated in Collins, Gaudí, Fig. 19.
7. Puig Boada, El Templo de la Sagrada Familia, p. 22.
8. S. Sellés y Baró, «El parque Güell,» Anuario de la Asociación de Arquitectos de Cataluña, (1903).

the Doric colonnade, and the upper plaza which is symmetrically divided by the axis; the other follows horizontally the wide *paseo,* and on its northeast end there is another entrance to the park. This roadway-*paseo* which is part of a network leading to all parts of the park has an extension of some three kilometers. The major roads of the park have grades of six per cent or less and are wide enough for vehicles while also serving as walkways. These are more or less horizontally oriented in sunny sites protected from the wind and are flanked by benches of stone. Other narrower roads with grades up to 12 per cent are reserved exclusively for pedestrians who may wish to shorten their path. In addition, there are several very steep and stepped short-cuts which abbreviate the distances to an even greater extent.

In this country-like development, as in all road layout work, certain parts had to be excavated and others filled in. Gaudí resolved the second condition in an original manner. Instead of the customary embankments, he constructed viaducts with underlying porticos which could also be used for protection from the rain and sun.

The services provided for the inhabitants (which the colony never had) are located close to the roads. Included among such facilities were two entrance pavilions—one to be used by the gate-keeper and as a waiting room for the park with telephone, washrooms, and a window through which residents could speak with persons outside, and the other to be used as the caretaker's cottage. In addition there was a garage for the cars used for internal transportation in the park; the magnificent stairway; the market place with its pseudo-Doric columns; the upper plaza, called the Greek Theater, to be used for festivals and open-air shows; a tiny hill where the community's church was to have been placed; stairs, access passages, and retaining walls to maintain multiple levels—all resolved in a structurally logical manner within the new esthetic created by Gaudí; an ingenious drainage systeme for the great plaza, involving ground absorption and conduits leading to a 1,200 cubic meter cistern where the water was made available for irrigation and other daily needs; there also was a system for pumping highly potable magnesium water to the surface for drinking; and finally, the surrounding wall which lent protection and security to the enclosure. All of these aspects of the park will be studied further in another chapter (XLVII - 189).

Here we should mention the planning of the blocks, which were divided into triangular lots, each having an area of 30,000 to 35,000 palms, of which only a sixth part was buildable, with the rest to be used as garden.

The elevation of the buildings was limited by ideal planes at 45 degrees inclination from the outside property boundaries. These boundaries could be outlined in masonry walls up to 40 centimeters in height, topped by open metal fences to maintain the feeling of one single garden.[9]

It is clear that here we are dealing with a complete urbanization plan in which numerous details were foreseen and the majority carried out, establishing Gaudí's position as an urban planner. But the most admirable part of this development as far as structure and esthetics are concerned is the manner by which these details were harmoniously realized in collaboration with the existing geological elements and vegetation, leading to extremely original and surprising artistic groupings.

9. The majority of the informative details on this park come from S. Sellés y Baró who it is assumed must have obtained them from Gaudí himself.

XXXI. GAUDÍ AND MUSIC

138. MORE FEELING THAN TECHNIQUE (Figs. 166, 167)

Before beginning, let us state clearly that music did not figure among the techniques mastered by Gaudí. Given the economic limitation of his parents, it is very probable that he did not even take singing lessons—one of the current «ornamental» studies for children of his day. We cannot attribute to our architect even an average standing among musicians no matter how far we stretch that classification, as he was neither a composer nor played an instrument; but we can—in fact we must—attribute to him a place as collaborator in and visionary force behind one of the most grandiose musical projects ever imagined which, had it become a reality, would have aroused general admiration and wonder.

Gaudí was more a man of space than of time. He had more feeling for the plastic arts than for literature and music, which does not mean that he did not possess refinement and cultural preparation in these two fields as well. We know from his fellow student J. Bassegoda that in his early years in Barcelona he did not often go to the theater but that he did often attend concerts and that he enjoyed hearing the *Misa del Gallo* (Christmas Eve Mass) at the cathedral with the music of Vilanova which he later criticized.[1] In his first years out of school he used to attend the opera at the Liceo,[2] but according to the musicologist Rev. Baldelló, who was a friend of the architect, this seems to have been more due to social obligations as a man of the world than to his affection for the music. In later years he did not even attend the concerts of the popular Municipal Band with any regularity, nor those of the Orfeó Català, despite his friendship and admiration for the director Luis Millet.[3] Deep inside he must have lamented this complacence, for he only attended the highly outstanding musical events. Though Gaudí did not consider himself to be musical, Rev. Baldelló tells us that he acquired valuable ideas from Gaudí whose intuition involved things about musical esthetics not to be learned in books.

Gaudí did have his musical ideas. On principle he found all of the art of the north to be cold, inexpressive, and lacking in light. Not even Bach escaped this prejudice, and he even blamed him for the part his chorales played in the Protestant Reformation. *The Seasons* left him indifferent, and he said that *The Wine Song* was one of drunkards compared to *La Verema* (The Vintage) of Clavé which he found to be more serene and balanced. When he heard Bach's *Passion According to St. Matthew* performed he was unenthusiastic, but left with an intense impression of mysticism, especially from the chorales and recitatives. The organist Schweitzer who had played that concert later visited the Sagrada Familia with Millet. When he asked Gaudí his opinion of the concert the response was favorable; but Gaudí attributed his pleasure to the fact that the director and his choral group had been able to infuse the music of Bach with the unique light of the Mediterranean. Schweitzer found this to be an ingenious observation.

The architect usually did attend the outstanding performances of the Orfeó Català such as the one just mentioned, and he considered choirs of human voices in a category superior to that of orchestras made up of instruments. We can recall his part in encouraging the children's choirs at the time of the Constantinian Festivities (XXIII - 102). Although he maintained that vision is the sense which perceives Glory, he did allow song as its aid.

When the Orfeó asked him to participate in the autograph album which it compiled in 1922, he acquiesced, his natural dislike for such activities being overruled by the affection which he felt toward the group and its director. On the page reserved for him he wrote «Al Cel tots en serem d'orfeonistes» (In Heaven we shall all be Orpheonists) with the date—St. Peter's Day 1922—and the signature A. Gaudí. To provide adequate [artistic] elaboration he had his assistant Quintana do a drawing of the legend of Orpheus which was completed in color by J. M. Jujol; the album is carefully preserved by the choral group which has granted us permission to reproduce the sheet (Fig. 166).

Gaudí did not enjoy classical polyphony such as that presented by the Sistine Chapel Choir from Rome in three concerts in May 1921 at the Palau de la Música Catalana for the simple reason that he could not apply it to the architecture of the Sagrada Familia.

He had no faith in works realized without effort, and this criterion carried over into the field of music. He once said that «musical *impromptus* are a lie; one does not improvise.» [4]

139. SPACE AND TIME

Architecture and Music are the arts of space and time respectively; each acts within its own medium in a manner similar to the other, with both depending on the same basic principles

1. Lluís Bonet Garí, «L'Espiritualitat en l'obra de Gaudi,» *Critèrion*, N.º 23, p. 42.
2. Ráfols, *op. cit.*, p. 24.
3. Rev. Francisco Baldelló, «Gaudi, músico,» lecture at the Centro de Estudios Gaudinistas. Since this book went to press, the content of the lecture has come out in the volumen *Petites biografies de grans barcelonins* by the Rev. Baldelló.
4. Bergós, *op. cit.*, p. 37.

166. Page, from the *Orfeó Cata-là* album, written and supervised by Gaudí in collaboration with the architects Jujol and Quintana.

of serenity, movement, composition, harmony, rhythm. It could be said that architecture is the music of space and music the architecture of time. Even dimension influences both in a similar manner. When amplified, the small pyramidal form which serves as a paperweight acquires the magnificence of the Pharaonic tombs. A light, intranscendental melody gains solemnity when amplified in scale. Puig Boada has said that «if we were to establish a parallel in music, we would have to situate Gaudí closer to Beethoven than to Wagner,» [5] and Rev. Baldelló adds that «all of his architectural composition is based on a freedom of rhythm, on a graceful alternation of binary and ternary cadences which do not obey the laws of isochronal rhythm (as we have seen in the preceding chapter). All of his architecture, especially the religious, reminds us of the perfect form of the Gregorian chant. The curves of the liturgical melody become living stone in the walls and the towers of the temple. That *Sanctus, Sanctus, Sanctus...* arranged in ascending progression passes through our eyes to resound silently in our ears as a melody sung in the liturgical service.» By using such procedures he was able to incorporate music into his architecture without ever having recourse to symbolical musical instruments, except in the case of the herald angels' trumpets.

The music for which he had the strongest feeling and which most took root in his spirit was the Gregorian chant with which he became acquainted in his last years; this was the music which seemed to fit most appropriately the liturgy which he imagined for his Temple. When Father Gregorio M. Sunyol gave lessons on the Gregorian chant in 1916 Gaudí attended them all—as he himself put it, in order to «learn architecture.» Music for him was the human voice, and above all childrens' voices with their heightened emotional quality. For this reason he had carefully worked out the best possible arrangement for liturgical chants, in designing the Sagrada Familia. The presbytery contained a section reserved for the priests and the people around to take part in the singing, thus integrating the very meaning of the Church; the men were separated from the boys, and in a separate gynaeceum were the women, with all sections enjoying the finest of acoustic conditions.

140. ACOUSTICAL STUDIES

Gaudí had taken physical—as opposed to musical—acoustical considerations into account from the time he built the Palacio Güell. Here the organ was the object of special study as it was to be situated in a very narrow space in the central salon, next to the altar which could be easily opened up into it. This organ was used both for religious functions and society concerts, and the space allotted it had room for the keyboard console and the register, but not for the pipes, which are an essential part of such instruments. Gaudí solved this problem

5. *El Templo de la Sagrada Familia,* 1952, pp, 91-92.

167. Picture of those attending the Advanced Course in Gregorian Chants taught by Father Gregorio M. Sunyol in 1916. Seated in first row: Rev. J. Masvidal, Luis Millet, Fr. G. M. Sunyol, Rev. F. Baldelló, Rev. J. Cogul; second row: Srta. Montserrat Guiu, Rev. C. Galadies, Rev. H. Anglés, Rev. C. Sabater, Rev. A. Batlle, J. de Moragas, A. Gaudí, P. J. Teixidor, J. Barberá, V. de Moragas, A. Capmany; third row: Rev. Raich, Rev. Pujol, Julita Farnés, Rev. J. Colomer, V. M. de Gibert, F. Pujol, E. Daniel, Cumellas Ribó, F. Figueras.

by placing the pipe tubes in the salon arcade which proved to be acoustically advantageous, for when singers were used they, too, were placed on the upper floor.

The success of Gaudí's solution is corroborated by the expert opinion of the specialist «Noemis,» writing in a publication on electric organs; in dealing with the Güell palace he writes that in the upper arches of the salon «they have placed the sweetly pleasant sounding Koulen bombardons in a manner which calls attention to the great 16-foot sounding pipes which have been arranged with the greatest taste and originality by said architect [Gaudí]. All of these pipes respond marvelously, even in the most rapid passages, despite the fact that the artist plays them from a great distance and despite the extremely surprising and strange distribution as arranged by the artist.»[6]

The music critic Gibert says that in this cupola Gaudí realized the idea which Wagner set forth in Parsifal of joining music with architecture, and he sums it up by saying that «it was Gaudí who built the dome of Montsalvat.»[7]

Gaudí developed his musical sentiments most fully in the bell towers of the temple which he conceived as a magnificent three-part instrument which would broadcast music throughout the city and would accompany certain liturgical ceremonies and processions outside of the temple. He planned to have three types of bells: the ordinary ones, tuned to the notes E, G, and C—most easily obtained in such bells—and others which would contain all of the notes of the scale and would be tubular; of this second kind some would be played by percussion and others would be sounded by injecting air. The first would sound like a piano and the second more like a reed organ. It was his contention that the piano only plays, whereas the reed organ sings and comes much closer to the word. The tubular bells, some 84 in number, would be fixed in the bell towers and would be sounded by electrically activated hammers controlled by a keyboard, or by a system of compressed air.

Once Gaudí had invented this musical program for his bell towers, he realized that he would have to confront complex technical problems in the fabrication and tuning of the bells. As was his custom, he proceeded to document his work with studies already carried out in the field but he was unable to find anything of use in the published literature. Therefore he decided to analyze the problem for himself.[8]

141. TUBULAR BELLS (Figs. 168, 169)

Gaudí observed that bells consist of two geometric parts: one, the hyperbolic part, gives it its characteristic appearance, and the other, the spherical, is the helmet which encloses its upper part. Each of these parts produces its own particular sound. From afar, that of the helmet is lost, but it serves to enhance the clarity of the dominant sound. Actually, the hyperbolic form is not a true one because designs using circular arcs similar to the hyprbola were developed to simplify the procedures of bell-making and to adapt then to the abilities of the workers.

Ordinary bells cannot be tuned to pitch and must be constantly checked while they are being turned and accordingly shortened or increased in interior diameter, thus becoming more slen-

6. Noemis, Organos eléctricos, p. 92.

7. Vicente M. de Gibert, «Gaudí, músico potencial,» La Vanguardia, (June 17, 1926).

8. In his research he availed himself of a foreign library service. This is explained in greater detail in my book, Conversaciones con Gaudí..., p. 62.

168. Tubes with which he tried out the sound of the percussive bells. Detail of Fig. 107.

169. Hammer which he used to strike the tubes.

der and apt to crack. We have already seen how he explained the cause and effect of deterioration in bells (XXI - 91). It was for this reason that he resolved the problem by giving the bells a tubular form which allows for easier tuning and the maintenance of a geometrically hyperbolical form engendered by extremely open hyperbolas whose asymptotes form a seven-degree angle which Gaudí felt to have advantageous tangential properties.[9]

The day that he explained all this to me he was trying out two tubes in a reduced scale model of the bells: the diameter and longitude of one were double that of the other and produced the same note at a one- or two-octave interval. He struck them with two small hammers of known weight, made from coins of ten and two céntimos. An assistant played notes on a reed organ to confirm the sounds. Gaudí showed me the tube with which he carried out his experiments and the little book in which he had taken down the results, listing each note obtained along with its appropriate flats or sharps, as determined by using different instruments (pipes lent by the Liceo, a reed organ, violin, etc.) to approximate the results.

The master spoke of the diverse sounds simultaneously perceived in a single chime or blow of the tuning fork where numerous secondary tones, difficult to distinguish, follow the principal one. As a general rule, he told me, the principal sound in the high notes is the low one, and in the low notes, the high; in unattuned ears the principal and secondary sounds can become confused.

Gaudí was very familiar with these phenomena. He added that the very high pitches, as well as the very lowest ones, are difficult to perceive because they approach those vibrations which the ear has trouble capturing. To enhance the appreciation of these extreme sounds, the masters of the organ accompanied them with the same note one or two octaves higher or lower, depending on the situation, augmenting by this simultaneity the audibility of the note.

The complete hyperbolic tube with two open ends gives two different notes when struck because of the different density of the metal produced between the upper and lower end in the casting process. In addition, if the tube is not placed horizontally but is rather vertical or inclined, the vibration of the upper part is more prolonged than the lower one because the force of gravity attracts and contains all that faces downward; on the other hand, the duration of the upper vibrations is favored by their oscillating position. From these facts Gaudí deduced that it would be preferable for the bell tubes to be semi-hyperbolic and face upward. The hammer would strike by a spring mechanism which would ideally recoil immediately from the bell surface.

They experimented with using less bronze in the bells and were successful in producing a better tone in the process. Then they placed one of the small-scale bells in one of the bell towers, all of which were built completely hollow to house the long tubes.[10] It was calculated that the bass F bell would be 20 meters long[11]; it and the rest of the fixed bells which were to be struck by electrically activated hammers would broadcast their sounds to the city by means of the inclined soundingboards which perforate the towers. The Nativity façade towers were to hold the tubular bells which we have discussed. Those of the Passion would house the pipe-like tubes resembling those of a grandiose organ. The principal façade would contain the regular bells in various sizes and tones.

Gaudí spent several years refining these studies, consulting those experts whom he believed could enlighten him on certain points. One such specialist was the maestro Francisco Pujols, the second director of the Orfeó Català, whom he consulted on numerous occasions,[12] and also the industrial metallurgist Miguel Carreras,[13] whose help he sought in order to furnish the temple with grandiose musical effect. The bells of the Sagrada Familia would, of course, have served for the usual chiming of the hours, holidays, or deaths, but they would have attained maximum splendor in disseminating magnificent concerts throughout the city —concerts which Gaudí spoke of with warm words and visionary anticipation, describing his dreams for the future.

His friend the conductor Millet has recorded his impressions of one such conversation in which the prophecy took on life-like proportions as the architect expressed it: «Standing at his side I listened silently and attentively, taking in every word along with every sparkle of those tiny eyes—the most penetrating that I had ever seen... He spoke of the immensely tall interior galleries of the temple designed for the use of future confraternities, with room for a brotherhood of ten thousand. He said: 'These galleries would open onto the exterior. Imagine, imagine: for the high religious festivals, processions will approach along the great avenues of the future city, and the harmony of ten thousand voices (for by then popular religious singing will have emerged victorious and every confraternity member will be a singer) will reverberate through the air from the exterior galleries, justly and gloriously as accompaniment to the psalmody of the good brothers.' Oh, the poetic vision of the great artist! How he moved those who listened to him! What pleasure he awakened with his precise and luminous words, with his refulgent and unwavering faith which would burst into a wrathful flame at the slightest contradictory observation.»[14]

9. Told to me by Gaudí himself, Ibid., pp. 59-62.

10. This tubular bell was not exactly hyperbolic. It had been commissioned by an enthusiast and supporter of the idea from whom Gaudí borrowed it for these experiments, Ibid., p. 63.

11. Puig Boada, op. cit., p. 126.

12. Lluís Millet, «Antoni Gaudí,» (Obituary), Revista musical catalana, (May-July, 1926).

13. Rev. Baldelló, Petites biografies de grans barcelonins, p. 82.

14. Lluís Millet, op. cit.

It would at first seem that it would be more difficult to connect literature and architecture than it was to relate music in the last chapter. Although he loved good literature, Gaudí did not like to show his admiration for men of letters, and at times he spoke unfavorably of certain literary displays. Nevertheless, he was the complete artist, and the present study of his esthetic theory would be incomplete without reference to the influence of literature on him and on his most famous work.

142. AN ASSIDUOUS READER (Figs. 170 - 172)

From his earliest years Gaudí showed singular erudition as far as architectural literature is concerned. Even if we did not know from his own statements the excitement with which he awaited the new acquisitions of the library at the School of Architecture, and his careful reading and marginal annotations in his copy of the *Dictionnaire* of Viollet-le-Duc (VI - 17), his knowledge would be apparent in the «Notes on Ornamentation» where he shows an extraordinary acquaintance with art history; this is true also of the «Memorial» which accompanied his project of lampposts for the Plaza Real. In both documents he supports his ideas with principles taken from his extensive reading.

He was not only attracted by technical and esthetic writings, but also by books of history, general culture, and the literary classics which he had enjoyed since his youth along with his taste for dramatic performances and the opera.

We know of his literary inclinations from Arturo Masriera who knew Gaudí in his student days (1876) and refers to him as a «man of letters of extremely exquisite taste, educated at Ixart's side and his inseparable companion, an insatiable reader of the classics of all ages and nations.»[1] In spite of this laudatory evidence, Gaudí did not generally show off his literary erudition or sensibilities except in occasional allusions to the classics when the conversation suggested it. At times I heard him make lucid comments on Shakespeare's *Hamlet* and its fantastic apparitions born of the northern mists in comparing it to the Mediterranean clarity and realism of the Greek tragedies.

All in all, it does not seem that he ever possessed a personal library commensurate with his affinity for reading. In addition to the School library he was a devotee of the reading room at the Barcelona Ateneo where we have seen that he made friends with the bibliophile and bookdealer Palau Dulcet; in spite of their good relationship, it seems that Gaudí did not usually buy books from him.[2]

The books in Gaudí's studio at the Sagrada Familia during the last years in which I knew and visited him there with some frequency scarcely constituted a library: rather, there were a few modest bookshelves with a discreet number of volumes, among which were the *Ceremonial de Obispos* and Father Prospère Gueranger's *L'Année Liturgique*—his guides in liturgical and even esthetic matters in the building of the Temple—as well as religious books which he read regularly. He also had books by his favorite authors of the Catalan literary movement and he subscribed to the *Clàssics Grecs i Llatins* collection which had been begun around 1923 by the «Fundació Cambó». An unexpected title was *Ripios Aristocráticos* by Antonio de Valbuena, a quasi-burlesque anti-aristocratic satire with poetic pretensions published at the end of the last century,[3] whose very presence in his tiny library constitutes a proof of his avidity as a reader. In the year 1915, the artist Luis Bracons designed a bookplate for him, but I don't believe that he ever used it.

Conscientious and reflective as Gaudí was in general, there can be no doubt that he was solidly educated in technical, scholarly, and literary matters. The first two are clearly apparent in his architectural works and were also evident in his conversation; as for the third which he chose to conceal, we have eloquent testimony in the superlatives used by his friend the poet and critic Masriera in describing him as a «man of letters of extremely exquisite taste.» Perhaps it was because of this solid formation that he judged so severely certain literary displays and that he would sometimes employ the word «literati» in a pejorative sense, referring to those who put their writing at the service of personal ambition more than at the service of culture. Of such persons he said that their purpose in writing books was to climb up on top of them, as on a footstool, in order to reach things unreachable by any other means. For Gaudí only good things were valid, and for him personally literature only counted as an esthetic diversion or as an element to enrich and unify his plastic conceptions.

143. A CARELESS WRITER

Such discrimination against the literary field was intuitive with him. Even as an adolescent, his friends Toda and Ribera, who cultivated literary romanticism, could never get Gaudí to write a

170. An *ex libris* for Gaudí designed by Luis Bracons.

1. Arturo Masriera, «De mi rebotica,» *La Vanguardia*, (June 19, 1914).
2. Told to me by Juan Matamala.
3. Item provided by the architect Quintana.

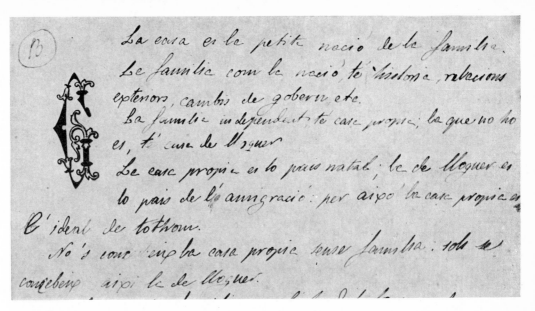

171. Portion of the manuscript on the *casa pairal*.

single line (III-7). From this came his fame as an «anti-literate,» which he himself fomented. This passive attitude toward literary activity reveals that of all that he had learned, there was nothing that he felt he had to say with the pen. He was a faithful learner, but once the teachings were assimilated he felt it fruitless to repeat them in writing; he did not, however, refuse to include them in his work after revising what he had learned, thus converting them into architecture. He himself told me that he «never wrote anything.» [4] He wrote very few letters, and the style though clear in concept is much too overblown in its expression. He had the ability and sensitivity of a writer but not the discipline necessary to translate his ideas into words and to subject them to a determined order.

Nevertheless, we know of three manuscripts written when he was about 24 years old which reveal a certain enjoyment of writing. The most extensive of these is the «Notes» which we have discussed and which, in spite of their stylistic and methodological faults, show interest in expressing his ideas in didactic form. When he was 62, I heard him say that he did not feel himself capable of preparing a lecture. [5] Nevertheless, in his youth he had sufficient perseverance to prepare the «Notes» with one, or perhaps even two, rough drafts, judging from the absence of corrections observed in the final manuscript. It is lacking in literary value, but the significance is in the dedication that it implies in his writing a 67-page treatise in the course of which, however, perhaps because of weariness, the concepts lose clarity or remain quite sketchy—as he himself admitted.

Another document which serves us in this respect is the memorandum submitted to the Mayor of Barcelona along with the lamppost project for the Plaza Real which he entitled «Descriptive Notes on the Project.» In these notes, perhaps because they were directed to the highest municipal authority, we can observe a more careful style, including some of the traditional bureaucratic phraseology, in which he sets forth clearly the historic-urbanistic, technical, and economic facts on which he draws in the document.

Neither of these two manuscripts, both written in Spanish, reveals any literary intent, but rather a desire for descriptive effectiveness which was more successful in the second; but there exists a third manuscript written in Catalan, not previously published (App. V), where we can perceive a literary sensibility not found in the earlier ones. It is a commentary on the *casa pairal* which he portrays as the home and the continuance of family traditions which are linked to the hygienic and social conditions of the residence. In describing the traditional *casa* he is carried away by an intimate feeling for family life. At one point, won over by a sort of twilight poetry, he imagines young maidens in the garden next to the street leaning over the openwork railing and «supporting their arms on it to watch the passers-by.» The evocation of this very natural feminine curiosity was not exactly what he wanted, and later he crossed out the words indicated here in quotes (they nevertheless remain legible) to continue the description of a stairway «from the top of which we discover the garden and there, among the foliage of the poplars and the plane trees, stands the house.»

In spite of the precision, and at times the bluntness, of his judgments, Gaudí's emotions were easily stirred. We have seen his eyes moisten with tenderness, and in his explanations he would mix poetry with scientific concepts in such a way that, had it been faithfully recorded, it would have definitive literary value. But the architect was not comfortable with the pen. It was not his way. Instead he talked; he talked a lot, clearly and effectively. And his conversation was warm with truth and feeling—a sort of spoken literature with impressive plastic force.

4. Martinell, *op. cit.*, pp. 77-78. But see note on p. 44. — G. R. C.
5. *Ibid.*, p. 26.

172. Tympanum of the central portal of the Nativity façade with the inscription «Gloria in Excelsis Deo...»

I remember the real and graphic description which he gave me of the marvelous future Temple in my last conversation with him. The effect was the same as that which the maestro Millet described in the passage transcribed at the end of our last chapter.

144. THE TEMPLE AS A POEM

In the two preceding sections we have seen that Gaudí was fond of reading, but not at all of writing. Given his sense of observation, his facility for synthesis, and his communicative character, this situation must have produced some sort of spiritual pressure or an expansive drive which impelled him otherwise to externalize his ideas of synthesis obtained through reading, observation of nature, and reflection. Had he felt the vocation of writer there can be no doubt that he would have left beautiful and profound thoughts on paper, but he did not choose to do so. The vacillating and tentative pages which he did leave us, in spite of their importance due to their very rarity, are not really a fair indication of what he might have written.

The repeatedly cited «Notes on Ornamentation» are, as we have said, nothing but an attempt at didactic literature; those entitled «Descriptive Notes on the Project,» are more an example of what we could call «administrative» literature; and the brief essay on «La Casa Pairal,» his most purely literary piece, fits in this category more for its sentiment than for its style. We do not know of any other noteworthy productions from his pen, but it is obvious from his conversation that he was not lacking in novel ideas. His words were always «edifying» to those who listened, and though they were never written out, their force was so persuasive that they were never forgotten.

So Gaudí was not destined to be a writer. His vocation was exclusively that of the architect which he pursued in an impassioned way, subordinating to it all of his other activities. He did not feel any need to translate the impressions and information received through reading into new literary forms, but these did influence his work as an architect, which he was fond of enriching with concepts borrowed from literature, so as to give it an elevated tone without subverting his original architectonic conception. In two early works, the Obrera Mataronense and the Casa Vicens, he decorated the living rooms with socially significant inscriptions. In the forged iron pinnacle of the Güell palace he alludes to the legend of Jaime I's conquest of Valencia, and on the lateral wall he depicts an episode of Verdaguer's *Atlántida;* in a more subtle manner, the simple vertical lines of the stones speak to us of the austerity and nobility of the owner. In his evocation of feudalism at the white Episcopal palace at Astorga, Gaudí sought to represent the purity and spiritual authority of the prelate; the house at Bellesguard was an homage of the earth itself to the last king of Barcelonan lineage who had his residence there, as well as to the elevation of the cross. All of this was done in a moderate but effective tone which subtly and unconsciously affects the observer and gives character to each building.

We have seen that the Sagrada Familia commission had a strong impact on the architect's professional and religious life. In this work he was able to unify the temple's grandiosity with the truths of faith, to which he hoped to give plastic form. The things which had most strongly impressed him in his readings and literary searchings took on new life in the shelter of the Expiatory Temple. Technical, historical, and liturgical texts and book of a mystic, hagiographic, or evangelic nature inflamed his spirit with religious-esthetic emotion, and he thought of nothing else but converting this emotion into stone—for the glory of God and the salvation of mankind. He was determined to use all resources at his command, including those of a literary nature, in order to intensify the religious impact. He wanted the temple to come alive and yet to maintain a humble character which would reflect spiritual light. For this reason he not only used representational scenes, but also conveniently placed inscriptions and legends, as well as electric reflectors, and he planned to include a jet of natural water and a torch of flames in the Gloria façade.

Gaudí was not awed by this grandiose vision which incorporated literature into architecture in a manner uncommon at that time. In Romanesque cloisters we find symbolic representations of man caught between vice and virtue as well as biblical scenes; Gothic temples display gargoyles in the form of monsters which represented sin and were therefore left outside by the artists; in the apse of the Sagrada Familia, Gaudí picked up this tradition in the snakes and reptiles which flee the radiance of the cross which will triumph in heaven. Gaudí went far beyond the symbolic-descriptive representations which he had theorized upon in his «Notes» and he converted the holy images, which he had criticized as beings only «an excuse to put up a pedestal or a little ornamented dais...,» into characters of the great poem which seethed in his mind. He paid no heed to the traditional ways, crippled in his day, wherein «religious nature is a bit indecisive... [and] religious objects are the slaves of a profane idea—art,» and he threw himself into the task of correcting the deficiency which he had observed that «those who make temples do not insist that they contain those characteristics proper to a terrible God who sacrifices himself for his creation, that they be mansions for the Omnipotence of the thousands of millions of solar systems, nor do they make the object that of achieving in an elevated manner which is the bloodless Sacrifice..»

Gaudí sought to convert his lament that «religious objects are the slaves of a profane idea —art,» into a victorious cry by which the architecture and every artistic detail of the new temple would, in addition to serving the liturgical needs of the services, be converted into a religious canticle—part of a great poem which would synthesize the truths and the great variety of faith; a poem in stone of imposing magnitude which would house the saving sacraments of Humanity, with each façade composed as a song to the life and glory of the Saviour. Each episode depicted was a stanza, and each detail, a verse of the grandiose poem; at times he engraved it in letters as an outlet for what little pure literary sediment still remained within his spirit.

Gaudí himself seemed to foresee this architectonic-literary dependence early in his career when he wrote: «Ornamentation is only a part [of the whole]: although essential in order to give character, it is, nevertheless, nothing more than the meter and rhythm of the poetry. A concept is expressed in many ways, but it becomes obscure and distilled when we introduce, willy-nilly, obligatory accesories which attack good intelligence and reason.»

He kept such literary parallels in mind in his architecture; despite the ornamental profusion of the artistic language employed in the Nativity façade, the characters are arranged to relate to frankly literary themes, and the composition of the masses is subjected to an overall rhythm and series of cadences suited to the subject matter. Using the same poetic nomenclature as he did in his «Notes,» we could say that he employed a smooth and optimistic poetic meter in the Nativity façade whereas that of the Passion became angular and pathetic in his plans. For the principal façade dedicated to the Glory of God, he envisioned a composition of grandiose cadences and rhythms, and at the summit of each of the temple's towers a luminous cross would reign triumphant as the symbol and content of the religion.

Such was the great poem that he conceived to be perpetuated as «petrified literature.» Gaudí's creative genius steered him clear of the pitfalls involved in mixing the literary and plastic arts. He was only able to execute the first canto of his magnificent vision, but even in this fragment—lacking still its polychrome finish—we can perceive the power of the decorative use of forms clearly inspired in literature. This novel solution was to become an important element in the evolution of Catalan architecture during the first quarter of the present century.

XXXIII. THE GENESIS OF A WORK OF ART

In the preceding chapters we have examined the principal theoretical motives behind Gaudí's art. In Part One we saw the events in his life as they affected his personality and character. It was from a combination of the theoretical and the personal that his work was produced. In his years of adolescence, of scholastic maturity, and in the initial professional years as well, certain characteristics appeared—some in a frank manner, others in seminal form—which would regulate his later life together with circumstantial factors which would determine how strongly he adhered to the theories we have mentioned. In all circumstances he would act with characteristic vitality and dynamism, and there was always a certain temperamental tension, coiled and ready to spring.

145. CREATIVE FORCES:

PASSION, GENIUS, FAITH, AND OPTIMISM. The basic source of Gaudí's creative activity was passion—a warm, decisive passion guided by faith and an ideal of beauty which encompassed small details as well as great works of art. His spirit was kindled by the flames of art and religion.

As we have seen, this passion was momentarily detoured along the sterile paths of human love, only to return resolutely to his double ideal. The struggles and contradictions involved in his first steps were all temperamental reactions originating in passion, as was the case with his characteristic stubbornness and impetuosiy in later years, perhaps born in part, of that unsatisfied amorous detour.

Passion is dynamism—the motor which drives the vehicle just as intelligence is the wheel which steers it. Gaudí was aware of his passionate temperament, and he valued it for its dynamic qualities while he feared it for its uncontrollability. Once, speaking of politicians, he said that they should be passionate men, but that in order to use passion to an advantage one had to know how to dominate it. A good politician must assume the leadership of his party and carry it to victory over the opposition. A person who cannot control his own party, and much less himself, will not be able to dominate the opposition. Gaudí ended the commentary by saying that throughout his lifetime he had made an effort to dominate his own character; usually he was successful, but at times the character was more clever than he.[1]

Gaudí's intelligence was so highly developed that we must call it *genius*; his technical and artistic solutions went beyond the current norms and were far ahead of his time. Later I will insist upon his genius as an architect, but here I will limit myself to the manner in which the sparks of genius influenced his character.

Gaudí was a modest man, opposed to awards and special attention, and his status as a genius superior to most men must have bothered him more than anything. Whenever he discovered an ingenious architectural solution with implications for the future he was more worried by the grave responsibility involved in such an unexpected advance than proud of it. In practical details, the great gap between his genial intuition and the everyday level of intelligence often caused him uncomfortable friction.

His privileged imagination and talent, moved by passion, led the genius to break the molds established by tradition. His works, out of scale in space and time, caused wonder, stupor, and controversy. But the genius is uncontrollable; his works are subtly based in reflection and calculation, but they appear to be intuitive and spontaneous. The grandiosity dictated by Gaudí's genius was sometimes offset, however, by the fact that it could not be carried out in reality and was therefore often left open to criticism as being unfinished work.

We have spoken of Gaudí's early religious indifference and of his dormant faith which was providentially awakened to become the most influential factor in his life. With his early crisis over, the theme of *faith* became foremost in his career, in conjunction with his architecture, and each reinforced the other.

I would like to mention yet another temperamental element—less important than those already cited—which influenced his life; this was the *optimism* which always gave a stability to his activities. He used to say that great undertakings are impossible without optimism, and even when his beloved Sagrada Familia project was about to be paralyzed because of economic difficulties, he did not fall into the depression that might be expected; his optimism showed him the advantageous side of this situation, which actually gave him additional time to work out certain structural problems and to solve them in a more perfect way.

---

1. Martinell, *op. cit.*, p. 17.

146. MODERATING ELEMENTS:

CLEAR-SIGHTEDNESS, PRUDENCE, REVISIONISM. Gaudí's character included certain moderating elements which contributed to his heightened creativity. One of these was his *clear-sightedness* or clarity of judgment which illuminated the professional aspects of his life and even the personal ones. Especially in those apparently insignificant details which are so susceptible to improvidence, his depth and precision of judgment were astounding. And of course his precision and profundity were even more pointed in transcendental cases.

Born of this clarity was the *prudence* which he practiced not only as a cardinal virtue but also as a way of life which helped him to foresee and avoid possible difficulties in the future. With the aid of prudence he was able to control and moderate the impulses of his passionate genius before carrying them into practice, and thus to avoid unfortunate consequences.

Another result of Gaudí's clear-sightedness was the development of his keen critical sensitivity. This in turn led to the *revisionism* which impelled him to revise all that was revisable, beginning with the historic architectural styles. While it is true that he made use of these styles, they did not serve him as a source of inspiration but rather as a regulatory norm providing the continuity and the guarantee of tradition after critical revision. Similarly rigorous criteria were later applied to his own original creations which he analyzed carefully and minutely before building them.

147. ESTHETIC IDEALS:

BEAUTY, GOODNESS, EXEMPLARINESS. The most coveted goal, and that which summarized all of Gaudí's artistic theories, was the creation of *beauty*. Light, color, and spatial qualities were valued as sources of beauty, and he saw them as his vocation. Every commission that he received inflamed his imagination to greater brilliance. His artistic ideas never obeyed profit motives, nor did they have erudition at their base, however much he may have made use of academic principles. Beauty was the goal in his life and his work and he sought to build things which were alive and linked to the society which they were to serve; in them he hoped to reach heights of perfection which would benefit his fellow men.

A moment arrived when his being was completely enveloped in mysticism, and beauty became only a relative end: something to awaken *goodness* through *exemplariness*. His very life was exemplary His conduct with friends, workers, and assistants (occasional intemperances notwithstanding) served as an edifying lesson in practical goodness.

148. IMPURITIES

UNPREDICTABLE SITUATIONS AND DIFFICULTIES. Gaudí's innate positive qualities and the spiritual potential which stimulated his creative ideas were menaced by a variety of perils, omissions, and a general nervousness. Most artistic ideals, pure and unadulterated in their conception, are contaminated when put into actual practice as a result of environmental, material, or technical problems.

The master's technical knowledge and his structural intuition removed some of these difficulties, and his fecund inspiration in these areas always offered an adequate solution. It was the environmental problems which he was least prepared to confront. His fervent involvement in every work he undertook gave a certain urgency to the work—an urgency which was perhaps prompted by the architect's authoritarian spirit, a sort of self-love, his lack of conformity to common practice, natural frictions of a personal type, and an unpredictable passion which could instantaneously eclipse his habitual moderation. A difficult client, bothersome bureaucratic red tape, or a worker unwilling to commit himself could exasperate the architect momentarily, but he was not long in regaining the composure with which he usually focused on his objective. He was, however, not always successful in attaining these objectives; this was not a sign of weakness, but rather of environmental difficulties which made perfection inaccessible. We will see several works which Gaudí could not complete because of situations which had nothing to do with him or with the works themselves. His vision of the artistic ideal was clear, and if he did not achieve it we must ask whether this was the result of personal failings or due to the excessive loftiness of the proposed ideal.

All works of art entail two creative processes—the conceptual and the physical. Gaudí was always able to resolve the first with firm, unvacillating ideas based on the essential study of the problem; in the physical creation he was just as firm so far as general lines and basic concepts, but he felt that an arbitrary firmness was detrimental to the flexibility necessary to achieve his architectonic conception. Enthusiasm for his work made him forget the recommendation expressed in his juvenile manuscript (IX-31) that projects should be made «realizable... economically speaking.» Discrepancies between budget and the means available cut short his participation in works such as the Teresan convent, the palace at Astorga, possibly the missions in Tangiers, the Güell colony church, the Casa Milá, and even the Sagrada Familia—works which, even without being complete, are impressive for their pure idealism and humanity: for the soul and body which give them life.

This lack of concern for budget was not a result of carelessness, but rather was the consequence of his elevated ideas of the architect's function. There came a moment in the creation of every work when his artistic ideals achieved such a level that the budget—which in his professional beginnings seemed of foremost importance—became only a secondary consideration.

Thus armed with his ideals — most of them positive, but others with their negative aspects — Gaudí battled his works and clients. He sought to control the first as far as possible. With the second this was often impossible and at times it was the clients who influenced him, helping to tame his indomitable spirit.

149.   A DESIRE FOR EXCELLENCE
150.   TALENT AND GENIUS
151.   AN ARCHITECTONIC SCHOOL

149.   A DESIRE FOR EXCELLENCE

If we accept Gaudí's view of life as guided by Providence, we must recognize the genius which lends value to his art as being a reward granted him for his desire for excellence that constantly impelled him to perfect his life and his work as an architect. His was an impassioned, sometimes dramatic, restlessness, reflected in his constant struggle to approach perfection. To approach, and nothing else, for he himself believed that perfection was not within the reach of man (XVI-61).

As we study the work of the master carefully, we can observe a constant ascent; at each successive level he would emerge with new resolution, to move onward to progressive excellence. Those solutions, which left the unprepared observers perplexed, were but small advances along his path—at first with inspiration as his guide, and later led by reflection. All of Gaudí's innovations had a potential for development comparable to the greater activity of chemical substances in their native state. Some of the problems which he so ably resolved were later carried further, to the point of becoming systematized, whereas others remained as mere potentialities.

150.   TALENT AND GENIUS

From his earliest works it was apparent that Gaudí was a talented architect with the touch of genius. It is the task of talent to perfect what is already known, and this is what he did in revising historical styles in an effort to improve them. In the eclectic environment which surrounded his entrance into the professional arena, an architect had the right to select the historic style which seemed most appropriate in each case, but not to interpret it: custom imposed respect for its canons. This produced a sterile and insincere art which the most talented architects fought to overcome, always limited by the stylistic barricades which prudent opinion considered indestructible.

Gaudí immediately stood out among these architects for his originality and daring solutions which were nevertheless well within the limits of his still-developing talents. But his restless spirit always promised him something more, and by dint of obsessive study and work his unique vision of architecture took shape. He had an ardent desire for infinity—as if his early esthetic theory regarding the radiance of Truth had been unintentionally directed toward the ideals of beauty and theology which were the guiding lights of his later years.

In his historical period and even later in his most personal stage the maestro was always pleased when he could find precedents for his creations which would prove their quality or shield him from charges of a vacuous quest for novelty.

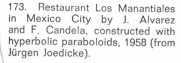

173.   Restaurant Los Manantiales in Mexico City by J. Alvarez and F. Candela, constructed with hyperbolic paraboloids, 1958 (from Jürgen Joedicke).

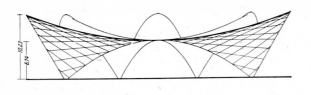

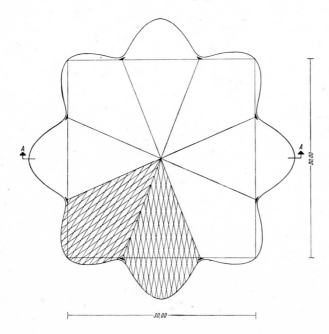

174. Plan and section of Fig. 173
(from Jürgen Joedicke).

Gaudí's genius first became apparent in his use of equilibrated structure, first in two- and later three-dimensional structures, where he resolved the chronic separation of mechanics and geometry by employing an ingenious method of funicular calculation. It was only logical that a new aesthetic with its accompanying forms and personal tectonics would be born as a result of these uncommonly novel and complex structures.

Assuming that talent perfects what is known, genius represents a leap into the future—it is ahead of its time. For this reason, the solutions of a genius often leave us perplexed, or are simply not to our liking since we are not prepared to understand them. Talent does not have to be original, but genius always is. El Greco was not understood in his time, and Philip II did without his services in decorating the Escorial because he did not like his painting of San Mauricio. Wagner had resolutely to battle musical opinion throughout Europe before his music could be accepted.

And so it was with Gaudí's architecture. The man on the street automatically asks what style it is in order to orient himself, and on finding that it does not correspond to any known style he remains disoriented, for he does not have the prerequisite knowledge necessary to enter into the new style and to be able to enjoy it. Apart from the fact that some people are somewhat pleased by it and others not at all, even the most ignorant feels the superiority of this architecture without understanding it; he does not exactly like it, but he does find it imposing in its content of the beyond.

The classification of Gaudí as a genius might seem to be subjective if it had not been demonstrated numerous times and accepted the world over. If necessary we could appeal to the test of time which has proved that his invention and work were well ahead of his time—and, as we have seen, this is an attribute of genius.

In 1878 Gaudí used parabolic arches in his project for Mataró, and then he employed them again in the Güell stables, a quarter of a century before Vierendeel published his calculations which showed them to be the most mechanically logical forms. Then he introduced spatially equilibrated structures in the model and crypt of the church for the Güell colony, and in the towers and models for the great Barcelona temple; such structures are frequently used today. The device which he planned to use to support the mushroom-shaped vaults of the Sagrada Familia where each column would support its part of the corresponding semi-hyperbolic reinforced concrete vaults was also a precedent for the future. We have seen that

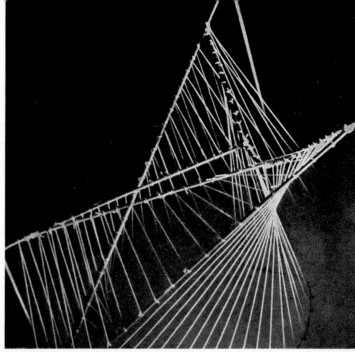

175. Phillips Pavilion for the Brussels World's Fair, 1958, by Le Corbusier (from *Le Poème Electronique, Le Corbusier*).

176. Metallic outline for the study of the pavilion (from *Le Poème Electronique, Le Corbusier*).

177. Large covered market in Cologne with equilibrated arches, by Theodor Teichen, 1937-39 (from Jürgen Joedicke).

178. Sports Palace in Rome with the cupola supported by inclined pillars following the lines of thrust, work of P. L. Nervi, 1957 (from Jürgen Joedicke).

employed patterns of color which can be classified as abstract in the Palacio Güell roof in the year 1889. The first declaredly abstract paintings were a Kandinsky water-color of 1910, and a Mondrian composition of 1911. Other examples of Gaudí's use of this sort of polychromy can be seen in the Güell stables, and were of course most fully developed in the park of the same name (1900-1914) still ahead of the surge of the abstract movement in painting.

Gaudí had been practicing the *functionalism* to which Le Corbusier gave status in 1923 from his earliest works; this becomes more apparent in the Casa Batlló with its stepped, subtly colored and tile-covered patio and its wide variety of functional window openings. Earlier, in León, and later in the Casa Milá, he distributed the apartments in an open manner, without bearing walls, in what would later come to be called the «flexible plan.» The underground stables which he employed in the Güell Palace were converted into garages in the Casa Milá before it was common to use the access ramps which have since become an almost indispensable element of all public garages.

This list of examples is only a sample, and could be amplified. It is the greatness of his work as a whole which impresses us more than the numerous innovative details. Fruition came after a long gestation period warmed in the light of optimism. His work is indifferent to and does not resemble anything around it, as it follows the ascending path of greater perfection toward the infinite; the Sagrada Familia towers were not the summit in the architect's mind, but only a step on which to elevate the highest peak of the luminous cross which would surmount his temple. There on high, ever upward, *Excelsior*, the architectural genius planned to unite his ideals of faith and art as a legacy for ages to come.

151.   AN ARCHITECTONIC SCHOOL (Figs. 173 - 178)

The characteristics discussed in the preceding chapters—*esthetic theory; equilibrated structures; decorative theory; geometric rhythms; synthetic spirit; stone textures; iron, wood, and ceramic ornamentation; the expressive use of space, plasticity, color, and light*—constitute the systems and principles of a school of Gaudinian architecture which exists despite the lack of any organized co-ordination.[1]

The inimitable originality of Gaudí would seem to belie the possibility of a school of followers; but when we consider that architecture, however unique and daring it may be, must meet practical requirements of *geometry, mechanics,* and *structure,* we can understand that, once known, these elements can be applied in the elaboration of new works which will necessarily be related to the works in which they were introduced.

Despite the fact that Gaudí did not publish his architectonic ideas and that many were never put into practice, it would not be difficult to compile an abundant inventory of Gaudinist principles which were later applied by followers of the master with great success. It was these followers, unassociated though they were, who make up the Gaudinist school. Some such works may have been created without direct influence from Gaudí, i.e., without any direct cause and effect relationship; but by the very fact of their existence, these related principles and forms give life to the school. Candela in Mexico with his paraboloid roofs; Le Corbusier and Vago in France with their parabolic surfaces and equilibrated arches; Nervi in Italy with his inclined supports; the legion of bridges throughout the world constructed with parabolic arches: all of these clearly show how the structural ideas first practiced by our architect, years ahead of his time, have proliferated.

Careful observation of the most characteristic elements of architecture of today based on new mechanical standards and on the systematic use of warped surfaces convinces us that such innovations have a common link which is essentially a school of Gaudinian principles which the master practiced or established in model form—in studies that were to be executed in more modern techniques foreseen by Gaudí and which he himself planned to adopt in his unfinished work.[2]

1. Martinell, «Escuela de Gaudinismo,» *Revista Gran Vía,* N.º 450 (November 26, 1960).

2. The architect Jorge Bonet Armengol has published an article entitled «Las teorías gaudinistas de la arquitectura moderna,» in the magazine *Templo,* (June, 1966) which is interesting for its objective compilation of data and for the author's skillful critique of Gaudí's relevance today. He had previously developed this theme in a lecture sponsored by the Centro de Estudios Gaudinistas. In another section of the same magazine, similar judgements are expressed by the architects José Luis Sert, José M. Sostres Maluquer, and the art historian A. Cirici-Pellicer.

part three / HIS WORK

152. THE PERSISTENCE OF NEO-CLASSICISM

When Gaudí graduated from the School of Architecture, the neo-classic architectural standards prescribed by the Academy of San Fernando and in general use since the last years of the preceding century still reigned supreme. At the beginning of the 19th century, Barcelona's *Junta de Comercio* (Chamber of Commerce), hoping to rid architectural education of the guild mannerisms with which it had become infested, proposed that Architecture be introduced as a course of study in the art school which the Junta sponsored. The architect Antonio Celles y Azcona, at that time studying in Rome on a pension awarded by the same civic organization, was asked to return to Barcelona to set up and teach the new program which was inaugurated in 1817 and followed the methods used in the Academy of Saint Luke in Rome and the Polytechnique in Paris.[1]

Celles was a proponent of the functional rationalism which had its origins in the last days of the reign of Louis XVI and the subsequent revolution, and whose esthetic ideal was confined to the classical styles; at first only the Roman was acceptable, though later more subtle Hellenic forms were allowed. His program did not include architectural history, leaving the students theoretically ignorant of other styles. A similar preference for the classic was shared by the guild schools which continued to exist. Evidence of this can be seen in the building with the lintelled Doric portico which was erected in the recently-urbanized Plaza de Palacio in the second or third decade of the century by Antonio Rovira y Riera, a product of the carpenters' guild training, and also in the new façade for the Casa de la Ciudad begun by José Mas, with masons' guild credentials, in 1830. Here an Ionic style column is employed similar to that which he used in the colonnade surrounding the open-air market place of San José (1836-1840).

The academically educated architects José Buxareu and Francisco Vila showed the same artistic orientation in their design for the Xifré houses on the avenue then open into the Plaza de Palacio; so, too, did Francisco Daniel Molina several years later (1848-1859) in his Plaza Real project which was inspired by the Paris *Palais Royal* and was the winning entry in a sharply contested competition; Miguel Garriga y Roca in the Liceo Theater (1848); and Rovira y Trias in the Corinthian colonnade or «loggia» bordering the garden of the Moya (now Comillas) Palace in 1856.

As we shall see, the endurance of neo-classicism was weakened as the century moved on, but it had its faithful cultivators throughout, as is apparent in the work of the architect J. Oriol Mestres, father of the illustrator Apeles, in the theater of the «Campos Eliseos» and the Samá Palace (both now demolished) and that of the *maestro de obras* José Fontseré Mestre in the façades of the Paseo de la Industria (now Martínez Anido), the Calle Pujadas, and the Paseo de Isabel II (today the Avenida del Marqués de la Argentera) across from the France railroad station, and in the Cascade in the Park of the Ciudadela.[2]

153. THE MEDIEVALIST VOGUE (Figs. 179, 180)

THE ROMANESQUE-GOTHIC. We have seen in Part One of this biography (IX-34) how, in the 1830's in Catalonia, there awoke—as a facet of the dominant Romanticism—an enthusiasm for historical studies in various fields of learning. One of these was archaeology under the motivation of Rogent in his capacity as director of the School of Architecture, and with the encouragement of the *Associació Catalanista d'Excursions Científiques,* in whose activities participated those young architects eager to study the artistic past of Catalonia in order to renew its present architectural vigor—by then exhausted by the near century-old reiteration of classic methods on their third time around in the history of architecture.

This archaeological development was not exclusive to Catalonia. Pablo Piferrer and later F. Pi y Margall, J. M. Cuadrado, and P. de Madrazo had seconded it in their work *Recuerdos y Bellezas de España,* illustrated with 558 lithographs by the print-maker Javier Parcerisas, which first appeared in 1839. Three years later, J. Pérez de Villamil, under the financial protection of the Marquis of Remisa, a Catalan financier living in Madrid, published in Paris his three volumes of large format lithographs entitled *España Artística y Monumental,* with text by Patricio de la Escosura. These works were imbued with the Romantic flavor which Piranesi had introduced in his engravings of Rome at the end of the preceding century.

Although the most notable figure and virtual guiding light of Catalan architectural Romanticism was Rogent, it would be unfair to forget the work of José Casademunt, Celles' successor as director of architectural studies at the Lonja where he added new subjects of a more technical and scientific sort. Casademunt was deeply moved by the demolition of the Gothic church

1. Martinell, *La escuela de la Lonja...* (Barcelona, 1951), pp. 56-57.
2. Adolfo Florensa, «José Fontseré y Mestre y el Parque de la Ciudadela,» in Miscel·lània Fontseré. Barcelona; Gili, 1969, pp. 175-82.

and cloister of Santa Catalina, ordered by the City in 1837. He carried out a careful survey and description of the monuments before their destruction in a study sponsored by the *Junta de Comercio*, thanks to which we today have some indication of their beauty.[3]

Manuel Milá y Fontanals, professor of Literature at the University and active in the restoration of Catalan letters, was joined by several of his sympathetic colleagues in urging their friend Rogent to use the Romanesque style in his project for the university (1859); Rogent was understandably receptive to the idea and adapted medieval forms to the Castilian Renaissance proportions which prevail in that building.[4] A project for the restoration of the church at Ripoll sponsored by the bishop of Vich, Doctor Morgades, in 1865 led Rogent to study those architectural examples contemporary with the ruined monastery still standing in Catalonia and in the neighboring French counties of Cerdeña and Rosellón, and to delve more deeply into the general study of the little-known Romanesque style.

Rogent's interpretation of the Romanesque was based on prints of noble buildings of a type known as «Byzantine» whether or not it really was. (Similarly, in such prints the Catalan medieval style was labelled «Lemosín».) To him we are indebted for the conscientious recreation of medieval styles, though it must be admitted that archaeological accuracy was often sacrificed to personal interpretations based on the Romantic taste of the times.

Among the medievalizing architects who followed Rogent, we should mention Juan Martorell who at times worked within the historic Gothic style, and at others interpreted the styles of the Middle Ages in a personal manner as in the Romanesque-Byzantine church for the Jesuits on the Calle de Caspe, and the svelte neo-Gothic church of the Salesas, as well as in his unsuccessful competition design for the Barcelona cathedral façade. Other followers of this personalizing tendency—usually within a general Gothic framework—were Doménech y Montaner, Granell, Gallissá, Font y Gumá, Puig y Cadafalch, and Gaudí who was outstanding for his independent ways.

MUDÉJARISM. The Romance tales of medieval battles which gave rise to the term Romanticism always revolve around the basic «Moors vs. Christians» plot. It was logical that in the evocative art of this period the Moslem element would not be missing: like Christian art, it too had its cultivators.

The best example of this style is found in Madrid, across from the Prado Museum, and was erected by the son and heir of the Catalan potentate Xifré in 1862-65; it was later furnished with authentic Arabic antiquities.[5]

When the City of Barcelona proposed the erection of a monument to the glories of Spain in Africa in the Plaza Tetuán (1875)—a monument that was never built—second prize in the competition for its design was awarded to the architect A. Rovira y Rabassa, whose project was conceived in an Arabic style. Later, a large pavilion of similar characteristics and especially intricate detailing was constructed at the summit of Mount Tibidabo, right next to a tiny Gothic chapel—symbolic of the compatibility between the two styles; these were later replaced by a sumptuously decorated restaurant in the same Arabic idiom.

On the Paseo de Gracia were built two twin houses separated by a passageway which served as the entrance to the *Teatro Español;* one of these—No. 24—still exists today with

3. José Casademunt, *Santa Catalina,* (Barcelona: 1886).

4. Information provided by Gaudí himself.

5. J. M. Ramón de San Pedro, *Don José Xifré Casas,* p. 104.

179. Church of the Salesas in a freely interpreted Gothic style, work of the architect Juan Martorell whom Gaudí assisted on this project.

180. The Arabic pavilion and Neo-Gothic chapel which existed at the summit of Mount Tibidabo at the end of the 19th century. From *Barcelona a la Vista* in the author's archive.

its original Moslem details on all but the lower story. On one of the chamfered corners of the Layetana-Mallorca intersection there used to stand a luxurious Arabic chalet with extremely fine detailing—one of the most outstanding examples of the style in Barcelona. It contained a square interior patio with 12 arches covered by a dome and a white marble fountain in the center.[6]

The *Arenas* bullfight ring, built in the Plaza de España by Augusto Font in 1892 and still existing, is another example of what we are talking about, as was another chalet, demolished only a few years ago, which was located on one of the corners of the Layetana-Consejo de Ciento intersection.

On the outskirts of Barcelona in the 1870's and '80's there was a vogue for a type of home that was discreetly Arabicized on the outside and contained a grand interior patio covered with colored glass panes with a central fountain encased with ceramic tile inlay, columns of the same material, and galleries of polychromed horseshoe arches on each floor; all of this was completed by furniture which left no doubt about the Islamic tastes of the proprietors.

154. ECLECTICISM

When Gaudí finished his studies and began his professional work, the neo-classicism which we have seen at mid-century still prevailed, but with less intensity due to the numerous interferences by other historical styles which interested the young architects. Each of these styles seemed to be reserved—although not exclusively—for certain purposes. The Romanesque was usually employed in churches and religious buildings as was the Gothic, which could also be used in residential architecture; the Arabic in bathhouses and recreational establishments; the Renaissance style, though not widely applied, was considered appropriate to theaters and certain public buildings; and the neo-Egyptian was used for funerary monuments and a few scattered urban buildings.

The adoption of these styles basically represented a recognition of the creative impotence which was at the root of the eager search for a new architectural style—a search which was later to crystallize in Modernismo. Meanwhile, European architectural ideas were being widely diffused through the exchange of published articles and illustrations of constructed works, as well as prints which were easily available; this lent a certain unity to all European architecture despite its heterogeneous origins.

THE RENOVATING MOVEMENT: At first this harmony of forms affected only decorative applications, but caused no general renovating movement. The Romantic-Medievalist architects were not limited to servile archaeological reproduction, but also were interested in reviving those unjustly forgotten techniques of the past which were practicable in modern buildings, such as wrought iron, stained-glass work, ceramics, mosaic, and all artistic crafts which could give character and enhanced quality to their works.

At the same time they attempted to dignify materials in common use, such as rubble and brick, which the eclectics tended to hide with plaster or stucco work designed to look like stone. They gave these two materials an important artistic character of their own. Brick acquired an especially exciting and expressive richness through the great variety of decorative and structural solutions possible in its use. By using the natural coloring of materials effectively and combining them with ceramic tiles, and by experimenting with novel textural combinations, the young architects began to awaken a chromatic interest which had been neglected by the neo-classic practitioners.[7]

Thus when Gaudí began his career, some of the problems which he was so masterfully to overcome had already been set forth; others he would both initiate and solve. It was important nevertheless for his restless nature that in his novice architectural years he found himself confronted by a panorama rich in possibility. It was logical that he would reject the exhausted neo-classicism of the previous decades, and his architectural sensibilities soon led him to discover those elements of contemporary European architecture which responded to his own searchings and could be incorporated into the Catalan milieu.

6. F. Rogent y Pedrosa, *Arquitectura moderna de Barcelona*, (Barcelona: 1897), p. 163.

7. Many other Catalan architects besides Gaudí used brick in this period to give a monumental character to their work.

XXXVI. PRECOCIOUS ACTIVITY

155. AN ATTEMPT TO RESTORE POBLET (Figs. 12 - 14)

We have seen in the biographic part of the present study how the innate vocation of our architect was already apparent before he began the illusory and unsuccessful attempt to restore Poblet. The episode is of more human than artistic interest, but we include it here in fulfillment of the purpose of the book, which is to catalogue and describe his entire architural production, including works such as this one whose greatest importance lies in being at the symbolic root of his future work.

The project for the restoration of the famous monastery involved the structural consolidation and dignifying of the ruins, and the creation of a socially model town on the site. The vastness of the plan indicates how impossible it was in the hands of those three youths, 13 and 15 years old. Each one took charge of a certain aspect of the project; Gaudí chose to be responsible for the construction which was most in line with his interests.

I have consulted the original manuscript of the youths' memorial in the monastery archives,[1] and have found the parts which deal with construction—in contrast to the illusory nature of the whole—to be amazingly prudent and practical in its consideration of the preparation necessary for the work and the cost of same, as well as the direction of the operations in view of the future town to which the boys aspired (Appendix II).

The section on construction is divided into three parts, the first being headed simply «Plan.» This sets forth the idea of a concentration of necessary workers from the nearby towns within the monastery grounds so that all of the work could be done on the premises, and also in order to form a basis for the future town; to serve this small working community, a store and a café would be provided. The plan was to return the scattered artistic fragments to their original places with a view toward attracting tourists, and they even dreamed of a branch railroad line which would lead directly to the nascent town with its Physics, Chemistry, and Natural Science exhibits and local Art Museum.

In a second section headed «Parts,» Gaudí specifies who will do the work and how, and indicates the buildings which are in most urgent need of repair: «the kitchen, the former boys' dormitory for the use of the workmen, and the towers where the directors of the work would sleep.» Once lodging for the personnel was taken care of, they would repair the walls, the entrances and doorways, the non-artistic parts of the church, the cloister, the dome, the sacristy and the rest, finishing up with the defense towers. Meanwhile one or two of the buildings would have been converted into workshops, and later they would restore related buildings outside of the monastery walls such as the hospital, the bag-making factory, the abbot's palace, and others. He also considers the problem of water—a prime necessity for the work—with plans for piping it in and distributing it through the grounds; they intended to obtain the sand they would need from a nearby river bed.

The artistic work would come after the utilitarian, and would be of considerable scope: «In preparation for this, someone will have to be hired, or else one of the directors will go to Asia to charter a ship and load it with ebony and other expensive and precious woods. Four good sculptors would be sought to begin the restoration—two for the wood objects and the other two for the rest of the sculpture» and they even planned to set up looms for the service of the church and for everyday household needs—one for mourning velvets, another for damascene work, and three or four common ones; marble and jasper would be obtained from local quarries.

And finally, there is a section entitled «Expenses» in which he considers the economic aspect of the restoration, foreseeing the use of salvagable materials from the ruins themselves, the construction of a brick kiln, the purchase of two mules for cartage, payment of construction workers and day-laborers to work the fields (for which he planned to request a brigade of prisoners), other employees for various tasks, and the purchase of tools. To each entry he assigns a value; these add up to a total of 64,800 *reales* for the first year, from which he deducted the 37,520 which they hoped to obtain by various means specified in other parts of the memorial.

The study is accompanied by a general plan of the monastery copied from the one which illustrated a monograph published by Andrés Bofarull in 1848. This plan was drawn up during a judicial dispute between the town of Vimbodí and the monastery and is absolutely lacking in geometric accuracy.[2] It is, however, interesting to note, for it shows the boys' desire to document the restoration, and the central part of the map is higlighted in bold colors—an early indication of Gaudí's preference for polychromy.

---

1. Left by Eduardo Toda, its co-author, who kept it until his death. I am grateful to the reverend community of Poblet for allowing me to study the memorial and reproduce the colored drawing.

2. The second edition in 1870 was illustrated with the same plan, which would indicate that it was difficult to obtain an accurate plan of Poblet. One was finally mode in 1880 by the students of the Architecture School of Barcelona under the direction of Rogent.

We can see from the memorial just summarized that this was nothing more than pure youthful illusion; only the assemblage of the fragments of the Abbot Alferic's sepulchral stone, which has survived to this day, was accomplished. Nevertheless, we should keep in mind the fact that Gaudí, at 15, without ever having studied architecture beyond mere observation of construction work in progress, had a clear overall vision of the job that had to be done, including a series of practical details which reveal a mature understanding of the facts of life.

156. STUDENT PROJECTS (Figs. 19, 20, 22 - 24)

After spending the earlier years studying fundamentals, it is easy to imagine the enthusiasm with which the 22-year-old Gaudí entered the last three years of his academic work (1874-1877), each of which required a special course of Projects that involved a semblance of professional practice, even if in the form of a scholastic exercise.

Ráfols speaks of these projects which, at the time he wrote his biography, could be consulted in the archive of the School of Architecture. Some have unfortunately disappeared. Following Ráfols' order they were: a lamppost, a water tower, a patio for the Provincial *Diputación*, the Spanish pavilion at the Philadelphia Exposition, a monumental fountain for the Plaza de Cataluña, a general hospital for Barcelona, and a wharf presented in order to be allowed to compete for a school prize. Probably as an oversight he does not list the cemetery gate which he discusses and reproduces,[3] and which the present author saw along with the others in that same archive in his student days.[4]

When Gaudí passed the first year of Projects with an outstanding grade (to this year probably belong the first two projects cited above as well as the cemetery gate) he still had not taken Art Theory, a third year subject, nor Architectural History which belonged to the previous year. But the lack of Theory and History—which he would pass the following year— did not prevent his getting a good mark. That he was deserving of this grade can be apprecited by observing the cemetery gate (Fig. 20), designed in a freely interpreted Romanesque style, which we are able to reproduce from Ráfols. The fine proportion and the character so well suited to the theme must have compensated for the uncommon freedom of interpretation in the eyes of the professors. Another favorable factor was undoubtedly the clever solution of the iron gate which was made up of two extended sections with the structurally necessary diagonal tie rods boldly exposed. These would later reappear in the stylized dragon of the gate to the Finca Güell in «Les Corts» (Figs. 223, 224).

In the «Patio of a building for the *Diputación Provincial*,» which probably was done in the second course of Projects (Fig. 19), we see a correct design within the Renaissance tradition; the moldings and architectural details are carefully worked out, with one largescale drawing to illustrate «the unusual foliate interweaving... which decorated the architraves.» (Ráfols) That year he was hoping for another «*Sobresaliente*,» as a prerequisite for competing for his class prize, and when he did not obtain it he requested a special exam project; he was given the theme of a wharf and only earned a «*Notable*» grade.

Gaudí himself told me[5] that the last project of the third course, which took the place of a final exam, was a hospital which he designed without enthusiasm, giving rise to the incident we have mentioned before, and the setting up of a new project—the one for the monumental fountain—which earned the praise of Villar who sat on the jury (VI - 22). This professor for whom Gaudí had worked as an assistant was justified in his praise of the project, conceived as it was with grandeur, good taste, and liberal resourcefulness in the combination of circular and angular masses, arches, columns, and statuary with the play of water either in spurts or falling along parabolic paths—all harmonized in an elegant and sharply silhouetted monumental whole (Fig. 24). In this project, despite its limited scope, we get an early look at the fertile and imaginative potential which would be confirmed in the architect's later work.

Recently, the comprehensive exam project has been located in the drawing collection of the Barcelona School of Architecture. This project consists of a university auditorium developed on five sheets of paper, and worked out in a conscientious manner which reveals the new architect's capability. In Fig. 22, the transversal section is reproduced, showing the architectural proportions, the chromatic richness of the decoration, and the spectacular variety of ornamental motifs. Fig. 23 shows a detail of the dome in which we can appreciate the correct composition of the scene depicted and Gaudí's facile drawing style which animates the figures. In this last academic project he proved beyond a doubt his domination of structural masses, color, and design.

157. COLLABORATION IN THE WORKS OF OTHERS AND ERRONEOUS ATTRIBUTIONS (Figs. 18, 21, 181)

We have seen that his family's economic situation forced Gaudí to work as a salaried draftsman for several professional architects, taking part in their projects at various levels of responsibility. As I understand it, he worked merely as a draftsman or assistant; nevertheless, all of his biographers have insisted on inverting the terms of these collaborations, putting the

3. José F. Ráfols, *Antonio Gaudí*, (Barcelona: 1929), pp. 19, 267.

4. These projects, some of which were in watercolor while others were either drawings or ferrocyanide copies, had been claimed by Gaudí after graduation and presumably were lost in his atelier during the Civil War. [It now appears, however, that some of them had been returned to the School for an exhibition sometime after 1905, and they have recently been rediscovered there. The fountain, the wharf, the university auditorium, and the detail of the *Diputación* are now in the School. The cementery gate and the Diputación patio are illustrated in Ráfols book (our Figs. 19, 20). Preparatory drawings that may be related to the hospital and the Exposition pavilion are in the Museum in Reus (see App. V). Ed.]

5. Martinell, *Conversaciones con Gaudí...*, p. 69.

181. Reservoir for providing water to the Park cascade, calculated by Gaudí while working for Fontseré. (It has now disappeared). From *Barcelona a la Vista* in the author's archive.

young Gaudí on top. Most especially I am referring to his relationship with the architect Villar and the *maestro de obras* Fontseré, for whom he worked as an assistant. I believe that both have suffered from errors in historical perspective which are best set right.

Today the name of Gaudí shines in its own light, and the radiance fills not only his active years but also seems to turn everything he touched to gold. Villar and Fontseré, on the other hand, have been historically obscured, perhaps due in part to the very fame of this man who was once their assistant. When Gaudí worked for them, between the ages of 22 and 25, his natural talent was doubtlessly apparent but he was inexpert; Villar was an accredited professional, the diocesan architect for Barcelona, professor of the School of Architecture and its director for a short period; Fontseré, who was not an architect, possessed the title of *maestro de obras* and director of road-works—a highly regarded credential in those days— and he was an expert in architectural matters and water systems.[6] Given these circumstances of obvious professional hierarchy alone, it would be difficult to allow that two responsible professional men, engaged in works as important as the *camarín* at Montserrat and the Cascade of the Park of the Ciudadela would cede the initiative to an unproven draftsman in his early twenties, regardless of his capabilities.

It was Ráfols who first suggested attributing the *camarín* and the cascade to Gaudí, as well as other possible attributions, in a flourish of admiration—and perhaps also in reaction to a certain indifference of the moment—in the first attempt at an *in extenso* catalogue of Gaudí's work (1927). While strongly arguing in favor of these attributions, Ráfols prudently envelops them in doubts and question marks. The strange thing is that subsequent biographers and critics, rather than clearing up the doubts and answering the questions, have given the attributions the value of unimpeachable truths and, worse still, in one of the most recent publications on the subject these gratuitous attributions have produced offspring.[7] I hope to be able to clear up some of the more extreme cases of error.

---

6. Florensa, *op. cit.*

7. I must except Florensa who, in his cited study of Fontseré, attributes the Cascade to him while allowing the possibility that Gaudí contributed two small decorative elements.

THE CAMARIN AT MONTSERRAT. Bergós says that during his first year at the School of Architecture, Gaudí worked for the architect Villar (p. 19). This would have been either the year 1873-1874 or the following one, depending on whether by first year he means the year of entrance or the first year of the actual architectural curriculum; at that time Gaudí was either 21 or 22 years old. According to notes in the margin of the manuscript in the Reus Museum where he recorded his hours of work, he and his fellow student Cristóbal Cascante were working at the end of 1876 on what he calls the «camarín Villar,» which we can assume to be that of Montserrat.

Extensive research in the archives of this monastery [8] yields the information that on the 17th of April of 1876, the first stone of the work on the exterior of the *camarín* was laid, and from weekly quarrier lists which run from November 4, 1878 to April 25, 1880 it can be deduced that work continued until the latter date; the exterior was completely terminated in March 1885.

It is possible that Gaudí was working as a draftsman on the *camarín* exterior in 1876, and perhaps for some time thereafter. There is no evidence that he assumed direction of this phase of the work, and much less that of the interior decoration, despite the claims of some biographers.

The interior decoration for the *camarín* was already under consideration before 1884. The first known document referring to the subject is a letter from the architect Villar on October 31 of that year, in which he presents his preliminary budget for this decoration to the Abbot Muntades. It is significant to note that by that date Villar's ex-draftsman had replaced him as architect in charge of the Sagrada Familia church against the will of the former—a fact which would logically exclude any collaboration between the two architects.

The *camarín* so often cited as a work by Gaudí was begun in 1887 and was designed and directed by Villar's son who had finished his professional studies the year before and thus offered up his first work in homage to the Virgin. Interesting letters from the young Villar are preserved in the monastery archives, some with explanatory sketches of the work which prove his authorship of the project beyond a doubt (Appendix VII). In spite of this fact, one writer has gone so far as to see in one of the capitals «one of the first clear expressions of what was to be (Gaudí's) future sense of plasticity;» he sees it as a harbinger of the ornamental motifs of the Güell Palace, the Casa Calvet, and the Sagrada Familia, and, with an unwarranted tone of superiority, marvels that this «truly exceptional» detail had been overlooked by so many scholars.[9] We have seen that this capital «so rich in (Gaudinian) content» is well documented as being by the younger Villar without any help from Gaudí.

WORK IN THE PARK OF THE CIUDADELA. The ancient citadel (*ciudadela*) was ceded to the city of Barcelona in 1868 by the central government, and the decision was made in 1871 to transform it into a public park. To this end, a design competition was held which was won by José Fontseré; his victory over several architects, who were angered that the prize would go to a *maestro de obras,* led to a tense situation and super-vigilance over him on the part of Rovira y Trías who was then the municipal architect in charge of embellishment.[10] In spite of this rivalry, the municipal authorities recognized Fontseré's technical and artistic capabilities and expressed their confidence in him by appointing him as director of the park construction which was begun in the same year, and also by entrusting to him the project for the grand cascade whose foundations were laid in February, 1875, and which was finished in 1881.[11]

I have set forth the preceding chronology in order to be able to prove that the depository which Gaudí calculated for Fontseré and which served as his Resistance of Materials exam in June 1875, was indeed a reservoir for the park—as he himself told me [12]—but not a depository in this cascade as has been affirmed elsewhere.[13] The argument that the overall design of the cascade belongs to Gaudí and that he was inspired by the *Chateau d'Eau* in Marseilles is based solely on speculation regarding a yellowed photograph of the French monument found among his papers when he died, and is otherwise unfounded.

If such a supposition were to be true, the project would have to have been entrusted to him before February, 1875, i.e., before the depository calculation; the fact that this was submitted for Professor Torras' review indicates that Fontseré's confidence in his assistant was not such as to delegate a project of so great importance to him (VI-19). Gaudí himself expressed surprise that he was attributed with a greater part in this structure than the role of simple draftsman which he played for Fontseré.[14]

We must also remember the tense relationship between Fontseré and the municipal architect, Rovira y Trías, who insisted that he present detailed drawings of every modification of the approved overall plan «no matter how insignificant,» as another reason that he could not afford to delegate the important work to the inexperienced hands of another.

Another work which has been attributed to Gaudí without apparent artistic reason is the pedestal of the large sculptural groupings at the entrance to the park; these pedestals, along with the beginning of the iron gate that goes with them, were drawn on onionskin paper and signed by José Fontseré on June 1, 1875. A study of this project which is preserved in the

8. In June 1964, at which time I was aided by dom Reinald Bozzo O. S. B. I am grateful to the reverend community for permission to consult the archive.

9. Roberto Pane, *Antoni Gaudí*, (Milan; 1964), p. 63 and Fig. 5.

10. Florensa, *op. cit.*

11. *Ibid.*

12. Martinell, *Conversaciones con Gaudí...*, p. 70.

13. I have inspected the Cascade and interviewed those in charge of it, and there is no evidence of any depository, nor does it appear that there ever was one. On the other hand, it is documented that at the time a great reservoir and other facilities for the irrigation of the Park were built in the upper part of the nearby «Asilo del Parque,» with a capacity for 10,000 cubic meters of water. Within this another smaller steel reservoir was built; it was also taller, to give greater pressure to the cascade, and it is probably this one that Gaudí designed. This depository was dismantled when they started using electric motors for the Cascade according to the municipal engineer, Sr. Biroles.

14. According to Juan Prats who was told this by Gaudí himself. [Gaudí's signature has been found on a piece of sculpture of the Cascade. Reported by J. Bassegoda in *La Vanguardia Española,* 10 Nov. 1972. — G. R. C.]

Municipal Administrative Archives reveals no trace of intervention by the young Gaudí unless it be simply in the drafting work.[15]

The hand of Gaudí has also been imagined in the railing which marks off the small square surrounding the monument erected to Aribau in 1885—an attribution based on a certain decorative element which echoes the hyperboloid motif which our architect was fond of using in its strictly geometrical context. This is an attribution which makes neither critical nor historical sense; nevertheless, in one recently published work it appears to have been extended to the monument of the poet himself, which is well-known to be by the architect José Vilaseca and the sculptor Manuel Fuxá.[16] The author of the railing is unknown, but it seems most logical to attribute it to one of the architects working on the park at the time.

When the monument to Aribau was erected ca.1885, Gaudí had been out of school for eight years and was headed in other directions. After working on the Mataró co-operative he had built the Casa Vicens in the Barcelona suburb of Gracia, and «El Capricho» in Comillas, and had been placed in charge of the Sagrada Familia while taking on the Palacio Güell commission. As he busied himself with these works, his assistantship to Fontseré of ten years earlier was certainly a thing of the past; the pseudo-hyperboloids (decorated with lines which do not coincide with the generatrices which Gaudí most certainly would have emphasized) which motivated the completely arbitrary attribution were most probably the work of another architect.

RAILINGS OF THE SALON DE SAN JUAN. Ráfols suggested that these railings near the park with pedestals which include sculpted urns and cast-iron eaglets could have been designed by Fontseré's assistant. However, the fact that this area was developed as a sort of antechamber to the 1888 Exposition makes this even more unlikely than in the railing mentioned above, since by that time Gaudí had received two additional commissions — that of the Episcopal Palace at Astorga, and the Güell stables in «Les Corts.»

Ráfols' suggestion seems to have been based on the original and dynamic aspect of the eaglets which serve as handles for the urns and constitute the most personal element of the cold and uninteresting railing. These urns are actually quite similar to those which lined the Paseo de Colón before its present urbanization, which had eaglets in even more daring attitudes; it would seem more logical to attribute the San Juan sculpture to the author of these other urns, A. Rovira y Rabassa,[17] the son of the municipal architect Rovira y Trías who may have influenced the granting of the commission.

It should also be observed that in the hurry to find works attributable to Gaudí's hand the «plethoric richness» (Ráfols) of the Aribau railing—influenced more by the floral neo-Egyptian friezes cultivated by Vilaseca—is thrown in with the cold and uninteresting Renaissance and neo-Grecian railings of the cascade and the Salón de San Juan—further proof of the arbitrary quality of such attributions.

OTHER COLLABORATIONS. In addition to those works in which we now know that Gaudí intervened only as an efficient assistant but without directive responsibility or else not at all, Ráfols mentions his work for the engineer José Serramalera, in the firm of Padrós y Borrás, where—according to Bergós—he became acquainted with the technique of precise mechanical drawing. Ráfols says that he also worked briefly under Emilio Sala, one of the most active architects in Barcelona at the end of the nineteenth century.

Gaudí was a staunch defender of the rejected design for the façade of the Cathedral of Barcelona submitted by the architect Juan Martorell to the 1882 competition. According to Ráfols, he also fervently copied fragments of the project during the short time that it was on exhibit in the cathedral cloisters, and later reconstructed it in his studio with an exactness which revealed his extraordinary memory for forms.[18] Gaudí's drawing was used to illustrate leaflets that were distributed in support of the Martorell design.

Ráfols also tells us that in the same year, while working in Martorell's studio, «Gaudí collaborated in organizing the complete and detailed project for the church which the Benedictine monks planned to build at the monastery of Villaricos at Cuevas de Vera (Almería).»[19] This church, which was never built, was conceived along the same lines as the church of the Salesas in Barcelona which Martorell was in the process of building at that time, with the altar in the center of the chancel, an arrangement which Gaudí would later adopt in the Sagrada Familia.

15. In his book *Nueva Visión de Gaudí*, E. Casanellas includes the well-known *camarín* of Montserrat among the illustrations (plate II), and in plates IV and CIV he shows an overall view and a detail of the entrances to the Parque de la Ciudadela—apparently an original attribution—without any substantiating documentation. [That Gaudí probably did design the gate and the iron fence that surrounded the Park is documented, according to J. Basegoda in *La Prensa*, 17 Oct. 1970, p. 10. *L'ilustració catalana* for 20 Sept. 1880 also corroborates this. — G. R. C.]

16. Casanellas, *op. cit.*, plates VIII and IX. The album *La Renaixensa*, 1883-85, gives the names of the authors of the monument referred to.

17. According to Rovira himself who told me so when he was my professor at the School of Architecture.

18. *Op. cit.*, p. 30.

19. *Idem.*

158.   «LA OBRERA MATARONENSE» (Figs. 163, 182 - 188)

We have noted that the commission for the street lamps in the Plaza Real was Gaudí's first of an official nature after he finished his studies. However, it is probable that even before taking his comprehensive exam he was at work on the project dreamed up by his friend Salvador Pagés for the group of workers under his leadership in Mataró. The city commissioned the lamppost model on February 27, 1878, and the Mataró plans are dated the following March 29. Although physically possible, it is unlikely that he would have designed the plans for the workers' residences and the layout of the 30 little houses and so carefully drawn them up in only a month's time; the drawings are co-signed by his fellow classmate Emilio Cabañas, a native of Mataró, who probably lent his name for administrative convenience.[1] The design was exhibited at the Paris Exposition, as we have seen (IX-32), in a general display of the co-operative's activity.

The poet Joaquín M. Bartrina, who was a classmate of Gaudí at the Escolapian School in Reus, was also a friend of the co-operative's manager Pagés whose ideas he seems to have shared; early in 1878, the poet was commissioned to write a prospectus on «La Obrera Mataronense»—our basic source for its characteristics, especially those of an urbanistic nature which we can assume were provided by Gaudí himself.[2]

The society was constituted in 1865. Its activities were originally carried out in rented quarters in the Barcelona suburb of Gracia; after a period of initial hardships, the Franco-Prussian war brought prosperity to the group which then decided to construct its own locale in Mataró in order to avoid having to be constantly on the move. The first stone was laid «on St. Stephen's Day» in 1874, and four years later they had acquired 20,534 square meters of property, on 2,307 of which they planned to construct the residences, the factory, and all of the necessary facilities, leaving the rest for gardens.

THE DISTRIBUTION. Thirty houses were planned which—since the society as a whole still could not manage to pay for them—would be built by each person at his own expense within the general established plan and at a moderate price. The houses were located southwest of the factory «so that the easterly winds dominant in this region would not carry the factory fumes their way...»

«Each of the cottages will be situated in a manner similar to the one which has already been constructed and that which is now being built, in the center of a planned area with its placement following a system of alternation in relation to the length of the lot in order that circulation not be hindered, i.e., across from the space left between two houses there will stand another with an open space or road in between which will be one-and-a-half time as wide as the height of each house...»

The layout for these thirty houses whose plan is preserved in the Municipal Archives of Mataró and reproduced here (Fig. 163) is one of several that we now know of by Gaudí. The residences were surrounded by a low iron fence with a diagonally rectangular grill and a masonry base; each house was placed in the center of a large garden and was entered by way of two piazzas—one sheltered from the open air and exposed to the wintertime sun, and the other a summer entrance way, completely open.

THE BUILDINGS. Besides the overall urbanization, Gaudí designed a model house with a distribution novel for the time, replacing the common block apartment house type with the «English» type as it is called in the municipal report. The elevation is simple, with discreetly painted ornamentation. The sinuous plant motif of the upper frieze is the same as that which adorns the base of the columns of the Plaza Real street lamps.

Of greater importance and originality is the drawing for the social hall which is preserved by the architect Brullet [3]—a carefully executed watercolor rendering of the lower floor, main floor, and semi-basement in detail, as well as the main and back garden façades. These plans reveal a more careful study than had been previously suspected, without any exceptional elements other than the spiral stairway which leads from the garden to the upper floor. These plans were drawn on a scale of 1 : 50 in May 1878, and are signed by Gaudí alone who numbered them 14 and 15 in the numbering system that we have indicated. The dominant style is reminiscent of neo-classicism, with novel uses of exposed brick and elements of cast iron. The pattern of vertical rectangles which we will see him use often in later works appears in the window openings of the upper story on the main façade.

This project was not carried out, and in the Municipal Archives there exist other plans of July 1883, signed by Gaudí alone and lacking the correlative numeration of the others; these were perhaps related to the hall with wooden parabolic arches which we will discuss later.

1. I am grateful to my friend the architect M. Ribas Piera for the photocopy of the plans for the development and the residence, which were jointly signed by Gaudí and Cabañas, which suggests a collaboration never cited before. Cabañas was two years older than Gaudí, and it was he who lent him Viollet's *Dictionnaire* which Gaudí returned in worn-out condition and filled with marginal annotations. According to the *Diccionario biográfico de artistas de Cataluña*, he got his degree in 1875 and in 1880 was named municipal architect of Mataró.

2. J. M. Bartrina, «La Sociedad Cooperativa mataronense,» in *Obras en prosa y en verso*, (Barcelona-Madrid: 1881), pp. 219-258.

3. He acquired them in 1950 from the descendents of the architect Cabañas.

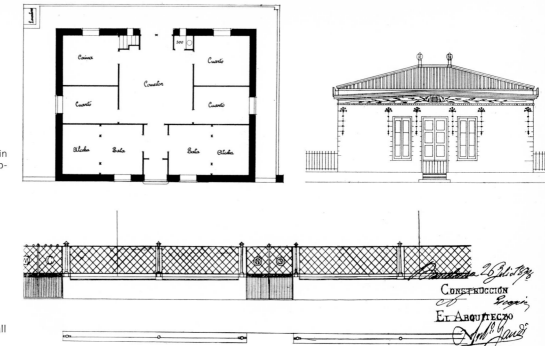

182. Project for a small house in «La Obrera Mataronense» co-operative.

183. Project for a property wall for the co-operative.

184. Ground and first floor plans for «La Obrera Mataronense» social hall.

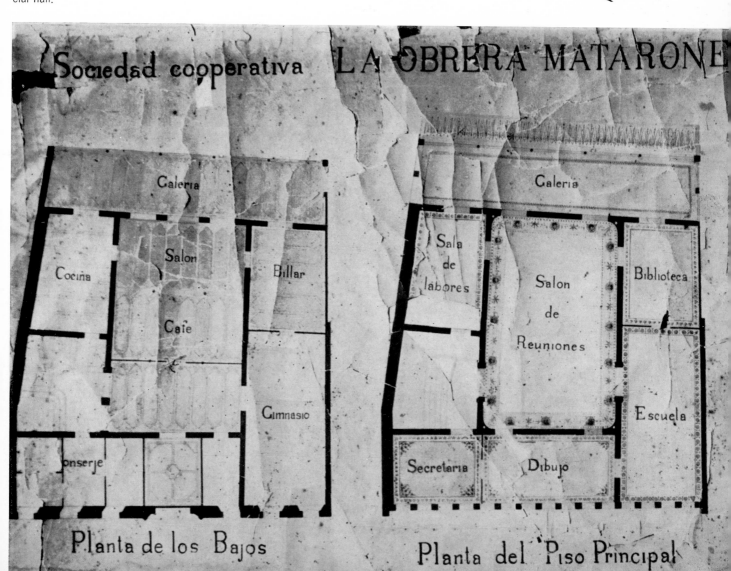

There also exists from the same year and with the same signature, another plan for a family residence with a wide porch. This was possibly the house of the manager, Salvador Pagés, about which we have no information other than that it was located on the Calle de la Cooperativa next to the houses of the highway.

WHAT REMAINS. Relatively important elements of this venerable co-operative are still standing, including one of the halls built prior to Gaudí's involvement.[4] The most interesting extant example of our architect's activity here is the dozen parabolic wooden arches which support the light roof of flat tiles which covers the 12-meter wide machinery hall. Six of these arches were built in the first stage, and the rest were added later;[5] now all are clipped at the edges due to a cutting back of one of the façades when the adjacent street was widened. The construction work is extremely good, involving short three-ply laminated wood planks that are secured with bolts to form the highly graceful and economical parabolic profile.

These arches are usually presented as the first appearance of the structurally equilibrated forms resulting from the containment of mechanical thrusts—forms essential to the theory which the master was later to develop more fully. Here, however, they are employed more in a decorative or intuitive manner than in a strictly structural one. The parabola is the form of arch which results from a system of loads evenly distributed along the arch's span; but the outer edges of the arches at Mataró bear no stress at all and could structurally become straight. Gaudí later adopted this solution in the atrium of the Güell Colony church, and his failure to do so in the co-operative was undoubtedly guided by other considerations.

4. The plan of one of these buildings is preserved in the Municipal Archives. It is signed by the architect Julio Marial on June 29, 1877; he must have been the technical builder of the co-operative before Gaudí finished his studies.
5. M. Ribas Piera, «Consideraciones sobre Gaudí, a través de sus obras urbanísticas», *Cuadernos de Arquitectura* N.º 63 (1966).

185. Project for the garden façade of «La Obrera Mataronense» social hall.

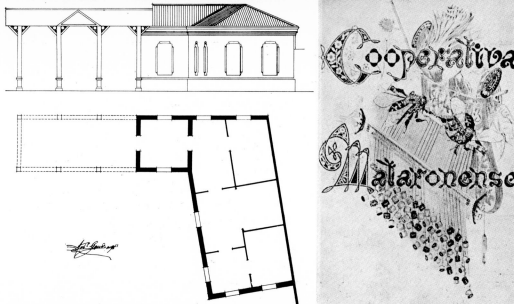

186. Project thought to be for a residence for the director of the co-operative which was built but does not exist today .

187. Emblem for «La Obrera Mataronense» probably designed by Gaudí.

188. Wooden parabolic arches in an industrial shed of «La Obrera Mataronense».

Another element which should be attributed to Gaudí is the small circular pavilion that was to have been used for sanitary facilities. This has also been cut back in recent years, but it shows certain incipient characteristics which were later to be expanded in some of the maste's better-known works.[6]

A TAKING-OFF POINT. We have just seen how Gaudí, not yet 25 and filled with youthful enthusiasm, began his professional career within the architectural norms of the day in spite of the fact that an innovational restlessness was already taking hold of him. His initial moderation runs counter to the «architectural revolutionary» title frequently given him and rather leads us to consider his work as a conscious evolutionary continuum.

Gaudí's work in Mataró—except for the six wooden parabolic arches, where he was more concerned with structure than with decoration—placed him solidly within the architectural tradition of his time. However, when he was presented with his first frankly ornamental theme, he showed himself to be more capable of interpreting the budding restlessness inside of him—a restlessness which later was to flower little by little in the formation of his original and highly personal architectural style.

This can be seen in the beautiful standard which he designed for the co-operative, symbolizing the concept of work in an original composition terminating in a busy bee which replaces the customary lance. Even more eloquent proof of his creativity was his conversion of the bleaching room for a special party celebrated on July 28, 1885, the eve of the town's Patron Saint's day. The elaborate decoration which was widely acclaimed was executed by the architect himself using plants, electric lighting—quite uncommon in those days—and «water in the form of a capricious waterfall,»[7] this last revealing the originality of Gaudí's resources and his aptitude for ornamentation which was, it must be admitted, to be the basis of the greatest part of his future fame.

159. THE MODEL LAMPPOST (Figs. 26, 161, 162, 189, 190)

The buildings for the Mataró co-operative, with their utilitarian purpose and the scanty economic means available, did not provide an appropriate setting for the introduction of the sumptuous themes which the architect was eager to attempt. It was in the coincident project for lampposts for public lighting which were commissioned by the City of Barcelona in 1878 that he was able to develop—on however small a scale—the decorative aspect which he so enjoyed.

BACKGROUND INFORMATION. In Chapter VIII we saw the care which he took to make his first work in Barcelona a success, along with the personal and anecdotal side of the project. Here we will be concerned with the description and technical aspect of the work.

The memorandum which Gaudí presented to the Mayor indicates that before proceeding to work on the project he investigated «various European capitals» where he found «a very pleasant innovation» consisting «in that the upper part of the lamps is made of white opal and thus the light is reflected to the ground, giving the lamp a grand appearance at night.» Such was the case in the lamps at the intersections of la Canebière in Marseille, whose advantages were communicated to him by M. Vaud, the municipal architect of that city. Another result of this research was his preference for «a crown-shaped arrangement of gas lamps, [found] both in this country and abroad; as four arms arranged naturally would form a cross rather than a crown, these lamps preferably consist of 3, 5, 6, 7, 8, etc. arms —five or more placed at the same level form a continuous line or crown of illumination...»[8]

BASIC CRITERIA. Once he had determined the most important factors to be considered, he attacked the problem directly, keeping in mind the funds at his disposal for the job, with «the fixed and unwavering idea of making a street lamp of noble simplicity but not flimsy, with each part given the required emphasis in regard to the strict fulfillment of the purpose for which it is being created.»

He shows himself to be a definite partisan of using materials in their natural state, and of creating forms which frankly reveal their structural function.

THE PROJECT. It was from these basic concepts that Gaudí developed the small wrought iron ensembles placed on stone bases where we can detect the true beginning of his later great works—a beginning which is more clearly seen if we let ourselves be guided by the words of the architect himself in the memorandum which accompanied the project. He says: «From a triangular pedestal with chamfered edges, in polished dark marble of the so-called «Santa Cruz» variety, rises the tapering form of the post whose upper part bears the arms of the lamps and which is capped by a mercantile emblem; the form of this post is derived from the structural need of a column with an embedded base and the details were worked out to facilitate those industrial operations necessary for the polishing and finishing of the iron...» He goes into great detail concerning the lamps, which could number either three or six without altering the design, and in the latter case he arranges them on two alternating levels to give greater playfulness to the pattern formed by the joining circles which were attached to a special piece composed of two truncated cones united along their smaller sections.

6. This is illustrated in Collins, *Gaudí,* Fig. 12, as is a cross-section of the machinery shed (Fig. 1).

7. *Ibid.,* transcription from *La Voz del Litoral,* August 2, 1885.

8. [Quotations in Section 159 are from the memorial eliminated from the English edition. Ed.]

189. One of the two lampposts existing in the Plaza Real in Barcelona, inaugurated in October, 1879.

190. The upper part of the lamp-post in the Plaza Real with six arms and the caduceus of Mercury.

«The truly important ornamental part is the top of the supporting shaft which synthesizes the historical tradition of Barcelona,» which, he says, is essentially a maritime and commercial one —here condensed in an explicit manner to give «monumental character to an object which is to serve as an ornament for the streets of Barcelona.» Thus it seemed most appropriate to him «to terminate the most important part of the lamppost with the easily understood symbol of Mercury's winged caduceus—a form which, in addition, lends itself perfectly to metal construction;» and he adds that «the background colors of the column will display the heraldic polychromy of the city's coat of arms.»

In addition to these general outlines, the architect supplies interesting data on how the poles were to be painted in colors which surprise us today when we see them in their present state. The decoration of the metallic elements was sunken so as not to be an obstacle to wheel polishing, «the edges being gold and red; the caduceus, gold with black enamel; the two serpents that uphold it will have gold and blue scales with golden tongues hanging out that are speckled with red, the color of their gullets.» In order to avoid discomforting reflections from the polished iron in bright sunlight, he designed the upper part of the arms to be red with gold stripes. Beneath the dome of each lamp and above the transparent side crystals, a crown of blue glass completed the polychrome effect.

THE EXECUTION. Gaudí always insisted on the perfect execution of all details as an important element in the final success of each work, and it was for this reason that he felt that every job should be closely supervised by the architect himself; he planned to cover the metal parts not with the usual coat of protective paint alone, but rather—in order to prevent a loss in quality—«with a long-lasting moisture-proof varnish which will shield it from the effects of humidity, as has been done in an infinite number of cases and most recently in the delicate iron framework of one of the installations which I directed for the current International Exposition with great success.» From bills that we have been able to study, it becomes apparent that the painting and gilding work was carried out; it is unfortunate that the original polychrome has been lost, and with it an example of Gaudí's early preference for color which would have given the lamps much greater importance.

PLACEMENT. We have seen in the biographical section (VIII - 28) that when the lamps were commissioned no specific location was indicated; rather, they were to go wherever needed. The architect was nevertheless concerned about their placement, not only for the design of the posts themselves, but also for the enhancement of the buildings whose facades they might illuminate. Thus he proposed that the four lampposts which were situated in front of the Casas Consistoriales «which require prompt substitution» be replaced by four of the new three-light street lamps; or they could be placed in front of the *Diputación* building, the Lonja, the Palace of the Civil Government, or the Cathedral. In discussing Gaudí as urbanist we have listed other possible locations (XXX - 134); and we have seen how it was decided that the two six-light lamps be installed in the Plaza Real, and two more without the gilding and helmets, in the Plaza de Palacio where they still stand; two others placed at the entrance to the Barceloneta were later removed

The lamps in the Plaza Real were inaugurated during the solemn festivities of the Virgen de la Merced (the patroness of Barcelona) in October 1879 and earned high praise from the press. One satirical weekly [9] even published in first-page caricature and judged the lamps artistically superior to the cast-iron sculpture of the Three Graces which adorned the center of the plaza (Fig. 26). Thus the master's earliest works achieved the distinction of caricature, as would so many of his later creations; for the International Exposition of 1888, the lampposts were reproduced in engraved illustrations of the plaza.[10]

The opalesque domes on each individual lamp, which at first had seemed so desirable, turned out not to be able to resist the heat of the gas and were frequently broken; with rain this inconvenience was further complicated. As each little dome cost 18 pesetas, the City Engineer, Juan Nadal, after consultation with Gaudí, ordered that they be replaced by more durable metal ones.

The four lampposts commissioned in addition to the original two were ordered on February 22, 1879, and finished on May 15 of the following year. On September 3, the City accepted them and authorized the Gas Company to put them in place.

COLLABORATORS. We have seen that these street lamps were assembled in the spacious carpentry workshop of Eudaldo Puntí at No. 9 on the Calle de la Cendra, and from the bills of other craftsmen who participated in the work we know that they included the marble worker Manuel Pons, the Valls Brothers' foundry, the glaziers Eudaldo and Ramón Amigó, the tinsmith Luis Cerdá, the gilder Vilaplana y Serrado, the painter Juan Parera, and, in the capacity of model-maker, the sculptor Lorenzo Matamala.

As detailed material on this project is at our disposal and because we are here dealing with Gaudí's first decorative work—a work which, as we shall see, ties up neatly with his last ones (XLVIII - 191)— we have gone into greater detail than will be possible in discussing other works. At the same time, the explanation of the master's meticulous procedure which we have given here can be equally well applied to those works which we must describe more briefly.

9. *L'Esquella de la Torratxa*, September 27, 1879.
10. *Organo Oficial de la Exposición*, Vol. I.

160. FURNITURE (Figs. 191 - 194)

In spite of the fact that the two commissions which we have seen in the same year that he finished his studies were certainly enough for the self-fulfillment of the novice architect, he simultaneously undertook a variety of other projects, some of them commissioned and others on his own initiative.

TWO TABLES FOR HIMSELF. Ráfols and Bergós both speak of the table which he designed for his own office immediately after graduating from the School of Architecture—a table reminiscent of the so-called «Secretarial» type adapted to his own needs and comfort, which

191. Desk for **Gaudí's** office.

192. Side view of a bench for the chapel of the Marquises of Comillas.

193. Prayer stool for the same chapel.

could be closed by roll-top latched covers and had compartments, a shelf on top, and little low cupboards on either side. The eight legs necessitated by the two cupboards were reduced to four by supporting them on brackets extending out from each of the desk legs. The result is an ingenious piece of furniture, functional in spirit and pleasing to look at, with no great overall esthetic pretensions though the architect's good artistic taste is evident in the turned legs and the carved low-relief ornamentation which decorates some of the surfaces (Fig. 191).

In this desk, Gaudí seems to have been more concerned about the utilitarian aspects than the esthetic ones, though in theory he linked both aspects into an ideal whole; however, in the «Notes on Ornamentation» at the museum in Reus he speaks of the same desk in a way in which esthetic principles were of prime concern. On September 22 he notes: «The surfaces—two large ones and a central one that is narrow and long, a formal indication of the contrasting ideas of central and lateral—are of sheets of polished and smooth-edged iron, and black enamel is used as a contrast; the objects are without relief, and therefore those represented should be too...» He follows this with several descriptive and symbolic considerations which we have quoted in XXVI-118.

His words are a good indication of the careful attention which he gave to each detail, no matter how insignificant, and of his delight in the combination of various materials, something we have already seen in the lamps for the Plaza Real.[1]

THE ORATORY FOR THE COMILLAS PALACE (SANTANDER). Probably through the architect Martorell for whom he was working as an assistant and who was the architect in charge of this oratory, Gaudí was commissioned to do several pieces of furniture—arm-chairs, benches, prie-dieux—in the same Gothic style as the chapel itself. These pieces were designed along severe lines and enriched with carving in limited spots which contrast with the over-riding simplicity of the other elements. The carving is stylized and geometric, yet inspired in natural forms. As Gaudí himself pointed out, some of the carved surfaces were decorated with twisting convoluted patterns which made them specially agreeable.[2]

THE COMELLA SHOWCASE. We have seen that while he was assembling the lampposts in Puntí's workshop Gaudí came into contact with the Comella firm which asked him to con-

1. These allusions to his own table which are somewhat unclear at times, open that part of the manuscript which was begun on September 22, 1878, and ends before the section which follows, written on March 20, 1879. It is not included in our Appendix IV.

2. Bergós, p. 43, says that the work even surprised the carvers. Gaudí told me that when Alfonso XII visited the oratory he spent a long while looking at this work; Gaudí believed the reason to be the especial attractiveness of those surfaces.

194. Display case for the Comella glove shop which was included in the Paris Exposition of 1878. From a drawing in the Reus Museum.

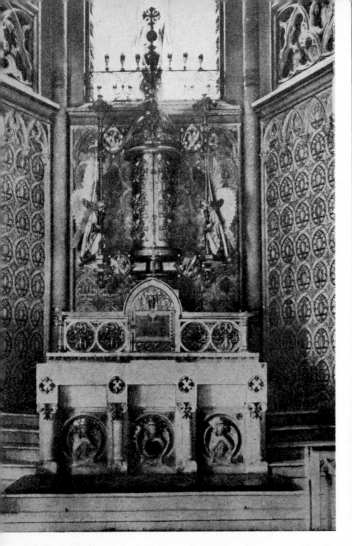

195. Altar for the nuns of Jesus and Mary in Tarragona.

196. Altar for the Bocabella family which is now preserved by their descendants.

struct a showcase to display their glove wares at the Paris Exposition that year (1878). The quality of his work on the lamps undoubtedly motivated the showcase commission. The master designed a cabinet-like pedestal above which was to be raised the main section, with a rectangular base and a double-pitched roof—all in glass with fine metal mountings reinforced by carved wooden buttresses at the corners which would be connected to the pedestal. Inside, he developed the glass and metal display-shelf apparatus in an attractively varied manner.

OTHER FURNITURE. Also in 1878, Gaudí designed an announcing apparatus for which we do not have the particulars,[3] and another table for his own dining room was built in 1885. In addition to those we have mentioned, he probably did other furniture pieces in his early years, and we can assume that they were similar in character.

161.   ALTARPIECES (Figs. 195 - 198)

A work which has recently been rediscovered is the altar which he built between 1879 and 1881 for the Sisters of Jesus and Mary in San Andrés de Palomar; the details were published after this book went to press.

We have seen that the architect's niece attended the boarding school which the same religious order maintained in Tarragona (IX - 32); and he constructed the altar for the chapel there in 1880-1882. The work can be studied from the photographic illustration provided by Ráfols in his biography (Fig. 195). The table was of alabaster with freely interpreted Gothic lines without ostentatious originality. Four small columns subdivided the frontal into three sections which were decorated with angels inscribed in circles, and the tabernacle which housed the Host was cylindrical and sveltely silhouetted, terminating in a cupola and a metal pinnacle topped by a cross. This was flanked by the four symbols of the evangelists surmounted by two kneeling angels with resplendent wings.

We know of another project, for a neo-Gothic building in Alella, conceived on the same lines—without archaeological pretensions in a solidly modern spirit.[4] Outstanding in the composition are the almond-shaped form in the center which contains the crucifix and the

3. Ráfols, op. cit., p. 267.
4. First published in Collins, Gaudí, Pl. 15.

197. Hood of the altarpiece for the Bocabella family, with artificial cloth leaves as decoration.

198. Project for a reliquary in the Reus Museum.

canopy placed above it which extends on out beyond the grouping. In this project, which dates from the year 1883, the word *Sanctus* is repeated over and over—early evidence of the predilection for this symbolic word which Gaudí would confirm later in the Sagrada Familia.

Ráfols dates the extremely simple altarpiece for the oratory of the Bocabella residence to 1885. The most notable element here is the rectangular upper hood in the Gothic style which sheds interesting light on the master's techniques.[5] The cyma or exterior part of the molding which forms the natural wood-colored hood is composed of a series of carved leaves which is repeated over and over; the lower concave molding is filled in with a garland of cloth leaves which were originally a close imitation of real ones, though now they have lost their gloss. This technique of naturalistic application is the only such case that we know of in his work, and it shows his strong desire to obtain a feeling of life—to the point of attempting the scenographic effects already sustained in his youthful notes (XXVIII - 121 and Appendix IV).

162. UNREALIZED DESIGNS (Figs. 198 - 203)

The early professional years of every architect usually yield a greater proportion of unrealized projects than do the years of full professional activity. With his characteristic dynamism and eagerness to work, the young Gaudí was no exception.

The museum at Reus preserves the drawing for a 30 cm.-high reliquary for an unknown destination, signed by Gaudí and dated in Barcelona in 1878. It is a full-sized drawing carefully delineated and colored. The reliquary is well composed, and the circular central section serves as a background for the Virgin with the inscription *Ave María* framing her head (Fig. 198). The three almond-shaped compartments to contain other relics were topped by crosses and were inscribed with the word *Sanctus* and a place reserved for the name of the saint. We also have evidence of a project for a flower stand commissioned by Comella in 1878. The next year, on the 250th anniversary of the death of the rector-poet of Vallfogona, F. Vicens García, the governors of that town proposed a literary competition and other acts to commemorate the event—a proposal which was supported by the *Associació Catalanista d'Excursions Científiques* of which Gaudí was a member.[6] It was undoubtedly because of this con-

5. This is preserved in the home of Bocabella's great grandson, Felipe de Dalmases (Calle Roger de Lauria, 31, 1.°), to whom I am grateful for the opportunity to study it.

6. *La Renaixensa*, July, 1879.

199. Drawing for the parade to honor the rector-poet of Vallfogona.

200. Overall view of the project for the illumination of the *Muralla de Mar*.

201. Project for a lamppost for the *Muralla de Mar*.

202. Sketch of a lamppost for the *Muralla de Mar*.

203. Project for a hunting pavilion for the Güell family in Garraf.

nection that Gaudí collaborated—we assume without remuneration—in the planning of an allegorical parade for the festivities, of which he made elaborate drawings, this one of which is preserved in the Reus Museum. It appears that the celebration was cancelled because the artists' and writers' enthusiasm found no response in the local community.[7]

ILLUMINATION OF THE MURALLA DEL MAR. In 1881, perhaps encouraged by the success of his lamps in the Plaza Real, Gaudí drew up a plan for the electric illumination of the *Muralla del Mar* (Sea Wall), in collaboration with the engineer José Serramalera, of the firm Padrós and Borrás, where the architect had worked four years earlier as a draftsman. The engineer took care of the technical electrical part, and the architect concerned himself chiefly with the structural artistic aspect in which it appears as if he wished to counter the numerous small-scale works he had realized to that point; probably considering the general effect of the lights as seen by ships arriving at sea, he designed sumptuous 20 meter-high lamps with inscriptions and emblems commemorating the glories of Catalonia. He made two studies for these lamps: one was completed and the other remained in sketch form. He probably rejected the second design since the first shows the series of lamps in perspective—all of the same type.

We can assume that the large scale, the luxury, and above all the costly estimate were the reasons that the design proposed to the City Council was not accepted. If we recall the economic hassles occasioned by the small lampposts (VIII - 29), despite their relative unimportance, the situation becomes more clear. If our speculation is valid, we have here the first occasion of Gaudí's ideas being rendered impractical by their very grandiosity, a situation which would be repeated in the future.

A CASINO AND A HUNTING PAVILION. In the young Gaudí's activities we can detect an understandable desire to busy himself with works that were equal to his creative drive. In spite of his general dislike for contests (as seen in a letter to a friend who had told him of an imminent competition for the design of a theater in Reus), he decided to take part in one which had been set up for the design of the Casino de San Sebastián. He submitted his entry on February 26, 1881, «with great corner towers and decorative elements which flutter a bit in the robust squareness of the overall architectural design.» [8] On learning that his project had not been chosen, he demanded its immediate return «as he had been commissioned to build a similar establishment.»

We have no evidence of a building with the mentioned characteristics, unless it could be a hunting pavilion which he designed for Güell at Garraf —a possible pretext for the demand on the competition jury. This building, never realized, was to have been dominated by an octagonal brick tower, the rest being a combination of brick and rubble masses.

We do not know whether or not Gaudí drew up the project for the Casa Consistorial, including the pavement for the Salón de Ciento and the main stairway, which Ráfols (p. 55-56) says was commissioned in 1887 by the Mayor of Barcelona, F. de P. Rius y Taulet «in recognition of his demonstrated competence in the art of decoration.» The same biographer tells us that this commission (of which we can find no record in the Administrative Archives) was later rescinded.

7. *La Campana de Gracia,* September 21, 1879.

8. Ráfols, *op. cit.,* p. 30.

XXXIX. WORKS OF ARABIC INFLUENCE

163. THE CASA VICENS
164. VILLA QUIJANO IN COMILLAS: «EL CAPRICHO»
165. THE FINCA GÜELL IN «LES CORTS»
166. TWO EXPOSITION PAVILIONS?

163. THE CASA VICENS. 1883-1885 (Figs. 87, 124, 204 - 213)

This was Gaudí's first commission for an artistically oriented residence. In spite of its small dimensions (some 10 by 16 meters), the architect was able to make the two floors for living quarters with semi-basement and loft seem larger than it actually is. The lot, at Nos. 24 and 26 on the Calle Carolinas (then the Calle de San Gervasio) in the former town of Gracia which was still separate from Barcelona, was situated between two walls, one belonging to a convent. The area available for the establishment of a garden, though not very large, was expanded to the maximum by the skillful placement of the building. Gaudí backed the chalet-like house against the property wall on the convent side so that the garden was kept all in one piece, and thus appeared to be larger; in order to screen the opposite wall faced by the house he built a parabolic arch topped by a graceful arcade in natural brick, setting the stage for plays of water and vegetation which served as background to an enlarged perspective of the garden as seen from the house. The house itself was conceived as a colossal vine which would climb up the adobe wall of the convent.[1]

The main parts of the house were contained on the lower floor, slightly above ground level, which was entered from the street by way of a small atrium. On this floor the daytime rooms were distributed around the dining room; these included a covered gallery with unglazed windows, a smoking parlor, and a living room. On the second story were the bedrooms, and the two floors were connected by a circular staircase located on a central patio next to the property wall—the only part of the house which does not have an exterior view. The semi-basement was for the use of the caretaker and also for servants' quarters.

STRUCTURE. Gaudí had a reputation for complicating things, but in this case the structure is extremely simple. He divided the building into bays parallel to the property wall, with wooden cross-beams supported on this, the interior bearing wall, and the parallel façade. The loft beams have the same horizontal distribution and follow the slope of the roof which can be clearly seen on the garden façade. The smoking parlor and the semi-basement are covered with *tabicada* vaults.

This house was bought in 1925 by the doctor Antonio Jover who added a bay on the convent side and several out-buildings on the side opposite the street; at the same time he bought up the lot next to the garden which allowed for the latter to be expanded. The garden was redone in harmony with the style of the house and the ancient tower of Santa Rita on the

1. Told to me by Sra. Jover de Herrera, the present owner of the house, who knows it as a part of the family tradition.

204. Section of the Casa Vicens drawn by the author.

205. Schematic plan of the Casa Vicens in its original state. With the aid of a plan by the architect Antonio Pineda and indications by the Sra. Jover de Herrera.

   A. Later amplification of the original work.

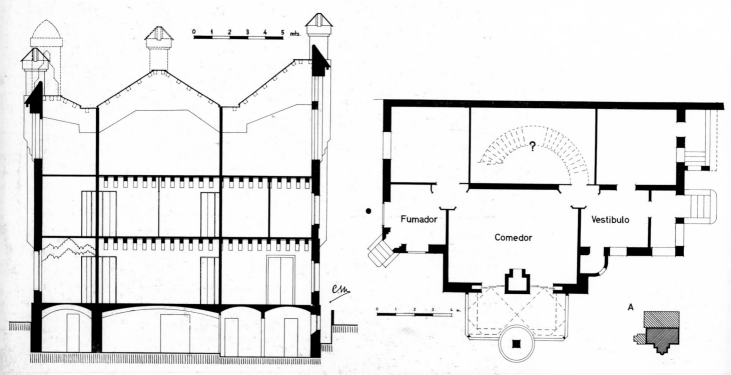

206. Casa Vicens. Garden gate and fence in its original state.

207. Casa Vicens. Street façade. Note the greater abundance of ceramic facing in the upper parts than the lower.

corner of the newly-acquired property. The expansion was directed by the architect J. B. Serra, who carefully continued the decoration of the façades and even consulted with Gaudí himself on several details. In this way an ensemble of Gaudinian unity was retained although in some aspects the original essence of the small house was spoiled. For example, the fountain which was located in front of the central section of the tiny polygonal tribune was removed, the tribune itself was transformed from a space open to the exterior and protected only by some wooden blinds into a common glassed gallery, an interior ventilation patio was eliminated, and the stairway that had existed in that patio was taken away.[2]

The present owner, Sra. Jover de Herrera, is reworking the grounds under the direction of the architect Antonio Pineda, in order to restore its original character.

DECORATION. We have seen that in placing this house against the wall of the neighboring convent, Gaudí planned to imitate a great vine crawling up the partition. Whether or not this is true, it is indeed certain that he wanted to achieve an overall effect of rich color—a goal which was constant throughout his work. Within the architectural eclecticism of his day, this necessarily led him to orientalism, in the chromatic sense if not the purely formal stylistic. The basic material for the façades was a common ochre-colored rubble combined with brick; at times its reddish hue is exposed, and at others it is covered with ceramic tiles—white and blue ones, and others decorated with flowers resembling the plants on the lot. He combined these materials in a way that reflects the structural and functional realities of the house; thus he does not conceal the various openings and smoke outlets, but rather emphasizes them as elements of the façade decoration. This decoration was regulated by geometric patterns similar to those which he used in other works of this same period. In the bulk of the building horizontal rectangular bands dominate, following the brick layers that alternate with the rubble construction. In the upper part the bands become vertical and are regulated by the windows—a rhythm which recalls that which we saw in the upper story of the Mataró houses. These two overall patterns are accompanied and pulled together by the square or checkerboard arrangement of the white and green tiles which cover the chimneys and other elements which jut above the roof to produce an effect of great plasticity and space. He used the same net-like pattern in the iron fence and gate that enclosed the garden and was decorated with highly naturalistic cast-iron palm leaves.[3]

On the interior, the dining room sets the decorative tone, with bracketed wooden ceiling beams alternating with polychrome floral reliefs, and mural decoration by the painter Torrecasana. The tribune which opens off of the dining room formerly had a fountain on the exterior fashioned from a graceful baptismal font in the Renaissance style.

Another adjoining room is the smoking parlor whose structural *tabicada* vaulting and tie rods are concealed by a false stalactitic ceiling which is the most outstanding Arabic note of the entire building (Fig 211). The general feeling of the decorative program is frankly cheerful with an abundance of floral elements, birds, and inscriptions praising the concepts of love and home.

ARTISTIC SIGNIFICANCE. I have deliberately avoided using the term «Mudéjar» which is usually applied to this work because I don't believe that it is appropriate. The «Mudéjar» style is correctly defined as «the grafting of elements of Christian tradition onto Arabic art,»[4] and I can not understand why these works of the master in which no such grafting work is apparent should be so labelled. The inverse phenomenon, where oriental art influenced the traditional Spanish styles, was called «Mozárabe.» However, this term is equally misleading, for aside from the influence of bright Islamic polychromy and the use of ceramic tile, we find in this house no other oriental forms than those of the smoking room ceiling. On the other hand, elements of structural sincerity which was never a part of Arabic art are extremely numerous —i. e., the emphasis on the use of materials in their natural state, the undisguised use of industrial techniques, and the absolute disdain for formulas as seen in the use of chimneys as essential elements in the plastic composition of the façade.

The most important aspect of this house is its overall expressive strength and the harmonious manner in which all of its volumes and colors are united, especially in the roof towers and the walkways which, as J. M. Martorell has said, define «a single whole, a perfectly defined space with is own expression and filled with the mystery which characterizes all architectural space.»[5]

164. VILLA QUIJANO IN COMILLAS: «EL CAPRICHO.» 1883-1885 (Figs. 122, 214 - 219)

This is a vacation villa on the outskirts of Comillas (in the province of Santander) next to the palace of the Marquis of that name. It is situated on sloping terrain and its wandering plan can be inscribed in a rectangle 15 by 36 meters. The building consists of one single main floor which opens onto the garden level in the back, with semi-basements on the main façade where the uneven ground level permits; there is also a small upper-story loft containing several rooms.

208. Casa Vicens. Garden façade in its original state.

2. J. M. Martorell, in *Gaudí*, (Centro de Estudios Gaudinistas), published by the Colegio Oficial de Arquitectos, 1960. [The author neglects to mention that at the same time a widening of the street forced the elimination of the steps and projections on that side (observable in Figs. 205, 205A), the changing of the entrance from the street to garden side, the redesigning of the street façade (as in Fig. 207), and the extension of the fence (Fig. 206) around the entire new property several hundred feet. These changes are pointed out in the caption to plate 12 in my book on Gaudí. — G. R. C.]

3. Bergós says that these leaves were cast from the natural ones that existed on the property before work was begun. *Op. cit.*, p. 73.

4. José Ramón Mélida, *Vocabulario de términos de Arte*, (Madrid: 1887), p. 373.

5. Martorell, *op. cit.*

209. Casa Vicens. Cascade in the garden, which no longer exists.

210. Casa Vicens. Tribune over the garden.

211. Stalactite ceiling in the smoking room of the same house.

212. Structure and decoration of the dining room ceiling.

213. Corner cupboard in the Casa Vicens.

The main entrance is a cut-away corner where four stone columns, which support the characteristic tower which we will discuss in a moment, form a small portico which serves as an antechamber to the hexagonally shaped vestibule. The interior distribution is based on a large hall with rooms on either side and one at the end; some of these rooms have caissoned ceilings (artesonados) which foreshadow those which we will see in the Palacio Güell. Next to the vestibule is a very small circular staircase which leads to the semi-basement and to the upper floor where there is a cylindrical tower containing another, wider circular stair—this one with a hole in the center, just as those he would later employ in the Sagrada Familia and the one which he had seen in the bell tower of his native Reus. The windows of the villa are of a double thickness of glass, and the carpentry work is everywhere extremely fine.

THE EXTERIOR APPEARANCE. On the front where the semi-basement serves as a lower floor, the basement section of the façade is made of stone with the horizontal joints emphatically marked with deep outlining bands in between each stone course, interrupted only by the windows of this floor. The general impression is one of grand sturdiness with rusticated surfaces which end in a bold strip of torus molding which indicates the beginning of the main floor of the building.

The main part of the house is built entirely of exposed brick, relieved every nine courses with horizontal strips of glazed tiles—leafy green ones alternating with yellow flowered ones. There are two small semi-octagonal corner balconies which are interesting for their wooden benches, built-in to the wrought iron railings.

The corbeling system in the eaves shows a certain delight in a rich coronation that is somewhat excessive to modern taste. The steeply sloping roof is subdivided into various sections, with its louvers, ventilators, and chimney stacks covered with brightly colored tiles lending movement to this upper part of the building.

The most characteristic element of the villa is the cylindrical tower which rises above the robust stone columns of the porch with their highly original capitals of floral and zoomorphic motifs united by a stone cupola and arches. The sturdy aspect of this portico is in contrast to the slender cylindrical tower which is circled at the top by a cast-iron railing at the edge of a corbeled platform. The tower is not supported by the columns, but rather by the little stone cupola which is especially braced for the purpose with two iron crossbars. The tower is completely covered with the same sort of tiles that we have already seen—some green and in low relief, others with yellow flowers in high relief—arranged here in a checkerboard pattern. The upper part of the tower is widened through a system of corbeled brackets to make room for an observation deck, as in an Arabic minaret, and a pinnacle—consisting of four slender cast-iron columns with highly stylized wide Doric capitals which support consoles terminating in a small bulbous cupola—lightens the top of the tower.

GENERAL CONSIDERATIONS. We do not know why this villa is called «El Capricho.» It is true that its characteristics when compared with the severe neo-Gothic palace and pantheon chapel or oratory of the Marquis of Comillas are somewhat capricious: the informal outline of the plan, the picturesque quality of the roof, the coquettish suggestiveness of certain details such as the corner balconies and, especially, the tower are all products of an optimistic and carefree inspiration which, seen superficially in a region of mountainous sobriety, might appear to be capricious. Yet the name is not altogether accurate, for the functional objectives of the villa are fully satisfied, and its decoration is consistent with the esthetic principles set forth in the Casa Vicens. There the structure was more simple; here it is complicated by the difficulties of bracing the roof frame, the louvers, circular staircases, the minaret tower, and an attached coach house.

The esthetic principles are the same, but the materials at Comillas are richer. Nevertheless, the result obtained in Barcelona is more agile and spontaneous than in the villa, where the overall grace never quite overcomes a certain rigidity.

Gaudí never visited this construction site; he entrusted the direction of the work to his friend the architect Cristóbal Cascante who had been a classmate and co-assistant to Villar and who was at the time working as a builder in Comillas. Though he was an effective director, it is possible that the work suffered to some degree from the lack of the author's personal presence. Gaudí would perhaps have asserted his authority and foresight in the modification of some details of the eaves and of the columns below the tower, which Bergós says he originally designed to be inclined and more slender. He may have adopted the heavy columns and the braced cupola which we see today in order to simplify Cascante's job; the forms are hardly in line with his nascent structural ideas.

In order to adapt to the slope of the terrain the small posterior esplanade which serves as a garden, there exist a number of buttresses in the form of benches, jardinieres, and a stairway; given the circumstances of construction, these must have been proposed by Cascante though they were, or course, worked out by Gaudí, whose hand can be detected, less in the decorative aspect than in the comfortableness of the reentering dihedral angled benches and the carefully worked-out drainage apparatus.

214. Comillas. Villa Quijano, exterior view of the façade.

215. Comillas. Villa Quijano, plan outline. (Author's plan.)

A. Coach house (now garage).

B. Storerooms of the lower floor along the façade, and basement for the rest of the house.

C. Small entrance portico.

When Gaudí was commissioned to do these buildings for the property which the Güells owned outside of Barcelona between Les Corts de Sarriá and Pedralbes, he was already working for that family on the house on the Calle del Conde del Asalto, but we will study this work first because of its stylistic relationship with those just examined, representing as it does an evolution of certain principles which he set forth in the earlier works. As a result of subsequent urbanization, these structures which originally were situated in the open country have lost their former unity; the most important group now stands in the vicinity of the Law School in the Ciudad Universitaria, next to the Avenida de la Victoria. Here we will study the Dragon Gate, the gate-house, and other details.

THE DRAGON GATE. This was the first important manifestation of Gaudí's amazing gift for giving artistic expression to wrought iron. In the previous works which we have discussed he primarily employed cast iron, but from this point on he would prefer the forge.

This gate is the main entrance to the gardens, and it is mounted in stone and brick with a small side door for the entrance of pedestrians. It is placed between two jambs; that near the turning axis is rather high—over 10 meters—in order to accommodate the built-in hinge and act as a counterweight for the gate when opened. The other jamb is part of a small wall which contains the pedestrian entrance gate. The masonry parts have stone foundations two meters high, the rest being built of brick which is used in an extremely intricate and careful manner. The bands are alternately reddish and yellowish in tone, and the mortar of the joints is inlaid with tiny fragments of a polychrome vitreous substance which, when hit by the sunlight, produce sparkling reflections. The pinnacles and the intermediate emblem of the tall pillar-jamb are of sculpted stone in forms which anticipate the Art Nouveau contours which would soon become firmly established in Gaudí's work.

216. Comillas. Villa Quijano, *artesonado* ceiling of one of the rooms.

217. Comillas. Villa Quijano, corner balcony with a railing that serves also as a seat, mixed structure of iron and wood as is the upper frame for vines.

218. Comillas. Villa Quijano, entrance portico and minaret tower with abundant polychrome ceramic decoration.

219. Comillas. Villa Quijano, capital of one of the portico columns.

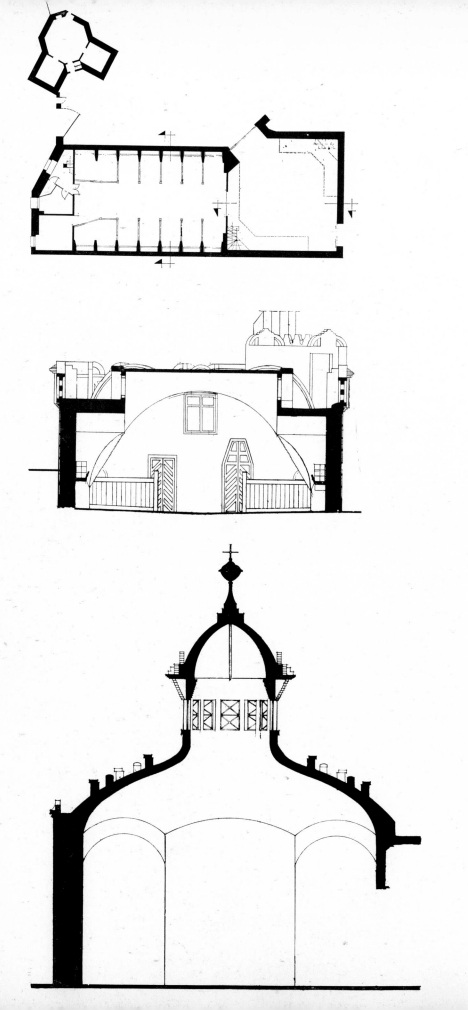

220. Finca Güell in Les Corts. Plan of the gatekeeper's pavilion, the stables, the riding-school and the entrance gate. (J. Bassegoda.)

221. Finca Güell in Les Corts. Section of the stables. (Bassegoda.)

222. Finca Güell in Les Corts. Section of the riding-school. (Bassegoda.)

223. Finca Güell. Dragon Gate in the bordering wall.

224. Finca Güell. Detail of the Dragon Gate.

225. Stairway exit from the roof of the old Güell residence in Les Corts.

228. Finca Güell. Wall with imbrications, corbelled parabolic openings and an upper railing with a triangular-hexagonal rhythm.

229. An open gallery-passage-wall in the gate-house which is now closed off.

226. Supporting pillar of the entrance gate with ornamentation that heralds the *modernista* style.

227. Finca Güell. Vault and lantern of the riding-school from the exterior, covered with polychrome ceramic and brick.

The most interesting part of this entranceway is, of course, the five-meter wide iron gate whose lower section is composed of two superimposed square net patterns, the first acting as a structural framework with diagonal diamond patterns of slender T-rods inscribed with small *repoussé* squares which form the second network of squares parallel to the diagonal of the first. The upper half of the gate is competely free in form imitating a mythological dragon who guards the entrance, with his wing conveniently placed to double as a brace for the correct suspension of the gate. The forged-iron work on this dragon is especially noteworthy for its delicate technique and ingenuity. When the gate was well cared for, the dragon would lift one of its feet when the door was opened, as if in defense of the enclosure.

THE GATE-HOUSE AND STABLES. The gatekeeper's residence is located to the left of the entrance and is divided into three parts: a central octagonal one-story dome-covered building flanked by two domed square towers containing upper floors. To the right is the pavilion which served as a stable—a rectangular hall with transverse parabolic arches which sustain *tabicada* vaults, and a contiguous square enclosure covered by a circular vault which terminates in a lantern; the smaller room served as a riding school, and the two sections are united by a continuous exterior.

STRUCTURE AND DECORATION. In these buildings, despite their modest function, Gaudí experimented for the first time with more personal structural solutions, cutting loose from tradition while using forms which are stylistically more manifestly Arabic in nature. Given the low height of the walls, he decided to build them of adobe masonry (which also serves as an excellent thermic insulator) mixed with brick and reinforced with pillars visible on the outside and bands of a single thickness of brick which form rectangles 1.70 and 2.44 meters long by 33 cm. high. The adobe masonry is mounted on a rubble base to protect it from the ground humidity, and is shielded on the exterior by cement slabs which are impressed with molds of semi-circular patterns (Fig. 229). The window jambs are of brick in the form of arches achieved by gradually advancing brick courses; in the crest of the wall is displayed a great profusion of ingenious combinations of brick, in small decorative arches of corbeled bands, and in openwork cornices and triangular networks which make up hexagonal motifs, decorated with polychrome ceramic inlays in a wide variety of artistic solutions.

Especially noteworthy is the roofing system which makes ample use of the *tabicada* vaults—some in cylindrical or pseudo-ellipsoidal form such as those which rest on the parabolic arches of the stables. These are the first such arches that Gaudí employed for structural reasons,[6] and they spring from corbeled horizontal brick courses which develop into strap or *tabicada* arches of great thickness. The other vaults are surfaces of revolution which are visible on the exterior in somewhat varied form to give greater expressive force; they are covered with polychromatic mosaic for decorative effect.

The roofs of these two pavilions are practicable and develop the great feeling for space and color which was suggested in the Casa Vicens; here it appears with even greater plasticity and richness of forms and hues, and we have a preview of some of the qualities which will be most evident in the roof of the Casa Milá.

OTHER ELEMENTS. Part of the Finca Güell, along with the seignorial mansion, was given over to King Alfonso XIII as a Barcelona residence, and in adapting this house to its new use, the roof terrace stairway exit and a smoke extractor which Gaudí had opened in the already existing house were removed. The stairway exit had also served as a small observation deck, with a platform rising above the level of the terrace accessible by means of several stairs which continued parallel to the stairway below. This exitway had, in addition, a stone bench at either side. It was built of brick with pillars and arches expressively arranged in ascending quarter circles, with the interlying surfaces faced in decorative patterns of white and colored tiles (Fig. 225).

The smoke extractor or ventilating tube was rather tall, with a bold silhouette and ceramic appliqués, and joined the *mirador* in giving an optimistic note to the terrace.

In one of the surrounding walls of the *finca* there was a brick portal with ceramic decoration which had to be destroyed for urbanistic reasons; this door was later reconstructed in another section of the urban development using the same bricks and retaining the same dimensions and distribution.

166. TWO EXPOSITION PAVILIONS? (Fig. 554)

I regret that I must answer this question negatively; I have stated it as a question merely by way of a transition between previous biographers and the results of my investigations which indicate that neither the pavilion for the Naval Exposition at Cádiz in 1887, nor that of the Universal Exposition in Barcelona in 1888 can be included among our architect's works. Writers on the subject unanimously attribute both pavilions to Gaudí without reference to archival documentation. Because of suspicions of a stylistic nature, I made inquiries at the Transatlantic Company (which sponsored both pavilions) and found that in their offices they have no records prior to 1936, a year in which all of their archives and documents were destroyed. From information requested from Cádiz, I learned that the author of the pavilion for that city was the *maestro de obras* García Cabezas.[7] Keeping in mind the fact that the Cádiz pavilion was dismountable, it is logical that once the exposition was over, the Transatlantic Company would have used the same pavilion at Barcelona the following year, as revealed by the official organ *La Exposición* which says, «at the left of this walk is the installation of the Transatlantic Company, the same that figured in the Naval Exposition of Cádiz...»

Gaudí, however, took part in the erection of the pavilion referred to and carried out some modifications—of which we speak in Appendix VIII.

6. We have seen that the parabolic wooden arches at Mataró are not strictly adapted to their function, and those of the Palacio Güell, which might be previous to these in Les Corts, are used more in a generic than a specifically equilibrated sense.

7. I am grateful to don Eduardo Buisen, repesentative of the company, for his interest in my research.

XL. THE PALACIO GÜELL. 1885-1890

167.   DESCRIPTION (Figs. 36 - 39, 230 - 232)

The location of this aristocratic mansion on a street such as that of the Conde del Asalto—in no way distinguished for its nobility—is explained by the fact that it was built as an extension of the Güell residence on the Ramblas, with which it was connected in the rear; the annex soon became the main building, however, due to the palatial elegance given it by the architect and the successful distribution of all its facilities in a relatively small area (18 × 22 meters).

The palace consists of six floors beginning with a basement in which the stables, a room for the groom, and a harness room were located—rooms which were reached by a gently sloping ramp for animals and a more pronounced spiral-shaped one for the servants. This basement is extremely well ventilated by means of a patio and air shafts which rise up to the roof terrace.

The lower floor at street level has a double doorway for the facile movement of coaches; here the main stairway begins between the two vestibules, and there is a coach house in the rear from which the ramps go down to the basement. This floor has the gatekeeper's rooms to one side, and on the other the servants' stairway built of iron in an ingenious hanging arrangement (Fig. 237). In the front vestibule there is a small stone platform reached by four low steps which served for the comfortable mounting of horses.[1] The main stairway leads to a mezzanine which was used for administrative offices, archives, a library, and a waiting room; from the latter the grand stairway ascends to the *piano nobile*.

It is from this point up that the building acquires its palatial character, with the subsidiary rooms being distributed around a central salon which is as high as the building itself, replacing the traditional interior patio. The grand staircase opens onto the front corridor along which are distributed the vestibule, a passage hall leading into the principal hall or salon, and the receiving room. Along the corridor which runs parallel to the back façade are the dining room, the «private» room, the billiard parlor, a dressing room, a pantry with a dumbwaiter communicating with the kitchen on the top floor, and other associated rooms. Between the front and back corridors stands the square salon which receives light indirectly through windows in the bearing walls which parallel the façades, and also from the high windows in the cupola. An altar table is located in this salon in a tiny cupboard-like structure which is usually closed; when it is opened, the hall becomes an oratory with a little sacristy and an organ whose pipes are placed in the upper galleries of the salon which could become tribunes for choirs when necessary, with fine acoustical results. The organ bellows had an independent access from the roof in order to avoid the danger of bothersome noises. The salon was the central room of the house where parties, family reunions, and the concerts of which the Güells were so fond were held.

On the next floor up, behind the tribunes which border on the salon, are the bedrooms of the house with their dressing tables, sanitary equipment, and other facilities; and on the upper floor there were 11 bedrooms for the servants, a laundry-room, and the kitchen. The roof terrace has a conical spire 15 meters high in the center which covers the salon cupola, and has four vaults flaring out to form clerestories for illumination. Around this center point are distributed the 18 ventilating tube projections which we will discuss later.

168   STRUCTURE AND DECORATION (Figs. 86, 91, 92, 125, 126, 138, 143, 147, 233 - 254)

It has been said that the architectural aspect of this palace was determined by the Italian origin of Güell's mother (from the Bacigalupi family, natives of Genoa who settled in Barcelona), and that Gaudí was seeking to evoke a type of Venetian palace. It seems more logical, when we consider the large number of possible solutions that he drew up for the façade,[2] that he was concerned with finding a solution of his own which would fit the character of the proprietor and the program established in conjunction with him.

It goes without saying that the house is solidly built. In addition to the exterior bearing walls there are massive supporting pillars of brick in the basement which flare out at the top in mushroom capitals to reduce the span of the arches and vaults which rest upon them. The façades and other bearing walls below the principal floor are constructed of gray polished marble from Garraf with columns of the same material where dictated by structural needs or artistic design.[3] The façade is both severe and noble, accentuated by the main-floor tribune which is supported by brackets with equilibrated profiles; the tribune stretches across the entire façade, rising a story higher on either end. The lower floors and tribune follow a vertical

---

1. A similar arrangement to this which Pane says was for climbing into coaches, was found in the feudal castles and noble mansions of medieval times. The Cathedral of Tarragona shows signs of one that existed next to the façade in the days when the canons rode horses.

2. Ráfols says that he made «many projects until he settled on the one that he considered definitive.» (*op. cit.*, p. 48) and Bergós details the fact that the studies and variations totalled 25 different drawings (*op. cit.*, p. 77). These projects, 25 in number, were drawn up by Berenguer under Gaudí's direction. This information was provided by Camps Arnau on December 22, 1961; he had been told this by Berenguer himself.

3. In cutting this stone at the quarry —which was owned by Güell—a continuous triple-spiral saw was provided by the owner—the most precise and adequate instrument known at the time. J. Puiggari in *Monografía de la Casa Palau y Museu del Excem. Sr. D. Eusebi Güell y Bacigalupi*, (Barcelona: 1894).

rectangular pattern which lightens the overall severity; this pattern is itself relieved by the two catenary entrance arches which enhance the expressiveness of the façade without the aid of a single sculpted ornament, except for an isolated series of fleurs-de-lis at the second-story level.

The most important decorative element of the façade is the latticework cylinder between the two parabolic entrance arches—a masterpiece of wrought-iron work which represents the coat of arms of Catalonia surrounded by ribbon-like lambrequins and surmounted by a helmet with an eaglet on top; equally beautiful are the intricately wrought flowers of the screen below.

The entrance gates within the arches are also outstanding examples of ironwork, and the first such gates to be used in Barcelona.[4] The movable parts are simply patterned in a twining manner ingeniously designed to keep people on the outside from looking in, while the stationary upper parts are more free in form and include the proprietor's initials on different shields surrounded by sinuous ironwork which recalls the movement of a whiplash—a motif later basic to the Art Nouveau. Other decorative pieces of wrought iron on the façade reflect the same characteristic refinement of technique and sobriety of form.

In the interior of the lower floor we find more ironwork of a similar nature, harmonizing well with the walls and columns of gray polished marble. Another notable aspect of the decoration is the set of three beautiful square panels in the ceiling of each of the two vestibules, each with a slightly pyramidal profile and a different patterned combination of brick placed on edge centering about a square marble keystone

The interior doors are of finely carved wood, some being inlaid with small plaques of repoussé iron. On the principal floor we see sumptuous woodwork whose interlacing recalls Arabic patterns which contrast with, but do not disturb, the medieval evocations of the palace as a whole. Some of the artesonado ceilings of the principal floor are outstanding for their carpentry work, the wide variety of the wood employed, the rich inventiveness of the solutions, and the technical perfection achieved. In the vestibule, eucalyptus was used, and in the receiving room, beech; both are combined with gilded ironwork in meter-high relief.

Characteristic of the central salon—nine meters square by 17.5 meters high—are the entrance doors, the oratory with its tortoise-shell facing and paintings on copper, and most especially the parabolic dome which is pierced to receive points of light from the exterior; this cupola is supported without pendentives, through direct intersection involving an ingenious corbel structure which reduces the diameter of the dome. An elegant feature of the room is the stairway (originally adorned with a bust of the proprietor's father—Fig 36) which leads to the tribune which is actually an extension of the salon and is bordered by a lacerywork railing in wood of Arabic inspiration.

An especially attractive element of the piano nobile is the series of tall slender parabolic arches along the main façade; despite their similar form, these graceful arches contrast with those of the main façade which project a sensation of resistance. Here we see Gaudí trying out the expressive possibilities of his new aesthetic ideas. There are similar arches in the tribune of the dining room; all of these arches are supported by gray marble columns—there are 127 throughout the palace—with hyperbolic capitals which either interweave or geometrically intersect the arches.

The rear façade is more staid in design, its only decorative elements being the large dining room tribune, the shuttered upper balcony, and a cleverly artistic conical plant shelter. The completely bare side façade which borders the terrace at the level of the principal floor was formerly decorated by a large fresco painting by Alejo Clapés depicting the mythological theme of Hercules in search of the Hesperides, but it has since disappeared. At the back of this terrace a gallery of slender columns and glassed-in pseudo-arches served as a passageway to the building on the Ramblas.

The bedrooms of the upper story were decorated with elegant sobriety and rich materials. Especially interesting is one room where wrought iron is used in combination with the stone arches and columns, where the metal extends the decoration of the stone capital into the arch space and the wall itself in anticipation of modernista motifs (Fig. 240). Also anticipatory of this style are some of the furniture pieces of the mansion which were skillfully combined with examples of both ancient and modern art.

The roof terrace is an essential part of the house, for it is here that the chimneys and ventilators from the lower floors emerge, converted by Gaudí into interesting conically shaped decorative motifs. Some of these projections are covered with polychrome tile fragments which enhance their powerful expressiveness, and when combined with the central cone—which caps the cupola and is perforated with cave-like openings and covered with greenish stone fragments—these constitute the most optimistic ornamental note of the entire palace.

4. These were used in some of the European capitals and were known in Barcelona through architectural magazines.

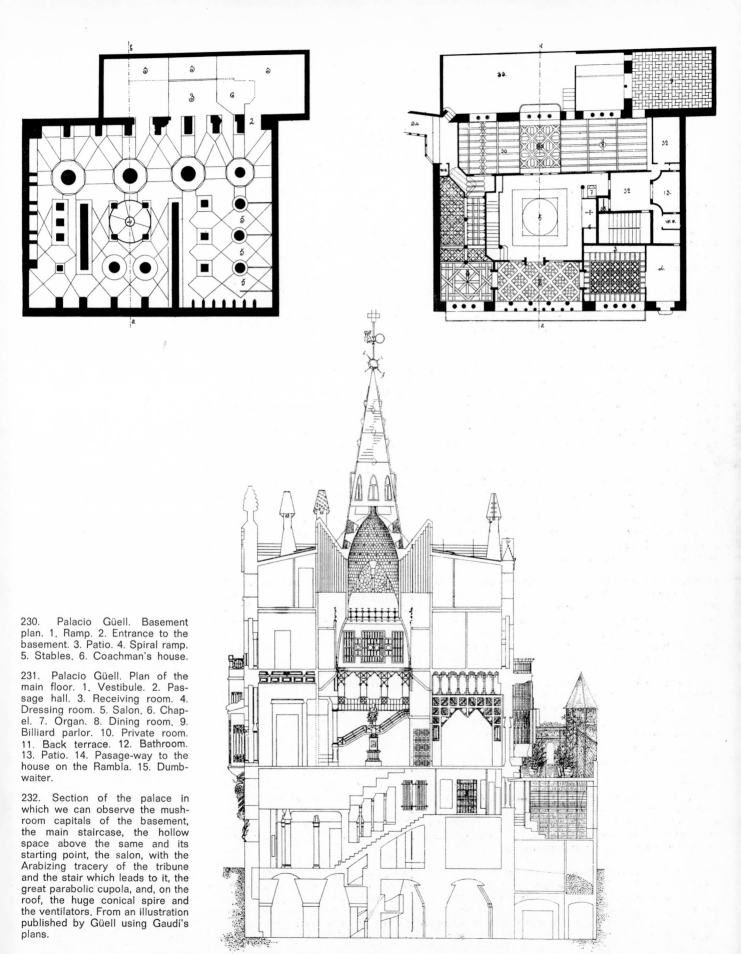

230. Palacio Güell. Basement plan. 1. Ramp. 2. Entrance to the basement. 3. Patio. 4. Spiral ramp. 5. Stables. 6. Coachman's house.

231. Palacio Güell. Plan of the main floor. 1. Vestibule. 2. Passage hall. 3. Receiving room. 4. Dressing room. 5. Salon. 6. Chapel. 7. Organ. 8. Dining room. 9. Billiard parlor. 10. Private room. 11. Back terrace. 12. Bathroom. 13. Patio. 14. Pasage-way to the house on the Rambla. 15. Dumbwaiter.

232. Section of the palace in which we can observe the mushroom capitals of the basement, the main staircase, the hollow space above the same and its starting point, the salon, with the Arabizing tracery of the tribune and the stair which leads to it, the great parabolic cupola, and, on the roof, the huge conical spire and the ventilators. From an illustration published by Güell using Gaudí's plans.

233. Palacio Güell. Street façade with a vertical rectangular rhythm except for the catenary arches of the entrance.

234. Palacio Güell. Extremely sober posterior façade with ingeniously resolved tribune and balcony.

We know from Gaudí himself that this termination for the building—simply decorative and pointed—was the first of its kind in Barcelona. It is not visible from the ground, but can be seen from the neighboring buildings.

169. PRESS COVERAGE 1891 (Figs 36 - 39)

Though most writers give 1889 as the termination date for this building and the date 1888 is sculpted in the upper part of the façade, we can assume that the finishing touches—which must have been considerable in a building of such quality and category, especially in regard to the furnishing—went on far into 1890 at least; this is supported by press reports dating from 1891 which are concerned with the palace as something «recently built.»

The illustrated magazines accompanied their reports with engravings (photographs were still not used at that time), displaying more than usual interest. In general, the articles focused on the building and its noble proprietor without mentioning the name of the architect at all. The name Gaudí was not yet known by the public. This was the first building in which he showed signs of his extraordinary architectural personality, and therefore it is not surprising that, though generally received with respect, certain critical reservation would become apparent.

La Ilustración Hispano-Americana, in an article illustrated with two full-page engravings which omits the name of the architect, describes it as a building «of robust and even heavy workmanship, whose original architecture departs entirely from anything ever seen before in this city...» (January 11, 1891). In a later issue the report is continued, accompanied by four half-page illustrations; this time the architect is named, and he is ranked with Doménech y Montaner as a leader in the architectural renaissance. This article also includes the names of those who collaborated in the work, such as the painter Alejo Clapés,[5] the architect Oliveras «who did the prodigious ornamentation,»[6] Puntí «who executed true works of art in the wooden elements,»[7] and Oñós and Gabarró the ironsmiths. In a third issue, *Ilustración* completed its coverage with a generally superficial description which nevertheless goes into some detail concerning the central dome which sticks up above the roof terrace: «from the summit of the cupola emerges the vigilant bat which since the days of Jaime el Conquistador has protected the arms of Catalonia with its wings: there stands the symbol of the powerful soul of this land, giving life to that immense mountain of stone.» (February 1, 1891). The article ends with the observation that this work—here illustrated with three more prints—was built completely with Catalan materials and labor.

THE ORGAN. No mention is made in these articles of the organ which had been commissioned from the manufacturer Aquilino Amezua of Azpeitia who had come to Barcelona to install the grand organ in the Universal Exposition's Palace of Fine Arts. (No Catalans were able to do the job at that time.) If the salon was the center of the palace, it could also be said that the organ was the heart of the salon, given the Güell family's love of music. The daughters were very fond of playing the organ, and took lessons from the great organist Gigou of Paris who supervised the installation.

At first it was planned that the organ would be only manual, but later an electric system was added in order to make it possible to carry out the architect's idea of placing the pipes in the upper tribunes (XXXI - 140). As finally installed, it consisted of one pedal and two manual keyboards; «the harmonies of the instrument were perceived by means of a mechanical system, simple but perfectly refined, wherein the tones descend from above, gently reflected by the fantastic salon cupola.»[8]

The fine musical instrument which the aristocrat and his family wanted was successfully achieved through the use of expensive materials: «an extravagance of money and good taste, such that I believe unequalled» (Noemis). According to Juan Rogent, who has carefully studied the question, the organ was designed and planned by Gaudí; he adds that «the musical life of Barcelona for half a century was linked to the Palacio Güell, and dominated by the gentle voices of the organ, whether it was classical music or religious to accompany the solemn celebration of the liturgical offices in the contiguous oratory.»[9] For many years of this century the palace was unoccupied, and since then it has been used for purposes it was not originally meant for. As a result the organ is in need of careful restoration.[10]

170 SIGNIFICANCE OF THE WORK

From the press articles transcribed it can be ascertained that this palace's appearance on the Barcelona urban scene was greeted with general surprise—a surprise mixed with admiration, and yet not without cautious reservations. The young architect who had proven himself in Gracia and Les Corts with two works whose polychrome vibrancy seemed to overshadow their structural importance made his debut in the center of the city with unexpected daring and a new language which the critics were not prepared to understand; even less could they predict where such novel solutions would lead. Everyone sensed that this was no trivial matter; this new architectural manifestation, even though agnostic, had an imposing superiority

5. The author of the paintings on the doors of the salon and of the great fresco on the lateral façade.

6. He directed the carving of the chimney and the dining room scaffolding. He was a friend of Gaudí's who argued with him about decoration and attended anticlerical gatherings.

7. The carved ceilings, doors and details of the salon and dining room.

8. Noemis, *Organos eléctricos,* p. 92.

9. Juan Rogent y Massó, «Proyecto y presupuesto de orientación para la restauración del órgano del palacio Güell, Propiedad de la Excma. Diputación de Barcelona, May, 1954.» An unpublished document which I am grateful to the author for his permission to consult.

10. At the death of its builder, the palace passed on to his daughter, Doña Mercedes who generously arranged to cede it to the Barcelona *Provincial Diputación.* [Eusebio Güell's office on the mezzanine floor was for many years the headquarters and research archive of the *Amigos de Gaudí* of Barcelona. — G. R. C.]

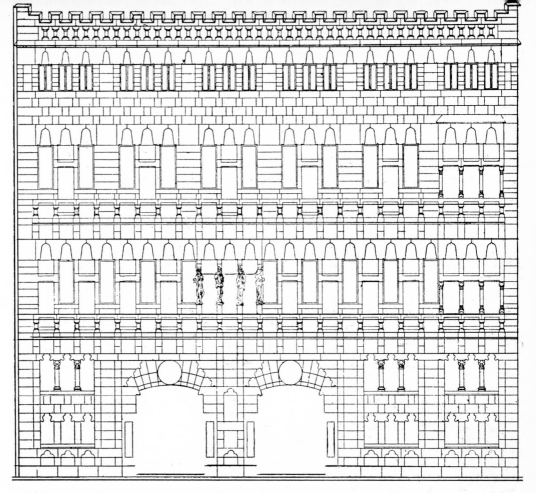

235. One of the 25 façade projects for the Palacio Güell drawn up by Berenguer at Gaudí's direction. From Ráfols.

which foretold something unsuspected. In retrospect we know that the Palacio Güell was the first firm step in the evolution of Gaudí's later style. But his contemporaries could not possibly know this, and it is not surprising that there were problems of lack of comprehension.

The almost unknown audacious architect who had just built that «robust and even heavy work,» was the same one who, out beyond the old city walls in the neighborhood of San Martín, had been put in charge of an already begun temple whose basic design he was striving to change. The prelate of Astorga had commissioned him to build a new bishop's palace. All of these commissions bear witness to the worth of the original artist who so elegantly took his first steps in the «City of the Counts.»

What Gaudí did, could be liked or disliked; the aspect of the house could be criticized as gloomy and the atmosphere as less than gay, but some of the details deserve nothing less than unconditional praise: the two catenary entrance arches, still more decorative than structural; the novel grating and coat of arms in wrought iron; the ramps descending to the basement, used here for the first time; the suspended iron stairway for the servants; the simple and majestic development of the grand staircase, with its magnificent spatial effect; the extremely beautiful parabolic arcades of the *piano nobile;* some of the *artesonado* ceilings of the same story; the cupola with its delicate interior coating of hexagonal pieces and its ingenious system of support; and the roof terrace with its central pinnacle and diverse projections in forms and colors which are far ahead of their time in originality and beauty. Some of these and other details were bound to upset Gaudí's own unprepared generation With our hindsight we can see them as clear examples of the architect's creative potential, and as eloquent lessons in good building and compositional practice.

Despite the numerous lessons that can be learned from this building, there are two elements of the solution which are not clearly justified: the first is an empty space near the ceiling of the ground-floor wall opposite the stairway which connects with the wrought-iron grille of the façade shield and is inaccessible and without practical function; the second is the central summit cone which, being invisible from the street, does not realize its full potential for beauty.

Such perplexing details are more than compensated, however, and there can be no doubt that this palace marks the first definitive step, the conscious and transcendental beginning of Gaudí's path; despite the restrained forms, we can find here the seed of the dynamic originality which would inspire his later works.

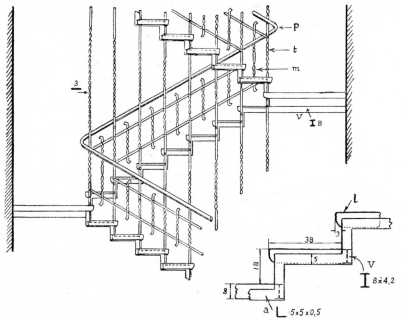

236. Palacio Güell. Basement pillars and vaults with spiral access ramp.

237. Palacio Güell. Secondary hanging-stairway. From Bergós.

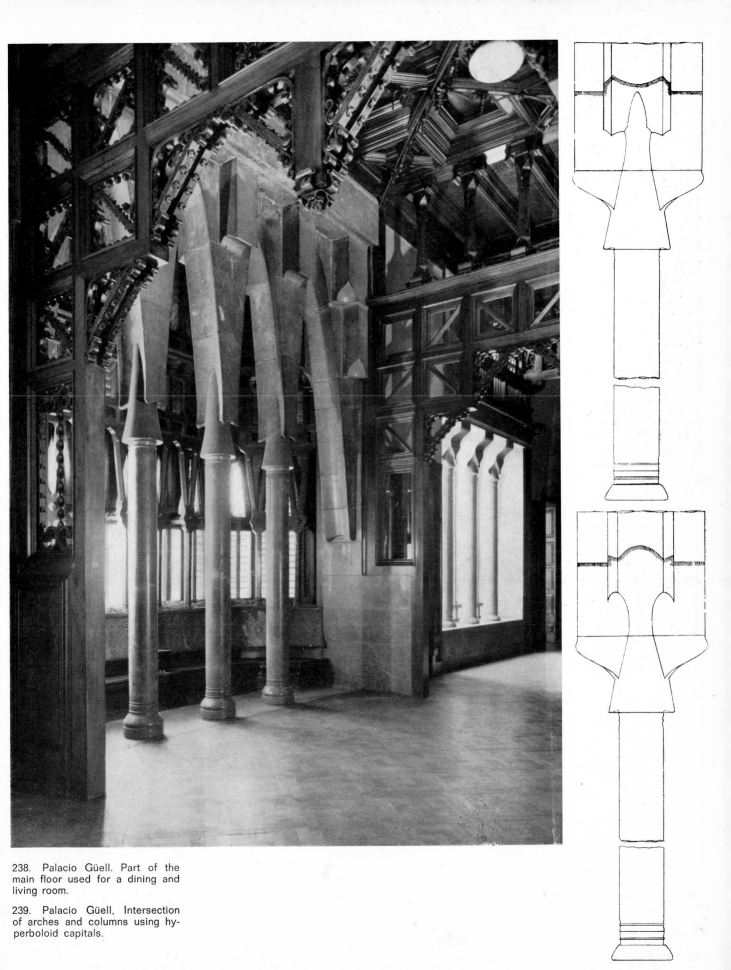

238. Palacio Güell. Part of the main floor used for a dining and living room.

239. Palacio Güell. Intersection of arches and columns using hyperboloid capitals.

240. Palacio Güell. Bedroom furnished in the days of the original owner with a pre-*modernista* divan and an arch decorated with wrought iron.

241. «Hercules seeking the Hesperides.» Detail of the mural painting by Alejo Clapés which has now disappeared from the lateral façade of the house.

242. Wrought-iron detail of the entrance portal.

243. Grating of the Palacio Güell in wrought iron with a sinuous rhythm which is regular in the lower part and free in the upper section.

244. Palacio Güell. Vestibule with an arrangement for comfortably mounting a horse, and the main staircase, in the period of the Güell family.

245. Palacio Güell. Cupola of the central salon with upper galleries used for choirs and organ pipes.

246. Palacio Güell. Decoration of a capital in wrought iron with forms that are *modernista* in spirit before the *modernista* period.

247. Palacio Güell. *Artesonado* ceiling of one of the main floor rooms.

248. Palacio Güell. Tracery-railing of wood with shell inlays which borders the upper tribune of the central salon.

249. Palacio Güell. Central element of the upper edge of the façade with one of the ventilators.

250. Palacio Güell. Roof terrace, pinnacle of the cone which protects the cupola, with its cross of St. George and the symbolical bat.

251. Palacio Güell. Roof terrace, base of the protective cone over the cupola, with parabolic openings.

252. Palacio Güell. A chimeny on the roof terrace.

253. Palacio Güell. Partial view of the roof terrace with a variety of chimneys and ventilators.

254. Palacio Güell. View of the
terrace from across the street,
with its dominant conical spire,
ventilators, and façade crests.

171. THE CRYPT
172. THE APSE

Gaudí began working on Güell's palace more than a year after he had been put in charge of the work on the Sagrada Familia church—still very much in its beginnings when he took over—which in his hands would vary a great deal from the initial idea. Bocabella had planned to take as his model for the new temple the church at Loreto (76 by 100 meters) where the sacred family of Nazareth was venerated—a plan which he later changed in favor of a neo-Gothic structure whose design was entrusted to the diocesan architect, F. de P. del Villar y Lozano. The first stone was laid on Saint Joseph's Day, 1882, and work began on the crypt which, once finished, would contain an exact copy of the house in Nazareth where Jesus's family lived.[1]

171. THE CRYPT. 1882-1891 (Figs. 255 - 261)

Villar had designed the pillars of this crypt as clustered columns of two different sizes, the tallest being those of greater diameter: departing from a common socle, the bases of the taller columns were on a lower level, and their capitals were larger with somewhat lower collars, though the abaci were all at the same height. From above these abaci would spring the circular arches, and the crypt would receive light through three round bull's-eye openings 90 cm. in diameter located in each of the seven chapels above the fascia running along at the height of the capitals (Fig. 255).[2]

On August 25, 1883, the excavation of the crypt area was completed, and Bocabella contracted the builder Macario Planella to lay the foundations and construct the walls, pillars, and other elements up to the springing of the arches. This first stage of construction must have been of short duration since hardly two months after the contract was signed, the disagreements arose which were to lead to Villar's resignation (X - 35). According to the latter's report, the «boundary walls, chapel compartments, and, in part, the pillars of the great crypt of the church...»[3] had already been built, but the limited span of time leads us to believe that these were actually only just begun.

According to the biographers, Gaudí took charge on the following November 3. It was then that the new director began to influence the construction work and the plans with which he was apparently in disagreement. He liked neither the work as it was proceeding nor the ad-

1. A pamphlet handed out in 1877 contains engravings of the façade and the interior of this church. Archive of the author.

2. Original plans of Villar, with the indicated characteristics. Archive of the author (donated by O. Planella.)

3. F. de P. Villar, *Diario de Barcelona*, May 17, 1885.

mts.
3
2
1
0

255. Sagrada Familia. Villar's project for the crypt.

ministrative setup, and therefore wished to cancel the previous stage, annulling the contract with Planella without excluding the possibility of drawing up another one with the same builder afterwards (X - 36). The critical point in the dispute seems to have come in February 1884, but opportune intervention by Rogent led to a solution agreeable to both parties involving the formalization, on March 28, of the continuation of the contract subject «to the plans, details, and orders of the new architect-in-charge, don Antonio Gaudí, and any variations in the project, changes in the structural system, etc. will be the object of additional conditions...» [4]

Gaudí would have liked to locate the axis of the temple along the diagonal of the block, [5] but he was forced to adhere to what had already been built; as for the pillars formed of clustered columns, he would have preferred that they be cylindrical, to the point that he even thought of constructing the one which had not yet been begun in that manner. He consulted the architect Martorell on this, and the latter agreed; later, however, he thought better of the idea and followed the type established so as not to introduce «civil war among the columns» adding with insight: «a marriage between cripples is preferable to marital strife.» [6] He decided to heighten the arches by making them pointed, and in order to rid the crypt of its subterranean dinginess he surrounded it with a moat-like ditch and, doing away with the chapel imposts, he converted the bull's-eyes into large windows. With authorization to devise a new project, we have seen that from the first moment he imposed his own criteria in both the administrative and architectural sense, designing the capitals according to his personal taste within the Gothic spirit and solving in his own way any new problems which might arise.

Although the crypt was not entirely finished until 1891, services were held for the first time on St. Joseph's Day, 1885, at that Saint's altar designed by Gaudí in severe Gothic with the image of the Saint some two meters high standing out against a rectangular background with the inscription *Sancte Josephus* at the level of his head, and *Ora Pro Nobis* written vertically on either side. It is logical to assume that for this solemn occasion at least one of the fan-like access stairways would have been completed; it was planned that these stairways would continue upward in the finished temple to provide access to the various tribunes and the roof. The central stairwell would eventually house an elevator.

The central well of the first flight is used as a sacristy, with beautiful doors whose ornamentation is an extension of the gigantic polished steel hinges which flower out to fill the panels

4. «Pliego de Condiciones...» original signed by José M. Bocabella and Macario Planella; in the archive of the author as a donation by D. Octavio Planella, Appendix IX.

5. Bergós, *op. cit.*, p. 40.

6. Martinell, *op. cit.*, p. 85.

256. Sagrada Familia. View of the crypt as modified by Gaudí.

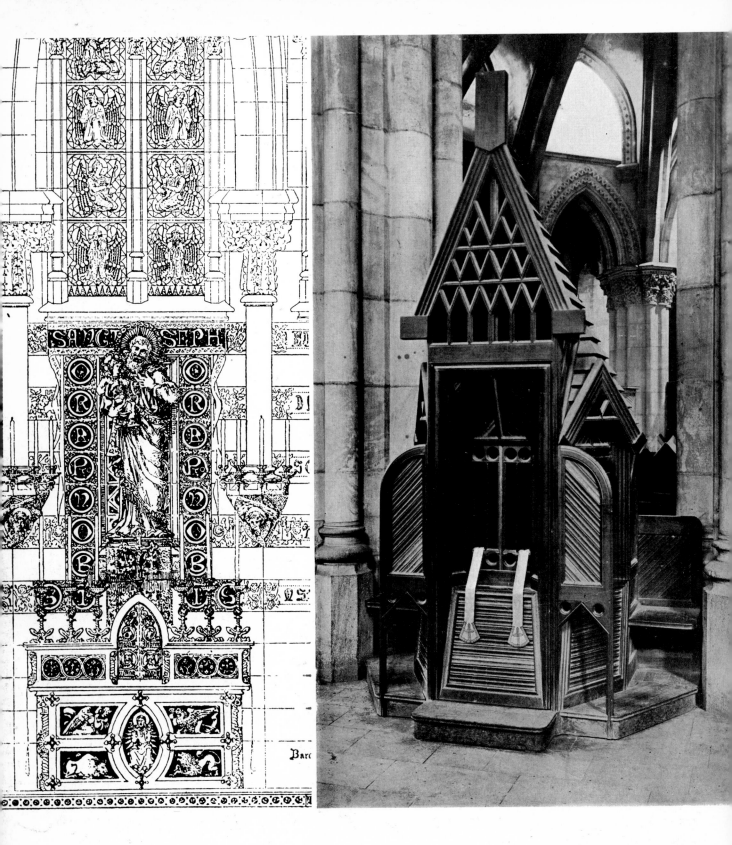

257. Sagrada Familia. Altar of St. Joseph in the crypt, designed by Gaudí.

258. Sagrada Familia. Interesting carpentry work on the confessional of the crypt.

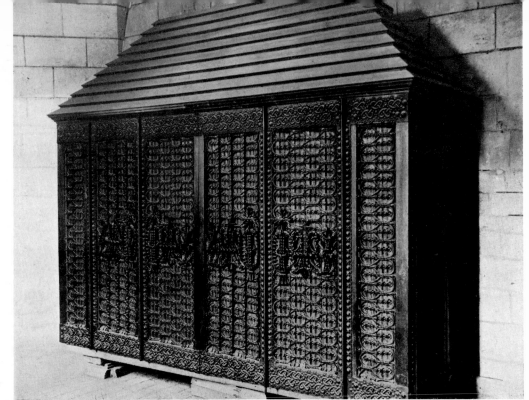

259. Sagrada Familia. Cupboard for liturgical ornaments.

260. Sagrada Familia. Door to the sacristy in the crypt.

261. Sagrada Familia. Ceremonial candlestick.

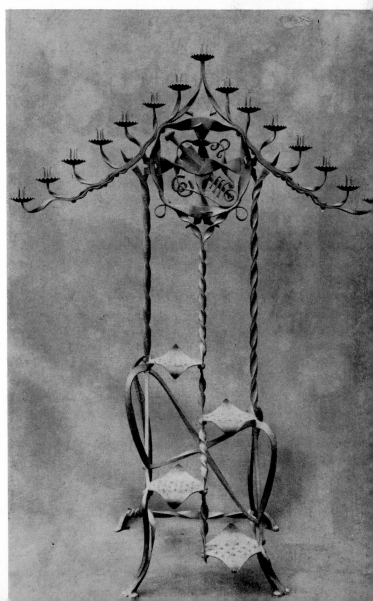

with an attractive combination of metal and wood. The apsidal altars were dedicated to the Holy Family of Jesus Christ: the Immaculate Conception, Saint Joseph, Saint Joachim and Saint Anne, Saint Elizabeth and Saint Zachariah, Saint John the Baptist, Saint John the Evangelist, and the Sacred Heart.[7] One chapel was used for the tomb of the Bocabella family, and another later housed that of Gaudí himself.

Despite several details where the originality of the architect can be observed, the general feeling of the crypt lies well within the historical Gothic style, in the technical aspect as well as the esthetic. A more advanced and markedly personal stylistic criterion is evident in the furniture which he designed with a view toward maximum liturgical purity.

172. THE APSE. 1891-1893 (Figs. 49, 264, 265)

While the crypt was being built, Gaudí worked out his design for the new church which had been entrusted to him. His plans were based on a liberal interpretation of Gothic norms, but his overall conception was more spatial and plastic than was usual in buildings based on that historical style, and the ornamental details were extremely personal.

From documentation through his extensive reading—then a more important influence than it was to be in later years—and through the direct study of certain churches which he had the opportunity to visit on his trips to the center of the peninsula and to the south of France, Gaudí arrived at the conclusion that the Gothic was an unfulfilled style based more on formulas and «industrial» repetition than on artistic considerations—a conclusion which he sustained throughout his lifetime. As a result, he dispensed with virtuousity of moldings, the superabundance of idle capitals, the useless imposts, and strangulated clusters unsuited to

7. Puig Boada, *El Templo de la Sagrada Familia*, (Barcelona: 1952), p. 26.

262. Sagrada Familia. Candlesticks and cross in wrought iron.

stone, and concerned himself with the classical concept of corporeality, concentrating on the relationship between solids and voids which the Gothic had forgotten in its abuse of decorative accessories.[8]

These were the principles which guided him as he began construction of the apse on top of the chapels of the crypt. He was obliged to follow the same arrangement, but he did so with a different spirit. We can see this immediately in the working of the exterior stone which has lost the cold, smooth finish of the crypt and acquired a less fine but more excitingly expressive texture.

Another characteristic element is the range of large windows which generally follow the traditional pointed Gothic form, here combined with a very simple molding, cut by imposts, arches, and circles of elementary composition. The upper termination of these apsidal chapels is free-form within the Gothic spirit, replacing the traditional gables with slender spires decorated with naturalistic plant motifs and simple, robust moldings.

In addition to the natural forms just mentioned which reproduce common grasses found on the property amplified to a giant scale, we should also note the zoomorphic gargoyles (seasnails, frogs, lizards, snakes...) which were cast from nature and greatly enlarged, in accordance with medieval symbolism which prescribed animals representing sin for this spot. The animals here appear to be descending, fleeing from the radiance of the cross with which Gaudí planned to terminate the highest pinnacle at the axis of the temple.

The present aspect of the apse—with construction still incomplete—is that of an airy battlement flanked and surmounted by two stair masses and the buttresses whose pinnacles exhibit floral motifs similar to those mentioned above.

8. Bergós, *op. cit.*, p. 83.

263. Sagrada Familia. Wrought-iron lectern.

264. Sagrada Familia. Gargoyles and freely interpreted molding of the apse.

265. Sagrada Familia. Naturalistic pinnacles of the spires of the apse.

173. THE EPISCOPAL PALACE IN ASTORGA. 1887-1893 (Figs. 43, 44, 133, 266 - 277)

The bishop's palace at Astorga was the third important work to be entrusted to Gaudí, coming after that of the expiatory temple and the palatial mansion for the Güell's; he received the commission in 1887.

Although his intensive and absorbing work schedule obliged him to obtain first details of the Astorgan job by mail, it did not keep him from getting down to work on those parts of the project which did not depend on local data. Gaudí was eager to make of architecture something vital and expressive; given the fact that he was dealing here with the residence for the lord who would exercise spiritual domain over the entire diocese, it seemed most fitting that the exterior should evoke a feudal castle without the military defense walls and watchtowers. Once again he turned to the Gothic, here as an evocation of feudal medievalism, in spite of the Renaissance predominance in the architectural environment of Astorga, and of his esthetic and structural reservations regarding the style in general.

In this work the architect's creative intellect becomes evident in a total concept which combines the character, in this case symbolic, with the utilitarian, structural, and artistic aspects in a synthesis which is clear in both the project and the actual building. The distribution recalls, to some extent, that of the Palacio Güell with an important central room around which are arranged the other facilities from the main floor to the roof which was open to considerable illumination. To facilitate the entrance of light—perhaps a lesson learned from the Güell palace which suffers from a lack of light in the central salon—he widened the section

266. Episcopal Palace at Astorga. Project for the main façade.

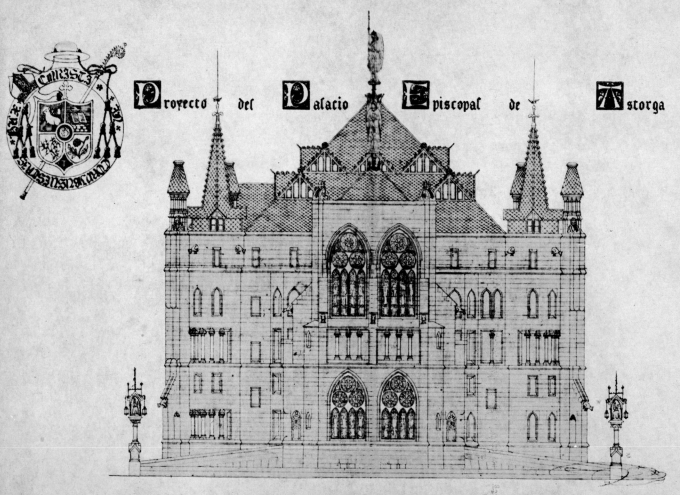

of the upper story to make room for clerestories in the great central section of the roof; unfortunately this part of the building was never completed.

The composition of the building was basically a square nucleus with a cylindrical tower at each corner. A projecting section contained the entrance portico and the throne room above it; another projecting section on the opposite side held the oratory which terminated in a triple apse, and there were various additional projections along the other sides. There are basements surrounded by an illumination and ventilation ditch, a lower floor, main floor, and a third-story attic. This arrangement gives an overall impression of motion where verticality and chiaroscuro effects predominate, along with the triple arch of the bold portico, modified somewhat from the original plans.

In his later years Gaudí considered building-plans to be merely a provisional orientation, subject always to improvement; but since in this case the work was to be subsidized by the state, a complete set of drawings was required with attached documentation which was to be submitted to the Ministry, examined by the Academy of San Fernando, and inspected by the official architects. These considerations led Gaudí to draw up the project in a precise and life-like manner, and perhaps even influenced him to stick to the compass-constructed arches of the Gothic style instead of using parabolic forms such as those adopted in the Güell house, so that the learned councils would not take his originality as an artistic transgression and therefore oppose his case.

In spite of these precautions, we have already seen in the biographical part of this study (XIII - 47) how Gaudí was angered by the amendments imposed by the Architectural Section of the Academy due to differences in viewpoint. Perhaps they were disturbed by the arrangement of the building on an animated plan instead of the usual rectangle, and by other unusual solutions which he later meticulously revised along the lines of the observations which caused him so much consternation.

267. Episcopal Palace at Astorga. Section.

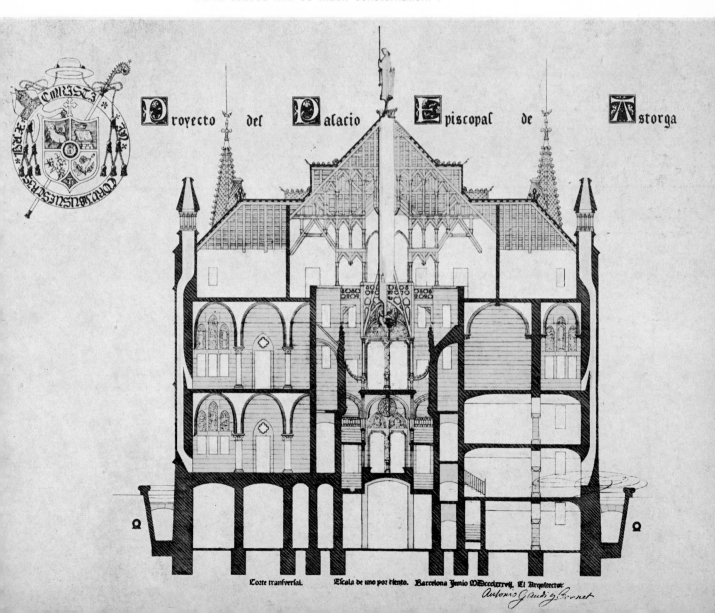

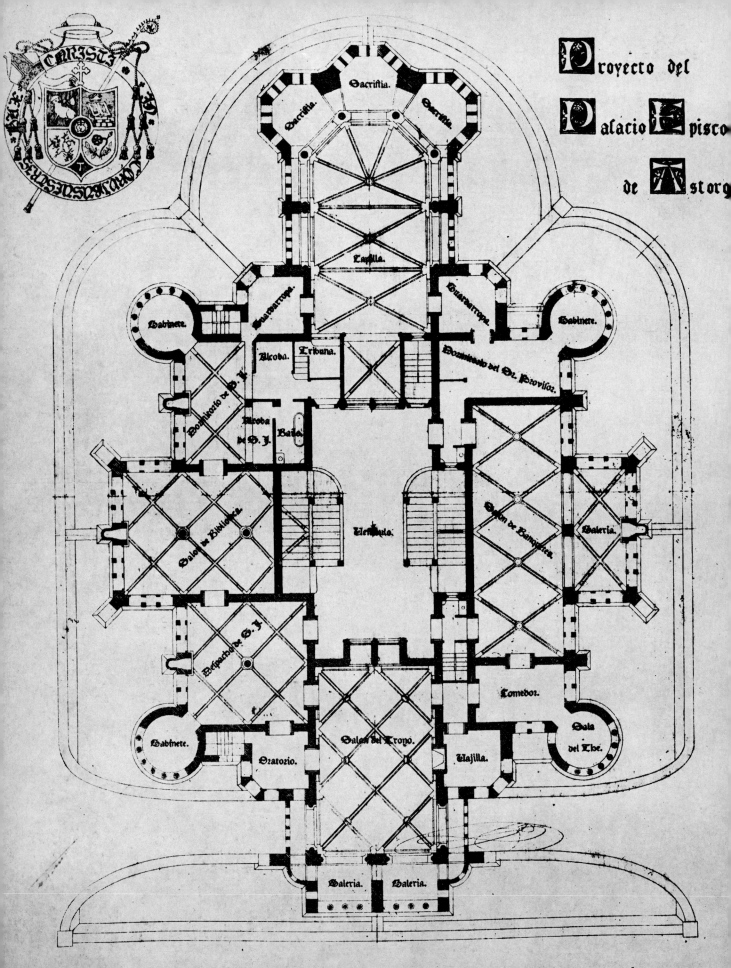

Proyecto del
Palacio Episcopal
de Astorga

Planta del piso Principal. Escala de uno por ciento. Barcelona Junio MDccclxxxvii. El arquitecto,
Antonio Gaudí Cornet

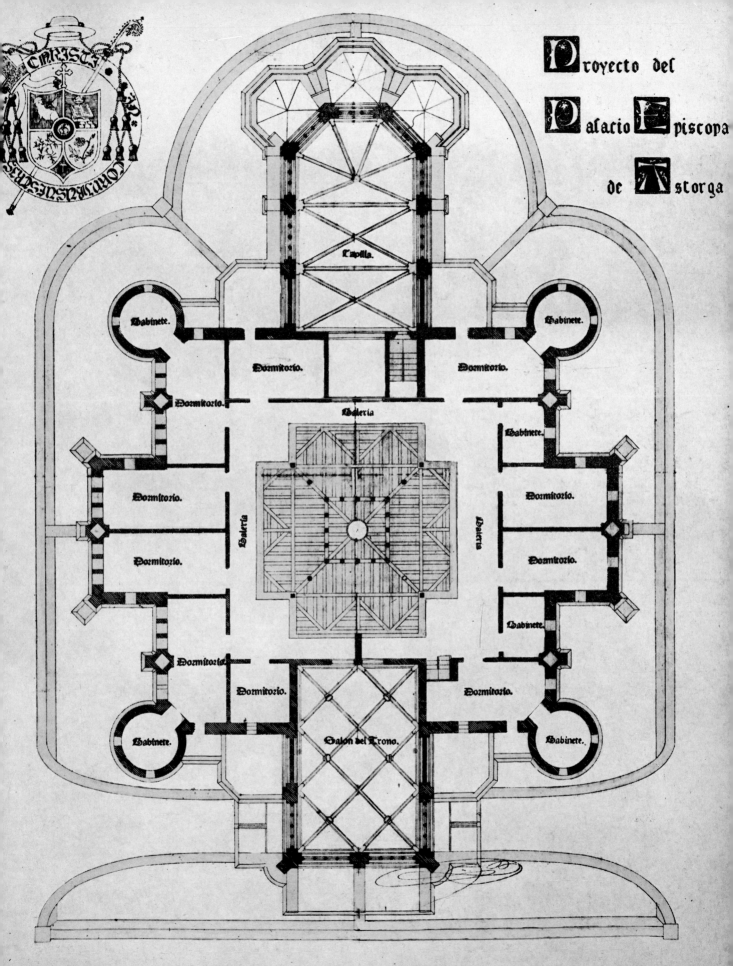

Proyecto del Palacio Episcopal de Astorga

Planta del Sotabanco. Escala de uno por ciento. Barcelona Junio MDccclxxxvij. El Arquitecto.
Antonio Gaudí y Cornet

[overleaf]

268. Episcopal Palace at Astorga.
Main-floor plan.

269. Episcopal Palace at Astorga.
Plan at cornice level.

270. Episcopal Palace at Astorga.
Details of the project preserved in
the bishopric.

271. Episcopal Palace at Astorga.
Partial view with the portico mod-
ified from the plans shown in
Fig. 266.

It must be noted that the merits and beauties of this building are somewhat obscured by the reality of its uninhabited state which deprives it of human warmth. It is symptomatic that the Astorgan prelates who have directed the diocese since the death of Bishop Grau in 1893, and most especially since it was roofed in 1907, have not taken up residence in the building. Perhaps their official duties have taken precedence over the everyday pastoral needs of the people? Or perhaps the numerous windows on the front façade of the palace are excessive in the raw Astorgan cold?

The recent establishment of an Archaeological Museum on the lower floor is only a first step toward the life which should animate this delightfully beautiful building, but at the same time it is an indication of serious deviation, after 70 years, from the original purpose.

The three angels included in the original design were constructed in zinc in 1913 by the Royal Asturian Mining Company with the aid of the architect Ricardo Guereta; since they could not be placed on the roof as planned, they were placed on pedestals 1.75 meters high and distributed around the palace.[1]

STRUCTURE AND ARTISTIC VALUE. We have seen the reasons why the architect of the project did not continue to supervise the work after the death of Bishop Grau in 1893, and why the bishop Julián Diego y Alcolea in 1907 entrusted the roof to the Madrid architect Luis de Guereta who ignored the original plans.

1. Information provided by the Rev. Augusto Quintana, Director of the Museo de los Caminos, installed in the semi-basement of the palace.

272.   Semi-basement of the Astorgan Episcopal Palace with spiral brick arches and *tabicada* vaults.

273.   Episcopal Palace at Astorga. Figure of an angel in zinc, 3.10 meters high, designed by Gaudí for the top of the building and executed in 1913 under the direction of the architect Guereta.

274.   Semi-basement of the episcopal palace in the part which underlies the apse of the chapel above.

275. Episcopal Palace at Astorga. Exterior view in which its grandiosity, which surpasses its actual size, is apparent on this snowy day.

276. Interior detail of the Astorgan Episcopal Palace.

277. Episcopal Palace at Astorga. Capital with a star-shaped abacus.

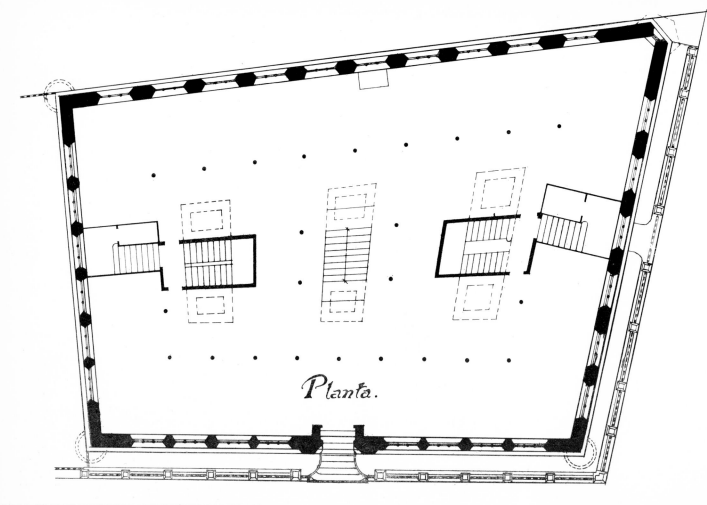

Planta.

Although the projected roof that was never constructed was a most important element of the whole, the state of the work when Gaudí left it was so far advanced that it was irrevocably stamped with his own character, making it one of the most important examples of the neo-Gothic style in Spain.

This building represents the moment of greatest Gothicistic influence in Gaudí's work, perhaps in part due to chronological circumstance, but also because of willful decision on his part. He allowed himself to be caught up in the general norms of the style, but he used his independent, revisionist feeling for structural sincerity to give certain elements a dose of modernity which lends new vibrancy to his work. The bishop, who was concerned that the work be a success, and who felt himself a collaborator in the undertaking, had suggested the use of artificial stone which he considered to be very modern. Gaudí dissuaded him: for a work such as this, pure unadulterated materials were called for, even though they might appear more modest. He was not opposed to the use of exposed brick, much less when it could be converted into a polychromatic element through the use of a ceramic varnish from Jiménez de Jamuz, to the south of Astorga. He took advantage of this red glaze—a derivative of an ancient Mudéjar art [2]—to enhance the especially carved bricks which he used abundantly for the pillars and arches which characterize the main floor interiors, in a manner never before employed in this area. He also used unadorned brick for the main transverse and diagonal ribs formed with square sections on edge, and in the exposed brick *tabicada* vaults resting on cut stone pillars.

The rest of the structure consists of bearing walls and pillars—generally made of stone and not too high—which support ogival ribs of varnished brick except in the oratory where the ribs are of stone with infilling of *tabicada* tile vaulting.[3]

For the exterior, the architect chose the white granite of the Bierzo mountains so that the palace would stand out against the dark background of the cathedral and the ash-green base of the city walls, and also because «the palace had to represent, first of all, the whiteness of the episcopal vestment; besides the liturgical significance, this would here have the advantage of marking a contrast, and therefore, of fixing a center point of radiation.» [4]

This palace, even though it is incomplete and unused, is of great interest for the esthetic significance of its structure—based on a historic style, but freely interpreted by the genius of Gaudí. In spite of the architect's strong personality, however, we can detect the general decorative influence of Viollet-le-Duc which appears most concretely in the tracery of the railing above the porch, and in the French Gothic flavor of the star-shaped abaci of the capitals on the main floor—a faithful reproduction of the eight-pointed stars of those in the lower chapel of the Sainte Chapelle at Paris (XIII century). Beyond such decided stylistic borrowing, the architect introduces personal solutions which liven up the work, such as the construction of trilobate arched openings in advancing courses, and, above all, in the trumpet-like arches of the porch—a first sign of the expressionism which would abound in his later works—forming a circular mass with a balcony above, which differs from the rectangular structure projected in the original design.

The overall, slightly scenographic, composition is integrated by numerous vertical masses which give it the unity which was a constant concern of the architect; and, had the roof which he designed been built, the whole would have acquired even greater strength. The complexity of elements and the discreet scenography mentioned give this palace a sense of grandiosity far superior to its actual dimensions which are rather small.

174. THE CASA FERNÁNDEZ Y ANDRÉS IN LEÓN. 1891-1893 (Figs. 46, 134, 278 - 284, 555)

A UTILITARIAN BUILDING. This house was called «the house of Los Botines» from the deformation of the last name of the founder of the business, Homs y Botinás. His successors, Simón Fernández and Mariano Andrés, bought the property in order to put up the building, giving rise to agitated lawsuits with the city; after protracted disputes, the case was decided in favor of the new proprietors.[5]

Gaudí, who was commissioned to do the project on the recommendation of his friend Güell, signed the plans in Barcelona in December 1891; on the 31st of that month they were approved by the City of León; excavation was immediately begun for the basement foundations, and finished by April 4.[6]

Meanwhile, we have already seen (XIV - 53) how the winter months were used to accumulate materials so that once the good weather arrived work could be begun. The actual construction work took only ten months—a fact that earned the admiration of the Leonese people.

This was a large building whose lower floor and basements were to be used for a textile business with the four upper stories serving as living quarters. It was situated on an almost rectangular lot with all sides clear. In order to make the building as practical as possible,

2. L. Alonso Luengo, *Gaudí en Astorga*, p. 10.

3. The decoration of some of these walls and vaults, so out of place in the sense of the architecture of the build-in, was done during the later phase of completion.

4. Alonso Luengo, *op. cit.*, p. 16.

5. The suit, brought by the City government, seems to have been provoked by the neighbor to the west who did not look kindly on the new building. The press and public opinion were filled with the case.

6. From an unpublished document of which more will be said later, deposited in the building itself. (See note 7.)

281. Protective fence around the surrounding ditch.

282. Casa Fernández Andrés. Partial view showing the original stone texture.

283. Casa Fernández Andrés.
Overall view.

284. Casa Fernández Andrés. Detail of a window on the lower floor.

the architect employed for the first time what later came to be known as the flexible plan in the two stories dedicated to the business; the roofs of these stories are supported by means of 26 wrought-iron stanchions. There are no internal bearing walls except for the two stairwells which border the two side entrances and constitute the only non-utilizable space in the two extremely wide warehouses of the lower floor and basements; the floors are interconnected by a central stair and a cargo elevator. On the upper floors he employed the traditional bearing walls which also serve to distribute the rooms and rest on the metal beams and stanchions of the lower floor which are especially arranged for this purpose. Access to the upper floors is by way of two entrances from the side streets and various stairways. The first floor of residences is divided into two parts—one for each of the two owners—and the three others are broken up into four parts for rental apartments. The building is bordered on the main façade and one side by an illuminating moat similar to those which he used in the crypt of the Sagrada Familia and the palace at Astorga.

Once the building was finished, it stood out as the most important non-religious structure in the city, and the warehouse that motivated it was superior by far to those of Madrid, Valladolid, and Asturias, according to our source of information, Sr. Martínez Galán. Despite the ill-omens of the construction period, the building today, after 70 years, still preserves its sturdiness without a single crack.

NEW RHYTHMS AND TEXTURES. Although Gaudí designed this building with practical and structural considerations foremost in his mind, he was also concerned with the esthetic aspect in accord with its practical purpose. He could not have done otherwise, considering the urban importance of its location in the most central square of the city and his own concept of architecture which could never be without artistic beauty. It appears that here he was interested in stressing the material character of the new building, as opposed to the spiritual aspect which he had emphasized in Astorga, while still staying within the realm of medieval evocations; to do this he modified the rhythms and texture—two of an architect's most valuable means of expression.

In the Episcopal Palace at Astorga, the unity of expression was achieved by a series of masses which outline a distinct vertical rhythm, subordinate to the pyramidal composition of the roof which was to have had a wide vertex angle serving as the axis for the building. In León he obtained this unity in a single cubic mass bordered by four extensive façades, and having a pyramidal roof of no more than common interest; he underlined the unity with the four pointed corner turrets which serve as boundary markers. On the façades a horizontal rhythm predominates in the three heavy string courses, and the regular distribution of the window openings. By using such elements he obtained an aspect of sobriety and impressive magnificence, complemented by the outline of the openings and the texture of the ashlar masonry. The windows of the ground floor are wide and each is subdivided into three bays with trilobate arches united by a multilobate archivolt. In the upper stories, the openings are simplified, and in the cylindrical turrets they become rectangular to avoid difficulties in carving the double curvature which appears in the arches of the original project. The ashlar masonry which outlines the openings and constitutes their splays is more finely worked than are the walls which are finished by hammering to achieve the contrasting roughness—an effect enhanced by the juxtaposition of unequal ashlars, of discontinuous joints and different sizes, which were a part of the original design. The ashlar masonry of the Astorga palace is not of extremely fine finish though it is generally smooth and of uniform size. In León Gaudí tried a more vigorous texture; on snowy days it catches the tiny flakes, completely transforming the aspect of the façades. This was the first important example of the variety of stonework textures which he would continue to exploit in all of his works. This sort of texture, using squared ashlars of various sizes and un-worked walls was soon to become fashionable, and others strove to achieve through fictitious applications the effect which Gaudí had obtained with ordinary procedures of construction.

The contrast between the horizontally cut stones of mixed sizes and the fine finishing of the window openings was complemented by the equally smooth string courses, also carefully finished, which mark bold sloping planes on which the openings of the respective floors rest; the lowest of them—also the widest—turns upward to form a rectangular hood over the main entrance.

In commemoration of the Catalan origins of the company's textile business, the center of the hood is presided over by a three-meter-high image of St. George, the patron of Catalonia —a sculpted stone figure which unexpectedly furnished us with a brief resumé of the building's history several years ago. In 1950, the new owners of the property, the *Caja de Ahorros y Monte de Piedad* bank of León, planned to replace the image of St. George with one of the Virgin; when they took down the first they found in its base several documents of the period of construction, the most interesting of which confirmed already mentioned data regarding the building and completed the list of the principal workmen who participated in the job.[7] From this document we know that the statue itself was executed in Barcelona by Antonio Cantó (who had supervised the stonecutting work as well) «following the model cast by the architect,» and that it was put in place on September 15, 1893.

7. This document was returned to its place when the St. George was put back; included were several issues of the León newspaper *El Campeón* with coverage of the long dispute over the property; a manuscript accrediting the works which describes the works which is transcribed in Appendix X. I am grateful to D. Ricardo Aller Pavía, the secretary of the firm which owns the building, for the photocopies of these documents (July, 1960).

A SLIGHT MODIFICATION OF METICULOUS PLANS. Despite what has been said of the relative unimportance of plans in Gaudí's general concept of his works, we can observe that the León drawings were carefully worked out and that he faithfully carried out the original design and its details. The execution and delineation of the drawings themselves were extremely fine, even though they were not to be subjected to the rigid control of the Astorga project.

However careful the preliminary studies may be, rare is the architectural work which does not require some changes at the moment of execution. We have already seen how the projected arches of the cylindrical turret windows were converted into lintels. For the protective iron grate of the surrounding illumination ditch, the faces were originally to have been consolidated by means of stone pillars terminating in lion-like figures;[8] these became instead iron reinforcements joined to the wall of the building in a simple and rational manner. The disappearance of these emblems on the fence was compensated for by the ironwork of the main door which replaced the wooden door of the original plan and contains a forged lion in its stationary upper section. The patterns on the two movable leaves recall those of the Güell palace, though they are quite different in outline. Another change was the conversion of the two medallions with heads protruding in a Plateresque manner, which were to have flanked the main door, into circular openings. The extremely simple upper cornice which was originally to have been straight was broken with smooth, rectangular offset sills at the foot of each skylight; below this cornice was placed a line of gargoyles which also was not foreseen in the plans. Finally, the rear right-hand tower which he designed with a polygonal plan was given cylindrical form like the others.

In spite of the apparent unimportance of these modifications, taken together they serve as a test for the perfection of the work, and reveal how the architect was concerned with every detail, becoming completely involved in the work either directly or through his collaborators during absences forced by the need to attend to his other works. They also show how carefully he followed the projected design in those days in respect to those elements which did not need modification—a practice he did not follow in his later works where he systematically ignored his plans in the execution of the decoration.

8. In some of the pillars of the project the form of this animal can be seen, and in others no. We can suppose that they all refer to the name of the city.

175. THE SCHOOL AND CONVENT OF SANTA TERESA. 1888-1890
  (Figs. 47, 88, 139, 149, 285 - 295)

In Part One we have seen how the architect was commissioned to do this work at No. 87 of the Calle Ganduxer which was to consist of three U-shaped halls, and how Gaudí only constructed the first—that perpendicular to the street and nearest to the mountain—which was to serve as a school and residence for the religious community. The church, which would have been a thing of great beauty according to those who remember the plans which disappeared in 1936, was located in the central hall. When it was later constructed, Gaudí refused to have

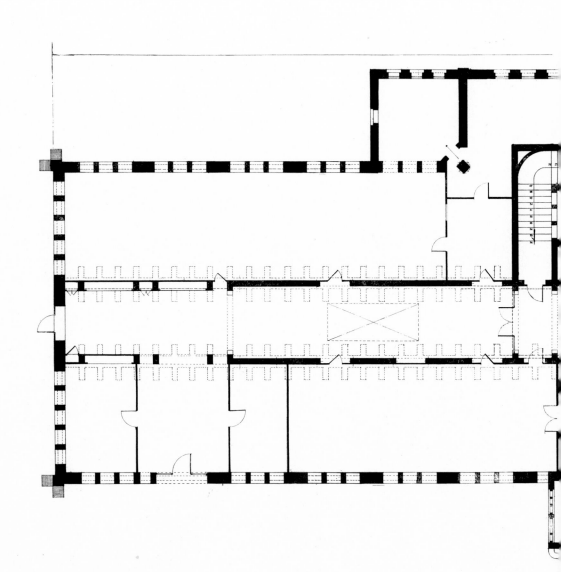

anything to do with it, apparently because he was not in agreement with proposed modifications in his original plan (XV - 57).

This group of buildings represented a new theme for the architect and, because of the especially strict budget which he had to follow, standards of great simplicity were established, especially in the materials employed. The shape of the building is rectangular, with its four floors divided into three bays running parallel to the main and rear façades. The interior bay is used as a corridor and patio.

Such an arrangement usually necessitates two interior bearing walls which divide the three bays; here these were only partially employed since they are replaced by corridors of extremely elongated parabolic arches on the second floor which rest on dual metal beams of the lower floor which are reinforced by natural brick corbels which project from either side of the underlying bearing wall. Above these parabolic arches rest the bearing walls of the two upper stories. On the main façade there is a small central projecting structure whose lower

285. School of Santa Teresa de Jesús. Ground floor plan by the architect Ll. Bonet Garí.

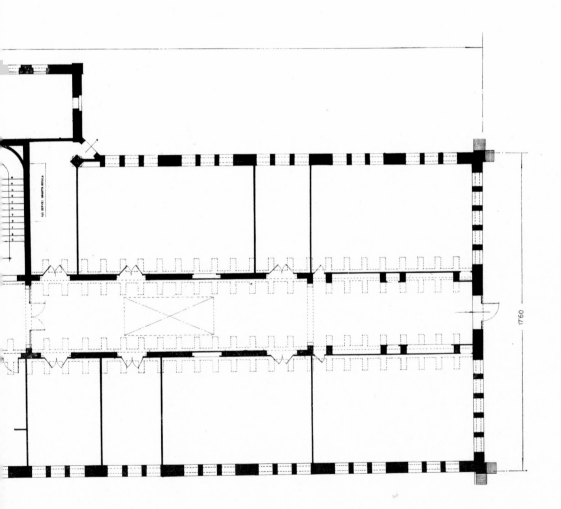

floor serves as an entrance portico, and which is only as tall as the third story of the building. On the opposite façade there is another projection, somewhat larger. The building is covered by a flat roof provided with a high-capacity insulating air chamber (top of Fig. 286).

The materials used are ordinary rubble, which is visible on the façade, and brick in the upper floor, the window jambs, and corners; he also employed brick in an original decorative manner which we will discuss further on.

RHYTHM AND EXPRESSION. It is apparent that Gaudí planned the composition and decoration of this building with the utmost simplicity in mind. The movement of the ground plan could not be more restrained, nor the construction materials more modest (with the exception of certain ceramic accessories which he applied in an ornamental-symbolic manner). The overall effect of the building depended solely on the combination of the ochre of the rubble and the reddish brick, just as that of the Casa Vicens had been based on the rhythm of its horizontal bands; here the rhythm is vertical and greatly simplified, the upper story accentuating the verticality with a range of pointed arches, some with windows and others blind, as well as the terminal gables that form part of the building's openwork cornice. At the corners there are brick spires rising above the rectangular body and recalling the corner turrets at León. Here as well as there these projections accentuate the limits of the mass and thus tend to unify the building. Each spire is topped with a four-armed cross.

Though the rubble walls are made up of a poor material which is usually covered with plaster, they have not been in any way. Here, without plaster, the rubble acquires a structural dignity which is enhanced by the artfully arranged common brick which brings out the effect desired by the architect.

The majority of the windows are surrounded by rectangles of layered brickwork which alternate with outlined rectangles of rubble. Within the window rectangles, parabolic arches are

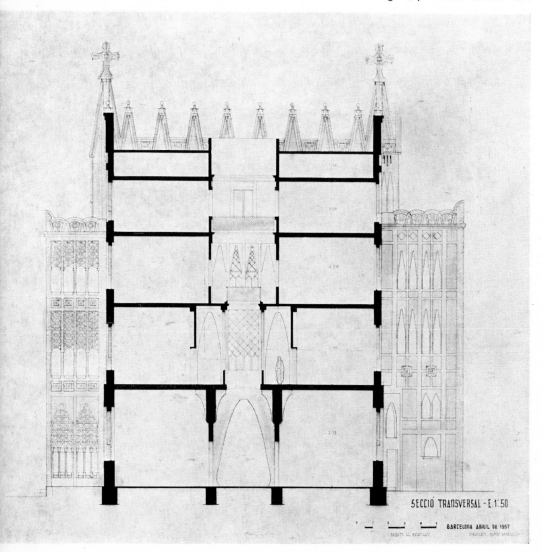

SECCIÓ TRANSVERSAL - E.1:50

BARCELONA ABRIL DE 1957

286. School of Santa Teresa de Jesús. Transverse section by the architect Ll. Bonet Garí.

formed by corbelled courses of brick. On the front and back façades, the ground floor windows are arranged in groups of three, corresponding to every two windows of the upper stories, and the parabolic form, protected by artistic iron gratings, is readily visible since the ground floor lacks the shutters which conceal the parabolic arches of the upper stories. On the upper floor, the windows are contained in mitered arches; between these there are smaller blind arches of similar form. This arch pattern, together with the narrow gables above, give the most emphatic note of Gothicism to the building.

The main door which opens into the small portico is also in the form of an extremely graceful and simple parabola obtained by corbelling brick courses except at the top where the arch is closed with radial bricks. In the upper corners of the interior, the arch spandrels are occupied by four pendentives which support a spherical dome covering the enclosure.

The beautiful entrance gate—a masterpiece of ironwork—is divided into three leaves of limited height, the center one topped by an elegant cross which centers the arch opening (Fig. 88). The inner door to the convent is made of perfectly joined rectangular panels. Two of the larger rectangles are occupied by square iron screens—the lower one serving as an interior peephole, and the upper one providing illumination.

The original intent of simplicity and economy in this building was generally maintained, but the ideal of perfection and beauty which guided the architect's fertile imagination, encouraging its decorative resourcefulness, led to greater sumptuosity in some details than the founder, Reverend Ossó, had wanted, giving rise to the economic disputes which we have noted

287. School of Santa Teresa de Jesús. View of the back before 1936 when the symbolic doctor's caps representing the Saint were removed from the pinnacles of the building.

(XV - 57). These details, without being exaggerated, give a tone of greater richness to the building. As examples we can cite the openwork crest at the top of the façades, and the two upper floors of the entrance portico whose surfaces are enlivened by a pattern of reticulated brick triangles which form hexagons in a way similar to that we have seen in the gatehouse of the Finca Güell; in the center of this decoration he placed the arms of the Carmelite Order. The corner elements mentioned earlier are further examples of his decorative use of brick, and also incorporate the Carmelite shield motif, on a somewhat smaller scale. The two brick courses which string along the façades are encrusted with pieces of glazed ceramics.

The interior is treated quite simply, with the brickwork of the door jambs and lintels and some of the parabolic structural arches left bare; placement of these elements is determined by their structural function. The artistic effect of the corridors of small parabolic arches, coated with plaster and mounted on pillars of exposed brick, is remarkable.

In addition to its general artistic and social interest, this work is also important as a lesson in the use of brick—a material which Catalan architects were involved in reviving at that time. Here Gaudí develops the method which he introduced on the Calle de las Carolinas and in Les Corts in a broader and more simple way.

RELIGIOUS SYMBOLISM. In this building we see for the first time in an obvious manner the religious symbolism which Gaudí was later to apply so abundantly, especially in the Sagrada Familia—evident proof that his religious convictions had been strengthened. This coincides with the period when Palau y Dulcet knew Gaudí at the Ateneo Barcelonés and felt «that St. Francis must have spoken as he does.»

288. One of the corners of the School of the Teresas where Gaudí first used the characteristic four-armed cross.

His personal religiosity had not been apparent in his works until this time. Despite its religious function, even the palace at Astorga was free of any emblems beyond the episcopal heraldry, and the St. George at León has more patriotic than mystical significance. Neither of these buildings displays the cross which was to become an essential part of his later works.

We have already noted the cross which dominates the decorative iron gate of the main entrance. He conceived the upper part of this central section as a sort of Carmelite coat of arms, with the schematic indication of a Monte Carmelo and the central star, the Saint's heart pierced by an arrow to one side and a thorn-crowned heart to the other, each in the middle of a radiating spiral (Fig. 88). The square screens of the wooden doorway are decorated with the letters S T (Santa Teresa) ingeniously arranged in a decoratively repetitive pattern (Fig. 289). On the edge of the entrance are written the words of the Saint «todo se pasa» («everything passes on») between inscriptions of Jesus' name; it has been interpreted that the wavy vertical ironwork to the sides indicates the love which the name of Jesus produces in the faithful.[1] The two brick bands which run along the façades are decorated with regularly placed square plaques of glazed ceramic—relief representations of Jesus' name. Between the two upper floors of the main façade entrance structure is a large redesigned coat of arms of the Order in polychrome relief, with the Monte Carmelo, the star, the cross, and the two hearts on either side; above is a representation of Santa Teresa's doctoral cap. The arms are repeated on a smaller scale at the corners as decoration for the pinnacles which are topped by the crosses which would hereafter characterize the master's works. These emblems, the T's (for Teresa) which decorate the openwork of the railings, and the red ceramic doc-

1. Bergós, op. cit., p. 89.

289. Entrance door to the school with the initials of the Saint on the peephole screen.

290. The entrance to the convent-school of the Teresas with brick decoration of Arabic influence.

toral caps which decorate the crest make up the symbolism of this building, as rich in mystical significance as it is simple in lines. [2]

The exterior of the building, then, displays the four corner crosses and another in the iron gate; there are 127 cases where the name of Jesus is written in ceramic, and 35 in wrought iron; the initial of Teresa appears in ceramic 87 times and in wrought iron, 6; there are 9 places where the initials ST can be found, five incidences of the arms of the Order in ceramic tile in addition to that of the door grating, and there were 91 doctoral caps before they were

2. The coats of arms of the Order and the Doctoral caps were destroyed during the Civil War 1936-39, and only the first have been replaced, though not in the original ceramic.

291. Structurally arranged arches of the lower floor.

removed. The perfect balance between symbolic content and decorative ends shows how well Gaudí had mastered ornamental technique, and the enthusiastic distribution shows his complete religious orthodoxy.

176.   A PROJECT FOR CATHOLIC MISSIONS IN AFRICA. 1892-1893 (Figs. 296, 297)

Of all of the works which Gaudí designed but did not get to carry out (except, of course, the Sagrada Familia) the one which disappointed him most was this one which he designed

292. School of Santa Teresa. Corridor of parabolic arches on the second floor.

293. Another view of the parabolic arches in the same building.

294. Iron window screens from the Teresas. From Bergós.

295. Teresan school. Interior patio that supports the pillars and parabolic arches of the upper floor.

for the African Missions in Tangiers—mainly because of the novelty of the theme and the grandiosity of his plans. He had a large-scale elevation of the vast building hanging in his Sagrada Familia office until he died. I saw it many times, and sometimes the master would allude to it, but unfortunately it never ocurred to me to find out the details of the situation; he undoubtedly would have furnished us with some extremely interesting data. Bergós, with whom he also used to discuss such things, mentions only the form of the towers in referring to this project [3]—a topic which Gaudí once talked to me about. Ráfols' notes, along with the photograph which he fortunately published before the elevation was destroyed during the Civil War,[4] furnish us with a somewhat lengthier description.

From a sketch of the ground plan,[5] (Fig. 297) and from the Ráfols illustration of the project which was carefully delineated with the shadows indicated in aquatint wash, we know that the plan had a quatrilobate outline, apparently with an entrance door between each of the four lobe corners surmounted by a circular tower ending in a point and rising above the contiguous buildings. Judging from the openings indicated in the façade, these buildings must have consisted of three or four stories, since the elevation shows a series of close, narrow openings on the ground floor which are repeated on what could be the third floor; the intermediary floors have very pointed angular openings in two alternating sizes.

Ráfols says that these outer buildings were «composed of schools and many other rooms,» and we can add, on seeing the project, that the surface of the exterior wall is not vertical, but rather slightly inclined toward the interior. The towers which we have mentioned have a similar slant which gives them conical caps; at the top there are naturalistic figures of an imprecise nature.

In the sketch of the plan there seem to have been four patios which separated the external rooms from the central nucleus which was a chapel with bell towers which predict those later

296. Project for a Franciscan Mission in Tangiers. Elevation.

3. *Op. cit.*, p. 91.
4. Ráfols, *op. cit.*, pp. 68, 87.
5. From the photograph hung in the Sagrada Familia.

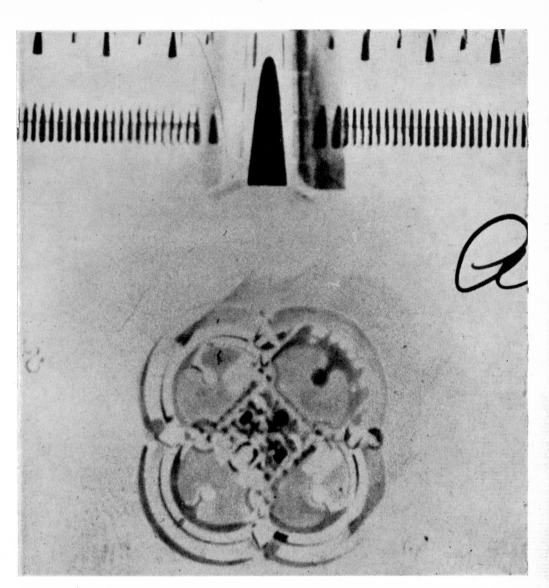

297. Plan of the project for the Mission in Tangiers.

erected at the Sagrada Familia; Gaudí himself often cited this relationship. The parabolic profile of these towers is not obvious. They appear more like the body of a very pointed cone, almost cylindrical at its base, which is united here with another larger and less pointed cone. It is possible that the blending surface of the two cones was paraboloid as in the Barcelona temple. There were 12 bell towers, all attached to the chapel, some with spirally arranged openings indicating an interior staircase. From the center rose another bell tower of greater height, and interspersed among these towers there appear several tall, slender spires which must have been ornamental elements of the chapel capping passageways between the towers.

It appears that Gaudí had made a first-hand study of the characteristics of the terrain where this building was to be built, on a trip which he made to Andalusia, Tetuán, and Tangiers in the company of the Marquis of Comillas [6] in the year 1887 when the Marquis was considering patronizing this religious and cultural legation directed by the Franciscans as the complement to a more extensive political and commercial endeavor which was never carried out. We have already seen in Part One that in Gaudí's opinion, the Marquis did not understand his architectural project, nor the great importance of the legation, and thus it was never realized (XVII - 65). It is not inconceivable that the noble gentleman—a fervent believer and a great economist—would not have appreciated the need for the 17 tall bell towers included in the project. Though there may have been other reasons for their disagreement, this could possibly have been the first concrete case in which a divergency of Gaudí's grandiose concept and the economic conditions served as a barrier to realization (XXXIII - 145).

Though we have called the elevation just studied a «project,» given the immensity of conception, it can really only be considered a «preliminary project» — especially when we compare it with the drawings which we have seen for the buildings at Astorga and León. As in those projects, the execution here was meticulous and careful, surprisingly so for a preliminary drawing of a project which was not certain to be carried out.

6. Ráfols, *op. cit.,* p. 68.

177. A GIGANTIC MANGER SCENE. 1891-1900 (Figs. 40, 48, 50, 52, 75, 101 - 103, 109, 111 - 114, 120, 172, 298 - 307, 309 - 312)

During the years that Gaudí was working on the crypt and the apse, his ideas and plans for the projected work on the expiatory temple were maturing considerably with regard to general distribution, sculpture, and symbolism. In addition to the main façade which would be oriented toward the south, he planned a façade to the east and another to the west—the latter facing the city as it slowly expanded outward.

Once the apse was terminated, he decided to begin work on one of the adjoining façades. Someone suggested that he begin on the west—facing the city—in order better to attract the public interest, but Gaudí was of the opposite opinion. He planned to dedicate the easterly façade, consisting of joyful forms and motifs, to the Birth of Jesus, whereas that on the west would be severe in sculptural forms and themes and dedicated to the Passion. He felt that it would be difficult for people to understand the meaning of the latter façade without the antecedent of the first, and so he began with the Nativity. Oriented toward the east, from whence each day's light is born, it would symbolically interpret the birth and childhood of the Lord, and would be the beginning stanza in the grand hymm in praise of His doctrine—a permanent tableau elevated here in the name of the city in a way similar to that in which Christian families commemorate the joyous Advent every year at Christmas-time with their home-made *pessebres,* or manger scenes.

A PROVIDENTIAL LEGACY. The façade was begun on a design of sober monumentality, but shortly afterwards the project was boosted by a legacy of considerable worth for those times—700,000 pesetas—which permitted and encouraged greater freedom in the work, especially because of the insistence of the administrator Dalmases, the son-in-law carrying on the work of the founder Bocabella, that the legacy be spent as quickly as possible.[1]

This coincidence was responsible for giving an unforeseen splendor to the design, and grandiosity to the scenes and symbols relating to the childhood of Christ. Gaudí based the façade composition on four square towers placed diagonally and grouped in two pairs which served as backdrops to the decorative sculpture. This arrangement left room for a great central portal and two smaller ones to the sides, with the sides of the squares forming the splays to the doorways. From these splays spring the archivolts—the central one being naturally higher—each of which is capped by a lantern. The composition has the general look of a Gothic triptych covered with naturalistic forms. The three portals are dedicated to the theological virtues of Faith, Hope, and Charity with appropriate episodes from Jesus' boyhood represented in each one.[2]

THE CHARITY PORTAL is divided into two parts by a pillar in the form of a bundle of palm fronds bound together by a spiral band which bears the names of the genealogy of Christ from Abraham to Joseph, the husband of Mary who gave birth to the Messiah. The lower part of this column is protected by a twined network of iron rods which is a masterpiece of light ironwork. The image of Jesus, accompanied by those of Joseph and Mary, tops the column. These are surrounded by inscriptions alluding to the Nativity; above is the star of the east with its luminous rays represented as spiraling forms extending down toward the Divine Child. Below, on each splay, great corbels decorated with plants and birds which evoke Christmas-time (Fig. 112) were intended to serve as pedestals for adoring shepherds and Wise Men.

To either side of the double door, heavy columns with helix striations adorned with heavy snow-covered palm capitals support two angels with trumpets—heralds of the Good Tidings. It is from these capitals that the pointed central gable covered with snowy icicles springs, sheltering the portico archivolt with its imprecise forms, evocative of the Holy Night; among these forms we can make out zodiacal constellations whose stellar positions indicate the date of the Birth of Christ. Between the archivolt and the gable vertex is a great lantern in which we witness the Coronation of the Virgin.

Above the gable rises a tall cypress (Fig. 101), symbol of incorruptibility, and on its trunk is the bleeding heart of Jesus, a symbol of Charity representing the one who loved the most. Around the holy symbol are the figures of angels who collect the Divine Blood in vessels to scatter it throughout the world. Below, other angels flanking the cross sculpted with the monogram of Jesus burn incense and sing the «Hossannah». Above the monogram, at the foot of the cypress, a pelican feeds her young; the ancients believed that she nourished them with her own blood. Two ladders lean against the cypress, and to either side there are two more angels, one bearing an amphora, and the other a bread basket.

---

1. Dalmases' insistence was based on the fear that the new bishop of Barcelona, Dr. Catalá, would use the legacy for other purposes.
2. Puig Boada, *op. cit.,* and Martinell, *La Sagrada Família,* (Barcelona: 1952). These representations which are only summarized in this text are amply described in these two books.

Gaudí planned that these sculpted forms should be painted, especially those inside of the portico and sheltered from the rain. The 1 : 25 scale model which he sent to the exhibition of his work in Paris in 1910 was polychromed.[3] In the model this central part was dominated by the intense blue of a winter's night dotted by white almond blossoms, the stars plated with shiny aluminum, and the numerous scenes which are now obscured highlighted in their respective colors to acquire full legibility. The cypress is decorated with pieces of green ceramic, and the doves that surround it are executed in white alabaster; high above in red mosaic stands the «tau» of the Greek alphabet, the initial letter of the word God (Fig. 307).

THE HOPE PORTAL is located to the south of the one we have just examined. In the tympanum we find Christ with Joseph in his workshop in Nazareth (Fig. 305); below and to the left is the flight into Egypt surrounded by plants and animals of the Nile region; to the right, on a similar background, is the Massacre of the Innocents; above are the images of Saints Joachim and Anne. Among other symbolic emblems, the upper gallery terminates in a lantern where we see the Marriage of the Virgin and St. Joseph. Even higher is an allegory of Montserrat: through the rocks of a grotto the boat of the Church passes, guided by the glorious Patriarch, while the Holy Ghost in the form of a dove flies toward a hillock with the words «Save Us»; all of this symbolic of the hope of the World Church invested in St. Joseph.

The dominant color in this door was to have been green, the symbolic color of Hope displayed in the leaves and vegetation of the Nile, with more purplish tones in the upper section signifying that the portal is also dedicated to St. Joseph.

3. The polychromy was done by Jujol at the master's instructions.

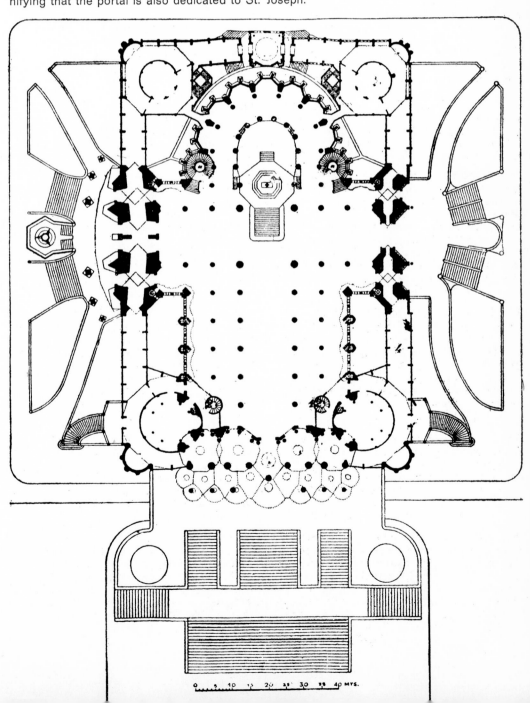

298. Plan of the Temple of the Sagrada Familia.

299. Central pillar of the portal of Charity with Jesus' family tree protected by a beautifully worked iron screen.

THE PORTAL OF FAITH is the other lateral doorway and has at its center the seated figure of Christ at about 12 years preaching in the temple (Fig. 306). To the left is the Visitation of Mary to St. Elizabeth, and to the right, St. Joseph and the Virgin admiring their Son on finding him with the Doctors; even more to the right is the adolescent Jesus in the carpenter's workshop. Above these are the figures of St. John preaching vehemently, and the priest Zacharias his father. The lintel of the portal is decorated with an extremely realistic bleeding-heart surrounded by thorns, flowers, and bees.

The upper gallery shows the Presentation of Jesus in the Temple, and ends in a pinnacle formed of thorns and clusters of grapes—a symbol of the Eucharist—inside of which there is a lampion with three large flames symbolizing the Trinity. From its center comes forth the Immaculate Conception, the sublime allegory of Faith.

The polycromy of this portal would have been in yellow and sienna tones, with the figures and animals painted in naturalistic colors.

300. Herald angels of the Nativity façade.

301. Evocation of the date of birth on this façade, represented by the signs and stars of the Zodiac.

The triptych which we have just seen was complemented by the two lateral lanterns of the cloister, and in the upper part by the bases of the bell towers which house the images of the apostles Barnabas, Simon, Judas, and Matthew to whom the towers are dedicated. There is very little continuity between this lower part of the façade proper and the bell towers that rise above; following the established chronological order, we will study the towers in a later section.

QUESTION MARKS. The attractiveness of this façade is due mainly to its smooth forms and the fine proportion of the elements. Nevertheless, when we examine them through the analytical magnifying glass, we are confronted with several questions which have no easy answer.

The two bell towers on the northern (right-hand) side are closer together than the other two, and therefore the Faith portal is somewhat narrower than the opposite one of Hope. My investigations have not come up with a convincing answer in regard to this anomaly. Someone has insinuated an error in planning—a suggestion which I must absolutely reject. The architect Quintana suggests that perhaps the widening of the distance between two of the bell towers could have been motivated by a desire to lengthen the principal nave.

293

302, 303, 304. Portals of Hope, Charity, and Faith in the Nativity façade.

294

305. Sagrada Familia. St. Joseph and the child Jesus. Detail of the Hope portal.

306. Sagrada Familia. Jesus among the doctors of the Temple. Detail of the Faith portal.

There is also no easy explanation for the presence of the two spirally striated columns, descendants of the Plateresque type known as *antorchadas* (a designation based on the process of twisting candles to make a torch) which are inscribed with the names of Joseph and Mary in *modernista* script. While not clashing esthetically, the traditional form seems to intrude somehow on the dominant expressionism and naturalism of the façade.

In the lower part of the towers where the cross-section moves toward a circular plan there appears a sort of opening which has both a stepped lintel and sill, with vertical jambs and a squared mullion in the center which is emphatically subdivided into drums. Whenever I heard Gaudí say that the slow growth of these towers was helpful in perfecting his work as it went along, I would think of these openings, so faithful to his structural principles, yet not to his esthetic ones—isolated from these by their discontinuous profiles, their ostentatiously subdivided mullions, and their location in an unnecessary place; all of these deviated from the spirit of unity which the master used to preach. Though the openings fulfill a utilitarian and decorative function, they were not continued as he went higher, leading us to believe that this may indeed have been one of those elements susceptible to greater perfection to which he often referred.

178. THE CLOISTER AND ROSARY PORTAL (Figs. 110, 116, 135, 155, 157, 308, 309)

A PERIPHERAL CLOISTER. Usually, the cloister of a church is to one side or, occasionally, in front in an atrium-like arrangement; here Gaudí put it around the building's periphery, with tiny spaces to serve as gardens which would keep the noises of the street at a distance. He designed two entrances through the grand portico of the main façade, and where the façade

307. Terminal cypress of the portal of Charity on the Nativity façade.

section meets the two lateral cloister wings there are four portals dedicated to the four most popular Marian cults of Catalonia: the two of the Nativity façade are dedicated to the Virgin of Montserrat and to Our Lady of the Rosary, the latter being the only completed portal of this series.

The cloister is small and is built on a foundation of semi-basements which were once used as the temple workshops and schools for Arts and Crafts. The cloister is covered with groin vaults which are extended to produce a series of gables along the lateral walls which are perforated by rose windows of three equilateral curved triangles (Fig. 309a).[4] The general inspiration is Gothic, and the parts next to the Nativity façade have already been erected. Once the church was functioning this would be used for liturgical acts or processions which did not require an exit into the streets. The posterior corners would cut through two large sacristies, and the wing next to the apse would be intersected by the chapel of the Assumption of the Virgin.

THE ROSARY PORTAL. The cloister would also serve for the processional recitation of the Holy Rosary, and Gaudí completed the portal dedicated to Our Lady of the Rosary so that it would serve as a guide to the interior decoration of the church. Like the rest of the interior, it was built of stone from Vilafranca which is easier to carve than that of Montjuich used for the exterior surfaces.

Being obliquely placed in relation to the axis of the cloister, this portal occupies a triangular space and is covered by an extremely slender conical lantern with a beautifully carved octagonal gallery visible from below, and another upper section opening onto the outside. The portal, softly illuminated by this lantern, looks into the cloister; the tympanum contains the im-

4. Puig Boada, *op. cit.,* p. 51.

308. Sagrada Familia. Rosary portal in the cloister.

ages of the Virgin and Child with those of St. Dominic and St. Catherine kneeling at her feet. All three are framed by garlands of finely sculpted roses which were to be painted in naturalistic colors. The jambs are decorated with images of David, Salomon, Isaac, and Jacob.

In the brackets from which the contiguous framing arch springs we see a man and a woman imploring the Virgin to help them conquer temptation as represented by monsters which are half man and half demon and offer an anarchist bomb to a worker—an allusion to the frequent terrorist assaults at the beginning of the century (Fig. 110)—and a sack of money to the woman in an attempt to undermine her purity through vanity. On another bracket we see sculpted the end of the *Ave María* whose last phrase is inscribed in the vault: the death of a good man is represented, surrounded by the three members of the Holy Family of Nazareth, and beneath it is the inscription *et in hora mortis nostrae, amen.*

The stonework of this portal and the tiny space which precedes it, as well as that of the lantern above and the beginning sections of the cloister are all of fine execution, with a great variety of ornamental themes set forth as a possible guide for the interior decoration of the temple which thus far remains completely smooth with the brackets, consoles, railings, and colonnettes only blocked out in primary forms awaiting their definitive decoration. Only one or two columns and two arch springers have been carved from the model. The upper part of the wooden door has an openwork pattern, and the whole is a model of perfectly executed carpentry work.[5]

179. RHYTHMS, SYMBOLS, AND SPACE (Figs. 130, 309a - 312)

In the general discussion of rhythms in Part Two we brought up the possibility that in this façade Gaudí may have resorted to a hidden framework in addition to the evident triangular

5. The door, which Gaudí probably supervised, was destroyed in 1936. The existing one is a faithful reproduction which was donated by the Barcelona Carpenter's Guild.

309. Sagrada Familia. Rosary portal, tympanum.

rhythm as a basis for calculating the relationship of the principal elements of the facade to each other and to the adjoining bell towers, in a manner similar to the Gothic practice of triangulation (XXIX - 130). This is only a hypothesis; what is not hypothetical is the visible triangular rhythm of the three gables of Gothic influence, the two lanterns of the cloister chapels, and the gables which have been begun on either side of the façade.

The rigidity of these triangles is softened by the lobed rhythms which give order to the exuberant ornamentation of the archivolts. This rhythm, common in medieval architecture, was also important to Modernismo, the style in vogue when the facade was erected; it is possible that this was a reason for its repeated presence here. If the architectural framework is Gothic, this is not true of the decoration which is completely naturalistic and without historical precedents (except for the two helicoidally striated columns already mentioned). All of the inscriptions which can be seen on the façade are carved in *modernista* script.

The spiral rhythm of the two columns between the central and lateral doorways is geometrized and distributed in six equal drums; the same rhythm reappears in a more naturalistic form in the central mullion of the double central portal in the band which binds the bundle of palm fronds forming the post, and also in the rays of light which descend from the star of the east.

The expressive qualities which the architect brings out in the stone forms are quite remarkable, as in the rays which seem to cut through the atmosphere, in the snowy icicles which seem about to melt, and in the incense which surrounds the monogram of Jesus with cloud-like granulated forms scattered along undulating lines.

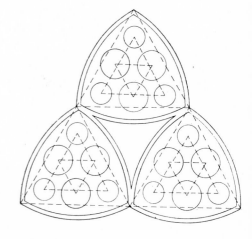

The graceful forms and poses of some of the angels, and the flourishes of the inscriptions fit well within the norms of Modernismo, without the effeminate daintiness which sometimes accompanied that style. As an example of his controlled elegance we can cite the pedestals that support the apostles of each tower, undulating in form but geometrically ordered in a manner which allows both variety and balance; this is echoed in the *miradores* above these figures, linked to the pointed canopies which terminate in lovely compositions using starfish forms and a dove (Fig. 103).

Most of the ornamental elements here have a symbolic significance as well—characteristic of the literary aspect of Modernismo. We have already seen that the very orientation of the façade was symbolic, and that it is, in turn, arranged in a symbolic manner with greater sublimity corresponding to physical height. At ground level the striated column nearest the sea has an aquatic turtle as its base, while the other has a land tortoise—both symbols of resistance. Higher up are the Christmas animals forming a base for the familiar manger scene, figures of kings and shepherds; above come less common representations: the Annunciation, the Betrothal, the Presentation; then come Faith, Hope, and Charity; the Sacred Heart; and finally the Eucharist which we will discuss later.

309a. Outline and triangular rhythm of straight lines and curves in the pinions of the cloister.

310. Decorative details of the façade *miradores*.

311. Lower part of the towers with mullioned openings, *miradores,* and a niche for the apostle St. Barnabas.

312. Sagrada Familia. Bridge uniting the two central towers of the Nativity façade.

SPATIAL VISION. All of the symbols and scenes that we have examined—as well as others we have omitted—can be observed from the outside of the church, as can the overall façade itself, but if the observer wishes to get inside of this tableau, he can do so quite comfortably while passing through the lanterns, galleries, *miradores,* and passageways which from below seem merely ornamental but which are actually quite functional. On coming into personal contact with the decorative forms, and on contemplating at close range the images, volumes, and unsuspected inner structure, we ourselves become absorbed within the dimension of movement and time which enlivens the space defined by the palpitating architecture. Anyone who has not climbed inside as if on a country outing, leaning over balconies, looking out from the *miradores,* and nearing St. Joseph's boat, ascended the spiral stairway of the bell towers, crossed the bridge behind the tall cypress, and surveyed from above the growing temple far below while coming close enough to reach out and almost touch the terminal crosses, cannot feel that he has really seen this façade. Only after we have intimately penetrated its inner substance, putting styles and theories aside and open only to esthetic emotions, can we truly say that we have seen and heard and touched this grandiose artistic florescence left to us by Gaudí. As we penetrate it, it will penetrate us as well, and on returning to the ground and looking up again at the magnificent «fragment» of the future temple, it may be that some of the surface symbolism will have vanished, but we will be left with a more complete, alive, and human reality.

180. CASA CALVET. 1898-1900 (Figs. 54, 95, 132, 313 - 330)

In our review of Gaudí's structures we have seen that—apart from several of his early altarpieces—each new work represented a different theme which the architect proceeded to study with great enthusiasm. For this building, which the sons of Pedro Mártir Calvet commissioned him to build at No. 48, Calle de Caspe, he was presented with a program almost identical to that which he had developed for Fernández and Andrés in León: the lower floor and basements were to be used for the business, the main floor for the home of the proprietor, and the upper stories for rented apartments. Although the program was the same, the lot and urbanistic circumstances were quite different, and this diversity produced a totally different house. The isolated property at León was more attractive than that in Barcelona which was wedged in between two other buildings—one in a series of houses in a row. In spite of this indistinct site, once the building was completed it was awarded the City prize in a newly-established competition which annually honored the best building of the year in Barcelona.

STRUCTURE AND STYLE.   This building is constructed within the finest structural standards of its day. The façade is of ashlar masonry, the interior walls of brick; the iron beams are

313, 314. Casa Calvet. Plan of one of the floors and the façade from the plans presented to the Ayuntamiento.

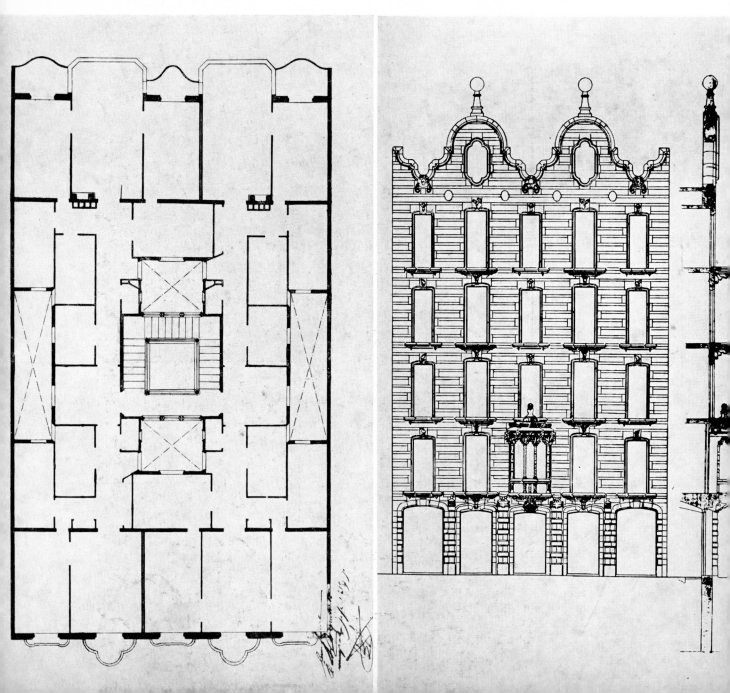

spanned by *bovedillas*, with the girders of the ground floor and basements resting on the bearing walls. The walls of the central light shaft rest on an ingenious arrangement of the first floor beams. However, apart from the great care taken with all of the details, the building displays no outstanding structural innovations. Of all of Gaudí's buildings, this is perhaps the most traditional and conservative, both in the distribution of the rooms and in the placement of the openings in the composition of the façades. The street façade and some of the decorative elements are based on two concepts which might seem to be mutually exclusive: simplicity and baroquism—a simple framework of rectangular patterns discreetly adorned with baroque motifs. Schematic simplicity and vivacious optimism in balanced harmony give this façade its special attractiveness, along with the simple and roughly-hewn texture of the ashlars contrasting with their smooth edges (another noteworthy tectonic method).

The major decorative details on the façade are the small tribune on a robust console containing the «parlante» coat of arms of the family over the entrance portal with its fine forms, agile composition, and graceful cupola on top, and the upper part of the façade itself with two baroque gables capped by wrought-iron crosses which have been mentioned before (XVII - 66). These gables surpassed the legal height, and when this transgression was noted by the municipal authorities, the architect threatened arbitrarily to cut off the façade at that point rather than modify his design, as we saw. The gables are pierced to make way for small, iron projections of a singularly interesting form that contain cleverly calculated iron apparatus for lifting furniture to the apartments. Between the gables and on either end of the

315. Casa Calvet. Main façade.

upper crest there are three other, non-projecting *miradores* which look onto the street and have wrought and cast-iron railings in the form of palm fronds, forms which allude to the heads of the martyrs which can be seen below: St. Peter Martyr in the center, and the patron saints of Vilassar de Dalt (St. Ginés the actor and St. Ginés the notary), the town where the father of the Calvets had been born and had established his textile factory.

It is unfortunate that these details are not easily visible from the street due to their position so high on the façade (we have already seen how the Señora Güell had trouble distinguishing the crosses, XVII - 66). Such invisibility does not conform to the usual standards which the master kept in mind regarding sculptural ornamentation; he also departed from his usual criterion of unity in terminating the façade with a double gable.

The balconies are distributed in five vertical rows; those in the outer and center rows are of slight projection with smoothly rounded edges; the others project to a greater extent and have a trilobate plan. All of the railings are of wrought iron with an elegant simplicity achieved by using prefabricated handrail profiles.

316. Casa Calvet. Elevator door with a circular rhythm superimposed on a square network.

317. Vestibule and beginning of the stairway with solomonic columns.

Perhaps the most interesting baroque detail of the façade is the door knocker at the entrance —a masterpiece of ironwork both technically and symbolically, with the cross—a symbol of goodness—striking a blow on the back of a louse—a symbol of evil—every time there is a knock on the door.

The posterior façade is boldly corporeal with projecting balconies, balustrade railings, and two enclosed tribune sections.

The stairway opens onto the two contiguous courts, integrating them into its composition —an innovation for that time. The back shaft is seen through three rampant arches, while communication to the front one is by way of three level arches (Fig. 320).

The dominant baroque element of the interior consists of the four solomonic columns of artificial reinforced granite surmounted by ornamental rampant arches adorned with grape leaves. Clusters of grapes are painted on the plaster of the spandrels and relieving arches. The stone parts of the stairway such as the pillars and the doorways to the floors and *anteescalera* are made of the same artificial stone as the solomonic columns; the staircase railing and elevator doors are of laminated steel strips forged in circles and combined to form an emphatically

318. Casa Calvet. Tribune.

319. Wrought-iron door-knocker.

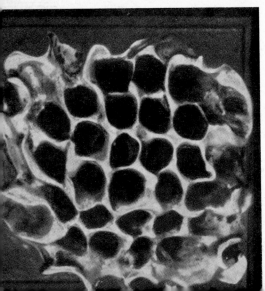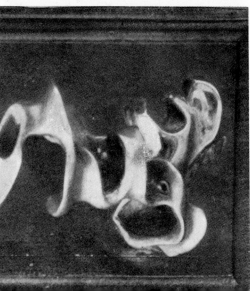

320. Vestibule patio which communicates with the stairway. We can read the slogan of the Floral Games: «Patria, Fe, Amor».

321, 322. Peephole and handle of the doors to the various floors.

323. Casa Calvet. Rear façade.

324. Property wall with openings which hide the next-door house from view and permit the passage of light at the same time.

325. Upper part of the main façade with its double gables and heads of the martyred saints.

geometric pattern (Fig. 316). Above the first arch of the stairway we read the inscription *Ave María Purissima, sens pecat fou concebuda* (Hail Mary Most Pure, conceived without sin), and the initials J M J; on the back court shaft the slogan of the Floral Games, *Patria-Fe-Amor* (Country, Faith, and Love), is repeated several times. Standing out against the restrained baroquism of the staircase and the entire house in general are the metal peepholes and doorknobs at the entrance to each floor (Figs. 321, 322). Their extremely free form was obtained when the architect capriciously put his fingers in wet plaster which, once it had set, served as a model for the metal worker.[1] This detail heralds the plasticity of Gaudí's forthcoming works.

In the apartments we should note the perfectly crafted doors with simply designed rectangular surfaces, and the wooden ceilings which replace the customary plastered type—a circumstance due to a plasterers' strike during the construction period which the architect countered by a change of material.

The shaft of the ventilating court which serves the apartments which border on the convent at No. 50 on the same street has a clever arrangement of small slanting arches which permit the passage of natural light while at the same time sheltering the nuns next door from view.

1. Information provided by D. Sebastián Buxó Calvet.

326. Casa Calvet. Expressionistic element of carpentry work.

327. Furniture in vestibule of the office at Casa Calvet.

This house was begun in 1898 (the plans presented to the city bear the date of March 29), and was finished the following year, judging from the date 1899 sculpted high on the façade and from the fact that it was awarded the City prize by jury decision on June 11, 1900, from among the buildings completed in the preceding year. In announcing their decision, the jurors referred not only to the originality, fine distribution, structure, and beauty of the building, but also to the «perfect hygienic conditions, especially in the ventilation and drainage of the latrine and sink pipes,» [2] indicating that the building must have been completely finished, structurally, when they made their decision public.

Earlier biographers have given 1904 as the date of termination. At the most a short lapse could be allowed for the installation of the offices and furniture of the ground floors, and for the completion of the profusely carved baroque carpentry work, but it is inconceivable that this period would reach four years — not even taking into account the movable furniture of the manager's office and that which is still preserved in the main floor salon, today inhabited by the widow Boyer who now owns the building. [3]

181. BELLESGUARD. 1900-1902 (Figs. 136, 331 - 346)

Gaudí was commissioned to do this country house by Doña María Sagués (the widow Figueras) a great admirer of the master's work, in 1900; this was two years after he had

2. *Anuario para 1901* of the Asociación de Arquitectos de Cataluña, p. 62.

3. The present owner of the house, Señora Boyer, is extremely interested in its care and conservation, as well as that of the furniture which she acquired with the building.

328. Casa Calvet. Sofa in the salon of the main apartment.

329, 330. Chairs for the office and dining room, Casa Calvet.

received the commission for the Güell Colony church, a project which he spent ten years preparing. From these preparatory studies there emerged the decidedly transformed architecture of Gaudí's mature years in which he no longer concerned himself with historic styles. Bellesguard is related to the Gothic but, conceived as it was in this transitional period, it seems constantly to evade those historical motifs which would tie it to tradition and to avoid all established patterns of form.

The site chosen by the widow Figueras was that known as Bellesguard where the palace of the last king of the House of Barcelona, Martin I, was erected in 1408 on the lower slopes of Mt. Tibidabo overlooking the arrival and departure of the ships at sea beyond the fruitful fields of the plain below, from which came the name Bell Esguard (Beautiful View) for the palace, perhaps at the suggestion of the chronicler Bernat Metge.[4] It was this historic tradition, revived even more by the remains of the ancient mansion located on the property, that led the architect to adopt a style which would evoke the glorious days of Catalonia and the regal events which were enacted on this site.

PREPARATORY LAYOUT. From the very beginning Gaudí planned to preserve and dignify what little remained of the old palace. In order to unify it with the new house as a part of the gardens, he diverted the old road which had passed between two ruined towers toward the nearby Vilana river bed; this necessitated the construction of a system of arches on inclined piers—a frank adoption of the new theory which he also applied lavishly in building Güell Park.[5] The restored archaeological ruins, with their merlons and open passageways, are located to the left of the entrance to the estate and are balanced by the mass of the groundkeeper's house to the right, also crowned with merlons, built later by the architect Su-

331. Bellesguard. Exterior view of the building.

332. Partial view of the roof.

333. The recently terminated building with neither fence nor surrounding wall, showing the new viaduct with its pillars and sustaining arches which can be seen today.

4. José M. Garrut, «Visita a la casa de campo Bellesguard,» in *Gaudí* (Barcelona, Centro de Estudios Gaudinistas, 1960).

5. These arches, which can be seen from the road across the river-bed from the property, not only display the same structural form as those of the Park, but also suggest a similar method of construction. [It now appears that the viaduct was not carried out—by Juan Rubió—until 1908, and that work on the house itself also lagged well after 1902. — G. R. C.]

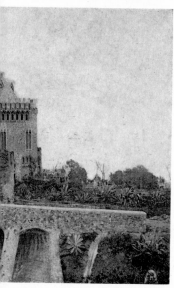

334. Detail of the upper window gallery and merlons with the roof in the background.

grañes. Beyond stands the house itself with its expressive agility and an amazing textural variety—the embodiment of the surrounding landscape and of the fortified palace tradition with its merloned crown and round-walks topped by the tall spire and four-armed cross similar to those which we saw for the first time at the Teresan convent; here both location and size are more ostentatious.

The layout of this developed estate, enclosed within an embattled wall, is centered on the motif of the home. This in turn has its center in the cross for which it serves as an integrated pedestal of stone from the surrounding land, thus achieving maximum harmony with the countryside and the extensive garden behind, later landscaped by the gardener Pedro Ballart Ventura.[6]

When Gaudí built the house, he designed the entranceway straight from the road to the door, the exterior gate, the merlons copying those of the ruined palace, water depositories, a wash room, and a motor-shed. The iron cross was put up later following Gaudí's design.[7]

EXTERIOR APPEARANCE. Harmony is achieved in the erect spire which rises above the whole, the diverse forms of the openings, and particularly in the general grayish color of the rubble—a merging of a variety of tonalities ranging from black to ochre. The overall plan of the building is square, with a protruding section which houses the entrance whose exterior corner supports the cross-bearing spire. The roof has the form of a truncated pyramid and an interesting structure which we will examine later; the façades present a variety of openings in which tall twin windows predominate, giving it a Gothic character in spite of its divergence from the general lines of that style. The merloned battlements of the upper-story gallery contribute to the fortified medieval castle look which the architect wanted for the building.

6. This information and that which follows was provided by the grandson of the gardener, Jorge Ballart, who has it by family tradition.

7. Information provided by Jorge Ballart.

311

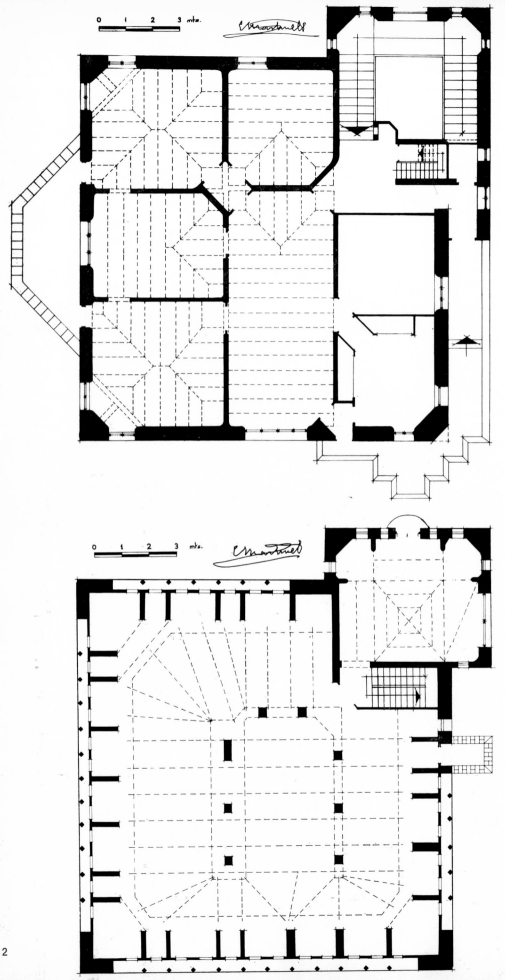

335. Bellesguard. Plan of the main floor and projection of the brick arches that sustain the ceiling. (Plan drawn by the author.)

336. Plan of the garret floor and projection of the structure which supports the roof. (Plan by the author.)

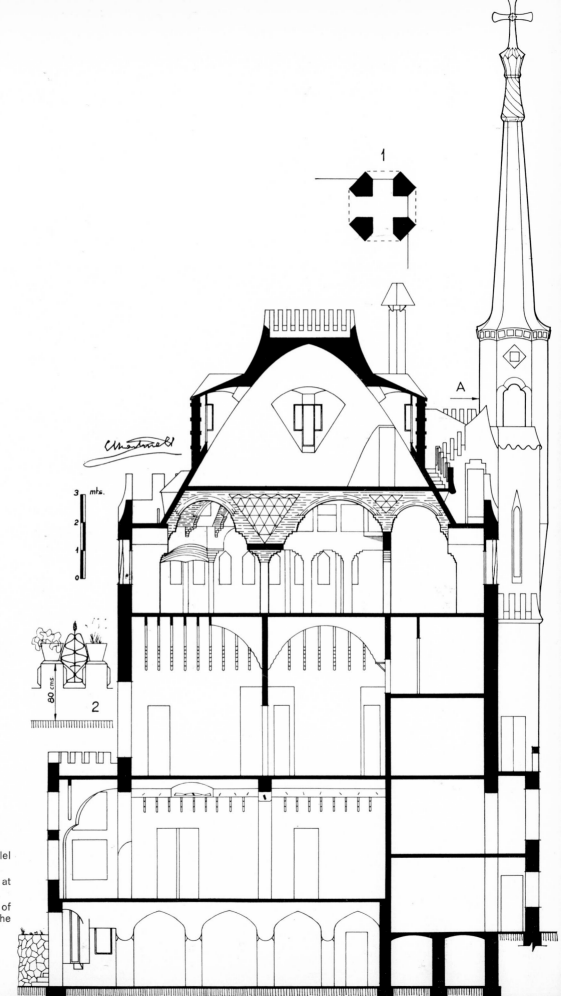

337. Bellesguard. Section parallel to the principal façade.

1. Plan of the corner tower at point A.
2. Detail of the balcony sill of the main floor. (Plan by the author.)

338. Bellesguard. Semi-basement before its present-day use.

339. Ceiling of the lower floor with vaults using tie rods.

340. Vestibule and stairway when the building was recently finished.

341. Ceiling of corner room of the main floor: flat tile deck on *tabicados* arches.

342. Bellesguard. Ceiling of the living room of the main floor.

The walls are of ordinary *opus incertum* rubblework with which he obtained a highly artistic texture which all alone sets the tone for the overall effect. Only the main windows, some of them with projecting stone jambs, provide a dominantly vertical pattern which goes well with the dominant spire. The symbolism of the cross which tops the spire is reinforced by the openwork cross motif below the sills of the taller window.

Standing apart from the general dominant rhythm is the semicircular arch of the entrance doorway bordered by octagonal, square, and hexagonal appliqués distributed in a geometric pattern—a variant of the textures employed elsewhere in the building. The wide window above the door has a five-lobed arch above which Gaudí planned to place a representation of the Three Kings in memory of King Martin; only the relief star, preserved in the glass window, was completed. He uses trilobate rhythms in several of the windows, but always in a less obvious manner than that which we have seen at Astorga and León.

The forged ironwork—always of interest in the master's works—is especially remarkable in the main floor window grates where he followed a course already insinuated at León using round iron bars which are here ingeniously intertwined as in basket weaving, with a minimum of riveted or soldered joints (Fig. 346). These interwoven grates, usually rectangular, are here and there enriched by the inclusion of circular motifs using the same basketry technique. The lower part of the door to the entrance vestibule (Fig. 345) is a variation on this type of ironwork. The upper semicircular part is of a completely different more complicated technique in which the devout salutation *Ave Maria Puríssima* is spelled out in hard-to-read letters

343. Bellesguard. Supporting structure of the roof with trilobed arches corbelled at the bottom and then becoming running arches higher up.

344. The springing of the supporting arches of the roof.

(especially those of the first word) which are followed by the more legible *sens pecat fou concebuda.*

Gaudí built the movable part of the entrance doorway in wood. This was later replaced by an iron one, under the supervisión of Sugrañes, and the one designed by Gaudí was adapted to the basement doorway on the side of the building.[8] Sugrañes, who acted with a certain independence as Gaudí's assistant, also did the stairway railing and the two polychrome tile benches which flank the entrance.

STRUCTURE. The structure of this tiny castle is interesting for the rational manner in which typical Catalan methods are employed to yield the artistic results proposed by the architect. The general impression that we get from an overall survey of the structural systems employed here is that he intended a comprehensive exhibition of the diverse ways in which masonry ceilings can be constructed without resorting to the customary beams (except in the servants' quarters where he used beams grouped together to form a mezzanine space).

The roof of the semi-basement or floor of the first floor is constructed of continuous thin shell masonry vaulting pierced by lunettes which are supported on massive cylindrical pillars. Because they are located in the basement and have the advantage of thicker walls, these vaults do not need tie rods. This is not the case, however, with the smaller ones forming the ceiling of the main floor, where the architect has made no attempt to conceal the tie rods of laminated steel bands twisted in spiral form. The roof of the second floor replaces vaults and tie rods with horizontal platforms of thin masonry which rest on diaphragm arches arranged in such a way that their thrusts are contained within themselves or absorbed by the exterior walls, while at the same time providing the decorative basis for each room. This decorative note is enhanced by several five-lobed arches and semi-arches placed across the corners in an original manner.

8. Acording to Jorge Ballart.

345. Bellesguard. Detail of the entrance and grating.

The clever solutions employed in the structure of the roof of the building make it extremely interesting. On this floor the interior bearing walls were replaced by brick pillars 30 centimeters on a side, some of which grow wider at the top and form board-like masonry platforms from which there spring a series of trilobate corbelled arches which, at a certain height, become true running arches over the central bay; over the lateral bays the arches are somewhat lower and rest on the vaults of the low walls next to the façades and perpendicular to them. The spandrels of these arches are not solid; instead they rather perforated to produce a triangular network of bricks which can be seen in a section drawing (Fig. 337), and photographs (Figs. 343, 344). Above these arches is extended the flat masonry surface which forms the faces of the roof pyramid, which is horizontal in the center to support another loft which is covered by four *tabicada* vaults (Fig. 337).

The square shaft which houses the stairway is resolved in a similar manner. Using a paradoxical phrase, we could say that the structural system adopted by the architect in this roof is one of simple complication. In order to give it the pyramidal form that he wanted without departing from the homogeneous masonry, he had to follow a course which presented special problems which he was able to solve so logically and with such facility that, once resolved, no trace remains of the difficulties. This «complication,» which exists for the spectator whereas Gaudí resolved it «simply,» is ample proof of the architect's admirable structural genius and of his clairvoyance in the unification of function, esthetics, and structure.

The roof exterior is faced with slate slabs taken from the site, which add a touch of attractive country coarseness to the aristocratic air of the whole. The roof pyramid is truncated by a small merloned platform which is reached by way of comfortable steps which accentuate the spatial concept of the roof, all of it accessible and visible from various viewpoints, which makes it a forerunner of the magnificent plastic concept of the Casa Milá roof terrace. The

346. Window screen for the servant's room on the lower floor with iron bars intertwined as if in basketry work.

passage and stairway railings of the roof consist of slender merlons which also supply the cresting for the building.

Part of this cresting, like some of the window jambs, is faced with artificial stone embellished with small rustic stones. This facing is used in pyramidal forms or moldings, depending on the case, and also in the small polygonal tablets that we have seen decorating the main entrance. Within his great textural variety, Gaudí's use of this system—which hides the brick of which the roof is built beneath stone appliqués which give the appearance of rubble—was only in this case; it is a rarity in the master's work, for, with few exceptions, he sought always to make evident the structure of his buildings.

In this case he did not glory in his usual technical sincerity, but the successful results compensate for the anomaly. The slate shingles which cover the inclined planes of the boardlike roof harmonize with the stone facings and the artificial pieces of small stones which border the Gothic-style openings with metal-reinforced artificial granite mullions.[9]

At Astorga, he would not allow the artificial stone suggested by his friend the bishop (XLII-173). There the work was imbued with hierarchical symbolism, whereas here he himself imposed a sort of romantic symbolism which led to this spread between a functional structure based on stone and brick employed in a modern fashion, and a historical evocation which he achieved with a superstructure of traditionally inspired forms and stone from the surrounding countryside, combined in a unified manner.

Such a procedure is admissible in all normal construction. We call attention to it in Gaudí's work because of the principle of purity which he usually practiced and which, in this case, he chose to sacrifice to the successful solution that he was able to come up with for the complex situation presented in this building—a solution which deserves careful study for its structural richness and originality.

9. The estate presently belongs to Dr. Luis Guilera Molas who has conserved it with exquisite care, and to whom I am grateful for the opportunity to study the work with maximum facility.

XLVI. GAUDÍ AND MODERNISMO

182. THE BAROQUE AND MODERNISMO (Figs. 6, 102, 103, 140, 302 - 304, 311)

Gaudí himself confessed to being a man of the Baroque. He never hid his admiration for that style so overflowing with dynamism and color which was scorned by the critics throughout the nineteenth century and well into the present day. In discussing the most outstanding of the sculptors from the 18th-century Bonifás family, Luis, he enthusiastically praised his work and proclaimed him to be his artistic brother. He judged Bonifás' work on the *camarín* of the Virgen de Misericordia in his native Reus to be among the most elegant anywhere, and he observed that just as he admired those works, the Baroque sculptor would admire his if he could see them, and if he were a contemporary, would create similar works.[1] In studying Gaudí's esthetic theory (XXIX - 132), we have seen his preference for three-dimensional forms and the importance which he gave to the expression of life in a work of art—both qualities which were standard in Baroque art.

The prevailing eclecticism of Gaudí's formative years did not include the Baroque; in spite of this we know that his early works were open to an overall exultant optimism, with certain details expressing his genius in forms paralleling those which would later be proper to Art Nouveau, or Modernismo as it was called in Spain. In spite of his brilliant imagination, he generally kept within the limits of planimetric composition. It was not until the last decade of the century that European architecture, tired of historic styles and the pendular oscillation of artistic taste, turned to the new baroque modes like Viennese Secessionism which is more a decorative than an architectural style.

Gaudí did not imitate anything. The wavy lines and languishing figures which came from Central Europe did not serve him as models; they did, however, represent a new esthetic of freedom and of the beyond which coincided with that of our architect who, from that moment on, would find the atmosphere more compatible with his own conceptions.[2]

This was the period when the Nativity Façade of the Sagrada Familia—begun within a Gothic framework with the flat surfaces that still characterized the apse—would swell into waves to contain all sorts of flora and fauna with both naturalistic and symbolic meaning, harmonizing

1. Martinell, *Conversaciones con Gaudí...*, p. 56.

2. See Ráfols, *Modernismo y Modernistas*, (Barcelona: 1949), and A. Cirici-Pellicer, *El arte modernista catalán*, (Barcelona: 1951).

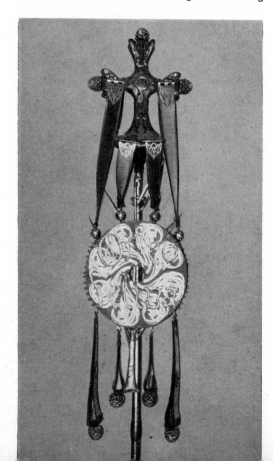

347. Standard of the *Orfeó* of San Feliu de Codinas.

with a literary mode which the architect did not share, but which, in reality, he dignified through the plastic strength of his expressive stone.

In speaking of this architectural expression we must distinguish between the surface Modernismo and the internal structural essence which is of much greater importance, though both are intimately united. Other, less united and possibly more attractive, elements such as the consoles and canopies of the apostles which we have mentioned elsewhere (XLIV - 179) constitute typical examples of Modernismo, and taken together they form a great, diffuse anthology of that artistic mode.

His *modernista* elements are not completely autonomous, in spite of their decisive character; they are parasites of a higher order. At the beginning of the century, however, he designed and completed several works which were conceived from the start within the norms of the apparent arbitrary freedom which characterizes Modernismo. Despite their obvious importance, these works which we will now study do not transcend the most valuable contribution of Gaudí's architecture, which is his structural and plastic theory.

183.   A STANDARD AND A GATEWAY (Figs. 347 - 352)

A STANDARD FOR A CHORAL SOCIETY (1901). We must place at the forefront of Gaudí's *modernista* work this standard which he designed for the «Orfeó Feliuà;» in spite of its reduced dimensions (175×50 cm), it is highly significant as a turning point. Around 1900 the town of San Feliu de Codinas founded this municipal choral society; the widowed Marquise of Tolrá presented the new group with a standard hose design was entrusted to our architect on the suggestion of her nephew, Emilio Carlos Tolrá.

Gaudí here created a completely original work, leaving aside the customary rectangular form and showy cloth fabric with embroidered or printed emblems such as he himself had used in the banner for La Obrera Mataronense. Here he resolved the problem by turning to those emblems which he considered most fitting—the cross, the millstone, and the palm symbolizing the martyrdom of San Feliu; he combined these in an original manner as if he intended to present a practical example of his slogan «*original* means to return to the origin.»

He placed the cross at the top of the shaft, projecting slightly forward so that it would be possible to hang from it the millstone of the saint's martyrdom (a symbol which also appears on the town's coat of arms); for this purpose he attached four double ribbons or bands, two of which hang from the arms and two from the foot of the cross. Four other doubled ribbons hang below the stone, and the ensemble is completed by the martyr's palm behind.

At the lower end of each of the four lower bands there are two pine cones: one open and facing downward, and another closed and facing upward. These, along with three others which

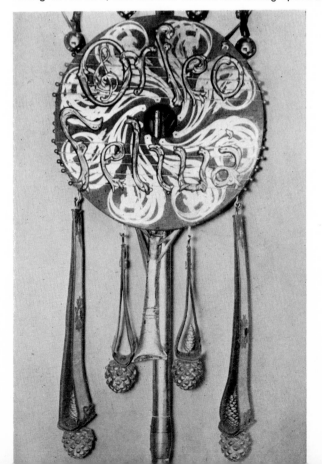

348. Lower half of the same standard.

terminate the arms and head of the cross, allude to the pine-nut market which was important to the town in ancient times and gave it the nickname *Sant Feliu dels pinyons* (of the pine nuts).

The aspect of this small work is both solemn and gay at the same time, and its Modernismo is manifest in the freedom of execution, the outline of the cross, and in the most visible element of the insignia—the millstone disc which is decorated with a motif of free *modernista* inspiration repeated eight times and radiating from the center in a spiral movement that widens on the outer edge. This pattern forms the background for the inscription «Orfeó Feliuà» in relief; each of the words is placed on a musical staff.

As important as the artistic appearance of this standard are the technique and the materials employed—ones not commonly found in the rest of Gaudí's work. The pole is a demountable brass tube in two pieces that screw together; in order to alleviate its weight, the cross is made of cork with axial iron reinforcements and external appliqués of brass plating which lend appropriate ornamental richness; the hanging ribbons or bands are of leather with applied silk and metal; the martyr's millstone, 50 cm. in diameter, 8 cm. thick. and with an 8 cm. hole in the middle, is also of cork and decorated with a superimposed brass plate. The inscription is obtained with a repoussé technique, and the musical staffs are made from metal wires. The palm on the back side of the cork disc is of forged brass, and the pine cones are of carved and gilded wood.

We have described this work in some detail, despite its less than architectonic nature, because here we can observe the care and skill which Gaudí applied to his every commitment, no matter how unimportant. This observation is reinforced by numerous other technical details of the standard which is carefully preserved in the Casa Consistorial at San Feliu.[3]

THE MIRALLES GATE AND WALL (1901-1902). Here structural Modernismo makes its first real appearance in Gaudí's architecture. Although these are only secondary elements of the house which Gaudí's friend the industrialist Hermenegildo Miralles, whom we have mentioned in Part One (XVII - 67), planned to construct, the architect created in them a highly personal work with a vigorous style which, as Ráfols says, «surpasses [that of] all of the contemporary *Modernistas* in movement and in life.» As he was dealing with uncomplicated structural elements—a surrounding wall and a simple entrance gate to the garden—he could perform on the decorative stage without mechanical preoccupations; he even seems to mock the latter in the trilobate, nonstructural profile of the arch and the *opus incertum* rubble which reveals no stereometric concern. Such apparent lack of preoccupation leads us to suspect that there may exist some hidden resource which guarantees the stability of the arch which seems so «anti-Gaudinist» in form and structural expression.

When confronted with this concession to the free, undulating lines of the period we can imagine the designer playfully giving rein to the movement of his pencil, momentarily escaping from the laws of mechanics in the simplicity of the entrance arches; as for the walls with their undulating surfaces, he was careful to increase their thickness at the base. The fabric of the wall is a harmonious, rusticated rubble terminating in an undulating contour which is protected by a somewhat projecting coping with a circular profile that is surmounted by a metallic screen which follows the undulation of the top of the wall. The most typicallly *modernista* element in this small ensemble is the panel between the two gateways which was probably meant to contain the title of the client's firm in papier-mâché relief. The iron gate of the smaller entrance is interesting for its three-dimensional effect and for its simplicity within the style. Contrasting with this predominance of curves was the grand rectilinear double-pitched marquee which projected 4.5 meters outward at its maximum point. This marquee, with its

3. I am grateful to the Ayuntamiento of Sant Feliu, and to my friend Martín Bonet for making the study of this work possible.

349, 350. Gate and wall of the Finca Miralles. Elevation and section. Plans from the Municipal Offices of Artistic Buildings, Barcelona.

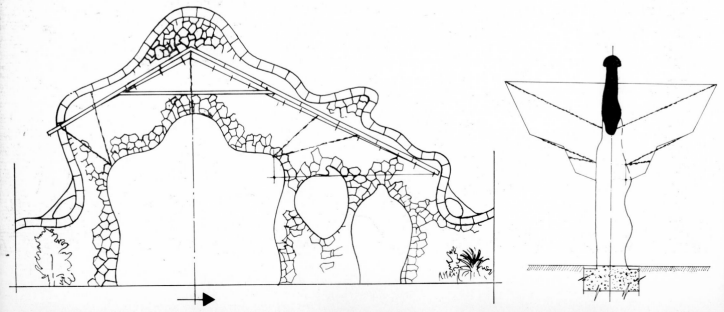

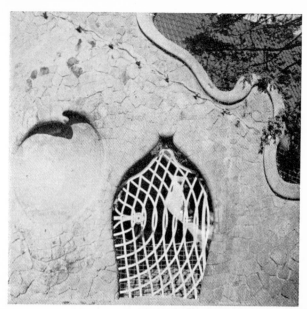

351. Lateral gate of the Finca Miralles.

352. Entrance portal to the Finca Miralles and part of the surrounding wall in original condition.

visible supporting framework and exposed truss rods which reduced the effect of the wind, was repeated on both sides of the opening (front and back). The roof was tiled with pieces of reinforced cement which rested on a net-like frame of metallic rods arranged diagonally, and which were laid in a manner similar to that of Roman roofing tile.

The pleasant contrast provided by the severe forms of the grand marquee which protect the undulating lines of the rest is another example of Gaudí's foresight in the introduction of new esthetic values.[4] The wooden gate in the center with its masonry pillars and lights, and the jardinieres and other structures within the fence were the work of Gaudí's collaborator, the architect Sugrañes.

184. A DEMOLISHED WORK AND TWO FRUSTRATED PROJECTS (Figs. 159, 353 - 357)

A SALON FOR THE «TORINO» BAR (1902). While the Miralles wall was being erected on the outskirts of Barcelona, the «Torino» Bar—for the retail sale of the vermouth of the same name—was being set up in the most central part of the new section of the city (at the intersection of the Paseo de Gracia and the Gran Vía); it was decorated in the exaggerated *modernista* tone then in vogue. The task of adapting the premises for this purpose was entrusted to Ricardo Campmany who put the municipal architect, Pedro Falqués, in charge of designing and executing a flashy marquee in wrought iron and glass; Puig y Cadafalch was to do the room, opening onto the street; and the decoration of another interior salon was placed in the hands of Gaudí. All of this was demolished years ago, which perhaps explains why none of the biographers or critics have discussed this work by the master; nevertheless, an illustration and various descriptions from the contemporary press afford us some idea of the salon's characteristics.[5]

Gaudí's room was rectangular, with a horizontal flat ceiling; his work was limited to the decoration of pre-existing plane surfaces, but this presented no obstacle to his success, according to the press acclaim when the bar was inaugurated.

The most attractive decorative element was the entrance door to the room with a pointed horseshoe arch opening of Arabic influence inscribed in a rectangle bordered by a zigzag pattern on either side. The door itself was of leaded glass, with a lozenge pattern below and *modernista* foliage in the upper part.

The rest of the decoration consisted of a variety of carefully balanced reliefs which covered the surfaces of the walls and the ceiling to obtain the desired plastic effect. The floor was the only part of the room without relief decoration; it is a patterned combination of glazed ceramic-tile squares in clear tones with hexagonal pieces which were probably made of potter's clay.

The lower part of the walls was covered with an ornate wainscot with a protective socle at ground level to prevent scraping with chairs. The dominant motif was the zigzag combined with subtler, less important floral themes. The decoration of the rest of the wall was also of a floral sort, with an overall square network in low relief discreetly contrasting with the background pattern.

Attached to the walls were decorative blue Venetian glass lamps of a color which reminds us of the glass crown that adorned the lamps in the Plaza Real. The placement of these fixtures demonstrates the master's preference for light sources next to walls; here this must have enhanced the effect of the surrounding reliefs.

At the top of the wall was a dark-colored frieze with a zigzag motif which ran all around the salon, above which was the ceiling, patterned in a clear hexagonal pattern where the architect's delight in draughting and geometry is apparent. In Figure 159 we can see the development of this rhythmic composition where two different ornamental motifs alternately occupy the six triangles of each hexagon; these are then joined in a manner such that no two similar triangles are contiguous. Such compositional subtleties underscore, and leave no doubt of, Gaudí's authorship of these tiles which are the forerunners of the concrete tiles used in the floors of the Casa Milá, and even of the original relief ceilings in that same house.

It is important to keep in mind that the plastic richness and sumptuosity obtained in this salon were achieved in spite of the inexpressive parallelepiped form which he had to work with, and the industrial nature of the papier-mâché pieces which he used, manufactured by his friend and client, Hermenegildo Miralles. Gaudí's close relationship with the industrialist and the natural attraction of any new plastic problem were both responsible for the high quality of the appliqués which made the room so successful; unfortunately no samples were preserved when the work was demolished. Whereas it has been largely forgotten until now, it nevertheless constitutes an important facet of the master's *modernista* work.[6]

THE GRANER CHALET. The opportunity soon came to escape from the obligatory planar forms of his previous works when his friend, the painter Luis Graner—for whom he supervised

353. Salon of the «Torino» bar. From an illustration in the magazine *Hispania*, November 15, 1902.

4. This marquee had to be dismantled years ago because its grand projection violated the municipal ordinances which went into effect in this area. Since the removal of the gate and the surrounding walls is also planned because of the future development of this zone, the city has agreed that the remainder be moved to Güell Park.

5. *Ilustración artística*, N.º 1091, (November 24, 1902) and *Hispania*, N.º 90, (November 15, 1902).

6. Martinell, «Otra obra de Gaudí olvidada en sus biografías,» *La Vanguardia*, (November 3, 1966).

the Sala Mercé music hall, ca. 1904 (XVII - 67) [7]—commissioned him to design a country house for the slopes of Tibidabo, near the Bonanova district; only the foundations were built, and part of the fence with «a crazy door combined with a bridge that crosses the nearby Pomaret river bed and honors Barcelona's Saint Eulalia according to plans drawn up by Gaudí.» [8] This bridge must have been supported on columns with the vaults distributed triangularly in a manner similar to the Güell Park viaduct (which I have indicated with the letter D in Figs. 165, 427).

From the sketch of the ground plan and the exterior which were kept in the archives at the Sagrada Familia until 1936, and which Ráfols was able to reproduce (Figs. 354, 355) [9] we can see that it was a highly fluid composition which surpasses even the Miralles gate in expression and dynamism. An extremely animated play of roofs connects to a cross-topped tower. We have no indication of the color of his plans for the project, but since it was to be a painter's home, we can imagine that the polychromatic effects, especially those of the roof, would have been outstanding—perhaps something along the lines of the Casa Batlló.

THE SANCTUARY OF THE VIRGIN OF MERCY. We recall that another work which the architect would have liked to realize, but which was frustrated midway in its conception, was that of the sanctuary of the Misericordia in Reus; we have discussed this project in Part One, indicating the personal conflicts which motivated the rejection (XVIII - 74). Gaudí made a model for this project which has unfortunately been lost, but we can get a general idea of his plans from a sketch which is in the Reus museum (Fig. 356). There we see an animated and optimistic silhouette, abounding in curves, a double bell gable on the façade, decorative pinnacles that stand out against the sky, and, apparently, a large image of the Virgin above the entrance portico—the *Ave Maria Mater Misericordiae* that we heard him refer to several times—as the principal element of the frontispiece. The rapid sketch gives no more details, but we know from other sources that beside the sanctuary he planned to represent the shepherdess Isabel Besora—to whom on this spot the Virgin appeared at the end of the XVI century—surrounded by her flock of sheep and lambs which would also serve as seats where people could rest; along the avenue leading from the city to the sanctuary he planned to represent the Mysteries of the Rosary. [10]

185. THE FIRST MYSTERY OF GLORY. 1900 - 1916 (Figs. 55, 56, 358, 359)

This work is interesting not only because it was designed and supervised for the most part by Gaudí, but also because it reflects a state of socio-religious opinion at the time. Although it does not exhibit *modernista* architectural characteristics—hardly suited to the representation of a Mystery in the midst of nature—we will study it here for chronological reasons.

On June 10, 1899, Ricardo Permanyer, the president of the *Lliga Espiritual de Nostra Dona de Montserrat,* asked the Abbot Deás for permission for his league to erect this Mystery. [11] On November 12 of the next year, he informed the abbot that the project had been commissioned to Gaudí, who accepted «with true enthusiasm, and even with gratitude, they say; he will undoubtedly create a work worthy to stand on the road to the Holy Grotto,» and he added that at an early date the architect would travel with several of the members of the *Lliga* to study the setting for the monument.

Before going on, we should mention that the basically religious meaning of this work also had its political overtones: this was a moment of political enthusiasm in which Catalanista aspirations were revived after almost two centuries of dormancy, and thus this first Mystery of Glory became for some the symbol of «all resurrection» as expressed in the description which accompanied it. In the letter just mentioned, Permanyer states that the work will be accomplished by Catalanista groups. Meanwhile a subscription was set up to raise funds; this apparently did not yield the hoped for results, since in February 1903 the *Lliga* ceded the initiative to a committee of well-known people from the cultural and financial worlds, apparently headed by Juan Mon y Bascós, who communicated the change to the abbot and told him of the colossal project which Gaudí was planning to begin immediately.

By April 27 they had collected 10,000 pesetas, and the architect was given the word to begin construction; he did this, entrusting the excavation in the rock, to form the cave which was to house the sepulcher, to the architect-contractor Jaime Bayó; foreseeing the expense which the undertaking would occasion, he asked Maragall for an allocution to promote contributions. Then he got José Llimona to do the sculpture work while, using the stone from the excavation, he built walls which served to widen the road, forming a little frontal square for better observing the Mystery.

Work proceeded slowly. On July 26, 1907, the same Sr. Mon wrote that Llimona had finished the statue of Christ, the most masterful ever to come from his hands, «which will require 30 men to put into place.» This optimistic note is offset by an undated letter from the same gentleman complaining to the abbot of a lack of donations. Gaudí, faced with this economic crisis, invested the remaining money in the casting of the colossal figure of Jesus which he erected in a spot which did not please some people—a reaction which appears to have motivated his retirement from direction of the job.

7. The architect Ll. Bonet Garí tells me that there existed a second theater in this *Sala* which was extremely well designed and is today used as a cinema. The floor was sloped to provide maximum visibility and the ceiling was vaulted with smoothly undulating longitudinal lines which favored the acoustics. The lights were colored and indirect to give a sensation of softness.

8. Ráfols, *Antonio Gaudí,* p. 117.

9. *Ibid.,* pp. 171, 172.

10. Guix Sugrañes, *op. cit.,* pp. 49, 50.

11. All of the data referring to the present works is from the archive of the monastery; see Note XVII-5.

354, 355. Sketch of a country house for the painter L. Graner. Plan and elevation. Ráfols.

356. Sketch of the project for remodeling the Sanctuary of the Misericordia in Reus. Overall view. Municipal Museum in Reus.

357. A separate detail for the same project in the Reus museum.

---

12. *Revista Montserratina*, 1916, pp. 509 ff.

13. The text of the inscription in bronze was written in Catalan. Translated it says: «The Spiritual League of the Virgin of Montserrat in the name of Catalan piety offers this Mystery, the symbol of all resurrection, XXIX of the month of the Rosary MCMXVI. It has been erected with the charity of our land, especially of Barcelona—the head and home of Cataluña—and the cities of Manresa, Tarrasa, and Sabadell which blossom at the foot fo the holy Mountain.»

After this retirement, Gaudí's place was probably taken temporarily by his assistant, the architect Juan Rubió, for in the mentioned letter, Sr. Mon states that Rubió had told him that 18,000 *duros* (90,000 pesetas) would be needed to complete the Mystery; he also states that they have no idea how to obtain the money and that they leave the affair in the hands of Providence. It seems that at the request of the monastery the *Lliga Espiritual* once again took over the work, and after a period of ups and downs, first the sepulcher and then the angel were erected—also sculpted by Llimona; early in 1916 the three Marys were put in place next to the tomb—these the work of Dionisio Renard after a design by Llimona. Only the crown, hair, and wounds of Christ were gilded, though Gaudí had originally envisioned the complete image in gold. Still to be done was the iron screen which was executed by the Ballarín firm from a design by Jerónimo Martorell,[12] who tried to follow Gaudí's technique closely. The bronze plaque of the Mystery with a dedication written by Maragall [13] was executed by the same Ballarín firm, and the Mystery was solemnly inaugurated on October 29, 1916, with the Christ image moved from the site where Gaudí had left it.

OTHER WORK AT MONTSERRAT. In my research in the Montserrat archives, I attempted also to document the supposed project for a Güell family pantheon in the monastery basilica (1895?), but without any success; nor was there evidence for a pantheon for the Marquis of Comillas which some have postulated. In a letter of January 23, 1887, the architect Villar the younger speaks of the project for a burial chapel for the Marquis of Tamarite, but similar projects for the above-mentioned families are unknown.

358. First Mystery of Glory on the mountain of Montserrat with the figure of Jesus where Gaudí put it.

359. The same Mystery with the image of Jesus where it is located today.

Also we must discard the idea of a subterranean church project which has been suggested by someone. The Reverend Bozzo who has been at the monastery since 1918 has never heard of such an idea, and he argues that once the important interior decoration and new façade of the church were finished at the end of the century, a new church would have no conceivable reason to exist.

On the other hand, Gaudí must have had many ideas of an imaginary nature; the architect Pericas drew a commercial illustration for the installation of a bell in the hole of the «roca foradada» on the mountain of Montserrat, inspired by an idea set forth by Gaudí, and Bergós explains his proposal to decorate the «Cavall Bernat» with a great crown and other emblems.[14]

186. THE MONUMENT TO DR. ROBERT. 1904-1910 (Figs. 115, 360 - 362)

Whereas in previous chapters I have eliminated certain works which, in my judgment, had been attributed without basis to the Reusian architect, in this chapter I have confirmed the authenticity of the salon of the «Torino» Bar, and now I will include a work which, with rare unanimity, has been overlooked by the cataloguers of his architectural work.

CONFIRMATION OF AUTHORSHIP. This monument was erected in memory of Bartolomé Robert, M. D., an outstanding scientific and political figure in the period which followed the loss of Spain's colonies in 1898, Mayor of Barcelona in 1899, and a *diputado* to the Spanish *Cortes,* who died in 1902 at the height of his popularity. The idea for the monument was initiated by his fellow deputy, the architect Doménech y Montaner, who was then chosen to do the monument; the model was made in collaboration with Llimona who was to execute the sculptured parts.[15]

The monument was paid for by a popular subscription organized by a special committee established for that purpose. Therefore it is difficult, if not impossible, to find any archival material in official institutions.

We do not know why Doménech's idea was not followed, nor do we know why the sculptor was given full authority to carry out the work as he saw fit. But it was Llimona who entrusted the architectural part of the monument to his good friend Gaudí. The two were co-founders of the Cercle Artistic de Sant Lluc, and were, at the time, collaborating on the Mystery at Montserrat. It is probable that Gaudí gladly accepted the job on the condition that his name remain in the background to avoid a straining of his relationship with his colleague Doménech.

For this reason it is not surprising that the contemporary press reports do not mention the name of the architect in their coverage of the laying of the first stone on January 31, 1904, nor of the inauguration of the monument on November 13, 1910, despite their accounts of the sculptor and of the important people in attendance.[16] I myself remember perfectly well that during my student years when the monument was being built, and later when it was unveiled in the Plàza de la Universidad, it was understood that the architecture was the work of our genial master.

Proof of this can also be found in the «Spain» volume of *Les Guides Bleus,* published in 1935, and advised by the distinguished Barcelonans Joaquín Folch y Torras conservator of the mu-

14. Bergós, *op. cit.*, p. 151.
15. Buenaventura Bassegoda, *Estatuas de Barcelona*, (Barcelona: 1903).
16. *Ilustració Catalana*, n.º 389, (November 20, 1910), published the portrait of Doménech as the «initiator» of the idea and did not mention the architect of the work.

360. The monument to Dr. Robert which stood in the Plaza de la Universidad in Barcelona from 1910 to 1940.

seums of Barcelona; Manuel Ribé, major-domo of the city government, a mayor's delegate, and Chief of Traffic Police for 25 years; and Manuel Marinel·lo, the secretary of the Society for the Attraction of Foreigners—all of whom approved the attribution of this monument to Llimona and Gaudí.[17] Cirici Pellicer makes the same attribution in his book on Modernismo.[18]

If this and the style of the monument itself—so completely out of line with Doménech's work, and so much in harmony with Gaudí's—were not enough, I consulted the sculptor Antonio Ramón González, who was once a student of Llimona and delights in recalling their conversations. I was told that his celebrated master repeatedly cited Gaudí's authorship of the architectural part of the monument which he defended against the critical opinions of some people.[19]

THE MONUMENT. The arguments adduced so far, however valuable to the case, are only of secondary importance when we consider the evidence to be found in the expressive quality of the monument itself, and its similarity to certain parts of the Casa Milá which was under construction at the same time.

It was said at the time of its inauguration that the movement of the masses in the work was intended to evoke the silhouette of the helmet of King Jaime the Conqueror and the legendary bat which we saw on the pinnacle of the Güell Palace—symbols proper to the period which do indeed fit the general form of the work. From contemporary press descriptions, and from recollections revived with photographs, we can tell that the stone came from Garraf (that stone so pleasing to Gaudí, probably from the quarry owned by his friend Güell), and that the work had not only a commemorative and decorative purpose, but that it also served as a public utility, with seven fountains which flowed from breast-like protuberances into a great decorative font where the passer-by could drink or fill water jugs, a low trough for dogs, and several stone benches where people could sit, as well as an interior room, accessible by way of a small door, where gardening tools were stored. This was just the sort of utilitarian touch with which Gaudí enjoyed humanizing his works. The monument had its greatest symbolic significance in the bust of Robert at the top, receiving counsel from a muse in the form of an extremely *modernista* feminine figure who speaks into his ear. In front, there was a group of magnificent bronze figures—among the sculptor's best—representing a harvester, the valiant poetry of Verdaguer, work shared with reading, and an enthusiastic youth raising the Catalan flag which is also in bronze and bears the four-armed cross which Gaudí often included in his works. On the back he recalls Robert's educational work as a professor with a group representing Medicine presenting a group of sick persons to the studious spirit of youth.

THE STYLE. The characteristic undulating curves of Modernismo dominate the principal lines of this work, highlighted by a play of subtle chiaroscuro effects also proper to that style. Here these are not employed with such reckless freedom as we saw in the Miralles gateway, but rather are regulated by a rhythm which runs smoothly from the rampant lateral arches to the robust marquee in front, passing through the wavy capitals of the slanted columns. Both capitals and columns show a striking resemblance to those which we will see in the Casa Milá. Apart from these purely plastic forms, we can note certain naturalistic details which are also related to Modernismo: the already mentioned breasts pouring forth water, a group of pine trees at the back of the monument recalling the then popular «Pine of the Three Branches,» and the mountainous terrain on which the forward group is situated, with provision for the growth of natural grass. All in all, the monument was an interesting example of Modernismo, emphasizing the virile and the expressionistic rather than the arbitrarily effete qualities of the style.

The monument was erected at the same time as the Batlló and Milá houses which we will study later, and tectonically it partakes of both: fine finishing like that of the Batlló house is seen in the lower part and in the smooth surfaces of the undulating capitals; in the upper part of the monument we see the sharp edges and rougher textures employed in the Casa Milá façade. In the monument the vigorous working of the three-dimensional surfaces is combined with the accentuated joints of the large ashlar masonry which emphasizes the structural reality of the work.

In addition to their interest as original and decisive forms, these structural details, which usually are not the concern of sculptors, indicate the collaboration of an architect working in perfect harmony with Llimona. Elsewhere I have written: «another characteristic of the monument was the harmony between the sculpture and the architecture, despite the fact that the sculptor and the architect did not profess the same esthetic ideas. Llimona worked within the classicistic idiom and always remained faithful to that tradition whether expressing himself softly or energetically. Gaudí, on the other hand, had much freer ideas and experimented with more daring forms—some of which he applied in this monument. In spite of this divergence, the two artists had the talent to unite their respective tendencies into a united and harmonious whole.»[20]

17. Marcel Monmarche, director, *Les Guides Blues: Volume Espagne*, (París, 1935), p. 41.

18. *El arte modernista catalán*, p. 157.

19. Statement of said professor González on February 19, 1965. See my article in *Destino*, N.º 1441, (March 20, 1965). This same authorship of the monument is recognized by the official chronicler of the city, D. Joaquín M. de Nadal. I have subsequently received a letter from González in which he says: «I am pleased to confirm what I have already told you in conversation, namely: that when I was a student of the sculptor José Llimona, from 1928 to 1934, the date of his death, I repeatedly heard him say that the architecture of the monument to Dr. Robert (for which he had done the sculptures) had been designed and executed by the architect Gaudí. I even recall that he once grew very indignant when a newspaper article appeared that attacked the architecture, saying that any critic who showed so little understanding of the work of such an eminent architect was hardly suited to the job.»

20. In the *Destino* article cited.

361. Detail of the monument to Dr. Robert in which we can appreciate Gaudí's characteristic structure as it harmonizes with Llimona's sculpture.

362. Side view of the same monument, with the four-armed cross characteristic of Gaudí at the top of the Catalan flag. The general silhouette evokes the helmet of Jaime I El Conquistador.

The monument to Dr. Robert which stood in the Plaza de la Universidad for some 30 years is not lost to Barcelona. The magnificent statues modeled by Llimona and the coarse ashlars designed by Gaudí are still preserved by the City, awaiting the day when urbanistic circumstances will allow the reconstruction of this beautiful work by two such eminent artists.

187. TWO MODEST WORKS (Figs. 363 - 366)

A STORAGE SHED (1904). Two short years after the «Torino» salon, we find Gaudí at work on another project, also overlooked by previous biographers, which is notable for the insight into his character provided by his acceptance at the height of his fame of this rather unimportant commission which, in contrast to the accentuated artistic quality of the previously mentioned job, presented no new structural or decorative problems.

In August 1904 he drew a design for a shed at 278 Calle de Nápoles for the industrial ironsmith José Badía; the latter, along with his brother Luis, did much of the admirable wrought-iron decoration in Gaudí's work. Their collaboration, which Gaudí turned into a friendship, was what motivated the great architect to take on the modest work without compensation; in spite of its simplicity, the project deserves attention as the harbinger of his personal architecture to come soon after.[21]

In this small building we see for the first time—though still designed with ruler and compass—the free forms which he was soon to trace free-hand and with greater mobility in designing the two houses that he built on the Paseo de Gracia. The outline of the shed door and window openings is not absolutely continuous, but it does approach that which he designed the following November for the remodeling of the Casa Batlló, and it looks even more like the sort of arrangement which he would adopt a year later in the Casa Milá. He also ignored the usual solutions in the 7.7-meter-long cornice, curving it up over the door to give added importance to the entrance. This undulation was then systematically employed in the two subsequent houses.

The storage shed was covered with a tiled sawtooth roof, receiving light through the vertical faces. The inclined surfaces of the roof were covered with flat tiles except in the first bay which was covered with a warped flagstone surface linking the second bay with the undulating cornice. The wall of the façade was built of ordinary rubble which he left exposed, and the openings were bordered with on-end bricks that were chamfered on the exterior corners. The window was protected by a webbed metal grate with two superimposed networks representing the four stripes of the Catalan flag; this was reinforced by two thick iron rings with crosses alluding to the cross of St. George—all projecting convexly toward the

21. Information contained in document N.º 9987 of the Archivo Administrativo Municipal, and additional data supplied by the present owner, Emilio Badía, the nephew of the builder.

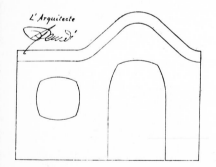

L'Arquitecte
Gaudí

363. Project for a shed for the blacksmith Badía on the Calle de Nápoles. Archivo Administrativo Municipal.

364. Old photograph of shed for the blacksmith José Badía, presently transformed.

street. The warehouse maintained its original aspect until 1957 when it was completely remodeled to its present-day condition.[22]

THE SCHOOLS OF THE SAGRADA FAMILIA. The building for these schools is a very simple work put up in 1909 to the side of the spot where he planned to erect the main façade of the church. Its provisional character led Gaudí to employ an economical procedure and to rely to the maximum on the structural properties of the humble materials used.

The walls, set on a base of rubble, were constructed of simple thin-wall tile without any exterior plastering; in order to increase the rigidity of these partitions and to resist at the same time the thrust of the inclined beams, he gave a smooth undulation, which varied according to the height, to the ground plan of the two long façades, and designed the other two with a slight outward convexity. Using such a simple procedure he was able to increase considerably the resistance of these roof-bearing elements which were not of heavy construction. The small structure is subdivided into three classrooms by means of two interior partitions. In the center, running lengthwise, is a horizontal steel I-beam which supports a system of sloping wooden beams whose ends describe an undulating line where they meet the façade which has the girder line as its median height. Since the beams are straight, it is evident that when one end goes up, the other goes down; the beams become a system of generatrices of a conoid whose directrices are the horizontal girder and one of the external undulating walls. By covering the beams with thin-shell tile masonry, a roof was obtained which had both the required drainage slopes and a certain elasticity to avoid the cracks which are usually a problem in roof terraces. It was an extremely economical structure which then cost only about 4,000 pesetas;[23] it continues in service today, after restoration that was necessary as a consequence of damage suffered in the Civil War period.

This pavilion constitutes proof of what the master always said: beauty and structural logic transcend all historic styles. It is certain that he did not propose to work in any determined style, nor did he submit to the arbitrary curves so dear to the esthetics of the time; these undulations, the result of a structural purpose, perhaps influenced by the studies which he had just carried out in the church for the Güell Colony, while not exponents of *modernista* decorativism, do fit perfectly within this style with which they coincide chronologically.

22. Information provided by Sr. Badía.
23. A fact supplied by the architect of the temple, F. de P. Quintana.

365. Schools of the Sagrada Familia, plan. From Ráfols.

366. View of htis school. Note small size, expressive forms, and modest materials.

188. THE CHURCH AT THE COLONIA GÜELL
189. THE PARK GÜELL

The master's prolific activity which we have seen up to this point was to be, in the overall picture, a sort of preparatory gestation period for the birth of the structural theory of equilibrated forms—an outstanding characteristic of Gaudi's architecture which he had intuitively foreseen from his earliest days. In this theory we have the convergence of his multiple observations of esthetic and structural details which had been building up for some time; the union was effected by his intense desire to find the perfect solution for his favorite work, the Sagrada Familia.

188. THE CHURCH AT THE COLONIA GÜELL. 1898-1916 (Figs. 83, 84, 128, 142, 153, 367 - 382)

When Gaudi received the commission for this original church from his friend Güell who wanted it to provide the finishing touch to his model industrial colony just built at Santa Coloma de Cervelló (to the south of Barcelona), he found himself confronted with a theme similar—although on a smaller scale—to that which had occupied him for years in the great temple. He therefore decided that it would be advantageous to study this smaller project carefully in every detail and use it as a sort of dress rehearsal; the results of these studies which seemed logical to him represented a new, unprecedented case in architectural history, and he was prudent enough to want to test for possible oversights as we have indicated in Part One (XVII - 69).

367. Church of the Güell colony. Idea for the whole sketched over a photograph of the funicular model inverted.

THE FUNICULAR MODEL. Given the bountiful comprehension of his client, instead of working out this project for the new church on paper as is customary, Gaudí proceeded to construct an upside-down model, made of cords and small weights with the latter representing the loads to be supported and the cords representing the arches and pillars of the new building; a dome was to occupy the greater part of the central nave, and another would cover the presbytery with two towers flanking the main portal and a small bell tower to one side. In this manner he obtained a tangible model of the structural complex proposed, with the lines of force of the principal supporting elements, vaults, and cupolas reflected in the carefully disposed hanging funicular model, its shape regulated by the anticipated loads, as represented by the little sacks of weighed gunshot suspended in their corresponding places.

The delicate exploratory work involving the adjustment of weights and the cord lengths lasted over 10 years. He was aided in his work by the architect José Canaleta, his assistant Francisco Berenguer, the Alsatian engineer Eduardo Goetz, and the official sculptor Juan Bertrán. He gave a certain solidity and body to the funicular form thus obtained by attaching tissue paper to the cords which filled in the holes to give an expression of the logically resultant volume. When good photographs of the exterior and interior were turned right-side up and the sacks blotted out by retouching, the complementary details, such as convenient openings and decoration, could be sketched in on top of the model forms.

While work was going on from 1908-1914, this model served as a guide in the same way that plans usually do in the construction process.[1] Work was suspended after only the crypt, the porch, part of the bell tower, the walls, and part of the door in the upper part had been built.

1. Bergós, *op. cit.*, p. 170, says that the model was preserved until 1916 when it started to unravel and get out of shape. The photographer A. Mas had been foresighted enough to take photographs of it before this occurred. Régulo Casas, the priest of this church—which is now a parish church—says in a pamphlet about it that the model was completely destroyed during the Civil War.

368. Funicular model for the static study of the church of the Colonia Güell, with weights and thrusts in the opposite direction to those of the executed work.

STRUCTURE. Knowing how the model was arrived at, it is easy to deduce that the supporting elements would be generally inclined, with a tendency to distribute themselves in a conical manner that would be obvious on the exterior. Due to the topography of the site (a small hill surrounded by pines) which Gaudí chose for the church, the posterior part of the crypt is backed against the earth and its exterior walls are therefore invisible. He emphasized the visible inclined supports of the front section by chamfering their edges at complex angles which merge with the vaults and the small vertical walls containing the window openings (see Fig. 376).

These angular supporting members are constructed of a combination of hard-fired blackish brick and small stones of the same color in horizontal rows, forming roughly textured triangular surfaces most of which are flat though some suggest a hyperbolic paraboloid form. The angular projections of the outside walls are concave on the interior; the spaces produced inside are utilized for such necessary church functions as confessionals and other similar things.

The vaguely parabolic form of the walls is more obvious in the entrance doors that lead to the crypt (Fig. 380) and to the upper floor where the door jambs are warped in form and carved into the stone itself. From this point on he used the hyperbolic paraboloid profusely in his studies and models—more so than in his actual work—considering it to be the geometrical form most suitable to structural needs.

In the interior of the crypt, the pillars have the slope indicated by the model, and the thickness necessitated by their corresponding loads. Those near the entrance doorway are plastered from top to bottom, others only partially, and some are of completely exposed brick in a variety of textures. In the center of the nave there are four basalt pillars, each roughly hewn from a single piece of stone with basalt bases and capitals put in place with leaded joints. These are impressive in their vigorous expressiveness, and are surmounted by a mass of exposed brick from which arches of on-edge brick spring.

369. Church of the Colonia Güell. Plan of the crypt and the entrance portico.

370. Plan of the crypt and projection of the dual system of arches which supports the ceiling. Plans by Ll. Bonet Garí.

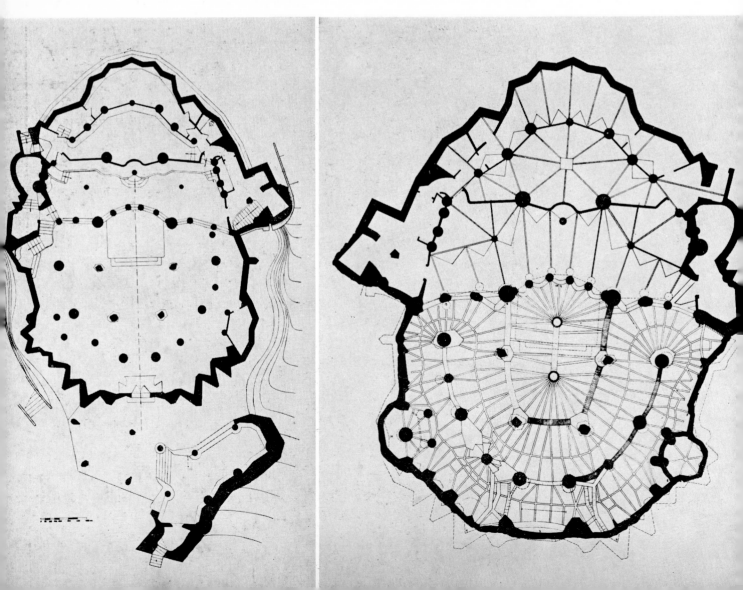

The roof of the main nave is supported by a double system of arches comparable to the common girder and beam system. From the stanchions (some branching into tree-like forms) there spring numerous robust rough brick arches of low rise—the majority curved, but some polygonal—upon which are supported an entire web of strap arches, 10 cm. thick running in various directions and very close together. By filling in the spandrels, these secondary arches line up horizontally at the same height, and on them the roof platform rests (see Fig. 374). This ceiling is not vaulted as usually claimed. Rather Gaudí used a system which recalls that employed in the second story at Bellesguard where the flat floor rested on thick partition arches.

Behind the nave and the main altar there is an elevated space for the choir which is reached by means of a passage through highly artistic slanting arches; the roof of this space is constructed of wide, slightly arched vaults on metal beams, due to the lowness of the roof at this point. Beyond the choir-loft is the sacristy which is covered by a vault which appears to be spherical and very shallow (in reality it is made up of eight cylindrical sectors connected in a cloister vault) and which is also supported on metal beams.

THE PORCH. As we have just seen in the conscientious preparatory studies for this church, Gaudí liked to subject his structural ideas to rigorous calculations and tests; once sure of the results, his active imagination would move on to variations or interpretations of what was established, in order to expand, from his experience and structural intuition, the repertoire of solutions applicable to any one case.

From what can be deduced from the photographs of the funicular model, Gaudí planned to have a porch to the crypt which would serve to support the access stairway to the upper story. This was actually carried out in reality, but many of the details were resolved differently than in the original plan, perhaps because of the terrain or as a result of experience acquired in the construction of the crypt itself. Although both crypt and porch share a similarity of texture and equilibrated forms, the latter are much more apparent, much more daring, and more agile in the porch than in the interior. We must, of course, realize that the crypt was

371. Exterior of the crypt of the Colonia Güell with an interesting variety of textures.

only to serve as the lower part of an upper structure which never got beyond the project stage, but nevertheless, the elements of the porch are a much fuller embodiment of the new structural theory.

The roof is sustained by slanting pillars. The least inclined are located in front of the door and are carved from basaltic stone like the four interior ones; from their capitals spring various arches in a palm-like manner, which connect with other pillars or end in the crypt façade. The spaces between the arches are filled with «board» vaults in hyperbolic paraboloid form; the edges of the tetrahedron which generates these surfaces are not usually visible, but rather are manifest in fragments which intersect the bearing arches with parabolic or hyperbolic forms.

This concave-convex play of forms constitutes one of the most original aspects of this work. Such convexities were not common in vaults, and Gaudí used them in order to prove the great potential of such forms, which in recent times have been used in large reinforced concrete structures. The master's predilection for this warped surface which he used so often in his models if not in his buildings has already been mentioned. In this tiny atrium we can see the embryo of the surfaces which he would employ in his later architecture.

TEXTURES AND ARTISTIC EXPRESSION. The unity of mechanical needs and structural solutions, which was the original end of the new theory, had logically to be coupled with the appropriate textures which would give the church the desired artistic expression. Here the architect hoped to express the dignity of the church concept within a naturalistic idiom which would harmonize with its rural environment. The discontinuation of the work frustrated the grandiose overall concept, and it is perhaps for this reason that the textures of the small part that was completed seem so intensely expressive, compensating in part for the missing church.

372. Sketch for the interior design of the church at the Colonia Güell, worked out on a photograph of funicular model inverted.

It is immediately apparent that the architect's idea was to leave the materials he used exposed while enriching their expressiveness with certain details of workmanship. Nevertheless, the lower parts of some walls and pillars on the interior were plastered and smoothed to protect the church visitors from unpleasant scraping against rough surfaces. The two round pillars closest to the entrance are almost completely stuccoed, with their cylindrical forms changing half-way up into prismatic ones which connect to the exposed bricks at the top. The passage from the cylinder to the prism is effected through smooth cut-away curves which give the upper part of the columns a somewhat lesser volume.

The interior is dominated by the natural brick textures of the walls, pillars, and arches. In some pillars, both on the interior and in the porch, he used semicircular bricks especially made to order. These semicircles are arranged in undulating rows of either single or double thickness which are offset to give beautiful chiaroscuro effects (Fig. 379). He also used these rounded bricks in horizontally advancing rows to form arch springers. The railing of the stairway that leads to the sacristy is of common voussoir-laid brick, and it originates in a spiral curve which synthesizes sober materials and elegant form (Fig. 373).

373. Access stairway to the back part of the crypt with interesting examples of unadorned brick textures.

374. Top of the columns and springing of the arches that support the flat-tile ceiling of the crypt at the Colonia Güell.

The most outstanding tectonic note of the interior is provided by the four central columns of roughly hewn basalt which are imposing in their strength and expression; their bases and capitals are roughly modeled in a similar fashion.

The texture of the exterior surfaces reveals a great concern with obtaining determined artistic effects from rustic materials of obvious coarseness. He employs clinker brick in horizontal bands with preference in the structurally active elements, and black rocks to achieve intentionally irregular and projecting surfaces in structurally neutral places.

These forms and texture do not imitate nature, as someone has said, but rather are conceived to harmonize with it, which is something quite different. The most expressive decorative elements are the rounded or quadrangular window openings with blunt vertices, protected on the outside from rain by novel angular brick flashings covered in part with glass mosaics. These windows are glazed (the present polychromy is not that which was placed there by Gaudí [2]), and they are protected by tenuous metallic screens fashioned from discarded needles taken from the colony's textile machines combined in the triangular pattern which generates hexagons seen in other of the master's works. At the extremities and vertices of these dihedral flashings there are small polychrome mosaic tablets with religious symbols.

In the porch we see a résumé of the already mentioned textures, with the additional feature of several extremely inclined brick pillars twisting in a helix form, and other pillars covered with tiny stone mosaics in a manner similar to that which we have seen on some parts of the Bellesguard exterior. The most far-reaching innovation in this portico is the one already mentioned of the hyperbolic paraboloid «board» vaults made up of triangular pieces, some of incrusted white tile, and some of darker tones which compose crosses. The brick arches, through corbelling in the springers and voussoir masonry at the center, generally follow equilibrated forms of rectangular cross section, but are decorated with small superimposed paraboloids with no structural or geometric relation to the arches except that of lending greater mobility and increased harmony in relation to the vaults. Perhaps they were also intended as an example of how easily these newly invented warped surfaces could be applied as a decorative element in construction.

189.   THE PARK GÜELL. 1900-1914 (Figs. 62, 85, 96 - 98, 121, 137, 144, 145, 150, 151, 156,
       165, 383 - 432)

While he was building the small church for his friend Güell, the latter also asked him to work out an urbanization of his Montaña Pelada property. We have seen that in his work at

2. The stained glass windows by Gaudí were destroyed in the Civil War.

375. Pillar, exterior walls, and windows with a variety of textures and grilles in hexagonal rhythm.

the Colonia Güell, Gaudí had just developed a new architectural concept, overflowing with possibilities; although there he was able to apply it in only a limited manner because of the nature of the building and its dimensions, here he had the opportunity for ample development of its potential, given the variety of materials at his disposal and the extensive area which he had to work with (over 37 acres).

The great diversity of elements which went into this park make it one of his most complete works; it is a synthesis of architecture, sculpture, polychromy, nature, space, and light, which here come together in a single artistic vision. The architect presents us with a sampling of the multiple possibilities of his new theory—possibilities which he was anxious to put into practice once he had tested them in the crypt which we have just seen. He not only had at his disposal a varied topography which served as a motif in itself for decorative solutions, but

376. Partial view of the walls and vaults of the portico with different textures and polychrome decoration of glass fragments and ceramic mosaic. Especially interesting is the motif above the doorway.

377. Interior view of the crypt of the church with the robust basalt pillars and the dual system of arches that sustains the flat-tile ceiling.

378, 379. Exterior and interior views of the portico of the Colonia Güell with its structural inclined pillars and decorative textures.

380. Another view of the same portico with a pillar that is unusually slanted.

381, 382. Small light-openings and various textural shades on the exterior walls of the crypt.

also he was able to take advantage of the quarries on the property for construction materials, and of the magnificent panorama over the city and the sea which he captured as a background for his work, thus extending it beyond its natural boundaries.

The peaceful site and the beauties contained therein are more to be enjoyed as a whole than to be analyzed and broken down under various headings; nevertheless, the nature of the present study imposes such a division, and we will therefore briefly examine here the principal elements of the park other than those we have already considered in the chapter on urbanism in Part Two (XXX - 137).

STRUCTURE AND TEXTURES. We have seen in Part One (XIX - 77) that once work was begun on this park in 1900, it went rapidly, and probably got ahead of the presentation of plans and other bureaucratic steps in the municipal offices, for the definitive layout was not officially approved until January 30, 1906.[3] As could be expected of the master, the park structure was perfect; in this case within a framework of maximum economy. This qualification should be kept in mind when we look at certain details which might indicate that Gaudí used materials and processes which were not in keeping with the growing interest awakened by his work, and that he rejected a guarantee of perenniality in the interest of saving money. We know that this aspect worried him, and I have spoken of it elsewhere.[4] Economic considerations led him to use laminated iron bands in some of the small guard rails and as a skeletal armature for some of the elements such as the backs of some stone seats; he also used appliqués of low quality artificial stone, and mosaic tile revetments in vulnerable places. These few elements, after more than half a century of resisting the elements and man's abuse, have required maintenance; this has been taken care of by the city ever since it acquired the park in 1922.

Some of the conservation work carried out by the city has made it possible to study the structural procedures which Gaudí used, e.g., the floor of the grand plaza in the section corresponding to the Doric colonnade which has no slope for drainage. Instead, drainage is accomplished by absorption into the ground itself which is set on a series of «board» vaults in the form of spherical skull-caps; in the pendentives of these shallow vaults are the drains which pass through the pierced centers of the columns below. These drains were filled with a large, rocky gravel in the bottom and smaller stones on the surface to filter the water from the ground formed of tamped earth. The columnar drains connect with a network of underground pipes which lead to a 1,200 cubic meter subterranean deposit located in front of the Doric porch.

Another of the elements whose structure has been revealed in this manner is the parabolic spire with a cross on top which is part of the caretaker's pavilion: it is hollow and constructed of a first interior layer of brick four centimeters thick, a layer of concrete reinforced with 10 mm. thick rods, three layers of tile, and an exterior appliqué of cement molded with the relief of the helixes which finally were incrusted with blue and white ceramic mosaic.[5]

The entire park was built according to ingenious and original methods, not only structurally, but also mathematically: the calculation was based on the criterion of least resistance in all pillars and retaining walls, as we will see more clearly in our examination of the different parts.

The general construction is of undisguised rubble taken from quarries on the same mountain set up where excavation work was necessary in order to lay out the roadways. With this ochrish-white stone he obtained a marvelous variety of textures ranging from the smoothly faced rubble of the walls, through the daring, almost violent projections which give character to some of the pillars and vaults, to the rustic ashlared surfaces and helicoidally striated columns which expand in diameter as they become part of the vault. Staying within the limits of the rough stone material it would be possible to catalog an extensive repertory of textures—some mixed with cement and used to face brick forms or metallic armatures—all used to give a different sort of expression.[6]

In the Doric colonnade, he used a system of facing which appears to be a gray colored artificial stone over three thicknesses of tile with the cylindrical lower part of each column being encased in white ceramic tile mosaic; the vaults are decorated with extremely interesting polychrome plaques which we will discuss later.

The revetments of tile mosaic are without a doubt one of the textures which lends most to the spectacular character of the work; this is due chiefly to the bold and varied polychrome patterns which we will be able to observe in examining the individual parts of the park.

ENCLOSING WALL, BUILDINGS, AND STAIRWAY. The park is surrounded by a wall which contains seven gates, two of which are always closed.[7] The most interesting part, artistically, is that which runs along the Calle de Olot where the park has its main entrance. In this section of the wall, Gaudí ingeniously employed artistic effects in satisfying the need to make the wall impregnable. The lower half of the wall is built of common rubble, and from that point up the surface leaves off being vertical and is carried on in corbelled bands of great rusticity which support the stepped double curvature of the upper coping-flashing. The cop-

3. Archivo Administrativo del Ayuntamiento, document 2100 of the Comisión de Fomento. In the same archive there is evidence that on September 7, 1905, a complaint was filed against the work of Sr. Trías for building without a permit, which had only been requested on the second of that month. On October 4, the case was passed on to the chief architect of Urbanization and Construction, who found favorably for the defendent on April 23, 1908.

4. Martinell, *Conversaciones con Gaudí...*, p. 22.

5. Information provided by Luis Montero, chief conservations of the Park.

6. Speaking of the columns, the architect Salvador Sellés, in the article cited in Note 8, Chapter XXX, says «many of them are hollow.» Buenaventura Bassegoda y Amigó who also visited the work during construction mentions «hollow pillars and *tabicada* vaults, both elements covered with coarse rocks held together with cement.» *(Diario de Barcelona*, January 14, 1903). At present, the procedure used in construction of some of the vaults and columns can be seen, and the rubble does not reveal a solid structure, as we will see in porticos A and D. It would be interesting to take borings that would show the composition of this mixed construction which is invisible today and can only be deduced from observation and the mentioned eye-witness accounts. This system recalls the stone facings seen at Bellesguard which, as we have said (XLV - 181), did not correspond to Gaudí's customary structural honesty.

7. Some of the descriptive details in this text are taken from Eladio Guzmán's «Hojas del Parque Güell,» published in *Ayer y Hoy*, the bulletin of the school located in the Park where Sr. Guzmán was a teacher (Nos. 25-32, from November, 1960, to June, 1961).

383. Park Güell. View of the main stairway showing the great harmony between architecture, polychromy, and vegetation.

384. Spherical vaults that support the great plaza and serve as drains for it.

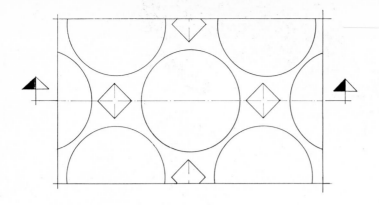

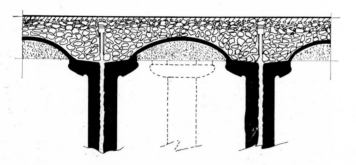

385, 386. Supporting and drainage structure of the great plaza, above the hypostyle hall. Plan and section of the columns. Drawing by Luis Montero.

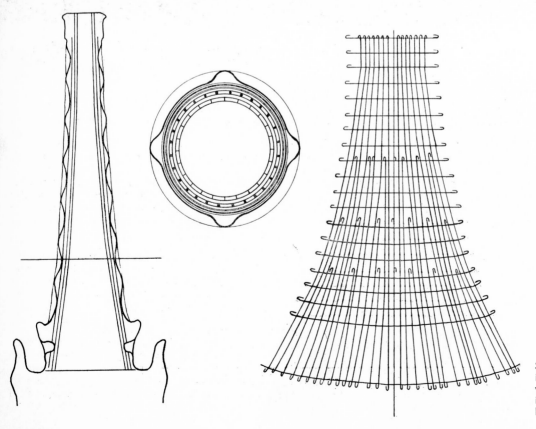

387. Spire of the entrance, pavilion. Vertical section, plan, and development of the interior reinforcing framework. Drawings by Luis Montero.

388. Güell Park. Entrance pavilion used for general services for the projected colony, seen from inside the park with former wooden gates.

389. The same pavilion showing the roof and spire faced with polychrome mosaic.

ing is faced with ceramic mosaic which is slippery, therefore making it impossible to get a good hold on it; this along with the upper distribution of the wall itself makes the wall impossible to scale.

The mosaic which covers the coping is patterned in alternating red and white rectangular sections, embellished every eight meters by discs that are two meters in diameter. These discs—14 in all—are also covered with mosaic decoration with the inscriptions *Park* and *Güell* alternating on every other one.

This wall is interrupted at the main entrance gate where it runs into the two pavilions on either side of the gateway—one a gatehouse for the caretaker, and the other a service pavilion for the use of those who were to live in the small community: a waiting room, a receiving window, sanitary facilities, and other similar things. Both pavilions have oval ground plans with continuous perimeter walls unlike anything seen in his previous work. The rubble walls are in ochre tones and contain rounded openings, some banded in blue and white mosaics which effectively contrast with the rest of the surface.

Most notable in these pavilions are the domed roofs, each terminating in a ventilating cupola surrounded by a circular lookout passage with a merloned railing which recalls the somewhat more rigid one on the roof at Bellesguard. The cupolas are joined to the façades by means of large trilobate gables of *modernista* influence; the whole roofing complex is covered with mosaic in chromatically delicate and forcefully imaginative tones.

In the composition of the roofs of these buildings, Gaudí intentionally sought to accentuate the impression of unity which is further emphasized in one of them by the spire which upholds a cross at its summit. This 10-meter-high spire—whose geometric characteristics we have examined in our discussion of the master's rhythms (XXIX - 131)—is a masterpiece of graceful form and structural equilibrium, both highlighted by the blue and white coloring which so marvelously combines with the blue background of the sky frequently streaked by white clouds.

Another notable aspect of the spire is its terminal cross which rests on an open ironwork frame of helicoidally twisted iron which displays the mechanical influence of gravity on the elegance of a supporting element; perhaps, too, we have the symbolic representation of gravity conquered by the cross in the ascending rhythm of the spire's double helix which branches into smaller helixes formed of laminated iron bands.

The main entranceway opens between the two pavilions with iron gratings and entrance gates taken from the garden of the Casa Vicens, works which were not used when the garden was sold and redesigned. There are similar plans to transfer the portal from the Finca Miralles, which has been threatened by urban expansion, to the second most important entrance to the park (that on the east side) and to reproduce its original marquee.[8]

Inside the park, the old family residence of the Güells still exists—an adaptation of the already existing Muntané house which today has been converted into a school. The building itself is rather common, but the door of the oratory, strongly stamped with Gaudí's personal style, and the area which precedes it, including a parabolic brick arch of regular dimensions, warrant special attention (Fig. 398).

Beyond the two pavilions as one enters the park there unfolds a sumptuous and colorful stairway, to the right of which is a small structure planned to shelter two or three horse-drawn carriages. This structure is covered by an ingenious subterranean ring vault with a parabolic profile, supported on a single mushroom-capital pillar of rubble. A central door, some three meters wide, is separated from two narrower lateral ones by means of columns, and all three are covered by arches (Fig. 399). In general the tiny area is remarkable for its spacious effect, and for the structural solutions arrived at without stylistic prejudice.

The stairway consists of two freely developed symmetrical sections interrupted by landings and separated by a waterfall and rough zoomorphic sculptures covered with mosaic—the most outstanding being an especially expressive dragon. The lateral retaining walls to either side of the stairs have a special ceramic facing which is unique in Gaudí's work for its pattern, texture, and color.

The pattern is composed of a combination of rectangles and squares which are harmoniously arranged. The texture is provided by an alternation of concave and convex surfaces (the convex corresponding to the rectangles, the concave to the squares) with the former being covered with mosaic tile and the latter with larger ceramic tiles which have been shattered without losing their original design. The rectangles are always white, with reds and yellows dominant in the square pieces though blue is also frequent. The upper edge of these retaining walls is bordered by an openwork railing of rubble which is surmounted by a series of boldly polychromed tiled merlons.

THE GREEK THEATER. In a concavity of the terrain, above and behind the main entrance, Gaudí designed a huge plaza which was destined to serve as a recreational area for the colony. He called it the «Greek Theater» because of its similarity to those ancient open-air natural amphitheaters built in the mountainside, sometimes—as here—with a magnificent

8. Information provided by the Building Conservation Service of the city.

390. Variety of rough stone textures along roadway C.

391. Textures of compressed rubble and rough ashlar masonry.

392. Textures in ordinary rubble masonry and mosaics in the surrounding wall.

393. Textures of rusticated ashlar masonry in the buttresses, ordinary rubble on top of rock carved *in situ*, and small stone revetment on reinforced masonry framework at the back of the grand plaza.

394. Upper part of the roof and the chimney of the caretaker's pavilion with a horizontal section through the merlons. Drawings by Luis Montero.

395. Central decorative element of the stairway.

396. The caretaker's pavilion.

397. Double entrance stairway of the Güell Park with its rich forms and abundant natural and applied polychromy.

398. Chapel door from the old Güell residence that was located in the park. The monogram of Jesus in wrought iron is placed in the upper part of the arch.

399. Coach shelter.

400. Surrounding wall adjoining the main entrance.

view beyond. Half of this plaza, which measures some 86 meters long by 40 meters
ts on solid ground; the other half is supported by a colonnade in which Gaudí
his own personal interpretation of the Doric order, in harmony with the name of the
in homage to classicism, as well as by way of contrast to the extremely free solu-
ch he was to employ in the rest of the park.

ed to use the covered space of the colonnade as a bazaar or market place. The noble
ppearance is enhanced by the proportions of the six-meter-high, 1.30-meter-in-diam-
umns in relation to the two-meter-wide entablature [9] which runs along the exterior
apitals in a stepped arrangement. Between the columns, reinforced concrete lintels
e ceiling into a quadrangular network with inscribed spherical helmets which vault
d spaces with smooth surfaces and which are covered with white ceramic tile mosaic.

9. Dimensions taken by Bergós, *op. cit.*, p. 105.

401. Robust and elegant forms of the Doric colonnade which supports the grand plaza.

At each vertex of the network there is a column, except that, in order to leave more free space, Gaudí left out two consecutive columns in one place and one in two other places, to leave six open squares in the first case and four in the other two. Where the four columns are missing, he decorated the spaces which would have been occupied by their capitals and the centers of the nearby vaults with mosaic plaques in bold colors designed by the architect Jujol to fit Gaudí's specifications; a collage process is used to combine the rich polychrome of the Venetian glass with different tonalities of mat and shining white—predicting to some extent artistic trends which were still to come.

All of the interior columns are vertical, with the same diameter at the top as at the bottom. Those on the outside are slightly tapered and slant inward, exaggerating the practice of the ancient Greeks. Above, the archaistic Doric pediment is adapted to the octagonal semi-

402. Inclined Doric columns at the perimeter of the colonnade with octagonal abaci and en-ressaut entablature.

polygon of the exterior side of the capital giving a certain modernity to the Hellenic forms, and serving as a base for the magnificent undulating bench of the upper plaza. On the back wall of the market area, next to the mountain, there is a tiny spring which we have mentioned elsewhere (XXX - 137).

A MARVELOUS BENCH. The large upper plaza—the so-called Greek Theater—has been left completely bare except on the periphery: in the mountain side it is bordered by a semicircular walk elevated to serve as a *mirador,* and on the other sides is bounded by the continuous and original undulating bench whose secondary elements and the desire on the part of some to see it as an *objet d'art* can not cover up the unavoidable and essential *truth* which we have discussed elsewhere (XXVII - 119). For Gaudí, the *truth* of this artistic work was the *bench* itself, and the secondary considerations were all subordinate to the primary truth: first, the form which was chosen for its utility; second, the facing, for comfort and for conservation; third, the colors, for attractiveness.

The sinuous form of the bench was determined by the distribution of the columns below, and at the same time responded to his preference for the sensation of *life* implied in the curved line and necessary to the work of art. In designing the seat and back he worked out and carefully applied the profiles best suited to comfort and the drainage of rain water. Another advantage of the wavy outline is that it creates small semiprivate hemicycles along its path which encourage small groups of visitors to chat together. Once the primary substance of the bench—the *truth*—was obtained, he provided for its conservation with a ceramic facing which was both waterproof and hygienic and at the same time extremely beautiful because of its striking color. In the interests of economy, he acquired tile, factory remnants and unusable tag ends that were either whole or broken; he asked for and accepted any glazed piece that they could give him, and he then arranged them as he saw fit, selecting certain

403. Mosaic decorative motifs in the ceiling of the hypostyle hall.

workmen to act as his collaborators in the vast project for protecting and decorating the work. As time went on, the workers learned to share Gaudí's insight and sensitivity and were able to draw nearer and nearer to the perfection which he sought in undertaking the mammoth task.

In his previous works for the same patron, (in the roof terrace of the Palacio Güell and in Les Corts) Gaudí had done something similar, but on a smaller scale where he was perhaps able to intervene in a more intimately personal manner, whereas here he was forced to work through supervised workmen who grew more sophisticated as they worked. Cirici Pellicer, who has studied this decoration quite carefully, believes that work must have progressed from right to left because of a growing perfection in that direction as far as distribution on symmetrical axes, contrasts in coloration, the use of black as a color (something not allowed by the neo-classicists), relief textures, and what seem to be «liturgical signs» on the backs of the benches comparable to those in the paintings of Miró, but «before Miró.» [10]

Recently these nearly invisible and incoherent inscriptions on ceramic pieces of unknown origin have been seen as a sort of ideological abstraction, without the incentive of coloration. This seems to be an obsessive belaboring of the importance of the marks. We must remember that Gaudí was an artist who was fond of light and clarity, and thus incapable of obscuring his work with occult codes of Celtic origin as one author would have us believe.

There has been a great deal written about these polychrome patterns. Every critic seems able to appreciate them according to his own particular point of view, which bears remarkable witness to the breadth of the master's work. Nevertheless, guided by his own statements, I feel that we must classify these mosaics as pure and simple decoration. Gaudí's purpose here was to *decorate* a bench in an economical and permanent manner, using colors that

10. In a visit to the park on May 2, 1958, organized by the Centro de Estudios Gaudinistas and led by Cirici, he made many interesting observations regarding this polychrome decoration, classifying it among the best of abstract painting.

404. Three-dimensional decorative motif in the same ceiling.

405. Decorative insert in the ceiling of the hypostyle hall.

406, 407, 410. Decorative details of the winding bench made of fragments of polychrome tile, usually appreciated as examples of abstract painting.

408. Partial view of the sinuous bench which borders the grand plaza.

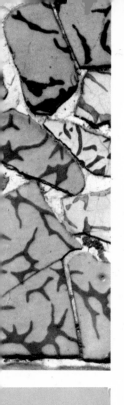

409. Partial view of the grand plaza.

would animate the conversation or the mid-morning snacks of those good Barcelonans who sought diversion there; his purpose was not to *paint* paintings, nor to expound the hieroglyphics of abstract themes—something which Gaudí, the lover of things concrete, always decried, and something which the frequenters of the park would not have understood. It is reasonable to suppose that, just as he planned to use the color of the surrounding vegetation to his artistic advantage, he also saw the variegated movement of the many visitors as an effective complement to its beauty; the public would complete the decorative program with the excitement of real life and at the same time serve as admirers for the famous bench.

As I have already stated earlier in this book, in such cases regarding semantic subtleties I am more inclined to look at the facts involved than the labels. I have gone rather deeply into the analysis of this marvelous bench in order to show how Gaudí achieved originality in a very simple way: by going back to the beginning, using workmen whose good taste he trained and supervised without taking into account artistic trends or hidden meanings. Again we have proof of the extraordinary genius of this man who with such simple and elementary means was able to create what is possibly the most beautiful and original bench in the world.

Except for its earliest years, the so-called Greek Theater has been used more for popular festivals and folkloric exhibitions than for legitimate theatrical performances.

PORTICOS AND ROADWAYS. The same creative genius which we have just observed can be seen in the rustic porticos which are another enchanting aspect of the park. We have seen that the irregular terrain of the property necessitated considerable excavation and leveling of the roadbeds, and that part of the problem was resolved by a series of porticos constructed in the coarse stone extracted from the excavations themselves. The practical purpose of these porticos was to provide shelter from the sun or rain while appreciably increasing the beauty of the gardens, but they also introduced a new sort of architecture in which the rusticity of the natural stone employed (direct from the quarry with very little finishing) is combined with highly refined forms determined by precise static calculations.

Calculation (which was absent in the design of the bench) plays an important part in the porticos, yet Gaudí employed its fruits with such perfection and naturalness that it passes com-

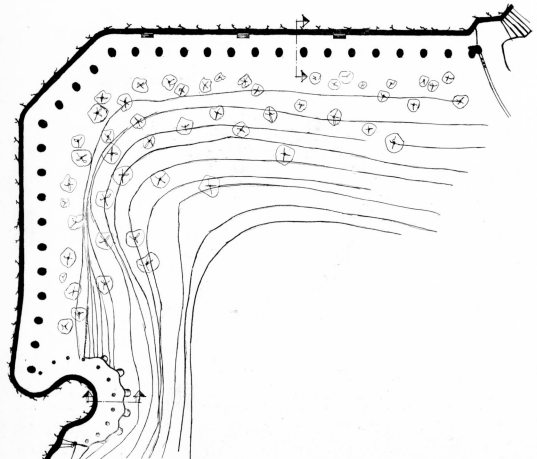

411. Plan of Portico A, at the extreme west of the old Güell residence. Plan and sections in collaboration with Professor Ruiz Vallés of the School of Architecture, and the students Batlle, Canosa, Carretero, Erice, Garreta, Masuet, and Santamaría.

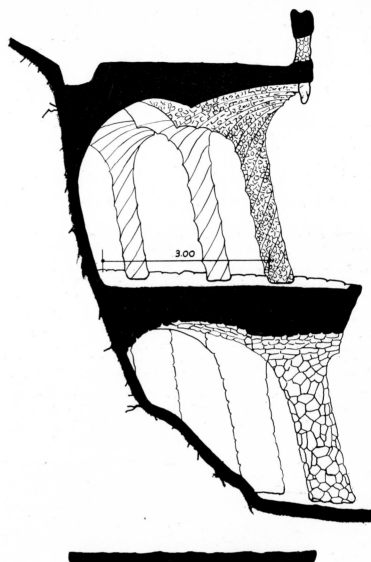

412. Section of the circular ramp of Portico A. The upper columns are spirally striated and prolonged to the mushroom-like upper parts.

413. Section of the long galleries of Portico A. The inclined columns and the vertical stone colonnettes are capped by mushroom capitals which join with the continuous barrel vault.

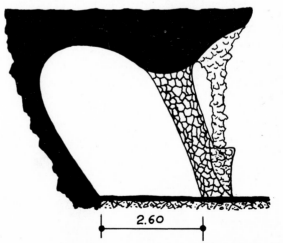

pletely unnoticed by the average visitor, and even by the expert eye until attention is deliberately called to it. The architect built four porticos altogether which are closely tied in to the walkways of the park, and he amused himself by devising a variety of equilibrated solutions within the same overall appearance of structural rusticity so characteristic of the park.

Before we begin our study of these interesting porticos, we should notice the walkway that forms a hemicycle in the upper part of the Greek Theater and is backed by a retaining wall formed of vertical vaults of ordinary rubble which rest on buttresses of carefully arranged rubblework which approaches ashlar masonry (Fig. 393). These vaults are partly supported by the cliff which has the same concave curve configuration. Capping everything is a series of jardinieres which grow out of the buttresses and give a festooned look to the wall. The variety of textures in this wall is magnificient, ranging from the cliff itself to the graved revetment covering the reinforced frame structure of the jardinieres, with numerous grades of rubble in between. At its east end, this hemicycle opens onto a wide walk that is decorated on either side with stone balls of varying size which, besides lending an original motif to the park, reflect the playful spontaneity and flexibility which prevail throughout.

Let us look first at the portico which we have designated with the letter A on the general plan (Fig. 165); this was located next to the former Güell residence, in a part of the park reserved for their own private use. The plan follows two perpendicular lines which meet at a chamfered corner, and the portico is braced against a higher cliff that is retained by a steeply sloping wall and by thirty inclined columns which mushroom out at the top and are joined to the wall on the inside by means of interior vaulting. The structure is completely determined by calculations of the earth loads that the portico is designed to support. At the exterior bases of the columns there are grafted stone pedestals from which there rise climbing vines

414. Exterior view of the two levels of the circular ramp of Portico A, showing the diversity of stone textures in the facings.

in stone and other capricious forms which help to support a widened upper roadway. At one end, next to the Greek Theater, there is a door of laminated iron which was designed by Gaudí's assistant Berenguer,[11] and can be closed to bar entrance to this private, pine-shaded area; on the other end, following a rocky projection of the cliff, the portico becomes a descending spiral passageway and the slanted columns—here smaller in diameter—outline a conical form which widens out in the bottom passage composed of bigger columns. The upper columns are coated with tiny stones and their trunks are striated in a helix form which expands in the inclined fungiform capitals to receive the rubble vault. The columns of this portico are among those which are supposed to be hollow.

Portico B is partially straight and partially curved, with 15 round interior columns and 15 external ones on the uphill, concave side and 17 on the convex, downhill side. The exterior pillars are rounded on the inside and trapezoidal on the outside; the stone junctures are for the most part carefully arranged in rectangular patterns, the slant of the exterior pillars being achieved by advancing the horizontally placed stones toward the interior. When this portico was built, a massive carob tree which stood in its path was spared, and for years it extended its branches outward; now only the trunk remains.[12] The roof of this gallery is based

11. This was told me by Juan Matamala.

12. The respect for existing trees in the layout of the gardens was later developed in an even more rigid and systematic manner by the landscape architect Forestier.

415. Straight galleries of Portico A with their mushroom-like columns and capitals of rubble which appears more superimposed than structural.

on an iron framework of double segmented arches which unite each pillar to the next, and divide the ceiling into rectangular bays in the straight section, and into trapezoids in the curve. Each double arch has an infilling which assists in the action of the arch, and the other rectangular and trapezoidal spaces were resolved in a similar manner to form vaults with sharply projecting stones hanging in the manner of stalactites.

The portico marked with the letter C develops along a curve, is open on both sides, and is supported by three rows of columns that are distributed triangularly and are united at the top by ribs which form polygonal arches while outlining triangular spaces. These spaces are filled by the rustic stone webbing which makes up the vaults, the ribs being made of steel that has been coated with tiny stones. The columns of the central row are vertical with stones in rectangular bond similar to ashlar masonry but with a very coarse finish which gives the look of rubble and which is accentuated by rough, projecting ashlars which lend still another texture. The exterior columns are inclined toward the center, responding to the thrust of the vaults; their bond is similar but more emphatic and lies in rows normal to the perpendicular. On the inside of five of these columns there are seats in the form of easy chairs with backs and arms, and on the exterior there is a *mirador*.

Above this portico is a road which is decorated with menhirs of natural stone topped with flower pots that are also of stone and are extremely ornamental in a forceful naturalistic way.

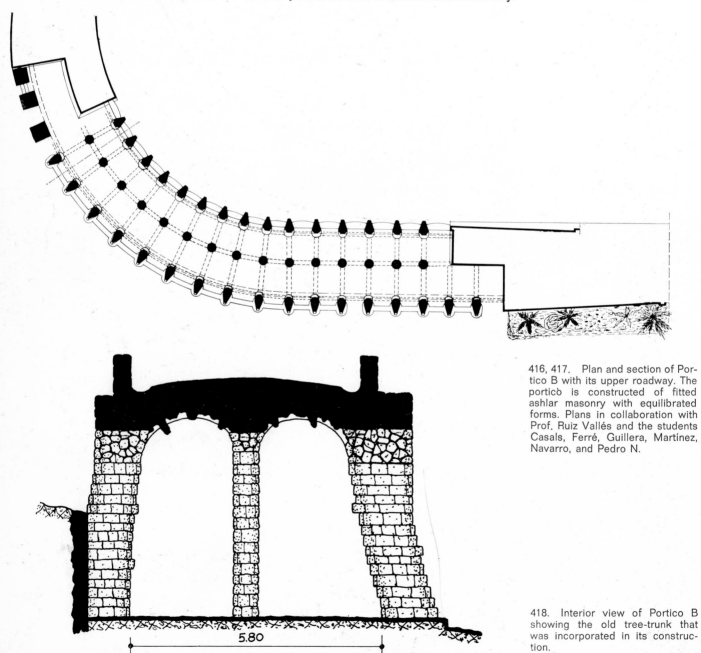

416, 417. Plan and section of Portico B with its upper roadway. The portico is constructed of fitted ashlar masonry with equilibrated forms. Plans in collaboration with Prof. Ruiz Vallés and the students Casals, Ferré, Guillera, Martínez, Navarro, and Pedro N.

5.80

418. Interior view of Portico B showing the old tree-trunk that was incorporated in its construction.

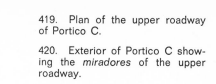

419. Plan of the upper roadway of Portico C.

420. Exterior of Portico C showing the *miradores* of the upper roadway.

421. Interior of Portico C showing seats at the foot of the columns.

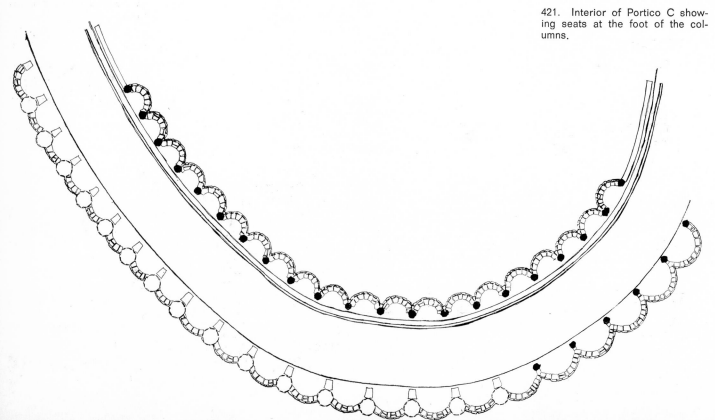

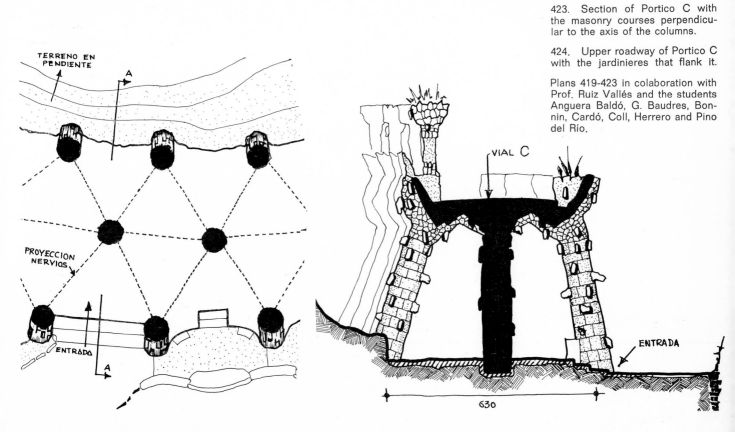

TERRENO EN PENDIENTE

A

PROYECCION NERVIOS

ENTRADA

A

VIAL C

ENTRADA

630

422. Detail of the plan of Portico C with the projection of the triangular vaults.

423. Section of Portico C with the masonry courses perpendicular to the axis of the columns.

424. Upper roadway of Portico C with the jardinieres that flank it.

Plans 419-423 in colaboration with Prof. Ruiz Vallés and the students Anguera Baldó, G. Baudres, Bonnin, Cardó, Coll, Herrero and Pino del Río.

425. Rustic seat in Portico C.

426. Inclined columns, *miradores*, and upper-level jardinieres of Portico C.

At intervals on the mountain side there are built-in stone benches, somewhat back from the roadway, with flat slabs from the quarry serving as seats and backs, the latter braced from behind by iron rods covered with cement and tiny rocks. On the other side—that which faces the sea—there is a series of subtly placed openwork rubble *miradores* which, from the outside, look like woven straw flower baskets.

Portico or gallery D slopes downhill and supports a walkway with jardinieres on the side that faces the main entrance of the park; below, it is made up of a single nave with two rows of alternating columns which occupy the vertices of a series of juxtaposed triangles arranged along the curve of the viaduct (Figs. 427, 429). These columns are inclined and terminate in a mushroom fashion, widening to vault the interior in conjuction with the others and forming a semihexagonal pattern that is almost invisible, the only break being that indicated by the extremely free textural differences. A little more than halfway up, the columns divide, with a small vertical exterior branch serving to maintain the width of the upper roadway. This portico, with its triangular distribution, recalls the structure of the projected bridge which was never built over the Pomaret river-bed.

The present state of the porticos makes it difficult to detect evidence of the structural system noted by Sellés and Bassegoda [13] where hollow pillars of terra-cotta tile are covered with rustic stone. From observing the appearance of the appliqués, however, it seems possible that

13. Monograph and article cited.

427. Plan of Portico D showing the triangular distribution of the columns and a projection of the semihexagonal intersections of the vaults.

428. Section and elevation of Portico D with inclined columns with mushroom-like capitals which become vaults and vertical stalks which extend the width of the upper roadway.

Plans 427, 428 in collaboration with Prof. Ruiz and the students Movilla, Pellicer, Recasens, Sarabia, and Villanueva.

2.50

1.75

429. View of Portico D with its expressive stone revetment.

430. Exterior view of the same portico.

such a method was used in porticos A and D, but not in B and C where the pillar masonry gives an indication of solidity. In other parts of the park the same appliqué structure can be observed, indicating a diversity of procedures which may have been employed in those sections that are now invisible, and which might even be used to establish the relative chronology of construction.

The imaginative solutions adopted by Gaudí in these four porticos—employing the simplest of means to obtain forcefully expressive results—are clear evidence of the master's creative power and structural ingenuity.

THE UNREALIZED ORATORY. The master must have been pleased at having been able to create so much beauty, but most probably he experienced nostalgic feelings about the small chapel which he could never build because the garden suburb was frustrated at the project stage. We know from his young friend at the time, Dr. Alfonso Trías, that he planned to make the church look like a rose. We do not know how he planned to achieve this resemblance, but after the wealth of technical solutions and the display of imagination that we have just seen, we have no doubts that he would have admirably succeeded in his goal.

As hope for the proposed colony faded, the oratorio became a Calvary, perhaps as a symbol of this painful episode. On the hillock to the west of the park, which the chapel would have occupied, are erected three prismatic and sober crosses; the center one is larger and its silhouette stands out against the sky—an emblem of sacrifice and redemption.

THE SIGNIFICANCE OF THIS WORK. Apart from its originality and its valuable beauty, the park which we have briefly described has a special significance within the master's work, being a sort of showroom for what could be accomplished with his new theory that was first put into practice in the Güell Colony church. In the park, the new theory presents itself to us in a rural setting, but it is not without a certain nobility—a nobility which remained constant in spite of the humble materials employed and the wide range of the life-giving solutions.

We will next see how the new theory was applied to an urban environment, where the techniques were more refined, but the demanding obstacles were greater. After that we will see how he introduced it into the grandiose, slowly growing Temple of the Sagrada Familia where the visionary architect purified and perfected all of the teachings of his later life. Few of his marvelous experiments were actually carried into the Temple, but realizing that he would not have time to translate his ideas into stone, he built a number of intelligent and carefully executed scale models. The rustic nobility of the modest materials in Güell Park served to demonstrate facets of the theory which its creator did not have a chance to carry over into his urban and religious work. The park—aside from its tangible reality—is a promise of possibility, an extensive repertory of ideas capable of giving life to vast monumental conceptions and even cities.

431. Calvary placed on the small hill where Gaudí hoped to erect a chapel.

432. Study for the cross which was to have occupied the chapel site.

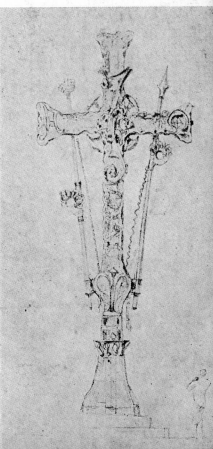

190. THE CASA BATLLÓ. 1904-1906 (Figs. 57, 82, 433 - 449)

We have already seen some of the administrative problems relating to this work and to the Casa Milá, which arose because of the architect's independent behavior (XVIII - 70). Here we will examine the architectural aspects of this building in the midst of the Paseo de Gracia (then the most distinguished street in all of Barcelona). Although it was only a remodeling, this house quickly drew attention to itself—much more so than the Casa Calvet which was his previous building within the city proper and which had been honored with the City prize (XLV - 180).

IMPRECISE PLANS. Between the Casa Calvet and the Casa Batlló, a transcendental change had come over the master's work. We have seen evidence of it in his work at the Colonia Güell and Güell Park which go far beyond his previous personalisms and cement the principles of a whole new architectural theory. We can see it, too, in his manner of drawing up the plans for his projects which were required by the municipal authorities. Those for the Casa Calvet were plans delineated with care and easily understandable to any other professional architect, but those for the Casa Batlló (and even more emphatically in those of the Casa Milá) give only an idea, almost freehand, of what he planned to do, and lend themselves to a diversity of possible interpretations, especially concerning the details. In these projects—which can be studied in the Municipal Administrative Archives [1]—we get the feeling of premeditated vagueness, as if he didn't want to be limited to predetermined solutions in working out the three-dimensional free forms that he was pursuing in the façades; in the floor plans he is more precise.

COMPOSITIONAL UNITY IN THE FAÇADES. The project involved the remodeling of a normal and uninteresting house, and the idea was to give it an attractive façade within the taste of the times; he was also to equip the main floor to serve as a residence for the owner's family, and to modernize the rest which would be used as rented apartments with a business office located on the ground floor.

The original façade was of a common four-story type with four rectangular balconies per floor. In order to take away the monotony and to enhance the overall unity, he erected five stone arches on the ground floor, and gave the second a continuous tribune which continued upward at either end to the fourth floor (like the tribune of the Palacio Güell) where it ended in balconies with robust railings. He added a floor to which he gave an exaggerated roof over the front bay and a small tower which was originally planned for the center of the façade, but moved to the side, next to the tiny terrace, in the course of construction. Thus, with the boldly

1. Document 9612 of the Comisión de Ensanche. [Recently Gaudí's own personal drawing of the façade has been rediscovered. It is elaborate, detailed, and much closer to the final design except at the cresting of the building.— G. R. C.]

433. Casa Batlló. Distribution of the main floor as it was carried out. 1. dining room; 2. grand staircase and landing; 3. waiting room with fireplace; 4. salon with adjoining oratory.

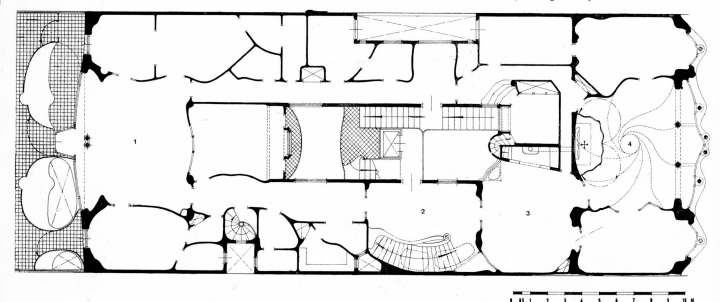

original forms of the new lower elements in Montjuich stone and the roof which has scales of ceramic tile like a great reptile, the whole acquired a unified tone which was accentuated by the presence of the terminal cross of the small turret, the expressive cast-iron forms of the balcony railings, and the unrelieved parts of the façade which are covered with richly colored glass mosaic, abounding in discreetly protruding disc forms; the surface is subtly undulated to give a greater richness, and also to avoid uniform reflection of the sun at certain times of day.

The tribune which is the most expressive element of the façade has a central window and two lateral ones in rounded forms that are subdivided by naturalistic, bone-like mullions which give the impression of strength; their articulations are camouflaged with plant-like forms. These undulating masses—a rhythm new to architecture—with no distinction between supporting and supported elements, pass, with no other breaks but the occasional ones necessary to liven up the chiaroscuros, from one component to another, never losing the unified character which the architect was seeking.

STRUCTURE AND DISTRIBUTION. The remodeling nature of the task spared Gaudí some structural problems while creating others which were perhaps even more delicate, such as the tedious work of offsetting the upper floors of the façade in order to leave room to construct the arches on the first floor and the tribune on the second. In some places, to avoid overburdening the house's good wooden beam system he employed a procedure adapted from reinforced concrete—a material just coming into use at the time—which he jokingly referred to as «reinforced wood.» This consisted in driving thick screws into the upper face of the beams and then imbedding their projecting heads in the three layers of the flat masonry flooring above. The screws acted as stirrups to resist the sheer forces and obliged the floor deck to work in compression, like mixed T-beams. He had to calculate carefully the torsion stress on the steel girder that was needed on the ceremonial staircase landing because of the double curvature of its form, and in the lower part of the light shafts he installed horizontal tubes that communicated with the façade in order to facilitate ventilation.[2] In constructing the upper floor of the new work he employed thin masonry tile arches to support the roof which was also of thin-shelled board-like masonry vaulting. The metal framework which supports the stairwell clerestory is interesting in its use of I-beams bent in parabolic arches (Fig. 445).

As for interior distribution, he was concerned chiefly with the story on which the owners were to live, the others being only slightly modified. The remodeling of this main floor began with the spacious vestibule on the ground level which served as an entrance to the stairs to the rented apartments and led to the ceremonial staircase in the back—an oak wood stairway which followed a majestic curve. This stair leads to the main floor reception area, opening onto the waiting room which in turn serves as an entrance to the living room; this salon corresponds to the central part of the tribune, and there are bedrooms on either side which look out of the end windows of the extensive and continuous structure which is actually divided into three sections for practical purposes. One of the bedrooms is separated from the salon by a glass and wood partition with bold three-dimensional forms. The ceiling

2. This information regarding the construction was told to me on April 25, 1955, by the architect Jaime Bayó, who served as builder for the work.

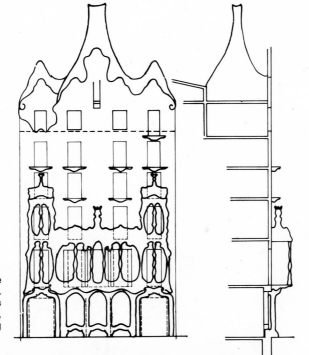

434. Project for remodeling the façade as approved by the City. The thick lines indicate the parts remodeled and the dotted lines, what has disappeared. Tracing from the approved plans.

435. Rear façade showing the rich polychromy of the upper parts and the clerestories which illuminate the lower floor.

436. Tribune of the main floor whose forms are generally expressionistic, but naturalistic in the mullion colonnettes.

is also three-dimensional and flowing, with smooth concave grooves, or wide striae, which begin at the edge and come together in a spiral roll toward the center where the chandelier is installed.

This room (Fig. 442) contained the family oratory which could be closed off when desired in an arrangement similar to that seen in the Güell Palace, although here the general forms are much freer. The altarpiece was composed of a Holy Family group by the sculptor Llimona, a crucifix by the sculptor Mani, and a highly original frame and two candelabra by Gaudí himself—all of which constituted a small ensemble of great artistic quality.[3] Most of the altarpiece was reproduced for the chapel of the Holy Family in the crypt of the Sagrada Familia.

Another important room was the dining room situated in the back with an exit onto the spacious rear terrace from which the posterior façade, with its undulating polychromed galleries built on tie-bar vaults,[4] can be seen.

FUNCTIONALISM AND SPACE. Gaudí was constantly concerned about these two concepts —concepts which were not prime concerns of his contemporaries—and his interest became more apparent as his personality became more independent. In this work—despite the fact that he was remodeling and could have resorted to routine structural procedures—he installed what was perhaps the first stepped patio wider in the upper part—a type which was much later made obligatory by the municipal ordinances. In the interior patio-shafts he increased the window surface area in the lower floors where the light was less intense. Each window has a special device in its lower part which allows ventilation of the room without opening the window itself. The light shaft was faced with ceramic slabs in various shades of blue —lighter in the lower parts and darker in the upper to establish a balanced light throughout.

3. This is presently located in Madrid in the home of D. Felipe Batlló, the previous owner of the Barcelona building.

4. It is unfortunate that the dining room and its two contiguous rooms had to be modified to suit the needs of the present owners; in other respects they have treated Gaudí's work with maximum respect.

437. Beginning of the principal stairway.

438. Transverse section through the patio and secondary staircase. Plans by L. Bonet Garí.

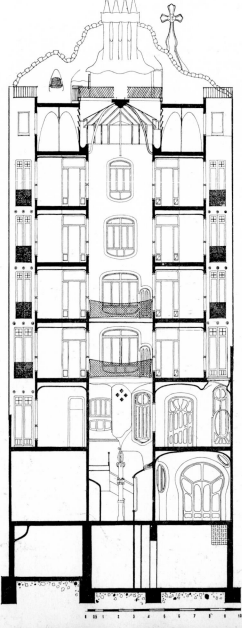

439. Detail of the central light shaft and secondary staircase.

440. Apartment door with tiled decoration which compensates chromatically for the natural light.

441. Waiting room of the main floor with fireplace and entrance door to the salon.

442. Salon of the main floor. Note interesting glasswork in the screen in the background and the oratory door to the right.

443. Oratory adjoining the salon with it doors open.

444. Protective screen of a patio skylight.

445. Clerestory for the light shafts and stairwell with parabolic frames.

446. Access corridor to the back rooms of the roof terrace with parabolic diaphragm arches.

447, 448. Carpentry details of the dining room.

449. Dining room, with furniture designed by Gaudí.

In the rooms of the ground floor and the basement, the window openings are provided with white tiled devices which reflect the interior light of the rooms.[5]

The spatial sense of this building is evident in numerous details, the most outstanding being the roof, with the opening that is cut in the façade to make the Paseo visible from the roof terrace. Then there is the location of the little side terrace and the turret with its cross; the parabolic *tabicada* arches in the corridor outside the servants' quarters (Fig. 446); the two polychromed chimney groups at opposite ends of the roof; and other details which can be observed in a careful study of the house.

It was for this house that the architect designed the pavement of relief concrete floor tiles which, because of the length of time involved in their manufacture, could not be used until the construction of the Casa Milá (XXIX - 132).

191.   THE CASA MILÁ, «LA PEDRERA.» 1906-1910 (Figs. 58 - 60, 89, 99, 100, 117, 141, 146, 152, 158, 159, 450-483)

This is, without a doubt, the most important nonreligious urban project that Gaudí built. In it, completely free of historical prejudices, he applied his structural and esthetic concepts in the architecture of an apartment house just as he had previously applied them in the Colonia Güell and the Park.

Here he had a lot some 34 by 56 meters to work with, more or less rectangular in form, and cut back at the chamfered northern corner of the Paseo de Gracia and the Calle de Provenza (which marked the borderline of the two townships before the nearby village of Gracia was incorporated into Barcelona). There was room on the site for a double building with independent entrances—one on the corner and the other off the Calle de Provenza—while preserving a united exterior front.

AN ORIGINAL DESIGN.   Three versions of the plans of this building are known, allowing us to follow the evolution of the design: a preliminary project, which I own, at a scale of 1:200 without façade drawings;[6] the official project on a scale 1:100 presented to and approved by the city with plans, a section and the façade;[7] and drawings which I myself have done of the plans, façade, and façade section from the work as it was finally carried out.[8]

These drawings confirm something which we have already noted: that Gaudí's carelessness in respect to the presentation drawings in his later work was definitely limited to the façades;

5.   Other functional details of this patio are studied in my book *Gaudinismo* (Barcelona: 1954), pp. 38, 39.

6.   This consists of plans of the basement, semi-basement, ground floor, five upper floors, and a section at a scale of 1:200 in ferrocyanide copies that have come in to my archive through the donation of my late friend the architect F. de P. Quintana.

7.   Archivo Administrativo. Sección de Ensanche, document 10,526.

8.   These plans were drawn up by the author for the Amigos de Gaudí at the time of their exhibition of Gaudí in the Salón del Tinell in 1956. They have since been extensively exhibited and reproduced. — G. R. C.

450.   Casa Milá. Preliminary project for the semi-basement in which can be seen the outline of the descending coach ramps leading from the entrance to the basement. The author's archive.

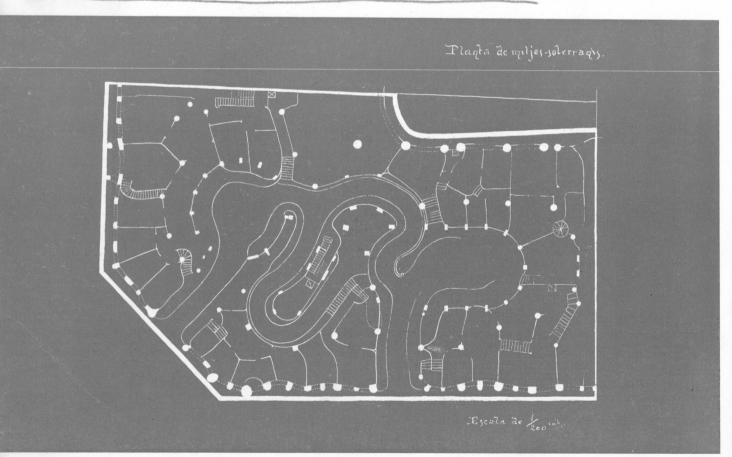

Planta de miljes-soterraris.

Escala de 1/200 inб.

the plans are meticulously worked out and delineated, even in what I have called the preliminary project which, given its precision, must have been preceded by conscientious study and previous sketches.

Although the vast structure was planned for rented apartments, Gaudí allowed for the possibility of unforeseen future adaptations. Considering that the cost would be quite substantial he decided to do without bearing walls which, in addition to elevating the cost, impose a similar arrangement on every floor; he adopted instead a system of pillars and girders such as that which he had used earlier in the basements and ground floor of the building in León. Taking advantage of the freedom of movement provided by this system, he amused himself by adopting different solutions for each floor, even in the preliminary drawings. Each of the floors of the double building was divided into a total of four apartments—two in each building—all facing onto the street. The rooms were rounded in form, some completely oval or circular, and the sinuous corridors had direct access to the balconies which could thus be reached without passing through the rooms.

This latter detail was not included in the plans approved by the city. In these, the profusion of curved surfaces in the rooms is diminished; as finally built, they became almost rectangular polygons. On the other hand, he retained throughout the idea of several balconies on a lower level than the apartment floors so as not to obstruct the window view of the street.

In the project presented to the authorities, the facade rhythm is completely indistinct, whereas in the work as completed there is a manifest rhythm of undulating horizontal bands which is echoed in the small-scale horizontal undulations of the capitals and imposts. The window grilles of the lower floor, which today no longer exist, displayed an undulating vertical rhythm like that of the majority of the projecting elements of the roof. These rhythms gave the finished work a cohesive composition not apparent in the officially approved design.

RAMPS AND STAIRWAYS. Another of the building's innovations was the placing of the stables in the basement (an idea that he had already used in the Güell Palace); here, thanks to the possibility of wider descent ramps, he extended the facility to include horse-driven coaches which were then still fashionable. It was the first instance in Barcelona—and possibly one of the first in the world—of the ramp system which was later so often used in multiple-story garages. This novelty and the unusual forms of the building which became more apparent as it grew, gave rise to a variety of imaginative fantasies on the part of the man in the street. One of these involved the fantastic notion that the residents could reach their

451. Casa Milá. Preliminary project for the second floor in which can be seen the majestic patio stairways and rounded rooms independent of the balcony accesses. The author's archive.

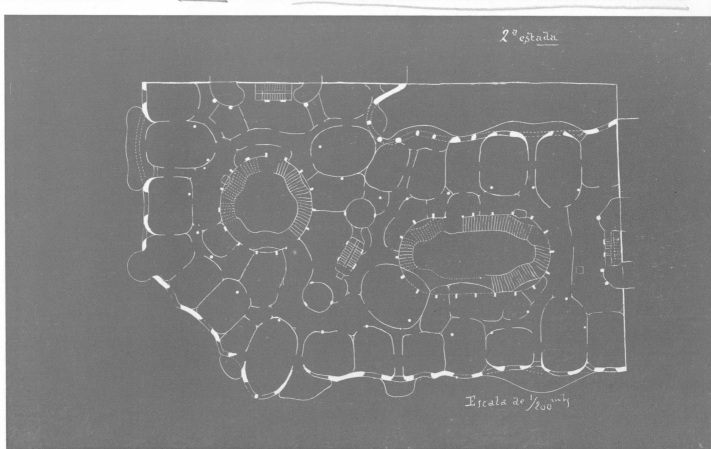

rooms in their coaches by means of ramps. This idea probably never crossed the architect's mind, but the public imagination may have been spurred on by his plans for majestically developed stairways which were designed to surround the two spacious patios.

These stairways are carefully detailed, with even the precise number of steps, in the floor plans and section of the preliminary project and also in the official plans, which would suggest that he was definitely set on the idea. The stairways would have been highly original and magnificent, with each flight serving to shelter the one below. In the extensive development of the stairs, ample space was provided for the steps which were broken by long landings —of a different size on each floor—which served as entrance vestibules to the apartments. Since the patios were bordered only by pillars and windows, with no continuous surface on which the stairs could lean, these staircases would be drawn into the interior of the patio at certain points to respect the privacy of the apartments along the way. The gracefully undulating structures were to have been provided with isolating screens which would shield them from the nearby windows as can be seen in the section which was built in the patio that is entered from the Calle de Provenza (Fig. 468).

Such details can be clearly seen in the indicated drawings, and we are also aided by the only two sections of the stair that were actually built—those leading to the first floor of each of the two houses. The Calle de Provenza stairway is covered with a marquee that is cleverly suspended from standard braced iron rods to create an admirable mixture of the industrial and the artistic. The stairway in the other patio was originally designed to be independent from and run in a direction opposite to the section leading to the first floor. Had the planned design been carried out, the result would have been two distinct stair groups whose expressive vigor and strength could be compared to that of the roof with its multiple levels and emerging forms.

In its present state the house has three stairways which were originally to have been used by the servants; here he employed several noteworthy technico-artistic or functional solutions such as in the doors to each floor where the typical peepholes were replaced by relatively wide grated wickets which allowed messages to be received without opening the door. There are also two elevators.

DECORATION AND SPACE. The most striking parts of the house are the façades and the pinnacles whose three-dimensional forms have been said to constitute as a whole the larg-

452. Casa Milá. Plan as it was built. The dotted parts distinguish the different apartments which face onto the front and rear façades.

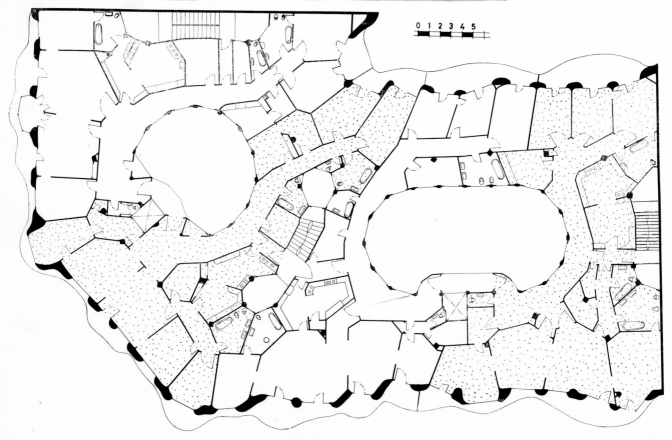

0 1 2 3 4 5

est work of abstract sculpture ever realized.[9] Indeed, putting aside the subtleties of nomenclature, this double house does produce the effect of a grandiose sculpture which some giant hands have modelled into smooth forms, converting the usual subdivided apartment house façade into a single mass of gently undulating horizontal bands which attenuate the inevitable division into stories.

Some say that these undulations were meant to imitate the waves of the sea, while others say that the overall effect was modelled on certain natural rock formations. I discard the first hypothesis for lack of any plastic relationship and also for lack of a logical motive; the second holds up insofar as it is meant as an interpretation of continuous forms in nature, but not as imitative naturalism. Whenever he specifically wanted to imitate Montserrat or other natural forms in the Sagrada Familia, and also in the Batlló house, Gaudí was able to be quite precise. The more or less wave-like rock strata occasionally found in nature always have something of the chaotic—a quality which we do not find in the Casa Milá, despite its nickname of «La Pedrera» (the stone quarry). Despite its geological strength, this ensemble has nothing chaotic about it; each and every part—even the smallest detail—exudes rhythm and harmony.

The plasticity of this building, as I see it, represents an interesting point in the architect's esthetic evolution. Here he leaves the naturalism that was still present in the Casa Batlló behind and he turns toward expressionism in those early years of the century when all Europe was looking for new architectural forms—long before Mendelsohn built his Einstein Tower (1920) along similar expressionistic lines. At first he tried out a sort of sentimental expressionism—that of the sculptor who models things with his hands (and the sort that was also to be employed by Mendelsohn); but he very shortly moved on to the geometrized expressionism evident in his sketches for the Passion façade and for the monument to the Bishop Torras as well as in the pinnacles of the towers of the Sagrada Familia which unite an agile conception with the scientific and purifying discipline of geometry.

The smooth surfaces of the Milá façade came prior to this final stage and were possibly inspired in nature where he found the clue to the solution of a problem which constantly preoccupied him—that of designing functional openings in continuous surfaces without falling into the arbitrary divisions of «supporting» and «supported» elements (XXV - 112). The overall unity is enhanced by a minimum of decorative details reduced to tenuous undulations which are recalled in the capitals of some of the columns, discreet moldings, and the works *Ave Ma-*

9. Subirachs, lecture cited (XXVIII-126).

453. Project for the Casa Milá façade as approved by the City. It was later modified by removing the cross and adopting another rhythm.

ria Gratia Plena Dominus Tecum and a rose at the top of the façade which do not interfere in any way with the dominant simplicity. The only superimposed ornamental elements are the wrought-iron balcony railings which harmonize extremely well with the stone, as do the projecting bodies on the roof which are more accusedly *modernista* in nature, yet conceived in the same rhythms as the house itself, making them an integrated extension of it. The same criterion can be observed in some of the interior detailing, among which we must not overlook the great variety of expressive ceilings in relief—a veritable exposition of originality which lends pleasing chiaroscuros and character to every room—and the relief pavements of hexagonal cement tiles (Figs. 159, 479).

The delicately carved columns designed for the main floor which was reserved for the owners' apartments would have contributed a great deal to the decorative richness of the interior. When Gaudí gave up direction of the work, only two of these columns had been completed. These were later covered with plaster making the original decoration invisible; only recently has it come to light as a result of the remodeling of that floor (Fig. 476).

There hardly exist any straight lines or plane surfaces in the decoration of the Casa Milá. Gaudí used three-dimensional surfaces that were still shaped according to his feelings rather than according to geometry; the result is an overall impression of fleshy *morbidezza* in the undulating horizontals and the vertical supporting elements. He has established a relationship of resistance in the latter and softness in the former which enhances their plastic balance. This together with the play of light and shadows which varies at every hour of the day, gives the building a mysterious breath of life.

This can be seen not only in the continuity of the façades, but also in the other volumes which are distributed so that they embrace the space and involve it in the plastic whole of the build-

454. Section of the Casa Milá approved by the City. The mansard is conceived as a continuous vault, and the roof terrace is reduced to a central passage.

455. Upper part of the façade with the group of the Virgin, in a drawing provided by the sculptor Juan Matamala who collaborated in the model. The group was elongated to compensate for the effect of foreshortening.

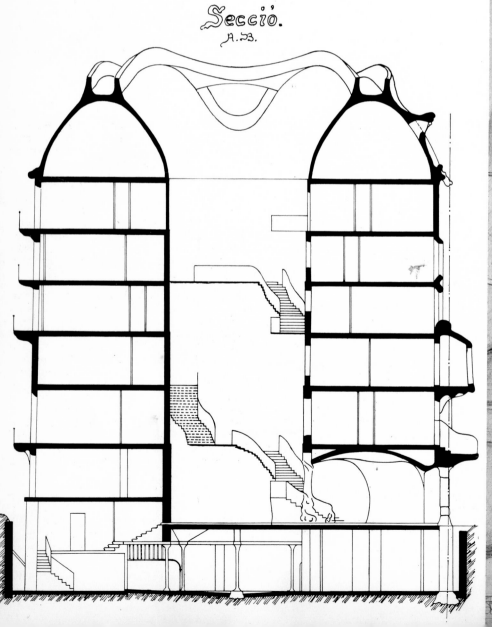

Secció.
A.53.

mansard Roof → double slope lower being longer + steeper then the upper

girder = large iron or steel beam for compound structure for bearing loads esp in bridge-building

ing: from the ups and downs of the pinnacles and chimneys of the roof top, the mansard roof and exterior passageway, to the iron and glass screens of the entrances which, more than separating, unite the street with the interior patios. In the main tribune-gallery and also in those of the other floors there are built-in benches which alternate with jardinieres for live plants, and there are steps which connect the various levels, merging the space with the architectonic elements. The effect is accentuated by the perforation of the tribune space roof which is covered by a clerestory which allows light to pass through to the upper balcony; the tribune is paved with glass tiles mounted on a simple network of T-beams for the same purpose. Similar solutions in other parts of the façade and numerous interior details instill a certain movement which generates a fourth dimension. Gaudí did not call it that, but it did form a part of his esthetic.

AN IMAGE OF THE VIRGIN. In the vaguely drawn façade approved by the city officials, the Paseo de Gracia edge of the chamfered corner is highlighted by a circular turret that runs from the second to the sixth floor and then is extended in a helicoidal spire which terminates in a cross. The Calle de Provenza edge appears to be rounded, and the upper molding which serves as a cornice rises sharply up from the façade, displaying a niche which frames an image of the Virgin. Judging from the placement of the cross next to the main street, its higher elevation, and the elaborate cylindrico-conical base, we would assume that the architect originally intended to give hierarchical preference to the cross over the image.

Nevertheless, in the transformation which these superficially *modernista* façades underwent in the course of construction, all trace of the turret and the cross disappeared, and the original design of the image was changed as Gaudí decided to move it to the center of the chamfered corner façade in the company of two angels whose wings would form a canopy. The gently undulating molding at the top of the facade contains the words of the angelic salutation relating to the Virgin who was to have at her feet the initial M and a rose—both of which were actually sculpted there. The idea grew so dear to Gaudí that his whole concept of the work became that of a pedestal for the image of the Virgin—a monument to the Virgin of the Rosary, the patron of the building's proprietress, that would compensate in part for the scarcity of such monuments in Barcelona.[10] Judging from what can be deduced from the plans, the idea was not there from the beginning, but rather—as we have said—arose as work progressed.

The sculptor Carlos Mani had already worked up a model for the Virgin-and-angels group which Gaudí first planned to execute in stone, gilded metal, and glass; later he decided to cast them in bronze and gild them in the fire.[11] They were designed to stand out against the background of the mansard roof and the tall projections behind, but the whole project was thwarted by the «Semana Trágica» events already indicated (XVIII - 73) which caused the omission of this final touch which, in addition to its spiritual beauty, would have complemented the existing decoration of the building and enhanced the sense of space.

STRUCTURE. We have seen that the structure of the building is based on freestanding pillars which support a steel framework and a series of small terra-cotta tile vaults *(bovedillas)* by which Gaudí achieved what we would call a «flexible plan;» he was also able in this way to reduce the cost of construction which also accounted for the high coefficients of wear allowed in the materials.[12] The pillars are generally made of brick and portland cement, except for some which are made of ashlar masonry to acommodate heavier loads, or of iron where a smaller section was necessary, as in that which passes through the ballroom on the first floor.[13]

The steel framework is based on a system of girders on pillars riveted together at the abutting joints (Fig. 475). Girders also run along the façades and side walls so that the house is belted in on each floor. The beams do not rest on the girders, but are rather joined to them with brackets which somewhat increases the height of the story above. When the loads required it, two or more coupled beams were used. The floor of the circular patio rests on a radial frame which is resolved in an interesting manner (Fig. 462). The laminated strips and pieces needed for the work were provided by the Torras firm and worked over in the workshop set up on the construction site under the supervision of Gaudí or his assistants. The façades were worked out during construction on a model that was one-tenth the actual size and built in the basement of the building itself according to the directions of the architect; the forms were then copied directly from the model. The hard limestone used for the resistant elements that act as pillars came from the Masllorens quarries in Tarragona, and another less hard type of stone from Vilafranca was used for the rest. When the stones were put in place, only the joining edges were smoothed; the surfaces were left rough until they could be carved in accordance with the forms determined by the model.

The projecting elements on the roof and some of the lower forms were held on by means of laminated strip steel rods that anchored in the girders of the floor, bent at an angle on the other end, imbedded deeply in the stone, and then filled in with mortar. Gaudí had his stonecutters copy those forms established in the model, and for the wavy horizontal edges he fixed steel rods along the wall in the pattern he wanted them to follow before the stone was

10. Bergós, *op. cit.,* p. 115.
11. Fact supplied by Juan Matamala.
12. Bergós, *op. cit.,* p. 115.
13. I am indebted to the architect-builder of the work, Jaime Bayó, for the technical data relating to the construction; these were communicated to me on the 20th and 25th of April, 1955.

456. Development of the façade
of the Casa Milá as it was constructed, with its section and plan,
showing the outline (dotted) of the
Virgin and angels group which was
not carried out. Drawing by the
author.

worked on.[14] After the surface had been sculpted, he would look again at the work and order any retouching that he thought was called for.

At times unforeseen protuberances had to be left, in putting the final touches on the wall, to avoid exposing the steel rods; in spite of this precaution and of the fact that the rods were previously coated with minium, the humidity has produced a number of chips in the thinnest areas of the rock.

From the official plans and from the preliminary project which have been discussed, we can deduce that Gaudí originally planned to cover the building with a continuous *tabicada* barrel vault of parabolic profile which would vary according to the width of the bays, but in the actual construction he followed another system, using parabolic *tabicada* arches that are all varying subject to the same relationship between width and height (Fig. 463). These arches rested on

14. Fact supplied by J. Matamala.

457. Exterior view of the Casa Milá in its early years, with grilles protecting the lower openings.

the floor beams which served as tie rods, and the closeness of one to another permitted them to be covered with stepped thin masonry surfaces *(soleras)* whose height varied with that of the arches.

The arches were five centimeters thick and needed a maximum thickness of 15 centimeters at the base, but Bayó—who did the calculations—made some of them 25 centimeters thick to insure greater security.[15] When Gaudí saw the results of the calculations, however, he decided to adhere to them in order to prove the effectiveness of the *tabicada* structure. For the same reason, he wanted to employ as many diverse arrangements of the horizontal and vertical rows as possible to demonstrate that by using good mortars the laws regulating joints normal to the intrados can be ignored. Though the arches were generally of the *tabicada* sort, those which supported the water tank were reinforced with strap arches 10 centimeters thick made of thin bricks of a type known as *pitxolí*.

15. The architect Bayó was professor of the subject «Resistance of Materials» at the School of Architecture.

458. Partial view of the façade as it is today, with the vigorous shadows of its projections and expressive iron railings.

These arches were all exposed; for many years they served as support for the mansard and also formed a garret used for storage; when the building changed hands, the whole floor was converted into rented apartments. The transition from garret to apartments was accomplished insofar as possible without destroying the expressive quality of these arches which were in places converted into decorative elements in the new apartments.[16]

The emerging bodies of the roof—the stairwell exits which at the same time serve as ventilators—rest on clusters of beams some 20 centimeters above those of the last floor; these projections are covered with parabolically curved vaults. The external forms are superimposed and based on models which—like the chimneys—were supervised by Gaudí himself without the intervention of assistants. The models were first worked up in plaster and then translated into reality, at which time they were subject to further modification.[17]

16. The architect F. J. Barba Corsini was in charge of the adaptation.

17. Bayó did not recall if the edges of these projecting forms were really constructed on the framework which their appearance indicates. The sculptor Juan Matamala who worked on the model recalls that Gaudí worked out these models using wires as directrices.

459. Tribune and entrance portico of the chamfered corner of the Casa Milá.

460. Three different versions of the grilles of the semibasements, today disappeared.

461. Supporting prop of the stairway of the patio next to the Calle de Provenza.

462. Framework supporting the floor of the circular patio. The sectors between the radial elements are covered with pseudo-conical prefabricated vaults.

HIS COLLABORATORS. In this work Gaudí collaborated with the architects Bayó, who worked as his builder, José Canaleta, who did the steel calculations along with Bayó, and Domingo Sugrañes, who supervised the progress of the work. Bayó had the feeling that Canaleta might have drawn up the plans that were presented to the city. This may have been the case for the ground plans, but the sketchy execution of the façade drawing does not indicate delegated work.

Another collaborator who deserves special mention is José María Jujol who, according to what I was told by Bayó, was taken on as Gaudí's assistant on Bayó's recommendation when he had him as a student at the School of Architecture. He immediately won the master's friendship and confidence, to the point that he was given great responsibility in the decorative area. The majority of the balcony ironwork in the Casa Milá is Jujol's, though Gaudí designed the first railing which was that above the corner tribune. This information comes to us from Juan Matamala, who adds that Jujol drew up the others in a similar style in life-size charcoals on large pieces of paper which were sent to the iron workshops of the brothers José and Luis Badía who also worked on the steel supports for the house.[18] Jujol was allowed to design the patterns for the interesting relief ceilings of the apartments once the model was established by Gaudí (who also personally directed the work on the most important ones), and he was put in charge of the polychromy of the balcony ironwork; this was originally to have been gilded, but it was later painted in ochre and reddish tones instead.

When Gaudí resigned from the work, several details of the decoration were pending, and he recommended his assistant to decorate the apartment of the Milá family; they requested a sample of his work, and rejected it because of the extremely wild coloring.[19]

18. In his statements to me of May 3, 1955, the masterr ironsmith Luis Badía did not recollect Jujol's intervention in these balconies, but only that of Gaudí when he made the first as a model. He attributed to Jujol the first grating of the ground floor on the Calle de Provenza which was not continued because it was too expensive. Those which were put up instead, all the same, he believed to be based on a model by Gaudí.

19. Story told to me by Sra. Milá on May 5, 1955.

We have already mentioned the sculptors Carlos Mani and Juan Matamala who did the models for the image of the Virgin and the sculpted façades, assisted by Juan Bertrán. The painter Alejo Clapés was entrusted with the pictorial decoration of the entrance vestibules which were to have been executed in mosaic; due to the highly irregular manner in which the work was terminated, they were painted in oil instead and some of the chimney groups remained simply plastered and without mosaic covering.

In appears that the painter Xavier Nogués intervened in the full-size drawings of the two large iron gates designed by Gaudí himself on a reduced scale. That of the corner entrance, which was carried out after Gaudí left the work, is not so perfectly executed as the one on the Calle de Provenza.

463. *Tabicada* diaphragm arches of the mansard before its present-day use for apartments.

464. Partial view of these arches as they are employed today. Remodeling directed by the architect Barba Corsini.

192. A GRANDIOSE PROJECT FOR THE UNITED STATES (Fig. 484)

This project, which never went beyond several small-scale but substantial drawings, has never been mentioned in the literature on Gaudí. The sculptor Matamala copied and interpreted the drawings by Gaudí himself before they were destroyed, and to him we are indebted for the graphic documentation of this little-known conception by the master (Fig. 484) and for the following information conveyed to him by the architect.

In 1908, an American businessman who admired the daring originality of Gaudí's architecture proposed that he design a colossal hotel building for the United States, with the understanding that its originality and exoticism should override its functional qualities. The businessman wanted a building that would impress people with its advanced form and daring structure.

465. The patio and the entrance to the stairway from the building entrance.

466. Vestibule and stairway entrance from the patio, showing the decorative jardinieres and illumination screen for the ramp which leads to the basement of Casa Milá.

The architect conceived of a group of parabolic domes some 200 to 300 meters high, with four grand dining rooms arranged in a cross-shaped distribution, all with exterior views and dedicated to four of the continents. The vaulting was to have been achieved with ingeniously arranged columns, and the exterior walls would have been double (in a manner similar to that employed in the towers of the Sagrada Familia) with the space in between to be used for elevators, stairways, and other related facilities.

The project was never carried out, but nevertheless the drawings which convey his basic ideas show that he had a broad and profound concept of the overall work from the beginning. In the drawing by Matamala we can see some detail which is conceived to harmonize with the general structure of the imposing exterior.

467. Casa Milá. View of the patio showing the Calle Provenza entrance and traces of polychromy on the floor levels.

20. [I am quite suspicious of this whole incident, as I have pointed out in my preface to Descharnes and Prévost, *Gaudí: The Visionary* (N. Y. C., 1971), where it is also discussed and illustrated. In any case, the drawing reproduced here is not by Gaudí but is Juan Matamala's version of the matter. Sr. Matamala has several drawings by Gaudí which he associates with the project, one of which is illustrated in Descharnes and Prévost. — G. R. C.]

468. The same patio with the grand staircase covered by a marquee.

The idea for this building came while Gaudí was working on the Casa Milá, and there is a certain plastic coincidence; however, the general mass of the hotel is so simplified in form as a result of the very grandiosity of the building that the rhythm is much more serene and equilibrated than that of the Barcelona apartments. Matamala's sketch provides us with an excellent example of the potential of the master's theory in an urban environment.

Sixty years after its conception, this grandiose project remains—as far as we are concerned—an unsurpassed milestone with forward-looking implications which would most certainly have been complemented by a version of the polychromed geometric ornamentation which the master applied to all of his latest works.[20]

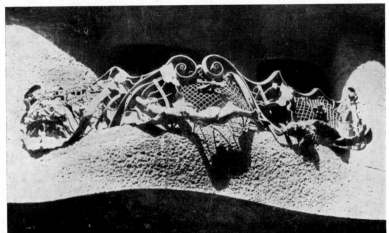

469. Balcony of the main floor in wrought iron with a translucent floor. Compare Fig. 89.

470. Wrought-iron railing of one of the balconies of Casa Milá.

471. Iron grating of the chamfered corner of the building from the interior.

472. Detail of the ironwork on the Calle de Provenza grating which was directly worked on by Gaudí.

473. Semi-basement grille designed by the architect and now removed.

474. Corbel of a tribune projection at the chamfered corner.

475. Main floor during remodelling, showing the structure of the ceiling and arrangement of the columns.

476. Inclined column decorated with reliefs discovered during recent remodelling work (1966) in the apartment originally inhabited by the Milá-Segimón family.

477. Modelled ceiling of the mezzanine apartment, which opens into the next-door room.

478. Modelled ceiling in the vestibule of one the floors.

479. Hexagonal floor tiles with reliefs alluding to the Earth, the Sea, and the Heavens.

480. Modelled ceiling and decorated moldings of Casa Milá.

481. Casa Milá. Stairwell exit with helicoidal rhythm on the roof.

482. Group of chimneys, ventilators, and a stairwell exit on the roof.

483. Casa Milá. General view of the roof with its variety of levels resolved by steps, showing the mansard as seen from one of the patios.

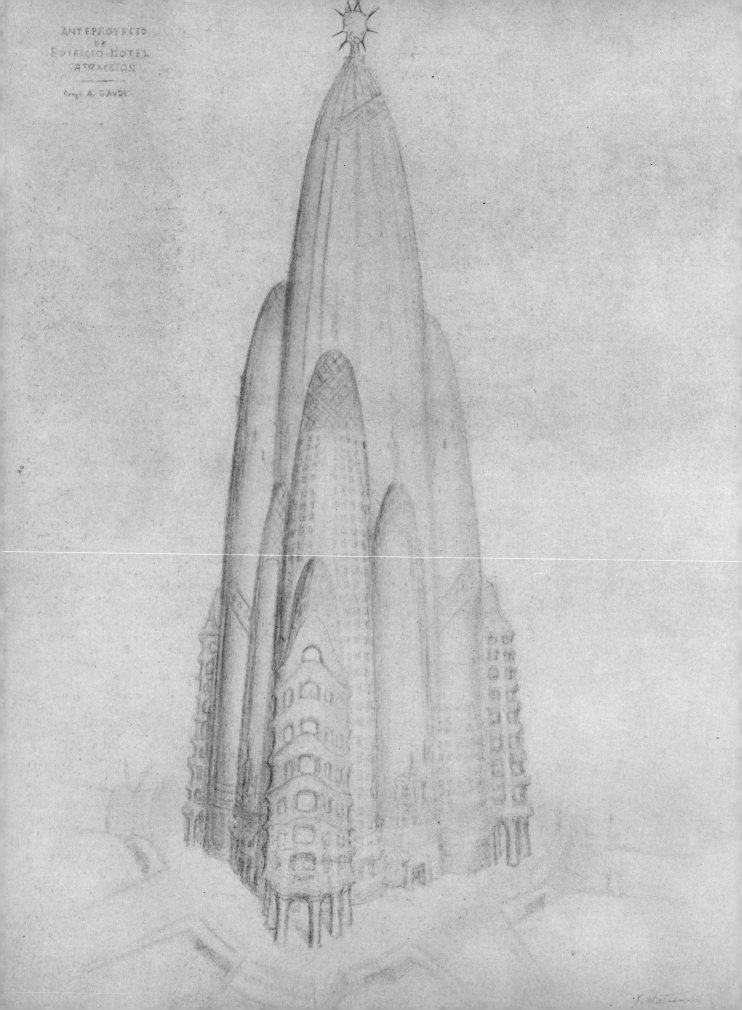

ANTEPROYECTO
DE
EDIFICIO-HOTEL
ATRACCION

Arq. A. GAUDÍ

XLIX. RESTORATION AND CREATION

193. RESTORATION OF THE CATHEDRAL OF MALLORCA. 1904-1914 (Figs. 94, 129, 485 - 499).

At the beginning of the present century, the young bishop of Mallorca, who had been born in his island diocese and served as the canon in charge of the works of the cathedral, decided that his temple needed a liturgical reformation which would free it of the additions and corruptions which had accumulated through the tolerance of past ages. He sought a profound and conscientious restoration which would remove elements which, by tradition, seemed permanent, and because of the importance of the project he sought someone with uncommon preparation and sensitivity to direct the work. In 1899, on a visit to the Sagrada Familia which lasted over three hours (XX - 85), he was impressed by Gaudí's liturgical and artistic knowledge, but it was not until the following year or perhaps the next, when passing through Barcelona on a return trip from Rome through Southern France where he had visited various cathedrals, that he presented his plan to the architect and asked his participation. Gaudí, surprised by the boldness of the plan already agreed upon by both the bishop and the chapter «believed that it could never become a reality—a project so beautiful would be difficult to execute.» [1]

Perhaps its difficult nature was the incentive for his acceptance, as well as the opportunity it presented to install in the great Mallorcan cathedral the standards which he had worked out for his expiatory Temple: to leave the nave of the church free for the worshippers, and place the choir up next to the altar, in the presbytery—a space reserved purely for the «presbyters.» In mid March of 1902 Gaudí went to Palma to study the restoration on the spot, and it seems that before the year was up, he had submitted three models in which he foresaw the removal of the choir from the center of the nave and its transferral to the presbytery; the enlargement of the presbytery itself; the removal of the Baroque altarpiece of the time of the Bishop Cepeda (1745) behind which was preserved another Gothic one, blessed by the Bishop Balle in 1346; the inclusion of an episcopal cathedra; pulpits, tribunes for the singers, and other details which we will examine further.

THE CHOIR. In the middle of 1904, assisted by the architect Rubió, he began the restoration work by moving the choir—which was located in the center of the nave in the monastic manner—to the presbytery, and by removing the main altarpiece. This latter move uncovered the elevated apsidal chapel of the Trinity (Fig. 486), where the kings of Mallorca were buried, and also the ancient episcopal throne which Gaudí decided to restore. The choir had Gothic stalls from the XIV century, with backs from the beginning of the sixteenth, whose dark hue he planned to liven up with trimmings and paintings which would harmonize with the ceramic facing which he planned for the presbytery walls. These polychrome touches in the choir stalls were entrusted to his assistant Jujol who accompanied the paintings with the fragmented gospel inscription *La Sang d'Ell, sobre nosaltres* (His Blood is on Our Hands) which did not please the canons at all; nor did they appreciate the paintings themselves, for which reason work was suspended. The choir seats were placed on either side of the presbytery and along the back wall in those parts not occupied by the cathedra and the sacristy doors.

THE EPISCOPAL THRONE. Once the XIII-century cathedral and the XIV-century niche and ornamental frame which surround it were visible again as a result of the removal of the Baroque retable, it is logical that they would be restored and made serviceable; this was done by leaving zones of the wall free on either side with inscriptions in gilded wrought iron. The dais on which the throne is raised was bordered by a railing which was also of wrought iron and by two ancient stone colonnettes skillfully converted into candlesticks and topped by two antique wooden angels. Thus by showing maximum respect for what already existed and making minimal additions, Gaudí was able to ennoble appreciably this key area of the cathedral.

Reverend Sagristá relates that when the architect was about to put up the railing, it was discovered that the iron rods that were to be imbedded in the hard limestone of the floor did not coincide with the holes which had been previously drilled—much to the dismay of the highly expert master ironsmith who was perhaps the victim of an error in the copy of the plans he received, making his work useless. Seeing the consternation of the elderly craftsman, Don Antonio ordered that the rods be slightly altered, resolving the problem in a different way which made them serviceable while maintaining the same high artistic quality.

THE PRESBYTERY AND THE MAIN ALTAR. The presbytery was enlarged by bringing it one bay forward, and the back walls of the apse next to the cathedra were covered above the

1. Emilio Sagristá, *Gaudí en la Catedral de Mallorca*, (Castellón de la Plana: 1962), p. 8. The major part of the information in this section is from the same source.

484. Project for a grand hotel in the United States, attributed to Gaudí by Juan Matamala whose sketch this is.

485. Cathedral of Mallorca. Presbytery restored by Gaudí seen from the apse.

choir-stall level with metallic reflecting majolica tiles decorated with laurel branches which were arranged in the triangular-hexagonal pattern which we have seen before. The resultant triangular spaces were occupied by the coats of arms of the bishops of the diocese. This decoration, perhaps based on the ancient polychromy of that site, gives a definite sumptuosity to this part of the presbytery without which it would be very dull (Fig. 129).

At the front of this area and elevated on three steps, he placed the extremely simple ancient altar table which was formed of a stone slab supported by six tiny columns in the Romanesque style (Fig. 486). At each corner of the stone steps there stands a quatrilobate col-

486. Cathedral of Mallorca. Presbytery seen from the nave.

2. These four columns with angels of stone and the other two with angels of wood were found in the oratory of Son Seguí owned by the Oleza family which agreed to return them to the cathedral. Sagristá, *op. cit.*, p. 14.

umn, all four with stone angels on top; these—along with the two that we have seen next to the episcopal throne—belong to the Gothic presbytery. They were expropriated from the cathedral as the centuries passed, and it was the architect's idea to return them as candlesticks with additional wrought-iron ornamentation.[2]

Above the table there hangs from the triumphal arch a great heptagonal baldachin which replaced a more simple square and horizontally hung canopy put up in 1904 for the inauguration of the restoration work.

487. Cathedral of Mallorca. Ceramic facing of the walls of the presbytery where the choir was transferred.

It was felt that the altar should have a more solemn baldachin, for which Gaudí developed two ideas: one in wrought iron, resting on the ground, which seems to have been preferred by the bishop and which left the Trinity chapel unobscured;[3] the other, also of iron and the one which was finally chosen, was designed to show the hierarchical importance of that place. The baldachin as built is very bold, and links ancient tradition with a modern sense of spatial sculpture. Its seven-sided form evokes the gifts of the Holy Ghost, and its 50 lamps (seven times seven plus one), the Pentecost; it is hung in an inclined position with the front vertex higher. Above the highest vertex stands Christ on the cross with the Virgin and St. John on either side recalling God's salvation of humanity. Other ornamental elements lend beauty or symbolism to the fixture which is accompanied by an ancient brocade canopy hanging somewhat higher and directly over the altar.

In spite of its many years of service and its sumptuous appearance, it should be noted that the entire baldachin is not of wrought iron as was planned, but only one side, the others being of painted wood and assorted lesser materials, as is also the case with the cross and the images that top the fixture. In the original design, the interior, inferior, and exterior faces were to have been «of colored glass which would filter the light of the electric bulbs inside. In the maquette that was put in place, only one face—the interior one on the back side—is completed in this fashion.» Sagristá, who wrote the passage quoted, feels that the canopy was only a trial model. We note that he adds that it was put in place with great haste and unforeseen accidents on the night of December 7, 1912, the eve of the inauguration, which leads us to believe that perhaps rather than a maquette it may have been only provisional in nature though later circumstances made it definitive.[4]

A wooden bench for the officiants was built for the altar along beautifully severe lines and with perfect craftsmanship; the design was carefully worked out to accommodate the vestments and ornaments of the priests.

The bishop's faldstool displays similar characteristics though it is more highly decorated and has no back in accordance with liturgical prescription. The benches and stools for the sub-cantors are simpler, and again reveal the furniture-making talents of the architect.

3. Sagristá, *op. cit.*, p. 40. The sketch of the unrealized project is held by the Rev. Guillermo Puigcerver of Palma de Mallorca (Fig. 489).
4. This episode is related in Chapter XXIII, section 104.

488. Cathedral of Mallorca. Episcopal throne.

489. Cathedral of Mallorca. Sketch of the unrealized baldachin, property of Rev. Guillermo Puigcerver.

TRIBUNES AND PULPITS. On either side of the presbytery Gaudí placed a tribune for the singers. Each one is composed of a lower part built of Plateresque elements taken from the front wall of the antique choir, and an upper part of carved wood—leftover accessories from the Gothic stalls.

He also made use of the Plateresque front wall elements in restoring the pulpits which were moved and altered somewhat (that of the Gospel side being made larger than that of the Epistle) when the presbytery was enlarged. Gaudí chose symbolically corresponding sculpted scenes and designed other appropriate new ones for the sounding boards which he planned to construct above the octagonal shaft which formed the mass of the larger pulpit. The sounding board was also to have been octagonal: «On the rim there should be angels with their wings spread... to form the parabolic curves of the sounding board; above this flared structure of rather small diameter would rise a colonnade with the twelve apostles; above these would be the four symbolic beasts of the Gospels, and between them the double banded orb and the cross—the symbol of Christ the Redeemer.»[5] Such symbolism did not get beyond the artist's imagination and graphic loquacity. In their place he left provisional sounding boards, with forms appropriate to their acoustic purpose.

WINDOWS AND OTHER DETAILS. It was Bishop Campins' idea that the *Regina* invocations of the Rosary liturgy should be the theme developed in the glass of the rose window and the eight large windows of the royal chapel. Of the eight windows, Gaudí only restored two. According to the painter J. Torres García,[6] who was called in to collaborate along with Ivo Pascual and Jaime Llongueras, the first thing that Gaudí did on receiving the commission was to study carefully the windows of the Barcelona churches where he observed that the enamel gave an opaque quality to the shading. In order to avoid this in his own windows, he thought up a system of composing his colors based on the superimposition of glass layers in the primary colors—red, yellow, and blue—toned down as needed in a manner comparable to that used in threetone printing. After trying out the system in fragments of the *Regina Apostolorum* window and that of the *Martyrs* with satisfactory results, he restored the

5. Sagristá, *op. cit.*
6. In his work *Universalismo Constructivo*, (Buenos Aires: 1944), p. 562.

rose window with the *Regina Angelorum* theme and then those dedicated to the *Virgins* and to the *Confessors*; he did not execute any others after that for the system was too expensive —again, according to Torres García.

In addition to what has been mentioned, his restoration work included the illumination of the basilica by means of wrought-iron candelabra, hanging lighting fixtures, and a bank of seven lamps in the Trinity chapel; the modification of small utilitarian windows which he changed on the exterior by putting up iron gratings; and some liturgical furniture which hasn't been mentioned, such as an ingenious folding stair by which the priest could reach the Holy Sacrament at those times when it was on public display (Fig. 94), another canopy, the novel bell (Fig. 495), and others.

He also saw to it that good use was made of the elements leftover from the restoration work: the Plateresque door which served as the entrance to the choir was placed at the entrance to the All Saints' Chapel; the Baroque altarpiece was transferred to another church in the city. The Gothic altar of the Bishop Balle from the mid XIV century which had both a front and back face was placed above the inner part of the Mirador portal with the two fronts placed above two brackets of stone to form a very noble Gothic tribune. The figures which remained in the altarpiece were placed on pedestals and covered with canopies constructed ex *profeso* above the arches that connect the choir and the lateral naves, cleverly concealing the small dimensions of these arches which are given an elevated aspect.

490. Cathedral of Mallorca. Lectern of wood and wrought-iron.

491. Model of the sepulcher of Jaime II for the royal chapel.

492. Cathedral of Mallorca. Baldachin with lamps.

194. OPINIONS AND DISAGREEMENTS

When it was decided, on the prelate's initiative and with the acquiescence of the chapter, that the cathedral should be restored, one of the premises of the commitment was that things should be returned to the way they were before the choir was put in the nave, giving maximum dignity to the remains of the temple and a minimum of innovation. The plan could be summed up in the slogan «restoration, but not reform.»

The transfer of the choir from the nave to the presbytery was nothing new. It had been done at Santa María del Mar in Barcelona at the end of the eighteenth century, and the Cathedral of Gerona chapter had planned to do the same in a project drawn up by Pedro Costa which never got beyond the planning stage. But in reality it was a daring idea, and to carry it out a bishop with Campins' pluck and an architect of Gaudí's reputation acting in fullest accord were needed. The bishop's proposal coincided with the architect's point of view. On studying the problem *in situ*, Gaudí immediately distinguished three different aspects to be considered: the apse represented the Church triumphant; in the crossing he saw the Church militant; in the nave, the Church of the faithful.[7] His enthusiasm served his vision and the liturgy, and these considerations soon became more important than style, just as we might expect for an architect who believed that beauty was above such prejudices.

7. Torres García, *op. cit.*, p. 162.

493, 494. Cathedral of Mallorca. Tribune and pulpit for which existing elements were used.

Gaudí respected the archaeological remains; whatever fragments he could save he restored with fullest dignity. He respected the body of the cathedral, although the historically knowledgeable Sagristá feels that he was not quite able to penetrate completely the spirit of the first architect «Mestre Nicolau,» and laments that he would take away the candlelight passages which Sagristá feels were historically important. But Gaudí was also very much in agreement with the line put forth by the bishop in his pastoral letter which said: «The clearest and most authentic document by which we can discover the extraordinary design of the cathedral is, wihtout a doubt, the cathedral itself,» and there can be no doubt that Gaudí could see the cathedral more clearly than all the archival documents and that his new liturgical adaptation was more in accord with the structural fact than with the scholarly data. An example of how he penetrated the structural essence of the cathedral is that the architect Rubió, who was his most efficient aid from the first moments of the restoration, spent his time on the island making an extremely complete graphic-static study of the great temple in whose columns suspicious deformations had appeared; the study was expanded under the master's supervision, to include the architectonic whole.

If there was possible disagreement with the way the architect adapted the ancient elements, such disagreement goes without saying for the cases where he designed new ones even though they too were adaptations, carried out in the architect's own personal manner. It could not be otherwise: had these details been designed according to archaeological standards, following the styles of past centuries the relative archaeological fidelity would have been unable to compensate for the lack of synchronism between the liturgical restoration that was proposed—a work of our time—and the forms adopted—a cold imitation of the past. The fears of those who were frightened by the fact that the architect of the crypt at the Colonia Güell should be called to work in a Gothic cathedral were quite unjustified. For a work of such magnitude they were precisely in need of an architect with Don Antonio's freedom of movement.

The new details which he created are in the style of his time which was well suited to the Mallorcan cathedral. The wrought-iron work which the master used so prodigiously here acquires a special tone that is adapted to the spirit of the simplified architecture. Even Reverend Sagristá, who is extremely particular, approves of the Gaudinian ironwork of the cathedral and he especially praises the beauty and harmony of the candelabra attached to the six Gothic columns of the presbytery. The same could be said of the furniture which is conceived with a sobriety fitting its use. If we compare these furniture pieces with others designed by Gaudí—even other liturgical ones—we will see how subtly these exquisite models were adapted to the place for which they were designed.

The simple fact is that even in a project of pure liturgical restoration Gaudí could not help but be creative. While he subjected himself completely to what was prescribed in terms of liturgy, he maintained his creative rhythm in the architectural field as was demanded by his professional sincerity—even in such cases as this where he was working within a historical framework.

Gaudí's exalted feelings were at least understood by someone. In the beginning the authority of the bishop backed him up and the protests were silenced to a certain extent. In spite of this, others were unleashed once the choir was transferred, by those who had «always» seen it in the old place (how it dismayed the little old lady who could no longer move her chair up next to the customary place!). Reaction was divided, not only in Palma but also on the peninsula where public opinion was horrified to hear that the choir of a cathedral could be taken out of the central nave in spite of the inconveniences suffered because of this arrangement copied from the monastic churches. The arguments even reached the press. Nevertheless, other cathedrals have since followed the example: the Romanesque one at Santiago de Compostela and recently the Gothic one at Tarragona have —as in Palma— returned their central naves to the worshipping people.

Another motive for disagreement was the painting in the choir stalls and the painted inscription; these displeased the canons but were defended by the architect, producing another important schism. The revetment of the presbytery with hexagons of shining tile also seemed inappropriate to the scholarly conception of a medieval church.

Fortunately, the first stage—which was inaugurated on December 8, 1904—was carried out in less than a year and could be praised from the pulpit with general approval, tacit or expressed, putting a damper on the dissenters for the moment. After that, work progressed slowly; Don Antonio became more difficult, and the disagreements less disguised. Regarding the canopy misfortune of December 1912, Sagristá wrote: «Those who did not intimately live those years can not realize the responsibility and difficulties of the canon Don Martín Llobera who was the capitular depository, warden of the chapter, and major-domo to Bishop Campins; in order to understand his position one has to have breathed in the stirred-up air when opinion turned against the good bishop who had initiated the reform, hired Gaudí, and retained him against the storm winds and high seas.» [8]

495. Bell.

496. Wrought-iron detail.

497. Wooden seat and wrought-iron railing.

498. Stained glass window of the cathedral with the *Regina Virginum*, in which we can see Santa Rosa of Lima, Santa Teresa, and Santa María de Cervelló.

8. Sagristá, *op. cit.*

A short time later the master angrily left Mallorca—without a scene and probably not considering his work terminated. It is possible that he would not have returned anyway, but the death of Campins which came shortly thereafter (1915) dispelled once and for all any thoughts of possible continuation.

195. PULPITS FOR BLANES. 1905 (Fig. 500)

These pulpits disappeared during the Civil War (1936-1939), but are known to us through photographs in which we can see a close relationship to those which were never finished in Palma. They were commissioned by Joaquín Casas Carbó to carry out a project initiated by his father-in-law.[9] On taking on the commitment in 1905 (not 1912 as Ráfols says) Gaudí proposed that the antique pulpits might be restored, but the priest Reverend Vall-llovera —who wanted to shift their location—insisted that they be newly-made.

Gaudí designed two pulpits, both on the same general lines, with that of the Gospel being larger than that of the Epistle—as was the case in Palma. The first was hexagonal in plan with sculpted parchment rolls bearing the names of the evangelists on the four most visible faces; the two posterior faces were simple wooden tablets which supported the foot of the sounding board. This board was sharply inclined toward the audience for acoustical reasons. It was circular in shape, slightly undulated, and divided into seven sectors with Latin inscriptions indicating the gifts of the Holy Ghost in polychrome relief. In the center there was a white dove, and the edge of the sounding board was also undulated and relieved with seven tongues of fire. The Epistle pulpit, as I have said, was somewhat smaller and different in several other points. In spite of Gaudí's personal style, both harmonized with the Gothic nave of the church and its Baroque altarpiece as well.

These pulpits were not only interesting as works of art in themselves, but also for their relationship to those of the cathedral of Mallorca whose sounding boards were never completed. This is corroborated by a photograph of the latter in their smooth state on which Gaudí had written in pen: «their ornamentation will be very similar to the Blanes pulpits.»

196. THE TOWERS OF THE SAGRADA FAMILIA. 1901-1926 (Figs. 51, 76, 102, 103, 118, 160, 501 - 510)

The temple of the Sagrada Familia was the master's work of fulfillment, and at each stage it reveals his current architectural preoccupations. In previous chapters (XLI, XLIV) we have looked at the crypt, the apse, and the Nativity façade; here we will examine the growth of the four towers—Gaudí's most highly personal creation—and the outstanding characteristics of this most attractive note of the present-day Barcelona skyline.

THE SQUARE BEGINNINGS. When the architect began this eastern façade, he visualized the four towers as square in plan with the corners normal to the façade plane. At the base the sides of these square towers served as splays for the three portals. They do not become distinguishable as towers until they reach the bases of the small side gables and the square corners are pointed sharply outward. The master did not like this arrangement and decided at that point to make them round.[10] I have already explained (XXVIII - 122) the perfect manner by which he accomplished this change in plan which resulted in the very beautiful *modernista* details of the projecting *miradores* which converted the oversight into a practical advantage.

THE CIRCULAR STAGE. Once the circular plan was obtained—as if in announcement of the innovations that we will see as we climb higher—one reads the inscription *Sursum Corda* from which a series of small mullioned windows with trilobate arches start upward in a helicoidal arrangement. They bid farewell, so to speak, to the traditionally influenced forms of the lower section which serve as a base for the slender campaniles which emerge with remarkable smoothness from the imperceptible transition.

Above are the twelve tall openings which are also spirally arranged and separated by robust pillars which stress the structure of each tower. Above these is repeated the word *Sanctus, Sanctus, Sanctus...*; every group of three being dedicated to the Father, Son and Holy Ghost. Don Antonio planned to paint the first one—alluding to the Father—yellow, this being the color which best represents light; the second—referring to the Holy Ghost— would be orange; and the third—to the Son—would be red, the color used in the liturgy to symbolize martyrdom. The Holy Ghost was in the middle to represent its function as the link between the Father and the Son, and thus, too, the color is that which results from a mixture of the other two.

The harmony of formal expression became greater as he moved upward, and the symbolism kept pace by becoming more and more purified. In the lower part of the façade, the symbols are more abundant and allude to human themes. The *Sanctus* inscriptions are placed at the point where the vertical walls of the cylindrical masses merge with the parabolic parts—a merger which represents, according to Gaudí, the union of gravity and light; the first is directed toward the earth and the second soars upward. The inscriptions themselves are a hymn

9. J. M. Garrut, «Una obra poco conocida de Antonio Gaudí,» *Templo*, (February, 1955). This is the source for my information regarding this work.

10. In my book, *La Sagrada Familia*, (Barcelona: 1952). I have spoken of the progress of these towers whose change of plan Gaudí communicated previously to J. Rubió, who then told me about it.

to the Trinity which would be intoned by anyone who read it: as one reads them in an upward progression—looking towards the heavens—they lead to the *Hosanna in Excelsis* of the pinnacles.

PARABOLIC BODIES. Above the vertical walls of the twelve tall openings, the world-famous parabolic structures begin. This is the most architecturally interesting part of the temple, for it summarizes the new structural theory which he was never able to apply to more complex structures. In his enthusiastic search for antecedents for his works, Gaudí said that these towers were the perfection of the Gothic campaniles with set-back floors. In reality, however, he had developed a new clearly defined system of structural equilibrium which the Gothic architects could never have achieved except by trial and error or by accident. Twelve vertical structural elements resting on the pillars between the tall slender openings rise uninterruptedly upward as they converge slowly together at the top; they are united by stone plaques which slant downward and serve as sounding boards for the bells. These plaques follow a helicoidal distribution which parallels the interior staircase.

The clear arrangement which has been indicated is really not so simple as it would seem, for there is another, similar, internal wall that is separate from the exterior and at the same time connected to it by the spiral staircase which permits ascent to the top; the two tower pairs are linked between themselves in three places and are twice united to each other by stairs which bridge the central space. The towers are completely hollow, prepared to receive the huge tubular bells.[11]

THE PINNACLES. The growth of the towers was a slow process. In 1905, there arose the financial crisis which occasioned the pathetic article by Maragall, and the silhouette of the four eternally truncated towers became endemic to the Barcelona cityscape. Meanwhile, the ar-

11. The domed structure of these towers is something we have seen in a less elongated form in the church of the Colonia Güell, and he also planned to adopt it in the Sagrada Familia sacristies. It was also to have been the general form for a grand hotel in the United States (See Chapter XLVIII, section 192).

499. Iron protective grating which serves to modify the outline of the existing window opening of a room adjoining the Mallorca Cathedral.

500. Pulpit in Blanes.

501. Sagrada Familia. Rear view of the upper part of the towers.

502. Interior of one of the bell towers seen from above.

chitect—who was the only one who could already «see» the finished towers—worked untiringly on the perfection of their pinnacle design. In the school year 1914-1915, I was working as a draftsman in the office of Juan Rubió who still maintained his contact with Gaudí. One day he told me, somewhat shocked, that the esteemed master was planning to build the pinnacles of the towers... in brick! He added understandingly that «whatever he comes up with will be valuable,» but he could not imagine that humble material as the summit to such a noble stone building. For his part, Gaudí was concerned only with finding the architectural expres-

503. Sagrada Familia. Frontal view of the upper part of the towers.

504. Detail of the expressionist geometric pinnacle forms.

505. Cylindrical body with helicoidally positioned openings and the inscription *Sanctus, Sanctus, Sanctus.*

506. Parabolic body with 12 tall openings to serve as sounding boards.

507. Hexagonally pyramidal pinnacle base with inscriptions and textures of brick and mosaic.

508. Expressionistic geometric forms of the pinnacles.

424

sion best suited to his idea which had nothing to do with pre-established categories of materials. It is possible that he would have changed his mind at a later stage of the construction, but as it turned out he employed black, hard-fired brick in combination with glazed ceramic tile in the first hexagonal section of the polychrome pinnacles, producing a magnificent effect and a note of color which is bold and refined at the same time.

The pinnacle begins with a six-sided pyramidal section whose edges are emphasized by a string of hexagonal plaques, each of which contains a letter of the words *Hosanna* and *Ex-*

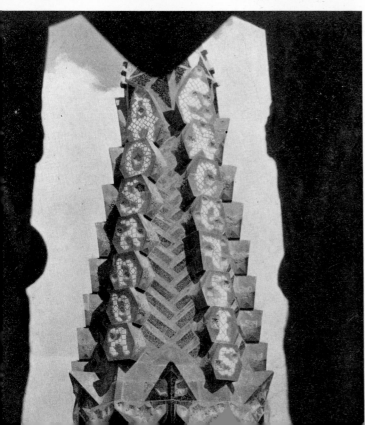

509. Exterior view of the Nativity façade.

510. The same façade seen from the west.

511. Interpretation of a note by Gaudí regarding the chapel of the Assumption of the Virgin. Drawing by the author.

512. Alabaster and metal lamp for the crypt.

513. Transverse section of the Temple.

514. Model of the internal structure.

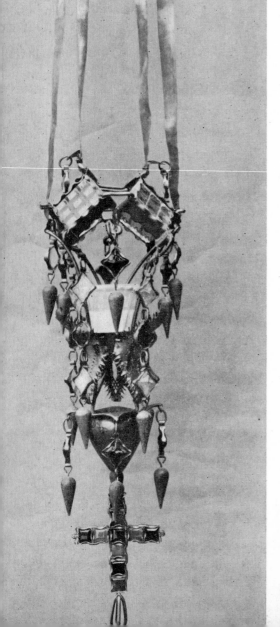

515. Window model resolved with hyperboloids and paraboloids.

516. Exterior model of the Temple with the nave body and cloister of marked Gothic influence.

517. The whole Temple. Drawing by Ll. Bonet Garí.

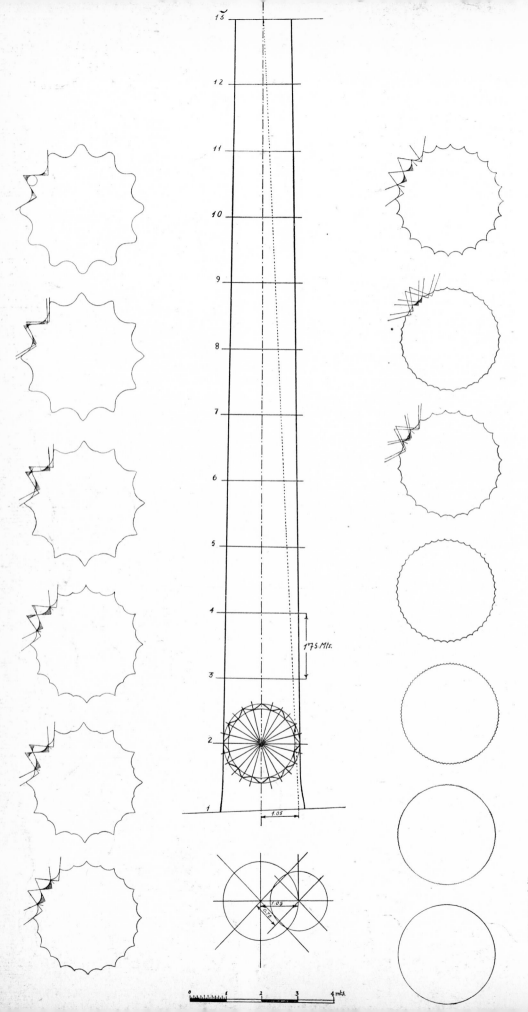

518. Inclined column of the central dome, 21 meters high, and its horizontal sections at various heights arranged from top to bottom and from left to right. Puig Boada.

519. Plaster model of these columns designed by Gaudí after several years of study.

520. Sketch of the monument to the Bishop Torras y Bages (Detail of Fig. 81).

celsis which are alternately repeated. He unites the stone part of the towers with the cross of the vertex through a succession of highly controlled geometric forms which harmonize perfectly with the rest, in spite of the fact that they are based on a different system which constitutes the ultimate development in Gaudí's architecture. All of the surfaces obey geometric forms which have been defined in the illustration reproduced before (Fig. 160). Outstanding among these is a semi-regular polyhedron obtained by irregularly truncating the vertices of a cube or a regular octahedron, which contains a sphere that protrudes through the polyhedral faces. Such polyhedrons were supposed to contain double electric lights to symbolize the evangelic doctrine preached by each of the apostles to whom the bell towers were dedicated; one light—for the Glory of God—would be aimed at the cross which would culminate the tall central dome, and the other—to light the way of man—would shine down on the ground. The top is an elongated chamfered triangular pyramid which curves into the shape of a crozier that is linked to a golden cross inscribed within a red square set on edge. The polychromy of these finials is achieved with Venetian glass mosaic that alternates with bits of glazed ceramic and other textures of applied stones; some of these, such as the projecting cubes, stand completely apart and lend vivacity to the contours.

A CYCLE COMES TO A CLOSE. The last geometric form which Gaudí constructed here in these summits of his temple—*the chamfered triangular pyramid*—is the same basic form that he used in the pedestals of his earliest work—the lampposts of the Plaza Real. In both works we find the same tendency toward unity and simplification (naturally more success-

521. Graphic-static drawing of the Passion portal previous to the drawing which he later realized (Fig. 81).

ful in the last than in the first). The equilateral triangle is the most simple and the most unified form that can be generated by straight lines (which are themselves more easily constructed than curves). This spirit of synthesis, which must have influenced his novice mind on creating his first work which was to serve for public illumination and on ground level, would bear fruit 47 years later (in a mind by then laden with experience) when he put the final touch on his bell towers with their double searchlights, also meant for illumination. There is another coincidence: in the Plaza Real, the triangular pyramids of stone are combined with circular medallions of wrought iron and, in the upper part, with forms generated by circles (the only unitary curvilinear form). At the top of the Sagrada Familia, the rectilinear triangle is similarly combined with circular and spherical parts which silhouette the upper cross to form a unified whole.

In the very early work—which only marked a beginning—the forms end right there, static; in the other—in spite of being his last—the forms seem rather restless, anxious to go beyond and fulfill the promise of excellence which could be achieved, as was demonstrated by another intermediary work which was never more than a sketch: the monument to the Bishop Torras y Bages which he designed to stand in front of the Passion façade (Fig. 520). In this monument, he adopted the triangular pyramid form which, instead of twisting into the form of a crozier as it does in the Temple, twists here into a helix which forms a pinnacle that is at the same time dynamic and novel.

However different the esthetic expression of the two extreme works, and even of the intermediary sketch, it is of great interest to observe how at the end of the line of ingenious works he remains faithful to the standards of his earliest years and, without suspecting his approaching death, closes the cycle of his professional life with this coincidence of forms.

POSTHUMOUS TERMINATION. Of the four towers, Gaudí himself only completed the southernmost one—that dedicated to St. Barnabas. He was pleased with it, and planned to terminate the others in the same manner, the only change being in the polychromy which he wanted to gild more profusely. It was not possible for him to carry out his proposal; the tower was finished at the beginning of 1926, and he died on June 10 of the same year. Sugrañes, who had executed the first pinnacle at the instructions of Don Antonio, completed the three remaining bell towers with absolute fidelity to the orders that he had previously received without a single change—not even in the coloring, which Gaudí had planned to vary.

We have said that the architect did not like to climb up to the construction site. He gave instructions to Sugrañes who was in charge of putting them into practice while the maestro observed the results from the ground. After many years of close association, there was an absolute, mutual understanding between director and collaborator, so that once the towers were concluded, Sugrañes proceeded to terminate the lanterns of the façade gables which were still not finished. These were included in the 1:25 scale model made by Juan Matamala under Gaudí's supervision, and sent to Paris in 1910, with the tall central cypress covered with pieces of green ceramic tile and surrounded by white alabaster doves, parts of which had already been prepared in the master's lifetime. We can say, then, with all surety, that such elements as were terminated by Sugrañes in collaboration with Quintana are actually works of Gaudí, built according to his instructions.

The sculptor Matamala also executed the projected stone images, some of which Gaudí had begun to work out, such as that of Jesus working as a carpenter—the first one he finished. This was followed by those of St. Joseph and the Virgin finding the boy in the temple; the Christ figure having been done by the master himself, as were the four herald angels. Then Matamala did the apostles—Barnabas, Simon, Thaddeus, and Matthew—for the niches of the towers. The groups of the Visitation, Betrothal, and Coronation of Mary, along with those which occupy the pinnacles of the lanterns and other parts of the façade, were also terminated, leaving out some of the details foreseen by Gaudí, for reasons of economy.

Work was extended until 1935 which is the date when we could consider the master's part of the building done. Then the problem was posed of undertaking the continuation of the work. Sugrañes, who had stayed on as director in charge, planned to carry on with the building of a sacristy, as this was the last of the studies which Gaudí left well-defined in model form and explicit in its structural characteristics; this also would have provided a covered space which could have been used for services of worship. The Civil War which broke out shortly thereafter, and the death of Sugrañes in that war, put an end to the plan.

197. LITURGY, ART, AND SYMBOLISM

We know that while Gaudí was erecting the impressive architectural structure which we have just examined he thought constantly of the grand temple of which this was only a part. Without the total idea of the temple, what he did would have been unjustified and, besides, it would have lacked the sap that was necessary to its growth. As soon as he took over the work, he became convinced that the most essential thing for a church was that it adapt itself with the greatest possible perfection to the practice of divine worship, and to this he added that it should have a maximum of splendor and artistic value as a tribute to the Lord.[1]

He accepted the Gothic temple type already established by the previous architect, with a ground plan in the shape of a Latin cross with five longitudinal naves and three transversal ones with a lobated apse and an ambulatory aisle. It was to be 95 meters long, 60 meters wide, and 45 meters high. The focal point of the church was the main altar which was to be without an altarpiece and only Christ on the cross which would occupy the forward part of the presbytery—placed in the apse and surrounded by the ambulatory while elevated two meters off the ground. In this section there were 200 seats for the priests who constituted the choir of the temple. There were seven other altars in the apsidal chapels, and those of the Holy Sacrament and the Assumption of the Virgin completed the total of 10 that the church would contain. Also planned were a baptistery, triforia for the singers in the apse, and gynaecea for the women's choir in the high tribunes of the lateral naves. Two large sacristies were located in the triangular spaces left between the apse and the cloister which surrounded it; inside the church 14,000 worshippers could comfortably be seated.

The windows and vaults were to be decorated with religious scenes and symbols which would enhance the attractiveness of the naves, but the splendor reached its greatest spectacularity on the exterior, in the three façades of which only one now exists. Another, on the opposite side was—as we know—dedicated to the Lord's Passion with the appropriate accompanying scenes, and the main façade, oriented to the south, was to depict—as in all great temples—the Last Judgment, a summation of the life and death of man, with heaven as the prize for virtue and hell as the punishment for vice. There he planned to depict humanity's struggle to reach the prize through work and virtue, showing the fruits of Redemption and the Grace of the Holy Ghost, sanctified humanity, and Glory—all of this within a grand portico 20 meters high with representations of the gifts of the Holy Ghost, the capital sins and their opposing virtues, the sacraments, and similar themes. In front of the façade he planned to erect two monuments—one, on the side of the baptistery, to water, with a very tall fountain, and the other, a monumental cresset in front of the confessional chapel, to fire; these would represent man's two means of purification, fire and water, which, along with the earth that sustains them and the air that surrounds them, comprise the four natural elements.

Each façade was to have four bell towers some 100 meters high which all together would represent the twelve apostles who spread Christ's teachings; the episcopal attributes of the pinnacles were to indicate that these were the first bishops in the world to support the new doctrine. On a lower level, in the apse, there would be images of the holy founders, and above the transept crossing, the great dome, 170 meters high, terminating in a 15-meter-high cross with a lamb in the center, surrounded by four other domes of lesser height dedicated to the four evangelists whose symbols they would display. Above the apse another dome would be raised, this one dedicated to the Virgin and some 140 meters in height, crowned by a luminous star to recall her title *Stella Matutina*.

Gaudí wished to make of this building a stone hymn in praise of the glory of the Lord (which explains the abundant use of symbols.) It was to serve as a pedestal for the supreme hierarchical figure of Christ the Lord, whose symbol it would raise on high. The attractive forms of the whole would be highlighted with notes of color and metallic reflectors abundant in gold —similar to the pinnacles of the completed towers—and with bright electric lights which at night would produce an impressive artistic effect in converging on the terminal cross.

The cross itself would be four-armed with a radiant glazed surface; from the arms and from the head luminous rays would shoot upward on the most solemn occasions to outline a cross in space, protectively hovering over the peaceful city. Beyond its religious function, the illuminated temple would also serve as a monumental stand for the great, radiant, sun-like cross which in the dark night would recall in an ostensible manner the soft voice of Jesus Christ who said to all mankind: *I am the Light of the World.*

This monumental stand was nothing less than a great temple which presented innumerable problems which he wished to resolve in the most perfect manner possible. From the begin-

1. For a detailed description of the Temple as Gaudí imagined it see the book by Puig Boada *(El Templo de la Sagrada Familia)* which is copiously documented, and also my more summary book, *La Sagrada Familia.*

ning he proposed to eliminate the difficulties of the Gothic structures, and after a great deal of study he was able to replace them with his equilibrated structures. The new theory led him to slanting arborescent pillars, to mushroom columns, to vaults that first were parabolic and later hyperbolic, and which contained within them a new and personal style—created by him alone—which he could offer to the glory of God by incorporating it in the base of the holy emblem.[2]

198. PLANS AND MODELS (Figs. 81, 511 - 521)

This great temple, conceived, coddled, and perfected for a period of over 40 years, was the marvelous vision of an architect with a great deal of faith; but it was virtually nothing more than an image in the architect's mind which came out only when his impassioned words made it almost visible. To enhance our understanding of and nostalgia for the unrealized and beautiful vision, he left behind a portentous fragment as a model which invites continuation.

The architectural work of the master was ended with the terminal cross of the tower of St. Barnabas or, if you will, with the last façade details that Sugrañes and Quintana completed according to his instructions; the rest must mark the new phase which he foresaw would bring rejuvenating life to benefit his work.

He worked on some of the future problems to guide future architects in case they had no better ideas.[3] He could have built the temple in horizontal zones, but he preferred to do it as he did in order to leave future architects free even to vary the plan if they believed it appropriate. It is also possible that he had a logical desire to terminate the part begun instead of beginning others.

The great architect left no plans of the work which he did not carry out, but what he did build, along with several sketches and clearly defined three-dimensional models, were sufficient data to allow the drawing up of complete plans of his plastic vision and of his solution to the structural problems posed by its execution.[4] But these were not really plans: they were simple idea-sketches or studies of details for the execution of models or perhaps one or two general drawings for publicity purposes.

A FAÇADE AND THREE MONUMENTS. The most precise general drawing which he left was that of the Passion façade. It is a drawing both valuable and surprising in its expressive strength, with a composition based on hyperbolic paraboloids which confirms his predilection for these forms in the moment when he drew up the design, and the aptness that he attributed to them for all plastic ends. This drawing has a precedent in another one which studies the thrust funiculars of the portico and indicates a previous solution (Fig. 521).

In this drawing, which is preserved in photographs (the original was lost in the Civil War), we note two of the master's outstanding qualities. One is his aptitude for representing masses with their three-dimensional form and of light and dark contrasts. The other is his skill in distributing the paraboloids which gives a sort of muscularity to the volumes which are invested with a skeletal rigidity that symbolizes the pathetic qualities of Calvary. In spite of the ambitious scope of the idea of molding the divine tragedy into stone, it must be recognized that the solution he designed was worthy of its objective and that, had Gaudí himself been able to carry it out, it would probably have been developed even further.

To stand in front of this façade, he designed the monument to his friend, the bishop Torras y Bages, with similar geometric control—perhaps even more purified; he sketched his idea for this monument to the side of the mentioned façade drawing. The form is pyramidal, with a triangular base of three inclined stanchions forming an aedicule which houses the seated figure of the prelate. Above this, the extremely elongated pyramid twists into a helix which leads up to the pinnacle where three radially symmetrical but indistinct elements can be distinguished, possibly alluding to the episcopal office or to religious themes. The monument culminates in the fish—the Greek ICHTYS, symbol of Jesus Christ, God, the Immortal Savior. It never fails to amaze me that writers have absolutely ignored Gaudí's commemorative monuments, and have left this theme of his esthetic evolution virtually untouched in their studies. Here we will briefly review this interesting theme.

Aside from his idea for a monument to Jaime I, we have seen his work on that for Dr. Robert, where he made use of intuitively modelled expressionistic forms similar to those of the Batlló and Milá houses. The Casa Milá itself—as we recall—was planned as a pedestal for a monument to the Virgin. After these works, he began to geometrize his decorative surfaces as can be seen in the Güell Park and in the Sagrada Familia. This was more the case in the former, though it is perhaps not so obvious, due to the rusticity of the textures employed. The geometry of the latter's towers was extremely rigid, but also not too apparent due to the simplicity of their almost cylindrical volumes. Nevertheless, one discerns an enthusiastic predilection for geometry which he adopted in some of his models of the period, e.g., those of the columns and the new design for the sacristy, and also in his drawings for the Passion façade and this monument to the bishop where the geometry has become more agile and dynamic, an excellent indication of what the architect was capable of doing within these

2. On the structural mechanics of the Temple, see Bergós, *op. cit.*, p. 147.

3. Martinell, *Conversaciones con Gaudí...* p. 25. I heard him express this idea many times.

4. In the unfortunate days of our Civil War, much of the study material was lost from the workshops of the Temple. After the war, the architect Quintana, working in collaboration with the architects Puig Boada and Bonet Garí who constituted the administrative committee, was able to reconstruct Gaudí's scale models from fragments that remained and to draw up complete plans that reflect the master's ideas.

norms. He was not able to develop this potential fully until he reached the pinnacle of the St. Barnabas tower. The apparently insignificant drawing of a monument thus has the double significance of illustrating a phase in Gaudí's development which is scarce in examples, and of being the antecedent of the famous tower tops.

This monument was conceived for the Passion side, and we have already seen that he planned two others in front of the main façade—one to water and one to fire—for which we have less graphic documentation than for the one to the bishop. It is interesting to observe that the brief sketches which he left show similar characteristics and the same elongated triangular pyramid configuration—the geometric form which we have already seen in the base of the lamps of the Plaza Real and later adopted in the pinnacles of the bell towers.

DESIRE FOR EXCELLENCE. The maestro did not have time to develop the most interesting of his theories fully. Although he left us a great deal in the four towers, the Güell Park, the Colonia Güell, and the Casa Milá, his structural and plastic ideas for the Temple which he saw as the culmination of his life's work had to be expressed in models which represent the substrata of his experience as a builder and of his meditations as a reflective and conscientious person.

The highly valuable models which Gaudí left had to be considered «terminated» once he was gone, but those of us who knew his way of working know that they were actually still «in progress.» He rarely seemed pleased with what he was doing; he always felt that it could be better. On our repeated visits we could observe the progress of his studies which he continued to perfect, even after an acceptable solution had been reached. One of the models which stood for the longest time on the studio table was that of the interior columns for the temple which he gradually modified until he more or less settled on a star-shaped plan with parabolic points moving along an ascending double helix. Had he lived longer, we can suppose that he might have found another, even more perfected solution.

In spite of his persistent desire to improve, some of Gaudí's models were close to definitive —although he himself would never have allowed such a characterization. These include the mentioned columns, the sacristy cupola, and some windows, all of which could be imitated today in worthy homage to the master. The other models—those with a decided neo-Gothic air—would have been of historical interest had they survived, showing as they did how far the master's feelings about the Temple had progressed.

The models that Gaudí constructed over the years for the future resolution of his grandiose vision can be classified into those which looked stylistically backward—those which the author himself later voided—and those which looked forward. These latter deserve to be studied—not only objectively as works of art, but also in a practical sense as an arsenal of possibilities capable of vitalizing present-day artistic trends.

199. FURTHER POSSIBILITIES

In this respect, it is worth-while to consider the numerous structural and esthetic possibilities inherent in Gaudí's studies, as the complement to our examination of his completed works.

Besides their essential structure, we can find in his models the germ of a fertile decorative theory which has not been taken advantage of. In these models we can see a new and pleasing geometry which provides a logical area for study—to be assimilated and used in the creation of original designs, rather than coldly imitated.

Some of these models constitute the final touch to certain aspects of his work. They help us to understand the origin of his ideal of perfection which was animated by the overall rhythm of his theory, as well as where it was going. These models, part of the temple of his dreams, are more valuable for their potential than for what they represent in themselves. Without our understanding of this potential, they would become inert material—mere archaeological artifacts unsuited to a living architecture such as that which Don Antonio practiced and desired in the continuation of his work.

We have repeatedly noted the importance that he gave to the materials he used, to the manner of applying them, and to the quality of certain imponderables which could influence the final result. All of this, which Gaudí considered so spontaneously, would require an absolute and profound understanding of the model on the part of anyone who would follow in his footsteps. But above all, a spirit of modernity would be needed, the same spirit which made the architect Gaudí a man ahead of his time. Gaudinian theory can not survive if its impetus toward the future is changed into a nostalgia for the past. Anyone who should decide to undertake this effort of comprehension would find his labor rewarded by the numerous possibilities afforded by the decorative use of directrices and generatrices, and would have at his command a whole new artistic language. Four decades after the death of this architectural genius, his decorative procedures are still perfectly applicable; and the theory behind them is a gold mine of ornamental possibilities comparable to the ancient arabesque, yet suited to the most modern conceptions.

In ending this overall review, I would like to insist once more on the vision of the future which inspired the master's latest creative ideas. In this Part Three, the reader will have noticed an attraction toward the future which grew progressively stronger from Gaudí's childhood on, beginning with the *eclecticism* of the early years, growing into the *revisionism* of his own historic styles, later overcoming these in his enthusiastic search for *functional expressionism,* and his stage of contemporary *modernismo* which finally led into the ingenious *esthetic-structural theory* which positively projected him into the future—a fact confirmed and emphasized by the study models where he worked on the ideas he would never carry out.

200. THE FOLLOWERS (Figs. 522 - 550)

Gaudí always said that he had no students; that the two who called themselves such were lacking the necessary «coppersmithery» or developed sense of space (he did not mention names). We will thus put aside the idea of a methodical, intentional and didactically oriented professional influence. He also used to say that he wasn't a lecturing man, that he felt himself incapable of preparing a talk,[1] which corroborates his aversion to pedagogical activity; but, on the other hand, whether or not he set out to do so, his presence, his words, and his example in addition to the dazzling novelty of his architectural work, could not help but influence those around him. Those who were his assistants and collaborators, or visitors to his studio, or even other architects who simply admired his architecture at a distance, felt themselves inescapably attracted to the master's methods and theories which they unconsciously incorporated into their own work.

FRANCISCO BERENGUER (Figs. 522, 523). A typical case of personal adaptation can be seen in the work of his friend and compatriot Francisco Berenguer, son of the teacher who in the Reus of his childhood taught him to read his first words. Berenguer was an architecture student, but he did not finish his studies, becoming instead Gaudí's efficient collaborator in the construction of the Sagrada Familia. He had an admirably deep understanding of his friend's style, as can be seen in the fact that his own most famous work, the «Bodegas Güell» in Garraf is frequently mistaken for one of the master's works; it is indeed worthy of such an attribution because of its daring solutions, structural details, and textures in the Gaudinian manner. The work of this architect (and he certainly was an architect, despite the lack of an academic degree) is strongly influenced by the master's standards which he not only knew, but *felt;* thus he acquired the elusive spontaneity which at times makes it difficult to distinguish the work of the two. This can be seen in several of the Colonia Güell buildings, as well as in the altarpiece to San José de Calasanz at Montserrat where he deftly applied Gaudinian norms of proportion, ornamentation, and liturgical detail.

JUAN RUBIÓ BELLVER (Figs. 524, 525). Rubió, also from Reus, worked for years as his collaborator in the Temple offices, in charge of the graphic-static studies of the roof supports before they decided on equilibrated forms; he was also Gaudí's reliable assistant in the

1. Martinell, *op. cit.,* p. 26.

522, 523. F. Berenguer. Two views of the Bodegas Güell in Garraf.

restoration of the cathedral of Mallorca, and he would have been in charge—in collaboration with Sugrañes—of the Misericordia sanctuary in Reus had the design of this reformation been entrusted to Gaudí. Rubió never gave up his own personality, but he did incorporate Gaudinian methods in an obvious manner in some of his works, such as the house called «El Frare Blanc» on the Avenida del Tibidabo with its bold brick projections which are cleverly counterbalanced on the interior; the Golferics house on the Avenida de José Antonio, in exposed rubble and polished, made-to-order brick with an extremely spacious stairway hall; the tiny rough stone chapel of St. Michael in Ripoll; the Santo Cristo asylum in Igualada with textures which recall those of the Güell Park. All of these show a definite Gaudinian influence: Rubió fully accepted the master's ideas up to the point of the three-dimensional surfaces of the Casa Milá, but according to his own statements, he was not favorably impressed with Gaudí's later solutions.

JOSÉ MARÍA JUJOL (Figs. 526-528, 530). Jujol was another assistant who earned the master's complete confidence, especially in ornamental chromatic details. He had a great facility for color, and a portentous domination of forms which he could express with a maximum of manual ability. We have already noted his intervention in Gaudí's decorative projects. Apart from this, his formal concepts also coincided with Gaudí's, and his mind was a fertile source of free structural and ornamental solutions. The great architect found that he could better influence his assistant by stimulating the free development of his dynamic polychrome conceptions than by the dictating of specific motifs.

Jujol was not from Reus, but he had been born in Tarragona—a fact favoring his chromatic and plastic sense, according to Gaudí's theory. As works of Gaudinian influence, we can mention the church of Vistabella near Tarragona, the Gisbert house in Sant Joan Despí, the house at No. 322 on the Avenida del Generalísimo in Barcelona, and a wrought-iron faldstool for Montserrat.[2]

DOMINGO SUGRAÑES. Another native of Reus, Sugrañes was the master's collaborator in the later years. His conscientious and capable understanding of Gaudí's ingenious architectural procedures is only sporadically reflected in his own works. On the estate of Ciriaco Bonet at Salou, he built some interesting roofs on thick platforms similar to those of the second floor at Bellesguard.

JOSÉ CANALETA. This was another of the collaborators who showed little interest in following the Gaudinian path. Nevertheless, he was the author of the two commemorative lamps for the Balmes Centennial in Vich of which we have spoken (XIX - 83, Fig. 64). Even if they were suggested by Gaudí himself, Canaleta's part must have been substantial at a time when he was also working with the master on the Colonia Güell and the Casa Milá.

2. This was sponsored in 1920 by Pedro Mañach who, at the recommendation of the abbot Marcet, asked Gaudí to design it; the latter declined and recommended Jujol as a substitute. Information provided by the monastery and the donor's widow.

524. Juan Rubió. «El Frare Blanc» country house, Barcelona.

525. Juan Rubió. Chapel of San Miguel de la Roqueta in Ripoll.

OTHER FOLLOWERS. In addition to these architects who received the personal influence of the master through their direct collaboration with him and an intimate contact with his work, there were others who (overcoming a certain indifference or hostility which for some surrounded the architect) appreciated the structural or esthetic advantages of the Gaudinian theory and did not hesitate to adopt the new equilibrated forms in their work. Among these were José Puig y Cadafalch, who used equilibrated vaults and arches in the building that he designed for the Codorniu Wine Company in San Sadurní de Noya where one floor is supported in its central zone by iron rods hanging from those arches—a system which recalls that of the hanging staircase in the Palacio Güell; Jerónimo Martorell, whom we saw working in the Gaudinian mode in the Mystery of Glory at Montserrat, shortly thereafter designed the auditorium for the Caja de Ahorros in Sabadell with showy equilibrated arches, and in 1909, he completed a shelter-refuge in Ull de Ter for the Centre Excursionista de Catalunya in Gaudinian forms which still survives; Luis Moncunill Parellada, who built the Masía Freixa in Tarrasa (which later became the Municipal School of Music) with parabolic arches and *tabicada* vaults of accentuated Gaudinian influence; Rafael Masó, who showed his admiration for Don Antonio in many details of his personal work in Gerona and in several

526. J. M. Jujol. Stairway in the Gisbert house at San Joan Despí.

527. J. M. Jujol. Church of Vistabella.

interesting studies which were never realized; and José M. Pericas, who showed the same influence in his first work—the chapel of the Immaculate at Montserrat, ca. 1906—and later in the parish church of Nuestra Señora del Carmen in Barcelona. Although he does not follow Gaudí's structural norms, we can also include Salvador Valeri who shared the master's plastic and chromatic sensibilities.

Those of us who were young architects and frequented Don Antonio's studio during the last years of his life, attracted by our own admiration for him, were logically carried by this same admiration to adopt his principles when they were applicable to our works. Thus, Luis Bonet Garí, in 1929, built the chapel of San Miguel del Cros in Argentona with decoratively effective hyperbolic and parabolic vaults; Puig Boada used Gaudinian forms in the chapel of the Santísimo in the parish church of Gelida, ca. 1928, and later in the sanctuary of Sant Joan de l'Erm; recently he designed the parish church at Balaguer. The works of Bergós include the hermitage of San Antonio near Seo de Urgel, the altar of the Holy Sacrament in the church of San Lorenzo at Lérida, and the house at No. 2 of the Rambla de Cataluña in that same city—all with striking characteristics of the master's work. In 1917, I myself began to

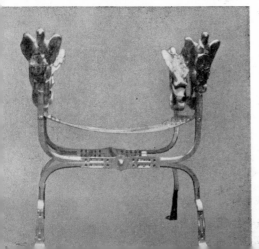

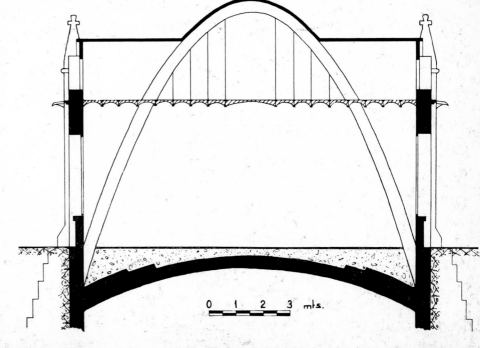

use equilibrated arches in large naves for reasons of economy as has already been mentioned (XXII - 93); some of these naves were covered with *tabicada* vaults resting on the arches, and the results were always economically and esthetically successful. Further influenced by Gaudí's procedures, I also employed vertical *tabicada* vaults in underground and surface level depositories, finding them structurally more advantageous than other current methods.[3]

The work of Gaudí was not only influential in a directly esthetic or structural manner; some architects with a desire for modernity were influenced, perhaps even stimulated, by the expressionism or naturalism of the master, and were liberated by him from historical styles so that they could create with their works a Catalan architectural environment comparable to the contemporary European movements; without imitating Gaudí, they linked his style and Modernismo with the later rationalist trends. Active here in addition to some of the above-mentioned names were Granell, Balcells, Goday, and Puig Gairalt.[4]

3. Such structures can also be found in several private buildings: in the co-operative wine-cellars of Rocafort de Queralt, Nulles, Pinell de Brai, Gandesa, San Cugat del Vallès, and Sant Guim, the last three covered with *tabicada* vaults. The vertical vaults are in these wine-cellars and sixteen other structures.

4. Ribas y Piera, «Consideraciones sobre Gaudí a través de sus obras urbanísticas,» *Cuadernos de Arquitectura*, N.º 63, 1966.

After Gaudí died in 1926, there was a period in which he seemed forgotten in the onslaught of new architectural trends and of the Civil War which produced a relative scarcity of Gaudinian examples. Meanwhile, the intimate circle of friends and admirers awaited the opportunity to revive his memory and re-evaluate his work in conjunction with the forthcoming centennial of his birth, and the 25th anniversary of his death. It was as a result of these commemorations that the name of the architect took its rightful place in history; the fame and content of his work spread abroad and has since awakened extensive interest in the younger generations who have taken up the flag. Although further removed from the maestro himself, they have brought his architecture up to date and applied it in their own buildings.

Besides those of us already mentioned who knew the master personally, we should mention the names of several Gaudinians among more recent generations of Barcelona architects: Bonet Armengol in 1955 developed an interesting structure for the church of Vinyoles d'O-

532. Jerónimo Martorell. Caja de Ahorros in Sabadell. Braced parabolic arches of the auditorium.

533. J. Masó. Sketch of inkstand in embossed metal and enamel.

534. Jerónimo Martorell. Refuge in Ull de Ter.

535. J. Masó. Entrance to a factory in Gerona.

536. Luis Moncunill. Masía Freixa in Tarrasa.

537. Salvador Valeri. Casa Comalat on the Avenida del Generalísimo, 442, in Barcelona. Rear façade.

538. Salvador Valeri. Torre Sant Jordi in Barcelona.

[overleaf]

539. Luis Bonet Garí. Interior of the church of San Miguel del Cros in Argentona.

540. I. Puig Boada. Parish church of Balaguer. Interior.

541. Juan Bergós. Votive hermitage of San Antonio in Seo de Urgel.

542. Isidro Puig Boada. Chapel of the Most Holy in the parish church of Gelida.

543. I. Puig Boada. Exterior view showing the bell tower of the parish church in Balaguer.

445

rís based on hyperboloid and paraboloids which he later carried even further in the Barcelona parish church of San Medín; José Anglada, Daniel Gelabert, and José Ribas working as a team have built the market of La Sagrera in Barcelona with a series of hyperbolic clerestories; Martinell Taxonera covered the presbytery of the parish church of Puerto de la Selva with paraboloids; Dapena Alfonsin, Mas Trilla, and perhaps others of whose activity we are unaware, have also shown analagous tendencies in their work.

We can observe that the earliest of these Gaudinian manifestations were usually based on the structural equilibrated forms which constituted the dominant characteristic of the master's

544. C. Martinell. Warehouses in Sant Guim with a triple nave of equilibrated arches covered with *tabicada* vaults. 1922.

545, 546. C. Martinell. Equilibrated side and central arches of the central nave of the Pinell de Brai wine cellar. 1919.

theory. The more recent ones display the decorative geometric structures which he worked out in his later years and developed in instructive models.

Meanwhile, technicians around the world have made the basic norms of Gaudinism their own, as we have already seen in Part Two (XXXIV - 151). I am not insinuating that they are his followers, nor do I believe that this is the place to wonder how the Gaudinian theories could have been transplanted from the tiny, almost hermetic world of our architect to the world-wide technical arena. The fact is that what Gaudí brought to light at the beginning of the century is now accepted and practiced by the great masters of modern architecture. Be

it mere imitation or be it coincidence of principles with a half-century lag, it can not be denied that this important aspect of present-day structure follows the direction quietly indicated by our architect.

201. STUDIES AND PUBLICITY

Gaudí's structural theory has not only been continued by his followers. His esthetic ideas have always aroused interest, and have been critically analyzed and studied with a great variety of insights. We notice, however that the extent of his fame has gone far beyond the just comprehension of his merits to produce occasional demonstrations of pseudo-cultural enthusiasm which may on the one hand extend the master's fame, but on the other disorient opinion by their erroneous interpretations of his work and ideas.

We must not forget that Gaudí's work requires a certain depth of understanding that can not be based solely on appearances. In spite of several valuable studies, much remains to be done in this area. In the preceding pages, I have tried to bring out the most interesting aspects of his work and his life, without pretending to be exhaustive. Each single work is worthy of a monograph of its own, and we hope that more such specific studies will be

547. Jorge Bonet Armengol. Vault of the church of San Esteban in Vinyoles d'Oris built with hyperboloids and paraboloids. 1955.

548. Jorge Bonet Armengol. Parish church of San Medín with a roof of warped forms of Gaudinian influence.

549. Jorge Bonet Armengol. Parish church of San Medín in Barcelona. Interior.

realized in the coming years by qualified persons and organizations—similar to the work already begun by the Centro de Estudios Gaudinistas.[5]

I would be most pleased if this study would be followed by others which extend, amend, or perfect the various themes covered here from other points of view. In a similar manner, I would not be at all disturbed if the present book were soon found to be out-of-date as regards study and documentation. Gaudí is one of those great men destined to have multiple biographers and studies of his work—not by those seeking mere prestige, but by those who seriously and conscientiously wish to diffuse his esthetic and structural theories. The fame of the architect has been established on an international scale, and any propagandistic activity would now be counter-productive, if not damaging to the artistic content of his work. What is needed now are more intelligent and scholarly studies of his theory without any personal axes to grind.

202.   THE TEMPLE BEGUN

The most profound and spectacular trail which Gaudí left behind was «his» temple which was only just begun—the church which is optimistically referred to as «unfinished» when

5.   The Centro de Estudios Gaudinistas was created as the result of a proposal by myself, within the Cercle Artístic de Sant Lluc and its «Amigos de Gaudí» section, chiefly in order to separate scholarly study of Gaudí's work from mere publicity activities. Later it became a part of the Historical Studies-Section of the Colegio Oficial de Arquitectos de Cataluña y Baleares. Its activities have included numerous lectures, visits to the master's buildings, and radio programs directed by specialized architects and professionals. The work of the years 1958-1960 was published by the Colegio de Arquitectos; and in the year 1960-61 it sponsored a contest for students of architecture to design Gaudinian projects and decoration, with prizes donated by the Barcelona School of Architecture.

550. José Anglada, Daniel Gelabert, and José Ribas. Hyperbolic lanterns of the La Sagrera market, Barcelona, 1966.

the end is not even a glimmer on the horizon. I have said elsewhere that this infant work is the most transcendental artistic problem ever to confront Barcelona,[6] and I do not say this as a complaint. But the great difficulty is the only negative side of this work of world-wide importance whose prestige honors Barcelona and all of Spain. It is a work which touches us with a mixture of joy and sadness; because of the beauty it contains and the sveltness of its towers, and because of the enormous amount that remains to be done and the difficulty of ensuring a worthy continuation. And something graver still: the seed of controversy which surrounded the master's work seems to have invaded the decision on the continuation of the temple. Not even Gaudí himself when he lived succeeded in making the work pleasing to everyone, but he, with his genius, at least knew how to overcome his detractors. Today, without the master's prestige it is logical that the disagreements persist.

When the Centro de Estudios Gaudinistas heard of this diversity of opinion in 1959, it opened the subject for discussion with a lecture by the architect Oriol Bohigas on «Problems concerning the Continuation of the Sagrada Familia,»[7] and at various subsequent meetings to discuss the same topic, the following positions were defined:

A) Continuation of the work with absolute adherence to Gaudí's models.

B) Adaptation of Gaudí's principles to modern techniques and needs, giving free rein to present and future architects.

C) Complete abandonment of Gaudí's plans, and the construction of a simple parish church; or the discontinuation of work altogether, leaving what has been accomplished as a monument to his architecture.

Position B was that most favored by those in attendance,[8] and also that based on the master's own desires as he foresaw the contribution of new generations of architects who would revitalize his own ideas with their youth.

At present, construction continues on the Passion façade under the supervision of the architects Quintana (lately deceased), Bonet Garí, and Puig Boada who are basing their work on Gaudí's drawings.

203. HIS EXAMPLE

After this analysis of Gaudí's life and work, we are struck by the exemplariness of both—a quality which must surely impress every sensitive person who has studied them with us.

His austere life is edifying—a mirror of persistence in the struggle to control his indomitable character and to harness it at the service of the kindness which—in spite of his genius—he practiced on his subordinates, workmen, and friends. He set a standard of generosity and and kept nothing for himself, even renouncing his salary in the work which took most of his energy and to whose perfection he gave himself completely.

In his professional work he was no less exemplary. The esthetic sparks which radiated out from his youthful years he protected, developed, and perfected through the painful years as a salaried draftsman and into his own architectural career where he translated them into works. His thirst for perfection was insatiable, and without disdaining the past he looked toward the future, quietly immersing himself in his work without presumption or complaint.

6. «La Sagrada Familia y su continuación. Conveniencia de un Centro de Estudios Gaudinistas,» lecture in the «Antonio Gaudí Chair» on March 23, 1957, published in *Ensayo* N.º 8, (Bulletin of The Escuela de Artes y Oficios Artisticos in Barcelona).

7. January 27, 1959, in the auditorium of the Fomento de las Artes Decorativas.

8. See, *Gaudí*, by the Centro de Estudios Gaudinistas (Barcelona: 1960); lecture by Sr. Bohigas and the following meetings.

More aware of facts than of social repercussions, he became the sort of architect who only cares about the perfection of his work and is unconcerned by hopes for glory.

I imagine that it would be extremely difficult to find another case of similar professional dedication with so much integrity and balance. Gaudí's edifying exemplariness and the path which he blazed during his lifetime will serve as guides for those who feel worthy to follow.

At the beginning of this section we mentioned synthesis. For Gaudí, synthesis was the sign of perfection. Just as he wanted to give his works that all-important sense of unity, so he was unable to separate his personal life from the professional. All was one and the same, ruled by evangelical standards of sacrifice and renunciation and impelled by faith and charity which helped him to conquer all impurities.

APPENDICES

GAUDÍ'S SCHOOL TRANSCRIPT
ARCHIVE OF THE INSTITUTO DE TARRAGONA

In the City of Reus on this 14th day of September of the year 1862, the Professors signing this statement proceeded to examine (for entrance purposes) the pupil D. Antonio Gaudí y Cornet.—*Questions on Christian Doctrine.*—What is the Baptism? Can an unbaptized person receive the other Sacraments? Why? What does the water signify? How many types of baptism are there? Which one is by water? Which one is by blood? By fire? etc. —*Questions on Castilian Grammar*—What is a preposition? What use is the Castilian language? Why is the article not used with proper nouns? Conjugate the verb *dispertarse.* Sentence, maxim or period: When you enter the church you will take off your hat.—*Arithmetic Problems.*—6789356 ×38=257995528. Addition of four integers.

Signature of the pupil, Antonio Gaudí. Signed and Sealed. Signatures of the Honorable Professors.— As a result of the examination he was admitted. Franco. S. Bru. Elías Jové del Castillo. Valentín Oliver Escolapio. Signed and Sealed.

SUMMARY OF THE REST OF THE TRANSCRIPT

First Grade. 1863-64 (11 years)
First Year Latin and Castilian . . . . mediano (average)
Christian Doctrine and Religious History . . . . mediano
Arithmetic Principles and Problems . . . . suspenso (suspended)
Idem. (Special Examination) . . . . reprobado (failed)

Second Grade. 1864-65 (12 years)
Descriptive Geography . . . . suspenso
Idem. (Special Examination) . . . . mediano

Third Grade. 1865-66 (13 years)
First Year Greek . . . . notablemente aprovechado
            (remarkably diligent)
Geometry and Arithmetic . . . . notable-sobresaliente
            (remarkable-outstanding)
Principles of Arithmetic . . . . notablemente aprovechado

Fourth Grade. 1866-67 (14 years)
Psychology . . . . notablemente aprovechado
Descriptive Geography and General History . . . . . . notablemente aprovechado
Religion and Ethics . . . . bueno (good)
Rhetoric and Poetics . . . . notablemente aprovechado

Fifth Grade. 1867-68 (15 years)
Mathematics . . . . notablemente aprovechado
Christian Doctrine and Religious History . . . . aprobado (passed)

[I am indebted to my friend D. Joaquín Avellá, the director of the Instituto de Tarragona, for facilitating my research in the archive of the school. I am also grateful to my good friend José Batalla Doménech who transcribed the documents referring to Gaudí; see Avellá, «Gaudí en los Archivos del Instituto de Tarragona,» *Diario Español,* (Tarragona: July 2, 1960.) C. M.]

ARCHIVE OF THE INSTITUTO BALMES IN BARCELONA

1868-69 School Year, Special Student (16 years)
June 3. Basic Physics . . . . aprobado
June 25. Natural History . . . . aprobado

MEMORIAL IN THE ARCHIVES OF THE REAL MONASTERIO DE POBLET
POBLET. ITS RESTORATION PLAN

Many and small are the towns around Poblet. If its restoration is to be undertaken, the workers employed should definitely live in the monastery, inhabiting the ancient buildings and workshops. There they would form the basis for the establishment of a community: once the work was over, a house and a parcel of land could be given either free or at a low price to each of the families, and they would establish a permanent town on the edge of the monastery.

The restoration must not go beyond the confines of Poblet; that is, all of the objects, artistic or otherwise, which need to be constructed must be made within the monastery walls, calling in artists to take charge of the work and inviting them to stay on with their families; therefore craftsmen must be sought whose social position allows for an easy change of domicile, so the various elements necessary to establish a town can be gathered together.

A general store could be set up at the monastery's expense where the workers could stock up on the things they need. The goods would be bought at wholesale prices and sold retail to the community, benefiting the monastery which would thus regain half the day's wages in profits.

A café could be established where the people would come together and grow to love the nascent town; it would also attract neighbors from nearby towns to gather in the monastery on holidays. Poblet houses many notable artistic beauties which will be destroyed by the inflexible hands of time unless someone comes to their aid, and there are many more treasures to be found scattered throughout the various towns of the province of Tarragona which must be returned to the monastery in the course of restoration. These would attract a large number of artists interested in studying the Renaissance genius which is so well illustrated in Poblet, and they would doubtless establish their homes there, thus increasing the size of the rapidly developing town.

[Two paragraphs omitted in English edition. Ed.]

PARTS

While two day-laborers would busy themselves with clearing the debris from the church, cloisters, halls, etc. leveling out the floors where needed and tearing down whatever was beyond repair, the masons could work on restoring the kitchen, the former boys' dormitory for the use of the workmen, and the towers where the directors of the work would sleep.

Once the walls and portals are repaired and the necessary doors put in place, the non-artistic part of the church could be restored; then the cloister, the dorne, the sacristy, and so on, with all of the areas of the enclosure—ending with the defense towers.

Once this was completed, three master-masons would fix up one or two of the buildings to serve as workshops for the technical trades—for the locksmiths, iron workers, carpenters, etc.; then they could finish the churches and chapels and finally the hospital, the bag-making factory, the abbot's palace, and the rest outside the walls.

Since water would be urgently needed, the large stream which passes by the monastery and flows into the river could be used. Later it would be necessary to discover the ancient pipelines which are surely to be found in their proper places. The water could be made to pass through a temporary conduit made of roofing-tile, which would run through the two plazas, the church, the cloister, and the nuns' locutorium before ending up in the river. Thus it would serve all parts of the monastery. Sand to make mortar can be found in the nearby river-bed.

Once the functional parts are terminated, work should immediately begin on the artistic restoration. In preparation for this, someone will have to be hired or else one of the directors will go to Asia to charter a ship and load it with ebony and other expensive and precious woods. Four good sculptors would be sought to begin the restoration—two for the wooden objects and the other two for the rest of the sculpture.

A velvet-loom would be set up to manufacture the mourning velvets for the church; another would be used to weave damascene hangings, and there would be three or four common looms to make the canvas and cotton materials for the daily use of the monastery.

When necessary, marble and jasper would be extracted from the quarries.

EXPENSES

The expenses of the restoration of the non-artistic parts of the monastery would be minimal. Since the monastery has not been liberated from the ruins which surround it on all sides and which have fallen from walls and roofs which have been torn down or caved in, it is logical that these walls and roofs can be rebuilt with the same stone that was used in the first place. Erection of a brick-maker's kiln outside of the cloister within the monastery itself will eliminate the necessity of using horses to transport such materials. Two mules owned by the monastery will be enough for the daily transportation of whatever is required by a team of 10 or 12 workmen.

First of all, a call should go out for at least three master-masons, one master-carpenter, a lock-smith, and a brick-maker—all with their corresponding apprentices and assistants.

For a moderate sum of three of four *reales,* one of the day-laborer's wives could be hired to run the grocery store.

A shepherd and an assistant would be paid to look after the cattle.

Caring for the other domestic animals—which is really more fun than work—could be taken care of by the directors themselves, or perhaps one of the day-laborers could be put in charge of them.

The sale of guidebooks, catalogues, etc. would be in the hands of the directors.

In order to cultivate the lands bought by and ceded to the monastery, a brigade of prisoners could be requested from the government for the first year, while two men will clear out the existing ruins; help would be provided in some of this work, such as cleaning the tombs, pantheons, the palace of King Martin, etc. by the directors of the works.

PRINCIPAL AND FIRST YEAR EXPENSES

	Principal	Productive
Mule	800 rs.	400
Donkey	200 rs.	
Hens	30 rs.	20
Locksmith's materials	200 rs.	
Carpenter's materials	600 rs.	
Printing	800 rs.	1 600
1 Cart	200 rs.	
Shovels, Picks, etc.	1 000 rs.	
Grocery Store	10 000 rs.	5 000
Various expenses	1 170 rs.	500
Unforeseen	10 000 rs.	
Total	25 000 rs.	Total 7 520

DAILY WAGES FOR 300 DAYS

3 Masons 8 reales		7 200
1 Carpenter 10 reales		3 000
3 Apprentices 4 reales		3 600
1 Grocery clerk 4 reales		1 200
2 Laborers 8 reales		4 800
20 Laborers for 6 months 6 reales		18 000
Masonry materials		1 000
Grain for Cereals (?)		1 000
Total		39 000

Principal	25 000 rs.	Taxes	30 000 rs.
Wages	39 800 rs.	Productive	7 520 rs.
	64 800 rs.		37 520 rs.

Expenses	64 800
Income	37 520
	27 280

[The memorial for the restoration of Poblet as planned by the youths Gaudí, Toda, and Ribera is preserved in the archive of the monastery at Poblet to whose reverend Abbot and Community I am indebted for help in my research. It is twelve pages long and is accompanied by the sketch of the general plan reproduced in the text (Fig. 12). I have transcribed only the parts that refer to the restoration work—i.e., that part in which Gaudí was probably most directly involved. C. M.]

APPENDIX III

NOTES FROM GAUDÍ'S TRANSCRIPT
IN THE ARCHIVES OF THE SCHOOL OF SCIENCE IN BARCELONA

October 11, 1869. A request in his own hand asking that he be allowed to register out of turn (not having been able to make the journey in time due to «political circumstances») for the subjects of Advanced Algebra, Geometry, Plane and Solid Trigonometry, Analytical Geometry—Plane and Solid. He states that he is 17 years old, a native of Reus, and that he wishes to study those subjects required for entrance into the Architecture program. (In the document the final s of the word «subjects» is crossed out.)

In the application for registration, which was allowed that very day, he repeats that he is a native of Reus, as he does in each of his successive applications; he gives his residence as Plaza de Moncada, 12, storefront, with Pancracio Barnusell of the same address as his guarantor.

In the regular 1869-70 examination period he passed Advanced Algebra and Analytic Geometry.

1870-1871 School Year. He is living at No. 10 Calle Espadería. Guarantor: Francisco Gaudí at the same address, 13 January 1871. He was registered for Differential Calculus, Rational Mechanics, Descriptive Geometry, and General Chemistry. He passed Calculus and Descriptive Geometry and was suspended in Rational Mechanics.

1871-1872 School Year. 19 years old, living at No. 16, Calle Montjuich de San Pedro, 4th floor. Guarantor: Francisco Gaudí Serra of the same address, September 25, 1871. He was registered in Geography, Geodesy, Physics, and Natural History. He passed the last one.

September 25, 1873. He requests a certificate of studies completed. Completion of Advanced Algebra, Plane and Solid Trigonometry, Plane and Solid Analytical Geometry, Descriptive Geometry, and Integral and Differential Calculus. He was given it the same day.

October 14, 1874. He asks to be allowed to take a second exam in Rational Mechanics which he had suspended the previous September. He is allowed and passes.

RESUMÉ OF GAUDÍ'S ACADEMIC TRANSCRIPT IN THE ARCHIVES
OF THE ESCUELA TECNICA SUPERIOR DE ARQUITECTURA DE BARCELONA

Entrance Year	Regular Exam	Special Exam	Year
Line Drawing		aprobado	73-74
Figure		aprobado	73-74
Preparatory Year			
Plaster casting		aprobado	74-75
Architectural detailing		aprobado	74-75
Shading and Perspective	aprobado		74-75
First Professional Year			
Stereotomy	aprobado		74-75
Resistance of Materials	aprobado		74-75
Properties of Materials	aprobado		75-76
History of Architecture	aprobado		75-76
Drawing of Architectural Groupings		aprobado	73-74
Second Professional Year			
Applied Construction Materials	notable		75-76
Art Theory	aprobado		75-76
Hydraulics	aprobado		74-75
First Year of Projects		sobresaliente	74-75
Third Professional Year			
Machines and Engines	aprobado		74-75
The Study of Building from a Social Point of View	aprobado		75-76
Technology	aprobado		76-77
Second Year of Projects		notable	75-76

Application of the Physio-Natural Sciences
    to Architecture . . . .   aprobado   76-77
Topography . . . .   aprobado   76-77
Architectural Law . . . .   aprobado   76-77
Third Year of Projects . . . .   notable   76-77

Comprehensives

First Exercise, October 22, 1877 . . . . .
Second Exercise (Final), January 4, 1878 . .   approved by a majority
Title issued in Madrid, March 15, 1878.

[The suspensions which Gaudí himself claimed are not listed in the transcript. They may be in the exam lists which I have not had the opportunity to consult. C. M.]

[Appendix IV in the Spanish edition is Gaudí's memorial about the design of street lamps, approximately 4 pages in length, here omitted. G.R.C.]

APPENDIX IV

NOTEBOOK IN THE MUNICIPAL MUSEUM IN REUS

«ORNAMENTATION»
August 10, 1878

I propose to study ornamentation seriously.

My goal is to make it interesting and intelligible.

Have spoken with Oliveras; seems to have no clear idea of where he is headed.

Visits to Cathedral during July to make casts of the dome, but annoying without direct results.

Examination of Alhambra photographs, observing that the columns, being small in diameter, have been shortened by adding moldings to the shaft which extends the length of the capitals; I believe that the application of colors, especially to the base, aids in giving the effect of a very short shaft section. Idem in the various halls where small columns are used for supporting the vaults in order to enlarge the room or member, giving play to the imagination just as the Gothic canopies do. Idem the superimposed bands with lines traveling in opposite directions, that is, if the interior one follows the design or motif in a longitudinal direction, the exterior follows the latitude—this last occuring in the Arabic inscriptions.

To be interesting, ornamentation should represent objects which remind us of poetic ideas, and which constitute motifs.

Such motifs are historical and legendary ones, those representing activities, emblems, fables, and those related to man and his life, actions, and passions. Naturalistic motifs can represent the animal, plant, and topographic kingdoms.

They can also be geometric in the forms of the masses, surfaces, and lines, or in combinations of all of these with contrasts which can be employed by Proportion—one of the principal properties of Beauty.

In order that an object be very beautiful, it is necessary that its form contain nothing superfluous, but only the material conditions which make it useful; we must take into account both the material and the use which will be made of it, and from this the general form will arise; concern for the preservation of the object and material will determine many parts of the form, and the others will be determined by contrast, i.e., giving it a form which, while pleasant in itself, makes its neighboring ones much more pleasant still. And if satisfactory forms do not emerge from this process—due to adverse dynamic or atmospheric conditions—then we can call to our aid purely ornamental motifs to elevate the form, perhaps concealing its structural and material parts and bringing out the form dictated solely by the complete satisfaction of some need. These are circumstances which are precisely determined by the «character» of the object.

It could be said that character is the criterion for ornamentation.

Nowadays, the character of an object depends on the nationality, the customs, and the splendor of him who uses it; public objects must have a serious character which differs from that of an everyday object used in the home. The character of a public object must correspond to its purpose; in embellishing it, the gravity, grandiosity of form, and simplicity must not be diluted by means of softer and easily decipherable ideas, but rather, geometry should be used; the former are preferable for private themes.

Geometric ornamentation is especially suited for public and religious buildings; Greek temples and other buildings exhibit rectangular plans, conical columns, square metopes, triangular pediments; the ornamentation consists of innumerable meanders which decorate the members, palmettes—which are no more than lines perpendicular to the horizontal band that they follow, etc. Cathedrals have the circular arches of the near-parabolic vaults, the combination of circles in the openwork, the pyramidal pinnacles, and other terminations as well as the geometric forms of the tracery.

When the forms are dryly geometric and are frequently repeated, they have need of a good contrast: an object very free in form which is not subjected to any general shape. In the temple of Apollo at Phigelia the accentuated form of the corner abaci, new squares and the lower circular molding, the meander of the abacus and the gorge, and the heavy striations of the column shaft with repeated base moldings, all make necessary the introduction of palmettes which resemble nature as closely as possible and call, in addition, for stilettos which dominate and unite the neutral surfaces of the moldings enumerated.

When a close-fitting gorge is attached to the cusp of the fluting below the simple and structurally determined form of the Doric capital, only the most conventional form from nature is needed; the painted palmettes constitute the most daring element, in comparison with the meander of the abacus and with the neighboring lines as the principal ornamentation—not in formal richness, but in content—the themes of the metopes, those of the tympanum, and the corners and crest of the pediment. By way of contrast we have the monument to Lysicrates with exaggeratedly geometric forms: the square socle contains some steps consisting of prisms and more prisms, above which there is a heavy cylinder—which only serves to give it the appearance of being larger than it is—and the cones of the columns; nothing could come after so much pure geometry, which is so imposing as such, but the most precisely represented nature; but the temple of Apollo could not be without its acanthus, with flowers and stems; the roof was justly converted into an unequalled tapestry of leaves in that model of size, material, line, composition, execution, and lighting—that marvelously Greek creation, the Erechtheum.

The capital of the Erechteum is so appropriate to the theme with which it deals that the moldings are enriched with chiaroscuro, the palmette gorges with carved work and other perennials, and the striations are more pronounced; as a consequence everything in it abounds with the indispensable geometric form, and the most frequent way of dominating so much movement and providing the culminating touch is a recollection of nature—something like the beginning of the clew to beauty and forms.

The Erechtheum is a temple whose interest is contained mainly in the porch where four to six columns constitute the principal element, since there is no major sculpture in the tympanum; its columns had to be as graceful as the human figure, yet rigid as those of the Parthenon, with their small size compensated for by a certain richness—not the richness of damask, but that of chiaroscuro relief and contour in every single part: small dimensions should be compensated by a display of carved and highly elaborate form, for common sense tells us that simple forms are characteristic of magnificence and that abundant ornamentation is more properly found in small masses.

Great masses in themselves are always an element of elevated ornamentation, e.g., the two-meter drums of the Parthenon columns—what ornamentation could possibly be wanted for them, or for the capital whose abacus was higher than an athlete's elbow, and whose echinus would have made his footprint look myopic?—what better ornamentation than to let this grandiosity shine forth in all of its purity?— and what could be more perfect than to create this, if possible, through subtle but energetic profiles which are delicate in parts to indicate the fineness and rich quality of the material, and elsewhere emphasize its grandiosity?

Ornamentation has been, is, and will be polychromatic; nature does not present us with any object that is monotonously uniform, not in the vegetable, geological, topographical, nor animal kingdom—the contrast is always more or less vivid; it follows that therefore we must necessarily color, partially or completely, all architectonic members; this coloration may disappear, but then the hand of time will see that it is replaced by that proper and precious one of antiquity. Who does not recall the golden tonality range of the stones of the Mediterranean regions? Does not a recently finished building display a repellent coldness? Who, for example, would dare to compare the brand-new façades of the University to the walls of the Lonja, those of the Diputación to the Ayuntamiento, the cold monuments of white marble in the Plaza de Palacio to the retrochoir of the Cathedral on the Plaza del Duque? Compare the Cathedral tones with the vestibule of the University or the recently-cut stones of the Diputación and you will be convinced that while the natural coloration of time is not present, painting is indispensable; this is equally adapted to the rigidity and severity of the great masses in the luxuriant hollows in the profuse ornamentation. This reminds me of something which proves how important color is, even in small masses: the St. George sculpture on the Diputación building is entirely monochrome, of the coldest color imaginable; the balcony on which it is placed is of the same material; but in the ornamentation of the pillars of the balustrade, the red cross of the Diputación stands out; comparing the two objects, the St. George comes out cold, confused, unpolished, and unfitting as the principal focus of the façade.

Architectural painting at certain points has the great advantage of lending energy to the outlines and structural elements, thus giving a clearer idea of the object.

The purpose of sculptural ornamentation is always to increase the importance of surfaces without weighing them down; the bosses, gargoyles, and moldings of the window-less lateral façade of the Belén church make it one great ornament; this is achieved because the smaller objects—understand that size is considered in relation to man's special criterion—are the more decorated, more profusely sculpted (the furniture, for example), not because cost was any obstacle (proved by the use of marble) but because it was logical. Some French buildings depart from this: the Opera where the attempt was made to give the exterior elevations great movement, as is commonly known, with the result being the dwarfing of the general lines —if these were defective in the first place, they were not improved by amending them with triturations which do no more than call on an overload that obfuscates the defects.

The ornamentation is only a part: although essential in order to give it character, it is, nevertheless, nothing more than the meter and rhythm of the poetry. A concept is expressed in many ways, but it becomes obscure and distilled when we introduce, willy-nilly, obligatory accessories which attack good intelligence and reason.

The most important requirement for an object that is to be considered beautiful is that it fulfill the purpose for which it is destined, not as if it were a matter of gathering together problems solved individually and assembling them to produce a heterogeneous result, but rather with a tendency toward a unified solution where the material conditions, function, and character of the object are taken care of and synthesized, and once the good solutions are known it is a matter of taking that one which is most fitting to the object as deduced from the need to attend to its function, character, and physical conditions.

Use. It can be said that use is the purpose for the creation of an object; character is the definition of its aesthetic-moral condition; the physical conditions are those which concern such matters as durability, conservation, etc.

We can group all of these into the broad definition of ornamentation and which we have indicated with character and physical laws.

Let us examine Character which, when public, can be Religious, Civil, or Military, and when private has to do with the family, its care, needs, and convenience, as well as the representation of it and its members.

Religious Character tends always toward the more grandiose, for its objective is a mystery, a quality which is achieved by infinite means, and obliges us today to consider religion in relation to society; the time is past when faith and enthusiasm could build an infinite number of cathedrals, perhaps indicating that religious nature is a bit indecisive, that religious objects are the slaves of a profane idea—art: those who make temples do not insist that they contain those characteristics proper to a terrible God who sacrifices himself for his creation, that they be mansions for the Omnipotence of the thousands of millions of solar systems, nor do they make the object that of achieving in an elevated manner which is the Bloodless Sacrifice (Holy Mass), but rather they seek to imitate the forms of other ages which, however magnificent they may have been for that time—we can still perceive something of that sacred incense—do not speak our language; what we see in the reproduction of those forms is more the memory of sculpted forms—reminiscences of the men over whom the idea soars revealing the Divinity to us in only a vague manner; i.e., in continuing the Gothic styles we adore the positive qualities and defects of the Middle Ages themselves, and its plastic forms bring to mind the history and tradition of its peoples; it could be said that they are more concerned with romantic ideas than religious ones, giving rise to religious protection of the art of past ages and an art which imposes itself as a style rather than an art which identifies with the religion in order to give it expression, as should be the case. Thus modern conceptions are those which we could call purely architectural—neither painting nor sculpture lends evidence of the mysteries of the holy religion; nor are the representations of the martyrs given their deserved place in the brilliant and sublime painting of the Renaissance; not even the formerly protected symbol is given its proper importance, but rather all is conceded, ridiculous as it seems, to the cabbage leaf, to the acanthus, to the openwork and to the molding—to all of these as purely plastic form. Perhaps such accessories, which as details do not conform to our way of life, are supposed to infuse religiosity? Where are those expressive reliefs which remind us here of martyrdom and there of mystery, charity, or contemplation? Now nothing but saints are represented, and even these are only an excuse to put up a pedestal or a little ornamented dais, i.e., as a pretext to introduce an irrelevant, purely plastic form. In addition, the methods of execution have completely changed: then all of the idealized embellishment of those churches could be realized at a much less exaggerated price, whereas the tiniest sculpture today, the most insignificant capital which will later be hidden in the shadows of the nave, cost a great deal due to the elevated cost of labor, and it has become impossible to lavish ornamentation (moldings, openwork, etc.). Even sculpture itself: therefore we are obliged to be reserved and even stingy once we have adopted the style, and we necessarily produce incomplete buildings which tell us nothing because the resources at our disposal are completely different. In spite of all of these sacrifices, can our modern buildings be compared with those of ancient times? Can we possibly compare the Sacre Coeur in Paris to the Cathedral of the same city, and is it not left even further behind by the mere mentioning of Rheims, Cologne, Strasbourg, Chartres where we have the grandiose portals, the seven towers, and the immense vaults; we must note that these are a result of the initiative of a population or of a prince, and that the Sacre Coeur is, or will be, a result of the effort of all Christianity, and all of this to obtain an enormous monument which will not express what we want, and can be placed only on a level with those which it wishes to imitate; this is because the conditions of those days of old have disappeared. On the other hand, we are ignoring those conditions which could give great results, letting them wander aimlessly in a hybrid and purposeless state, isolating them nowadays from their sublime manifestations. And don't say that there is no one who feels this genre sufficiently; suffice it to recall the Burial of St. Stephen in the last exposition in Madrid, the latest drawings of Rosales for the Four Evangelists, etc., etc. Decoration which, in the best way, so well suits the character of our own sacrosanct religion with its spirituality; just as Paganism is preponderant in sculpture, i.e., in tangible forms, in the earthly viewpoint with its demi-gods and heroes, Christianity is suited as a mold for its conceptions, to trace them spiritually in an impalpable atmosphere in a building without relief, but rather all expression, all moral affections. Note that this is perfectly realizable—that there exist highly qualified painters is undeniable; there are innumerable youths who would place themselves under their tutelage in order to learn the secrets of art, and one day become masters themselves. The price and cost of such a decorative system could be made more reasonable, and could be made effective in relation to the ceremonies and rites and customs which we could call religious.

In the centuries of Gothic architecture, we know that the custom of sermons was not general, only at the time of the Reformation did the preaching Orders emerge, and the custom began to be established; thus, at that time the church was only a place for prayer and the exercise of religious ceremonies: it was not a seat of learning like today where one goes to be instructed and morally fortified by means of the lectures. Before, the principal purpose was ceremony, but now another has been added, that of discourse; therefore satisfaction of the needs for fulfilling this purpose is required. We must also mention the nightly functions, which are now more frequent because of our daily occupations; it is unnecessary to recount the advantages of paintings when artificial lighting is used, nor the sustenance which such graphic scenes give to the spoken word. That most easily distracted sense—hearing—is made more attentive when guided by sight; this is a situation even more worthy of being considered insofar as not so many years ago, and even to this day in some cultures, the custom was observed of drawing all curtains during the sermon to make the church almost completely dark—a darkness which would aid the imagination to see vaguely scenes related to the holy discourse. All that has been mentioned was nothing more or less than the ideal of some of the Renaissance churches, was later confused with completely opposite ideas, i.e., the application of forms and members so exaggeratedly revealed that, logically, the chiaroscuro of painting seemed to be phantasmagoric and seen through a gaseous substance; in addition, the requisite order of the ornamentation obstructed the sites most *a propos* to receive such paintings which found themselves relegated to the most inconvenient places in respect to light and visibility. Let us continue to consider these problems so relevant to our day and instead of complaining alone, let us try to find solutions to them—no small task.

Today, all that tends to elevate the cost of labor tends to lower the cost of the materials. Everyone knows that since the beginning of this century, the daily wage has doubled, tripled, and quadrupled in all branches of industry. Doubtless this is due to the introduction of machinery which produces great quantity in a short period of time. If only it were possible for us to employ machines, the cost of labor would be reduced; in regard to materials, their price has definitely gone down due to the ease with which they can now be extracted and transported. The Romans, who needed large buildings, did not hesitate to use the machines of their time in constructing their baths and circuses, i.e., the slaves: the military organization was not able to absorb the great abundance of craftsmen, and so they were used in the manufacture of rubble and concrete. How much better we could make such works today, having as we do the powerful machines with which to break up the stone and form the concrete, the strong portable engines to cover great heights, and everywhere around quarries to produce hydrolized limes which are so well-suited to the manufacture just indicated; this is not to mention the stone finishing which can also be obtained by means of machinery. We save on the system and we are miserably stingy with the sculpture; i.e., let us not lavish money on meaningless things, but stick to what is morally and materially indispensable. Products modeled in terracotta and glazed, or in majolica, can be of great service in giving both character and durability, and they can be obtained at a very reasonable and convenient price; then we would be in the position of freely possessing elements with which to give great character to religious buildings. It should not be seen as an obstacle that the secondary industries will have to be created, because they produce markets for products which would be difficult for industry to produce. For our part let us see that the means are normalized in order to have greater elements; those who have worked for a few years in this cause have seen the coming of painted windows; the casting of iron has not been around long either, nor the process for sawing marble, etc. Right here we have several factories for the mechanical production of roof tiles which require special machines. Now we come to the materials that best give character to religious buildings, beginning with...

The exterior character of churches.

The position generally given to churches can be said to be in harmony with their importance and their use; we can impute nothing to their general placement.

The exterior should be in harmony with the interior, and an attempt should be made to make the predominant form that of the pyramid.

The materials used for this purpose are: unfinished ashlar masonry, statuary in some cases, brick and terracotta for relief and ornamentation, bronze in some places, in others iron and lead, and, sparingly, wood. In the general forms—grand portals sheltering statuary, buttresses acknowledging the thrusts of the vaults and arches—complete harmony between the structural system and the representation of religious ideas; do not conceal the great masses, but rather, on the contrary, keep their magnitude in mind, dissolving, if necessary, their imposing effect by means of fitting and simple ornamentation. The forms of the exterior should mirror those of the interior; arches and vaults of equilibrated form, brick ribs, and rubble or *tabicada* spandrels can be raised on great pillars; domes can play an important part in providing high windows, well-suited to illuminate the paintings on the walls and the vaults themselves; on the exterior, materials of glazed terracotta can satisfactorily cover all of these forms.

As to the form of the plan and the means of covering it, we will recommend the spherical form inscribed in a square—producing four pendentives and four pillars to support them—as an extremely open form; considering the structure, in each of the corners a quarter squinch can be employed which receives the upper thrusts; these can also be sustained by two other pendentives to achieve the square, these forming a cross with the central dome into whose four cavities would fit four independent chapels which would enhance the effect of the whole. Taking the dome as the means to cover a square space, it is natural that this element can be applied in a number of ways, depending on the grandiosity of the project—from the most simple church with one single cupola to the more grandiose forms with a combination of domes.

The main nave of the church has something to do with the unity of the Divinity, and a central dome would also serve to indicate this same unity.

A church without a cupola does not have the grand exterior and interior importance of the crossing and its transept.

The semi-spherical dome with a lantern takes on notable grandiosity and spirituality; it causes the heaviness and massiveness of the form to disappear; a rib vault has esthetic need of a key at the crossing to emphasize an important point and the succession of points in the overall perspective.

The large nave of the church grows by comparison to the lateral naves, in the same way in which a cupola becomes larger next to barrel vaults.

The cupola—the place from which the light comes—lifts one to great ideas and thoughts; its construction on four pillars produces a natural horizontal division which gives it even greater height.

But the greatest advantage of the spherical cupola is that it is able to absorb the thrusts by means of an iron ring to the extent that the materials have acquired the necessary consistency, and then, although that ring destroys the unity of the cupola, it can be built with material prepared by machine, and aided by molds and structural frames.

By studying the thrusts and counter-forces, these could be applied as part of general structural studies to give extremely valuable results; it is known that they did not directly apply such theories in medieval times for they were not understood; they built their buildings intuitively and practically, but we could well take advantage of such advances in order to create structures appropriate to the progress of our times, taking advantage of our facilities and avoiding the inconveniences which can possibly not be overcome.

Returning to the exterior character of religious buildings we can say, in respect to placement:

Being surrounded with private or public buildings and all the rest, it should have a plaza in front of the entrance, our cities have a great deal of outdoor life, and as a consequence the church should have greater richness than the other buildings, and also in relation to other times when the particular circumstances required less dignity. To maintain the quality of the temple it is necessary to give it an external appearance that is refined and worthy, so long as it not be overloaded with ornamentation. We can see that this was already done in the Middle Ages which did not neglect the great monuments in any way: if some of our Cathedrals today exhibit a rather unpleasant or uncared-for appearance, it is due to the later additions which they have suffered.

[This continues for 12 more pages in the Spanish edition. Some of those portions omitted here can be found, also originally translated by Miss Rohrer but then more freely rendered in the 1973 issue of *VIA* (magazine of the Graduate School of Fine Arts of the University of Pennsylvania). For analysis of the contents, see IX-31 and XXV-110.—G.R.C.]

DIARY NOTES FROM THE END OF NOVEMBER 1876 TO THE BEGINNING OF JANUARY 1877

[The Notes on Ornamentation are followed by 26 blank pages; on page 93 of the notebook a series of daily notations begins. C. M.]

...... my board and the hour of Señores Padrós y Borrás. I missed class.
22. Half hour for Sr. Villar at Montserrat and study of the Wardrobe which...... they accept and are supported by the data that they can yield 9.2 %.
The Grabulosa plan has been held up by City Hall.
23. Morning, ½ hour Fontseré and 2 hours Villar, section.
24. One hour Fontseré. Candelabrum detail and Villar *Camarín* 2 and ½.
25. 3 ½ Villar on the *Camarín*, 2 ½ Serrallach Pavilion for a summer house.
Much work is necessary to get out of trouble.
26. Pavilion delivered to Serrallach in pencil only. Sta. Malera Wardrobe overall and detail.
27. The section of the Memorial for the remodeling of Sr. Grabulosa's house required by the City and working out of the plans and two façades and sections, all day long from 8 in... 5 in the A [?].
I skipped class saying that I was sick as I was needed by Fontseré.
Saturday presentation of plans in the City Offices. The Junta [?] dealt with the streetcar in order to form a company and they gave me an album of the Firm which...
29. One hour Serrallach and delivery of... Masnou altar plan. Cf. Laurent album...

December 1. 1 hour Fontseré. Detail Candelabrum. 3 Hours *Camarín* Villar.
Laurent Views... which are in the book of Memorial and in the newspapers of this...
2. ½ hour Fontseré Candelabrum.
3. 1 hour Fontseré Candelabrum and Malera Wardrobe detail have gone several days without working enough hours to finish for Villar.
4. 3 hours Montserrat Section, Malera Wardrobe and 1 ½ Vilardell display window.
5. ¾ Fontseré Candelabrum Malera Wardrobe and Padrós and Borrás sheet again.
6. One hour Fontseré Candelabrum 3 hours Villar Section Montserrat altar, Malera Wardrobe. Another solution sought for Hospital project since the project not accepted in the Generality.
7. Half hour Fontseré if we do it in Villar he will say...
8. Study of the ironwork of the Casa Cokoril la Bolesca and writing of Padrós and Borrás communication and measurement of the stone of the Grabulosa house and agreement on several improvements from here on and later search for the origin of the crystal pieces that are to be built tomorrow.
10. Sta. Malera Wardrobe and Administration to...
11. 4 hours Fontseré candelabrum with... pedestal, presentation of Malera Wardrobe detail. Visit Gustá and Casa Fontseré.
12. ... to know the Saint Gaubaint crystal factory delegation and Marseilles depository.
13. ... a note from Aracoli demanding ... in pay or he will not go to the Administration.
Nothing
Received twelve *duros* on the Fontseré account.
14. Absolutely nothing.
15. One hour Villar cupola.
16. Villar 2 hours Cupola and altar. Visit Grabulosa.
17. Villar altar two hours, Paredes Iranzo trip.
18. Villar three hours, Ateneo armchair.

19. Villar five hours.
20. Villar four hours altar.
21. Villar three hours *camarín*.
22. Villar 3 hours *camarín*.
23. Villar 2 hours *camarín*.
24. Trip to Casa Antúnez with Pedro Borrás.
25.
26.
27. 2 ½ Villar the two sections, visit governor and before Junta resolution of a grand summer house the Villa Arcadia and Office of Public Works Sr. Brugada we must come another day to see the Plaza Antúnez plan and who owns the road of the...
28. Five hours Villar Montserrat Section, Vilardell house takes more measurements than the store ... and visit ... for idem, and for doing the façade of the same one hour.
29. Six hours Montserrat section, visits to the Commandant Marien, fortification of the Port to the Assistant of the Works Buyada [?] three for the Villa Arcadia and visit to the Grabulosa house and letter to Captain Diego González.
30. 8 hours Villar, Montserrat Section, someone should talk to Villar to fill the vacuum of his words, this makes him very uncommunicative with me.
31. 4 hours Villar. Montserrat Section, visit to this monastery seems like he has no set idea. I must give him what is needed to build the lower part of the three apses with details on a scale of 1:10 and with plan and all that is needed to formulate an idea. One hour Fontseré in the copy of the Candelabrum.

1877

January 1. Nothing. Casa Pisch [?] Committee and layout of the Villa Arcadia to ... an aviary and a watchtower to support ... of steam, idea for the distribution of the Hospital for two ... present project elsewhere in another solution.
2. Exposition in Padró and Borrás' of the Villa Arcadia Project, an hour and a half Fontseré on the candelabrum.
3. 2 ½ hours candelabrum Fontseré, visit Grabulosa.
4. 18 *duros* collected from Grabulosa and 10 *duros* given to Marine, at same time five *duros* for the permit for exterior doors for the same Grabulosa, two hours Fontseré for candelabrum lunch at the *fonda de Cataluña* invited by the newly-titled architects.
5. I visit the animals and eat breakfast at the Liceo restaurant the Aragonese continue to work and as a result Barraquer has been put in charge of their military direction—he being the nephew of the other.
6. Nothing, passed the day without doing anything.
9.

[Here it is cut off. C. M.]

APPENDIX V

TWO OTHER MANUSCRIPTS AND OTHER OBJECTS THAT BELONGED
TO GAUDÍ IN THE MUSEO MUNICIPAL DE REUS

1. NOTES ON THE *CASA PAIRAL* (THE FAMILY HOME) [Written in Catalan.—G.R.C.]

The house is the small nation of the family.

The family, like the nation, has its history, external relations, changes of government, etc.

The independent family has its own home; that which is not independent must rent a home.

One's own home is his native country; a rented home is the country of emigration; thus to own his own home is every man's dream.

One cannot imagine his own home without family; only a rented house can be imagined in that manner.

The family home has been given the name *casa pairal*. On hearing this name, who does not recall some beautiful place in the country or in the city?

The spirit of luxury and changing customs have caused the disappearance of the majority of the *casas pairals* from our city; those which remain are so oppressed and in such poor condition that they, too, will soon be gone.

551. Gaudí's notes on the decoration of architectural supports. In the Municipal Museum at Reus.

Estracto de los asuntos históricos para
la decoración de los *soportes* de la *S.E.*

Pasage... Romana —

Roger de Flor propuso la expedición a Federico de Sicilia. 20 galeras y ...
y otros, en... total 36, 1500 caballos y 4000 almogávares tuvieron, jefes —
... ... Ximenes de Arenós, ... Juan de Atones, Corberán de ...
... Pedro de Aros, ... Pedro de Lagran y jefe de los almogávares Berenguer de
... y Berenguer de Ronfort, Victoria de Artaqui entre los turcos
Filadelfia, Thira, Anria, Hierro — Ramón Muntaner Alcaide de Castellón
de Ampurias, G. de Fonsy, Berenguer de Rocafort de Albarazat
... se salvaron en Andrinópolis ———— ... Heraclea ...
... Pedro Llopis — Galipoli — ... ...

Atenas — Berenguer ... — Alfonso ...

Artaqui — Andrinópolis — Galipoli — Atenas

The need for the *casa pairal* is not only the need of a particular family and period; it is the need of all men and all times.

Independence of the room, good orientation, and the abundance of air and light that are usually lacking in urban rooms are now sought in the infinite number of free-standing single-family houses in the outskirts where, strange though it seems, the majority of families have their everyday homes.

In order to find these qualities, inhabitants of foreign cities do not have to worry about being distant from the center of the same, even though it would be easy for them due to the numerous means of communication which we, too, are fortunately beginning to have at our disposal.

(Stranger still: the most capable is the least called upon to serve.)

It is proper, then, that we take advantage of the means available to us and that we think in terms of the true family home; by uniting the urban residence and the single-unit country house we get the *casa pairal*. To this end, let us imagine a house neither large nor small —a house that we could refer to as common; were it enlarged and embellished it would become a palace, made smaller and economizing on the materials it would be the modest home of a comfortable family.

Let us imagine a lot in the New Section of Barcelona as large as the proprietor's means allow, and situated in a more or less beautiful neighborhood, depending on his fortune and position; it is surrounded by a wall which encloses the garden landscape or by its height prevents visibility from the street; the wall is capped by an openwork crown (where at sunset we can see the young maidens supporting their arms on it to watch the passers-by.) [the words in parentheses have been crossed out in the manuscript. C. M.] A small loggia near the door interrupts the terrace. On one side of the property there is a long ramp which serves as a carriage road; at the front there is a stairway, from the top of which we discover the garden, and there among the foliage of the poplars and the plane trees, there stands the house. The rooms are grouped according to their necessary orientation to form a picturesque ensemble, with the wide windows of the bedrooms, the office, and the family living room on the south; the winter dining room and the parlors on the west, and on the north the study, the summer dining room, and other rooms. Separate from this group and in the same direction there is the kitchen and its related secondary rooms. Between the bedroom and the study shaded by acacia and weeping willow trees, we come upon a porch decorated with terracotta pieces in which the sparrows make their nests. In the opposite corner we find a greenhouse of iron and glass—a winter garden which is linked to the receiving rooms and can be used as a salon for large family parties. On the interior, simplicity has been systematized, guided by good taste and determined by the satisfaction of certain needs and comforts. Everything is formal. We find representations of the family memories, the historical gestures, the legends of the land, the delicate conceptions of our poets, and the spectacles and scenes of mother nature; all that has meaning and is appreciated. In a word, from son to son.

All in all, the house that we imagine has two objectives: first, by its hygienic conditions to make strong and robust beings (of those who grow up and develop therein), and second, by its artistic conditions to endow them as far as possible with our proverbial integrity of character.

In a word, to make the sons who are born there true sons of the *casa pairal*.

2. EXTRACT OF THE HISTORIC EVENTS FOR THE DECORATION OF THE SUPPORTS FOR THE F. E.

Passage to Rumania.
Roger de Flor proposed the expedition to Federico of Sicily 10 galleons and 2 ships and other vessels, total 36, 1,500 horses and 4,000 light troops, 1,000 persons. Leaders—Ferran Ximenis de Arenas—Juran de Aones, Don Corberan de Alet, Don Pedro de Aros, Don Pedro de Logran, and leaders of the light troops, Berenguer de Entenza and Berenguer de Rocafort, Victory of Artaqui over the Turks, Philadelphia, Thirras, Anira, «Iron»—Ramón Alguer de Castellón de Ampurias, G. de Tous and Berenguer de Roudor del Llobregat only met each other in Andrianopolis... Heraclea, Siscar. Pedro Llopis—Galipoli—Apro—Fuilla—Spoll—Negroponte—Athens—Beranger Estanyol—Alfonso Fedanio. Artiqui—Andrianopolis—Galipoli—Athens.

[At the foot of the sheet there are various pencil sketches of decorative motifs associated with the names mentioned above. See Fig. 551. C. M.]

[In the Spanish edition, the author read the title as «...de los soportes de la I. E. (¿Iluminación eléctrica?).» One can see, however, by comparing other capital letters in the photograph, that it is «... de la F. E.» I have always assumed that this was a sheet of notes corresponding to Gaudí's lost architectural school project for a Spanish Pavilion at our Centennial Exposition in Philadelphia (Filadelfia Exposición) of 1876. (See Note 107a in my 1960 book on Gaudí.). It appeared to me to be the supports for a stand decorated with names from Catalan history that had been associated with the expedition by Roger de Flor to Philadelphia in Asia Minor in 1304.—G.R.C.]

3. SHEET OF PAPER with fragments of the concepts which are repeated in the notebook transcribed in the previous appendix—possibly preparatory notes for it. Published in Casanelles, *La Nueva Visión de Gaudí* (Barcelona, 1965) and translated in the English edition of same.

4. SHEET OF PAPER noting the cost per bed, in francs, of various foreign hospitals with very quick sketches of two hospitals with the layout of pavilions.

5. SHEET OF PAPER folded into four small faces with a pencil drawing of a capital and geometry notes, also in pencil and difficult to decipher. (Published by Collins.)

6. DRAWING-PROJECT for the parade in honor of the Rector of Vallfogona (Fig. 199).

7. THREE SHEETS OF FIGURE DRAWINGS and plant sketches. (Published by Ráfols).

8. VERY TINY SKETCHES of the project for remodelling the Sanctuary of the Misericordia in Reus (Figs. 356, 357).

9. PHOTOGRAPHIC PORTRAIT of Gaudí by Audouard and Cia., Rambla del Centro, 17, 1.° (Fig. 27).

10. EXHIBITOR'S PASS No. 2221 allowing D. Antonio Gaudí free entrance to the fairgrounds of the Universal Exposition in Barcelona 1888; the owner's picture is affixed (Fig. 45).

11. A VERTICAL CARD with the inscription «Ant.° Gaudí, architect» in carefully executed lettering; centered at the bottom: «Office - Barcelona - Call - 11 - 3.» On the back, a meticulously rendered drawing of the Comella display case and quick sketches of same (Fig. 194).

12. DRAWING-PROJECT for a reliquary 30 cm., high, colored in green and blue. At the bottom it says, «actual size. Barcelona 1878, A. Gaudí.» (Fig. 198).

13. OFFICIAL COMMUNICATION from the Ayuntamiento of Barcelona and a Diploma of Honor on painted parchment commemorating the prize awarded the Casa Calvet for the year 1899.

14. THE TIE that he was wearing when he was run over on June 7, 1926.

15. A SMALL RELIGIOUS PRINT he carried with him on that same day.

[These objects were given to the museum by the architect Domingo Sugrañes, Gaudí's collaborator in his latest years and executor of his will. C. M.]

APPENDIX VI

REPORT OF THE ROYAL ACADEMY OF SAN FERNANDO ON THE PROJECT FOR THE EPISCOPAL PALACE AT ASTORGA REVISED IN ACCORDANCE WITH ANOTHER PREVIOUS REPORT

Presented by the Excmo. Sr. Marqués de Cubas

Most Excellent Sub-Secretary of Grace and Justice.

Most Excellent Sir: The Architectural Division of this Royal Academy, having examined the project for the construction of the Episcopal Palace at Astorga as expanded by its author D. Antonio Gaudí y Cornet in response to a previous report issued by this advisory body on February 24 of the present year, finds: that a new document No. 6 has been added to the original set of plans, containing a notebook of observations concerning the mentioned report of this Royal Academy; a sheet of onionskin paper with several details of structure at various scales, and a diagram showing the loads acting on a lateral chapel buttress, one in the tribunal gallery, and another in the archives of the same, and the graphic-static representations that determine the resulting pressure curves in these fundamental supports. In the mentioned report issued on February 24, the following observations were made regarding the original project:

On the Memorial: that the great amount of combustible material which was used in the roof of the central part of the building be protected from the contingencies of fire, using modern fire-proofing procedures, and that it also be made safe from atmospheric fire through a system of lightning rods which will require additional drawings and budget entries; that this be accompanied by a structural study of the most substantial parts of the palace to confirm their solidity and appropriate placement. In his additions to the Memorial which constitute part of the new Document No. 6, the author of the project states that his design was controlled by conditions of strict economy which had resulted in the choice of wood as a structural material, and that it would be protected by the four lightning rods on the corner towers.

This Division must insist, in conformity with its original report, on the necessity for preparing the large central wooden frame through appropriate saturation, non-combustible paints, etc., etc., to protect it against fire, and also on the establishment of a complete system for the prevention of ignition by lightning which, as has been stated, can be the subject of a separate project and supplementary budget.

On the Plans. In the original report, this Division recommended in regard to this second document: that the project be expanded to include a plan of the roofing and framework, with detailed sections that would clarify the resistance qualities of the most essential parts of the material structure; in addition the Division added that the ditch surrounding the building which serves to insulate, illuminate, and drain the partially underground basement floor (Plan 10) should be wider and clear in its narrowest part, and the floor of the ditch should be slightly lower than the floor of the basement, as should be the drainage pipes indicated in Plan 11; it was also found necessary to widen the stairs which were too small and insufficient for a building of this sort. For reasons of climate and hygiene, the Division also recommended the elimination of the extreme intercolumniation in the colonnades of the corner rotundas of the palace (Plans 6, 7, 8, and 9) and also that the thrusts of the strongly depressed vaults of the basement be more carefully studied.

The second supplementary Memorial states: that regarding the new plan requested, the various structural details in the second notebook of the expanded document 6 will serve the same purpose; that the partial expansion of the ditches and an increase in their depth would be too expensive for the limited budget allowed for the project; that the widening of the flights of stairs would mean the narrowing of the central passageway of the vestibule and would destroy the effect and arrangement of the central supports of the building, proposing to obviate these inconveniences by replacing the projected stone railings with iron ones which would give a total width of 1.8 meters to the stairs; that in regard to the colonnades at the corners of the Palace, which were to take the place of projecting bodies or balconies, two or three of them can be eliminated; as far as the depressed vaults of the basements, he responded that the thrusts have no adverse effect as can be seen in the accompanying additional study of their resistance.

[One more page of this Report and its signatures are here omitted, but will be found in the Spanish edition.—G.R.C.]

APPENDIX VII

TWO LETTERS FROM THE ARCHITECT FRANCISCO DE P. DEL VILLAR Y CARMONA IN THE ARCHIVES OF THE REAL MONASTERIO DE MONTSERRAT

Very Most Reverend Father Abbot of Montserrat
Barcelona, January 23, 1883.

My Dear Most Highly Respected Sir: I am writing to forward the measurement information that you requested as I am now working on the surface calculations. The area turns out to be, as you can see, 39.1564 m² which, when multiplied by the rate of 10 pesetas per square meter, comes to a total of 391.564 pesetas.

Please excuse the oversight that I did not give you prior warning of the fact that the workmen and Pellarin would be coming up to the Monastery, but as I was able to begin work four days earlier than I had expected (since Pellarin was actually contracted to begin on the 26th) I preferred to have him leave earlier and thus get a head start on the work.

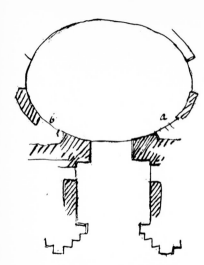

552. Marginal diagram in a letter from the architect Villar.

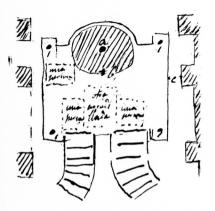

553. Marginal diagram in a letter from the architect Villar.

Regarding the distribution of work and time, I would like to follow a strict schedule since March 25 and the last minute rush are fast approaching; thus I feel that it would be desirable, unless you have a better idea, for Pellarin to start working at point *a*, in order to allow time for the stonecutters and sculptors to finish the rose window at point *b* where the scaffolding can be left up until Pellarin gets around to that point, at which time it can be dismantled. Also, the minute that Pellarin arrives he should finish and polish the *camarín*, for which he will need some iron pieces from you to be used in joining his work with the carpentry elements at the opening of the *camarín*.

Working in this manner will make it possible for the mosaic workers and stonecutters to work at the same time, and we will be able to finish one of the portal rose windows in time for the inauguration, something that is highly desirable from all points of view: besides the fact that the general public will be able to see what the other doors will be like, the discerning individual will be able to judge the overall value of the work with more data.

I have given Pellarin orders to show you the coat of arms that I have designed and to follow your orders concerning the colors of the cross of San Benito and the letters which make up that part, and also in the modification of the heraldry in any way you think would be best.

Tomorrow I shall begin to work on the detailing of the bell-tower railing which, along with the estimate, I will forward to you later this week, God willing.

I am not sending along the statement of the prices for the supports of the eaglets at the *camarín* entrance because the models have to be somewhat modified.

Regarding the construction of the sepulchral chapel of the Marquise of Tamarite, I can now assure you (although extraofficially) that it will go ahead; it seems that she and her executors have postponed writing to you because she first wants to come to Barcelona to see about modifying the burial practices in some way. We shall see, and I will write to you in any case although I imagine that they will let you know shortly or it will be done by common agreement.

My father has asked me to send his greetings to you and the entire Community, and says that he has not written to you because he is still awaiting a call from the Captain-General; when that situation is verified he will let you know immediately.

Finally, I ask you to pass along my greetings to all of the Fathers, especially to Father Buera. I am as always your devoted and humble servant who kisses your ring.

Francisco del Villar.

Very Most Reverend Father Abbot of Montserrat
Barcelona, February 9, 1887 *

My Dear Sir and Beloved Father.

This morning Pablo Berenguer stopped by for a visit, and from him I learned that you are well and that things are going smoothly at the Monastery, which gives me great satisfaction. He informed me of the progress of the work, and said that you were worried by the size of the Virgin's pedestal once executed in relation to the plans; I should like to point out, however, that once it is put in place it will not appear so large and I am sure that it will be exactly as you wanted it.

I should like to tell you how I designed it in view of the necessity for people to climb up to kiss the Virgin's hand. The projection of the head of the image is at point *a*, and the curved form of the pedestal which you already have was continued in the stone base in order to better show off the image. The overall rectangular form was chosen in case you or your successors in the centuries to come should someday wish to put up a baldachin; this could be done with the greatest of ease (there is more than enough altitude) and this motivated the forms numbered 1. The hand of he Virgin projects to point *b* (after the image is given a quarter-turn to facilitate the kissing of the hand), and there is a little more than a meter beween it and the edge of the pedestal to allow the circulation of persons who climb up to kiss the hand; there will always be three persons there—one who is starting back down, one who is kissing (and kneels down for a moment), and one who has just come up to carry out the ritual: a total of .60 square meters per person has been allowed, which is the minimum space necessary to avoid confusion.

Space *c* which is the area between the pedestal and the base of the walls will not be .20, but just under .25, at the feet because above the legs the room will be greater since the colonnettes will be set back.

* I presume that this year date is in error; judging from the relation of this letter to the previous one and others in the same archive, it was written in 1883. C. M.

By arranging things in this manner, I think that we will clearly indicate that the public should not climb up anywhere else except by way of the stairs in the pedestal; yet the Brothers can have free access to clean the area and to carry out the above mentioned ritual.

Regarding the form of the stairway itself, that will have to be worked out on the spot, and thus I hope that by this Saturday the pedestal can be mounted just as indicated in the small plan in your possession, so that we can best determine what form should be given to those stairs.

On Saturday, God willing, I will come up with Rosell to finish assembling the opening to the *camarín,* and on Monday I have arranged to meet Sr. Batalla at the monastery to begin to put up the railings; for this reason I hope that you will advise Miguel, the locksmith, so that everything will be ready for the fitters or Sr. Batalla to begin work on Monday or Tuesday.

Please pardon the dryness of this letter, but if I were not careful these letters would be interminable; even trying to be concise I always fear that I am forgetting something that I should tell you.

I will leave the other small details to be discussed when I have the pleasure of kissing your ring.

Your Most Devoted Servant.

Francisco del Villar.

I know that Pellarin is making bells, which is rather irresponsible: please hurry him a bit and pardon my frankness.

APPENDIX VIII

NEWS ITEMS CONCERNING THE PAVILION AT THE CADIZ EXPOSITION, 1887, AND LACK OF NEWS ITEMS ABOUT THAT IN BARCELONA, 1888

CÁDIZ PAVILION

Diario de Cádiz, March 23, 1887, published a letter from the Marquis of Comillas to the President of the Provincial Diputación of Cadiz, announcing a contest sponsored by the Compañía Trasatlántica in relation to the Maritime Exposition to be held the following August, in which he offers, among other things: «First, to the Directing Committee, FREE TRANSPORTATION of materials of and for the Exposition on their boats from port to port.»

The same *Diario,* in its issue of September 18, 1887, has a short article entitled «El Pabellón de la Trasatlántica» from which we transcribe the following fragments of interest to our discussion.

«They (the Compañía Trasatlántica) knew what they were doing when they entrusted this project to the distinguished Master Builder *Sr. García Cabezas,* so well-known for his competence, initiative, and good taste.»

The Pavilion as it stands constructed shows how justly deserved his reputation is.»

[This represents only ¼ of the original article, which is reprinted in full in the Spanish edition.—G.R.C.]

BARCELONA PAVILION

In the numerous resumés and descriptions of the 1888 Barcelona Exposition which I have read, the Trasatlántica pavilion is praised, but no mention is made of its author; nor does any reference to the pavilion exist in those archives of the company which escaped destruction in 1936. One of the most complete accounts is that of J. Ixart in his book *El año pasado. Letras y Artes en Barcelona, 1889,* which tells us that the pavilion was «covered with plastercasts of the Alhambra ornamentation,» and that «the whiteness of its walls ... give it, at a distance, the look of one of those small ivory scale models of the mentioned palace.» But here again the name of the architect of the little palace is not given. (It should be remembered that Ixart and Gaudí were good friends.)

554. Pavilion of the Compañía Trasatlántica at the Barcelona Universal Exposition, 1888. From *La Ilustración Hispano-Americana*, August 26, 1888.

From an article by B. Bassegoda Amigó published in *La Vanguardia* of Barcelona (March 14, 1929) we know that Gaudí had a hand in putting up this pavilion in Barcelona, probably because of his friendship with the director of the Trasatlántica, the Marquis of Comillas who was the brother-in-law of his friend Eusebio Güell. At that time, the architect was busy with the termination of multiple and painstaking details of the Palacio Güell, the termination of the crypt of the Sagrada Familia, and with the tedious modifications of the project for the Episcopal Palace in Astorga required by the Academy of Fine Arts. In such circumstances he was not very pleased by this simple and impersonal task.

Nevertheless, Gaudí improved the Cádiz pavilion of García Cabezas in several of its façade details. Not so with the four tall corner towers which were added and which rob the ensemble of its unity while dwarfing the central cupola. Such circumstances, along with the absence of the polychromy so characteristic of the Arabic style, both contrary to Gaudí's own esthetic principles, suggest that these towers were requested, if not imposed, by the greater importance of the Barcelona exposition and the desire to avoid the appearance of a mere repetition.

This would also suggest the possibility that Gaudí himself was interested in keeping his name out of the reference to a work that was not conceived by him and in which he had not even wanted to participate.

APPENDIX IX

SPECIFICATIONS FOR THE CRYPT OF THE EXPIATORY TEMPLE
OF THE SAGRADA FAMILIA

[I have left out those conditions of a technical sort which have nothing to do with the change in the directing architect of the work, which is the point of the present transcription. The document is in my personal archive. C. M.]

1st.   The work will be subject to the plans for the project drawn up by the architect D. Francisco de P. del Villar, to these specifications, and to the disposition of the mentioned architect.

13th.   If the Commission or the directing architect should vary the project completely or in part, as is their privilege, or the type of materials, quality of the stone, dimensions of the same, etc., this must only be done by indemnification of materials gathered together or work prepared, and the establishment of new prices which will be agreed upon by the Commission, the architect, and the contractor.

14th.   If, instead of ashlar masonry facing, it be resolved to build the pillars, arches, and vaults of solid ashlar masonry, the stones, ashlars, and voussoirs will be completely finished on all sides, that is, they will sit flat in their beds without the necessity of stone wedges in all parts of the construction where ashlar masonry sits on ashlar masonry. The arches and the vaults must be worked out in such a way that only a single bed of mortar will be necessary. The joints will be no thicker than the single sheets of lead plating used to avoid chipping at the edges. Once this is established, only the case of the previous condition needs to be considered.

21st.   If the necessity for a work stoppage should arise, the contractor must be given a month's prior notice in order to minimize his damages and to limit the accumulation of materials.

22nd.   Once both parties have agreed on the date of stoppage, a liquidation of the work completed will follow; as far as economic effects, every stoppage will be considered to be a termination of the work, without this implying recision of the contract because the contracted commitment is understood to include the total work; exceptions will be made in the case of determined motives which cause the stoppage, or in the case that the stoppage should last for more than a year.

23rd.   Work must always proceed with sufficient speed so that, excepting periods of forced stoppages, the masonry and stone-cutting sections will be finished within the time-limit set in each partial agreement, leaving everything compltely terminated and ready for services in all of the chapels at the same time, at the end of the period which results from the sum of the partial agreements.

24th.   The contractor can not make any changes, modifications, or addition whatsoever, under penalty of having to return things to their original state at his own expense.

27th.   The directing architect will put on a practical foreman at the expense of the Commission, who will constantly supervise the quantity and quality of the materials that enter the work area and the progress of the laborers' work.

28th.   The contractor must gather with sufficient anticipation the necessary materials in proportionate quantity and quality to the work contracted in the jugdment of the director.

29th.   A supervisor of plans and other office work will be named by the director, and his salary of two hundred twenty five pesetas per month for eight hours per day of work be paid by the contractor from whose own salary this amount will be discounted at every fifteen-day pay period, and for every such period 10 % of the pay will be withheld as a guarantee against possible imperfections in the work whose reparation will be taken care of by the contractor who will follow the directions of the architect.

33rd.   In clarification of conditions 21 and 22, grounds for recision of the contract will consist of: cases which cause absolute stoppage of the works by one of the parties for reasons beyond his control, e.g., an act of God, death of the contractor, etc. In such cases a final liquidation will be made with the endorsement of the directing architect.

34th.   The contractor will be in charge of the protection or vigilance of the construction while work proceeds, and in cases of partial stoppages the salary of the warden will be taken care of by the Commission.

35th.   Conservation and reparation of the construction work will be the job of the contractor during the course of the work and six months thereafter, in everything that concerns natural settling or the quality of the work, but not the imperfections which result from extraneous causes.

36th.   Stoppages resulting from workers' strikes will not be considered as negligence in complying with these conditions on the part of the contractor.

Additional Conditions

1st.   The part of the Crypt contracted today will consist of: the foundation; the stone base;

the walls up to the arches and vaults, including the inset pillars between the chapels; the complete termination of the central chapel, including the two free-standing pillars and the part of the arches and vaults in the lateral nave that rests on these two pillars and the inset ones of the same chapel and the foundations and walls of the longitudinal part of the Crypt contained within the clearing for the crossing and the general floor.

Barcelona, August 25, 1883

José María Bocabella

The Contractor,
Macario Planella

2nd.   In the future, the contractor must follow the plans, details, and orders of the new directing architect D. Antonio Gaudí, and any variations of the project, change in the structural system, etc., will be the object of additional conditions so that they will be included in the liquidations, and those which do not demand an express condition can be formalized simply by a note from the directing architect.

3rd.   In order to resolve those disagreements which may arise in applying condition 13, or in the interpretation of any of the others, two competent persons will be named for each case being aired—one by the Commission and another by the contractor; if these two are not able to come to an agreement, a third will be named and his decision, once reached, will not be appealable by either side.

4th.   Applying condition 14, it has been agreed that the price be 55 *duros* per cubic meter of Montjuich stone, instead of the 44 *duros* previously assigned, for which increase the contractor will present valid arguments in view of the graphic data drawn up by the directing architect.

5th.   Condition 29 has been inoperative to this date as the contractor himself has executed the service provided for in said condition insofar as it refers to his parts of the contract in accord with the previous director and approval of the Commission.

Barcelona, March 28, 1884

José María Bocabella

The Contractor,
Macario Planella

6th.   In compensation for office work carried out by the contractor, he is exempted from paying the foreman's salary mentioned in condition 29.

Barcelona, March 28, 1884

José María Bocabella

The Contractor,
Macario Planella

APPENDIX X

COPY OF THE DOCUMENT CONTAINED IN THE FOOT OF THE IMAGE
OF SAINT GEORGE IN THE BUILDING THAT GAUDÍ CONSTRUCTED IN LEÓN

[From a photograph provided in July 1960 by D. Ricardo Aller Pavía, secretary for the Caja de Ahorros y Monte de Piedad in León, the present proprietors of the building (Fig. 555).]

FERNÁNDEZ Y ANDRÉS

Let all who read this document know that as an historical datum, the building in [which] it is deposited has been built at the expense of Don Mariano Andrés González Luna and Don José and Don Aquilino Fernández Riu, the latter two being sons of Don Simón Fernández y Fernández who died on July 29, 1891, the buyer in conjunction with the first-named of the land on which the building is situated, from the heirs of the most excellent Duke of Uceda.

Excavation work was begun on the 4th day of January, 1892, and terminated on the 4th day of the following April, on which day the foundations were begun.

The plans for the work were drawn up by the architect Sr. D. Antonio Gaudí y Cornet, a native of Reus (Tarragona), and work was supervised in his absence by his assistant Don Claudio Alsina.

The stone-cutting work was executed by the master stonecutter, D. Antonio Cantó, assisted by a large team.

FERNÁNDEZ y ANDRÉS.

Sepan cuantos leyeren este documento, que como dato histórico depositamos en este lugar, que el edificio en que queda archivado, ha sido construido á expensas de D. Mariano Andrés González Luna y Don José y D. Aquilino Fernández Riu, hijos ... los dos últimos de Don Simón ... Ander y Fernández, fallecido en 29 de Julio de 1893, comprado en ... el primero á los herederos del Excmo. Señor Duque de ... el solar en que está emplazado.

Iniciáronse los primeros trabajos de excavación el día cuatro de ... de 1892 que terminaron ... de Abril siguiente en que se ... pararon los cimientos.

Los planos de la obra han sido ejecutados ... el Arquitecto D. Antonio Gaudí y Cornet natural de Reus (Barcelona) secundado en sus ausencias por su Ayudante D. Claudio Alsina ...

Los trabajos de cantería fueron ejecutados por el Maestro en el ramo D. Antonio Cantó, auxiliado de un personal escogido.

El ramo de Albañilería estuvo á cargo del Maestro D. Mariano ... procedente de Barcelona como el anterior á cuyas órdenes ... oficiales Catalanes y de la provincia con el correspondiente número de operarios.

Los trabajos de Carpintería estuvieron confiados al Maestro D. ... auxiliado de un buen personal de oficiales de la provincia ... la mayoría de las puertas y ventanas de los cuatro pisos fueron construidas en Barcelona en los talleres de "Casas, Planas y Ca." ... herraje por el maestro Sr. Hijo de Ignacio Damians.

Los techos fueron decorados por los Hermanos ... Vila.

... que rodea el edificio en sus lados Este y Sur así como la barandilla de las ... escaleras fueron ejecutadas en Gijón en los talleres de y ... Nessler, ... y Ca. así como el Ascensor para la carga y descarga de bultos y ... por el cerrajero D. Bernardo Valle ó las rejas de los sótanos.

Y por último el San Jorge que se coloca hoy en este sitio en cuyo pedestal se deposita este documento fué tallado en Barcelona con arreglo al modelo variado por el Sr. Arquitecto por D. Antonio Cantó.

El tiempo empleado en la construcción fué de diez meses.

Para que sirva de dato á la posteridad consignamos los particulares que dejamos reseñados de cuya verdad y exactitud dan fe los que suscriben firmando la presente acta en esta de ... á quince días de Septiembre de mil ochocientos noventa y tres =

Aquilino Fernández Riu

José Fernández Riu

Mariano Andrés

555. Document contained in the pedestal of the image of Saint George which decorates the façade of the Casa Fernández Andrés in León.

The masonry team was headed by the master-mason D. Mariano Padró who comes from Barcelona as does the formerly mentioned master and who had under him several Catalan craftsmen as well as those from this province and a corresponding nucleus of workmen.

The carpentry was entrusted to the master D. Juan Coll who was aided by a goodly staff of local craftsmen, although the major part of the doors and windows of the four stories was constructed in Barcelona in the workshops of Casas, Planas, and Cía. The hardware was by the master Sr. Hijo de Ignacio Damians.

The ceilings were decorated by the Vila Brothers.

The grating which bounds the building to the east and the south, and the railing of the two stairways, were executed in Gijón, in the workshops of Nessler, Raviada, and Cía. as was the cargo elevator; the basement window grilles were done by the locksmith D. Bernardo Valero of this city.

And finally, the Saint George, which is today placed in this site and in whose pedestal this document is deposited, was cast in Barcelona by D. Antonio Cantó according to the model established by the architect.

The time taken for construction was 10 months.

We hereby consign the information which we have outlined here in order that it serve as a datum for posterity; its truth and accuracy is attested to by those who subscribe to it by signing the present document here in León on this fifteenth day of September of eighteen ninety three.

Aquilino Fernández Riu   Mariano Andrés

José Fernz. Riu

[The Spanish edition contained two additional appendices: 1) a classification of Gaudí's buildings by styles, here omitted. 2) a discussion of the project for a hotel of 1908 (Fig. 555) which has been moved to XLVIII-192 (Fig. 484) in this edition. —G.R.C.]

SOURCES FOR THE PRESENT STUDY

ARCHIVES CONSULTED

Academia de Bellas Artes de San Fernando in Madrid. Academia de Bellas Artes de San Jorge in Barcelona. Amigos de Gaudí de Barcelona. Archivo Histórico de Barcelona. Archivo Administrativo Municipal de Barcelona. Archivo Municipal de Mataró. Archivo Municipal and Museum of Reus. Institute of Tarragona. Balmes Institute of Barcelona. School of Sciences in Barcelona. Escuela Técnica Superior de Arquitectura de Barcelona. Monastery of Montserrat. Monastery of Poblet. Compañía Trasatlántica. Orfeó Català. Caja de Ahorros of León. Juan Rogent y Massó.

PERSONAL REFERENCES

From Gaudí himself between January 23, 1915 and January 22, 1926; Luís Badía, Rev. Francisco Baldelló, Jaime Bayó Font, Sebastián Buxó Calvet, J. M. Camps Arnau, Felipe de Dalmases, Bernardo García Galán, Antonio Ramón González, Isidro Magriñá, Juan Antonio and Helena Maragall, Juan Matamala Flotats, Ricardo Opisso, J. M. Pericas, Juan Prats, Rev. Gaspar Puigneró Bofill, Francisco de P. Quintana, Juan Rubió, Rosario Segimón Vda. de Milá, A. Trías Maxenchs and Joaquín Vilaplana.

BRIEF BASIC BIBLIOGRAPHY

1903. Salvador Sellés y Baró, «El parque Güell,» *Anuario de la Asociación de Arquitectos de Cataluña.*

1913. Juan Rubió, «Dificultats per arribar a la sintesis arquitectónica,» *Anuario de la Asociación de Arquitectos de Cataluña.*

1917. Domingo Sugrañes, «La estabilidad en la construcción del Templo de la Sagrada Familia,» *Ibérica* (Observatorio del Ebro: March 31).

1923. Domingo Sugrañes, «Disposición estática del Templo de la Sagrada Familia,» *Anuario de la Asociación de Arquitectos de Cataluña.*

1927. Francisco de P. Quintana, «Les formes guerxes del Temple de la Sagrada Familia,» *La Ciutat i la Casa,* (Barcelona), III, N.º 6.

1928. José F. Ráfols, *Gaudí,* (Editorial Canosa, Barcelona). This was published in Catalán, translated into Castilian in 1929. Revised edition in 1952 (Editorial Aedos, Barcelona, 1952), with another edition in 1960.

   Francisco Folguera, *L'Arquitectura Gaudiniana,* contained in Rafols' *Gaudí* volume of 1928 and 1929.

1929. J. Puig Boada, *El Temple de la Sagrada Familia,* (Editorial Barcino, Barcelona). Second edition in Castilian, (Ediciones Omega, Barcelona, 1952).

1949. José F. Ráfols, *Modernismo y modernistas* (Ediciones Destino, S. L., Barcelona.)

1951. À. Cirici Pellicer, *El arte modernista Catalán,* (Aymà, Editor, Barcelona).

1952. Santiago Rubió, *Cálculo funicular del hormigón armado: Generalización de los métodos de cálculo y proyecto del arquitecto Gaudí a las estructuras de hormigón armado,* (Ediciones G. Gili, Buenos Aires).

1954. Joan Bergós, *Antoni Gaudí, l'home i l'obra* (Ariel, Barcelona).

1960. Bohigas Guardiola, Bonet Armengol, Cirici Pellicer, Garrut Roma, Gili Moros, Martinell Brunet, Martorell Codina, Puig Boada, Quintana Vidal, Ribas Piera, and Sostres Maluquer. Lectures of the Centro de Estudios Gaudinistas (1958-1959) with a prologue by Solá Morales in the volume *Gaudí* published by the Colegio Oficial de Arquitectos de Cataluña y Baleares.

1960. James Johnson Sweeney and José Luis Sert, *Antoni Gaudí,* (The Architectural Press, London).

1960. George R. Collins, *Antonio Gaudí,* (Braziller, New York).

PUBLICATIONS OF THE AUTHOR THAT AMPLIFY ASPECTS OF THE PRESENT STUDY

Books and Pamphlets

1951. *Gaudí i la Sagrada Familia, comentada per ell mateix.* Aymà S.L., editors. Revised and expanded edition: *Conversaciones con Gaudí,* Ediciones Punto Fijo, Barcelona, 1969. (See Chapter XXI, this volume, Notes 1,2.)

1952. *La Sagrada Familia,* Aymà S.L., Barcelona.

1953. *Significación de Gaudí en la arquitectura española.* Premiated in the *Certamen del Centro de Lectura de Reus,* 1952. Libro del Certamen, pp. 93, 130. Reus.

1953. *La raiz reusense de la obra de Gaudí.* Premiated in the same *Certamen;* in the same book, pp. 271, 299.

1954. *Gaudinismo.* Amigos de Gaudí. Barcelona.

1955. *Antonio Gaudí.* Electra Editrice, Milan.

1957. *La Sagrada Familia y su continuación. Conveniencia de un Centro de Estudios gaudinistas.* Lecture on the *Cátedra Antonio Gaudí* in the School of Architecture, Barcelona, published in *Ensayo,* N.º 8. Barcelona. Separately printed.

Articles

1915. «El temple de la Sagrada Familia.» *La Crónica de Valls,* Feb. 6. (Valls)

1916. «Arquitectura catalana. El templo de la Sagrada Familia.» *La Tribuna,* Feb. 28. (Madrid)

1922. «L'escultor Bonifàs al temple de la Sagrada Familia.» *La Crónica de Valls,* Aug. 22. (Valls)

1926. «L'originalitat de Gaudí.» *La Publicitat,* July 13. (Barcelona)

1927. «El mestratge intim de Gaudí.» *El propagador de la devoción a San José,* June 1. (Barcelona)

1951. «Contenido de arquitectura de Gaudí.» *Diario ilustrado,* N.º 24. (Lisbon)

1952. «Gaudí y la Eucaristía.» *Paz cristiana,* N.º 1. (Barcelona)

1952. «Grandeza y humildad de Gaudí.» *Reus,* N.º 11 (Reus)

1953. «Lo decorativo y lo estructural en la obra de Gaudí.» *Cupola,* N.º 39. (Barcelona)

1953. «Gaudí o la superación.» *Ateneo,* N.º 40. (Madrid)

1953. «El legado de Gaudí.» *Destino,* N.º 813, 814, 815. (Barcelona)

1956. «El sentido de la unidad en la arquitectura de Gaudí.» *Ensayo,* N.º 6. (Barcelona)

1957. «El gran templo de la Sagrada Familia.» *Gaceta ilustrada,* N.º 26. (Barcelona)

1960. «Escuela de gaudinismo.» *Revista Gran Vía,* N.º 450. (Barcelona)

1961. «Valoricemos debidamente la obra de Gaudí.» *Destino, N.º 1271.* (Barcelona)

1965. «El monumento al doctor Robert, obra de Gaudí olvidada en sus biografías.» *Destino,* N.º 1441. (Barcelona)

1965. «Las farolas de la plaza Real, primera obra de Gaudí, estrenada por la Merced, en 1879.» *Destino,* N.º 1468. (Barcelona)

1966. «El camarín de la Virgen de Montserrat y sus autores.» *La Vanguardia,* April 28.

1966. «Otra obra de Gaudí olvidada en sus biografías. Salón en el desaparecido bar Torino.» *La Vanguardia,* Nov. 3.

1966. «Gaudí, hombre de letras.» *La Vanguardia,* Dec. 18.

[Rather than trying supplement or update this bibliography from the Spanish edition, we wish to refer the reader to the following:

1. For a handy, classified and annotated working bibliography of approximately 60 titles, see the listing inserted by the undersigned at the rear of Descharnes and Prévost, *Gaudí: the Visionary,* New York, Viking Press, 1971.

2. A comprehensive bibliography, comprising some 1800 entries published throug the year 1971 (with subject index) has been published as *Papers X* of the American Association of Architectural Bibliographers (The University Press of Virginia, Charlottesville, 1973), entitled «Antonio Gaudí and the Catalan Movement, 1870-1930.» It was compiled by the undersigned with the assistance of Maurice E. Farinas and is based on the files of the Archive of Catalan Art and Architecture, Department of Art History, Columbia University, NYC. Fifty-eight of Martinell's publications, including some that appeared later than this book, are listed and described on pp. 79-85 of *Papers X.* -G.R.C.]

INDEX AND CHRONOLOGICAL LIST OF GAUDI'S WORKS

(This inventory also serves as a list of the illustrations of Gaudi's works and projects in this volume. Questionable works are marked «(attrib.).» Major collaborating architects are indicated in parentheses. The dates are those used by Sr. Martinell in the text. — G. R. C.)

168, 169, 189, 290-296, 435, 437. figs. 40, 48, 50, 52, 75, 101-103, 109, 111-114, 120, 130, 140, 172, 298-307, 309A-312.
Cloister and Rosary Portal. pp. 137, 164, 172, 296-301. figs. 110, 116, 135, 155, 157, 308, 309.

1901-26
Towers and spires. pp. 76, 80, 109, 110, 112, 126, 129, 130, 136, 141, 144, 147, 151, 158, 164, 169, 173, 175, 184, 185, 189, 194, 196, 228, 288, 289, 387, 400, 420-438. figs. 51, 76, 102, 103, 118, 501-510.

1911-17
Façade of the Passion. pp. 126, 146, 158, 189, 387, 436-438. figs. 81, 521.

c. 1916
Façade of the Glory. pp. 189, 436.

c. 1925
Sacristies. pp. 420, 435, 437.

1882-1926
Projects, plans, models. pp. 86, 88, 89, 91, 94, 95, 98-102, 104, 105, 134, 136, 170, 172, 183, 188-191, 194, 264, 334, 371, 387, 437-439. figs.

32, 33, 52, 68-70, 72, 81, 103, 104, 106-108, 154, 164, 298, 309, 511, 513-521.
Furniture and smaller objects. pp. 110, 116, 138, 140. figs. 90, 93, 258, 259, 261-263, 512.

Works of questionable or indeterminate date

Essay on the *Casa Pairal* (the family home). pp. 44, 46, 187, 188, 464-466. fig. 171.
Barcelona, Reliquary for the Bocabella family. p. 51.
Barcelona, Small theatre in the Rambla de los Estudios. p. 77.
Manresa, Consulted on restoration of the Cathedral (A. Soler y March). p. 78.
Montserrat, Underground church (attrib.). pp. 78, 328.
Montserrat, Bell in cleft of rock (attrib.). pp. 78, 328. figs. 55, 56.
Montserrat, Pantheon for the Comillas family (attrib.). p. 327.
S. Feliu de Codines, Consulted on design of textile factory. p. 77.

INDEX OF PERSONAL NAMES

INDEX OF PLACES

SOURCES OF THOSE PHOTOGRAPHS
AND DRAWINGS NOT ACKNOWLEDGED IN CAPTIONS

Abadía de Montserrat, 18, 358, 359.
Abadía de Poblet, 12.
Aleu, Foto, 91, 92, 95, 193, 199, 201, 211, 212, 224, 236, 277, 328, 373, 377, 378, 379, 380, 396, 414, 464, 490, 497.
Amatller, Instituto, 229, 230.
Amigos de Gaudí, 62, 184, 185, 188, 213, 281, 284, 313, 314, 381, 382, 491.
Anglada, José, 549.
Archivo Municipal Administrativo, 363.
Author's archive, 28, 49, 119, 160, 180, 181, 255, 309a, 545.

Badía, Emilio, 93, 364, 525.
Balear, Foto, 428, 492, 493, 494, 495, 497, 498.
Ballart, J., 166, 290, 346.
Bergós, J., 541.
Bonet Armengol, J., 547, 548, 549.
Bonet Garí, Luis, 539.
Bonet, Martín, 347, 348.
Branguli, 74.
Busquets, P. Pedro, 55.

Canosa, Emilio, 514.
Catalá Roca, F., 101, 102, 111, 116, 172, 252, 300, 301, 305, 306, 312.
Cementos y Cales Freixa, S. A., 405, 406, 407, 410.
Colegio de Arquitectos, 57, 97, 265, 299, 338, 435, 436, 440, 441, 458, 465, 467, 468, 526, 528, 537, 538.
Cuyás, N., 324.

Escofet, 479.
Escuela T. S. de Arquitectura, 22, 23.
Exakta, Laboratorio fotográfico, León, 42, 46, 266, 267, 268, 269, 270, 271, 272, 273, 274, 283.

Ferrán, A., 511.
Fornas, Jordi, 58, 76, 99, 303, 304.
Francés Estroch, F., 544.

Gaseta de les Arts, 106.
Godes, 21.
Gómez Moreno, 44.
Gomis-Prats, 83, 85, 87, 89, 98, 112, 113, 114, 118, 223, 228, 245, 247, 250, 251, 264, 310, 311, 374, 383, 390, 391, 393, 400, 401, 408, 418, 425, 426, 431, 437, 444, 445, 446, 471, 481, 482, 483, 501, 502, 503, 504, 505, 506, 507, 516.
Guix Sugrañes, José M., 2, 41.

Hauser y Mener, 52.
Huelin, Foto, 79, 460, 462, 472, 474, 477, 478, 480.

Imperio, Foto, 214, 216, 217, 218, 219.
Instituto Municipal de Historia, 3, 16, 26, 35, 36, 50, 52, 59, 60, 63, 66, 69, 70, 72, 104, 105, 241, 257, 353.

Junta Templo de la Sagrada Familia, 48, 65, 71, 297.

Martinell Taxonera, 469, 470.
Martínez, 4.
Mas, Ampliaciones y Reproducciones, 238, 246, 318, 323, 325, 326, 327, 461, 463, 486, 488, 521.
Mas, Archivo, 14, 17, 51, 54, 68, 75, 81, 82, 84, 86, 88, 90, 100, 107, 109, 110, 115, 168, 206, 208, 209, 210, 226, 229, 233, 234, 240, 242, 243, 244, 256, 258, 259, 260, 261, 262, 263, 287, 292, 293, 308, 309, 340, 352, 360, 361, 362, 367, 368, 388, 402, 439, 443, 457, 459, 520, 522.
Maspons+Ubiña, 177, 196, 197, 248, 249, 254, 333, 339, 341, 342, 343, 399, 475.
Mateu y Cochet, 29.
Monistrol, Fotos, 532.
Montero, Luis, 384.
Museo de los Caminos, Astorga, 43.
Museo de Historia, Barcelona, 15, 533.
Museo de Reus, 45.

Pérez Moya, from Baldelló, 167.
Plasencia, 398, 403, 404, 409, 420, 424.
Puig Boada, 73, 298, 540, 542, 543.

Quintana, Ramón, 345.

Ràfols, 191, 195, 225, 296.
«Raymond», 10, 527.
Ricart, N., 13.
Ro Foto, 536.

Sanahuja, Amadeo, 5, 7, 27, 194, 198, 356, 357.
Segarra, 80.
Servicio Municipal de Parques y Jardines, 397, 429.
Sunyer, Pedro, 514.

Templo de la Sagrada Familia, 96, 207, 227, 253, 275, 276, 282, 288, 289, 295, 307, 331, 351, 371, 376, 388, 395.
Toldrá Viazo, A., 179, 315, 332, 524, 529.

Vilá, Ernesto, 189, 190, 324.
Vilaseca, Salvador, 8.

Zerkowitz, 6, 9, 430, 508, 509, 510.

326009

326009